Get the eBook FREE!

(PDF, ePub, Kindle, and liveBook all included)

We believe that once you buy a book from us, you should be able to read it in any format we have available. To get electronic versions of this book at no additional cost to you, purchase and then register this book at the Manning website.

Go to https://www.manning.com/freebook and follow the instructions to complete your pBook registration.

That's it!
Thanks from Manning!

The Well-Grounded Java Developer, Second Edition

Praise for the First Edition

At the cutting edge of Java development...learn to speak Java 7 and next-gen languages.
—Paul Benedict, Corporate Personnel & Associates

Buy this book for what's new in Java 7. Keep it open for lessons in expert Java.
—Stephen Harrison, PhD, FirstFuel Software

A great collection of knowledge on the JVM platform.

—Rick Wagner, Red Hat

How to become a well-grounded Java developer—and how to stay that way.
—From the Foreword by Dr. Heinz Kabutz, *The Java Specialists' Newsletter*

The Well-Grounded Java Developer

Second Edition

BENJAMIN J. EVANS, JASON CLARK,
AND MARTIJN VERBURG

MANNING

SHELTER ISLAND

Manning Publications Co.
20 Baldwin Road
PO Box 761
Shelter Island, NY 11964

Development editor:	Elesha Hyde
Technical development editor:	Jonathan Thoms
Review editor:	Mihaela Batinić
Production editor:	Deirdre Hiam
Copy editor:	Pamela Hunt
Proofreader:	Jason Everett
Technical proofreader:	Michael Haller
Typesetter:	Gordan Salinovic
Cover designer:	Marija Tudor

ISBN 9781617298875
Printed and bound by CPI Group (UK) Ltd,
Croydon, CR0 4YY

brief contents

contents

foreword

Well-grounded? You mean, "well-rounded"? Two years of pandemic would do that without the need for a book.

Merriam-Webster defines *well-grounded* as "having a firm foundation." I like that. We want to have a firm foundation in Java—a practical knowledge of what we need to know to call ourselves Java experts. This book picks up where *Effective Java* stops.

This is the second edition of a great book. The first taught us all that we needed to know for Java 7. That seems like eons ago. Java 7 belonged to another age, when features were added to the language at best every three years. Back then, it was easy to keep versions apart. Java 5? Generics and enums. Java 7? `try-with-resource`. Java 8? Streams and lambdas. Those comfortable easy days ended when Oracle introduced the six-month cycle. Records—were those Java 14, 15, or 17? Enhanced Switch? Was that already in Java 11?

The fast release cycle is great for programmers who work for adventurous companies. Every six months, they get new toys to play with. They might even get to try out previews of what will come next. The myriad of new features is wonderful for programmers, but not so nice for authors. Before the ink has dried, a new feature release makes a bunch of things obsolete.

Ben, Jason, and Martijn have done a fantastic job with this new Java book. The basic premise remains the same. In my words: "If you wanted to hire a professional Java programmer, what would you expect them to already know? What skills would they need to prove they are well grounded?"

This new version of the book is as current as is possible with the six-month release cadence. At the same time, the authors don't overwhelm us with new stuff. The stark reality is that most enterprises are still stuck on an older version of Java. Even with Java 18 released, a lot of banks, insurance companies, and government departments are still on Java 8.

This book is about 200 pages longer than the previous edition. The fonts are a bit larger—well, we have all aged by nine years, haven't we? But the margins are smaller. Quite a few of the sections have completely new content. This is one case where the new edition does not make the old one obsolete. Both belong on a serious Java programmer's bookshelf.

Benjamin J. Evans, Jason R. Clark, and Martijn Verburg are Java experts. They hold senior Java positions at Red Hat, New Relic, and Microsoft. Let's take advantage of their collective wisdom. This book will help us discover areas of weakness that we can then improve on. In the end, with enough work, we can call ourselves *Well-Grounded Java programmers.*

HEINZ KABUTZ
THE JAVA SPECIALISTS' NEWSLETTER

preface

The first edition of this book started life as a set of training notes written for new graduate developers in the foreign exchange department of a bank. One of us (Ben), looking at the existing books on the market, found a lack of up-to-date material aimed at Java developers who wanted to level up. Partway through writing that material, he found he was writing that missing book and enlisted Martijn to help.

That was more than 10 years ago—we were writing as Java 7 was being developed—and the world is very different now. In response, the book has changed substantially since the first edition. So, although our original primary goals were to introduce topics like

- Polyglot programming
- Dependency injection
- Multithreaded programming
- Sound build and CI practices
- What's new in Java 7

when we came to write the second edition, we found that we needed to make some changes, including

- Trimming down polyglot a bit
- Adding a new emphasis on functional programming
- Enhancing the discussion of multithreading
- Putting a different spin on build and deploy (including containers)
- Talking about what's new in Java 11 and 17

One very important change was that the first edition included Scala as one of three non-Java languages discussed (the others being Groovy and Clojure—Kotlin didn't really exist at the time we wrote it). At that time, many of the developers exploring Scala were looking for "Java, but a better mousetrap," which is essentially the view of Scala that we presented in the first edition.

However, since then, the world has moved on. Java 8 and 11 became hugely dominant, and the "better mousetrap" crew are mostly writing Kotlin (or just sticking with Java). Scala, in the meantime, has become a very powerful statically typed, FP-first JVM language. This is great for the folks who want that, but it has come with costs, such as an ever-more-complex runtime and a language that has less and less in common with Java as time goes by.

This development is sometimes abbreviated to the phrase that "Scala wants to be Haskell on the JVM," although this is not entirely accurate and is more a convenient conversational shorthand than anything else. So, after having made the decision to drop Groovy from the second edition, we thought long and hard about whether to keep Scala or replace it with Kotlin.

Our eventual conclusion was basically that Scala is heading in its own, FP-heavy direction, and that we wanted to present a language that was more approachable to Java developers who were coming fresh to non-Java languages, such as Kotlin. This left us with a dilemma. The parts of Scala that are easily accessible to Java folks are very similar to Kotlin (with near-identical syntax in some cases), but the philosophy and direction of travel of the two languages are totally different. We felt that explaining what Scala *is* in sufficient depth—so that the coverage was distinct from Kotlin— would take up far too much space in the book.

Therefore, our eventual decision was to drop from three to two additional languages to make space and give extra depth to the coverage of the remaining languages (Kotlin and Clojure). For this reason, although we make the occasional comment about Scala, we don't devote entire sections (let alone chapters) to it.

Clojure is a very different story—and, indeed, a very different language—than either Kotlin or Java. For example, in chapter 15 we struggle a bit because many of the concepts that we're introducing in the other languages (e.g., higher-order functions and recursion) have already been introduced and are just "part of the landscape" in Clojure. Rather than follow the template used by Java and Kotlin, the discussion goes in a different direction. Clojure is, fundamentally, a much more functionally oriented language, and we would just end up repeating ourselves a lot if we were to follow the exact same structure as for the other languages.

In this book, we hope that the theme of software development as a social activity rings out clearly. We believe that the technical aspects of the craft are important, but the more subtle concerns of communication and interaction between people are at least as important. It can be hard to explain these facets easily in a book, but that theme is present throughout.

Developers are sustained throughout their careers by their engagement with technology and the passion to keep learning. In this book, we hope that we've been able to highlight some of the topics that will ignite that passion. It's a sightseeing tour, rather than an encyclopedic study, but that's the intention—to get you started and then leave you to follow up on those topics that capture your imagination.

We take you from the new features of the recent versions of Java through to best practices of modern software development and the future of the platform. Along the way, we show you some of the highlights that have had relevance to us on our own journey as Java technologists.

Concurrency, performance, bytecode, and class loading are some of the core techniques that fascinated us the most. We also talk about new, non-Java languages on the JVM for two reasons:

- Non-Java languages continue to gain importance in the overall Java ecosystem.
- Understanding the different perspectives that different languages bring makes you a better programmer in any language you write in.

Above all, this is a journey that's forward looking and puts you and your interests front and center. We feel that becoming a well-grounded Java developer will help to keep you engaged and in control of your own development and will help you learn more about the changing world of Java and the ecosystem that surrounds it. We hope that the distilled experience that you're holding in your hands is useful and interesting to you and that reading it is thought provoking and fun. Writing it certainly was!

acknowledgements

We would like to thank the following people for their contributions to the book:

Elesha Hyde, for being a most excellent development editor; Jonathon Thoms, for his great work in the technical reviews; Alex Buckley, for a very detailed discussion of the class loading process; Heinz Kabutz, for excellent suggestions and discussions (and even PRs!) about the details of the concurrency chapters, as well as another wonderful foreword; Holly Cummins, not only for helping inspire the original edition but also for her consistently grounded and practical advice; Bruce Durling, for discussion of the Clojure material; Dan Heidinga, for detailed feedback on the current state of Project Valhalla; Piotr Jagielski, Louis Jacomet, József Bartók, and Tom Tresansky for corrections regarding some of the details about how Gradle really works; and Andrew Binstock, for a very meticulous close reading of several chapters and sound advice, as always.

We would also like to thank the staff at Manning: Mihaela Batinić, our reviewing editor; Michael Haller, our technical reviewer; Deirdre Hiam, our project editor; Pamela Hunt, our copyeditor; and Jason Everett, our proofreader. To all the reviewers: Adam Koch, Alain Lompo, Alex Gout, Andres Sacco, Andy Keffalas, Anshuman Purohit, Ashley Eatly, Christian Thoudahl, Christopher Kardell, Claudia Maderthaner, Conor Redmond, Dr. Irfan Ullah, Eddú Meléndez Gonzales, Ezra Simeloff, George Thomas, Gilberto Taccari, Hugo da Silva Possani, Igor Karp, Jared Duncan, Javid Asgarov, Jean-François Morin, Jerome Meyer, Kent R. Spillner, Kimberly L Winston-Jackson, Konstantin Eremin, Matt Deimel, Michael Haller, Michael Wall, Mikhail Kovalev, Patricia Gee, Ramanan Natarajan, Raphael Villela, Satej Kumar Sahu, Sergio Edgar Martínez Pacheco, Simona Ruso, Steven K Makunzva, Theofanis Despoudis, Troi Eisler, Yogesh Shetty, and William E. Wheeler, your suggestions helped make this a better book.

From Jason

Thanks are due to many different people across many years.

To Mrs. Nimmo, thank you for all the extra credit in middle school English for my silly little stories. It's no exaggeration that your encouragement set me on a lifelong path of writing.

To Mom, thank you for your infectious love of reading, which I'm so glad to have inherited.

To Dad, thank you for sharing your love of computers. It has provided me not only with a career but the chance to write and share that joy with others.

To Ben, thank you first and foremost for your friendship. It has been a blast to be drawn deeper into the JVM by your awesome curiosity and enthusiasm. And, of course, thanks for asking me along on this second edition. It was more work than any of us expected, but a better book in the end as well!

And last but not least, thanks to my wife, Amber, and my kids, Coraline and Asher, for their continued love and support throughout the strange and wonderful process that is making a book.

From Martijn

Firstly I'd like to thank Ben and Jason for inviting me to be part of this second edition. My contribution was *very* minimal in comparison to theirs, and they were most gracious in insisting my name still be on the cover!

To Kerry, you've been a mountain of support during the whirlwind career moments of the past decade, not to mention reacting with a smile when I said, "It's just a few edits this time around, I promise!"

To Hunter, your enthusiasm for life reminds me why I got into the creative joy of programming in the first place. I hope you'll find that same joy in life no matter what path you take.

To the fine folks of the Java Engineering Group at Microsoft, the Eclipse Adoptium Community, the London Java Community, the Java Champions Community, and too many others to mention. You inspire me every day, and I always walk away each day having learned something new and added another five things on my list to read for the next day!

From Ben

To my parents, Sue and Martin, for their unwavering faith that we would find, and make, our own way on the path less traveled.

To my wife, Anna, for her illustrations, her artistic vision, and her tireless support and understanding through yet another book.

In memory of Marianito, who, partway through the development of this book, discovered that laptops that have been left open make a marvelously warm spot upon which to sleep.

To Joselito, who overcame some of his fear by being curious about why I would sit and be so fascinated by the screen that was so much less interesting than the one in the other room that has spaceships and explosions on it.

about this book

Who should read this book?

Welcome to *The Well-Grounded Java Developer*. This book is aimed at turning you into a Java developer for the next decade, reigniting your passion for both the language and platform. Along the way, you'll discover new Java features, ensure that you're familiar with essential modern software techniques (such as test-driven development, and container-based deployments), and start to explore the world of non-Java languages on the JVM.

To begin, let's consider the description of the Java language provided by James Iry in a wonderful blog post, "A Brief, Incomplete, and Mostly Wrong History of Programming Languages" available at http://mng.bz/2rz9:

> *1996—James Gosling invents Java. Java is a relatively verbose, garbage collected, class-based, statically typed, single dispatch, object-oriented language with single implementation inheritance and multiple interface inheritance. Sun loudly heralds Java's novelty.*

Although the point of Java's entry is mostly to set up a gag where C# is given the same writeup, this is not bad as descriptions of languages go. The full blog post contains a bunch of other gems, and it's well worth a read in an idle moment.

This does present a very real question: why are we still talking about a language that is now over 26 years old? Surely it's stable, and not much new or interesting can be said about it?

If that were the case, this would be a short book. We are still talking about it because one of Java's greatest strengths has been its ability to build on a few core design decisions, which have proven to be very successful in the marketplace:

- Automatic management of the runtime environment (e.g., garbage collection, just-in-time compilation)
- A simple syntax and relatively few concepts in the core language
- A conservative approach to evolving the language
- Additional functionality and complexity in libraries
- Broad, open ecosystem

These design decisions have kept innovation moving in the Java world—the simple core has kept the barrier to joining the developer community low, and the broad ecosystem has made it easy for newcomers to find pre-existing components that fit their needs. These traits have kept the Java platform and language strong and vibrant—even if the language has had a historical tendency to change slowly. It turns out that the mix of strong consistency and evolutionary change has won quite a few fans among software developers.

How to use this book

The material in this book is broadly designed to be read end-to-end, but we understand that some readers may want to dive straight into particular topics, so we have done our best to also accommodate that style of reading.

We strongly believe in hands-on learning, so we recommend that readers try out the sample code that comes with the book as they read through the text. The rest of this section deals with how you can approach the book if you are more of a standalone chapter style of reader.

The Well-Grounded Java Developer is split into the following five parts:

- From 8 to 11, and beyond
- Under the hood
- Non-Java languages on the JVM
- Build and deployment
- Java frontiers

Part 1 (chapters 1–3) contains three chapters on the most recent versions of Java. The book as a whole uses Java 11 syntax and semantics throughout and calls out specific uses of post-11 syntax.

Part 2 (chapters 4–7) contains a first peek behind the curtain. It is a truism of art that one needs to know the rules before one can credibly break them. These chapters outline how one first bends, and then breaks, the rules of the Java programming language.

Part 3 (chapters 8–10) covers polyglot programming on the JVM. Chapter 8 should be considered required reading because it sets the stage by discussing the categorization and use of alternative languages on the JVM.

The following two language chapters cover a Java-like OO-functional language (Kotlin) and a truly functional one (Clojure). Those languages can be read stand-alone, although developers new to functional programming will probably want to read them in order.

Part 4 (chapters 11–14) introduces build, deployment, and testing as they are done in modern projects, and they assume that the reader has at least a basic understanding of unit testing as showcased in, for example, JUnit.

Part 5 (chapters 15–18) builds on topics that have been introduced earlier to delve deeper into functional programming, concurrency, and the internals of the platform. Although the chapters can be read standalone, in some sections, we assume that you've read the earlier chapters and/or already have familiarity with certain topics.

This book is firmly aimed at Java developers who wants to modernize their knowledge base in both the language and the platform. If you want to get up to speed with what modern Java has to offer, this is the book for you.

If you are looking to brush up on your techniques and understanding of topics such as functional programming, concurrency, and advanced testing, this book will give you a good grounding in those topics. This is also a book for those developers who are curious about what non-Java languages can teach them and how broadening their horizons will make them a better programmer.

About the code

The initial download and installation you'll need is Java 17 (or 11). Simply follow the download and installation instructions for the binary you need for the OS you use. You can find binaries and instructions online at your usual Java vendor, or at the vendor-neutral Adoptium project, run by the Eclipse Foundation, at https://adoptium.net/.

Java 11 (and 17) runs on Mac, Windows, Linux, and pretty much any other modern OS and hardware platform.

> **NOTE** If you're concerned about details of Java licensing and so on, you can head to appendix A where a full discussion can be found.

This book contains many examples of source code both in numbered listings and in line with normal text. In both cases, source code is formatted in a `fixed-width font like this` to separate it from ordinary text.

In many cases, the original source code has been reformatted; we've added line breaks and reworked indentation to accommodate the available page space in the book. Additionally, comments in the source code have often been removed from the listings when the code is described in the text. Code annotations accompany many of the listings, highlighting important concepts.

You can get executable snippets of code from the liveBook (online) version of this book at https://livebook.manning.com/book/the-well-grounded-java-developer-second-edition. The complete code for the examples in the book is available for download from the Manning website at https://www.manning.com/books/the-well-grounded-java-developer-second-edition, and from GitHub at https://github.com/well-grounded-java/resources.

However, most readers will probably want to try out the code samples in an IDE. Java 11/17 and the latest versions of Kotlin and Clojure are well supported by recent versions of the main IDEs:

- Eclipse IDE
- IntelliJ IDEA Community Edition (or Ultimate Edition)
- Apache NetBeans

liveBook Discussion Forum

Purchase of *The Well-Grounded Java Developer, 2nd Edition* includes free access to liveBook, Manning's online reading platform. Using liveBook's exclusive discussion features, you can attach comments to the book globally or to specific sections or paragraphs. It's a snap to make notes for yourself, ask and answer technical questions, and receive help from the author and other users. To access the forum, go to https://livebook .manning.com/book/the-well-grounded-java-developer-second-edition/discussion. You can also learn more about Manning's forums and the rules of conduct at https:// livebook.manning.com/discussion.

Manning's commitment to our readers is to provide a venue where a meaningful dialogue between individual readers and between readers and the authors can take place. It is not a commitment to any specific amount of participation on the part of the authors, whose contribution to the forum remains voluntary (and unpaid). We suggest you try asking the authors some challenging questions lest their interest stray! The forum and the archives of previous discussions will be accessible from the publisher's website as long as the book is in print.

Other online resources

https://github.com/well-grounded-java/resources

about the authors

BEN EVANS is a Java Champion and Senior Principal Software Engineer at Red Hat. Previously he was Lead Architect for Instrumentation at New Relic, and co-founded jClarity, a performance tools startup acquired by Microsoft. He has also worked as Chief Architect for Listed Derivatives at Deutsche Bank and as Senior Technical Instructor for Morgan Stanley. He served for six years on the Java Community Process Executive Committee, helping define new Java standards.

Ben is the author of six books, including *Optimizing Java* and the new editions of *Java in a Nutshell* and his technical articles are read by thousands of developers every month. Ben is a regular speaker and educator on topics such as the Java platform, systems architecture, performance and concurrency for companies and conferences all over the world.

JASON CLARK is a principal engineer and architect at New Relic where he has worked on everything from Ruby instrumentation libraries to container orchestration platforms. He was previously an architect at WebMD building .Net-based web services.

A regular conference speaker, Jason contributes to the open-source project Shoes, aiming to make GUI programming easy and fun for beginners and students.

 **MARTIJN VERBURG** is the Principal SWE Group Manager for the Java Engineering Group at Microsoft. He is the co-leader of the London Java User Group (aka the LJC) where he co-founded Adopt-OpenJDK (now Eclipse Adoptium), the world's leading (non-Oracle) OpenJDK distribution. Martijn is the co-author of the first edition of *The Well-Grounded Java Developer,* and sits on numerous Java standards bodies (JCP, Jakarta EE, et al).

about the cover illustration

The figure on the cover of *The Well-Grounded Java Developer*, titled "A Posy Seller," is taken from Sylvain Maréchal's nineteenth-century compendium of regional dress customs, published in France.

In those days, it was easy to identify where people lived and what their trade or station in life was just by their dress. Manning celebrates the inventiveness and initiative of the computer business with book covers based on the rich diversity of regional culture centuries ago, brought back to life by pictures from collections such as this one.

Part 1

From 8 to 11 and beyond!

These first three chapters are about ramping up to Java 17. You'll ease in with an introductory chapter that covers some quality-of-life changes that came in with Java 11. You'll see how the Java ecosystem and release cycle has changed since Java 8, including the following, and what that means to developers:

- var keyword
- Collections factories
- New HTTP client with HTTP/2 support
- Single-file source code programs

From there, you'll get a deep dive on one of the biggest changes in the Java landscape in many years—the addition of a full module system. You'll see why this dramatic change was necessary. It's been carefully designed for incremental adoption, and along with understanding the concepts, you'll come away knowing how to start taking advantage of it in your applications and libraries.

Under the new release cycle, Java 17 brings together a significant batch of new language features, including

- Text blocks
- Switch expressions
- Records
- Sealed types

By the end of part 1, you'll be thinking and writing naturally in Java 17, ready to use this new knowledge throughout the remainder of the book.

Introducing modern Java

This chapter covers

- Java as a platform and a language
- The new Java release model
- Enhanced Type inference (var)
- Incubating and preview features
- Changing the language
- Small language changes in Java 11

Welcome to Java in 2022. It is an exciting time. Java 17, the latest Long-Term-Support (LTS) release shipped in September 2021, and the first and most adventurous teams are starting to move to it.

At the time of writing, apart from a few trailblazers, Java applications are more or less evenly split between running on Java 11 (released September 2018) and the much older Java 8 (2014). Java 11 offers a lot to recommend, especially for teams that are deploying in the cloud, but some have been a little slow to adopt it.

So, in the first part of this book, we are going to spend some time introducing some of the new features that have arrived in Java 11 and 17. Hopefully, this discussion will help convince some teams and managers who may be reluctant to upgrade from Java 8 that things are better than ever in the newer versions.

3

Our focus for this chapter is going to be Java 11 because a) it's the LTS version with the largest market share and b) no noticeable adoption of Java 17 has occurred yet. However, in chapter 3, we will introduce the new features in Java 17 to bring you all the way up to date.

Let's get underway by discussing the language-versus-platform duality that lies at the heart of modern Java. This is a critically important point that we'll come back to several times throughout the book, so it's essential to grasp it right at the start.

1.1   *The language and the platform*

Java as a term can refer to one of several related concepts. In particular, it could mean either the human-readable programming language or the much broader "Java platform."

Surprisingly, different authors sometimes give slightly different definitions of what constitutes a language and a platform. This can lead to a lack of clarity and some confusion about the differences between the two and about which provides the various programming features that application code uses.

Let's make that distinction clear right now, because it cuts to the heart of a lot of the topics in this book. Here are our definitions:

- *The Java language*—The Java language is the statically typed, object-oriented language that we lightly lampooned in the "About this book" section. Hopefully, it's already very familiar to you. One obvious point about source code written in the Java language is that it's human-readable (or it should be!).
- *The Java platform*—The platform is the software that provides a runtime environment. It's the JVM that links and executes your code as provided to it in the form of (not human-readable) class files. It doesn't directly interpret Java language source files but instead requires them to be converted to class files first.

One of the big reasons for the success of Java as a software system is that it's a standard. This means that it has specifications that describe how it's supposed to work. Standardization allows different vendors and project groups to produce implementations that should all, in theory, work the same way. The specs don't make guarantees about how well different implementations will perform when handling the same task, but they can provide assurances about the correctness of the results.

Several separate specs govern the Java system—the most important are the Java Language Specification (JLS) and the JVM Specification (VMSpec). This separation is taken very seriously in modern Java; in fact, the VMSpec no longer makes any reference whatsoever to the JLS directly. We'll have a bit more to say about the differences between these two specs later in the book.

> **NOTE** These days the JVM is actually quite a general-purpose and language-agnostic environment for running programs. This is one reason for the separation of the specs.

One obvious question, when you're faced with the described duality, is, "What's the link between them?" If they're now separate, how do they come together to make the Java system?

The link between the language and platform is the shared definition of the class file format (the .class files). A serious study of the class file definition will reward you (and we provide one in chapter 4)—in fact, it's one of the ways a good Java programmer can start to become a great one. In figure 1.1, you can see the full process by which Java code is produced and used.

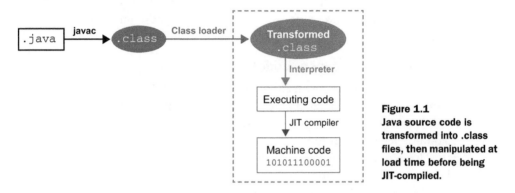

Figure 1.1
Java source code is transformed into .class files, then manipulated at load time before being JIT-compiled.

As you can see in the figure, Java code starts life as human-readable Java source, and it's then compiled by `javac` into a .class file and loaded into a JVM. It's common for classes to be manipulated and altered during the loading process. Many of the most popular Java frameworks transform classes as they're loaded to inject dynamic behavior such as instrumentation or alternative lookups for classes to load.

> **NOTE** Class loading is an essential feature of the Java platform, and we will learn a lot more about it in chapter 4.

Is Java a compiled or interpreted language? The standard picture of Java is of a language that's compiled into .class files before being run on a JVM. If pressed, many developers can also explain that bytecode starts off by being interpreted by the JVM but will undergo just-in-time (JIT) compilation at some later point. Here, however, many people's understanding breaks down into a somewhat hazy conception of bytecode as basically being machine code for an imaginary or simplified CPU.

In fact, JVM bytecode is more like a halfway house between human-readable source and machine code. In the technical terms of compiler theory, bytecode is really a form of intermediate language (IL) rather than actual machine code. This means that the process of turning Java source into bytecode isn't really compilation in the sense that a C++ or a Go programmer would understand it, and `javac` isn't a compiler in the same sense as `gcc` is—it's really a class file generator for Java source code. The real compiler in the Java ecosystem is the JIT compiler, as you can see in figure 1.1.

Some people describe the Java system as "dynamically compiled." This emphasizes that the compilation that matters is the JIT compilation at runtime, not the creation of the class file during the build process.

> **NOTE** The existence of the source code compiler, javac, leads many developers to think of Java as a static, compiled language. One of the big secrets is that at runtime, the Java environment is actually very dynamic—it's just hidden a bit below the surface.

So, the real answer to "Is Java compiled or interpreted?" is "both." With the distinction between language and platform now clearer, let's move on to talk about the new Java release model.

1.2   *The new Java release model*

Java was not always an open source language, but following an announcement at the JavaOne conference in 2006, the source code for Java itself (minus a few bits that Sun didn't own the source for) was released under the GPLv2+CE license (https://openjdk .java.net/legal/gplv2+ce.html).

This was around the time of the release of Java 6, so Java 7 was the first version of Java to be developed under an open source software (OSS) license. The primary focus for open source development of the Java platform since then has been the OpenJDK project (https://openjdk.java.net), and that continues to this day.

A lot of the project discussion takes place on mailing lists that cover aspects of the overall codebase. There are "permanent" lists such as core-libs (core libraries), as well as more transient lists that are formed as part of specific OpenJDK projects such as lambda-dev (lambdas), which then become inactive when a particular project has been completed. In general, these lists have been the relevant forums for discussing possible future features, allowing developers from the wider community to participate in the process of producing new versions of Java.

> **NOTE** Sun Microsystems was acquired by Oracle shortly before Java 7 was released. Therefore, all of Oracle's releases of Java have been based on the open source codebase.

The open source releases of Java had settled into a feature-driven release cycle, where a single marquee feature effectively defines the release (e.g., lambdas in Java 8 or modules in Java 9).

With the release of Java 9, however, the release model changed. From Java 10 onward, Oracle decided that Java would be released on a strict, time-based model. This means that OpenJDK now uses a *mainline* development model, which includes the following:

- New features are developed on a branch and merged only when they are code complete.
- Releases can occur on a strict time cadence.

- Late features do not delay releases but are held over for the next release.
- The current head of the trunk should always be releasable (in theory).
- If necessary, an emergency fix can be prepared and pushed out at any point.
- Separate OpenJDK projects are used to explore and research longer-term, future directions.

A new version of Java is released every six months ("feature releases"). The various providers (Oracle, Eclipse Adoptium, Amazon, Azul, et al.) can choose to make *any* of those releases a Long-Term Support (LTS) release. However, in practice, all of the vendors follow having one release every three years being named as the LTS release.

> **NOTE** As of late 2021, discussions are underway to reduce the LTS gap from three years to two years. We may well see the next LTS version as Java 21 in 2023 as opposed to Java 23 in 2024.

The first LTS release was Java 11, with Java 8 retrospectively included in the set of LTS releases. Oracle's intention was for the Java community to upgrade regularly and to take up the feature releases as they emerge. However, in practice, the community (and enterprise customers in particular) have proved to be resistant to this model, preferring instead to upgrade from one LTS release to the next.

This approach, of course, limits the uptake of new Java features and stifles innovation. However, the realities of enterprise software are what they are, and many people still view an upgrade of the Java version as a significant undertaking.

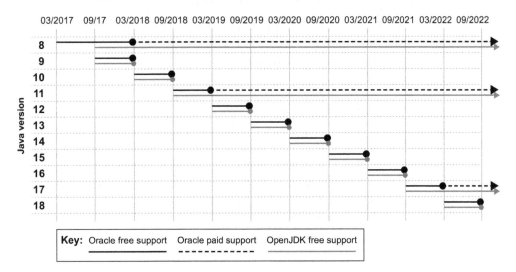

Figure 1.2   The timescale of recent and future releases

This means that whereas the release road map shown in figure 1.2 contains a major release every six months, the only releases that have significant usage are the LTS versions—Java 17 (which was just released in September 2021), Java 11 (which was released in September 2018), and the pre-modules release, Java 8, which is more than seven years old. Java 8 and Java 11 have roughly equal market share, with Java 11 recently having taken over 50% and rapidly accelerating. Java 17 adoption is expected to be much quicker than the move from Java 8 to Java 11 because the most difficult hurdles introduced by the module system and security restrictions will have already been overcome with the earlier migration.

The other significant change in the new release model is that Oracle has changed the license for their distribution. Although Oracle's JDK is built from the OpenJDK sources, the binary is not licensed under an OSS license. Instead, Oracle's JDK is proprietary software, and as of JDK 11, Oracle provides support and updates for only six months for each version. This means that many people who relied on Oracle's free updates are now faced with a choice:

- Pay Oracle for support and updates, or
- Use a different distribution that produces open source binaries.

Alternative JDK vendors include Eclipse Adoptium (previously AdoptOpenJDK), Alibaba (Dragonwell), Amazon (Corretto), Azul Systems (Zulu), IBM, Microsoft, Red Hat, and SAP.

> **NOTE** Two of the authors (Martijn and Ben) helped found the AdoptOpenJDK project, which has evolved into the vendor-neutral Eclipse Adoptium community project to build and release a high-quality, free, and open source Java binary distribution. See adoptium.net for more details.

With the licensing changes and with so many providers, picking the correct Java for you and your team is a choice that you should make with care. Thankfully, leaders in the Java ecosystem have written some very detailed guides, and appendix A distills them down for you.

Although the Java release model has changed to use timed releases, the vast majority of teams are still running on either JDK 8 or 11. These LTS releases are being maintained by the community (including major vendors) and still receive regular security updates and bug fixes. The changes made to the LTS versions are deliberately small in scope and are "housekeeping updates." Apart from security and small bug fixes, only a minimal set of changes are permitted. These include fixes needed to ensure that the LTS releases will continue to work correctly for their expected lifetime. This includes things like the following:

- The addition of the new Japanese Era
- Time zone database updates
- TLS 1.3
- Adding Shenandoah, a low-pause GC for large modern workloads

One other necessary change is that the build scripts for macOS needed to be updated to work with a recent version of Apple's Xcode tool so that they will continue to work on new releases of Apple's operating system.

Within the projects to maintain JDK 8 and 11 (sometimes called the "updates" projects), some potential scope still exists for new features to be backported, but it is minimal. As an example, one of the guiding rules is that newly ported features may not change program semantics. Examples of permissible changes could include the support for TLS 1.3 or the backport of Java Flight Recorder to Java 8u272.

Now that we've set the scene by clarifying the difference between the language and platform and explaining the new release model, let's meet our first technical feature of modern Java. The new feature we're going to meet is something that developers have been asking for since almost the first release of Java—a way to reduce the amount of typing that writing Java programs seems to involve.

1.3   *Enhanced type inference (var keyword)*

Java has historically had a reputation as a verbose language. However, in recent versions, the language has evolved to make more and more use of *type inference*. This feature of the source code compiler enables the compiler to work out some of the type information in programs automatically. As a result, it doesn't need to be told everything explicitly.

> **NOTE**   The aim of type inference is to reduce boilerplate content, remove duplication, and allow for more concise and readable code.

This trend started with Java 5, when generic methods were introduced. Generic methods permit a very limited form of type inference of generic type arguments, so that instead of having to explicitly provide the exact type that is needed, like this:

```
List<Integer> empty = Collections.<Integer>emptyList();
```

the generic type parameter can be omitted on the right-hand side, like so:

```
List<Integer> empty = Collections.emptyList();
```

This way of writing a call to a generic method is so familiar that many developers will struggle to remember the form with explicit type arguments. This is a good thing—it means the type inference is doing its job and removing the superfluous boilerplate content so that the meaning of the code is clear.

The next significant enhancement to type inference in Java came with version 7, which introduced a change when dealing with generics. Before Java 7, it was common to see code like this:

```
Map<Integer, Map<String, String>> usersLists =
                    new HashMap<Integer, Map<String, String>>();
```

That is a really verbose way to declare that you have some users, whom you identify by userid (which is an integer), and each user has a set of properties (modeled as a map of string to strings) specific to that user.

In fact, almost half of the source is duplicated characters, and they don't tell us anything. So, from Java 7 onward, we can write

```
Map<Integer, Map<String, String>> usersLists = new HashMap<>();
```

and have the compiler work out the type information on the right side. The compiler is working out the correct type for the expression on the right side— it isn't just substituting the text that defines the full type.

> **NOTE** Because the shortened type declaration looks like a diamond, this form is called "diamond syntax."

In Java 8, more type inference was added to support the introduction of lambda expressions, like this example where the type inference algorithm can conclude that the type of s is a `String`:

```
Function<String, Integer> lengthFn = s -> s.length();
```

In modern Java, type inference has been taken one step further, with the arrival of *Local Variable Type Inference* (LVTI), otherwise known as var. This feature was added in Java 10 and allows the developer to infer the types of *variables,* instead of the types of *values,* like this:

```
var names = new ArrayList<String>();
```

This is implemented by making var a reserved, "magic" type name rather than a language keyword. Developers can still in theory use var as the name of a variable, method, or package.

> **NOTE** An important side effect of using var appropriately is that the domain of your code is once more front and center (as opposed to the type information). But with great power comes great responsibility! Make sure that you name your variables carefully to help future readers of your code.

On the other hand, code that previously used var as the name of a type will have to be recompiled. However, virtually all Java developers follow the convention that type names should start with a capital letter, so the number of instances of preexisting types called var should be vanishing small. This means that it is entirely legal to write code like that shown in the next listing.

> Listing 1.1   Bad code

```
package var;

public class Var {
  private static Var var = null;
```

```
  public static Var var() {
    return var;
  }

  public static void var(Var var) {
    Var.var = var;
  }
}
```

And then call it like this:

```
var var = var();
if (var == null) {
  var(new Var());
}
```

However, just because something is *legal*, does not mean it is *sensible*. Writing code like the previous listing is not going to make you any friends and should not pass code reviews!

The intention of var is to reduce verbosity in Java code and to be familiar to programmers coming to Java from other languages. It does not introduce dynamic typing, and all Java variables continue to have static types at all times—you just don't need to write them down explicitly in all cases.

Type inference in Java is *local*, and in the case of var, the algorithm examines only the declaration of the local variable. This means it cannot be used for fields, method arguments, or return types. The compiler applies a form of *constraint solving* to determine whether any type exists that could satisfy all the requirements of the code as written.

> **NOTE** var is implemented solely in the source code compiler (javac) and has no runtime or performance effect whatsoever.

For example, in the declaration of lengthFn in the previous code sample, the constraint solver can deduce that the type of the method parameter s must be compatible with String which is explicitly provided as the type of the parameter to Function. In Java, of course, the string type is final, so the compiler can conclude that the type of s is exactly String.

For the compiler to be able to infer types, enough information must be provided by the programmer to allow the constraint equations to be solved. For example, code like this

```
var fn = s -> s.length();
```

does not have enough type information for the compiler to deduce the type of fn, and so it will not compile. One important case of this is

```
var n = null;
```

which cannot be resolved by the compiler because the null value can be assigned to a variable of any reference type, so there is no information about what types n could conceivably be. We say that the type constraint equations that the inferencer needs to solve are "underdetermined" in this case—a mathematical term that connects the number of equations to be solved with the number of variables.

You could imagine a scheme of type inference that goes beyond just the initial declaration of the local variable and examines more code to make inference decisions, like this:

```
var n = null;
String.format(n);
```

A more complex inference algorithm (or a human) might be able to conclude that the type of n is actually String, because the format() method takes a string as the first argument.

This might seem appealing, but, as with everything else in software, it represents a trade-off. More complexity means longer compilation times and a wider variety of ways in which the inference can fail. This, in turn, means that the programmer must develop a more complicated intuition to use nonlocal type inference correctly.

Other languages may choose to make different trade-offs, but Java is clear: only the declaration is used to infer types. Local variable type inference is intended to be a beneficial technique to reduce boilerplate text and verbosity. However, it should be used only where necessary to make the code clearer, not as a blunt instrument to be used whenever possible (the "Golden Hammer" antipattern).

Some quick guidelines for when to use LVTI follow:

- In simple initializers, if the right-hand side is a call to a constructor or static factory method
- If removing the explicit type deletes repeated or redundant information
- If variables have names that already indicate their types
- If the scope and usage of the local variable is short and simple

A complete set of applicable rules of thumb is provided by Stuart Marks, one of the core developers of the Java language, in his style guides for LVTI usage at http://mng.bz/RvPK.

To conclude this section, let's look at another, more advanced, usage of var—the so-called *nondenotable types*. These are types that are legal in Java, but they cannot appear as the type of a variable. Instead, they must be inferred as the type of the expression that is being assigned. Let's look at a simple example using the jshell interactive environment, which arrived in Java 9:

```
jshell> var duck = new Object() {
   ...>     void quack() {
   ...>         System.out.println("Quack!");
   ...>     }
```

```
   ...> }
duck ==> $0@5910e440

jshell> duck.quack();
Quack!
```

The variable `duck` has an unusual type—it is effectively `Object` but extended with a method called `quack()`. Although the object may quack like a duck, its type lacks a name, so we can't use the type as either a method parameter or return type.

With LVTI, we can use it as the inferred type of a local variable. This allows us to use the type within a method. Of course, the type can't be used outside of this tight local scope, so the overall utility of this language feature is limited. It's more of a curiosity than anything else.

Despite these limitations, this does represent a glimpse at Java's take on a feature that is present in some other languages—sometimes referred to as *structural typing* in statically typed languages and *duck typing* in dynamically typed languages (particularly Python).

1.4 Changing the language and the platform

We think it's essential to explain the "why" of language change as well as the "what." During the development of new versions of Java, much interest around new language features often exists, but the community doesn't always understand how much work is required to get changes fully engineered and ready for prime time.

You may also have noticed that in a mature runtime such as Java, language features tend to evolve from other languages or libraries, make their way into popular frameworks, and only then get added to the language or runtime itself. We hope to shed a bit of light on this area and hopefully dispel a few myths along the way. But if you're not very interested in how Java evolves, feel free to skip ahead to section 1.5 and jump right into the language changes.

There is an effort curve involved in changing the Java language—some possible implementations require less engineering effort than others. In figure 1.3, we've tried to represent the different routes and show the relative effort required for each.

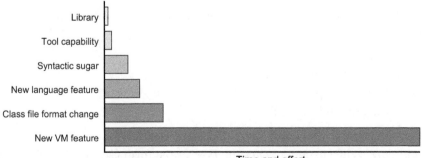

Figure 1.3 The relative effort involved in implementing new functionality in different ways

In general, it's better to take the route that requires the least effort. This means that if it's possible to implement a new feature as a library, you generally should. But not all features are easy, or even possible, to implement in a library or an IDE capability. Some features have to be implemented deeper inside the platform. Here's how some recent features fit into our complexity scale for new language features:

- *Library change*—Collections factory methods (Java 9)
- *Syntactic sugar*—Underscores in numbers (Java 7)
- *Small new language feature*—try-with-resources (Java 7)
- *Class file format change*—Annotations (Java 5)
- *New JVM feature*—Nestmates (Java 11)
- *Major new feature*—Lambda Expressions (Java 8)

Let's take a close look at how changes across the complexity scale are made.

1.4.1   Sprinkling some sugar

A phrase that's sometimes used to describe a language feature is "syntactic sugar." That is, the syntactic sugar form is provided because it's easier for humans to work with despite the functionality already existing in the language.

As a rule of thumb, a feature referred to as syntactic sugar is removed from the compiler's representation of the program early in the compilation process—it's said to have been "desugared" into the basic representation of the same feature.

This makes syntactic sugar changes to a language easier to implement because they usually involve a relatively small amount of work and only involve changes to the compiler (javac in the case of Java).

One question that might well be asked at this point is, "What constitutes a small change to the spec?" One of the most straightforward changes in Java 7 consisted of adding a single word—"String"—to section 14.11 of the JLS, which allowed strings in a switch statement. You can't really get much smaller than that as a change, and yet even this change touches several other aspects of the spec. Any alteration produces consequences, and these have to be chased through the entire design of the language.

1.4.2   Changing the language

The full set of actions that must be performed (or at least investigated) for *any* change follows:

- Update the JLS.
- Implement a prototype in the source compiler.
- Add library support essential for the change.
- Write tests and examples.
- Update documentation.

In addition, if the change touches the JVM or platform aspects, the following actions must occur:

- Update the VMSpec.
- Implement the JVM changes.
- Add support in the class file and JVM tools.
- Consider the impact on reflection.
- Consider the impact on serialization.
- Think about any effects on native code components, such as Java Native Interface (JNI).

This isn't a small amount of work, and that's after the impact of the change across the whole language spec has been considered!

An area of hairiness, when it comes to making changes, is the type system. That isn't because Java's type system is terrible. Instead, languages with rich static type systems are likely to have a lot of possible interaction points between different bits of those type systems. Making changes to them is prone to creating unexpected surprises.

1.4.3 JSRs and JEPs

Two main mechanisms are used to make changes to the Java platform. The first is the *Java Specification Request* (JSR), which is specified by the *Java Community Process* (JCP). This is used to determine standard APIs—both external libraries and major internal platform APIs.

This was historically the only way of making changes to the Java platform and was best used to codify a consensus of already mature technology. However, in recent years, a desire to implement change faster (and in smaller units) led to the development of the *JDK Enhancement Proposal* (JEP) as a lighter-weight alternative. Platform (aka umbrella) JSRs are now made up of JEPs targeted for the next version of Java. The JSR process is used to grant extra intellectual property protections for the whole ecosystem.

When discussing new Java features, it is often useful to refer to an upcoming or recent feature by its JEP number. A complete list of all JEPs, including those that have been delivered or withdrawn, can be found at https://openjdk.java.net/jeps/0.

1.4.4 Incubating and preview features

Within the new release model, Java has two mechanisms for trying out a proposed feature before finalizing it in a later release. The aim of these mechanisms is to provide better features by gathering feedback from a much wider pool of users and potentially changing or withdrawing the feature before it becomes a permanent part of Java.

Incubating features are new APIs and their implementation, which in their simplest form are effectively just a new API shipped as a self-contained module (we will meet the details of Java modules in chapter 2). The name of the module is chosen so that it makes it clear that the API is temporary and will change when the feature is finalized.

> **NOTE** This means that any code that relies upon a nonfinalized version of an incubating feature will have to make changes when the feature becomes final.

One very visible example of an incubating feature is the new support for version 2 of the HTTP protocol, usually referred to as HTTP/2. In Java 9, this was shipped as the incubator module `jdk.incubator.http`. The naming of this module, and the use of the `jdk.incubator` namespace rather than `java` clearly marked the feature as nonstandard and subject to change. The feature was standardized in Java 11 when it was moved to the `java.net.http` module in the `java` part of the namespace.

> **NOTE** We will meet another incubating feature in chapter 18 when we discuss the Foreign Access API, which is part of an OpenJDK project codenamed Panama.

The main advantage of this approach is that an incubating feature can be isolated to a single namespace. Developers can quickly try out the feature and even use it in production code, providing they are happy to modify some code and recompile and relink when the feature becomes standardized.

Preview features are the other mechanism that recent Java versions provide for shipping nonfinalized features. They are more intrusive than incubating features because they are implemented as part of the language itself, at a deeper level. These features potentially require support from the following:

- The `javac` compiler
- Bytecode format
- Class file and class loading

They are available only if specific flags are passed to the compiler and runtime. Trying to use preview features without the flags enabled is an error, both at compile time and at runtime.

This makes them much more complex to handle (compared to incubating features). As a result, preview features can't really be used in production. For one thing they are represented by a version of the classfile format that is not finalized and may never be supported by any production version of Java.

This means that preview features are suitable only for experimentation, developer testing, and familiarization. Unfortunately, in almost all deployments, only fully finalized features can be used in code that is destined for production.

Java 11 did not contain any preview features (although a first preview version of *switch expressions* arrived in Java 12), so it's hard to give a good example of one in this section. We'll dig more into preview versions in chapter 3 when we discuss Java 17, though.

1.5 Small changes in Java 11

Since Java 8, a relatively large number of new small features have appeared in successive releases. Let's take a quick tour through some of the most important ones—although this is by no means all the changes. You're most likely to see these features for the first time when moving to Java 11.

1.5.1 Collections factories (JEP 213)

An often-requested enhancement is to extend Java to support a simple way to declare *collection literals*—a dumb collection of objects (such as a list or a map). This seems attractive because many other languages support some form of this, and Java itself has always had array literals, as shown here:

```
jshell> int[] numbers = {1, 2, 3};
numbers ==> int[3] { 1, 2, 3 }
```

However, although it seems superficially attractive, adding this feature at the language level has some significant drawbacks. For example, although `ArrayList`, `HashMap`, and `HashSet` are the implementations that are most familiar to developers, a primary design principle of the Java Collections are that they are represented as interfaces, not classes. Other implementations are available and are widely used.

This means that it would run counter to the design intent to have a new syntax that directly couples to specific implementations, no matter how common. Instead, the design decision was to add simple factory methods to the relevant interfaces, exploiting the fact that Java 8 added the ability to have static methods on interfaces. The resulting code looks like this:

```
Set<String> set = Set.of("a", "b", "c");

var list = List.of("x", "y");
```

Although this method is a little more verbose than adding support at language level, the complexity cost in implementation terms is substantially less. These new methods are implemented as a set of overloads as follows:

```
List<E> List<E>.<E>of()
List<E> List<E>.<E>of(E e1)
List<E> List<E>.<E>of(E e1, E e2)
List<E> List<E>.<E>of(E e1, E e2, E e3)
List<E> List<E>.<E>of(E e1, E e2, E e3, E e4)
List<E> List<E>.<E>of(E e1, E e2, E e3, E e4, E e5)
List<E> List<E>.<E>of(E e1, E e2, E e3, E e4, E e5, E e6)
List<E> List<E>.<E>of(E e1, E e2, E e3, E e4, E e5, E e6, E e7)
List<E> List<E>.<E>of(E e1, E e2, E e3, E e4, E e5, E e6, E e7, E e8)
List<E> List<E>.<E>of(E e1, E e2, E e3, E e4, E e5, E e6, E e7, E e8, E e9)
List<E> List<E>.<E>of(E e1, E e2, E e3, E e4, E e5, E e6, E e7, E e8, E e9,
   E e10)
List<E> List<E>.<E>of(E... elements)
```

The common cases (up to 10 elements) are provided, along with a varargs form for the unlikely use case that more than 10 elements are required in the collection.

For maps, the situation is a little more complicated, because maps have two generic parameters (the key type and the value type) and so, although the simple cases can be written like this:

```
var m1 = Map.of(k1, v1);
var m2 = Map.of(k1, v1, k2, v2);
```

there is no simple way of writing the equivalent of the varargs form for map. Instead, a different factory method, ofEntries(), is used in combination with a static helper method, entry(), to provide an equivalent of a varargs form, as shown next:

```
Map.ofEntries(
    entry(k1, v1),
    entry(k2, v2),
    // ...
    entry(kn, vn));
```

One final point that developers should be aware of: the factory methods produce instances of immutable types, as follows:

```
jshell> var ints = List.of(2, 3, 5, 7);
ints ==> [2, 3, 5, 7]

jshell> ints.getClass();
$2 ==> class java.util.ImmutableCollections$ListN
```

These class are new implementations of the Java Collections interfaces that are immutable—they are not the familiar, mutable classes (such as ArrayList and Hash-Map). Attempts to modify instances of these types will result in an exception being thrown.

1.5.2 *Remove enterprise modules (JEP 320)*

Over time, Java Standard Edition (aka Java SE) had a few modules added to it that were really part of Java Enterprise Edition (Java EE) such as

- JAXB
- JAX-WS
- CORBA
- JTA

In Java 9, the following packages that implemented these technologies were moved into noncore modules and deprecated for removal:

- java.activation (JAF)
- java.corba (CORBA)
- java.transaction (JTA)

- java.xml.bind (JAXB)
- java.xml.ws (JAX-WS, plus some related technologies)
- java.xml.ws.annotation (Common Annotations)

As part of an effort to streamline the platform, in Java 11 these modules have been removed. The following three related modules used for tooling and aggregation have also been removed from the core SE distribution:

- java.se.ee (aggregator module for the six modules above)
- jdk.xml.ws (tools for JAX-WS)
- jdk.xml.bind (tools for JAXB)

Projects built on Java 11 and later that want to use these capabilities now require the inclusion of an explicit external dependency. This means that some programs that relied upon these APIs built cleanly under Java 8 but require modifications to their build script to build under Java 11. We will investigate this specific issue more fully in chapter 11.

1.5.3　HTTP/2 (Java 11)

In modern times, a new version of the HTTP standard has been released—HTTP/2. We're going to examine the reasons for finally updating the venerable HTTP 1.1 specification (dating from 1997!). Then we'll see how Java 11 gives the well-grounded developer access to the new features and performance of HTTP/2.

As you might expect for technology from 1997, HTTP 1.1 has been showing its age, particularly around performance in modern web applications. Limitations include problems such as:

- Head-of-line blocking
- Restricted connections to a single site
- Performance overhead of HTTP control headers

HTTP/2 is a *transport*-level update to the protocol focused on fixing these sorts of fundamental performance issues that don't fit how the web really works today. With its performance focus on how bytes flow between client and server, HTTP/2 actually doesn't alter many of the familiar HTTP concepts—request/response, headers, status codes, response bodies—all of these remain semantically the same in HTTP/2 vs. HTTP 1.1.

HEAD-OF-LINE BLOCKING

Communication in HTTP takes place over TCP sockets. Although HTTP 1.1 defaulted to reusing individual sockets to avoid repeating unnecessary setup costs, the protocol dictated that requests be returned in order, even when multiple requests shared a socket (known as *pipelining*; see figure 1.4). This means that a slow response from the server blocked subsequent requests, which theoretically could have been returned sooner. These effects are readily visible in places like browser rendering stalling on downloading assets. The same one-response-per-connection-at-a-time behavior can also limit JVM applications talking to HTTP-based services.

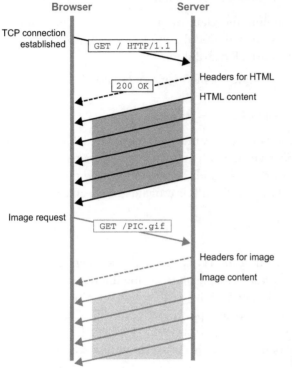

Figure 1.4   HTTP 1.1 transfers

HTTP/2 is designed from the ground up to multiplex requests over the same connection, as shown in figure 1.5. Multiple *streams* between the client and server are always supported. It even allows for separately receiving the headers and the body of a single request.

This fundamentally changes assumptions that decades of HTTP 1.1 have made second nature to many developers. For instance, it's long been accepted that returning lots of small assets on a website performed worse than making larger bundles. JavaScript, CSS, and images all have common techniques and tooling for smashing many smaller files together to return more efficiently. In HTTP/2, multiplexed responses mean your resources don't get blocked behind other slow requests, and smaller responses may be more accurately cached, yielding a better experience overall.

RESTRICTED CONNECTIONS

The HTTP 1.1 specification recommends limiting to two connections to a server at a time. This is listed as a *should* rather than a *must*, and modern web browsers often allow between six and eight connections per domain. This limit to concurrent downloads from a site has often led developers to serve sites from multiple domains or implement the sort of bundling mentioned before.

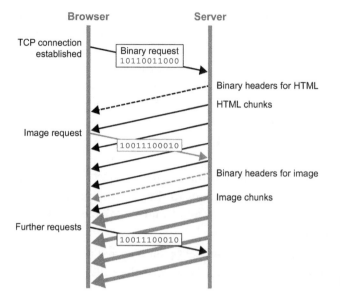

Figure 1.5   HTTP/2 transfers

HTTP/2 addresses this situation: each connection can effectively be used to make as many simultaneous requests as desired. Browsers open only one connection to a given domain but can perform many requests over that same connection at the same time.

In our JVM applications, where we might have pooled HTTP 1.1 connections to allow for more concurrent activity, HTTP/2 gives us another built-in way to squeeze out more requests.

HTTP HEADER PERFORMANCE

A significant feature of HTTP is the ability to send *headers* alongside requests. Headers are a critical part of how the HTTP protocol itself is stateless, but our applications can maintain state between requests (such as the fact your user is logged in).

Although the body of HTTP 1.1 payloads may be compressed if the client and server can agree on the algorithm (typically gzip), headers don't participate. As richer web applications make more and more requests, the repetition of increasingly large headers can be a problem, especially for larger websites.

HTTP/2 addresses this problem with a new binary format for headers. As a user of the protocol, you don't have to think much about this—it's simply built in to how headers are transmitted between client and server.

TLS ALL THE THINGS

In 1997, HTTP 1.1 entered a very different internet than we see today. Commerce on the internet was only starting to take off, and security wasn't always a top concern in early protocol designs. Computing systems were also slow enough to make practices like encryption often far too expensive.

HTTP/2 was officially accepted in 2015 into a world that was far more security conscious. In addition, the computing needs for ubiquitous encryption of web requests through TLS (known in earlier versions as SSL) are low enough to have removed most arguments over whether or not to encrypt. As such, in practice, HTTP/2 is supported only with TLS encryption (the protocol does, in theory, allow for transmission in cleartext, but none of the major implementations provide it).

This has an operational impact on deploying HTTP/2, because it requires a certificate with a lifecycle of expiration and renewal. For enterprises, this increases the need for certificate management. Let's Encrypt (https://www.letsencrypt.org), and other private options have been growing in response to this need.

OTHER CONSIDERATIONS

Although the future is trending toward the uptake of HTTP/2, deployment of it across the web hasn't been fast. In addition to the encryption requirement, which even impacts local development, this delay may be attributable to the following rough edges and extra complexity:

- HTTP/2 is binary-only; working with an opaque format is challenging.
- HTTP layer products such as load balancers, firewalls, and debugging tools require updates to support HTTP/2.
- Performance benefits are aimed mainly at the browser-based use of HTTP. Backend services working over HTTP may see less benefit to updating.

HTTP/2 IN JAVA 11

The arrival of a new HTTP version after so many years motivated JEP 110 to introduce an entirely new API. Within the JDK, this replaces (but doesn't remove) `HttpURL-Connection` while aiming to put a usable HTTP API "in the box," as it were, because many developers have reached for external libraries to fulfill their HTTP-related needs.

The resulting HTTP/2- and web socket–compatible API came first to Java 9 as an Incubating feature. JEP 321 moved it to its permanent home in Java 11 under `java.net.http`. The new API supports HTTP 1.1 as well as HTTP/2 and can fall back to HTTP 1.1 when a server being called doesn't support HTTP/2.

Interactions with the new API start from the `HttpRequest` and `HttpClient` types. These are instantiated via builders, setting configurations before issuing the actual HTTP call, as shown next:

```
var client = HttpClient.newBuilder().build();

var uri = new URI("https://google.com");
var request = HttpRequest.newBuilder(uri).build();

var response = client.send(
    request,
    HttpResponse.BodyHandlers.ofString(
        Charset.defaultCharset()));

System.out.println(response.body());
```

Constructs an HttpClient instance we can use to make requests

Constructs a specific request to Google with an HttpRequest instance

Synchronously makes the HTTP request and saves its response. This line blocks until the entire request has completed.

The send method needs a handler to tell it what to do with the response body. Here we use a standard handler to return the body as a String.

This demonstrates the synchronous use of the API. After building our request and client, we issue the HTTP call with the send method. We won't receive the response object back until the full HTTP call has completed, much like the older HTTP APIs in the JDK.

The first parameter is the request we set up, but the second deserves a closer look. Rather than expecting to always return a single type, the send method expects us to provide an implementation of the HttpResponse.BodyHandler<T> interface to tell it how to handle the response. HttpResponse.BodyHandlers provides some useful basic handlers for receiving your response as a byte array, as a string, or as a file. But customizing this behavior is just an implementation of BodyHandler away. All of this plumbing is based on the java.util.concurrent.Flow publisher and subscriber mechanisms, a form of programming known as reactive streams.

One of the most significant benefits of HTTP/2 is its built-in multiplexing. Only using a synchronous send doesn't really gain those benefits, so it should come as no surprise that HttpClient also supports a sendAsync method. sendAsync returns a CompletableFuture wrapped around the HttpResponse, providing a rich set of capabilities that may be familiar from other parts of the platform, as shown here:

```
var client = HttpClient.newBuilder().build();        Creates the client and
                                                      request as before
var uri = new URI("https://google.com");
var request = HttpRequest.newBuilder(uri).build();    Uses CompletableFuture.allOf
                                                      to wait for all the requests to
var handler = HttpResponse.BodyHandlers.ofString();   finish
CompletableFuture.allOf(
                                                      When the future completes,
    client.sendAsync(request, handler)                we use thenAccept to
        .thenAccept((resp) ->                         receive the response.
                    System.out.println(resp.body()),
    client.sendAsync(request, handler)                We can reuse the same
        .thenAccept((resp) ->                         client to make multiple
                    System.out.println(resp.body()),  requests simultaneously.
    client.sendAsync(request, handler)
        .thenAccept((resp) ->
                    System.out.println(resp.body())
).join();
```

sendAsync starts an HTTP request but returns a future and does not block.

Here we set up a request and client again, but then we asynchronously repeat the call three separate times. CompletableFuture.allOf combines these three futures, so we can wait on them all to finish with a single join.

This only scratches the two main entry points to this API. It offers tons of features and customization, from the configuration of timeouts and TLS, all the way to advanced asynchronous features like receiving HTTP/2 server pushes via HttpResponse.PushPromiseHandler.

Building off the futures and reactive streams, the new HTTP API in the JDK provides an attractive alternative to the large libraries that have dominated the ecosystem in the HTTP space. Designed with modern asynchronous programming at the forefront, `java.net.http` puts Java in an excellent place for wherever the web evolves to in the future.

1.5.4 Single-file source-code programs (JEP 330)

The usual way that Java programs are executed is by compiling source code to a class file and then starting up a virtual machine process that acts as an execution container to interpret the bytecode of the class.

This is very different from languages like Python, Ruby, and Perl, where the source code of a program is interpreted directly. The Unix environment has a long history of these types of *scripting languages*, but Java has not traditionally been counted among them.

With the arrival of JEP 330, Java 11 offers a new way to execute programs. Source code can be compiled in memory and then executed by the interpreter without ever producing a .class file on disk, as shown in figure 1.6.

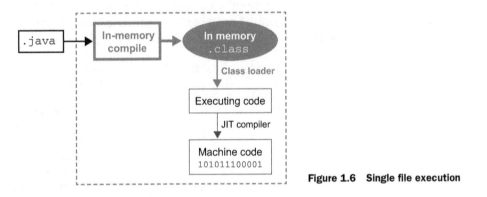

Figure 1.6   Single file execution

This gives a user experience that is like Python and other scripting languages.

The feature has some limitations, including the following:

- It is limited to code that lives in a single source file.
- It cannot compile additional source files in the same run.
- It may contain any number of classes in the source file.
- It must have the first class declared in the source file as the entry point.
- It must define the main method in the entry point class.

The feature also uses a `--source` flag to indicate source code compatibility mode— essentially the language level of the script.

Java file-naming conventions must be followed for execution, so the class name should match the filename. However, the .java extension should *not* be used because this can confuse the launcher.

These types of Java scripts can also contain a shebang line, as shown next:

```
#!/usr/bin/java --source 11

public final class HTTP2Check {
    public static void main(String[] args) {
        if (args.length < 1) {
            usage();
        }
        // implementation of our HTTP callers...
    }
}
```

Full code for HTTP2Check is provided in project resources.

The shebang line provides the necessary parameters so that the file can be marked executable and directly invoked, like this:

```
$ ./HTTP2Check https://www.google.com
https://www.google.com: HTTP_2
```

Although this feature does not bring the full experience of scripting languages to Java, it can be a useful way of writing simple, useful tools in the Unix tradition without introducing another programming language into the mix.

Summary

- The Java language and platform are two separate (if strongly related) components of the Java ecosystem. The platform supports many languages beyond just Java.
- After Java 8, the Java platform has adopted a new timed-release process. New versions arrive every six months and a Long-Term-Support (LTS) release comes out every two or three years.
- The current LTS versions are 11 and 17, with Java 8 still being supported for now.
- With its focus on backward compatibility, making changes to Java can often be difficult. Changes restricted to just the library or compiler are often much simpler than changes that also require updates in the virtual machine.
- Java 11 introduced many useful features that are worth upgrading for:
  - The var keyword to streamline variable definitions
  - Factory methods to simplify creating lists, maps, and other collections
  - A new HttpClient implementation with full HTTP/2 support
  - Single-file programs that can be run directly without compiling to class files

Java modules

2

This chapter covers

- Java's platform modules
- Changes to access control semantics
- Writing modular applications
- Multi-release JARs

As mentioned in chapter 1, versions of Java, up to and including Java 9, were delivered according to a feature-driven release plan, often with a major new capability that defined or was strongly associated with the release.

For Java 9, this feature was Java Platform Modules (also known as JPMS, Jigsaw, or just "modules"). This is a major enhancement and change to the Java platform that had been discussed for many years—it was originally conceived of as potentially shipping as a part of Java 7, back in 2009/2010.

In this chapter, we will explain the reasons modules are needed, as well as the new syntax used to articulate modularity concepts and how to use them in your applications. This will enable you to use JDK and third-party modules in your build as well as packaging apps or libraries as modules.

NOTE Modules represent a new way of packaging and deploying your code, and adopting them will make your applications better. However, if you just want to start using modern Java features (11 or 17), there is no need for you to adopt modules immediately unless you want to.

The arrival of modules has profound implications for the architecture of applications, and modules have many benefits to modern projects that are concerned about such aspects as process footprint, startup cost, and warmup time. Modules can also help to solve the so-called JAR Hell problem that can plague Java applications with complex dependencies. Let's get to know them.

2.1 Setting the scene

A *module* is a fundamentally new concept in the Java language (as of Java 9). It is a unit of application deployment and dependency that has semantic meaning to the runtime. This is different from existing concepts in Java for the following reasons:

- JAR files are invisible to the runtime—they're basically just zipped directories containing class files.
- Packages are really just namespaces to group classes together for access control.
- Dependencies are defined at the class level only.
- Access control and reflection combine in a way that produces a fundamentally open system without clear deployment unit boundaries and with minimal enforcement.

Modules, on the other hand

- Define dependency information between modules, so all sorts of resolution and linkage problems can be detected at compile or application start time
- Provide proper encapsulation, so internal packages and classes can be made safe from pesky users who might want to fiddle with them
- Are a proper unit of deployment with metadata that can be understood and consumed by a modern Java runtime and are represented in the Java type system (e.g., reflectively)

NOTE Before modules, within the core language and runtime environment, there was no aggregated dependency metadata. Instead, it was defined only in build systems like Maven or in third-party modules systems (such as OSGI or JBoss modules) that the JVM neither knows nor cares about.

Java platform modules represent an implementation of a missing concept within the Java world as it existed at version 8.

NOTE Java modules are often packaged as special JAR files, but they are not tied to that format (we will see other possible formats later).

The aim of the modules system is to make the deployment units (modules) as independent of each other as possible. The idea is that modules are able to be separately loaded and linked, although in practice, real applications may well end up depending on a group of modules that provide related capabilities (such as security).

2.1.1 Project Jigsaw

The project within OpenJDK to deliver the modules feature was known as *Project Jigsaw*. It aimed to deliver a full-featured modularity solution which included the following goals:

- Modularizing the JDK platform source
- Reducing the process footprint
- Improving the application startup time
- Having modules available to both the JDK and to application code
- Allowing true strict encapsulation for the first time in Java
- Adding new, previously impossible access control modes to the Java language

These goals were, in turn, driven by the following other objectives that are more closely focused on the JDK and Java runtime:

- Bringing the end of a single, monolithic runtime JAR (rt.jar)
- Properly encapsulating and protecting JDK internals
- Allowing major internal changes to be made (including changes that will break unauthorized non-JDK usage)
- Introducing modules as "super packages"

These secondary goals may require a bit more explanation because they are more closely connected to internal and implementation aspects of the platform.

MODULAR, NOT MONOLITHIC JAVA RUNTIME

The legacy JAR format is essentially just a zip file that contains classes. It dates back to the earliest days of the platform and is in no way optimized for Java classes and applications. Abandoning the JAR format for the platform classes can help in several areas—for example, enabling much better startup performance.

Modules provide two new formats—*JMOD* and *JIMAGE*—which are used at different times (compile/link time and runtime, respectively) in the program lifecycle.

The JMOD format is somewhat similar to the existing JAR format, but it has been modified to allow the inclusion of native code as part of a single file (rather than having to ship a separate shared object file as is done in Java 8). For most developer needs, including publishing modules to Maven, it's better to package your own modules as modular JARs rather than as JMODs.

The JIMAGE format is used to represent a Java runtime image. Until Java 8, only two possible runtime images existed (JDK and JRE), but this was largely an accident of history. Oracle introduced the *Server JRE* with Java 8 (as well as *Compact Profiles*) as a stepping-stone toward full modularity. These images basically removed some capabilities (e.g., GUI frameworks) to provide a smaller footprint specifically geared toward the needs of server-side applications.

A modular application has enough metadata that the exact set of dependencies can be known before program start. This leads to the possibility that only what is needed has to be loaded, which is much more efficient. It is possible to go even further and define a *custom runtime image* that can be shipped along with an application and that does not contain a full, general-purpose installation of Java but only what the application requires. We will encounter this last possibility at the end of this chapter when we meet the `jlink` tool.

For now, let's meet the `jimage` tool that's available to show details about a Java runtime image. For example, for a Java 15 full runtime (i.e., what used to be contained in a JDK), see the following code sample:

```
$ jimage info $JAVA_HOME/lib/modules
 Major Version:  1
 Minor Version:  0
 Flags:          0
 Resource Count: 32780
 Table Length:   32780
 Offsets Size:   131120
 Redirects Size: 131120
 Locations Size: 680101
 Strings Size:   746471
 Index Size:     1688840
```

or

```
$ jimage list $JAVA_HOME/lib/modules
jimage: /Library/Java/JavaVirtualMachines/java15/Contents/Home/lib/modules

Module: java.base
    META-INF/services/java.nio.file.spi.FileSystemProvider
    apple/security/AppleProvider$1.class
    apple/security/AppleProvider$ProviderService.class
    apple/security/AppleProvider.class
    apple/security/KeychainStore$CertKeychainItemPair.class
    apple/security/KeychainStore$KeyEntry.class
    apple/security/KeychainStore$TrustedCertEntry.class
    apple/security/KeychainStore.class
    com/sun/crypto/provider/AESCipher$AES128_CBC_NoPadding.class
    ... many, many lines of output
```

Moving away from `rt.jar` allows for better startup performance and to optimize for only what is needed by an application. The new formats are designed to be opaque to the developer and are implementation-dependent. It is no longer possible to just unzip `rt.jar` and get back the JDK's class library. This is just one step, however, in making the platform's internals less accessible to Java programmers, which was one of the goals of the modules system.

ENCAPSULATE THE INTERNALS

The contract between the Java platform and its users was always intended to be an API contract—that backward compatibility would be maintained at the interface level, *not* in the details of the implementation.

However, Java developers have not held up their end of the bargain and, instead, over time, have tended to use parts of the platform implementation that were never intended for public consumption.

This is problematic, because the OpenJDK platform developers want the freedom to modify the implementation of the JVM and platform classes to future-proof and modernize them—to provide new features and better performance without worrying about breaking user applications.

One major impediment to making breaking changes to the platform internals is Java's approach to access control as it exists in Java 8. Java only defines `public`, `private`, `protected`, and `package-private` as access control levels, and these modifiers are applied only at the class level and finer.

We can work around these restrictions in numerous ways (such as reflection or creating additional classes in relevant packages), and there is no foolproof (or expert-proof) way to fully protect the internals.

The use of the workarounds to access the internals was historically often for valid reasons. As the platform has matured, however, an official way of accessing almost all of the desired functionality has been added. The unprotected internals, therefore, represent a liability for the platform going forward without a corresponding benefit—and modularity was one way to remove that legacy problem.

To sum up, Project Jigsaw was a way to solve several problems at once—primarily to reduce runtime size, improve startup time, and tidy up dependencies between internal packages. These were problems that were hard (or impossible) to tackle incrementally. Opportunities for these types of "nonlocal" improvement do not come along very often, especially in mature software platforms, so the Jigsaw team wanted to take advantage of their circumstances.

THE JVM IS MODULAR NOW

To see this, consider the next very simple program:

```
public class StackTraceDemo {
    public static void main(String[] args) {
        var i = Integer.parseInt("Fail");
    }
}
```

Compiling and running this code produces a runtime exception, shown next:

```
$ java StackTraceDemo
Exception in thread "main" java.lang.NumberFormatException:
  For input string: "Fail"
    at java.base/java.lang.NumberFormatException.forInputString(
    NumberFormatException.java:65)
```

```
    at java.base/java.lang.Integer.parseInt(Integer.java:652)
    at java.base/java.lang.Integer.parseInt(Integer.java:770)
    at StackTraceDemo.main(StackTraceDemo.java:3)
```

However, we can clearly see that the format of the stack trace has changed somewhat from the form that was used in Java 8. In particular, the stack frames are now qualified by a module name (`java.base`) as well as a package name, class name, and line number. This clearly shows that the modular nature of the platform is pervasive and is present for even the simplest program.

2.1.2 *The module graph*

Key to all of modularity is the *module graph*, which is a representation of how modules depend on each other. Modules make their dependencies explicit via some new syntax, and those dependencies are hard guarantees that the compiler and runtime can rely upon. One very important concept is that the module graph must be a *directed acyclic graph* (DAG), so in mathematical terms, there cannot be any cyclic dependencies.

> **NOTE** It is important to realize that in modern Java environments, all applications run on top of the modular JRE; a "modular mode" and a "legacy classpath mode" don't exist.

Although not every developer needs to become an expert in the modules system, it makes sense that a well-grounded Java developer would benefit from a working knowledge of a new subsystem that has changed the way that all programs are executed on the JVM. Let's take a look at a first view of the modules system, shown in figure 2.1, as most developers encounter it.

In figure 2.1, we can see a simplified view of some of the main modules in the JDK. Note that the module `java.base` is always a dependency of every module. When drawing pictures of module graphs, the implicit dependency on `java.base` is often eliminated just to reduce visual clutter.

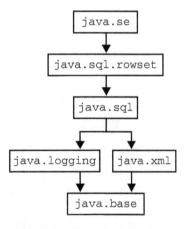

Figure 2.1 JDK system modules (simplified view)

The clean and relatively simple set of module boundaries that we can see in figure 2.1 needs to be contrasted with the state of the JDK in Java 8. Unfortunately, before modules, Java's top-level unit of code was the package—and Java 8 had almost 1,000 of them in the standard runtime. This would be essentially impossible to draw, and the dependencies within the graph would be so complex that a human would not be able to make sense of it.

Taking the premodular JDK and reshaping it into the well-defined form that we see today was not easy to achieve, and the path to delivering JDK modularity was long. Java 9 was released in September 2017, but development of the feature had begun several years before that with the Java 8 release train. In particular, there were several subgoals that were necessary first steps for the delivery of modules, including the following:

- Modularizing the layout of source code in the JDK (JEP 201)
- Modularizing the structure of runtime images (JEP 220)
- Disentangling complex implementation dependencies between JDK packages

Even though the finished modules feature did not ship until Java 9, much of the cleanup was undertaken as part of Java 8 and even allowed a feature known as *compact profiles* (which we will meet at the end of this chapter) to ship as part of that release.

2.1.3   *Protecting the internals*

One of the major problems that modules needed to solve was overcoupling of user Java frameworks to internal implementation details. For example, this piece of Java 8 code extends an internal class to get access to a low-level *URL canonicalizer.*

The following code is for demonstration purposes only, so we can have a concrete example to discuss modules and access control—your code should never access internal classes directly:

```
import sun.net.URLCanonicalizer;

public class MyURLHandler extends URLCanonicalizer {

    public boolean isSimple(String url) {
        return isSimpleHostName(url);
    }
}
```

A URL canonicalizer is a piece of code that takes a URL in one of the various forms permitted by the URL standard and converts it to a standard (canonical) form. The intent is that canonical URLs can act as a single source of truth for the location of content that can be accessed via multiple different possible URLs. If we try to compile it using Java 8, javac warns us that we're accessing an internal API, as shown next:

```
$ javac MyURLHandler.java
MyURLHandler.java:1: warning: URLCanonicalizer is internal proprietary API
  and may be removed in a future release

import sun.net.URLCanonicalizer;
              ^
MyURLHandler.java:3: warning: URLCanonicalizer is internal proprietary API
  and may be removed in a future release

public class MyURLHandler extends URLCanonicalizer {
                                  ^
2 warnings
```

However, by default, the compiler still allows access, and the result is a user class that is tightly coupled to the internal implementation of the JDK. This connection is fragile and will break if the called code moves or is replaced.

If enough developers abuse this openness, then this leads to a situation in which it is difficult or impossible to make changes to the internals, because to do so would break deployed libraries and applications.

> **NOTE** The URLCanonicalizer class needs to be called from several different packages, not just its own, so it has to be a public class—it can't be package-private—meaning it's accessible to anyone.

The solution to this very general problem was to make a one-time change to Java's model of access control. This change applies both to user code calling the JDK and to applications calling third-party libraries.

2.1.4 New access control semantics

Modules add a new concept to Java's access control model: the idea of *exporting* a package. In Java 8 and earlier, code in any package can call public methods on any public class in any package. This is sometimes called "shotgun privacy," after a famous quote about another programming language:

> *Perl doesn't have an infatuation with enforced privacy. It would prefer that you stayed out of its living room because you weren't invited, not because it has a shotgun.*

> —Larry Wall

For Java, however, shotgun privacy represented a major problem. More and more libraries were using internal APIs to provide capabilities that were difficult or impossible to provide in another way, and this threatened to harm the long-term health of the platform.

As of Java 8, there was no way to enforce access control across an entire package. This meant that the JDK team was unable to define a public API and know with certainty that clients of that API could not subvert it or directly link to the internal implementation.

The convention that anything in a package that starts java or javax is a public API and everything else is internal only is just that—a convention. No VM or class loading mechanism enforces that, as we've already seen.

With modules, however, this changes. The exports keyword has been introduced to indicate which packages are considered the public API of a module. In the modular JDK, the package sun.net is not exported, so the previous Java 8 URL canonicalizer code will not compile. Here's what happens when we try with Java 11:

```
$ javac src/ch02/MyURLHandler.java
src/ch02/MyURLHandler.java:3: error: package sun.net is not visible
import sun.net.URLCanonicalizer;
          ^
  (package sun.net is declared in module java.base, which does not export
```

```
      it to the unnamed module)
src/ch02/MyURLHandler.java:8: error: cannot find symbol
        return isSimpleHostName(url);
                 ^
  symbol:    method isSimpleHostName(String)
  location: class MyURLHandler
2 errors
```

Note that the form of the error message explicitly says that the `sun.net` package is now not visible—the compiler cannot even see the symbol. This is a fundamental change in the way Java access control works. Only methods on exported packages are accessible. It is no longer the case that a public method on a public class is automatically visible to all code everywhere.

However, this change may not be visible to many developers. If you're a Java developer who plays by the rules, you will never have called an API in an internal package directly. However, you might use a library or a framework that does, so it's good to understand what has actually changed and avoid the FUD.

> **NOTE** Proper encapsulation is not free, and premodular Java is actually a very open system. It is perhaps only natural that when confronted with the more structured system that modules provide, many Java developers find some of the extra protections constraining or frustrating. Let's meet the syntax that encodes these new semantics of Java modules.

2.2   Basic modules syntax

A Java platform module is defined as a conceptual unit, which is a collection of packages and classes that are declared and loaded as a single entity. Each module must declare a new file, called a *module descriptor*, represented as a module-info.java file, which contains the following:

- Module name
- Module dependencies
- Public API (packages exported)
- Reflective access permissions
- Services provided
- Services consumed

This file must be placed in a suitable place within the source hierarchy. For example, within a Maven-style layout, the full module name `wgjd.discovery` appears directly after src/main/java and contains module-info.java and the package root, as shown here:

```
src
  └── main
        └── java
              └── wgjd.discovery
                    ├── wgjd
```

```
|    └── discovery
|        ├── internal
|        |   ├── AttachOutput.java
|        |   └── PlainAttachOutput.java
|        ├── VMIntrospector.java
|        └── Discovery.java
└── module-info.java
```

This is, of course, slightly different from nonmodular Java projects, which often nominate src/main/java as the root of the package directories. However, the familiar hierarchical structure of packages under the module root is still visible.

> **NOTE** When a modular project is built, the module descriptor will be compiled into a class file, module-info.class, but that file (despite its name) is actually quite different from the usual sort of class file that we see in the Java platform.

In this chapter we will address the basic directives of the descriptor but will not be delving deeply into all of the capabilities that modules provide. In particular, we will not discuss the services aspects of modules.

A simple example of a module descriptor looks like this:

```
module wgjd.discovery {
  exports wgjd.discovery;

  requires java.instrument;
  requires jdk.attach;
  requires jdk.internal.jvmstat;
}
```

This contains three new keywords—module, exports, and requires—in a syntax that should be suggestive to most Java programmers. The keyword module simply declares the opening scope of the declaration.

> **NOTE** The name module-info.java is reminiscent of package-info.java, and they are somewhat related. Because packages are not really visible to the runtime, a workaround (hack?) was needed to provide a hook for annotation metadata that was intended to apply to the whole package. This hack was package-info.java. In the modular world, much more metadata can be associated with a module, and so a similar name was chosen. The new syntax actually consists of *restricted keywords*, which are described in the Java Language Specification like this:
>
> *A further ten character sequences are restricted keywords:* open, module, requires, transitive, exports, opens, to, uses, provides, *and* with. *These character sequences are tokenized as keywords solely where they appear as terminals in the* ModuleDeclaration *and* ModuleDirective *productions.*

In simpler language, this means these new keywords will appear only in the descriptor for the module metadata and are not treated as keywords in general Java source. However, it is good practice to avoid these words as Java identifiers, even if it is technically legal to use them. This is the same situation as we saw with var in chapter 1, and we will use looser language and refer to them as "keywords" throughout the rest of the book.

2.2.1   *Exporting and requiring*

The exports keyword expects an argument, which is a package name. In our example

```
exports wgjd.discovery;
```

means that our example discovery module exports the package wgjd.discovery, but because the descriptor does not mention any other packages, wgjd.discovery .internal is not exported and is not normally available to code outside the discovery module.

Multiple exports lines are possible in a module descriptor and, in fact, are quite usual. Fine-grained control is also possible with the exports … to … syntax that indicates only certain external modules may access a specified package from this module.

> **NOTE** A single module exports one or more packages that constitute the public API of the module and that are the only packages that code in other modules may access unless an override (e.g., command-line switch) is used.

The requires keyword declares a dependency of the current module and always requires an argument, which is a *module* name, rather than a package name. The java.base module contains the most fundamental packages and classes of the Java runtime. We can use the jmod command to take a look, as follows:

```
$ jmod describe $JAVA_HOME/jmods/java.base.jmod
java.base@11.0.3
exports java.io
exports java.lang
exports java.lang.annotation
exports java.lang.invoke
exports java.lang.module
exports java.lang.ref
exports java.lang.reflect
exports java.math
exports java.net
exports java.net.spi
exports java.nio
// ... many, many more lines of output
```

These packages are used by every Java program, and so java.base is always an implicit dependency of every module, so does not need to be explicitly declared in module-info.java. This is in much the same way that java.lang is an implicit import into every Java class.

Some of the basic rules and conventions for module names follow:

- Modules live in a global namespace.
- Module names must be unique.
- Use the standard `com.company.project` convention if appropriate.

One important basic modules concept is *transitivity*. Let's take a closer look at this concept, because it occurs not only in the context of modules but also in Java's more familiar library (i.e., JAR file) dependencies (which we will meet in chapter 11).

2.2.2 *Transitivity*

Transitivity is a very general computing term, not specific to Java at all, which describes the situation that occurs when a code unit requires other units to function correctly, and those units can themselves require other units. Our original code may never even mention these "one step removed" code units, but they still need to be present or our application will not work.

To understand why this is the case—and why it is important—consider two modules A and B where A requires B. There are two different possible cases:

- A does not export any methods that mention types from B directly.
- A includes types from B as part of its API.

In the case where A exports methods that return types that are defined in B, this would have the effect that A is not usable unless clients of A (those modules that require A) also require B. This is quite an unnecessary overhead on clients of A.

The modules system provides some simple syntax to solve this: `requires transitive`. If a module A requires another module transitively, then any code that depends on A will also, implicitly, pick up the transitive dependencies as well.

Although usage of `requires transitive` is unavoidable in some use cases, in general, when writing modules, minimizing use of transitivity is considered a best practice. We will have more to say about transitive dependencies when we discuss build tools in chapter 11.

2.3 *Loading modules*

If the first time you've encountered Java class loading is when we briefly mentioned it in chapter 1 and you have no other experience of it, don't worry. The most important thing to know right now is that the following four types of modules exist, some of which have slightly different behaviors when loaded:

- Platform modules
- Application modules
- Automatic modules
- Unnamed module

On the other hand, if you're already familiar with class loading, you should know that the arrival of modules has changed some of the details of the way that class loading operates.

A modern JVM has module-aware class loaders, and the way that the JRE classes are loaded is quite different than in Java 8. One key concept is the *module path,* which is a sequence of paths to modules (or directories that contain modules). This is similar to, but separate from, the traditional Java classpath.

> **NOTE** We will meet class loading properly in chapter 4 and introduce the modern way of doing things to both new and experienced readers.

The fundamental principles of the modular approach to class loading follow:

- Modules are resolved from the module path, not the old-school classpath.
- At startup, the JVM resolves a graph of modules, which must be acyclic.
- One module is the root of the graph and is where execution starts from. It contains the class with the main method that will be the entry point.

Dependencies that have already been modularized are known as *application modules* and are placed on the module path. Unmodularized dependencies are placed on the familiar classpath, and are coopted into the modules system via a migration mechanism.

Module resolution uses depth-first traversal, and because the graph must be acyclic, the resolution algorithm will terminate (and in linear time). Let's delve a little more deeply into each of the four types of modules.

2.3.1 *Platform modules*

These are modules from the modular JDK itself. They would have been part of the monolithic runtime (rt.jar) in Java 8 (or possibly ancillary JARs, such as tools.jar). We can get a list of the available platform modules from the --list-modules flag, as shown here:

```
$ java --list-modules
java.base@11.0.6
java.compiler@11.0.6
...
java.xml@11.0.6
java.xml.crypto@11.0.6
jdk.accessibility@11.0.6
...
jdk.unsupported@11.0.6
...
```

This code will provide an unabridged list, rather than the partial set that we saw in figure 2.1.

> **NOTE** The exact list of modules and their names will depend on the version of Java in use. For example, on Oracle's GraalVM implementation, some additional modules like com.oracle.graal.graal_enterprise, org.graalvm.js .scriptengine and org.graalvm.sdk may be present.

The platform modules make heavy use of the *qualified exporting* mechanism wherein some packages are exported only to a specified list of modules and are not made generally available.

The most important module in the distribution is `java.base`, which is always an implicit dependency of every other module. It contains `java.lang`, `java.util`, `java.io`, and various other basic packages. The module basically corresponds to the smallest possible Java runtime that an application could require and still run.

At the other end of the spectrum are the *aggregator modules,* which don't contain any code but which serve as a shortcut mechanism to allow applications to bring in a very broad set of dependencies transitively. For example, the `java.se` module brings in the entire Java SE platform.

2.3.2 *Application modules*

These types of modules are the modularized dependencies of an application, or the application itself. This type of module is also sometimes known as a *library module.*

> **NOTE** No technical distinction exists between platform and application modules—the difference is purely philosophical—and which class loader is used to load them, as we will discuss in chapter 4.

The third-party libraries that an application depends on will be application modules. For example, the Jackson libraries for manipulating JSON have been modularized as of version 2.10 and count as application (aka library) modules.

Application modules will typically depend upon both platform modules and other application modules. It is a good idea to try to constrain the dependencies of these modules as much as possible and to avoid requiring, for example, `java.se` as a dependency.

2.3.3 *Automatic modules*

One deliberate design feature of the modules system is that you can't reference the classpath from a module. This restriction seems to be potentially problematic—what happens if a module needs to depend on some code that has not yet been modularized?

The solution is to move the nonmodular JAR file onto the module path (and remove it from the classpath). When this is done, the JAR becomes an *automatic module.* The modules system will automatically generate a name for your module, which is derived from the JAR's name.

An automatic module exports every package that it contains, and automatically depends upon all other modules in the module path. Automatic modules do not have proper module dependency information, because they neither explicitly declare their dependencies nor advertise their API. This means that they are not first-class citizens in the modules system and do not provide the same level of guarantees as genuine Java modules.

It is possible to explicitly declare a name, by adding an entry for `Automatic-Module-Name` into the MANIFEST.MF file in the JAR. This is often done as an intermediate step when migrating to Java modules, because it allows developers to reserve a module name and start to gain some of the benefits of interoperating with modular code.

For example, the Apache Commons Lang library is not yet fully modularized, but it provides `org.apache.commons.lang3` as an automatic module name. Other modules can then declare that they depend upon this automatic module, even if the maintainers of it have not finished transitioning it to full modularity.

2.3.4   *Unnamed module*

All classes and JARs on the classpath are added to a single module, which is the unnamed module, or `UNNAMED`. This is done for backward compatibility but at the cost that the modules system is not as effective as it might be all the time that some code remains in the unnamed module.

For the case of completely nonmodular apps (e.g., Java 8 apps that are running on top of a Java 11 runtime), the contents of the classpath are dumped into the unnamed module, and the root module is taken to be `java.se`.

Modular code cannot depend on the unnamed module, and so in practice, modules cannot depend upon anything in the classpath. Automatic modules are often used to help resolve this situation. Formally, the unnamed module depends upon all modules in JDK and on the module path because it is replicating the premodular behavior.

2.4   *Building a first modular app*

Let's build a first example of a modular application. To do this, we need to build a module graph (which is, of course, a DAG). The graph must have a *root module*, which in our case is the module containing the entry point class of the app. The module graph of the application is the transitive closure of all modular dependencies of the root module.

For our example, we're going to adapt the HTTP site-checking tool we created at the end of chapter 1 to become a modular app. The files will be laid out like this:

```
.
└── wgjd.sitecheck
    └── wgjd
    |   └── sitecheck
    |       ├── concurrent
    |       |   └── ParallelHTTPChecker.java
    |       ├── internal
    |       |   └── TrustEveryone.java
    |       └── HTTPChecker.java
    |       └── SiteCheck.java
    └── module-info.java
```

We're breaking out certain concerns (e.g., the TrustEveryone provider) into their own classes rather than representing them as static inner classes, as we had to when all the code needed to live in a single file. We've also set up separate packages and will not be exporting all of them. The module file is very similar to the one we met earlier, shown here:

```
module wgjd.sitecheck {
  requires java.net.http;
  exports wgjd.sitecheck;
  exports wgjd.sitecheck.concurrent;
}
```

Note the dependency on the module java.net.http. To investigate what happens when a dependency is missed, let's comment out the dependency on the HTTP module and try to compile the project using javac as follows:

```
$ javac -d out wgjd.sitecheck/module-info.java \
    wgjd.sitecheck/wgjd/sitecheck/*.java \
    wgjd.sitecheck/wgjd/sitecheck/*/*.java
wgjd.sitecheck/wgjd/sitecheck/SiteCheck.java:8: error:
  package java.net.http is not visible
import java.net.http.*;
                 ^
  (package java.net.http is declared in module java.net.http, but
      module wgjd.sitecheck does not read it)
wgjd.sitecheck/wgjd/sitecheck/concurrent/ParallelHTTPChecker.java:4:
  error: package java.net.http is not visible
import java.net.http.*;
                 ^

// Several similar errors
```

This failure shows that simple problems with modules can be very easy to solve. The modules system has detected the missing module and is trying to help by suggesting a solution: add the missing module as a dependency. If we make that change, then, as expected, the module builds without complaint. However, more complex problems may require changes to the compilation step or manual intervention via a switch to control the modules system.

2.4.1 Command-line switches for modules

When compiling a module, a number of command-line switches can be used to control the modular aspects of the compile (and, later, execution). The most commonly encountered of these switches follow:

- list-modules—Prints a list of all modules
- module-path—Specifies one or more directories that contain your modules
- add-reads—Adds an additional requires to the resolution
- add-exports—Adds an additional exports to the compilation

- add-opens—Enables reflective access to all types at runtime
- add-modules—Adds the list of modules to the default set
- illegal-access=permit|warn|deny—Changes the reflective access rule

We have already met the majority of these concepts already—with the exception of the qualifiers related to reflection, which we will discuss in detail in section 2.4.3

Let's see one of these switches in action. This will demonstrate a common issue with module packaging and serves as an example of a real-world issue that many developers may encounter when starting to use modules with their own code.

When starting to work with modules, we sometimes find that we need to break encapsulation. For example, an application that has been ported from Java 8 may be expecting to access an internal package that is no longer exported.

For example, let's consider a project with a simple structure that uses the *Attach API* to dynamically connect to other JVMs running on a host and report some basic information about them. It's laid out on disc like this, just as we saw in an earlier example:

```
.
└── wgjd.discovery
    └── wgjd
    |   └── discovery
    |       ├── internal
    |       |   └── AttachOutput.java
    |       └── Discovery.java
    |       └── VMIntrospector.java
    └── module-info.java
```

Compiling the project gives the following series of errors:

```
$ javac -d out/wgjd.discovery wgjd.discovery/module-info.java \
  wgjd.discovery/wgjd/discovery/*.java \
  wgjd.discovery/wgjd/discovery/internal/*

wgjd.discovery/wgjd/discovery/VMIntrospector.java:4: error: package
  sun.jvmstat.monitor is not visible
import sun.jvmstat.monitor.MonitorException;
                  ^
  (package sun.jvmstat.monitor is declared in module jdk.internal.jvmstat,
    which does not export it to module wgjd.discovery)
wgjd.discovery/wgjd/discovery/VMIntrospector.java:5: error: package
  sun.jvmstat.monitor is not visible
import sun.jvmstat.monitor.MonitoredHost;
                  ^
  (package sun.jvmstat.monitor is declared in module jdk.internal.jvmstat,
    which does not export it to module wgjd.discovery)
```

These problems are being caused by some code in the project that makes use of internal APIs, as shown next:

```
public class VMIntrospector implements Consumer<VirtualMachineDescriptor> {

    @Override
    public void accept(VirtualMachineDescriptor vmd) {
        var isAttachable = false;
        var vmVersion = "";
        try {
            var vmId = new VmIdentifier(vmd.id());
            var monitoredHost = MonitoredHost.getMonitoredHost(vmId);
            var monitoredVm = monitoredHost.getMonitoredVm(vmId, -1);
            try {
                isAttachable = MonitoredVmUtil.isAttachable(monitoredVm);
                vmVersion = MonitoredVmUtil.vmVersion(monitoredVm);
            } finally {
                monitoredHost.detach(monitoredVm);
            }
        } catch (URISyntaxException | MonitorException e) {
            e.printStackTrace();
        }

        System.out.println(
                vmd.id() + '\t' + vmd.displayName() + '\t' + vmVersion +
                    '\t' + isAttachable);
    }
}
```

Although classes like VirtualMachineDescriptor are part of the exported interface of the jdk.attach module (because the class is in the exported package com.sun .tools.attach), other classes that we depend on (such as MonitoredVmUtil in sun .jvmstat.monitor) are not accessible. Fortunately, the tools provide a way to soften the module boundaries and provide access to a nonexported package.

To achieve this, we need to add a switch—--add-exports—to force access to the internals of the jdk.internal.jvmstat module, which means we are definitely breaking encapsulation by doing this. The resulting compilation command line looks like this:

```
$ javac -d out/wgjd.discovery \
  --add-exports=jdk.internal.jvmstat/sun.jvmstat.monitor=wgjd.discovery \
  wgjd.discovery/module-info.java \
  wgjd.discovery/wgjd/discovery/*.java \
  wgjd.discovery/wgjd/discovery/internal/*
```

The syntax of --add-exports is that we must provide the module and package name that we require access to and which module is being granted the access.

2.4.2 Executing a modular app

Until the arrival of modules, only the following two methods existed to start a Java application:

```
java -cp classes wgjd.Hello
java -jar my-app.jar
```

These should both be familiar to Java programmers as launching a class and the main class from within a JAR file. In modern Java, two more methods of launching programs have been added. We met a new way of launching single-source-file programs in section 1.5.4, and now we're going to meet the fourth mode: launching the main class of a module. The syntax follows:

```
java --module-path mods -m my.module/my.module.Main
```

However, just as for compilation, we may need additional command-line switches. For example, from our earlier example of introspection:

```
$ java --module-path out -m wgjd.discovery/wgjd.discovery.Discovery
Exception in thread "main" java.lang.IllegalAccessError:
  class wgjd.discovery.VMIntrospector (in module wgjd.discovery) cannot
    access class sun.jvmstat.monitor.MonitorException (in module
      jdk.internal.jvmstat) because module jdk.internal.jvmstat does not
        export sun.jvmstat.monitor to module wgjd.discovery
    at wgjd.discovery/wgjd.discovery.VMIntrospector.accept(
    VMIntrospector.java:19)
    at wgjd.discovery/wgjd.discovery.Discovery.main(Discovery.java:26)
```

To prevent this error, we must also provide the encapsulation-breaking switch to the actual program execution as follows:

```
$ java --module-path out \
  --add-exports=jdk.internal.jvmstat/sun.jvmstat.monitor=wgjd.discovery \
  -m wgjd.discovery/wgjd.discovery.Discovery

Java processes:
PID     Display Name     VM Version     Attachable
53407    wgjd.discovery/wgjd.discovery.Discovery    15-ea+24-1168    true
```

If the runtime system can't find the root module we asked for, then we expect to see an exception like this:

```
$ java --module-path mods -m wgjd.hello/wgjd.hello.HelloWorld
Error occurred during initialization of boot layer
java.lang.module.FindException: Module wgjd.hello not found
```

Even this simple error message is showing us that we have new aspects to the JDK, including

- Packages, including `java.lang.module`
- Exceptions, including `FindException`

This shows once again that the modules system really has become an integral part of the execution of every Java program, even if it is not always immediately obvious.

In the next section, we'll briefly introduce the interaction of modules with reflection. We assume that you're already familiar with reflection, but if you're not, feel free to skip this section for now and come back to it after you've read chapter 4, which contains an introduction to class loading and reflection.

2.4.3 Modules and reflection

In Java 8, developers can use reflection to access almost anything in the runtime. There's even a way to bypass the access control checks in Java and, for example, call private methods on other classes via the so-called setAccessible() hack.

As we've already seen, modules change the rules for access control. This also applies to reflection—the intent is that by default, only exported packages should be accessed reflectively.

However, the creators of the modules system realized that sometimes developers want to give reflective access (but not direct access) to certain packages. This requires an explicit permission and can be achieved by using the opens keyword to provide reflective-only access to an otherwise internal package. Developers can also specify fine-grained access by using the syntax opens … to … to allow a named set of packages to be opened reflectively to specific modules, but not more generally.

The previous discussion seems to imply that these types of reflective tricks are now ruled out. The truth is a little more complicated and is best explained via a discussion of the command-line switch --illegal-access. This switch comes with three settings—permit|warn|deny—and is used to control the strictness of checks on reflection.

The intent of the modules system has always been that over time, the entire Java ecosystem should move toward proper encapsulation, including reflection, and that at some point, the switch will default to deny (and will ultimately be removed). This change obviously could not happen overnight—if the reflection switch was suddenly set to deny, huge swathes of the Java ecosystem would break and *no one would upgrade.*

However, with the release of Java 17, it is now four years since Java 9 was released and this warning first started to appear. This is, surely, time enough and fair warning. Accordingly, the decision was made in Java 16 to change the default option of --illegal -access to deny and to remove the option's effect completely in Java 17.

> **NOTE** This change to reflective encapsulation semantics is one reason an
> application migrating directly from 8 to 17 may see more headaches than one
> that performs two upgrade hops (8 to 11 and then 11 to 17).

It is still possible to use the --add-opens command-line option, or the Add-Opens JAR manifest attribute, to open specific packages. This usage may be required for specific libraries or frameworks that have always used reflection and have not yet fully modularized. However, the brute force option to globally reenable access has been removed in Java 17.

One additional useful concept to help this transition is *open modules*. This simple declaration is used to allow for completely open reflective access—it opens all the module's packages for reflection but not compile-time access. This provides simple compatibility with existing code and frameworks but is a looser form of encapsulation.

For this reason, open modules are best avoided or used only as a transitional form when migrating to a modular build. In chapter 17, we will discuss the specific case of `Unsafe`, which is a great example to indicate some of the problems with reflection in a modular world.

2.5   *Architecting for modules*

Modules represent a fundamentally new way of packaging and deploying code. Teams do need to adopt some new practices to get the most out of the new functionality and the architectural benefits. However, the good news is there's no need to start doing that straightaway just to start using modern Java. The traditional, old-school methods using the classpath and JAR files will continue to work until such time as teams are ready to adopt modules wholeheartedly.

In fact, Mark Reinhold (chief architect for Java at Oracle) had this to say about the "need" for applications to adopt modularity.

> *There is no need to switch to modules.*
>
> *There has never been a need to switch to modules.*
>
> *Java 9 and later releases support traditional JAR files on the traditional class path, via the concept of the unnamed module, and will likely do so until the heat death of the universe.*
>
> *Whether to start using modules is entirely up to you.*
>
> *If you maintain a large legacy project that isn't changing very much, then it's probably not worth the effort.*
>
> —Mark Reinhold, https://stackoverflow.com/a/62959016

In an ideal world, modules would be the default for all greenfield apps, but this is proving to be complex in practice, so as an alternative, when migrating, follow a process like this:

1 Upgrade to Java 11 (classpath only).
2 Set an automatic module name.
3 Introduce a *monolithic module* consisting of all code.
4 Break out into individual modules as needed.

Typically, at step 3, way too much implementation code is exposed. This means that quite often, part of the work of step 4 is to create additional packages to house internal and implementation code and to refactor code into them.

If you are still using Java 8 and you aren't ready yet to migrate to a modular build, you can still do the following things to prepare your code for the migration:

- Introduce an automatic module name in MANIFEST.MF.
- Remove split packages from your deployment artifacts.
- Use `jdeps` and Compact Profiles to reduce your footprint of unnecessary dependencies.

To take the first of these, the use of an explicit automatic module name (as we discussed earlier in the chapter) will ease the transition. The automatic module name will be ignored by all versions of Java that do not support modules but will still allow you to reserve a stable name for your library and to move some code out of the unnamed module. It also has the advantage that consumers of your library are prepared for the transition to modules, because you have already advertised the name the module will be using. Let's take a closer look at the other two concrete recommendations.

2.5.1 *Split packages*

One common problem that developers encounter when they start to use modules is *split packages*—when two or more separate JARs contain classes belonging to the same package. In a nonmodular application, there is no problem with split packages because neither JAR files nor packages have any particular significance to the runtime. However, in the modular world, a package must belong to only one module and cannot be split.

If an existing application is upgraded to use modules and has dependencies that contain split packages, this will have to be remediated—there just is no way around it. For code that the team controls, this is additional work but not too difficult. One technique is to have a specific artifact (often using a -all suffix) that is generated by the build system alongside the nonmodular versions, with a single JAR containing all parts of the split package.

For external dependencies, remediation can be more complicated. It may be necessary to repackage third-party open source code into a JAR that can be consumed as an automatic module.

2.5.2 *Java 8 Compact Profiles*

Compact Profiles are a Java 8 feature. They are runtime environments that are reduced in size that must implement both the JVM and Java language specifications. They were introduced in Java 8 as a useful stepping-stone to the modularity story that would arrive in Java 9.

A Compact Profile must include all classes and packages that are explicitly mentioned in the Java language specification. Profiles are lists of packages, and they are usually identical to the package of the same name in the full Java SE platform. Very few exceptions exist, but they are explicitly called out.

One of the main use cases of profiles is as the basis for a server application or other environment, where deploying unnecessary capabilities is undesirable. For example, historically, a large number of security vulnerabilities were connected to Java's GUI features, especially in Swing and AWT. By choosing not to deploy the packages that implement those features in applications where they are not needed, we can gain a modest amount of additional security, especially for, for example, server applications.

NOTE At one time, Oracle shipped a cut-down JRE (the "Server JRE") that played a very similar role to Compact 1.

Compact 1 is the smallest set of packages on which it is feasible to deploy an application. It contains 50 packages, from the very familiar

- java.io
- java.lang
- java.math
- java.net
- java.text
- java.util

to some perhaps more unexpected packages that nonetheless provide essential classes to modern applications:

- java.util.concurrent.atomic
- java.util.function
- javax.crypto.interfaces
- javax.net.ssl
- javax.security.auth.x500

Compact 2 is significantly larger, containing packages such as those needed for XML, SQL, RMI, and security. Compact 3 is larger still and basically consists of the entire JRE, minus the windowing and GUI components—similar to the java.se module.

NOTE All profiles ship the transitive closure of types referred to by Object and all types mentioned within the language specification.

The Compact 1 profile is the closest to a minimal runtime, so in some ways it resembles a prototypical form of the java.base module. Ideally, if your application or library can be made to run with only Compact 1 as a dependency, then it should.

To help determine whether your app can run with Compact 1 or another profile, the JDK provides jdeps. This is a static analysis tool that ships with Java 8 and 11 for examining the dependencies of packages or classes. The tool can be used in a number of different ways, from identifying which profile an application needs to run under, to identifying developer code that makes calls into the undocumented, internal JDK APIs (such as the sun.misc classes), through to helping trace transitive dependencies. It can be very helpful for migrations from Java 8 to 11 and works with both JARs and modules. In its simplest form, jdeps takes a class or package and provides a brief list of packages that are the dependencies. For example, for the discovery example:

```
$ jdeps Discovery.class
Discovery.class -> java.base
Discovery.class -> jdk.attach
Discovery.class -> not found
   wgjd.discovery              -> com.sun.tools.attach     jdk.attach
   wgjd.discovery              -> java.io                  java.base
```

```
wgjd.discovery              -> java.lang              java.base
wgjd.discovery              -> java.util              java.base
wgjd.discovery              -> wgjd.discovery.internal  not found
```

The `-P` switch shows which profile is needed for a class (or package) to run, although, of course, this works only for a Java 8 runtime.

Let's move on to take a quick look at another migration technique that a well-grounded Java developer should be aware of—the use of *multi-release JARs*.

2.5.3 *Multi-release JARs*

This new capability allows the construction of a JAR file that can house libraries and components that can work on both Java 8 and modern, modular JVMs. For example, you can depend on library classes that are available only in later versions but can still run on an earlier version by using a fallback and stubbing approach.

To make a multi-release JAR, the following entry must be included in the JAR's manifest file:

```
Multi-Release: true
```

This entry is meaningful to JVMs only from version 9 upward, so if the JAR is used on a Java 8 (or earlier) VM, the multi-release nature will be ignored.

The classes that target post–Java 8 versions are referred to as *variant code* and are stored in a special directory in `META-INF` within the JAR, as shown next:

```
META-INF/versions/<version number>
```

The mechanism works by overriding on a per-class basis. Versions 9 and upward of Java will look for a class that has the exact same name in the `versions` directories as in the main content root. If one is found, the overridden version is used in place of the class in the content root.

> **NOTE** Java class files are stamped with the version number of the Java compiler that created them—the *class file version number*—and code created on a later Java release will not run on an older JVM.

The `META-INF/versions` location is ignored by Java 8 and earlier, so this provides a clever trick to sidestep the fact that some of the code contained in a multi-release JAR has too high a class file version to run on Java 8.

However, this does mean that the API of the class in the content root and any over-ridden variants must be the same, because they will be linked in exactly the same way for both cases.

EXAMPLE: BUILDING A MULTI-RELEASE JAR

Let's look at providing an example capability: getting the process ID of the running JVM. Unfortunately, this is somewhat cumbersome on versions of Java before 9 and requires some low-level hackery in the `java.lang.management` package.

Java 11 does provide an API for getting a PID from the Process API, so we want to set up a simple multi-release JAR that will use the simpler API when it is available and fall back to the JMX-based approach only if necessary.

The main class looks like this:

```
public class Main {
    public static void main(String[] args) {
        System.out.println(GetPID.getPid());
    }
}
```

Note that the capability that has a version-dependent implementation has been iso-lated into a separate class, GetPID. The Java 8 version of the code is somewhat verbose, as shown here:

```
public class GetPID {
  public static long getPid() {
    System.out.println("Java 8 version...");   ◁——  We include this line so we can see
    // ManagementFactory.getRuntimeMXBean().getName() returns the name that
    // represents the currently running JVM. On Sun and Oracle JVMs, this
    // name is in the format <pid>@<hostname>.

    final var jvmName = ManagementFactory.getRuntimeMXBean().getName();
    final var index = jvmName.indexOf('@');
    if (index < 1) {
        return 0;
    }

    try {
        return Long.parseLong(jvmName.substring(0, index));
    } catch (NumberFormatException e) {
        return 0;
    }
  }
}
```

We include this line so we can see that this is the Java 8 version.

This requires us to parse a string from a JMX method—and even then our solution is not guaranteed to be portable across JVM implementations. By contrast, Java 9 and later provide a much simpler standard method in the API, as shown in the following code snippet:

```
public class GetPID {
    public static long getPid() {
        // Use the ProcessHandle API, new in Java 9 ...
        var ph = ProcessHandle.current();
        return ph.pid();
    }
}
```

Because the ProcessHandle class is in the package java.lang, we don't even need an import statement.

We now need to arrange the multi-release JAR so that the Java 11 code is included in the JAR and is used in preference to the fallback version, if the JVM has a high enough version. One suitable code layout looks like this:

```
.
└── src
    ├── main
    │   └── java
    │       └── wgjd2ed
    │           └── Main.java
    │           └── GetPID.java
    └── versions
        └── 11
            └── java
                └── wgjd2ed
                    └── GetPID.java
```

The main part of the codebase needs to be compiled with Java 8, and then the post–Java 8 code is compiled afterward with a different Java version, before being packaged into a multi-release JAR "by hand" (i.e., using the command-line `jar` tool directly).

NOTE This code layout uses the convention that the Maven and Gradle build tools follow, which we'll meet properly in chapter 11.

Let's compile the code from the command line using JDK version `javac` but targeting our output to Java 8 via the `--release` flag:

```
$ javac --release 8 -d out src/main/java/wgjd2ed/*.java
```

Next, we build the Java 11 targeted code with a separate output directory for the variant code `out-11`:

```
$ javac --release 11 -d out-11 versions/11/java/wgjd2ed/GetPID.java
```

We also need a MANIFEST.MF file, but we can use the (Java 11) `jar` tool to automatically construct what we need as follows:

```
$ jar --create --release 11 \
      --file pid.jar --main-class=wgjd2ed.Main
    -C out/ . \
    -C out-11/ .
```

This creates a multi-release JAR, which is also runnable (with `Main` being the entry point class). Running the JAR gives the next output on Java 11:

```
$ java -version
openjdk version "11.0.3" 2019-04-16
OpenJDK Runtime Environment AdoptOpenJDK (build 11.0.3+7)
OpenJDK 64-Bit Server VM AdoptOpenJDK (build 11.0.3+7, mixed mode)

$ java -jar pid.jar
13855
```

and on Java 8:

```
$ java -version
openjdk version "1.8.0_212"
OpenJDK Runtime Environment (AdoptOpenJDK)(build 1.8.0_212-b03)
OpenJDK 64-Bit Server VM (AdoptOpenJDK)(build 25.212-b03, mixed mode)

$ java -jar pid.jar
Java 8 version...
13860
```

Note the extra banner we added to the Java 8 version so you can distinguish between the two cases and be sure that the two different classes are actually being run. For real-world use cases for multi-release JARs, we would want the code to either perform the same in both cases (if we're shimming a capability back to Java 8) or to fail in a graceful or predictable way if run on a JVM that doesn't support a capability.

One important architectural pattern that we recommend following is isolating JDK version-specific code into a package or group of packages, depending on how extensive the capability is.

Some basic guidelines and principles for the project follow:

- The main codebase must be able to be built with Java 8.
- Java 11 portion must be built with Java 11.
- Java 11 portion must be in a separate code root, isolated from the main build.
- The end result should be a single JAR.
- Keep the build configuration as simple as possible.
- Consider making the multi-release JAR modular as well.

The last point is especially important, and this continues to be true for more complex projects that will inevitably end up requiring a proper build tool, rather than just `javac` and `jar`.

2.6 *Beyond modules*

To conclude the chapter, let's take a quick look at what lies beyond modules. Recall that the entire point of modules was to introduce a missing abstraction into the Java language: the idea of deployment units with dependency guarantees that can be relied upon by the source code compiler and runtime.

This idea of modular dependency information that can be trusted has a number of applications to the modern world of deployable software. In Java, modules have seen slow but steady adoption as the tooling and ecosystem comes to fully support them and the benefits that they enable have become better understood.

Let's conclude this chapter by meeting a new capability that was added to the platform along with modules—*JLink*. This is the ability to package a reduced Java runtime along with an application. This provides the following benefits to applications that make use of it:

- Package the application and JVM into a single, self-contained directory.
- Reduce the footprint and overall download size of the application and JRE bundle.
- Reduce support overhead, because there is no need to debug interactions between a Java application and a host-installed JVM.

The self-contained directories that `jlink` produces can easily be packaged as deployable artifacts (such as a Linux `.rpm` or `.deb`, a Mac `.dmg`, or a Windows `.msi`), providing a simple installation experience for modern Java applications.

In some ways, the Compact Profiles technology in Java 8 provides an early version of JLink, but the version that arrived with modules is far more useful and comprehensive. As an example, we're going to reuse the discovery example from earlier in the chapter. This has a simple module-info.java:

```
module wgjd.discovery {
    exports wgjd.discovery;

    requires java.instrument;
    requires java.logging;
    requires jdk.attach;
    requires jdk.internal.jvmstat;
}
```

This can be built into a JLink bundle via a command like this:

```
$ jlink --module-path $JAVA_HOME/jmods/:out  --output bundle/ --add-modules
    wgjd.discovery
```

In our simple example, we have produced a JLink bundle that can be delivered as a TAR ball or packaged into a Linux package (such as .deb or .rpm). We can actually take this one step further and use *static compilation* to convert such a bundle into a native executable, but a full discussion of this is outside the scope of this book.

We should sound a word of caution: JLink is a great piece of technology, but it has some important limitations that you should be aware of:

- It will work only with an application with fully modularized dependencies.
- It does not work with nonmodular code.
- Even automatic modules are not sufficient.

This is because, to be absolutely sure that all of the necessary parts of the JRE are included in the bundle, JLink relies upon the strongly declarative information in the module graph and therefore requires a `module-info.class` for each dependency. Without this information, building a reduced JRE is very likely to be unsafe.

Unfortunately, in the real world, many libraries that applications depend upon are still not fully modularized. This sharply reduces the usefulness of JLink. To solve this problem, toolmakers have developed plugins to repackage and synthesize "true" modules from unmodularized libraries. We'll discuss these in chapter 11. However, to use these tools requires the use of a build system. This means we will defer real-world examples of JLink until later on, when we meet the build tools in chapter 11.

Summary

- Modules are a new concept in Java. They group packages and provide metadata about the whole unit, its dependencies, and its public interfaces. These constraints are then enforced by the compiler and runtime.
- Modules are *not* a deployment construct (e.g., a different file format). Modularized libraries and applications can still be distributed via JAR files and downloaded by standard build tools.
- Moving to modules requires changes in how we develop our Java applications.
  - New syntax in the module-info.java file controls how classes and methods are exposed within the module system.
  - Class loading is aware of the restrictions a module defines and handles loading nonmodular code.
  - Building with modules requires new command-line flags and a change to the standard layout for a Java project.
- Modules provide a number of benefits in return for this work.
  - Because of the more granular controls, modules are a fundamentally better way to architect applications for modern deployment and future maintainability.
  - Modules are key to reducing footprint, especially in containers.
  - Modules pave the way for other new capabilities (such as static compilation).
- Migrating to modules can be challenging, especially for legacy monolithic applications. Even three years after the first modular runtime was released, adoption remains patchy and incomplete.
- Tools such as multi-release JARs and Compact Profiles can help prepare existing Java 8 projects to integrate with the modular ecosystem, even if they can't move now.

Java 17

These represent the major new features that have been added to the Java language and platform since the release of Java 11, up to and including Java 17.

> **NOTE** To understand the changes in the Java release methodology since Java 8, it may be a good idea to review the discussion in chapter 1 or appendix A.

As well as the major, user-visible language upgrades, Java 17 contains many internal improvements (especially performance upgrades). However, this chapter focuses on the major features that we expect will change the way that you, the developer, write Java.

3.1 Text Blocks

Since the very first version, Java 1.0, developers have been complaining about Java's strings. Compared to other programming languages, such as Groovy or Scala or Kotlin, Java's strings have sometimes seemed a little primitive.

Java has historically provided only one type of string—the straightforward, double-quoted string in which certain characters (notably " and \) must be escaped to be used safely. These have, under a surprisingly wide array of circumstances, led to the need to produce convoluted escaped strings, even for very common programming situations.

The *Text Blocks* project has been through several iterations as a preview feature (we discussed preview features briefly in chapter 1) and is now a standard feature in Java 17. It aims to expand the notion of a string in Java syntax by allowing string literals that extend over multiple lines. In turn, that should avoid the need for most of the escape sequences that, historically, Java programmers have found to be an excessive hindrance.

NOTE   Unlike various other programming languages, Java Text Blocks do not currently support *interpolation*, although this feature is under active consideration for inclusion in a future version.

As well as helping to free Java programmers from the bother of dealing with excessive escaping of characters, a specific goal of Text Blocks is to allow readable strings of code that are not Java but that need to be embedded in a Java program. After all, how often do you have to include, for example, SQL or JSON (or even XML) in one of your Java programs?

Before Java 17, this process could be painful, indeed, and, in fact, many teams resorted to using an external templating library with all of its additional complexity. Since the arrival of Text Blocks, this is, in many cases, no longer necessary.

Let's see how they work, by considering an SQL query. In this chapter, we're going to use a few examples from financial trading—specifically foreign exchange currency trading (FX). Perhaps we have our customer orders stored in a SQL database that we will access with a query like this:

```
String query = """
        SELECT "ORDER_ID", "QUANTITY", "CURRENCY_PAIR" FROM "ORDERS"
        WHERE "CLIENT_ID" = ?
        ORDER BY "DATE_TIME", "STATUS" LIMIT 100;
        """;
```

You should notice two things. First, the Text Block is started and terminated with the sequence """, which was not legal Java prior to version 15. Second, the Text Block can be indented with whitespace at the start of each line—and the whitespace will be ignored.

If we print out the query variable, then we get exactly the string we constructed, as shown here:

```
SELECT "ORDER_ID", "QUANTITY", "CURRENCY_PAIR" FROM "ORDERS"
WHERE "CLIENT_ID" = ?
ORDER BY "DATE_TIME", "STATUS" LIMIT 100;
```

This happens because a Text Block is a constant expression (of type String), just the same as a string literal. The difference is that a Text Block is processed by javac before recording the constant in the class file as follows:

1 Line terminator characters are translated to LF (\u000A), that is, the Unix line-ending convention.
2 Extra whitespace surrounding the block is removed, to allow for extra indentation of Java source code, as per our example.
3 Any escape sequences in the block are interpreted.

These steps are carried out in the above order for a reason. Specifically, interpreting escape sequences last means blocks can include literal escape sequences (such as \n) without them being modified or deleted by earlier steps.

> **NOTE** At runtime, there is absolutely no difference between a string constant that was obtained from a literal versus a Text Block. The class file does not record in any way the original source of the constant.

For more details about Text Blocks, please see JEP 378 (https://openjdk.java.net/jeps/378). Let's move on and meet the new *Switch Expressions* feature.

3.2 Switch Expressions

Since its earliest versions, Java has supported *switch statements*. Java took a lot of inspiration for its syntax from the forms present in C and C++, and the `switch` statement is no exception, as shown next:

```
switch(month) {
  case 1:
    System.out.println("January");
    break;
  case 2:
    System.out.println("February");
    break;
  // ... and so on
}
```

In particular, Java's switch statement inherited the property that if a `case` doesn't end with `break`, execution will continue after the next `case`. This rule allows the grouping of cases that need identical handling, like this:

```
switch(month) {
  case 12:
  case 1:
  case 2:
    System.out.println("Winter, brrrr");
    break;
  case 3:
  case 4:
  case 5:
    System.out.println("Spring has sprung!");
    break;
  // ... and so on
}
```

Convenience for this situation, though, brought with it a dark and buggy side. Omitting a single break is an easy mistake for programmers, both new and old, and often introduced errors. In our example, we would get the wrong answer because excluding our first break would have resulted in messages for both winter and spring.

Switch statements are also clunky when trying to capture a value for later use. For example, if we wanted to grab that message for use elsewhere, instead of printing it, we'd have to set up a variable outside the switch, set it correctly in each branch, and potentially ensure after the switch that we actually set the value; something like this:

```
String message = null;
switch(month) {
  case 12:
  case 1:
  case 2:
    message = "Winter, brrrr";
    break;
  case 3:
  case 4:
  case 5:
    message = "Spring has sprung!";
    break;
  // ... and so on
}
```

Much like a missed break, we now must ensure every case properly sets the message variable or risk a bug report in our future. Surely, we can do better.

Switch Expressions, introduced in Java 14 (JEP 361), provide alternatives to address these shortcomings, while also acting to open future language frontiers. This aim includes helping to close a linguistic gap with more functionally oriented languages (e.g., Haskell, Scala, or Kotlin). A first version of Switch Expressions is more concise, as shown here:

```
String message = switch(month) {
  case 12:
  case 1:
  case 2:
    yield "Winter, brrrr";
  case 3:
  case 4:
  case 5:
    yield "Spring has sprung!";
  // ... and so on
}
```

In this revised form, we no longer set the variable in each branch. Instead, each case uses the new yield keyword to hand our desired value back to assign to the String variable, and the expression as a whole *yields a value*—from one case branch or another (and each case branch must result in a yield).

With this example in hand, the name of this new feature—*Switch Expressions* versus the existing *Switch Statement*—takes on more meaning. In programming languages, a *statement* is a piece of code executed for its side effect. An *expression* refers instead to code executed to produce a value. switch prior to Java 14 was only a side-effecting statement, but now it can produce values when used as an expression.

Switch Expressions also bring another even more concise syntax, which may well prove to be more widely adopted, as shown here:

```
String message = switch(month) {
  case 1, 2, 12  -> "Winter, brrrr";
  case 3, 4, 5   -> "Spring has sprung!";
  case 6, 7, 8   -> "Summer is here!";
  case 9, 10, 11 -> "Fall has descended";
  default        -> {
    throw new IllegalArgumentException("Oops, that's not a month");
  }
}
```

The -> indicates we're in a switch expression, so those cases don't need an explicit yield. Our default case shows how a block enclosed in {} can be used where we don't have a single value. If you're using the value of a switch expression (as we are by assigning it to message), multiline cases must either yield or throw.

But the new labeling format isn't just more helpful and shorter—it solves real problems. For one, multiple cases are directly supported by the comma-delimited list after the case. This solves the problem that previously required dangerous switch fall-through. A switch expression in the new labeling syntax never falls through, closing off that stumbling block for everyone.

The added safeguards don't end there. Another common way to mess up your switch statements is to miss a case you should have handled. If we remove the default line from the previous example, we get a compile error, as shown next:

```
error: the switch expression does not cover all possible input values
    String message = switch(month) {
                     ^
```

Unlike switch statements, Switch Expressions must handle every possible case for your input type, or your code won't even compile. That's an excellent guarantee to help you cover all the bases. It also combines nicely with Java's enums, as we can see if we rewrite the switch to use typesafe constants rather than ints as follows:

```
String message = switch(month) {
    case JANUARY, FEBRUARY, DECEMBER   -> "Winter, brrrr";
    case MARCH, APRIL, MAY             -> "Spring has sprung!";
    case JUNE, JULY, AUGUST            -> "Summer is here!";
    case SEPTEMBER, OCTOBER, NOVEMBER -> "Fall has descended";
};
```

This new capability is useful as a standalone feature, because it allows us to simplify a very common case of the use of `switch`, behaving a bit like a function, yielding an output value based on the input value. In fact, the rule for Switch Expressions is that every possible input value must be guaranteed to produce an output value.

> **NOTE** If all the possible enum constants are present in a switch expression, the match is *total* and it is not necessary to include a `default` case—the compiler can use the exhaustiveness of the enum constants.

However, for Switch Expressions that take, for instance, an `int`, we must include a `default` clause as it is not feasible to list all approximately four billion possible values.

Switch Expressions are also a stepping-stone toward a major feature, Pattern Matching, in a possible future version of Java, which we will discuss both later in this chapter and later in the book. For now, let's move on to meet the next new feature, Records.

3.3   *Records*

Records are a new form of Java class designed to do the following:

- Provide a first-class means for modeling data-only aggregates
- Close a possible gap in Java's type system
- Provide language-level syntax for a common programming pattern
- Reduce class boilerplate

The ordering of these bullet points is important, and in fact, Records are more about language semantics than they are about boilerplate reduction and syntax (although the second aspect is what many developers tend to focus on). Let's start by explaining the basic idea of what a Java record is.

The idea of Records is to extend the Java language and create a way to say that a class is "the fields, just the fields, and nothing but the fields." By making that statement about our class, the compiler can help us by creating all the methods automatically and having all the fields participate in methods like `hashCode()`.

> **NOTE** This is the way that the semantics "a record is a transparent carrier of the fields" defines the syntax: "accessor methods and other boilerplate are automatically derived from the record definition."

To see how it shows up in day-to-day programming, remember that one of the most common complaints about Java is that you need to write a lot of code for a class to be useful. Quite often we need to write

- `toString()`
- `hashCode()` and `equals()`
- Getter methods
- Public constructor

and so on.

For simple domain classes, these methods are usually boring, repetitive, and the kind of thing that could easily be mechanically generated (and IDEs often provide this capability), but until we had Records, the language didn't provide any way to do this directly. This frustrating gap is actually worse when we're reading someone else's code. For example, it might look like the author is using an IDE-generated hash-Code() and equals() that uses all the fields of the class, but how can we be sure without checking each line of the implementation? What happens if a field is added during refactoring and the methods are not regenerated?

Records solve these problems. If a type is declared as a record, it is making a strong statement, and the compiler and runtime will treat it accordingly. Let's see it in action.

To really explain this feature fully, we need a nontrivial example domain, so let's continue to use FX currency trading. Don't worry if you're not familiar with the concepts used in this area—we'll explain what you need to know as we go along. Later in the book, we're going to continue the theme of financial examples, so this is a good place to get started.

Let's walk through how we can use Records and a few other features to improve our modeling of the domain and get cleaner, less verbose, and simpler code as a result. Consider an order that we want to place when trading FX. The basic order type might consist of the following:

- Number of units I'm buying or selling (in millions of currency units)
- The "side"—whether I'm buying or selling (often called *Bid* and *Ask*)
- The currencies I'm exchanging (the *currency pair*)
- The time I placed my order
- How long my order is good for before it times out (the *time-to-live* or *TTL*)

So, if I have £1M and want to sell it for US dollars within the next second, and I want $1.25 for each £, then I am "buying the GBP/USD rate at $1.25 now, good for 1s." In Java, we might declare a domain class like this (we're calling it "classic" to call out that we have to do this with a class for now—better ways are coming):

```
public final class FXOrderClassic {
    private final int units;
    private final CurrencyPair pair;
    private final Side side;
    private final double price;
    private final LocalDateTime sentAt;
    private final int ttl;

    public FXOrderClassic(int units, CurrencyPair pair, Side side,
                          double price, LocalDateTime sentAt, int ttl) {
        this.units = units;
        this.pair = pair;  // CurrencyPair is a simple enum
        this.side = side;  // Side is a simple enum
        this.price = price;
        this.sentAt = sentAt;
        this.ttl = ttl;
```

```
    }

    public int units() {
        return units;
    }

    public CurrencyPair pair() {
        return pair;
    }

    public Side side() {
        return side;
    }

    public double price() {
        return price;
    }

    public LocalDateTime sentAt() {
        return sentAt;
    }

    public int ttl() {
        return ttl;
    }

    @Override
    public boolean equals(Object o) {
        if (this == o) return true;
        if (o == null || getClass() != o.getClass()) return false;

        FXOrderClassic that = (FXOrderClassic) o;

        if (units != that.units) return false;
        if (Double.compare(that.price, price) != 0) return false;
        if (ttl != that.ttl) return false;
        if (pair != that.pair) return false;
        if (side != that.side) return false;
        return sentAt != null ? sentAt.equals(that.sentAt) :
                                that.sentAt == null;
    }

    @Override
    public int hashCode() {
        int result;
        long temp;
        result = units;
        result = 31 * result + (pair != null ? pair.hashCode() : 0);
        result = 31 * result + (side != null ? side.hashCode() : 0);
        temp = Double.doubleToLongBits(price);
        result = 31 * result + (int) (temp ^ (temp >>> 32));
        result = 31 * result + (sentAt != null ? sentAt.hashCode() : 0);
        result = 31 * result + ttl;
        return result;
    }
```

```
    @Override
    public String toString() {
        return "FXOrderClassic{" +
                "units=" + units +
                ", pair=" + pair +
                ", side=" + side +
                ", price=" + price +
                ", sentAt=" + sentAt +
                ", ttl=" + ttl +
                '}';
    }
}
```

That's a lot of code, but it means that my order can be created like this:

```
var order = new FXOrderClassic(1, CurrencyPair.GBPUSD, Side.Bid,
                        1.25, LocalDateTime.now(), 1000);
```

But how much of the code to declare the class is really necessary? In older versions of Java, most developers would probably just declare the fields and then use their IDE to autogenerate all the methods. Let's see how Records improve the situation.

> **NOTE** Java doesn't provide any way to talk about a data aggregate other than by defining a class, so it is clear that any type containing "just the fields" will be a class.

The new concept is a *record class* (or usually just record). This is an immutable (in the usual "all fields are final" Java sense), transparent carrier for a fixed set of values, known as the *record components*. Each component gives rise to a final field that holds the provided value and an accessor method to retrieve the value. The field name and the accessor name match the name of the component.

The list of fields provides a *state description* for the record. In a general class, there might be no relation between a field x, the constructor argument x, and the accessor x(), but in a record, they are *by definition* talking about the same thing—a record *is* its state.

To allow us to create new instances of record classes, a constructor is also generated—called the *canonical constructor*—which has a parameter list that exactly matches the declared state description. The Java language also now provides concise syntax for declaring Records, in which all the programmer needs to do is to declare the component names and types that make up the record, like this:

```
public record FXOrder(int units,
                      CurrencyPair pair,
                      Side side,
                      double price,
                      LocalDateTime sentAt,
                      int ttl) {}
```

By writing this record declaration, we are not just saving some typing, we are making a much stronger, semantic statement. The FXOrder type *is* just the state provided, and any instance *is* just a transparent aggregate of the field values.

If we now examine the class file with javap (which we will meet properly in chapter 4), we can see that the compiler has autogenerated a bunch of boilerplate code for us:

```
$ javap FXOrder.class
Compiled from "FXOrder.java"
public final class FXOrder extends java.lang.Record {
  public FXOrder(int, CurrencyPair, Side,
                  double, java.time.LocalDateTime, int);

  public java.lang.String toString();
  public final int hashCode();
  public final boolean equals(java.lang.Object);
  public int units();
  public CurrencyPair pair();
  public Side side();
  public double price();
  public java.time.LocalDateTime sentAt();
  public int ttl();
}
```

This looks remarkably like the set of methods we had to write in the code for the class-based implementation. In fact, the constructor and accessor methods all behave exactly as before. However, methods like toString() and equals() use an implementation that might be surprising to some developers, as shown here:

```
public java.lang.String toString();
    Code:
       0: aload_0
       1: invokedynamic #51,  0          // InvokeDynamic #0:toString:
                                          // (LFXOrder;)Ljava/lang/String;
       6: areturn
```

That is, the toString() method (and equals() and hashCode()) are implemented using an invokedynamic-based mechanism. This is a powerful technique that we will meet later in the book (in chapters 4 and 16).

We can also see that there is a new class, java.lang.Record, that will act as the supertype for all record classes. It is abstract and declares equals(), hashCode() and toString() to be abstract methods. The java.lang.Record class cannot be directly extended, as we can see by trying to compile some code like this:

```
public final class FXOrderClassic extends Record {
    private final int units;
    private final CurrencyPair pair;
    private final Side side;
    private final double price;
```

```
    private final LocalDateTime sentAt;
    private final int ttl;

    // ... rest of class elided
}
```

The compiler will reject this attempt:

```
$ javac FXOrderClassic.java
FXOrderClassic.java:3: error: records cannot directly extend Record
public final class FXOrderClassic extends Record {
                 ^
1 error
```

The only way to get a record is to explicitly declare one and have `javac` create the class file. This also ensures that all record classes are created as final.

As well as the autogeneration of methods and boilerplate reduction, a couple of other core Java features also have special characteristics when applied to Records. First, Records must obey a special contract regarding the `equals()` method: if a record R has components c1, c2, ... cn, and if a record instance is copied as follows:

```
R copy = new R(r.c1(), r.c2(), ..., r.cn());
```

then it must be the case that `r.equals(copy)` is `true`. Note that this invariant is in addition to the usual familiar contract regarding `equals()` and `hashCode()`—it does not replace it.

At this point, let's move on to talk about some of the more design-level aspects of the Records feature. To do so, it's helpful to recall how enums work in Java. An enum in Java is a special form of class that implements a design pattern (*finitely many typesafe instances*) but with minimal syntax overhead—the compiler generates a bunch of code for us.

Similarly, a record in Java is a special form of class that implements a pattern (*Data Carrier* aka *Just Holds Fields*) with minimal syntax. All of the boilerplate code that we expect will be autogenerated for us by the compiler. However, although the simple concept of a Data Carrier class that just holds fields makes intuitive sense, what does that really mean in detail?

When Records were first being discussed, a lot of possible different designs were considered. For example:

- Boilerplate reduction of POJOs
- Java Beans 2.0
- Named tuples
- Product types (a form of *algebraic data type*)

These possibilities were discussed by Brian Goetz in his original design sketch (http://mng.bz/M5j8) in some detail. Each design option comes with additional secondary questions that follow from the choice of the design center for Records, questions such as:

- Can Hibernate proxy them?
- Are they fully compatible with classic Java Beans?
- Do they support name erasure/"shape malleability"?
- Will they come with Pattern Matching and destructuring?

It would have been plausible to base the Records feature on any one of the above four approaches—each has advantages and disadvantages. However, the final design decision is that Records are *named tuples.* This is partially driven by a key design idea in Java's type system— *nominal typing.* Let's take a closer look at this key idea.

3.3.1 *Nominal typing*

The nominal approach to static typing is the idea that every piece of Java storage (variables, fields) has a definite type and that each type has a name, which should be (at least somewhat) meaningful to humans.

Even in the case of anonymous classes, the types still have names—it's just that the compiler assigns the names and they are not valid names for types in the Java language (but are still OK within the JVM). For example, we can see this in jshell:

```
jshell> var o = new Object() {
   ...>    public void bar() { System.out.println("bar!"); }
   ...> }
o ==> $0@37f8bb67

jshell> var o2 = new Object() {
   ...>    public void bar() { System.out.println("bar!"); }
   ...> }
o2 ==> $1@31cefde0

jshell> o = o2;
|  Error:
|  incompatible types: $1 cannot be converted to $0
|  o = o2;
|      ^^
```

Notice that even though the anonymous classes were declared in exactly the same way, the compiler still produced two different anonymous classes, $0 and $1, and would not allow the assignment, because in the Java type system, the variables have different types.

> **NOTE** There are other (non-Java) languages where the overall shape of class (e.g., what fields and methods it has) can be used as the type (rather than an explicit type name). This is called *structural typing.*

It would have been a major change if Records had broken with Java's heritage and brought in structural typing for Records. As a result, the "Records are nominal tuples" design choice means that we expect that Records will work best where we might use tuples in other languages. This includes use cases such as compound map keys, or to simulate multireturn from a method. An example compound map key might look like this:

```
record OrderPartition(CurrencyPair pair, Side side) {}
```

Conversely, Records will not necessarily work well as a replacement for existing code that currently uses Java Beans. A number of reasons exist, notably that Java Beans are mutable whereas Records are not and that they have different conventions for their accessors. Records name their accessor methods the same as the field names (possible because field and method names are separately namespaced in Java) whereas Beans prepend `get` and `set`.

Records do allow some additional flexibility above and beyond the simple, single-line declaration form because they are genuine classes. Specifically, the developer can define additional methods, constructors, and static fields apart from the autogenerated defaults. However, these capabilities should be used carefully. Remember that the design intent of Records is to allow the developer to group related fields as a single, immutable data item.

One example of a use additional method that a record might create is a static factory method to simulate default values for some of the record parameters. Another example might be a `Person` class (with immutable date of birth) that might define a `currentAge()` method.

A good rule of thumb is: the more tempting it is to add a lot of additional methods and so on to the basic Data Carrier (or to make it implement several interfaces), the more likely it is that a full class should be used, rather than a record.

3.3.2 Compact record constructors

One important possible exception to the simplicity/"full class" rule of thumb is the use of *compact constructors*, which are described like this in the language specification:

> *The formal parameters of a compact constructor of a record class are implicitly declared. They are given by the derived formal parameter list of the record class.*

> *The intention of a compact constructor declaration is that only validation and/or normalization code need be given in the body of the canonical constructor; the remaining initialization code is supplied by the compiler.*

> —Java Language Specification

For example, we might want to validate orders to make sure that they don't attempt to buy or sell negative quantities or set an invalid time-to-live as follows:

```
public record FXOrder(int units, CurrencyPair pair, Side side,
                      double price, LocalDateTime sentAt, int ttl) {
    public FXOrder {
        if (units < 1) {
```

```
                throw new IllegalArgumentException(
                        "FXOrder units must be positive");
            }
            if (ttl < 0) {
                throw new IllegalArgumentException(
                        "FXOrder TTL must be positive, or 0 for market orders");
            }
            if (price <= 0.0) {
                throw new IllegalArgumentException(
                        "FXOrder price must be positive");
            }
        }
    }
}
```

One advantage that Java Records have over the anonymous tuples found in other languages is that the constructor body of a record allows for code to be run when Records are created. This allows for validation to occur (and exceptions to be thrown if an invalid state is passed). This would not be possible in purely structural tuples.

It might also make sense to use static factory methods within the body of the record, for example, to work around the lack of default parameter values in Java. In our trading example we might include a static factory like this

```
public static FXOrder of(CurrencyPair pair, Side side, double price) {
    var now = LocalDateTime.now();
    return new FXOrder(1, pair, side, price, now, 1000);
}
```

to declare a quick way to create orders with defaulted parameters. This could also be declared as an alternate constructor, of course. The developer should choose which approach makes sense to them in each circumstance.

One other use for alternate constructors is to create Records for use as compound map keys, as in this example:

```
record OrderPartition(CurrencyPair pair, Side side) {
    public OrderPartition(FXOrder order) {
        this(order.pair(), order.side());
    }
}
```

The type OrderPartition can then be easily used as a map key. For instance, we might want to construct an order book for use in our trade matching engine, like so:

```
public final class MatchingEngine {
    private final Map<OrderPartition, RankedOrderBook> orderBooks =
                                                    new TreeMap<>();

    public void addOrder(final FXOrder o) {
        orderBooks.get(new OrderPartition(o)).addAndRank(o);
        checkForCrosses(o.pair());
    }
```

```
public void checkForCrosses(final CurrencyPair pair) {
    // Do any buy orders match with sells now?
}

// ...
}
```

Now, when a new order is received, the addOrder() method extracts the appropriate order partition (consisting of a tuple of the currency pair and buy/sell side) and uses it to add the new order to the appropriate price-ranked order book. The new order might match against existing orders already on the books (which is called "crossing" of orders), so we need to check if it does in the checkForCrosses() method.

Sometimes we might want not to use the compact constructor and instead have a full, explicit canonical constructor. This signals that we need to do actual work in the constructor—and the number of use cases for this with simple Data Carrier classes is small. However, for some situations, like the need to make defensive copies of incoming parameters, this is necessary. As a result, the possibility of an explicit canonical constructor is permitted by the compiler—but think very carefully before making use of this approach.

Records are intended to be simple Data Carriers, a version of tuples that fits into Java's established type system in a logical and consistent manner. This will help many applications make domain classes clearer and smaller. It will also help teams eliminate many hand-coded implementations of the underlying pattern. It should also reduce or remove the need for libraries like Lombok.

Many developers are already reporting significant improvements when starting to use Records. They also combine extremely well with another new feature that also arrived in Java 17—Sealed Types.

3.4 Sealed Types

Java's enums are a well-known language feature. They allow the programmer to model a finite set of alternatives that represent all possible values of a type—effectively type-safe constants.

To continue our FX example, let's consider an OrderType enum to denote different types of order:

```
enum OrderType {
    MARKET,
    LIMIT
}
```

This represents two possible types of FX order: a *market* order that will take whatever the current best price is, and a *limit* order that will execute only when a specific price is available. The platform implements enums by having the Java compiler automatically generate a special form of class type.

NOTE   The runtime actually treats the library type `java.lang.Enum` (which all enum classes directly extend) in a slightly special way compared to other classes, but the details of this need not concern us here.

Let's decompile this enum and see what the compiler generates as follows:

```
$ javap -c -p OrderType.class
final class OrderType extends java.lang.Enum<OrderType> {
  public static final OrderType MARKET;

  public static final OrderType LIMIT;

  ...
  // Private constructor
}
```

Within the class file, all the possible values of the enum are defined as `public static final` variables, and the constructor is private, so additional instances cannot be constructed.

In effect, an enum is like a generalization of the Singleton pattern, except that instead of being only one instance of the class, there are a finite number. This pattern is extremely useful, especially because it gives us a notion of *exhaustiveness*—given a not-null `OrderType` object, we can know for sure that it is either the `MARKET` or the `LIMIT` instance.

However, suppose we want to model many different orders in Java 11. We must choose between two unpalatable alternatives. First, we can choose to have a single implementing class (or record), `FXOrder`, with a state field holding the actual type. This pattern works because the state field is of enum type and provides the bits that indicate which type is really meant for this specific object. This is obviously suboptimal, because it requires the application programmer to keep track of bits that are really the proper concern of the type system. Alternatively, we can declare an abstract base class, `BaseOrder`, and have concrete types, `MarketOrder` and `LimitOrder`, that subclass it.

The issue here is that Java has always been designed as an open language that is extensible by default. Classes are compiled at one time, and subclasses can be compiled years (or even decades) later. As of Java 11, the only class inheritance constructs permitted in the Java language are open inheritance (default) and no inheritance (`final`).

Classes can declare a package-private constructor, which effectively means "can only be extended by package-mates," but nothing in the runtime prevents users from creating new classes in packages that are not part of the platform, so this is an incomplete protection at best.

If we define a `BaseOrder` class, then nothing prevents a third party from creating a `EvilOrder` class that inherits from `BaseOrder`. Worse still, this unwanted extension can happen years (or decades) after the `BaseOrder` type was compiled, which is hugely undesirable.

    The conclusion is that until now, developers have been constrained and must use a
field to hold the actual type of the BaseOrder if they want to be future-proof. Java 17
has changed this state of affairs, by allowing a new way to control inheritance in a
more fine-grained way: the *sealed type*.

> **NOTE** This capability is present in several other programming languages in
> various forms and has become somewhat fashionable in recent years,
> although it is actually quite an old idea.

In its Java incarnation, the concept that sealing expresses is the idea that a type can be
extended, but only by a known list of subtypes and no others. Let's look at the new syntax for a simple example of a Pet class (we'll return to FX examples in a moment):

```
public abstract sealed class Pet {
    private final String name;

    protected Pet(String name) {
        this.name = name;
    }

    public String name() {
        return name;
    }

    public static final class Cat extends Pet {
        public Cat(String name) {
            super(name);
        }

        void meow() {
            System.out.println(name() +" meows");
        }
    }

    public static final class Dog extends Pet {
        public Dog(String name) {
            super(name);
        }

        void bark() {
            System.out.println(name() +" barks");
        }
    }
}
```

The class Pet is declared as sealed, which is not a keyword that has been permitted in
Java until now. Unqualified, sealed means that the class can be extended only inside
the current compilation unit. Therefore, the subclasses have to be nested within the
current class or non-public in the source file. We also declare Pet to be abstract
because we don't want any general Pet instances, only Pet.Cat and Pet.Dog objects.

This provides us with a nice way to implement the object-oriented (OO) modeling pattern we described earlier, without the drawbacks that we discussed.

Sealing can also be used with interfaces, and it's quite possible that the interface form will be more widely used in practice than the class form. Let's take a look at what happens when we want to use sealing to help model different types of FX orders:

```java
public sealed interface FXOrder permits MarketOrder, LimitOrder {
    int units();
    CurrencyPair pair();
    Side side();
    LocalDateTime sentAt();
}

public record MarketOrder(int units,
                          CurrencyPair pair,
                          Side side,
                          LocalDateTime sentAt,
                          boolean allOrNothing) implements FXOrder {

    // constructors and factories elided
}

public record LimitOrder(int units,
                         CurrencyPair pair,
                         Side side,
                         LocalDateTime sentAt,
                         double price,
                         int ttl) implements FXOrder {

    // constructors and factories elided
}
```

There are several things to notice here. First, FXOrder is now a sealed interface. Second, we can see the use of a second new keyword, permits, which allows the developer to list the permissible implementations of this sealed interface—and our implementations are Records.

> **NOTE** When you use permits, the implementing classes do not have to live within the same file and can be separate compilation units.

Finally, we have the nice bonus—because MarketOrder and LimitOrder are proper classes, they can have behaviors specific to their types. For example, a market order just takes the best price available immediately and does not need to specify a price. On the other hand, a limit order needs to specify the price that the order will accept and how long it is prepared to wait to try to achieve it (the time-to-live or *TTL*). This would not have been straightforward if we were using a field to indicate the "real type" of the object, because all methods for all subtypes would have to be present on the base type or force us to use ugly downcasts.

If we now program with these types, we know that any FXOrder instance that we encounter must either be a MarketOrder or a LimitOrder. What's more, the compiler can use this information, too. Library code can now safely assume that these are the only possibilities, and this assumption cannot be violated by client code.

Java's OO model represents the two most fundamental concepts of the relationship between types. Specifically, "Type `X IS-A Y`" and "Type `X HAS-A Y`." Sealed Types represent an object-oriented concept that previously could not be modeled in Java: "Type `X IS-EITHER-A Y OR Z`." Alternatively, they can also be thought of as

- A halfway house between `final` and open classes
- The enum pattern applied to types instead of instances

In terms of OO programming theory, they represent a new kind of formal relationship, because the set of possible types for o is the *union* of Y and Z. Accordingly, this is known as a *union type* or *sum type* in various languages, but don't be confused—they are different from C's `union`.

For example, Scala programmers can implement a similar idea using case classes and their own version of the `sealed` keyword (and we'll meet Kotlin's take on this idea later).

Beyond the JVM, the Rust language also provides a notion of *disjoint union* types, although it refers to them using the `enum` keyword, which is potentially *extremely* confusing for Java programmers. In the functional programming world, some languages (e.g., Haskell) provide a feature called *algebraic data types* that contain sum types as a special case. In fact, the combination of Sealed Types and Records also provides Java 17 with a version of this feature.

On the face of it, these types seem like a completely new concept in Java, but their deep similarity to enums should provide a good starting point for many Java programmers. In fact, something similar to these types already exists in one place: the type of the exception parameter in a multicatch clause.

From the Java Language Specification (JLS 11, section 14.20):

```
The declared type of an exception parameter that denotes its type as a union
with alternatives D1 | D2 | ... | Dn is lub(D1, D2, ..., Dn).
```

However, in the multicatch case, the true union type cannot be written as the type of a local variable—it is *nondenotable*. We cannot create a local variable typed as the true union type in the case of multicatch.

We should make one final point about Java's Sealed Types: they must have a base class that all the permitted types extend (or a common interface that all permitted types must implement). It is not possible to express a type that is "ISA-String-OR-Integer," because the types `String` and `Integer` have no common inheritance relationship apart from `Object`.

NOTE Some other languages do permit the construction of general union types, but it's not possible in Java.

Let's move on to discuss another new language feature that was delivered in Java 17—a new form of the instanceof keyword.

3.5   *New form of instanceof*

Despite being part of the language since Java 1.0, the instanceof operator sometimes gets a certain amount of bad press from some Java developers. In its simplest form, it provides a simple test: x instanceof Y returns true if the value x can be assigned to a variable of type Y and false otherwise (with the caveat that null instanceof Y is false for every Y).

This definition has been derided as undermining object-oriented design, because it implies a lack of preciseness in the types of objects and possibly in the choice of parameter types. However, in practice, in some scenarios the developer must confront an object that has a type that is not fully known at compile time. For example, consider an object that has been obtained reflectively about which little or nothing is known.

In these circumstances, the appropriate thing to do is to use instanceof to check that the type is as expected and then perform a downcast. The instanceof test provides a guard condition that ensures that the cast will not cause a ClassCastException at runtime. The resulting code looks like this example:

```
Object o = // ...
if (o instanceof String) {
    String s = (String)o;
    System.out.println(s.length());
} else {
    System.out.println("Not a String");
}
```

From the point of view of the developer, the new instanceof capability available in Java 17 is very simple—it simply provides a way to avoid the cast, as shown here:

```
if (o instanceof String s) {
    System.out.println(s.length());      ◁——— s is in scope on this branch.
} else {
    System.out.println("Not a String");  ◁——— s is not in scope on the "else" branch.
}

// ... More code      ◁——— s is not in scope once the if statement has ended.
```

However, although it might not seem that important, we get an important clue from the way that the JEP for this feature was named. JEP 394 was titled "Pattern Matching for instanceof," and it introduces a new concept—the *pattern*.

> **NOTE** It is very important to understand that this is a different usage of *pattern matching* than that used in text processing and regular expressions.

In this context, a pattern is a combination of the following two things:

1 A predicate (aka test) that will be applied to a value
2 A set of local variables, known as *pattern variables*, that are to be extracted from the value

The key point is that the pattern variables are extracted only if the predicate is successfully applied to the value.

In Java 17, the instanceof operator has been extended to take either a type or a *type pattern*, where a type pattern consists of a predicate that specifies a type, along with a single pattern variable.

NOTE We will meet type patterns in more detail in the next section.

As it stands, the upgraded instanceof does not seem to be very significant, but it is the first time that patterns have been seen in the Java language, and as we will see, more usages are coming! This is but the first step.

Having completed our tour of new Java 17 language features, it's time to look to the future and return to the subject of preview features.

3.6 *Pattern Matching and preview features*

In chapter 1, we introduced the concept of preview features, but we couldn't give a good example of one, because Java 11 didn't have any preview features! Now that we're talking about Java 17, we can carry on with the discussion.

In fact, all of the new language features that we've met in this chapter, including Switch Expressions, Records, and Sealed Types, went through the same lifecycle. They started out as preview features and went through one or more rounds of public preview before being delivered as final features. For example, sealed classes were previewed in Java 15, and again in 16, before being delivered as a final feature in Java 17 LTS.

In this section, we're going to meet a preview feature that extends Pattern Matching from instanceof to switch. Java 17 includes a version of this feature, but only as a first preview version (see chapter 1 for more details on preview features). The syntax is liable to change before the final release (and the feature may even be withdrawn, although this is most unlikely for Pattern Matching).

Let's see how Pattern Matching can be used in a simple case to improve some code that has to deal with objects of unknown type. We can use the new form of instanceof to write some safe code like this:

```
Object o = // ...

if (o instanceof String s) {
    System.out.println("String of length:"+ s.length());
} else if (o instanceof Integer i) {
    System.out.println("Integer:"+ i);
} else {
    System.out.println("Not a String or Integer");
}
```

This is quickly going to get cumbersome and verbose, though. Instead, we could introduce type patterns into a `switch` expression, as well as the simple `instanceof` Boolean expressions we already have. In the syntax of the current (Java 17) preview feature, we can rewrite the previous code into a simple form:

```
var msg = switch (o) {
    case String s      -> "String of length:"+ s.length();
    case Integer i     -> "Integer:"+ i;
    case null, default -> "Not a String or Integer";  <──
};
System.out.println(msg);
```

Null is now allowed as a case label to prevent the possibility of NullPointerException.

For those developers who want to experiment with code like this, we should explain how to build and run with preview features. If we try to compile code like the previous example that uses a preview feature, we get an error, as shown next:

```
$ javac ch3/Java17Examples.java
ch3/Java17Examples.java:68: error: patterns in switch statements are a
  preview feature and are disabled by default.

            case String s -> "String of length:"+ s.length();
                 ^
  (use --enable-preview to enable patterns in switch statements)
1 error
```

The compiler helpfully hints that we might need to enable preview features, so we try again with the flag enabled:

```
$ javac --enable-preview -source 17 ch3/Java17Examples.java
Note: ch3/Java17Examples.java uses preview features of Java SE 17.
Note: Recompile with -Xlint:preview for details.
```

The story is similar at runtime as well:

```
$ java ch3.Java17Examples
Error: LinkageError occurred while loading main class ch3.Java17Examples
    java.lang.UnsupportedClassVersionError: Preview features are not enabled
  for ch16/Java17Examples (class file version 61.65535). Try running with
  '--enable-preview'
```

Finally, if we include the preview flag, then the code will finally run:

```
$ java --enable-preview ch13.Java17Examples
```

The need to constantly enable the preview features is a pain, but it is designed to protect developers from having any code that uses unfinished features from escaping into production and causing problems there. Similarly, it's important to note the message about class file version that appeared when we tried to run a class containing preview features without the runtime flag. If we have explicitly compiled with preview features, we do not get a standard class file, and most teams should not be running that code in production.

The preview version of Pattern Matching in Java 17 also has functionality to integrate closely with Sealed Types. Specifically, patterns can take advantage of the fact that Sealed Types offer exclusivity of the possible types that can be seen. For example, when processing FX order responses, we may have the following base type:

```
public sealed interface FXOrderResponse
        permits FXAccepted, FXFill, FXReject, FXCancelled {
    LocalDateTime timestamp();
    long orderId();
}
```

We can combine this with a switch expression and type patterns, to give some code like this:

```
FXOrderResponse resp = // ... response from market
var msg = switch (resp) {
    case FXAccepted a  -> a.orderId() + " Accepted";
    case FXFill f      -> f.orderId() + " Filled "+ f.units();
    case FXReject r    -> r.orderId() + " Rejected: "+ r.reason();
    case FXCancelled c -> c.orderId() + " Cancelled";
    case null          -> "Order is null";
};
System.out.println(msg);
```

Note that a) we explicitly include a `case null` to ensure this code is null-safe (and won't throw a `NullPointerException`), and b) we do not need a default. The second point is because the compiler can examine all of the permitted subtypes of `FXOrder-Response` and can conclude that the pattern match is *total*, it covers every possibility that could ever occur and so a default case would be dead code under all circumstances. In the case where the match is not total, and some cases are not covered, a default would be needed.

The first preview also includes *guarded patterns*, which allow a pattern to be decorated with a Boolean guard condition, so the overall pattern matches only if both the pattern predicate and the guard are true. For example, let's suppose we want to see the details only of large filled orders. We can change the fill case in the previous example to some code like this:

```
case FXFill f && f.units() < 100 -> f.orderId() + " Small Fill";
case FXFill f                     -> f.orderId() + " Fill "+ f.units();
```

Note that the more specific case (small orders of less than 100 units) is tested first, and only if it fails does the match attempt the next case, which is the unguarded match for fills. The pattern variable is also already in scope for any guard conditions. We will return to Pattern Matching in chapter 18 when we discuss the future of Java and talk about some features that didn't make it in time for Java 17.

Summary

- Java 17 introduced a number of new features that developers will immediately be able to take advantage of in their own code:
  - Text Blocks for multiline strings.
  - Switch Expressions for a more modern switch experience.
  - Records as transparent carriers of data.
  - Sealed Types—an important new OO modeling concept.
  - Pattern Matching—although not fully delivered as of Java 17, it clearly shows the direction of travel of the language in the coming versions.

Part 2

Under the hood

This part of the book is all about exploring how the JVM *actually* works. You'll start off examining class loading. Many Java developers don't have a good understanding of how the JVM actually loads, links, and verifies classes. This leads to frustration and wasted time when an "incorrect" version of some class is executed due to some sort of classloader conflict.

Being able to dive into the internals of a Java class file and the bytecode it contains is a powerful debugging skill. You'll see how to use `javap` to navigate and understand the meaning of bytecode.

Next, you'll come to grips with the multicore CPU revolution occurring in hardware. The well-grounded Java developer needs to be aware of Java's concurrency capabilities. Chapters 5 and 6 will teach you how to get the most out of modern processors. First you'll look at concurrency theory and the building blocks Java has had for concurrent programming since 2006 (Java 5). You'll learn about the Java Memory Model and how threading and concurrency is implemented in that model.

Once you have some theory under your belt, we'll guide you through the features of the `java.util.concurrent` package, which provides modern structures for practical development of concurrent Java.

Performance tuning is often seen as an art, as opposed to a science, and tracking down and fixing performance issues often takes development teams extraordinary time and effort. In chapter 7, the final chapter in this part, we'll teach you to measure, not guess, and that "tuning by folklore" is wrong. You'll learn a scientific approach that quickly gets you to the heart of your performance issues.

In particular, we focus on garbage collection (GC) and the just-in-time (JIT) compiler, two major parts of the JVM that affect performance. Among other performance knowledge, you'll learn how to read GC logs and use the free Java VisualVM (jvisualvm) tool to analyze memory usage.

By the end of part 2, you'll no longer be a developer who thinks only of the source code sitting in your IDE. You'll know how Java and the JVM work under the hood, and you'll be able to take full advantage of what is arguably the most powerful general-purpose VM the planet has to offer.

Class files and bytecode

This chapter covers

- Class loading
- Reflection
- The anatomy of class files
- JVM bytecode and why it matters

One tried-and-true way to become a more well-grounded Java developer is to improve your understanding of how the platform works. Getting familiar with core features such as class loading and the nature of JVM bytecode can greatly help with this goal.

Consider the following scenarios that a senior Java developer might encounter: Imagine you have an application that makes heavy use of dependency injection (DI) techniques such as Spring, and it develops problems starting up and fails with a cryptic error message. If the problem is more than a simple configuration error, you may need to understand how the DI framework is implemented to track down the problem. This means understanding class loading.

Or suppose that a vendor you're dealing with goes out of business. You're left with a final drop of compiled code, no source code, and patchy documentation. How can you explore the compiled code and see what it contains?

All but the simplest applications can fail with a `ClassNotFoundException` or `NoClassDefFoundError`, but many developers don't know what these are, what the difference is between them, or even why they occur.

This chapter focuses on the aspects of the platform that underlie these concerns. We'll also discuss some more advanced features, but they are intended for those folks who like to dive deep and can be skipped if you're in a hurry.

We'll get started with an overview of class loading—the process by which the JVM locates and activates a new type for use in a running program. Central to that discussion are the `Class` objects that represent types in the JVM. Next, we'll look at how these concepts build into the major language feature known as reflection (or Core Reflection).

After that, we'll discuss tools for examining and dissecting class files. We'll use `javap`, which ships with the JDK, as our reference tool. Following this class file anatomy lesson, we'll turn to bytecode. We'll cover the major families of JVM opcodes and look at how the runtime operates at a low level.

Let's get started by discussing *class loading*—the process by which new classes are incorporated into a running JVM process. In this section, we will first discuss the basics of "classic" class loading, as it was done in Java 8 and earlier. Later in the chapter, we will talk about how the arrival of the modular JVM introduces some (small) changes to class loading.

4.1   *Class loading and class objects*

A .class file defines a type for the JVM, complete with fields, methods, inheritance information, annotations, and other metadata. The class file format is well-described by the standards, and any language that wants to run on the JVM must adhere to it.

> **NOTE**   A class is the fundamental unit of program code that the Java platform will understand, accept, and execute.

From the perspective of a beginning Java developer, a lot of the class loading mechanism is hidden from view. The developer provides either an executable JAR file or the name of the main application class (which must be present on the classpath), and the JVM finds and executes the class.

Any application dependencies (e.g., libraries other than the JDK) must also be on the classpath, and the JVM finds and loads them as well. However, the Java specifications do not say whether this needs to be done at application startup or later, as needed.

> **NOTE**   The API that the Java class loading system presents to the user is fairly simple—a lot of the complexity is hidden on purpose, and we will discuss the developer-available API later in the chapter.

Let's start with a very simple example:

```
Class<?> clazz = Class.forName("MyClass");
```

This piece of code will load a class, MyClass, into the current execution state. From the JVM's perspective, to achieve this a number of steps must be performed. First, a class file corresponding to the name MyClass must be found, and then the class it contains it must be resolved. These steps are performed in native code—in HotSpot, the native method is called JVM_DefineClass().

The actual process, at a high level, is that the native code builds the JVM's internal representation (which is called a *klass* and which is not a Java object—we will meet it properly in chapter 17). Then, provided the klass can be extracted from the class file successfully, the JVM constructs a Java "mirror" of the klass, which is passed back to Java code as a Class object.

After this, the Class object representing the type is available to the running system, and new instances of it can be created. In the previous example, clazz ends up holding the Class object corresponding to the type MyClass. It cannot hold the klass, because a klass is a JVM-internal object and *not* a Java object.

> **NOTE**   The same process is used for the main application class, all of its dependencies, and any other classes that may be required after the program has started.

In this section, we'll cover the steps from the JVM's point of view in a bit more detail and provide an introduction to class loaders, which are the objects that control this entire process.

4.1.1   Loading and linking

One way of looking at the JVM is that it is an execution container. In this view, the purpose of the JVM is to consume class files and execute the bytecode they contain. To achieve this, the JVM must retrieve the contents of the class file as a data stream of bytes, convert it to a useable form, and add it to the running state. This is essentially the process that we are describing here.

This somewhat complex process can be divided in a number of ways, but we refer to it as *loading* and *linking*.

> **NOTE**   Our discussion of loading and linking refers to some details that are specific to the HotSpot code, but other implementations should do similar things.

The first step is to acquire the data stream of bytes that constitute the class file. This process starts with a byte array that is often read in from a filesystem (but other alternatives are definitely possible).

Once we have the stream, it must be parsed to check that it contains a valid class file structure (this is sometimes called *format checking*). If so, then a candidate klass is created. During this phase, while the candidate klass is being filled in, some basic checks are performed (e.g., can the class being loaded actually access its declared superclass? Does it try to override any final methods?).

However, at the end of the loading process, the data structure corresponding to the class isn't usable by other code yet, and, in particular, we don't have a fully functional klass.

To get there, the class must now be linked and then initialized before it can be used. Logically speaking, this step breaks down into three subphases: verification, preparation, and resolution. However, in a real implementation, the code might not be cleanly separated out, so if you are planning to read the source code, you should be aware that the description provided here is a high-level or conceptual description of the process and does not have a precise correlation to the actual implementing code.

With this in mind, verification can be understood to be the phase that confirms that the class conforms to the requirements of the Java specifications and won't cause runtime errors or other problems for the running system. This relationship between the phases of linking can be seen in figure 4.1.

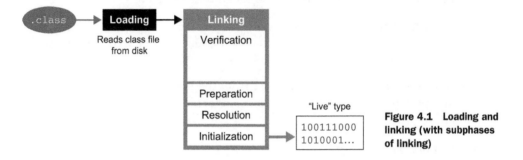

Figure 4.1   Loading and linking (with subphases of linking)

Let's meet each phase in turn.

VERIFICATION

Verification is quite a complex process, consisting of several independent concerns. For example, the JVM needs to check that symbolic information contained in the constant pool (discussed in detail in section 4.3.3) is self-consistent and obeys the basic behavior rules for constants.

Another major concern, and probably the most complex part of verification, is checking the bytecode of methods. This involves ensuring that the bytecode is well-behaved and doesn't try to circumvent the JVM's environmental controls.

Some of the main checks that are performed follow:

- Make sure bytecode doesn't try to manipulate the stack in disallowed or evil ways.
- Make sure every branch instruction (e.g., from an `if` or a loop) has a proper destination instruction.
- Check methods are called with the right number of parameters of the correct static types.
- Check local variables are assigned only suitably typed values.
- Check each exception that can be thrown has a legal catch handler.

These checks are done for several reasons, including performance. The checks enable the skipping of runtime checks, thus making the interpreted code run faster. Some of them can also simplify the compilation of bytecode into machine code at runtime (*just-in-time compilation*, which we'll cover in chapter 6).

PREPARATION

Preparing the class involves allocating memory and getting static variables in the class ready to be initialized, but it doesn't initialize variables or execute any JVM bytecode.

RESOLUTION

Resolution is the part of linking where the JVM checks that the supertype of the class being linked (and any interfaces that it implements) are already linked, and if they are not, then they are linked before the linking of this class continues. This can lead to a recursive linking process for any new types that have not been seen before.

> **NOTE**   A key phrase that relates to this aspect of class loading is the *transitive closure* of types. Not only the types that a class inherits from directly but also all types that are indirectly referenced must be linked.

Once all additional types that need to be loaded have been located and resolved, the JVM can initialize the class it was originally asked to load.

INITIALIZATION

In this final phase, any static variables are initialized and any static initialization blocks are run. This is a significant point because it is only now that the JVM is finally running bytecode from the newly loaded class.

When this step completes, the class is fully loaded and ready to go. The class is available to the runtime and new instances of it can be created. Any further class loading operations that refer to this class will now see that it is loaded and available.

4.1.2   Class objects

The end result of the linking and loading process is a `Class` object, which represents the newly loaded and linked type. It's now fully functional in the JVM, although for performance reasons, some aspects of the `Class` object are initialized only on demand.

> **NOTE**   `Class` objects are regular Java objects. They live in the Java heap, just like any other object.

Your code can now go ahead and use the new type and create new instances. In addition, the `Class` object of a type provides a number of useful methods, such as `get-Superclass()`, which returns the `Class` object corresponding to the supertype.

Class objects can be used with the Reflection API for indirect access to methods, fields, constructors, and so forth. A `Class` object has references to `Method`, `Field`, and various other objects that correspond to the members of the class. These objects can be used in the Reflection API to provide indirect access to the capabilities of the class, as we will see later in this chapter. You can see the high-level structure of this in figure 4.2.

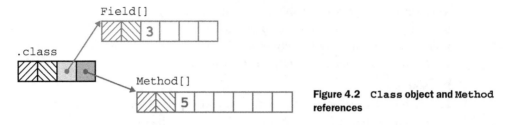

Figure 4.2   Class object and Method references

So far, we haven't discussed exactly which part of the runtime is responsible for locating and linking the byte stream that will become the newly loaded class. This is handled by class loaders—subclasses of the abstract class ClassLoader, and they're our next subject.

4.2   Class loaders

Java is a fundamentally object-oriented system with a dynamic runtime. One aspect of this is that Java's types are alive at runtime, and the type system of a running Java platform can be modified—in particular, by the addition of new types. The types that make up a Java program are open to extension by unknown types at runtime (unless they are final or one of the new sealed classes). The class-loading capability is exposed to the user. Class loaders are just Java classes that extend ClassLoader—they are themselves Java types.

> **NOTE**   In modern Java environments, all class loaders are modular. Loading classes is always done within the context of a module.

The class ClassLoader has some native methods, including the loading and linking aspects that are responsible for low-level parsing of the class file, but user class loaders are not able to override this aspect of class loading. It is not possible to write a class loader using native code.

The platform ships with the following typical class loaders, which are used to do different jobs during the startup and normal operation of the platform:

- BootstrapClassLoader (or *primordial* class loader)—This is instantiated very early in the process of starting up the JVM, so it's usually best to think of it as being a part of the JVM itself. It's typically used to get the absolute basic system loaded—essentially java.base.
- PlatformClassLoader—After the bare minimum system has been bootstrapped, then the platform class loader loads the rest of the platform modules that the application depends upon. This class loader is the primary interface to access any platform class, regardless of whether it was actually loaded by this loader or the bootstrap. It is an instance of an internal class.
- AppClassLoader—The application class loader—this is the most widely used class loader. It loads the application classes and does the majority of the work in most modern Java environments. In a modular JVM, the application class loader is no longer an instance of URLClassLoader (as it was in Java 8 and earlier) but, instead is an instance of an internal class.

Let's see these new class loaders in action, by adding some code to the top of the main method in SiteCheck from the wgjd.sitecheck module from chapter 2:

```
...
var clThis = SiteCheck.class.getClassLoader();
System.out.println(clThis);
var clObj = Object.class.getClassLoader();
System.out.println(clObj);
var clHttp = HttpClient.class.getClassLoader();
System.out.println(clHttp);
....
```

We recompile it with the following:

```
$ javac -d out wgjd.sitecheck/module-info.java \
        wgjd.sitecheck/wgjd/sitecheck/*.java \
        wgjd.sitecheck/wgjd/sitecheck/*/*.java
```

and run it like this:

```
$ java -cp out wgjd.sitecheck.SiteCheck http://github.com/well-grounded-java
```

Notice the use of the "starting module" syntax rather than an explicit starting class.

This produces the next output:

```
jdk.internal.loader.ClassLoaders$AppClassLoader@277050dc
null
jdk.internal.loader.ClassLoaders$PlatformClassLoader@12bb4df8
http://github.com/well-grounded-java: HTTP_1_1
```

The class loader for Object (which is in java.base) reports as null. This is a security feature—the bootstrap class loader does no verification and provides full security access to every class it loads. For that reason it does not make sense to have the class loader represented and available within the Java runtime—too much potential for bugs or abuse.

In addition to their core role, class loaders are also often used to load resources (files that aren't classes, such as images or config files) from JAR files or other locations on the classpath. This is often seen in a pattern that combines with try-with-resources to produce code like this:

```
try (var is = TestMain.class.getResourceAsStream("/resource.csv");
     var br = new BufferedReader(new InputStreamReader(is));) {
     // ...
}
// Exception handling elided
```

The class loaders provide this mechanism in a couple of different forms, returning either a URL or an InputStream.

4.2.1   *Custom class loading*

More complex environments will often have a number of additional *custom class loaders*—classes that subclass `java.lang.ClassLoader` (directly or indirectly). This is possible because the class loader class is not final, and developers are, in fact, encouraged to write their own class loaders specific to their individual needs.

Custom class loaders are represented as Java types, so they need to be loaded by a class loader, which is usually referred to as their *parent class loader*. This should not be confused with class inheritance and parent classes. Instead, class loaders are related by a form of *delegation*.

In figure 4.3, you can see the delegation hierarchy of class loaders and how the different loaders relate to each other. In some special cases, a custom class loader may have a different class loader as its parent, but the usual case is that it is the loading class loader.

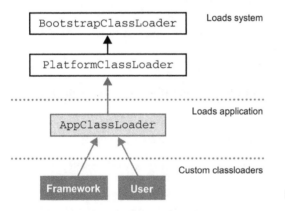

Figure 4.3   **Classloader hierarchy**

The key to the custom mechanism is found in the methods `loadClass()` and `findClass()`, which are defined on `ClassLoader`. The main entry point is `loadClass()` and a simplified form of the relevant code in `ClassLoader` follows:

```
protected Class<?> loadClass(String name, boolean resolve)
        throws ClassNotFoundException
    {
        synchronized (getClassLoadingLock(name)) {
            // First, check if the class has already been loaded
            Class<?> c = findLoadedClass(name);
            if (c == null) {
                // ...
                try {
                    if (parent != null) {
                        c = parent.loadClass(name, false);
                    } else {
                        c = findBootstrapClassOrNull(name);
                    }
```

```
        } catch (ClassNotFoundException e) {
            // ClassNotFoundException thrown if class not found
            // from the non-null parent class loader
        }

        if (c == null) {
            // If still not found, then invoke findClass in order
            // to find the class.
            // ...
            c = findClass(name);

            // ...
        }
    }
    // ...

    return c;
    }
}
```

Essentially, the loadClass() mechanism looks to see whether the class is already loaded and then asks its parent class loader. If that class loading fails (note the try-catch surrounding the call to parent.loadClass(name, false)), then the loading process delegates to findClass(). The definition of findClass() in java.lang .ClassLoader is very simple—it just throws a ClassNotFoundException.

At this point, let's return to a question that we posed at the start of the chapter and explore some of the exception and error types that can be encountered during class loading.

CLASS LOADING EXCEPTIONS

The meaning of ClassNotFoundException is relatively simple: the class loader attempted to load the specified class but was unable to do so. That is, the class was unknown to the JVM at the point when loading was requested, and the JVM was unable to find it.

Next up is NoClassDefFoundError. Note that this is an *error* rather than an exception. This error indicates that the JVM did know of the existence of the requested class but did not find a definition for it in its internal metadata. Let's take a quick look at an example:

```
public class ExampleNoClassDef {

    public static class BadInit {
        private static int thisIsFine = 1 / 0;
    }

    public static void main(String[] args) {
        try {
            var init = new BadInit();
        } catch (Throwable t) {
```

```
            System.out.println(t);
        }
        var init2 = new BadInit();
        System.out.println(init2.thisIsFine);
    }
}
```

When this runs, we get some output like this:

```
$ java ExampleNoClassDef
java.lang.ExceptionInInitializerError
Exception in thread "main" java.lang.NoClassDefFoundError: Could
  not initialize class ExampleNoClassDef$BadInit
    at ExampleNoClassDef.main(ExampleNoClassDef.java:13)
```

This shows that the JVM tried to load the BadInit class but failed to do so. Nevertheless, the program caught the exception and tried to carry on. When the class was encountered for the second time, however, the JVM's internal metadata table showed that the class had been seen but that a valid class was not loaded.

The JVM effectively implements *negative caching* on a failed class loading attempt—the loading is not retried, and instead an error (NoClassDefFoundError) is thrown.

Another common error is UnsupportedClassVersionError, which is triggered when a class loading operation tries to load a class file that was compiled by a higher version of the Java source code compiler than the runtime supports. For example, consider a class compiled with Java 11 that we try to run on Java 8, shown next:

```
$ java ScratchImpl
Error: A JNI error has occurred please check your installation and try again
Exception in thread "main" java.lang.UnsupportedClassVersionError:
  ScratchImpl has been compiled by a more recent version of the Java
    Runtime (class file version 55.0), this version of the Java Runtime
    only recognizes class file versions up to 52.0
    at java.lang.ClassLoader.defineClass1(Native Method)
    at java.lang.ClassLoader.defineClass(ClassLoader.java:763)
    at java.security.SecureClassLoader.defineClass(SecureClassLoader.java:142)
    at java.net.URLClassLoader.defineClass(URLClassLoader.java:468)
    at java.net.URLClassLoader.access$100(URLClassLoader.java:74)
    at java.net.URLClassLoader$1.run(URLClassLoader.java:369)
    at java.net.URLClassLoader$1.run(URLClassLoader.java:363)
    at java.security.AccessController.doPrivileged(Native Method)
    at java.net.URLClassLoader.findClass(URLClassLoader.java:362)
    at java.lang.ClassLoader.loadClass(ClassLoader.java:424)
    at sun.misc.Launcher$AppClassLoader.loadClass(Launcher.java:349)
    at java.lang.ClassLoader.loadClass(ClassLoader.java:357)
    at sun.launcher.LauncherHelper.checkAndLoadMain(LauncherHelper.java:495)
```

The Java 11 format bytecode may have features in it that are not supported by the runtime, so it is not safe to continue to try to load it. Note that because this is a Java 8 runtime, it does not have modular entries in the stack trace.

Finally, we should also mention LinkageError, which is the base class of a hierarchy containing NoClassDefFoundError, VerifyError, and UnsatisfiedLinkError, as well as several other possibilities.

A FIRST CUSTOM CLASS LOADER

The simplest form of custom class loading is simply to subclass ClassLoader and override findClass(). This allows us to reuse the loadClass() logic that we discussed earlier and to reduce the complexity in our class loader.

Our first example is the SadClassLoader, shown in the next code sample. It doesn't actually do anything, but it makes sure that you know that it was technically involved in the process and it wishes you well:

```
public class LoadSomeClasses {

    public static class SadClassloader extends ClassLoader {
        public SadClassloader() {
            super(SadClassloader.class.getClassLoader());
        }

        public Class<?> findClass(String name) throws
          ClassNotFoundException {
            System.out.println("I am very concerned that I
              couldn't find the class");
            throw new ClassNotFoundException(name);
        }
    }

    public static void main(String[] args) {
        if (args.length > 0) {
            var loader = new SadClassloader();
            for (var name : args) {
                System.out.println(name +" ::");
                try {
                    var clazz = loader.loadClass(name);
                    System.out.println(clazz);
                } catch (ClassNotFoundException x) {
                    x.printStackTrace();
                }
            }
        }
    }
}
```

In our example, we set up a very simple class loader and some code that uses it to try to load classes that may or may not already be loaded.

NOTE One common convention for custom class loaders is to provide a no-argument constructor that calls the superclass constructor and provides the loading class loader as an argument (to become the parent).

Many custom class loaders are not that much more complex than our example—they just override findClass() to provide the specific capability that is needed. This could include, for example, looking for the class over the network. In one memorable case, a custom class loader loaded classes by connecting to a database via JDBC and accessing an encrypted binary column to get the bytes that would be used. This was to satisfy an encryption-at-rest requirement for very sensitive code in a highly regulated environment.

It is possible to do more than just override findClass(), however. For example, loadClass() is not final and so can be overridden, and, in fact, some custom class loaders do override it precisely to change the general logic we met earlier.

Finally, we also have the method defineClass() that is defined on ClassLoader. This method is key to class loading because it is the user-accessible method that performs the "loading and linking" process that we described earlier in the chapter. It takes an array of bytes and turns them into a class object. This is the primary mechanism that is used to load new classes at runtime that are not present on the classpath.

The call to defineClass() will work only if it is passed a buffer of bytes that are in the correct JVM class file format. If not, it will fail to load because either the loading or verification step will fail.

> **NOTE** This method can be used for advanced techniques such as loading classes that are generated at runtime and that have no source code representation. This technique is how the lambda expressions mechanism works in Java. We will have more to say on this subject in chapter 17.

The defineClass() method is both protected and final and is defined on java.lang .ClassLoader, so it can be accessed only by subclasses of ClassLoader. Custom class loaders, therefore, always have access to the basic functionality of defineClass() but cannot tamper with the verification or other low-level class loading logic. This last point is important: being unable to change the verification algorithm is a very useful safety feature—a poorly written custom class loader cannot compromise the basic platform security the JVM provides.

In the case of the HotSpot virtual machine (which is by far the most common JVM implementation), defineClass() delegates to the native method defineClass1(), which does some basic checks and then calls a C function called JVM_DefineClass-WithSource().

This function is an entry point into the JVM, and it provides access into the C code of HotSpot. HotSpot uses the C SystemDictionary to load the new class via the C++ method ClassFileParser::parseClassFile(). This code actually runs much of the linking process, in particular, the verification algorithm.

Once class loading has completed, the bytecode of the methods is placed into HotSpot's metadata objects that represent the methods (they are called *methodOops*). They are then available for the bytecode interpreter to use. This can be thought of as a method cache conceptually, although the bytecode is actually held by the methodOops for performance reasons.

We have already met the `SadClassloader`. Now let's look at another couple of examples of custom class loaders, staring with a look at how class loading can be used to implement dependency injection.

EXAMPLE: A DEPENDENCY INJECTION FRAMEWORK

We want to highlight the following two primary concepts that are highly relevant to DI:

- Units of functionality within a system have dependencies and configuration information upon which they rely for proper functioning.
- Many object systems have dependencies that are difficult or clumsy to express in code.

The picture you should have is of classes that contain behavior and configuration and dependencies that are external to the objects. This latter part is what is usually referred to as the *runtime wiring* of the objects. In this example, we'll discuss how a hypothetical DI framework could use class loaders to implement runtime wiring.

> **NOTE** The approach we'll take is like a simplified version of the original implementation of the Spring framework. However, modern production DI frameworks have significantly higher complexity. Our example is for demonstration purposes only.

Let's start by looking at how we'd start an application under our imaginary DI framework, as shown here:

```
java -cp <CLASSPATH> org.wgjd.DIMain /path/to/config.xml
```

The class `DIMain` is the entry point class for the DI framework. It will read the config file, create the system of objects, and link them together ("wire them up"). Note that the class `DIMain` is not an application class—it comes from the framework and is completely general.

We can also see that the `CLASSPATH` for the application must contain three things: a) the JAR files for the DI framework, b) the application classes that are referred to in the config.xml file, and c) any other (non-DI) dependencies that the application has. Let's look at an example config file, shown next:

```xml
<beans>

 <bean id="dao" class="app.ch04.PaymentsDAO">
  <constructor-arg index="0" value="jdbc:postgresql://db.wgjd.org/payments"/>
  <constructor-arg index="1" value="org.postgresql.Driver"/>
 </bean>

  <bean id="service" class="app.ch04.PaymentService">
    <constructor-arg index="0" ref="dao"/>
  </bean>

</beans>
```

The DI framework uses the config file to determine which objects to construct. This example needs to make the dao and service beans, and the framework will need to call the constructors for each bean, with the specified arguments.

Class loading occurs in two separate phases. The first phase (which is handled by the application class loader) loads the class DIMain and any framework classes that it refers to. Then DIMain starts to run and receives the location of the config file as a parameter to main().

At this point, the framework is up and running in the JVM, but the user classes specified in config.xml haven't yet been touched. In fact, until DIMain examines the config file, the framework has no way of knowing what classes to load.

To bring up the application configuration specified in config.xml, a second phase of class loading is required. In our example, this uses a custom class loader.

First, the config.xml file is checked for consistency and to make sure it's error-free. Then, if all is well, the custom class loader tries to load the types from the CLASS-PATH. If any of these fail, the whole process is aborted, causing a runtime error.

If this succeeds, the DI framework can proceed to instantiate the required objects in the correct order (with their constructor parameters). Finally, if all of this completes correctly, the application context is up and can begin to run.

It is worth reiterating that this example is hypothetical and illustrative. It would be entirely possible to build a simple DI framework that worked in the manner described here. However, the actual implementation of real DI systems is much more complicated in practice. Let's move on to look at another example.

EXAMPLE: AN INSTRUMENTING CLASS LOADER

Consider a class loader that alters the bytecode of classes to add extra instrumentation information as they're loaded. When test cases are run against the transformed code, the instrumentation code records which methods and code branches are actually tested by the test cases. From this, the developer can see how thorough the unit tests for a class are.

This approach was the basis of the EMMA testing coverage tool, which is still available from http://emma.sourceforge.net/, although it is now rather outdated and has not been kept up-to-date for modern Java versions. Despite this, it's quite common to encounter frameworks and other code that use specialized class loaders that transform the bytecode as it's being loaded.

> **NOTE** The technique of modifying bytecode as it is loaded is also seen in the *java agent* approach, which is used for performance monitoring, observability, and other goals by tools such as New Relic.

We've briefly touched on a couple of use cases for custom class loading. Many other areas of the Java technology space are big users of class loaders and related techniques. Some of the best-known examples follow:

- Plugin architectures
- Frameworks (whether vendor or homegrown)

- Class file retrieval from unusual locations (not filesystems or URLs)
- Java EE
- Any circumstance where new, unknown code may need to be added after the JVM process has already started running

Let's move on to discuss how the module system affects class loading and modifies the classic picture that we've just explained.

4.2.2   *Modules and class loading*

The modules system is designed to operate at a different level from class loading, which is a relatively low-level mechanism within the platform. Modules are about large-scale dependencies between program units, and class loading is about the small scale. However, it is important to understand how the two mechanisms intersect and the changes to program startup that have been caused by the arrival of modules.

Recall that when running on a modular JVM, to execute a program, the runtime will compute a module graph and try to satisfy it as a first step. This is referred to as *module resolution*, and it derives the transitive closure of the root module and its dependencies.

During this process, additional checks are performed (e.g., no modules with duplicate names, no split packages). The existence of the module graph means that fewer runtime class-loading problems are expected, because missing JARs on the module path can now be detected before the process even starts fully.

Beyond this, the modules system does not alter class loading much in most cases. There are some advanced possibilities (such as dynamically loading modular implementations of service provider interfaces by using reflection), but those are not likely to be encountered often by most developers.

4.3   *Examining class files*

Class files are binary blobs, so they aren't easy to work with directly. But there are many circumstances in which you'll find that investigating a class file is necessary.

Imagine that your application needs additional methods to be made public to allow better runtime monitoring (such as via JMX). The recompile and redeploy seems to complete fine, but when the management API is checked, the methods aren't there. Additional rebuild and redeploy steps have no effect.

To debug the deployment issue, you may need to check that javac has produced the class file that you think it has. Or you may need to investigate a class that you don't have source for and where you suspect the documentation is incorrect.

For these and similar tasks, you must make use of tools to examine the contents of class files. Fortunately, the standard Oracle JVM ships with a tool called javap, which is very handy for peeking inside and disassembling class files.

We'll start off by introducing javap and some of the basic switches it provides to examine aspects of class files. Then we'll discuss some of the representations for method names and types that the JVM uses internally. We'll move on to take a look at the constant pool—the JVM's "box of useful things"—which plays an important role in understanding how bytecode works.

4.3.1 Introducing javap

From seeing what methods a class declares to printing the bytecode, javap can be used for numerous useful tasks. Let's examine the simplest form of javap usage, as applied to the class-loading example from earlier in the chapter:

```
$ javap LoadSomeClasses.class
Compiled from "LoadSomeClasses.java"
public class LoadSomeClasses {
  public LoadSomeClasses();
  public static void main(java.lang.String[]);
}
```

The inner class has been compiled out into a separate class, so we need to also look at that one:

```
$ javap LoadSomeClasses\$SadClassloader.class
Compiled from "LoadSomeClasses.java"
public class LoadSomeClasses$SadClassloader extends java.lang.ClassLoader {
  public LoadSomeClasses$SadClassloader();
  public java.lang.Class<?> findClass(java.lang.String) throws
    java.lang.ClassNotFoundException;
}
```

By default, javap shows the public, protected, and default access (package-protected) visibility methods. The -p switch also shows the private methods and fields.

4.3.2 Internal form for method signatures

The JVM uses a slightly different form for method signatures internally than the human-readable form displayed by javap. As we delve deeper into the JVM, you'll see these internal names more frequently. If you're keen to keep going, you can jump ahead, but remember that this section's here—you may need to refer to it from later sections and chapters.

In the compact form, type names are compressed. For example, int is represented by I. These compact forms are sometimes referred to as *type descriptors*. A complete list is provided in table 4.1 (and includes void, which is not a type but does appear in method signatures).

Table 4.1   Type descriptors

Descriptor	Type
B	Byte
C	Char (a 16-bit Unicode character)

Table 4.1 Type descriptors

Descriptor	Type
D	Double
F	Float
I	Int
J	Long
L<type name>;	Reference type (such as Ljava/lang/String; for a string)
S	Short
V	Void
Z	Boolean
[	Array-of

In some cases, the type descriptor can be longer than the type name that appears in source code (e.g., Ljava/lang/Object; is longer than Object, but the type descriptors are always fully qualified so they can be directly resolved).

javap provides a helpful switch, -s, which will output the type descriptors of signatures for you, so you don't have to work them out using the table. You can use a slightly more advanced invocation of javap to show the signatures for some of the methods we looked at earlier, as shown next:

```
$ javap -s LoadSomeClasses.class
Compiled from "LoadSomeClasses.java"
public class LoadSomeClasses {
  public LoadSomeClasses();
    descriptor: ()V

  public static void main(java.lang.String[]);
    descriptor: ([Ljava/lang/String;)V
}
```

and for the inner class:

```
$ javap -s LoadSomeClasses\$SadClassloader.class
Compiled from "LoadSomeClasses.java"
public class LoadSomeClasses$SadClassloader extends java.lang.ClassLoader {
  public LoadSomeClasses$SadClassloader();
    descriptor: ()V

  public java.lang.Class<?> findClass(java.lang.String) throws
    java.lang.ClassNotFoundException;
    descriptor: (Ljava/lang/String;)Ljava/lang/Class;
}
```

As you can see, each type in a method signature is represented by a type descriptor.

In the next section, we'll see another use of type descriptors. This is in a very important part of the class file—the constant pool.

4.3.3   *The constant pool*

The constant pool is an area that provides handy shortcuts to other (constant) elements of the class file. If you've studied languages like C or Perl, which make explicit use of symbol tables, you can think of the constant pool as being a somewhat similar JVM concept.

Let's use a very simple example in the next listing to demonstrate the constant pool, so we don't swamp ourselves with detail. The next listing shows a simple "playpen" or "scratchpad" class. This provides a way to quickly test out a Java syntax feature or library, by writing a small amount of code in run().

Listing 4.1   Sample playpen class

```java
package wgjd.ch04;

public class ScratchImpl {

    private static ScratchImpl inst = null;

    private ScratchImpl() {

    }

    private void run() {

    }

    public static void main(String[] args) {
        inst = new ScratchImpl();
        inst.run();
    }
}
```

To see the information in the constant pool, you can use javap -v. This prints a lot of additional information—much more than just the constant pool—but let's focus on the constant pool entries for the playpen, shown next:

```
#1 = Class #2 // wgjd/ch04/ScratchImpl

#2 = Utf8 wgjd/ch04/ScratchImpl

#3 = Class #4 // java/lang/Object

#4 = Utf8 java/lang/Object

#5 = Utf8 inst

#6 = Utf8 Lwgjd/ch04/ScratchImpl;
```

```
#7 = Utf8 <clinit>

#8 = Utf8 ()V

#9 = Utf8 Code

#10 = Fieldref #1.#11 // wgjd/ch04/ScratchImpl.inst:Lwgjd/ch04/ScratchImpl;

#11 = NameAndType #5:#6 // instance:Lwgjd/ch04/ScratchImpl;

#12 = Utf8 LineNumberTable

#13 = Utf8 LocalVariableTable

#14 = Utf8 <init>

#15 = Methodref #3.#16 // java/lang/Object."<init>":()V

#16 = NameAndType #14:#8 // "<init>":()V

#17 = Utf8 this

#18 = Utf8 run

#19 = Utf8 ([Ljava/lang/String;)V

#20 = Methodref #1.#21 // wgjd/ch04/ScratchImpl.run:()V

#21 = NameAndType #18:#8 // run:()V

#22 = Utf8 args

#23 = Utf8 [Ljava/lang/String;

#24 = Utf8 main

#25 = Methodref #1.#16 // wgjd/ch04/ScratchImpl."<init>":()V

#26 = Methodref #1.#27 // wgjd/ch04/ScratchImpl.run:([Ljava/lang/String;)V

#27 = NameAndType #18:#19 // run:([Ljava/lang/String;)V

#28 = Utf8 SourceFile

#29 = Utf8 ScratchImpl.java
```

As you can see, constant pool entries are typed. They also refer to each other, so, for example, an entry of type Class will refer to an entry of type Utf8. A Utf8 entry means a string, so the Utf8 entry that a Class entry points out will be the name of the class.

Table 4.2 shows the set of possibilities for entries in the constant pool. Entries from the constant pool are sometimes discussed with a CONSTANT_ prefix, such as CONSTANT

_Class. This is to make it clear that they are not Java types, in situations where they could be confused.

Table 4.2   Constant pool entries

Name	Description
Class	A class constant. Points at the name of the class (as a Utf8 entry).
Fieldref	Defines a field. Points at the Class and NameAndType of this field.
Methodref	Defines a method. Points at the Class and NameAndType of this field.
InterfaceMethodref	Defines an interface method. Points at the Class and NameAndType of this field.
String	A string constant. Points at the Utf8 entry that holds the characters.
Integer	An integer constant (4 bytes).
Float	A floating-point constant (4 bytes).
Long	A long constant (8 bytes).
Double	A double-precision floating-point constant (8 bytes).
NameAndType	Describes a name and type pair. The type points at the Utf8 that holds the type descriptor for the type.
Utf8	A stream of bytes representing Utf8-encoded characters.
InvokeDynamic	Part of invokedynamic mechanism—see chapter 17.
MethodHandle	Part of invokedynamic mechanism—see chapter 17.
MethodType	Part of invokedynamic mechanism—see chapter 17.

Using this table, you can look at an example constant resolution from the constant pool of the playpen. Consider the Fieldref at entry #10. To resolve a field, you need a name, a type, and a class where it resides: #10 has the value #1.#11, which means constant #11 from class #1. It's easy to check that #1 is indeed a constant of type Class, and #11 is a NameAndType. #1 refers to the ScratchImpl Java class itself, and #11 refers to #5:#6—a variable called inst of type ScratchImpl. So, overall, #10 refers to the static variable inst in the ScratchImpl class itself (which you might have been able to guess from the output above).

In the verification step of class loading, there's a step to check that the static information in the class file is consistent. The preceding example shows the kind of integrity check that the runtime will perform when loading a new class.

We've discussed some of the basic anatomy of a class file. Let's move on to the next topic, where we'll delve into the world of bytecode. Understanding how source code is turned into bytecode will help you gain a better understanding of how your code will run. In turn, this will lead to more insights into the platform's capabilities when we reach chapter 6 and beyond.

4.4 Bytecode

Bytecode has been a somewhat behind-the-scenes player in our discussion so far. Let's start by reviewing what we've already learned about it:

- Bytecode is an intermediate representation of a program, halfway between human readable source and machine code.
- Bytecode is produced by `javac` from Java source code files.
- Some high-level language features have been compiled away and don't appear in bytecode. For example, Java's looping constructs (`for`, `while`, and the like) are gone, turned into bytecode branch instructions.
- Each opcode is represented by a single byte (hence the name *bytecode*).
- Bytecode is an abstract representation, not "machine code for an imaginary CPU."
- Bytecode can be further compiled to machine code, usually "just in time."

When explaining bytecode, there can be a slight chicken-and-egg problem. To fully understand what's going on, you need to understand both bytecode and the runtime environment that it executes in. This is a rather circular dependency, so to solve it, we'll start by diving in and looking at a relatively simple example. Even if you don't understand everything that's in this example on the first pass, you can come back to it after you've read more about bytecode in the following sections.

After the example, we'll provide some context about the runtime environment, and then catalogue the JVM's opcodes, including bytecodes for arithmetic, invocation, shortcut forms, and more. At the end, we'll round off with another example, based on string concatenation. Let's get started by looking at how you can examine bytecode from a .class file.

4.4.1 Disassembling a class

Using `javap` with the `-c` switch, you can disassemble classes. In our example, we'll use the `ScratchImpl` class we met earlier. The main focus will be to examine the bytecode that makes up methods. We'll also use the `-p` switch so we can see bytecode from private methods.

Let's work section by section—there's a lot of information in each part of `javap`'s output, and it's easy to become overwhelmed. First, the header. There's nothing terribly unexpected or exciting in here, as shown here:

```
$ javap -c -p wgjd/ch04/ScratchImpl.class

Compiled from "ScratchImpl.java"

public class wgjd.ch04.ScratchImpl extends java.lang.Object {
  private static wgjd.ch04.ScratchImpl inst;
```

Next is the static block. This is where variable initialization is placed, so this represents initializing `inst` to `null`. The keen-eyed reader might guess that `putstatic` could be a bytecode that puts a value in a static field:

```
static {};

Code:
   0: aconst_null
   1: putstatic #10 // Field inst:Lwgjd/ch04/ScratchImpl;
   4: return
```

The numbers in the preceding code represent the offset into the bytecode stream from the start of the method. So byte 1 is the putstatic opcode, and bytes 2 and 3 represent a 16-bit index into the constant pool. In this case, the 16-bit index is the value 10, which means that the value (in this case, null) will be stored in the field indicated by constant pool entry #10. Byte 4 from the start of the bytecode stream is the return opcode—the end of the block of code.

Next up is the constructor:

```
private wgjd.ch04.ScratchImpl();

Code:
   0: aload_0
   1: invokespecial #15 // Method java/lang/Object."<init>":()V
   4: return
```

Remember that in Java, the void constructor will always implicitly call the superclass constructor. Here you can see this in the bytecode—it's the invokespecial instruction. In general, any method call will be turned into one of the JVM's five invoke instructions, which we'll meet in section 4.4.7.

The constructor invocation requires a target, which is provided by the aload_0 instruction. This loads a reference (an *Address*) and uses a shortcut form (which we'll meet properly in section 4.4.9) to load the 0th local variable, which is just this, the current object.

There's basically no code in the run() method, because this is just a scratchpad class for testing out code. This method immediately returns to the caller and does not pass a value back (which is correct, because the method returns void):

```
private void run();

Code:
   0: return
```

In the main method, we initialize inst and do a bit of object creation. This demonstrates some very common basic bytecode patterns that we can learn to recognize:

```
public static void main(java.lang.String[]);

Code:
   0: new #1 // class wgjd/ch04/ScratchImpl
   3: dup
   4: invokespecial #21 // Method "<init>":()V
```

This pattern of three bytecode instructions—new, dup, and invokespecial of a method called <init>—always represents the creation of a new instance.

The new opcode allocates memory for a new instance and places a reference to it on the top of the stack. The dup opcode duplicates the reference that's on top of the stack (so now there are two copies). To finish fully creating the object, we need to call the body of the constructor. The <init> method contains the code for the constructor body, so we call that code block with invokespecial.

When methods are called, the reference to the receiver object (if any) is consumed from the stack, along with any arguments to the method. This is why we need to perform a dup first—without it, the newly allocated object will have its only reference consumed by the invoke and will be inaccessible after this point.

Let's look at the remaining bytecodes for the main method:

```
 7: putstatic #10 // Field inst:Lwgjd/ch04/ScratchImpl;
10: getstatic #10 // Field inst:Lwgjd/ch04/ScratchImpl;
13: invokevirtual #22 // Method run:()V
16: return
```

Instruction 7 saves the address of the singleton instance that has been created. Instruction 10 puts it back on top of the stack, so that instruction 13 can call a method on it. This is done with the invokevirtual opcode, which carries out Java's "standard" dispatch for instance methods.

> **NOTE** In general, the bytecode produced by javac is a simple representation—it isn't highly optimized. The overall strategy is that just-in-time (JIT) compilers do a lot of optimizing, so it helps if they have a relatively plain and simple starting point. The expression, "Bytecode should be dumb," describes the general feeling of JVM implementers toward the bytecode produced from source languages.

The invokevirtual opcode includes checking for overrides of the method in the object's inheritance hierarchy. You might notice that this is a bit odd, because private methods can't be overridden. You might guess that the source code compiler could actually emit invokespecial instead of invokevirtual for private methods. In fact, this used to be the case and was changed only in recent versions of Java. For details, see the section on nestmates in chapter 17.

Let's move on to discuss the runtime environment that bytecode needs. After that, we'll introduce the tables that we'll use to describe the major families of bytecode instructions—load/store, arithmetic, execution control, method invocation, and platform operations. Then we'll discuss possible shortcut forms of opcodes, before moving on to another example.

4.4.2 The runtime environment

Understanding the operation of the stack machine that the JVM uses is critical to understanding bytecode. One of the most obvious ways that the JVM doesn't look like a hardware CPU (such as an x64 or ARM chip) is that the JVM doesn't have processor registers and instead uses a stack for all calculations and operations. This is referred to as the *evaluation stack* (it's officially called the *operand stack* in the VM specification, and we'll use the two terms interchangeably).

The evaluation stack is local to a method, and when a method is called, a fresh evaluation stack is created. Of course, the JVM also has a *call stack* for each Java thread that records which methods have been executed (and which forms the basis of stack traces in Java). It's important to keep the distinction between the per-thread call stack and the per-method evaluation stack clear.

Figure 4.4 shows how the evaluation stack might be used to perform an addition operation on two int constants. We're showing the equivalent JVM bytecode below each step—we'll meet this bytecode later in the chapter, so don't worry if it doesn't make complete sense right now.

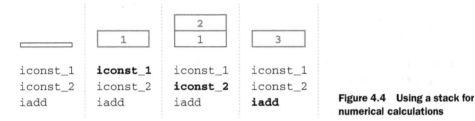

Figure 4.4   Using a stack for numerical calculations

As we discussed earlier in this chapter, when a class is linked into the running environment, its bytecode will be checked, and a lot of that verification boils down to analyzing the pattern of types on the stack.

> **NOTE**   Manipulations of the values on the stack work only if the values on the stack have the correct types. Undefined or bad things could happen if, for example, we pushed a reference to an object onto the stack and then tried to treat it as an int and do arithmetic on it.

The verification phase of class loading performs extensive checks to ensure that methods in newly loaded classes don't try to abuse the stack. This prevents a malformed (or deliberately evil) class from ever being accepted by the system and causing problems.

As a method runs, it needs an area of memory to use as an evaluation stack, for computing new values. In addition, every running thread needs a call stack that records which methods are currently in flight (the stack that would be reported by a stack trace). These two stacks will interact in some cases. Consider this bit of code:

```
var numPets = 3 + petRecords.getNumberOfPets("Ben");
```

To evaluate this, the JVM puts 3 on the operand stack. Then it needs to call a method to calculate how many pets Ben has. To do this, it pushes the receiver object (the one the method is being called on—petRecords, in this example) onto the evaluation stack, followed by any call arguments.

Then the getNumberOfPets() method is called using one of the invoke opcodes, which will cause control to transfer to the called method and the just-entered method to appear in the call stack. But, as the JVM enters the new method, it starts using a fresh operand stack, so the values already on the caller's operand stack can't possibly affect results calculated in the called method.

When getNumberOfPets() completes, the return value is placed onto the operand stack of the caller, as part of the process whereby getNumberOfPets() is removed from the call stack. Then the addition operation takes the two values and adds them.

Let's now turn to examining bytecode. This is a large subject, with lots of special cases, so we're going to present an overview of the main features rather than a complete treatment.

4.4.3 Introduction to opcodes

JVM bytecode consists of a sequence of operation codes (opcodes), possibly with some arguments following each instruction. Opcodes expect to find the stack in a given state and transform the stack, so that the arguments are removed and results placed there instead.

Each opcode is denoted by a single-byte value, so at most 255 possible opcodes exist. Currently, only around 200 are used. This is too many for us to list exhaustively (but a complete list can be found at http://mng.bz/aJaX). Fortunately, most opcodes fit into one of a number of basic families that provide similar functionality. We'll discuss each family in turn, to help you get a feel for them. Some operations don't fit cleanly into any of the families, but they tend to be encountered less often.

> **NOTE** The JVM isn't a purely object-oriented runtime environment. It has knowledge of primitive types. This shows up in some of the opcode families— some basic opcode types (such as store and add) are required to have a number of variations that differ, depending on the primitive type they're acting upon.

The opcode tables have the following four columns:

- *Name*—This is a general name for the type of opcode. In many cases, several related opcodes do similar things.
- *Args*—The arguments that the opcode takes. Arguments that start with i are (unsigned) bytes that are used to form a lookup index in the constant pool or local variable table.

> **NOTE** To make longer indices, bytes are joined together, so that i1, i2 means "make a 16-bit index out of these two bytes" via bit shifting and addition: ((i1 << 8) + i2)

If an arg is shown in brackets, it means that not all forms of the opcode will use it.

- *Stack layout*—This shows the state of the stack before and after the opcode has executed. Elements in brackets indicate that not all forms of the opcode use them or that the elements are optional (such as for invocation opcodes).
- *Description*—What the opcode does.

Let's look at an example of a row from table 4.3 by examining the entry for the get-field opcode. This is used to read a value from a field of an object.

getfield	i1, i2	[obj] -> [val]	Gets the field at the constant pool index specified from the object on top of the stack.

The first column gives the name of the opcode—getfield. The next column says that there are two arguments that follow the opcode in the bytecode stream. These arguments are put together to make a 16-bit value that is looked up in the constant pool to see which field is wanted (remember that constant pool indexes are always 16-bit). The stack layout column shows that the reference to the object is replaced by the value of the field.

This pattern of removing object instances as part of the operation is just a way to make bytecode compact, without lots of tedious cleanup and having to remember to remove object instances that you're finished with.

4.4.4   *Load and store opcodes*

The family of load and store opcodes is concerned with loading values onto the stack or retrieving them. Table 4.3 shows the main operations in the load/store family.

Table 4.3   Load and store opcodes

Name	Args	Stack layout	Description
load	(i1)	[] -> [val]	Loads a value (primitive or reference) from a local variable onto the stack. Has shortcut forms and type-specific variants.
ldc	i1	[] -> [val]	Loads a constant from the pool onto the stack. Has type-specific and wide variants.
store	(i1)	[val] -> []	Stores a value (primitive or reference) in a local variable, removing it from the stack in the process. Has shortcut forms and type-specific variants.
dup		[val] -> [val, val]	Duplicates the value on top of the stack. Has variant forms.
getfield	i1, i2	[obj] -> [val]	Gets the field at the constant pool index specified from the object on top of the stack.
putfield	i1, i2	[obj, val] -> []	Puts the value into the object's field at the specified constant pool index.
getstatic	i1, i2	[] -> [val]	Gets the value of the static field at the constant pool index specified.
putstatic	i1, i2	[val] -> []	Puts the value into the static field at the specified constant pool index.

As we noted earlier, a number of different forms of the load and store instructions exist. For example, a dload opcode loads a double onto the stack from a local variable, and an `astore` opcode pops an object reference off the stack and into a local variable.

Let's do a quick example of `getfield` and `putfield`. This simple class:

```
public class Scratch {
    private int i;

    public Scratch() {
        i = 0;
    }

    public int getI() {
        return i;
    }

    public void setI(int i) {
        this.i = i;
    }
}
```

will decompile the getter and setter as:

```
public int getI();
    Code:
        0: aload_0
        1: getfield        #7                  // Field i:I
        4: ireturn

  public void setI(int);
    Code:
        0: aload_0
        1: iload_1
        2: putfield        #7                  // Field i:I
        5: return
```

which shows how the stack is used to hold temporary variables before transferring them to heap storage.

4.4.5 *Arithmetic opcodes*

These opcodes perform arithmetic on the stack. They take arguments from the top of the stack and perform the required calculation on them. The arguments (which are always primitive types) must always match exactly, but the platform provides a wealth of opcodes to cast one primitive type to another. Table 4.4 shows the basic arithmetic operations.

The cast opcodes have very short names, such as `i2d` for an `int` to `double` cast. In particular, the word *cast* doesn't appear in the names, which is why it's in parentheses in the table.

Table 4.4   Arithmetic opcodes

Name	Args	Stack layout	Description
add		[val1, val2] -> [res]	Adds two values (which must be of the same primitive type) from the top of the stack and stores the result on the stack. Has shortcut forms and type-specific variants.
sub		[val1, val2] -> [res]	Subtracts two values (of the same primitive type) from the top of the stack. Has shortcut forms and type-specific variants.
div		[val1, val2] -> [res]	Divides two values (of the same primitive type) from the top of the stack. Has shortcut forms and type-specific variants.
mul		[val1, val2] -> [res]	Multiplies two values (of the same primitive type) from top of the stack. Has shortcut forms and type-specific variants.
(cast)		[value] -> [res]	Casts a value from one primitive type to another. Has forms corresponding to each possible cast.

4.4.6   *Execution flow control opcodes*

As mentioned earlier, the control constructs of high-level languages aren't present in JVM bytecode. Instead, flow control is handled by a small number of primitives, which are shown in table 4.5.

Table 4.5   Execution control opcodes

Name	Args	Stack layout	Description
if	b1, b2	[val1, val2] -> [] or [val1] -> []	If the specific condition matches, jump to the specified branch offset.
goto	b1, b2	[] -> []	Unconditionally jump to the branch offset. Has wide form.
tableswitch	{depends}	[index] -> []	Used to implement switch.
lookupswitch	{depends}	[key] -> []	Used to implement switch.

Like the index bytes used to look up constants, the b1, b2 args are used to construct a bytecode location within this method to jump to. They cannot be used to jump outside of the method—this is checked at class-loading time and would cause the class to fail verification.

The family of if opcodes is a little larger than you might expect—it has more than 15 instructions to handle the various source code possibilities (e.g., numeric comparison, reference equality).

> **NOTE**   The family of if opcodes also contains two deprecated instructions, jsr and ret, which are no longer produced by javac and are illegal in modern Java versions.

A wide form of the `goto` instruction (`goto_w`) takes 4 bytes of arguments and constructs an offset, which can be larger than 64 KB. This isn't often needed because it would only apply to very, very large methods (and such methods have other problems, such as being too large to be JIT compiled). There is also `ldc_w`, which can be used to address very large constant pools.

4.4.7 Invocation opcodes

The invocation opcodes comprise four opcodes for handling general method calling, plus the unusual `invokedynamic` opcode, which was added in Java 7. We'll discuss this special case in more detail in chapter 17. The five method invocation opcodes are shown in table 4.6.

Table 4.6 Invocation opcodes

Name	Args	Stack layout	Description
invokestatic	i1, i2	[(val1, ...)] -> []	Calls a static method.
invokevirtual	i1, i2	[obj, (val1, ...)] -> []	Calls a "normal" instance method.
invokeinterface	i1, i2, count, 0	[obj, (val1, ...)] -> []	Calls an interface method.
invokespecial	i1, i2	[obj, (val1, ...)] -> []	Calls a "special" instance method, such as a constructor.
invokedynamic	i1, i2, 0, 0	[val1, ...] -> []	Dynamic invocation; see chapter 17.

It's easiest to see the difference between these opcodes with an extended example, shown here:

```
long time = System.currentTimeMillis();

// This explicit typing is deliberate... read on
HashMap<String, String> hm = new HashMap<>();
hm.put("now", "bar");

Map<String, String> m = hm;
m.put("foo", "baz");
```

Let's use `javap -c` to look at the bytecode for this:

```
Code:
      0: invokestatic  #2  // Method java/lang/System.currentTimeMillis:()J
      3: lstore_1
      4: new           #3 // class java/util/HashMap
      7: dup
      8: invokespecial #4 // Method java/util/HashMap."<init>":()V
     11: astore_3
     12: aload_3
     13: ldc           #5 // String now
     15: ldc           #6 // String bar
```

```
17: invokevirtual #7 // Method java/util/HashMap.put:(
                     //Ljava/lang/Object;Ljava/lang/Object;)
                     //Ljava/lang/Object;
20: pop
21: aload_3
22: astore        4
24: aload         4
26: ldc           #8 // String foo
28: ldc           #9 // String baz
30: invokeinterface #10,  3 // InterfaceMethod java/util/Map.put:(
                     //Ljava/lang/Object;Ljava/lang/Object;)
                     //Ljava/lang/Object;
35: pop
```

As we discussed earlier, the Java method calls are actually turned into one of several possible invoke* bytecodes. Let's take a closer look:

```
0: invokestatic  #2 // Method java/lang/System.currentTimeMillis:()J
3: lstore_1
```

The static call to System.currentTimeMillis() is turned into an invokestatic that appears at position 0 in the bytecode. This method takes no parameters, so nothing needs to be loaded onto the evaluation stack before the call is dispatched.

Next, the two bytes 00 02 appear in the byte stream. These are combined into a 16-bit number that is used as an offset into the constant pool.

The decompiler helpfully includes a comment that lets the user know which method offset #2 corresponds to. In this case, as expected, it's the method System .currentTimeMillis().

On return, the result of the call is placed on the stack, and at offset 3, we see the single, argument-less opcode lstore_1 that saves this return value off into the local variable 1.

Human readers are, of course, able to see that the variable time is never used again. However, one of the design goals of javac is to represent the contents of the Java source code as faithfully as possible, whether or not it makes sense. Therefore, the return value of System.currentTimeMillis() is stored, even though it is not used after this point in the program.

This is "dumb bytecode" in action: remember that from the point of view of the platform, the class file format is the input format to the compiler that really matters—the JIT compiler:

```
 4: new           #3 // class java/util/HashMap
 7: dup
 8: invokespecial #4 // Method java/util/HashMap."<init>":()V
11: astore_3
12: aload_3
13: ldc           #5 // String now
15: ldc           #6 // String bar
17: invokevirtual #7 // Method java/util/HashMap.put:(
```

```
                                   //Ljava/lang/Object;Ljava/lang/Object;)
                                   //Ljava/lang/Object;
        20: pop
```

Bytecodes 4 to 10 create a new `HashMap` instance, before instruction 11 saves a copy of it into a local variable. Next, instructions 12 to 16 set up the stack with the `HashMap` object and the arguments for the call to `put()`. The actual invocation of the `put()` method is performed by instructions 17 to 19.

The invoke opcode used this time is `invokevirtual` because the static type of the local variable was declared as `HashMap`—a class type. We will see what will happen if the local variable is declared as `Map` in a moment.

An instance method call differs from a static method call because a static call does not have an instance on which the method is called (sometimes called the receiver object).

> **NOTE** In bytecode, an instance call must be set up by placing the receiver and any call arguments on the evaluation stack and then issuing the invoke instruction.

In this case, the return value from `put()` is not used, so instruction 20 discards it, as shown here:

```
        21: aload_3
        22: astore          4
        24: aload           4
        26: ldc             #8 // String foo
        28: ldc             #9 // String baz
        30: invokeinterface #10,  3 //InterfaceMethod java/util/Map.put:(
                                    //Ljava/lang/Object;Ljava/lang/Object;)
                                    //Ljava/lang/Object;
        35: pop
```

The sequence of bytes from 21 to 25 seems rather odd at first glance. The `HashMap` instance that we created at 4 and saved to local variable 3 at instruction 11 is now loaded back onto the stack, and a copy of the reference is saved to local variable 4. This process removes it from the stack, so it must be reloaded (from variable 4) before use. This shuffling occurs because in the original Java code, we created an additional local variable (of type `Map` rather than `HashMap`), even though it always refers to the same object as the original variable. This is another example of the bytecode staying as close as possible to the original source code.

After the stack and variable shuffling, the values to be placed in the map are loaded at instructions 26 to 29. With the stack prepared with receiver and arguments, the call to `put()` is dispatched at instruction 30. This time, the opcode is `invoke-interface`, even though the exact same method is actually being called. This is because the Java local variable is of type `Map`—an interface type. Once again, the return value from `put()` is discarded, via the `pop` at instruction 35.

As well as knowing which Java method invocations turn into which operations, you should notice a couple of other wrinkles about the invocation opcodes. First off is that invokeinterface has extra parameters. These are present for historical and backward compatibility reasons and aren't used these days. The two extra zeros on invoke-dynamic are present for forward-compatibility reasons.

The other important point is the distinction between a regular and a special instance method call. A regular call is *virtual,* which means that the exact method to be called is looked up at runtime using the standard Java rules of method overriding.

However, a couple of special cases exist, including calls to a superclass method. In these cases, you don't want the override rules to be triggered, so you need a different invocation opcode to allow for this case. This is why the opcode set needs an opcode for invocation of methods without the override mechanism—invokespecial—which instead indicates exactly which method will be called.

4.4.8   *Platform operation opcodes*

The platform operation family of opcodes includes the new opcode, for allocating new object instances, and the thread-related opcodes, such as monitorenter and monitorexit. The details of this family can be seen in table 4.7.

Table 4.7   **Platform opcodes**

Name	Args	Stack layout	Description
new	i1, i2	[] -> [obj]	Allocates memory for a new object, of the type specified by the constant at the specified index.
monitorenter		[obj] -> []	Locks an object. See chapter 5.
monitorexit		[obj] -> []	Unlocks an object. See chapter 5.

The platform opcodes are used to control certain aspects of the object lifecycle, such as creating new objects and locking them. It's important to notice that the new opcode allocates only storage. The high-level conception of object construction also includes running the code inside the constructor.

At the bytecode level, the constructor is turned into a method with a special name—<init>. This can't be called from user Java code, but it can be called by bytecode. This leads to the distinctive bytecode pattern that directly corresponds to object creation—a new followed by a dup followed by an invokespecial to call the <init> method, as we saw earlier.

The monitorenter and monitorexit bytecodes correspond to the start and end of a synchronized block.

4.4.9   *Shortcut opcode forms*

Many of the opcodes have shortcut forms to save a few bytes here and there. The general pattern is that certain local variables will be accessed much more frequently than others, so it makes sense to have a special opcode that means "do the general operation directly on the local variable" rather than having to specify the local variable as an argument. This gives rise to opcodes such as `aload_0` and `dstore_2` within the load/store family, which are 1 byte shorter than the equivalent byte sequences, `aload 00` or `dstore 02`.

> **NOTE** One byte saved may not sound like much, but it adds up over the entire class. Java's original use case was applets, which were often downloaded over dial-up modems, at speeds of 28.8 *kilobits* per second. With that speed of bandwidth, it was important to save bytes wherever possible.

To become a truly well-grounded Java developer, you should run `javap` against some of your own classes and learn to recognize common bytecode patterns. For now, with this brief introduction to bytecode under our belts, let's move on to tackle our next subject—reflection.

4.5   *Reflection*

One of the key techniques that a well-grounded Java developer should have at their command is *reflection*. This is an extremely powerful capability, but many developers struggle with it at first because it seems alien to the way that most Java developers think about code.

Reflection is the ability to query or *introspect* objects and discover (and use) their capabilities at runtime. It can be thought of as several different things, depending on context:

- A programming language API
- A programming style or technique
- A runtime mechanism that enables the technique
- A property of the language type system

Reflection in an object-oriented system is essentially the idea that the programming environment can represent the types and methods of the program as objects. This is possible only in languages that have a runtime that supports this, and it is a fundamentally dynamic aspect of a language.

When using the reflective style of programming, it is possible to manipulate objects without using their static types at all. This seems like a step backward, but if we can work with objects without needing to know their static types, then it means that we can build libraries, frameworks, and tools that can work with *any* type—including types that did not even exist when our code was written.

When Java was a young language, reflection was one of the key technological innovations that it brought to the mainstream. Although other languages (notably Smalltalk) had introduced it much earlier, it was not a common part of many languages at the time Java was released.

4.5.1 Introducing reflection

The abstract description of reflection can often seem confusing or hard to grasp. Let's look at some simple examples in JShell to try to get a more concrete view of what reflection is:

```
jshell> Object o = new Object();
o ==> java.lang.Object@a67c67e

jshell> Class<?> clz = o.getClass();
clz ==> class java.lang.Object
```

This is our first glimpse of reflection—a class object for the type `Object`. In fact, the actual type of `clz` is `Class<Object>`, but when we obtain a class object from class loading or `getClass()`, we have to handle it using the unknown type, `?`, in the generics, as follows:

```
jshell> Class<Object> clz = Object.class;
clz ==> class java.lang.Object

jshell> Class<Object> clz = o.getClass();
|  Error:
|  incompatible types: java.lang.Class<capture#1 of ? extends
   java.lang.Object> cannot be converted to java.lang.Class<java.lang.Object>
|  Class<Object> clz = o.getClass();
|                      ^----------^
```

This is because reflection is a dynamic, runtime mechanism, and the true type `Class<Object>` is not known to the source code compiler. This process introduces irreducible extra complexity to working with reflection because we cannot rely on the Java type system to help us very much. On the other hand, this dynamic nature is the key point of reflection—if we don't know what type something is at compile time and have to treat it in a very general way, we can exploit this flexibility to build an open, extensible system.

> **NOTE** Reflection produces a fundamentally open system, and as we saw in chapter 2, this can come into conflict with the more encapsulated systems that Java modules try to bring to the platform.

Many familiar frameworks and developer tools rely heavily on reflection to achieve their capabilities, such as debuggers and code browsers. Plugin architectures, interactive environments, and REPLs also use reflection extensively. In fact, JShell itself could not be built in a language without a reflection subsystem. Let's exploit this and use JShell to explore some of reflection's key features, as shown next:

```
jshell> class Pet {
   ...>    public void feed() {
   ...>        System.out.println("Feed the pet");
   ...>    }
```

```
  ...> }
| created class Pet

jshell> var clz = Pet.class;
clz ==> class Pet
```

Now we have an object that represents the class type of Pet that we can use to do other actions, such as creating a new instance, as follows:

```
jshell> Object o = clz.newInstance();
o ==> Pet@66480dd7
```

The problem we have is that newInstance() returns Object, which isn't a very useful type. We could, of course, cast o back to Pet, but this requires us to know ahead of time what types we're working with, which rather defeats the point of the dynamic nature of reflection. So let's try something else:

```
jshell> import java.lang.reflect.Method;

jshell> Method m = clz.getMethod("feed", new Class[0]);
m ==> public void Pet.feed()
```

Now we have an object that represents the method feed(), but it represents it as abstract metadata—it is not attached to any specific instance.

The natural thing to do with an object that represents a method is to call it. The class java.lang.reflect.Method defines a method invoke() that has the effect of calling the method that the Method object represents.

> **NOTE** When working in JShell, we avoid a lot of exception-handling code. When writing regular Java code that uses reflection, you will have to deal with the possible exception types in one way or another.

For this call to succeed, we must provide the right number and types of arguments. This argument list must include the *receiver object* on which the method is being called reflectively (assuming the method is an instance method). In our simple example, this looks like this:

```
jshell> Object ret = m.invoke(o);
Feed the pet
ret ==> null
```
The call returns null because the feed() method is actually void.

As well as the Method objects, reflection also provides for objects that represent other fundamental concepts within the Java type system and language, such as fields, annotations, and constructors. These classes are found in the java.lang.reflect package, and some of them (such as Constructor) are generic types.

The reflection subsystem also had to be upgraded to deal with modules. Just as classes and methods can be treated reflectively, so there needs to be a reflective API for working with modules. The key class is, perhaps unsurprisingly, `java.lang.Module`, and we can access directly from a `Class` object as follows:

```
var module = String.class.getModule();
var descriptor = module.getDescriptor();
```

The descriptor of a module is of type `ModuleDescriptor` and provides a read-only view of the metadata about a module—basically equivalent to the contents of `module-info.class`.

Dynamic capabilities, such as discovery of modules, are also possible in the new reflective API. This is achieved via interfaces such as `ModuleFinder`, but a detailed description of how to work reflectively with the modules system is outside the scope of this book—the interested reader should consult chapter 12 of Nicolai Parlog's book, *The Java Module System* (Manning, 2019), http://mng.bz/gwGG.

4.5.2   *Combining class loading and reflection*

Let's look at an example that combines class loading and reflection. We won't need a full class loader that obeys the usual `findClass()` and `loadClass()` protocols. Instead, we'll just subclass `ClassLoader` to gain access to the protected `defineClass()` method.

The main method takes a list of filenames, and, if they're a Java class, it uses reflection to access each method in turn and detect whether or not it's a native method, as shown next:

```java
public class NativeMethodChecker {

    public static class EasyLoader extends ClassLoader {
        public EasyLoader() {
            super(EasyLoader.class.getClassLoader());
        }

        public Class<?> loadFromDisk(String fName) throws IOException {
            var b = Files.readAllBytes(Path.of(fName));
            return defineClass(null, b, 0, b.length);
        }
    }

    public static void main(String[] args) {
        if (args.length > 0) {
            var loader = new EasyLoader();
            for (var file : args) {
                System.out.println(file +" ::");
                try {
                    var clazz = loader.loadFromDisk(file);
                    for (var m : clazz.getMethods()) {
                        if (Modifier.isNative(m.getModifiers())) {
                            System.out.println(m.getName());
                        }
                    }
                }
```

```
            } catch (IOException | ClassFormatError x) {
                System.out.println("Not a class file");
            }
        }
      }
    }
}
```

These types of examples can be fun to explore the dynamic nature of the Java platform and to learn how the Reflection API works. However, it's important that a well-grounded Java developer be conscious of the limitations and occasional frustrations that can occur when working reflectively.

4.5.3   *Problems with reflection*

The Reflection API has been part of the Java platform since version 1.1 (1996), and in the 25 years since its arrival, a number of issues and weaknesses have come to light. Some of these inconveniences follow:

- It's a very old API with array types everywhere (it predates the Java Collections).
- Figuring out which method overload to call is painful.
- API has two different methods, `getMethod()` and `getDeclaredMethod()`, to access methods reflectively.
- API provides the `setAccessible()` method, which can be used to ignore access control.
- Exception handling is complex for reflective calls—checked exceptions are elevated to runtime exceptions.
- Boxing and unboxing is necessary to make reflective calls that pass or return primitives.
- Primitive types require placeholder class objects, for example, `int.class`, which is actually of type `Class<Integer>`.
- The `void` methods require the introduction of the `java.lang.Void` type.

As well as the various awkward corners in the API, Java Reflection has always suffered from poor performance for several reasons, including unfriendliness to the JVM's JIT compiler.

> **NOTE** Solving the problem of reflective call performance was one of the major reasons for the addition of the Method Handles API, which we will meet in chapter 17.

There is one final problem with reflection, which is perhaps more of a philosophical problem (or antipattern): developers frequently encounter reflection as one of the first truly advanced techniques that they meet when leveling up in Java. As a result, it can become overused, or a *Golden Hammer* technique—used to implement systems that are excessively flexible or which display an internal mini-framework that is not really needed (sometimes called the *Inner Framework* antipattern). Such systems are often very configurable but at the expense of encoding the domain model into configuration rather than directly in the domain types.

Reflection is a great technique and one that the well-grounded Java developer should have in their toolbox, but it is not suitable for every situation, and most developers will need to use it only sparingly.

Summary

- The class file format and class loading are central to the operation of the JVM. They're essential for any language that wants to run on the VM.
- The various phases of class loading enable both security and performance features at runtime.
- JVM bytecode is organized into families with related functionality.
- Using `javap` to disassemble class files can help you understand the lower level.
- Reflection is a major feature and extremely powerful.

5

Java concurrency fundamentals

This chapter covers

- Concurrency theory
- Block-structured concurrency
- Synchronization
- The Java Memory Model (JMM)
- Concurrency support in bytecode

Java has two, mostly separate concurrency APIs: the older API, which is usually called *block-structured concurrency* or *synchronization-based concurrency* or even "classic concurrency," and the newer API, which is normally referred to by its Java package name, java.util.concurrent.

In this book, we're going to talk about both approaches. In this chapter, we'll begin our journey by looking at the first of these two approaches. After that, in the next chapter, we'll introduce java.util.concurrent. Much later, we'll return to the subject of concurrency in chapter 16, "Advanced Concurrent Programming," which discusses advanced techniques, concurrency in non-Java JVM languages, and the interplay between concurrency and functional programming.

Let's get started and meet the classic approach to concurrency. This was the only API available until Java 5. As you might guess from the alternative name, "synchronization-based concurrency," this is the language-level API that is built into the platform and depends upon the `synchronized` and `volatile` keywords.

It is a low-level API and can be somewhat difficult to work with, but it is very much worth understanding. It provides a solid foundation for the chapters later in the book that explain other types and aspects of concurrency.

In fact, correctly reasoning about the other forms of concurrency is very difficult without at least a working knowledge of the low-level API and concepts that we will introduce in this chapter. As we encounter the relevant topics, we will also introduce enough theory to illuminate the other views of concurrency that we'll discuss later in the book, including when we meet concurrency in non-Java languages.

To make sense of Java's approach to concurrent programming, we're going to start off by talking about a small amount of theory. After that, we'll discuss the impact that "design forces" have in the design and implementation of systems. We'll talk about the two most important of these forces, *safety* and *liveness,* and mention some of the others.

An important section (and the longest one in the chapter) is the detail of block-structured concurrency and an exploration of the low-level threading API. We'll conclude this chapter by discussing the Java Memory Model (JMM), and then using the bytecode techniques that we learned in chapter 4 to understand the real source of some common complexities in concurrent Java programming.

5.1   Concurrency theory primer

Let's get started on our journey into concurrency with a cautionary tale before we meet some basic theory.

5.1.1   But I already know about Thread

It's one of the most common (and potentially deadly) mistakes a developer can make: to assume that an acquaintance with `Thread`, `Runnable`, and the language-level basic primitives of Java's concurrency mechanism are enough to be a competent developer of concurrent code. In fact, the subject of concurrency is a large one, and good multi-threaded development is difficult and continues to cause problems for even the best developers with years of experience under their belts.

It is also true that the area of concurrency is undergoing a massive amount of active research at present—this has been going on for at least the last 5–10 years and shows no signs of abating. These innovations are likely to have an impact on Java and the other languages you'll use over the course of your career.

In the first edition of this book, we made the following claim: "If we were to pick one fundamental area of computing that's likely to change radically in terms of industry practice over the next five years, it would be concurrency." Not only has history borne out this claim, but we feel comfortable rolling this prediction forward—the next five years will see a continued emphasis on the different approaches to concurrency that are now part of the programming landscape.

So, rather than try to be a definitive guide to every aspect of concurrent programming, the aim of this chapter is to make you aware of the underlying platform mechanisms that explain why Java's concurrency works the way it does. We'll also cover enough general concurrency theory to give you the vocabulary to understand the issues involved and to teach you about both the necessity and the difficulty involved in getting concurrency right. First, we'll discuss what every well-grounded Java developer should know about hardware and one of the most important theoretical limitations of concurrency.

5.1.2   Hardware

Let's start with some basic facts about concurrency and multithreading:

- Concurrent programming is fundamentally about performance.
- There are basically no good reasons for implementing a concurrent algorithm if the system you are running on has sufficient performance that a serial algorithm will work.
- Modern computer systems have multiple processing cores—even mobile phones have two or four cores today.
- All Java programs are multithreaded, even those that have only a single application thread.

This last point is true because the JVM is itself a multithreaded binary that can use multiple cores (e.g., for JIT compilation or garbage collection). In addition, the standard library also includes APIs that use *runtime-managed concurrency* to implement multithreaded algorithms for some execution tasks.

> **NOTE** It is entirely possible that a Java application will run *faster* just by upgrading the JVM it runs on, due to performance improvements in the runtime.

A fuller discussion of hardware takes place in chapter 7, but these basic facts are so fundamental and so relevant to concurrent programming that we want to introduce them immediately.

Now let's meet *Amdahl's law*, named after an early IBM computer scientist, Gene Amdahl, sometimes called the "father of the mainframe."

5.1.3   Amdahl's law

This is a simple, rough-and-ready model for reasoning about the efficiency of sharing work over multiple execution units. In the model, the execution units are abstract, so you can think of them as threads, but they could also be processes, or any other entity that is capable of carrying out work.

> **NOTE** None of the setup for or consequences of Amdahl's law depend on the details of how the work is done or the precise nature of the execution units or how the computing systems are implemented.

The basic premise is that we have a single task that can be subdivided into smaller units for processing. This allows us to use multiple execution units to speed up the time taken to complete the work.

So, if we have N processors (or threads to do the work), then we might naively expect the elapsed time to be T1 / N (if T1 is the time the job would take on a single processor). In this model, we can finish the job as quickly as we like by just adding execution units and thereby increasing N.

However, splitting up the work is not free! A (hopefully small) overhead is involved in the subdividing and recombination of the task. Let's assume that this *communication overhead* (sometime called the *serial part* of the calculation) is an overhead that amounts to a few percent, and we can represent it by a number s ($0 < s < 1$). So, a typical value for s might be 0.05 (or 5%, whichever way you'd prefer to express it). This means that the task will always take at least s * T1 to complete—no matter how many processing units we throw at it.

This assumes that s does not depend upon N, of course, but in practice, the dividing up of work that s represents may get more complex and require *more* time as N increases. It is extremely difficult to conceive of a system architecture in which s *decreases* as N increases. So the simple assumption of "s is constant" is usually understood to be a *best-case* scenario.

So, the easiest way to think about Amdahl's law is: if s is between 0 and 1, then the maximum speedup that can be achieved is 1 / s. This result is somewhat depressing—it means that if the communication overhead is just 2%, the maximum speedup that can ever be achieved (even with thousands of processors working at full speed) is 50X.

Amdahl's law has a slightly more complex formulation, which is represented like this:

```
T(N) = s + (1/N) * (T1 - s)
```

This can be seen visually in figure 5.1. Note that the *x*-axis is a logarithmic scale—the convergence to 1 / s would be very hard to see in a linear scale representation.

Having set the scene with hardware and a first, very simple concurrency model, let's dive into the specifics of how Java handles threading.

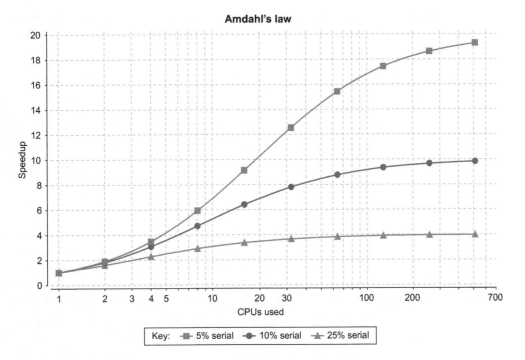

Figure 5.1 Amdahl's law

5.1.4 Explaining Java's threading model

Java's threading model is based on the following two fundamental concepts:

- Shared, visible-by-default mutable state
- Preemptive thread scheduling by the operating system

Let's consider the following most important aspects of these ideas:

- Objects can be easily shared between all threads within a process.
- Objects can be changed ("mutated") by any threads that have a reference to them.
- The thread scheduler (the operating system) can swap threads on and off cores at any time, more or less.
- Methods must be able to be swapped out while they're running (otherwise, a method with an infinite loop would steal the CPU forever).
- This, however, runs the risk of an unpredictable thread swap, leaving a method "half-done" and an object in an inconsistent state.
- Objects can be *locked* to protect vulnerable data.

The last point is absolutely crucial—without it there is a huge risk of changes being made in one thread not being seen correctly in other threads. In Java, the ability to lock objects is provided by the `synchronized` keyword in the core language.

NOTE Technically, Java provides *monitors* on each of its objects, which combine a lock (aka mutual exclusion) with the ability to wait for a certain condition to become true.

Java's thread-and-lock-based concurrency is very low level and often hard to work with. To cope with this, a set of concurrency libraries, known as `java.util.concurrent` after the Java package where the new classes live, was introduced in Java 5. This provided a set of tools for writing concurrent code that many programmers find easier to use than the classic block-structured concurrency primitives. We will discuss `java.util.concurrent` in the next chapter and will focus on the language-level API for now.

5.1.5   *Lessons learned*

Java was the first mainstream programming language to have built-in support for multithreaded programming. This represented a huge step forward at the time, but now, 15 years later, we've learned a lot more about how to write concurrent code.

It turns out that some of Java's initial design decisions are quite difficult for most programmers to work with. This is unfortunate, because the increasing trend in hardware is toward processors with many cores, and the only good way to take advantage of those cores is with concurrent code. We'll discuss some of the difficulties of concurrent code in this chapter. The subject of modern processors naturally requiring concurrent programming is covered in some detail in chapter 7 where we discuss performance.

As developers become more experienced with writing concurrent code, they find themselves running up against recurring concerns that are important to their systems. We call these concerns *design forces*. They're high-level concepts that exist (and often conflict) in the design of practical concurrent OO systems. We're going to spend a little bit of time looking at some of the most important of these forces in the next couple of sections.

5.2   *Design concepts*

The most important design forces, listed next, were catalogued by Doug Lea as he was doing his landmark work producing `java.util.concurrent`:

- Safety (also known as *concurrent type safety*)
- Liveness
- Performance
- Reusability

Let's look at each of these forces now.

5.2.1 *Safety and concurrent type safety*

Safety is about ensuring that object instances remain self-consistent, regardless of any other operations that may be happening at the same time. If a system of objects has this property, it's said to be *safe* or *concurrently typesafe*.

As you might guess from the name, one way to think about concurrency is in terms of an extension to the regular concepts of object modeling and type safety. In nonconcurrent code, you want to ensure that regardless of what public methods you call on an object, it's in a well-defined and consistent state at the end of the method. The usual way to do this is to keep all of an object's state private and expose a public API of methods that alter the object's state only in a way that makes senses for the design domain.

Concurrent type safety is the same basic concept as type safety for an object, but applied to the much more complex world in which other threads are potentially operating on the same objects on different CPU cores at the same time. For example, consider this simple class:

```java
public class StringStack {
    private String[] values = new String[16];
    private int current = 0;

    public boolean push(String s) {
        // Exception handling elided
        if (current < values.length) {
            values[current] = s;
            current = current + 1;
            return true;
        }
        return false;
    }

    public String pop() {
        if (current < 1) {
            return null;
        }
        current = current - 1;
        return values[current];
    }
}
```

When used by single-threaded client code, this is fine. However, preemptive thread scheduling can cause problems. For example, a context switch between execution threads can occur at this point in the code:

```java
public boolean push(String s) {
        if (current < values.length) {
            values[current] = s;
            // .... context switch here          The object is left in an inconsistent
            current = current + 1;               and incorrect state.
            return true;
        }
        return false;
    }
```

If the object is then viewed from another thread, one part of the state (`values`) will have been updated but the other (`current`) will not. Exploring, and solving, this problem is the primary theme of this chapter.

In general, one strategy for safety is to never return from a nonprivate method in an inconsistent state, and to never call any nonprivate method (and certainly not a method on any other object) while in an inconsistent state. If this practice is combined with a way of protecting the object (such as a synchronization lock or critical section) while it's inconsistent, the system can be guaranteed to be safe.

5.2.2   Liveness

A live system is one in which every attempted activity eventually either progresses or fails. A system that is not live is basically stuck—it will neither progress toward success or fail.

The keyword in the definition is *eventually*—there is a distinction between a transient failure to progress (which isn't that bad in isolation, even if it's not ideal) and a permanent failure. Transient failures could be caused by a number of underlying problems, such as

- Locking or waiting to acquire a lock
- Waiting for input (such as network I/O)
- Temporary failure of a resource
- Not enough CPU time available to run the thread

Permanent failures could be due to a number of causes. Some of the most common follow:

- Deadlock
- Unrecoverable resource problem (such as if the network filesystem [NFS] goes away)
- Missed signal

We'll discuss locking and several of these other problems later in the chapter, although you may already be familiar with some or all of them.

5.2.3   Performance

The performance of a system can be quantified in a number of different ways. In chapter 7, we'll talk about performance analysis and techniques for tuning, and we'll introduce a number of other metrics you should know about. For now, think of performance as being a measure of how much work a system can do with a given amount of resources.

5.2.4   Reusability

Reusability forms a fourth design force, because it isn't really covered by any of the other considerations. A concurrent system that has been designed for easy reuse is sometimes very desirable, although this isn't always easy to implement. One approach is to use a reusable toolbox (like `java.util.concurrent`) and build nonreusable application code on top of it.

5.2.5 *How and why do the forces conflict?*

The design forces are often in opposition to each other, and this tension can be viewed as a central reason that designing good concurrent systems is difficult, as explained by the following points:

- Safety stands in opposition to liveness—safety is about ensuring that bad things don't happen, whereas liveness requires progress to be made.
- Reusable systems tend to expose their internals, which can cause problems with safety.
- A naïvely written safe system will typically not be very performant, because it usually resorts to heavy use of locking to provide safety guarantees.

The balance that you should ultimately try to achieve is for the code to be flexible enough to be useful for a wide range of problems, closed enough to be safe, and still reasonably live and performant. This is quite a tall order, but, fortunately, some practical techniques can help with this. Here are some of the most common in rough order of usefulness:

1 Restrict the external communication of each subsystem as much as possible. Data hiding is a powerful tool for aiding with safety.
2 Make the internal structure of each subsystem as deterministic as possible. For example, design in static knowledge of the threads and objects in each subsystem, even if the subsystems will interact in a concurrent, nondeterministic way.
3 Apply policy approaches that client apps must adhere to. This technique is powerful but relies on user apps cooperating, and it can be hard to debug if a badly behaved app disobeys the rules.
4 Document the required behavior. This is the weakest of the alternatives, but it's sometimes necessary if the code is to be deployed in a very general context.

The developer should be aware of each of these possible safety mechanisms and should use the strongest possible technique, while being aware that in some circumstances, only the weaker mechanisms are possible.

5.2.6 *Sources of overhead*

Many aspects of a concurrent system can contribute to the inherent overhead:

- Monitors (i.e., locks and condition variables)
- Number of context switches
- Number of threads
- Scheduling
- Locality of memory
- Algorithm design

This should form the basis of a checklist in your mind. When developing concurrent code, you should ensure that you have thought about everything on this list.

In particular, the last of these—algorithm design—is an area in which developers can really distinguish themselves, because learning about algorithm design will make you a better programmer in any language.

Two standard texts (highly recommended by the authors) are *Introduction to Algorithms* by Cormen et al. (MIT, 2009)—don't be deceived by the title; this is a serious work—and *The Algorithm Design Manual* (3rd ed.), by Skiena (Springer-Verlag, 2020). For both single-threaded and concurrent algorithms, these books are excellent choices for further reading.

We'll mention many of these sources of overhead in this chapter and the subsequent ones (especially chapter 7, about performance), but now let's turn to our next subject: a review of Java's "classic" concurrency and a close look at why programming with it can be difficult.

5.3   *Block-structured concurrency (pre-Java 5)*

Much of our coverage of Java concurrency is about discussing alternatives to the language-level, aka block-synchronization-based, aka *intrinsic* approach to concurrency. But to get the most out of the discussion of the alternatives, it's important to have a firm grasp of what's good and bad about the classic view of concurrency.

To that end, for the rest of this chapter, we'll discuss the original, quite low-level way of tackling multithreaded programming using Java's concurrency keywords— synchronized, volatile, and so on. This discussion will take place in the context of the design forces and with an eye to what will come later on.

Following on from that, we'll briefly consider the life cycle of a thread and then discuss common techniques (and pitfalls) of concurrent code, such as fully synchronized objects, deadlocks, the volatile keyword, and immutability. Let's get started with an overview of synchronization.

5.3.1   *Synchronization and locks*

As you probably already know, the synchronized keyword can be applied either to a block or to a method. It indicates that before entering the block or method, a thread must acquire the appropriate lock. For example, let's think about a method to withdraw money from a bank account, as shown next:

```
public synchronized boolean withdraw(int amount) {        ◁─┐ Only one thread can try
    // Check to see amount > 0, throw if not               │ to withdraw from this
    if (balance >= amount) {                                │ account at once.
        balance = balance - amount;
        return true;
    }

    return false;
}
```

The method must acquire the lock belonging to the object instance (or the lock belonging to the `Class` object for `static synchronized` methods). For a block, the programmer should indicate which object's lock is to be acquired.

Only one thread can be progressing through any of an object's synchronized blocks or methods at once; if other threads try to enter, they're suspended by the JVM. This is true regardless of whether the other thread is trying to enter the same or a different synchronized block on the same object. In concurrency theory, this type of construct is sometimes referred to as a *critical section*, but this term is more commonly used in C++ than in Java.

> **NOTE** Have you ever wondered why the Java keyword used for a critical section is `synchronized`? Why not "critical" or "locked"? What is it that's being *synchronized*? We'll return to this in section 5.3.5, but if you don't know or have never thought about it, you may want to take a couple of minutes to ponder it before continuing.

Let's look at some basic facts about synchronization and locks in Java. Hopefully you already have most (or all) of these at your fingertips:

- Only objects—not primitives—can be locked.
- Locking an array of objects doesn't lock the individual objects.
- A synchronized method can be thought of as equivalent to a `synchronized (this) { … }` block that covers the entire method (but note that they're represented differently in bytecode).
- A `static synchronized` method locks the `Class` object, because there's no instance object to lock.
- If you need to lock a `Class` object, consider carefully whether you need to do so explicitly or by using `getClass()`, because the behavior of the two approaches will be different in a subclass.
- Synchronization in an inner class is independent of the outer class (to see why this is so, remember how inner classes are implemented).
- `synchronized` doesn't form part of the method signature, so it can't appear on a method declaration in an interface.
- Unsynchronized methods don't look at or care about the state of any locks, and they can progress while synchronized methods are running.
- Java's locks are reentrant—a thread holding a lock that encounters a synchronization point for the same lock (such as a `synchronized` method calling another `synchronized` method on the same object) will be allowed to continue.

> **NOTE** Non-reentrant locking schemes do exist in other languages (and can be synthesized in Java—see the detail of the Javadoc for `ReentrantLock` in `java.util.concurrent.locks` if you want the gory details), but they're generally painful to deal with, and they're best avoided unless you really know what you're doing.

That's enough review of Java's synchronization. Now let's move on to discuss the states that a thread moves through during its life cycle.

5.3.2 The state model for a thread

In figure 5.2, you can see the state model for a Java thread. This governs how a Java thread progresses through its life cycle.

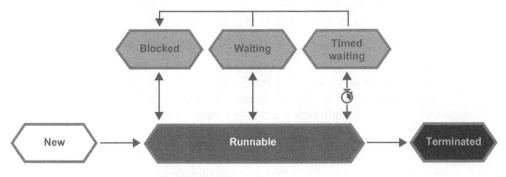

Figure 5.2   The state model of a Java thread

Java has an enum called `Thread.State`, which corresponds to the states in the above state mode and is a layer over the operating system's view of the thread state.

> **NOTE** Every operating system has its own version of threads, and they may differ in the precise details. In most cases, modern operating systems have reasonably similar thread and scheduling implementations, but this was not always the case (e.g., Solaris or Windows XP).

A Java thread object is initially created in the NEW state. At this time, an OS thread does not yet exist (and may never exist). To create the execution thread, `Thread.start()` must be called. This signals the OS to actually create a thread.

The scheduler will place the new thread into the run queue and, at some later point, will find a core for it to run upon (some amount of waiting time may be involved if the machine is heavily loaded). From there, the thread can proceed by consuming its time allocation and be placed back into the run queue to await further processor time slices. This is the action of the forcible thread scheduling that we mentioned in section 5.1.1.

Throughout this scheduling process, of being placed on a core, running, and being placed back in the run queue, the Java `Thread` object remains in the RUNNABLE state. As well as this scheduling action, the thread itself can indicate that it isn't able to make use of the core at this time. This can be achieved in two different ways:

1 The program code indicates by calling `Thread.sleep()` that the thread should wait for a fixed time before continuing.
2 The thread recognizes that it must wait until some external condition has been met and calls `Object.wait()`.

In both cases, the thread is immediately removed from the core by the OS. However, the behavior after that point is different in each case.

In the first case, the thread is asking to sleep for a definite amount of time. The Java thread transitions into the TIMED_WAITING state, and the operating system sets a timer. When it expires, the sleeping thread is woken up and is ready to run again and is placed back in the run queue.

The second case is slightly different. It uses the condition aspect of Java's per-object monitors. The thread will transition into WAITING and will wait indefinitely. It will not normally wake up until the operating system signals that the condition may have been met—usually by some other thread calling Object.notify() on the current object.

As well as these two possibilities that are under the threads control, a thread can transition into the BLOCKED state because it's waiting on I/O or to acquire a lock held by another thread. Finally, if the OS thread corresponding to a Java Thread has ceased execution, then that thread object will have transitioned into the TERMINATED state. Let's move on to talk about one well-known way to solve the synchronization problem: the idea of fully synchronized objects.

5.3.3 Fully synchronized objects

Earlier in this chapter, we introduced the concept of concurrent type safety and mentioned one strategy for achieving this. Let's look at a more complete description of this strategy, which is usually called *fully synchronized objects*. If all of the following rules are obeyed, the class is known to be thread-safe and will also be live.

A fully synchronized class is a class that meets all of the following conditions:

- All fields are always initialized to a consistent state in every constructor.
- There are no public fields.
- Object instances are guaranteed to be consistent after returning from any non-private method (assuming the state was consistent when the method was called).
- All methods provably terminate in bounded time.
- All methods are synchronized.
- No method calls another instance's methods while in an inconsistent state.
- No method calls any nonprivate method on the current instance while in an inconsistent state.

Listing 5.1 shows an example of such a class from the backend of a banking system. The class FSOAccount models an account. The FSO prefix is there to clearly indicate that this implementation uses fully synchronized objects.

This situation provides deposits, withdrawals, and balance queries—a classic conflict between read and write operations—so synchronization is used to prevent inconsistency.

Listing 5.1 A fully synchronized class

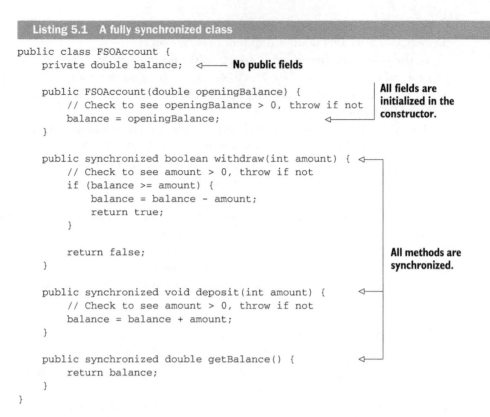

```
public class FSOAccount {
    private double balance;    ←——— No public fields

    public FSOAccount(double openingBalance) {
        // Check to see openingBalance > 0, throw if not
        balance = openingBalance;
    }

    public synchronized boolean withdraw(int amount) {
        // Check to see amount > 0, throw if not
        if (balance >= amount) {
            balance = balance - amount;
            return true;
        }

        return false;
    }

    public synchronized void deposit(int amount) {
        // Check to see amount > 0, throw if not
        balance = balance + amount;
    }

    public synchronized double getBalance() {
        return balance;
    }
}
```

All fields are initialized in the constructor.

All methods are synchronized.

This seems fantastic at first glance—the class is both safe and live. The problem comes with performance. Just because something is safe and live doesn't mean it's necessarily going to be very quick. You have to use `synchronized` to coordinate all the accesses (both get and put) to the balance, and that locking is ultimately going to slow you down. This is a central problem of this way of handling concurrency.

In addition to the performance problems, the code in listing 5.1 is quite fragile. You can see that you never touch `balance` outside of a synchronized method, but this is possible only to check by eye due to the small amount of code in play.

In real, larger systems, this sort of manual verification would not be possible due to the amount of code. It's too easy for bugs to creep into larger codebases that use this approach, which is another reason that the Java community began to look for more robust approaches.

5.3.4 *Deadlocks*

Another classic problem of concurrency (and not just Java's take on it) is the *deadlock*. Consider listing 5.2, which is a slightly extended form of the previous example. In this version, as well as modeling the account balance, we also have a `transferTo()` method that can move money from one account to another.

NOTE This is a naïve attempt to build a multithreaded transaction system. It's designed to demonstrate deadlocking—you shouldn't use this as the basis for real code.

In the next listing, let's add a method to transfer funds between two FSOAccount objects, like this.

Listing 5.2 A deadlocking example

```java
public synchronized boolean transferTo(FSOAccount other, int amount) {
    // Check to see amount > 0, throw if not
    // Simulate some other checks that need to occur
    try {
        Thread.sleep(10);
    } catch (InterruptedException e) {
        Thread.currentThread().interrupt();
    }
    if (balance >= amount) {
        balance = balance - amount;
        other.deposit(amount);
        return true;
    }

    return false;
}
```

Now, let's actually introduce some concurrency in a main class:

```java
public class FSOMain {
    private static final int MAX_TRANSFERS = 1_000;

    public static void main(String[] args) throws InterruptedException {
        FSOAccount a = new FSOAccount(10_000);
        FSOAccount b = new FSOAccount(10_000);
        Thread tA = new Thread(() -> {
            for (int i = 0; i < MAX_TRANSFERS; i = i + 1) {
                boolean ok = a.transferTo(b, 1);
                if (!ok) {
                    System.out.println("Thread A failed at "+ i);
                }
            }
        });
        Thread tB = new Thread(() -> {
            for (int i = 0; i < MAX_TRANSFERS; i = i + 1) {
                boolean ok = b.transferTo(a, 1);
                if (!ok) {
                    System.out.println("Thread B failed at "+ i);
                }
            }
        });
        tA.start();
        tB.start();
        tA.join();
        tB.join();
```

```
        System.out.println("End: "+ a.getBalance() + " : "+ b.getBalance());
    }
}
```

At first glance, this code looks sensible. You have two transactions being performed by separate threads. This doesn't seem too outlandish a design— just threads sending money between the two accounts—and all the methods are synchronized.

Note that we've introduced a small sleep into the transferTo() method. This is to allow the thread scheduler to run both threads and lead to the possibility of deadlock.

> **NOTE** The sleep is for demonstration purposes, not because it is something you'd actually do when writing code for a bank transfer. It's there to simulate code that would actually be there in practice—a delay caused by a call to a database or an authorization check.

If you run the code, you'll normally see an example of a deadlock—both threads will run for a bit and eventually get stuck. The reason is that each thread requires the other to release the lock it holds before the transfer method can progress. This can be seen in figure 5.3.

Threads need both x and y to progress.

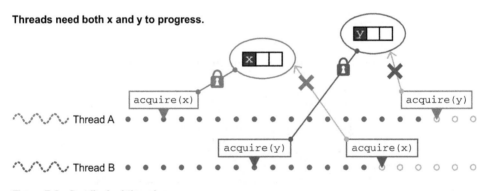

Figure 5.3   Deadlocked threads

Another way of looking at this can be seen in figure 5.4, where we show the Thread Dump view from the JDK Mission Control tool (we will have more to say about this tool in chapter 7 and will show you how to find this useful view then).

The two threads have been created as Thread-0 and Thread-1, and we can see that Thread-0 has locked one reference and is BLOCKED, waiting to lock the other. The corresponding thread dump for Thread-1 would show the opposite configuration of the locks, hence the deadlock.

> **NOTE** In terms of the fully synchronized object approach, this deadlock occurs because of the violation of the "bounded time" principle. When the code calls other.deposit(), we cannot guarantee how long the code will run for, because the Java Memory Model gives us no guarantees on when a blocked monitor will be released.

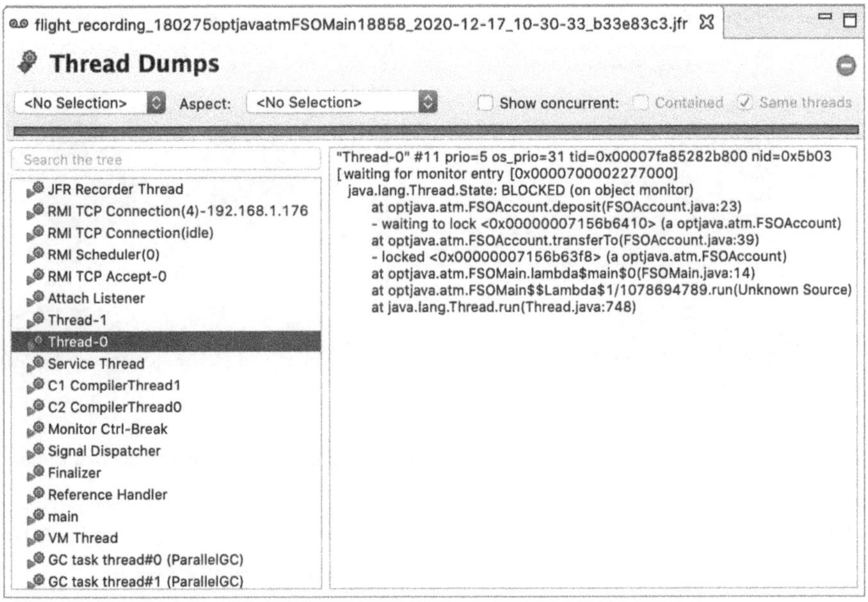

Figure 5.4   Deadlocked threads

To deal with deadlocks, one technique is to always acquire locks in the same order in every thread. In the preceding example, the first thread to start acquires them in the order A, B, whereas the second thread acquires them in the order B, A. If both threads had insisted on acquiring them in the order A, B, the deadlock would have been avoided, because the second thread would have been blocked from running at all until the first had completed and released its locks. Later in the chapter, we will show a simple way to arrange for all locks to be obtained in the same order and a way to verify that this is indeed satisfied.

Next, we'll return to a puzzle we posed earlier: why the Java keyword for a critical section is named synchronized. This will then lead us into a discussion of the volatile keyword.

5.3.5   Why synchronized?

A simple conceptual model of concurrent programming is timesharing of a CPU— that is, threads swapping on and off a single core. This classic view is shown in figure 5.5.

However, this has not been an accurate picture of modern hardware for many years now. Twenty years ago, a working programmer could go for years on end without encountering a system that had more than one or at most two processing cores. That is no longer the case.

Today, anything as big as or larger than a mobile phone has multiple cores, so the mental model should be different, too, encompassing multiple threads all running on different cores at the same physical moment (and potentially operating on shared

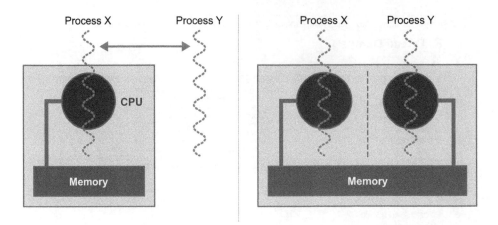

Figure 5.5   The single (left) and multicore (right) of thinking about concurrency and threads

data). You can see this in figure 5.5. For efficiency, each thread that is running simultaneously may have its own cached copy of data being operated on.

NOTE We will still present theoretical models of execution where our hypothetical computer has only one core. This is purely so that you can see that the nondeterministic concurrency problems we are discussing are inherent and not caused by particular aspects of hardware design.

With this picture in mind, let's turn to the question of the choice of keyword used to denote a locked section or a method.

We asked earlier, what is it that's being synchronized in the code in listing 5.1? The answer is: *the memory representation in different threads of the object being locked.* That is, after the synchronized method (or block) has completed, any and all changes that were made to the object being locked are flushed back to main memory before the lock is released, as illustrated in figure 5.6.

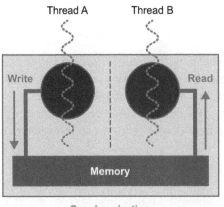

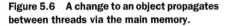

Synchronization

Figure 5.6   A change to an object propagates between threads via the main memory.

In addition, when a synchronized block is entered, after the lock has been acquired, any changes to the locked object are read in *from* main memory, so the thread with the lock is synchronized to the main memory's view of the object before the code in the locked section begins to execute.

5.3.6   *The volatile keyword*

Java has had the `volatile` keyword since the dawn of time (Java 1.0), and it's used as a simple way to deal with concurrent handling of object fields, including primitives. The following rules govern a volatile field:

- The value seen by a thread is always reread from the main memory before use.
- Any value written by a thread is always flushed through to the main memory before the bytecode instruction completes.

This is sometimes described as being "like a tiny little synchronized block" around the single operation, but this is misleading because `volatile` does not involve any locking. The action of `synchronized` is to use a mutual exclusion lock on an object to ensure that only one thread can execute a synchronized method on that object. Synchronized methods can contain many read and write operations on the object, and they will be executed as an indivisible unit (from the point of view of other threads) because the results of the method executing on the object are not seen until the method exits and the object is flushed back to main memory.

The key point about `volatile` is that it allows for only *one* operation on the memory location, which will be immediately flushed to memory. This means either a single read, *or* a single write, but not more than that. We saw these two sorts of operations in figure 5.6.

A volatile variable should be used to model a variable only where writes to the variable don't depend on the current state (the read state) of the variable. This is a consequence of `volatile` guaranteeing only a single operation.

For example, the `++` and `--` operators are not safe to use on a `volatile`, because they are equivalent to v = v + 1 or v = v - 1. The increment example is a classic example of a *state-dependent update*.

For cases where the current state matters, you must always introduce a lock to be completely safe. So, `volatile` allows the programmer to write simplified code in some cases, but at the cost of the extra flushes on every access. Notice also that because the volatile mechanism doesn't introduce any locks, you can't deadlock using volatiles— only with synchronization. Later in the chapter, we will meet some other applications for `volatile` and discuss the mechanism in more detail.

5.3.7   *Thread states and methods*

A `java.lang.Thread` object is just that: a Java object that lives in the heap and contains metadata about an operating system thread that either exists, used to exist, or will potentially exist in the future.

Java defines the following states for a thread object, which correspond to OS thread states on mainstream operating systems. They are closely related to the state model we saw in figure 5.2:

- NEW—the Thread object has been created, but the actual OS thread has not.
- RUNNABLE—The thread is available to run. The OS is responsible for scheduling it.
- BLOCKED—The thread is not running; it needs to acquire a lock or is in a system call.
- WAITING—The thread is not running; it has called Object.wait() or Thread.join().
- TIMED_WAITING—The thread is not running; it has called Thread.sleep().
- TERMINATED—The thread is not running; it has completed execution.

All threads start in the NEW state and finish in the TERMINATED state, whether the thread's run() method exits normally or throws an exception.

NOTE The Java thread state model does not distinguish between whether a RUNNABLE thread is actually physically executing at that precise moment or is waiting (in the *run queue*).

The actual creation of the thread is done by the start() method, which calls into native code to actually perform the relevant system calls (e.g., clone() on Linux) to create the thread and begin code execution in the thread's run() method.

The standard Thread API in Java breaks down into three groups of methods. Rather than include a lot of boilerplate Javadoc descriptions of each method, we will just list them and leave the reader to consult the API docs for more detail.

The first is a group of methods for reading metadata about the thread:

- getId()
- getName()
- getState()
- getPriority()
- isAlive()
- isDaemon()
- isInterrupted()

Some of this metadata (such as the thread ID obtained from getId()) will be fixed for the lifetime of the thread. Some of it, such as the thread state and interrupted state, will naturally change as the thread runs, and some of it (e.g., the name and daemon status) can be set by the programmer. This leads us to the second group of methods:

- setDaemon()
- setName()
- setPriority()
- setUncaughtExceptionHandler()

It is often better for the programmer to configure any appropriate properties for threads before starting them.

Finally, the following set of thread control methods are used to start new threads and interact with other running threads:

- `start()`
- `interrupt()`
- `join()`

Note that `Thread.sleep()` does not appear in this list, because it's a static method that targets only the current thread.

> **NOTE** Some of the thread methods with timeouts (e.g., `Thread.join()` with a timeout parameter) may actually result in the thread being placed into `TIMED_WAITING` instead of `WAITING`.

Let's take a look at an example of how to use the thread methods in a typical life cycle of a simple multithreaded application:

```
Runnable r = () -> {
    var start = System.currentTimeMillis();
    try {
        Thread.sleep(1000);
    } catch (InterruptedException e) {
        e.printStackTrace();
    }
    var thisThread = Thread.currentThread();
    System.out.println(thisThread.getName() +
        " slept for "+ (System.currentTimeMillis() - start));
};

var t = new Thread(r);          ◁──┘ The thread's metadata
t.setName("Worker");                  object is created.
t.start();         ◁────────┐  The operating system
Thread.sleep(100);          │  creates an actual thread.
t.join();       ◁───────────┐
System.out.println("Exiting");│  The main thread pauses and waits for
                              │  the worker to exit before continuing.
```

This is pretty simple stuff: the main thread creates the worker, starts it, then waits for at least 100 ms (to give the scheduler a chance to run) before reaching the `join()` call, which causes it to pause until the worker thread exits. In the meantime, the worker thread completes the sleep, wakes up again, and prints out the message.

> **NOTE** The elapsed time for the sleep will most likely not be exactly 1000 ms. The operating system scheduler is nondeterministic, and so the best guarantee that is offered is that the operating system will attempt to ensure that the thread sleeps for the requested amount of time, unless woken. However, multithreaded programming is often about dealing with unexpected circumstances, as we will see in the next section.

INTERRUPTING THREADS

When working with threads, it's relatively common to want to safely interrupt the work a thread is doing, and methods are provided for that on the Thread object. However, they may not behave as we'd first expect. Let's run the following code that creates a thread, hard at work, and then tries to interrupt it:

```
var t = new Thread(() -> { while (true); });    Creates and starts a new
t.start();                                      thread that will run forever

t.interrupt();  <---|  Asks the thread to interrupt
|-> t.join();       |  itself (i.e., stop executing)
|
Waits in our main thread for the other to complete
```

If you run this code, you may be surprised to find that our join() will block forever. What's happening here is that thread interruption is opt-in—the methods being called in a thread have to explicitly check the interrupt state and respond to it, and our naive while loop never makes such a check. We can fix this in our loop by doing the expected check, as follows:

```
var t = new Thread(() -> { while (!Thread.interrupted()); });
t.start();

t.interrupt();              Checks our current thread's interrupt
t.join();                   state instead of looping on true
```

Now our loop will exit when requested, and our join() no longer blocks forever.

It is common for methods in the JDK that are blocking—whether on IO, waiting on a lock, or other scenarios—to check the thread interrupt state. The convention is that these methods will throw InterruptedException, a checked exception. This explains why, for instance, Thread.sleep() requires you to add the Interrupted-Exception to the method signature or handle it.

Let's modify our example from the previous section to see how Thread.sleep() behaves when interrupted:

```
Runnable r = () -> {
    var start = System.currentTimeMillis();      Our Runnable must handle the checked
    try {                                         InterruptedException. When we interrupt,
        Thread.sleep(1000);                       it prints the stack, and then execution
    } catch (InterruptedException e) {  <-----    continues from here.
        e.printStackTrace();
    }
    var thisThread = Thread.currentThread();
    System.out.println(thisThread.getName() +
        " slept for "+ (System.currentTimeMillis() - start));
    if (thisThread.isInterrupted()) {
        System.out.println("Thread "+ thisThread.getName() +" interrupted");
    }
};

var t = new Thread(r);
```

```
t.setName("Worker");
t.start();           ◁──────── Creates the worker thread
Thread.sleep(100);
t.interrupt();       ◁──────────────┐ The main thread interrupts
t.join();                           │ the worker and wakes it up.
System.out.println("Exiting");
```

When we run this code, we see some output like this:

```
java.lang.InterruptedException: sleep interrupted
    at java.base/java.lang.Thread.sleep(Native Method)
    at examples.LifecycleWithInterrupt.lambda$main$0
     (LifecycleWithInterrupt.java:9)
    at java.base/java.lang.Thread.run(Thread.java:832)
Worker slept for 101
Exiting
```

If you look closely, you will see that the message `"Thread Worker interrupted"` does not appear. This reveals a pertinent fact about handling interrupts in our code: checks for the thread's interruption state actually reset the state. The code that throws the standard `InterruptedException` cleared that interrupt, because it's considered "handled" when the exception is thrown.

> **NOTE** We have the following two methods for checking the interrupt state: a static `Thread.interrupted()`, which implicitly looks at the current thread, and an instance level `isInterrupted()` on a thread object. The static version clears the state after checking and is what's expected for use before throwing an `InterruptedException`. The instance method, on the other hand, doesn't alter the state.

If we want to retain the information that our thread was interrupted, we have to handle that directly ourselves. For our simple example where we need the state only later in the thread's code, something like this would work:

```
Runnable r = () -> {
    var start = System.currentTimeMillis();  │ Sets up the state to record
    var wasInterrupted = false;    ◁─────────┘ a possible interruption
    try {
        Thread.sleep(1000);
    } catch (InterruptedException e) {
        wasInterrupted = true;     ◁────── Records the interruption
        e.printStackTrace();
    }
    var thisThread = Thread.currentThread();
    System.out.println(thisThread.getName() +
        " slept for "+ (System.currentTimeMillis() - start));
    if (wasInterrupted) {
        System.out.println("Thread "+ thisThread.getName() +" interrupted");
    }
};
```

```
var t = new Thread(r);
t.setName("Worker");
t.start();
Thread.sleep(100);
t.interrupt();
t.join();
System.out.println("Exiting");
```

In more complex situations, you may wish to ensure an InterruptedException is rethrown for callers, throw a custom exception of some sort, perform your own custom logic, or even restore the interrupt state onto the thread in question. All of these are possible, depending on your specific needs.

WORKING WITH EXCEPTIONS AND THREADS

Another issue for multithreaded programming is how to handle exceptions that may be thrown from within a thread. For example, suppose that we are executing a Runnable of unknown provenance. If it throws an exception and dies, then other code may not be aware of it. Fortunately, the Thread API provides the ability to add uncaught exception handlers to a thread before starting it, like this example:

```
var badThread = new Thread(() -> {
    throw new UnsupportedOperationException(); });

// Set a name before starting the thread
badThread.setName("An Exceptional Thread");

// Set the handler
badThread.setUncaughtExceptionHandler((t, e) -> {
    System.err.printf("Thread %d '%s' has thrown exception " +
                    "%s at line %d of %s",
            t.getId(),
            t.getName(),
            e.toString(),
            e.getStackTrace()[0].getLineNumber(),
            e.getStackTrace()[0].getFileName()); });

badThread.start();
```

The handler is an instance of UncaughtExceptionHandler, which is a functional interface, defined like this:

```
public interface UncaughtExceptionHandler {
    void uncaughtException(Thread t, Throwable e);
}
```

This method provides a simple callback to allow thread control code to take action based on the observed exception—for example, a thread pool may restart a thread that has exited in this way to maintain pool size.

NOTE Any exception thrown by `uncaughtException()` will be ignored by the JVM.

Before we move on, we need to discuss some other control methods of `Thread` that are deprecated and that should not be used by application programmers.

DEPRECATED THREAD METHODS

Java was the first mainstream language to support multithreaded programming out of the box. However, this "first mover" advantage had its dark side—many of the inherent issues that exist with concurrent programming were first encountered by programmers working in Java.

One aspect of this is the unfortunate fact that some of the methods in the original Thread API are simply unsafe and unfit to use, in particular, `Thread.stop()`. This method is essentially impossible to use safely—it kills another thread without any warning and with no way for the killed thread to ensure that any locked objects are made safe.

The deprecation of `stop()` followed close on the heels of its active use in early Java because stopping another thread required injecting an exception into the other thread's execution. However, it's impossible to know precisely *where* that other thread is in execution. Maybe the thread is killed in the middle of a `finally` block the developer assumed would run fully, and the program is left in a corrupted state.

The mechanism is that an unchecked `ThreadDeath` exception is triggered on the killed thread. It is not feasible for code to guard against such an exception with try blocks (any more than it is possible to reliably protect against an `OutOfMemoryError`), and so the exception immediately starts unwinding the stack of the killed thread, and all monitors are unlocked. This immediately makes potentially damaged objects visible to other threads, and so `stop()` is just not safe for use.

In addition to the reasonably well-known issues with `stop()`, several other methods also have serious issues. For example, `suspend()` does not cause any monitors to be released, so any thread that attempts to access any synchronized code that is locked by the suspended thread will block permanently, unless the suspended thread is reactivated. This represents a major liveness hazard, and so `suspend()` and `resume()` should never be used. The `destroy()` method was never implemented, but it would have suffered from the same issues if it had been.

> **NOTE** These dangerous thread methods have been deprecated since Java 1.2—over 20 years ago—and have recently been marked for removal (which will be a breaking change, to give you some idea of how seriously this is viewed).

The real solution to the problem of reliably controlling threads from other threads is best illustrated by the *Volatile Shutdown* pattern that we will meet later in the chapter. Now let's move on to one of the most useful techniques when handling data that must be shared safely when programming in a concurrent style.

5.3.8 *Immutability*

One technique that can be of great value is the use of immutable objects. These are objects that either have no state or that have only final fields (which must, therefore, be populated in the constructors of the objects). These are always safe and live, because their state can't be mutated, so they can never be in an inconsistent state.

One problem is that any values that are required to initialize a particular object must be passed into the constructor. This can lead to unwieldy constructor calls, with many parameters. As a result, many coders use a *factory method* instead. This can be as simple as using a static method on the class, instead of a constructor, to produce new objects. The constructors are usually made protected or private, so that the static factory methods are the only way of instantiating. For example, consider a simple deposit class that we might see in a banking system, as shown here:

```java
public final class Deposit {
    private final double amount;
    private final LocalDate date;
    private final Account payee;

    private Deposit(double amount, LocalDate date, Account payee) {
        this.amount = amount;
        this.date = date;
        this.payee = payee;
    }

    public static Deposit of(double amount, LocalDate date, Account payee) {
        return new Deposit(amount, date, payee);
    }

    public static Deposit of(double amount, Account payee) {
        return new Deposit(amount, LocalDate.now(), payee);
    }
```

This has the fields of the class, a private constructor, and two factory methods, one of which is a convenience method for creating deposits for today. Next up are the accessor methods for the fields:

```java
    public double amount() {
        return amount;
    }

    public LocalDate date() {
        return date;
    }

    public Account payee() {
        return payee;
    }
```

Note that in our example, these are presented in *record style*, where the name of the accessor method matches the name of the field. This is in contrast to *bean style*, when getter methods are prefixed with get and setter methods (for any nonfinal fields) are prefixed with set.

Immutable objects obviously can't be changed, so what happens when we want to make changes to one of them? For example, it's very common that if a deposit or other transaction can't take place on a specific day, that transaction is "rolled" to the following day. We can achieve this by having an instance method on the type that returns an object that is almost the same, but has some modified fields, as follows:

```
public Deposit roll() {
    // Log audit event for rolling the date
    return new Deposit(amount, date.plusDays(1), payee);
}

public Deposit amend(double newAmount) {
    // Log audit event for amending the amount
    return new Deposit(newAmount, date, payee);
}
```

One problem that immutable objects potentially have is that they may need many parameters to be passed in to the factory method. This isn't always very convenient, especially when you may need to accumulate state from several sources before creating a new immutable object.

To solve this, we can use the Builder pattern. This is a combination of two constructs: a static inner class that implements a generic builder interface, and a private constructor for the immutable class itself.

The static inner class is the builder for the immutable class, and it provides the only way that a developer can get hold of new instances of the immutable type. One very common implementation is for the Builder class to have exactly the same fields as the immutable class but to allow mutation of the fields. This listing shows how you might use this to model a more complex view of a deposit.

Listing 5.3   Immutable objects and builders

```
public static class DepositBuilder implements Builder<Deposit> {
    private double amount;
    private LocalDate date;
    private Account payee;

    public DepositBuilder amount(double amount) {
        this.amount = amount;
        return this;
    }
```

```
        public DepositBuilder date(LocalDate date) {
            this.date = date;
            return this;
        }

        public DepositBuilder payee(Account payee) {
            this.payee = payee;
            return this;
        }

        @Override
        public Deposit build() {
            return new Deposit(amount, date, payee);
        }
    }
```

The builder is a generic top-level interface, which is usually defined like this:

```
public interface Builder<T> {
    T build();
}
```

We should note a couple of things about the builder. First of all, it is a so-called SAM type (for "single abstract method"), and it could, technically speaking, be used as the target type for a lambda expression. However, the purpose of the builder is to produce immutable instances—it is about gathering up state, not representing a function or callback. This means that although the builder *could* be used as a functional interface, in practice, it will never be useful to do so.

For this reason, we do *not* decorate the interface with the @FunctionalInterface annotation—another good example of "just because you can do something, doesn't mean that you should."

Secondly, we should also notice that the builder is not thread-safe. The design implicitly assumes that the user knows not to share builders between threads. Instead, correct usage of the Builder API is for one thread to use a builder to aggregate all needed state and then produce an immutable object that *can* be trivially shared with other threads.

> **NOTE** If you find yourself wanting to share a builder between threads, take a moment to stop and reconsider your design and whether your domain needs refactoring.

Immutability is a very common pattern (not just in Java, but also in other languages, especially functional languages) and is one that has wide applicability.

One last point about immutable objects: the final keyword applies only to the object directly pointed to. As you can see in figure 5.7, the reference to the main object can't be assigned to point at object 3, but within the object, the reference to object 1 can be updated to point at object 2. Another way of saying this is that a final reference can point at an object that has nonfinal fields. This is sometimes known as *shallow immutability*.

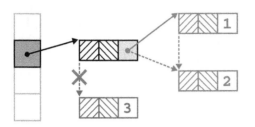

Figure 5.7 Immutability of value versus reference

Another way of seeing this is that it is perfectly possible to write the following:

```
final var numbers = new LinkedList<Integer>();
```

In this statement, the reference numbers and the integer objects contained in the list are immutable. However, the list object itself is still mutable because integer objects can still be added, removed, and replaced with the list.

Immutability is a very powerful technique, and you should use it whenever feasible. However, sometimes it's just not possible to develop efficiently with only immutable objects, because every change to an object's state requires a new object to be spun up. So we're sometimes left with the necessity of dealing with mutable objects.

In the next section, we'll discuss the often-misunderstood details of the Java Memory Model (JMM). Many Java programmers are aware of the JMM and have been coding to their own understanding of it without ever being formally introduced to it. If that sounds like you, this new understanding will build upon your informal awareness and place it onto firm foundations. The JMM is quite an advanced topic, so you can skip it if you're in a hurry to get on to the next chapter.

5.4 The Java Memory Model (JMM)

The JMM is described in section 17.4 of the Java Language Specification (JLS). This is a formal part of the spec, and it describes the JMM in terms of synchronization actions and some quite mathematical concepts, for example, a *partial order* for operations.

This is great from the point of view of language theorists and implementers of the Java spec (compiler and JVM makers), but it's worse for application developers who need to understand the details of how their multithreaded code will execute.

Rather than repeat the formal details, we'll list the most important rules here in terms of a couple of basic concepts: the *Synchronizes-With* and *Happens-Before* relationships between blocks of code:

- *Happens-Before*—This relationship indicates that one block of code fully completes before the other can start.
- *Synchronizes-With*—An action will synchronize its view of an object with main memory before continuing.

If you've studied formal approaches to OO programming, you may have heard the expressions *Has-A* and *Is-A* used to describe the building blocks of object orientation. Some developers find it useful to think of Happens-Before and Synchronizes-With as being similar, basic conceptual building blocks, but for understanding Java concurrency rather than OO. However, we should emphasize that no direct technical connection exists between the two sets of concepts. In figure 5.8 you can see an example of a volatile write that Synchronizes-With a later read access (for the `println()`).

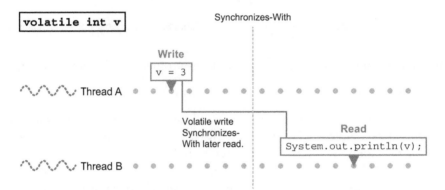

Figure 5.8   A Synchronizes-With example

The JMM has these main rules:

- An unlock operation on a monitor Synchronizes-With later locks operations.
- A write to a volatile variable Synchronizes-With later reads from the variable.
- If an action A Synchronizes-With action B, then A Happens-Before B.
- If A comes before B in program order, within a thread, then A Happens-Before B.

The general statement of the first two rules is that "releases happen before acquires." In other words, the locks that a thread holds when writing are released before the locks can be acquired by other operations (including reads). For example, the rules guarantee that if one thread writes a value to a volatile variable, then any thread that later reads that variable will see the value that was written (assuming no other writes have taken place).

Additional rules, which are really about sensible behavior, follow:

- The completion of a constructor Happens-Before the finalizer for that object starts to run (an object has to be fully constructed before it can be finalized).
- An action that starts a thread Synchronizes-With the first action of the new thread.
- `Thread.join()` Synchronizes-With the last (and all other) actions in the thread being joined.
- If X Happens-Before Y and Y Happens-Before Z, then X Happens-Before Z (transitivity).

These simple rules define the whole of the platform's view of how memory and synchronization works. Figure 5.9 illustrates the transitivity rule.

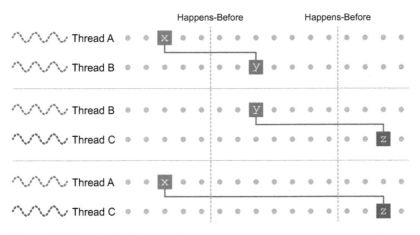

Figure 5.9   Transitivity of Happens-Before

NOTE In practice, these rules are the minimum guarantees made by the JMM. Real JVMs may behave much better in practice than these guarantees suggest. This can be quite a pitfall for the developer because it's easy for the false sense of safety given by the behavior of a particular JVM to turn out to be just a quirk hiding an underlying concurrency bug.

From these minimum guarantees, it's easy to see why immutability is an important concept in concurrent Java programming. If objects can't be changed, there are no issues related to ensuring that changes are visible to all threads.

5.5   *Understanding concurrency through bytecode*

Let's discuss concurrency through the lens of a classic example: a bank account. Let's assume that a customer's account looks like this and that withdrawals and deposits are possible by calling methods. We have provided both synchronized and unsynchronized implementations of the key methods:

```
public class Account {
    private double balance;

    public Account(int openingBalance) {
        balance = openingBalance;
    }

    public boolean rawWithdraw(int amount) {
        // Check to see amount > 0, throw if not
        if (balance >= amount) {
            balance = balance - amount;
            return true;
        }
```

```
        return false;
    }

    public void rawDeposit(int amount) {
        // Check to see amount > 0, throw if not
        balance = balance + amount;
    }

    public double getRawBalance() {
        return balance;
    }

    public boolean safeWithdraw(final int amount) {
        // Check to see amount > 0, throw if not
        synchronized (this) {
            if (balance >= amount) {
                balance = balance - amount;
                return true;
            }
        }
        return false;
    }

    public void safeDeposit(final int amount) {
        // Check to see amount > 0, throw if not
        synchronized (this) {
            balance = balance + amount;
        }
    }

    public double getSafeBalance() {
        synchronized (this) {
            return balance;
        }
    }
}
```

This set of methods will allow us to explore many common concurrency problems in Java.

NOTE There is a reason we are using the block form of synchronization at this stage, rather than the `synchronized` method modifier—we will explain why a bit later in the chapter.

We might also suppose that, if required, the class has two argument helper methods that look like this:

```
public boolean withdraw(int amount, boolean safe) {
    if (safe) {
        return safeWithdraw(amount);
    } else {
        return rawWithdraw(amount);
    }
}
```

Let's start by meeting one of the fundamental problems that multithreaded systems display that requires us to introduce some sort of protection mechanism.

5.5.1　Lost Update

To demonstrate this common problem (or antipattern), known as *Lost Update*, let's look at the bytecode for the rawDeposit() method:

```
public void rawDeposit(int);
    Code:
        0: aload_0
        1: aload_0
        2: getfield        #2   // Field balance:D      ◁─┐ Reads the balance
                                                           │ from the object
        5: iload_1
        6: i2d             ┐ Adds the deposit amount
        7: dadd            ◁─┘
                                                           ┐ Writes the new
        8: putfield        #2   // Field balance:D      ◁─┘ balance to the object
       11: return
```

Let's introduce two threads of execution, called A and B. We can then imagine two deposits being attempted on the same account at once. By prefixing the instruction with the thread label, we can see individual bytecode instructions executing on different threads, but they are both affecting the same object.

> **NOTE** Remember that some bytecode instructions have parameters that follow them in the stream, which causes occasional "skips" in the instruction numbering.

Lost Update is the issue that it is possible, due to the nondeterministic scheduling of application threads, to end up with a bytecode sequence of reads and writes like this:

```
A0: aload_0
    A1: aload_0                                            ┐ Thread A reads a value
    A2: getfield        #2   // Field balance:D      ◁─┘ from the balance.
    A5: iload_1
    A6: i2d
    A7: dadd

// ....            Context switch A -> B

        B0: aload_0                                        ┐ Thread B reads the same
        B1: aload_0                                        │ value from the balance as
        B2: getfield        #2   // Field balance:D  ◁─┘ A did.
        B5: iload_1
        B6: i2d
        B7: dadd                                           ┐ Thread B writes a new
        B8: putfield        #2   // Field balance:D  ◁─┘ value back to the balance.
        B11: return

// ....            Context switch B -> A
                                                           ┐ Thread A overwrites the
    A8: putfield        #2   // Field balance:D      ◁─┘ balance—B's update is lost.
    A11: return
```

The updated balance is calculated by each thread by using the evaluation stack. The dadd opcode is the point where the updated balance is placed on the stack, but recall that every method invocation has its own, private evaluation stack. So, at point B7 in the previous flow are *two* copies of the updated balance: one in A's evaluation stack and one in B's. The two putfield operations at B8 and A8 then execute, but A8 overwrites the value placed at B8. This leads to the situation where both deposits appear to succeed, but only one of them actually shows up.

The account balance will register a deposit, but the code will still cause money to vanish from the account, because the balance field is read twice (with getfield), then written and overwritten (by the two putfield operations). For example, in some code like this:

```
Account acc = new Account(0);
Thread tA = new Thread(() -> acc.rawDeposit(70));
Thread tB = new Thread(() -> acc.rawDeposit(50));
tA.start();
tB.start();
tA.join();
tB.join();

System.out.println(acc.getRawBalance());
```

it is possible for the final balance to be either 50 or 70—but with both threads "successfully" depositing money. The code has paid in 120 but has lost some of it—a classic example of incorrect multithreaded code.

Be careful with the simple form of the code shown here. The full range of nondeterministic possibilities may not show up in such a simple example. Do not be fooled by this—when this code is combined into a large program, the incorrectness will assuredly appear. Assuming that your code is OK because it's "too simple" or trying to cheat the concurrency model will inevitably end badly.

> **NOTE** There is an example (AtmLoop) that shows this effect in the source code repository, but it relies upon using a class we haven't met yet (Atomic-Integer) so we won't show it in full here. So, if you need to be convinced, please go and examine how the example behaves.

In general, access patterns like

```
A: getfield
B: getfield
B: putfield
A: putfield
```

or

```
A: getfield
B: getfield
A: putfield
B: putfield
```

will cause problems for our account objects.

Recall that the operating system effectively causes nondeterministic scheduling of threads, so this type of interleaving is always possible, and Java objects live in the heap, so the threads are operating on shared, mutable data.

What we really need is to introduce a mechanism to somehow prevent this and ensure that the ordering is always of the following form:

```
...
A: getfield
A: putfield
...
B: getfield
B: putfield
...
```

This mechanism is synchronization, and it is our next subject.

5.5.2 *Synchronization in bytecode*

In chapter 4, we introduced JVM bytecodes and briefly met monitorenter and monitorexit. A synchronized block is turned into these opcodes (we'll talk about synchronized methods a bit later). Let's see them in action by looking at an example we saw earlier (we're reproducing the Java code so it's close at hand):

```java
public boolean safeWithdraw(final int amount) {
    // Check to see amount > 0, throw if not
    synchronized (this) {
        if (balance >= amount) {
            balance = balance - amount;
            return true;
        }
    }
    return false;
}
```

This is turned into 40 bytes of JVM bytecode:

```
public boolean safeWithdraw(int);
    Code:
        0: aload_0
        1: dup
        2: astore_2
        3: monitorenter      <───┐  The start of the
        4: aload_0                  synchronized block
        5: getfield       #2  // Field balance:D
        8: iload_1
        9: i2d
       10: dcmpl
       11: iflt         29   <───┐  The if statement that
       14: aload_0                  checks the balance
       15: aload_0
```

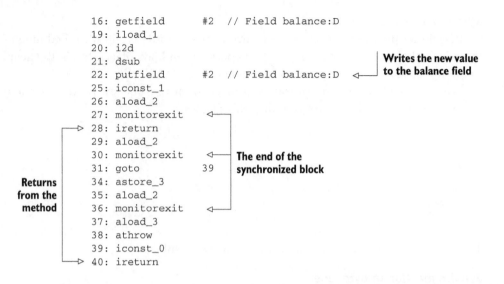

The eagle-eyed reader might spot a couple of oddities in the bytecode. First of all, let's look at the code paths. If the balance check succeeds, then bytecodes 0–28 are executed with no jumps. If it fails, bytecodes 0–11 execute, then a jump to 29–31 and a jump to 39–40.

At first glance, no set of circumstances will lead to bytecodes 34–38 being executed. This seeming discrepancy is actually explained by exception handling—some of the bytecode instructions (including `monitorenter`) can throw exceptions, so there needs to be an exception handling code path.

The second puzzler is the return type of the method. In the Java code, it is declared as `boolean`, but we can see that the return instructions are `ireturn`, which is the integer variant of the return opcode. In fact, no variant forms of instructions for bytes, shorts, chars, or booleans exist. These types are replaced by ints during the compilation process. This is a form of *type erasure*, which is one of the misunderstood aspects of Java's type system (especially as it is usually applied to the case of generics and type parameters).

Overall, the previous bytecode sequence is more complex than the nonsynchronized case but should be possible to follow: we load the object to be locked onto the evaluation stack and then execute a `monitorenter` to acquire the lock. Let's assume the lock attempt succeeds.

Now, if any other thread attempts to execute a `monitorenter` on the same object, the thread will block, and the second `monitorenter` instruction will not complete until the thread holding the lock executes a `monitorexit` and releases the lock. This is how we deal with Lost Update—the `monitor` instructions are enforcing the following ordering:

```
...
A: monitorenter
A: getfield
```

```
A: putfield
A: monitorexit
...
B: monitorenter
B: getfield
B: putfield
B: monitorexit
...
```

This provides the Happens-Before relationship between synchronized blocks: the end of one synchronized block Happens-Before the start of any other synchronized block on the same object, and this is guaranteed by the JMM.

We should also note that the Java source compiler ensures that every code path through a method that contains a monitorenter will result in a monitorexit being executed before the method terminates. Not only this, but at class loading time, the classfile verifier will reject any class that tries to circumvent this rule.

We can now see the basis for the claim that "synchronization is a cooperative mechanism in Java." Let's look at what happens when thread A calls safeWithdraw() and thread B calls rawDeposit():

```
public boolean safeWithdraw(final int amount) {
    // Check to see amount > 0, throw if not
    synchronized (this) {
        if (balance >= amount) {
            balance = balance - amount;
            return true;
        }
    }
    return false;
}
```

We've reproduced the Java code once again for easy comparison:

```
public boolean safeWithdraw(int);
    Code:
        0: aload_0
        1: dup
        2: astore_2
        3: monitorenter
        4: aload_0
        5: getfield      #2  // Field balance:D
        8: iload_1
        9: i2d
       10: dcmpl
       11: iflt          29
       14: aload_0
       15: aload_0
       16: getfield      #2  // Field balance:D
       19: iload_1
       20: i2d
       21: dsub
```

```
22: putfield      #2  // Field balance:D
25: iconst_1
26: aload_2
27: monitorexit
28: ireturn
```

The depositing code is very simple: just one field read, an arithmetic operation, and a write back to the same field, as shown here:

```
public void rawDeposit(int amount) {
      // Check to see amount > 0, throw  if not
      balance = balance + amount;
  }
```

The bytecode looks more complicated but actually isn't:

```
public void rawDeposit(int);
    Code:
       0: aload_0
       1: aload_0
       2: getfield      #2  // Field balance:D
       5: iload_1
       6: i2d
       7: dadd
       8: putfield      #2  // Field balance:D
      11: return
```

NOTE The code for rawDeposit() does not contain any monitor instructions—and without a monitorenter, the lock will never be checked.

An ordering like this, between two threads A and B, is entirely possible, as shown next:

```
// ...
 A3: monitorenter
// ...

A14: aload_0
A15: aload_0
A16: getfield      #2  // Field balance:D

// ... Context switch A -> B

 B0: aload_0
 B1: aload_0
 B2: getfield      #2  // Field balance:D
 B5: iload_1
 B6: i2d
 B7: dadd                                    Writes to the balance (via
 B8: putfield      #2  // Field balance:D  ◁— unsynchronized method)

// ... Context switch B -> A

B11: return
```

```
A19: iload_1
A20: i2d
A21: dsub
A22: putfield      #2  // Field balance:D
A25: iconst_1
A26: aload_2
A27: monitorexit
A28: ireturn
```

Second write to the balance (via synchronized)

This is just our old friend Lost Update, but now it occurs when one of the methods uses synchronization and one doesn't. The amount deposited has been lost—good news for the bank, but not so good for the customer. The inescapable conclusion is this: to get the protections provided by synchronization, *all* methods must use it correctly.

5.5.3   *Synchronized methods*

Until now, we have been talking about the case of synchronized blocks, but what about the case of synchronized *methods*? We might guess that the compiler will insert synthetic `monitor` bytecodes, but that's actually not the case, as we can see if we change our safe methods to look like this:

```
public synchronized boolean safeWithdraw(final int amount) {
    // Check to see amount > 0, throw if not
    if (balance >= amount) {
        balance = balance - amount;
        return true;
    }
    return false;
}

// and the others...
```

Instead of showing up in the bytecode sequence, the `synchronized` modifier for the method actually shows up in the method's flags, as `ACC_SYNCHRONIZED`. We can see this by recompiling the method and noticing that the `monitor` instructions have disappeared, as shown here:

```
public synchronized boolean safeWithdraw(int);
Code:
   0: aload_0
   1: getfield      #2  // Field balance:D
   4: iload_1
   5: i2d
   6: dcmpl
   7: iflt          23
  10: aload_0
  // ... no monitor instructions
```

When executing an invoke instruction, one of the first things the bytecode interpreter checks is to see whether the method is synchronized. If it is, then the interpreter proceeds down a different code path—first by trying to acquire the appropriate lock. If the method does not have the ACC_SYNCHRONIZED, then no such check is done.

This means that, just as we might expect, an unsynchronized method can execute at the same time as a synchronized one because only one of them performs a check for the lock.

5.5.4 *Unsynchronized reads*

A very common beginner's error with Java concurrency is to assume that "only methods that write data need to be synchronized; reads are safe." This is emphatically not true, as we will demonstrate.

This false sense of security for reads sometimes occurs because the code example being reasoned about is a bit too simple. What happens when we introduce a small ATM fee to our example—say, 1% of the amount being withdrawn?

```java
private final double atmFeePercent = 0.01;

public boolean safeWithdraw(final int amount, final boolean withFee) {
    // Check to see amount > 0, throw if not
    synchronized (this) {
        if (balance >= amount) {
            balance = balance - amount;
            if (withFee) {
                balance = balance - amount * atmFeePercent;
            }
            return true;
        }
    }
    return false;
}
```

The bytecode for this method is now a bit more complex:

```
public boolean safeWithdraw(int, boolean);
    Code:
        0: aload_0
        1: dup
        2: astore_3
        3: monitorenter
        4: aload_0
        5: getfield      #2  // Field balance:D
        8: iload_1
        9: i2d
       10: dcmpl
       11: iflt          49
       14: aload_0
       15: aload_0
       16: getfield      #2  // Field balance:D
       19: iload_1
```

Compares balance to amount

```
20: i2d
21: dsub
22: putfield        #2  // Field balance:D      ⟵──┐ The account balance
25: iload_2                                          is updated.
26: ifeq            45
29: aload_0
30: aload_0
31: getfield        #2  // Field balance:D
34: iload_1
35: i2d
36: aload_0
37: getfield        #5  // Field atmFeePercent:D
40: dmul                                            The fee is applied and the
41: dsub                                            balance updated again.
42: putfield        #2  // Field balance:D      ⟵──┘
45: iconst_1
46: aload_3
47: monitorexit
48: ireturn
49: aload_3
50: monitorexit
51: goto            61
54: astore          4
56: aload_3
57: monitorexit
58: aload           4
60: athrow
61: iconst_0
62: ireturn
```

Note that there are now two `putfield` instructions, because `safeWithdraw()` takes a boolean parameter that determines whether a fee should be charged. The fact that two separate updates occur is what raises the potential for a concurrency bug.

The code for reading the raw balance is very simple:

```
public double getRawBalance();
    Code:
        0: aload_0
        1: getfield        #2  // Field balance:D
        4: dreturn
```

However, this can be interleaved with the withdraw-with-fee code like this:

```
A14: aload_0
A15: aload_0
A16: getfield        #2  // Field balance:D
A19: iload_1
A20: i2d                                        The balance written with
A21: dsub                                       the amount (but not the
A22: putfield        #2  // Field balance:D  ⟵── fee) deducted
A25: iload_2
A26: ifeq            45
A29: aload_0
```

```
A30: aload_0
A31: getfield       #2  // Field balance:D

// ... Context switch A -> B

 B0: aload_0
 B1: getfield       #2  // Field balance:D
 B4: dreturn

// ... Context switch B -> A

A34: iload_1
A35: i2d
A36: aload_0
A37: getfield       #5  // Field atmFeePercent:D
A40: dmul
A41: dsub
A42: putfield       #2  // Field balance:D
```

The balance read while the full withdraw is still being processed

With an unsynchronized read, there is the possibility of a *nonrepeatable read*—a value that does not actually correspond to a real state of the system. If you're familiar with SQL databases, this may remind you of performing a read partway through a database transaction.

NOTE You might be tempted to think, "I know the bytecodes," and optimize your code based on that. You should resist this temptation for several reasons. For example, what happens when you have handed over your code and it is maintained by other developers who do not understand the context or consequences of seemingly harmless code changes?

The conclusion: there is no get-out clause for "just reads." If even one code path fails to use synchronization correctly, the resulting code is not thread-safe and so is incorrect in a multithreaded environment. Let's move on and take a look at how deadlock shows up in bytecode.

5.5.5   *Deadlock revisited*

Suppose the bank wants to add the ability to transfer money between accounts into our code. An initial version of this code might look like this:

```java
public boolean naiveSafeTransferTo(Account other, int amount) {
    // Check to see amount > 0, throw if not
    synchronized (this) {
        if (balance >= amount) {
            balance = balance - amount;
            synchronized (other) {
                other.rawDeposit(amount);
            }
            return true;
        }
    }
    return false;
}
```

This produces quite a long bytecode listing, so we have shortened it by omitting the by-now-familiar sequence for checking that the balance can support the withdrawal and some synthetic exception-handling blocks.

> **NOTE** There are now two account objects, and each of them has a lock. To be safe, we need to coordinate access to both locks—the lock belonging to `this` and that belonging to `other`.

We will need to deal with *two* pairs of `monitor` instructions, with each pair dealing with the lock of a different object:

```
public boolean naiveSafeTransferTo(Account, int);
    Code:
        0: aload_0
        1: dup
        2: astore_3
        3: monitorenter    <------ Acquires a lock on this object

        // Omit the usual balance checking bytecode

       14: aload_0
       15: aload_0
       16: getfield       #2  // Field balance:D
       19: iload_2
       20: i2d
       21: dsub
       22: putfield       #2  // Field balance:D
       25: aload_1
       26: dup
       27: astore         4
       29: monitorenter   <------ Acquires a lock on the other object
       30: aload_1
       31: iload_2
       32: invokevirtual #6  // Method rawDeposit:(I)V
       35: aload          4
       37: monitorexit    <------ Releases the lock on the other object
       38: goto           49

        // Omit exception handling code

       49: iconst_1
       50: aload_3
       51: monitorexit    <------ Releases the lock on this object
       52: ireturn

        // Omit exception handling code
```

Imagine two threads that are trying to transfer money between the same two accounts—let's call the threads A and B. Let's further suppose that the threads are executing transactions that are labeled by the sending account, so thread A is trying to send money from object A to object B and vice versa:

```
A0: aload_0
A1: dup
A2: astore_3
A3: monitorenter
```
> **The lock acquired on account object A (by thread A)**

```
// Omit the usual balance checking bytecode

B0: aload_0
B1: dup
B2: astore_3
B3: monitorenter
```
> **The lock acquired on account object B (by thread B)**

```
// Omit the usual balance checking bytecode

B14: aload_0
B15: aload_0
B16: getfield       #2  // Field balance:D
B19: iload_2
B20: i2d
B21: dsub
B22: putfield       #2  // Field balance:D
B25: aload_1
B26: dup
B27: astore         4
B29: ...
```
> **Thread B tries to acquire a lock on object A. It fails and blocks.**

```
A14: aload_0
A15: aload_0
A16: getfield       #2  // Field balance:D
A19: iload_2
A20: i2d
A21: dsub
A22: putfield       #2  // Field balance:D
A25: aload_1
A26: dup
A27: astore         4
A29: ...
```
> **Thread A tries to acquire a lock on object B. It fails and blocks.**

After executing this sequence, neither thread can make progress. Worse yet, only thread A can release the lock on object A, and only thread B can release the lock on object B, so these two threads are permanently blocked by the synchronization mechanism, and these method calls will never complete. By viewing the deadlock antipattern at a bytecode level, we can see clearly what actually causes it.

5.5.6 *Deadlock resolved, revisited*

To solve this problem, as we discussed earlier, we need to ensure that the locks are always acquired in the same order by every thread. One way to do this is by creating an ordering on the threads—say, by introducing a unique account number and implementing the rule: "acquire the lock corresponding to the lowest account ID first."

NOTE For objects that don't have numeric IDs, we will need to do something different, but the general principle of using an unambiguous *total order* still applies.

This method produces a bit more complexity, and to do it completely correctly, we need a guarantee that the account IDs are not reused. We can do this by introducing a `static int` field, which holds the next account ID to be allocated, and updating it only in a `synchronized` method, like this:

```
private static int nextAccountId = 1;

private final int accountId;

private static synchronized int getAndIncrementNextAccountId() {
    int result = nextAccountId;
    nextAccountId = nextAccountId + 1;
    return result;
}

public Account(int openingBalance) {
    balance = openingBalance;
    atmFeePercent = 0.01;
    accountId = getAndIncrementNextAccountId();
}

public int getAccountId() {
    return accountId;
}
```

We don't need to synchronize the `getAccountId()` method because the field is `final` and can't change, as illustrated here:

```
public boolean safeTransferTo(final Account other, final int amount) {
    // Check to see amount > 0, throw if not
    if (accountId == other.getAccountId()) {
        // Can't transfer to your own account
        return false;
    }

    if (accountId < other.getAccountId()) {
        synchronized (this) {
            if (balance >= amount) {
                balance = balance - amount;
                synchronized (other) {
                    other.rawDeposit(amount);
                }
                return true;
            }
        }
        return false;
    } else {
        synchronized (other) {
            synchronized (this) {
```

```
            if (balance >= amount) {
                balance = balance - amount;
                other.rawDeposit(amount);
                return true;
            }
        }
    }
    return false;
}
```

The resulting Java code is, of course, a little asymmetrical.

> **NOTE** By avoiding holding any locks for any longer than necessary makes it clear which parts of the code actually require locks.

The previous code produces a very long bytecode listing, but let's break it down by parts. First off, we check the ordering of the account IDs:

```
// Elide balance and account equality checks
13: aload_0
14: getfield     #8   // Field accountId:I
17: aload_1
18: invokevirtual #10  // Method getAccountId:()I
21: if_icmpge    91
```

If A < B (which it is), then we move on to instruction 24; otherwise, we jump ahead to 91, as follows:

```
24: aload_0
25: dup
26: astore_3          The start of
27: monitorenter  ◁── synchronized (this) {
28: aload_0
29: getfield     #3   // Field balance:D
32: iload_2
33: i2d
34: dcmpl             If insufficient funds exist, bails
35: iflt         77  ◁── out to offset 77 (further on)
```

Let's follow the branch where the sending account has sufficient funds to continue, so control falls through to bytecode 38, which is the start of the balance = balance - amount; statement in the Java code:

```
38: aload_0
39: aload_0
40: getfield     #3   // Field balance:D
43: iload_2
44: i2d
45: dsub
46: putfield     #3   // Field balance:D
49: aload_1
```

```
50: dup
51: astore          4      │ The start of
53: monitorenter      ◄────┘ synchronized (other) {
54: aload_1
55: iload_2
56: invokevirtual #9     // Method rawDeposit:(I)V
59: aload          4
61: monitorexit       ◄─────────────────┐
62: goto            73            │ The end of
// Omit exception handling code   │ synchronized (other) {
73: iconst_1
74: aload_3                │ The end of
75: monitorexit       ◄────┘ synchronized (this) {
76: ireturn
```

For completeness, let's show the code path used in the case of insufficient balance in the sending account. We basically just unlock the monitor on this and return this:

```
77: aload_3                │ The end of
78: monitorexit       ◄────┘ synchronized (this) {
79: goto            89
// Omit exception handling code
89: iconst_0
90: ireturn
```

Note that some of the instructions (such as invoke and monitor instructions) may throw exceptions, so we are, as usual, ignoring the bytecode handlers for those exceptions. The rest of the method looks like this:

```
91: aload_1
// ...
// Highly similar, but for the other branch
```

Let's look at what happens with two threads, remembering that the account ID of A < B.

We now have one additional complication: the local variables (used in instructions such as aload_0) are different between the two threads. To draw out this distinction, we'll slightly mangle the bytecode by labeling the local variable with the thread as well, so we'll write aload_A0 and aload_A1 for clarity:

```
A24: aload_A0
A25: dup
A26: astore_A3            │ The lock acquired on
A27: monitorenter    ◄────┘ object A by thread A

// Elide balance check

A38: aload_A0
A39: aload_A0
A40: getfield       #3    // Field balance:D

// ....            Context switch A -> B
```

```
        B91: aload_B1
        B92: dup
        B93: astore_B3          The lock attempted on object
        B94: monitorenter    ◁──┘ A by thread B: blocks

// ....              Context switch B -> A

        A43: iload_A2
        A44: i2d
        A45: dsub
        A46: putfield      #3    // Field balance:D
        A49: aload_A1
        A50: dup
        A51: astore        A4    The lock acquired on
        A53: monitorenter    ◁──┘ object B by thread A
        A54: aload_A1
        A55: iload_A2
        A56: invokevirtual #9    // Method rawDeposit:(I)V
        A59: aload         A4
        A61: monitorexit     ◁──────────┐
        A62: goto          73           │ The lock released on
                                          object B by thread A

// Omit exception handling code

        A73: iconst_A1
        A74: aload_A3            The lock released on object A by
        A75: monitorexit     ◁──┘ thread A: thread B can resume

// ....              Context switch A -> B

        B95: aload_B0
        B96: dup
        B97: astore        B4
        B99: monitorenter
        // ...
       B132: ireturn

// ....              Context switch B -> A

        A76: ireturn
```

This is, without doubt, a complex listing. The key insight is that A0 == B1, so locking these two objects will always induce a blocking call in the second thread. The invariant A < B ensures that thread B is sent down the alternate branch.

5.5.7 *Volatile access*

What does volatile look like in bytecode? Let's take a look at an important pattern—*Volatile Shutdown*—to help answer this.

The Volatile Shutdown pattern helps solve the problem of interthread communication that we touched upon earlier when we met the dangerous and deprecated stop() method. Consider a simple class that is responsible for doing some work. In

the simplest case, we will assume that work comes in discrete units, with a well-defined
"complete" status for each unit, as shown next:

```
public class TaskManager implements Runnable {
    private volatile boolean shutdown = false;

    public void shutdown() {
        shutdown = true;
    }

    @Override
    public void run() {
        while (!shutdown) {
            // do some work - e.g. process a work unit
        }
    }
}
```

The intent of the pattern is hopefully clear. All the time the shutdown flag is false,
work units will continue to be processed. If it ever flips to true, then the TaskManager
will, after it has completed its current work unit, exit the while loop and the thread
will exit cleanly, in a "graceful shutdown."

The more subtle point is derived from the Java Memory Model: any write to a volatile variable Happens-Before all subsequent reads of that variable. As soon as another
thread calls shutdown() on the TaskManager object, the flag is changed to true and
the effect of that change is guaranteed to be visible on the next read of the flag—
before the next work unit is accepted.

The Volatile Shutdown pattern produces bytecode like this:

```
public class TaskManager implements java.lang.Runnable {
  private volatile boolean shutdown;

  public TaskManager();
    Code:
       0: aload_0
       1: invokespecial #1              // Method java/lang/Object."<init>":()V
       4: aload_0
       5: iconst_0
       6: putfield      #2              // Field shutdown:Z
       9: return

  public void shutdown();
    Code:
       0: aload_0
       1: iconst_1
       2: putfield      #2              // Field shutdown:Z
       5: return

  public void run();
    Code:
       0: aload_0
```

```
 1: getfield      #2          // Field shutdown:Z
 4: ifne          10
 7: goto          0
10: return
}
```

If you look carefully, you can see that the volatile nature of shutdown does not appear anywhere except in the field definition. There are no additional clues on the opcodes—and it is accessed using the standard getfield and putfield opcodes.

> **NOTE** volatile is a hardware access mode and produces a CPU instruction that says to ignore the cache hardware and instead read or write directly from main memory.

The only difference is in how putfield and getfield behave—the implementation of the bytecode interpreter will have separate code paths for volatile and standard fields.

In fact, *any* piece of physical memory can be accessed in a volatile manner, and—as we will see later on—this is not the only access mode possible. The volatile case is merely a common case of access semantics that James Gosling and the original designers of Java chose to encode in the core of the language, by making it a keyword that can apply to fields.

Concurrency is one of the most important features of the Java platform, and a good developer will increasingly need a solid understanding of it. We've reviewed the underpinnings of Java's concurrency and the design forces that occur in multi-threaded systems. We've discussed the Java Memory Model and low-level details of how the platform implements concurrency.

This chapter isn't intended to be a complete statement of everything you'll ever need to know about concurrency—it's enough to get you started and give you an appreciation of what you'll need to learn more about, and stop you from being dangerous when writing concurrent code. But you'll need to know more than we can cover here if you're going to be a truly first-rate developer of multithreaded code. A number of excellent books about nothing but Java concurrency are out there. One of the best is *Java Concurrency in Practice* by Brian Goetz and others (Addison-Wesley Professional, 2006).

Summary

- Java's threads are a low-level abstraction.
- Multithreading is present even in the Java bytecode.
- The Java Memory Model is very flexible but makes minimal guarantees.
- Synchronization is a cooperative mechanism—all threads must participate to achieve safety.
- Never use Thread.stop() or Thread.suspend().

JDK concurrency libraries

In this chapter we'll cover what every well-grounded developer should know about `java.util.concurrent` and how to use the toolbox of concurrency building blocks it provides. The aim is that by the end of the chapter, you'll be ready to start applying these libraries and concurrency techniques in your own code.

6.1 Building blocks for modern concurrent applications

As we saw in the previous chapter, Java has supported concurrency since the very beginning. However, with the advent of Java 5 (which was itself over 15 years ago), a new way of thinking about concurrency in Java emerged. This was spearheaded by the package `java.util.concurrent`, which contained a rich new toolbox for working with multithreaded code.

> **NOTE**   This toolbox has been enhanced with subsequent versions of Java, but the classes and packages that were introduced with Java 5 still work the same way, and they're still very valuable to the working developer.

If you (still!) have existing multithreaded code that is based solely on the older (pre-Java 5) approaches, you should consider refactoring it to use `java.util.concurrent`. In our experience, your code will be improved if you make a conscious effort to port it to the newer APIs—the greater clarity and reliability will be well worth the effort expended to migrate in almost all cases.

We're going to take a tour through some of the headline classes in `java.util .concurrent` and related packages, such as the atomic and locks packages. We'll get you started using the classes and look at examples of use cases for them.

You should also read the Javadoc for them and try to build up your familiarity with the packages as a whole. Most developers find that the higher level of abstraction that they provide makes concurrent programming much easier.

6.2   *Atomic classes*

The package `java.util.concurrent.atomic` contains several classes that have names starting with `Atomic`, for example, `AtomicBoolean`, `AtomicInteger`, `AtomicLong`, and `AtomicReference`. These classes are one of the simplest examples of a *concurrency primitive*—a class that can be used to build workable, safe concurrent applications.

> **WARNING**   Atomic classes don't inherit from the similarly named classes, so `AtomicBoolean` can't be used in place of a `Boolean`, and an `AtomicInteger` isn't an `Integer` (but it does extend `Number`).

The point of an atomic is to provide thread-safe mutable variables. Each of the four classes provides access to a single variable of the appropriate type.

> **NOTE**   The implementations of the atomics are written to take advantage of modern processor features, so they can be nonblocking (lock-free) if support is available from the hardware and OS, which it will be for virtually all modern systems.

The access provided is lock-free on almost all modern hardware, so the atomics behave in a similar way to a volatile field. However, they are wrapped in a Class API that goes further than what's possible with volatiles. This API includes atomic (meaning all-or-nothing) methods for suitable operations—including state-dependent updates (which are impossible to do with volatile variables without using a lock). The end result is that atomics can be a very simple way for a developer to avoid race conditions on shared data.

> **NOTE**   If you're curious as to how atomics are implemented, we will discuss the details in chapter 17, when we talk about internals and the class `sun.misc .Unsafe`.

A common use case for atomics is to implement something similar to sequence numbers, as you might find provided by an SQL database. This capability is accessed by using methods such as the atomic getAndIncrement() on the AtomicInteger or AtomicLong classes. Let's look at how we would rewrite the Account example from chapter 5 to use an atomic:

```
private static AtomicInteger nextAccountId = new AtomicInteger(1);

private final int accountId;
private double balance;

public Account(int openingBalance) {
    balance = openingBalance;
    accountId = nextAccountId.getAndIncrement();
}
```

As each object is created, we make a call to getAndIncrement() on the static instance of AtomicInteger, which returns us an int value and atomically increments the mutable variable. This atomicity guarantees that it is impossible for two objects to share the same accountId, which is exactly the property that we want (just like a database sequence number).

NOTE We could add the final qualifier to the atomic, but it's not necessary because the field is static and the class doesn't provide any way to mutate the field.

For another example, here is how we would rewrite our volatile shutdown example to use an AtomicBoolean:

```
public class TaskManager implements Runnable {
    private final AtomicBoolean shutdown = new AtomicBoolean(false);

    public void shutdown() {
        shutdown.set(true);
    }

    @Override
    public void run() {
        while (!shutdown.get()) {
            // do some work - e.g. process a work unit
        }
    }
}
```

As well as these examples, the AtomicReference is also used to implement atomic changes but to objects. The general pattern is that some modified (possibly immutable) state is built optimistically and can then be "swapped in" by using a *Compare-and-Swap* (CAS) operation on an AtomicReference.

Next, let's examine how `java.util.concurrent` models the core of the classic synchronization approach—the `Lock` interface.

6.3 Lock classes

The block-structured approach to synchronization is based on a simple notion of what a lock is. This approach has a number of shortcomings, as follows:

- Only one type of lock exists.
- It applies equally to all synchronized operations on the locked object.
- The lock is acquired at the start of the synchronized block or method.
- The lock is released at the end of the block or method.
- Either the lock is acquired or the thread blocks indefinitely—no other outcomes are possible.

If we were going to reengineer the support for locks, we could potentially change several things for the better:

- Add different types of locks (such as reader/writer locks).
- Not restrict locks to blocks (allow a lock in one method and an unlock in another).
- If a thread cannot acquire a lock (e.g., if another thread has the lock), allow the thread to back out or carry on or do something else—a `tryLock()`.
- Allow a thread to attempt to acquire a lock and give up after a certain amount of time.

The key to realizing all of these possibilities is the `Lock` interface in `java.util` `.concurrent.locks`. This interface ships with the following implementations:

- `ReentrantLock`—This is essentially the equivalent of the familiar lock used in Java synchronized blocks but more flexible.
- `ReentrantReadWriteLock`—This can provide better performance in cases where there are many readers but few writers.

NOTE Other implementations exist, both within the JDK and written by third parties, but these are by far the most common.

The `Lock` interface can be used to completely replicate any functionality that is offered by block-structured concurrency. For example, listing 6.1 shows the example from chapter 5 for how to avoid deadlock rewritten to use `ReentrantLock`.

We need to add a lock object as a field to the class, because we will no longer be relying on the intrinsic lock on the object. We also need to maintain the principle that locks are always acquired in the same order. In our example the simple protocol we maintain is that the lock on the object with the lowest account ID is acquired *first*.

| Listing 6.1   Rewriting deadlock example to use `ReentrantLock` |

```
private final Lock lock = new ReentrantLock();

public boolean transferTo(SafeAccount other, int amount) {
    // We also need code to check to see amount > 0, throw if not
    // ...

    if (accountId == other.getAccountId()) {
        // Can't transfer to your own account
        return false;
    }

    var firstLock = accountId < other.getAccountId() ?
            lock : other.lock;
    var secondLock = firstLock == lock ? other.lock : lock;

    firstLock.lock();
    try {
        secondLock.lock();
        try {
            if (balance >= amount) {
                balance = balance - amount;
                other.deposit(amount);
                return true;
            }
            return false;
        } finally {
            secondLock.unlock();
        }
    } finally {
        firstLock.unlock();
    }
}
```

The firstLock object has a lower account ID. → `firstLock.lock();`

`secondLock.lock();` ← **The secondLock object has a higher account ID.**

The pattern of an initial call to `lock()` combined with a `try … finally` block, where the lock is released in the `finally`, is a great addition to your toolbox.

NOTE The locks, like much of `java.util.concurrent`, rely on a class called `AbstractQueuedSynchronizer` to implement their functionality.

The pattern works very well if you're replicating a situation that is similar to one where you'd have used block-structured concurrency. On the other hand, if you need to pass around the `Lock` objects (such as by returning it from a method), you can't use this pattern.

6.3.1 Condition objects

Another aspect of the API provided by `java.util.concurrent` are the *condition objects*. These objects play the same role in the API as `wait()` and `notify()` do in the original intrinsic API but are more flexible. They provide the ability for threads to wait indefinitely for some condition and to be woken up when that condition becomes true.

However, unlike the intrinsic API (where the object monitor has only a single condition for signaling), the Lock interface allows the programmer to create as many condition objects as they like. This allows a separation of concerns—for example, the lock can have multiple, disjoint groups of methods that can use separate conditions.

A condition object (which implements the interface Condition) is created by calling the newCondition() method on a lock object (one that implements the Lock interface). As well as condition objects, the API provides a number of *latches* and *barriers* as concurrency primitives that may be useful in some circumstances.

6.4   *CountDownLatch*

The CountDownLatch is a simple concurrency primitive that provides a *consensus barrier*—it allows for multiple threads to reach a coordination point and wait until the barrier is released. This is achieved by providing an int value (the count) when constructing a new instance of CountDownLatch. After that point, two methods are used to control the latch: countDown() and await(). The former reduces the count by 1, and the latter causes the calling thread to block until the count reaches 0 (it does nothing if the count is already 0 or less). In the following listing, the latch is used by each Runnable to indicate when it has completed its assigned work.

Listing 6.2   Using latches to signal between threads

```
public static class Counter implements Runnable {
    private final CountDownLatch latch;
    private final int value;
    private final AtomicInteger count;

    public Counter(CountDownLatch l, int v, AtomicInteger c) {
        this.latch = l;
        this.value = v;
        this.count = c;
    }

    @Override
    public void run() {
        try {
            Thread.sleep(100);
        } catch (InterruptedException e) {
            Thread.currentThread().interrupt();
        }
        count.addAndGet(value);       Updates the count value atomically
        latch.countDown();            ◄─── Decrements the latch
    }
}
```

Note that the countDown() method is nonblocking, so once the latch has been decremented, the thread running the Counter code will exit.

We also need some driver code, shown here (exceptions elided):

```
var latch = new CountDownLatch(5);
var count = new AtomicInteger();
for (int i = 0; i < 5; i = i + 1) {
    var r   = new Counter(latch, i, count);
    new Thread(r).start();
}

latch.await();
System.out.println("Total: "+ count.get());
```

In the code, the latch is set up with a quorum value (in figure 6.1, the value is 2). Next, the same number of threads are created and initialized, so that processing can begin. The main thread awaits the latch and blocks until it is released. Each worker thread will perform a sleep and then `countDown()` once it has finished. The main thread will not proceed until both of the threads have completed their processing. This situation is show in figure 6.1.

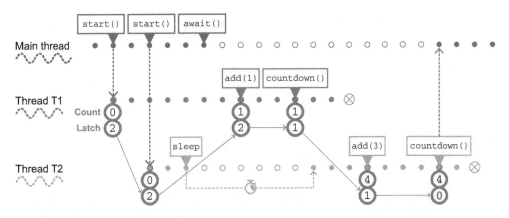

Figure 6.1   Using a CountDownLatch

To provide another example of a good use case for `CountDownLatch`, consider an application that needs to prepopulate several caches with reference data before the server is ready to receive incoming requests. We can easily achieve this by using a shared latch, a reference to which is held by each cache population thread.

When each cache finishes loading, the `Runnable` populating it counts down the latch and exits. When all the caches are loaded, the main thread (which has been awaiting the latch opening) can proceed and is ready to mark the service as up and begin handling requests.

The next class we'll discuss is one of the most useful classes in the multithreaded developer's toolkit: the `ConcurrentHashMap`.

6.5   ConcurrentHashMap

The ConcurrentHashMap class provides a concurrent version of the standard HashMap. In general, maps are a very useful (and common) data structure for building concurrent applications. This is due, at least in part, to the shape of the underlying data structure. Let's take a closer look at the basic HashMap to understand why.

6.5.1   *Understanding a simplified HashMap*

As you can see from figure 6.2, the classic Java HashMap uses a function (the *hash function*) to determine which *bucket* it will store the key-value pair in. This is where the "hash" part of the class's name comes from.

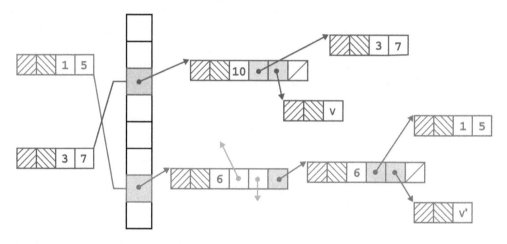

Figure 6.2   The classic view of a HashMap

The key-value pair is actually stored in a linked list (known as the *hash chain*) that starts from the bucket corresponding to the index obtained by hashing the key.

In the GitHub project that accompanies this book is a simplified implementation of a Map<String, String>—the Dictionary class. This class is actually based on the form of the HashMap that shipped as part of Java 7.

> **NOTE** Modern Java versions ship a HashMap implementation that is significantly more complex, so in this explanation, we focus on a simpler version where the design concepts are more clearly visible.

The basic class has only two fields: the main data structure and the size field, which caches the size of the map for performance reasons, as shown next:

```
public class Dictionary implements Map<String, String> {
    private Node[] table = new Node[8];
    private int size;

    @Override
```

```
public int size() {
    return size;
}

@Override
public boolean isEmpty() {
    return size == 0;
}
```

These rely on a helper class, called a Node, which represents a key-value pair and implements the interface Map.Entry as follows:

```
static class Node implements Map.Entry<String,String> {
    final int hash;
    final String key;
    String value;
    Node next;

    Node(int hash, String key, String value, Node next) {
        this.hash = hash;
        this.key = key;
        this.value = value;
        this.next = next;
    }

    public final String getKey()        { return key; }
    public final String getValue()      { return value; }
    public final String toString() { return key + "=" + value; }

    public final int hashCode() {
        return Objects.hashCode(key) ^ Objects.hashCode(value);
    }

    public final String setValue(String newValue) {
        String oldValue = value;
        value = newValue;
        return oldValue;
    }

    public final boolean equals(Object o) {
        if (o == this)
            return true;
        if (o instanceof Node) {
            Node e = (Node)o;
            if (Objects.equals(key, e.getKey()) &&
                    Objects.equals(value, e.getValue()))
                return true;
        }
        return false;
    }
}
```

To look for a value in the map, we use the `get()` method, which relies on a couple of helper methods, `hash()` and `indexFor()` as follows:

```
@Override
public String get(Object key) {
    if (key == null)
        return null;
    int hash = hash(key);
    for (Node e = table[indexFor(hash, table.length)];
            e != null;
            e = e.next) {
        Object k = e.key;
        if (e.hash == hash && (k == key || key.equals(k)))
            return e.value;
    }
    return null;
}

static final int hash(Object key) {          A bitwise operation to make
    int h = key.hashCode();                   sure that the hash value is
    return h ^ (h >>> 16);         ◄───────   positive
}
                                              A bitwise operation to make
static int indexFor(int h, int length) {      sure that the index is within
    return h & (length - 1);       ◄───────   the size of the table
}
```

First, the `get()` method deals with the irritating null case. Following that, we use the key object's hash code to construct an index into the array `table`. An unwritten assumption says that the size of `table` is a power of two, so the operation of `indexFor()` is basically a modulo operation, which ensures that the return value is a valid index into `table`.

NOTE This is a classic example of a situation where a human mind can determine that an exception (in this case, `ArrayIndexOutOfBoundsException`) will never be thrown, but the compiler cannot.

Now that we have an index into `table`, we use it to select the relevant hash chain for our lookup operation. We start at the head and walk down the hash chain. At each step we evaluate whether we've found our key object, as shown next:

```
if (e.hash == hash && ((k = e.key) == key || key.equals(k)))
    return e.value;
```

If we have, then we return the corresponding value. We store keys and values as pairs (really as `Node` instances) to allow for this approach.

The `put()` method is somewhat similar to the previous code:

```
@Override
public String put(String key, String value) {
    if (key == null)
        return null;
```

```
    int hash = hash(key.hashCode());
    int i = indexFor(hash, table.length);
    for (Node e = table[i]; e != null; e = e.next) {
        Object k = e.key;
        if (e.hash == hash && (k == key || key.equals(k))) {
            String oldValue = e.value;
            e.value = value;
            return oldValue;
        }
    }

    Node e = table[i];
    table[i] = new Node(hash, key, value, e);

    return null;
}
```

This version of a hashed data structure is not 100% production quality, but it is intended to demonstrate the basic behavior and approach to the problem, so that the concurrent case can be understood.

6.5.2 Limitations of Dictionary

Before we proceed to the concurrent case, we should mention that some methods from `Map` are not supported by our toy implementation, `Dictionary`. Specifically, `putAll()`, `keySet()`, `values()`, or `entrySet()` (which need to be defined, because the class implements `Map`) will simply throw new `UnsupportedOperationException()`.

We do not support these methods purely and solely due to complexity. As we will see several times in the book, the Java Collections interfaces are large and feature-rich. This is good for the end user, because they have a lot of power, but it means an implementor must supply a lot more methods.

In particular, methods like `keySet()` require an implementation of `Map` to supply instances of `Set`, and this frequently results in needing to write an entire implementation of the `Set` interface as an inner class. That is too much extra complexity for our examples, so we just don't support those methods in our toy implementation.

> **NOTE** As we will see later in the book, the monolithic, complex, imperative design of the Collections interfaces presents various problems when we start to think about functional programming in detail.

The simple `Dictionary` class works well, within its limitations. However, it does not guard against the following two scenarios:

- The need to resize `table` as the number of elements stored increases
- Defending against keys that implement a pathological form of `hashCode()`

The first of these is a serious limitation. A major point of a hashed data structure is to reduce the expected complexity operations down from $O(N)$ to $O(\log N)$, for example, for value retrieval. If the table is not resized as the number of elements held in the map increases, this complexity gain is lost. A real implementation would have to deal with the need to resize the table as the map grows.

6.5.3 Approaches to a concurrent Dictionary

As it stands, Dictionary is obviously not thread-safe. Consider two threads—one trying to delete a certain key and the other trying to update the value associated with it. Depending on the ordering of operations, it is entirely possible for both the deletion and the update to report that they succeeded when in fact only one of them did. To resolve this, we have two fairly obvious (if naïve) ways to make Dictionary (and, by extension, general Java Map implementations) concurrent.

First off is the fully synchronization approach, which we met in chapter 5. The punch line is not hard to predict: this approach is unfeasible for most practical systems due to performance overhead. However, it's worth a small diversion to look at how we might implement it.

We have two easy ways to achieve simple thread safety here. The first is to copy the Dictionary class—let's call it ThreadSafeDictionary and then make all of its methods synchronized. This works but involves a lot of duplicated, cut-and-paste code.

Alternatively, we can use a synchronized wrapper to provide *delegation*—aka forwarding— to an underlying object that actually houses the dictionary. Here's how we can do that:

```
public final class SynchronizedDictionary extends Dictionary {
    private final Dictionary d;

    private SynchronizedDictionary(Dictionary delegate) {
        d = delegate;
    }

    public static SynchronizedDictionary of(Dictionary delegate) {
        return new SynchronizedDictionary(delegate);
    }

    @Override
    public synchronized int size() {
        return d.size();
    }

    @Override
    public synchronized boolean isEmpty() {
        return d.isEmpty();
    }

    // ... other methods

}
```

This example has a number of problems, the most important of which is that the object d already exists and is not synchronized. This is setting ourselves up to fail—

other code may modify d outside of a synchronized block or method, and we find ourselves in exactly the situation we discussed in the previous chapter. This is not the right approach for concurrent data structures.

We should mention that, in fact, the JDK provides just such an implementation— the synchronizedMap() method provided in the Collections class. It works about as well and is about as widely used, as you might expect.

A second approach is to appeal to immutability. As we will say, and say again, the Java Collections are large and complex interfaces. One way in which this manifests is that the assumption of mutability is baked throughout the collections. In no sense is it a separable concern that some implementations may choose, or not, to express—all implementations of Map and List must implement the mutating methods.

Due to this constriction, it might seem as though we have no way to model a data structure in Java that is both immutable and conforms to the Java Collections APIs—if it conforms to the APIs, the class must also provide an implementation of the mutation method. However, a deeply unsatisfactory back door exists. An implementation of an interface can always throw UnsupportedOperationException if it has not implemented a certain method. From a language design point of view, this is, of course, terrible. An interface contract should be exactly that—a contract.

Unfortunately, this mechanism and convention predates Java 8 (and the arrival of default methods) and thus represents an attempt to encode a difference between a "mandatory" method and an "optional" one, at a time when no such distinction actually existed in the Java language.

It is a bad mechanism and practice (especially because UnsupportedOperationException is a runtime exception), but we could use it something like this:

```
public final class ImmutableDictionary extends Dictionary {
    private final Dictionary d;

    private ImmutableDictionary(Dictionary delegate) {
        d = delegate;
    }

    public static ImmutableDictionary of(Dictionary delegate) {
        return new ImmutableDictionary(delegate);
    }

    @Override
    public int size() {
        return d.size();
    }

    @Override
    public String get(Object key) {
        return d.get(key);
    }

    @Override
    public String put(String key, String value) {
```

```
        throw new UnsupportedOperationException();
    }

    // other mutating methods also throw UnsupportedOperationException

}
```

It can be argued that this is something of a violation of object-oriented principles—the expectation from the user is that this is a valid implementation of Map<String, String>, and yet, if a user tries to mutate an instance, an unchecked exception is thrown. This can legitimately be seen as a safety hazard.

> **NOTE** This is basically the compromise that Map.of() has to make: it needs to fully implement the interface and so has to resort to throwing exceptions on mutating method calls.

This is also not the only issue with this approach. Another drawback is that this is, of course, subject to the same basic flaw as we saw for the synchronized case—a mutable object still exists and can be referenced (and mutated) via that route, violating the basic criteria that we were trying to achieve. Let us draw a veil over these attempts and try to look for something better.

6.5.4   *Using ConcurrentHashMap*

Having shown a simple map implementation and discussed approaches that we could use to make it concurrent, it's time to meet the ConcurrentHashMap. In some ways, this is the easy part: it is an extremely easy-to-use class and in most cases is a drop-in replacement for HashMap.

The key point about the ConcurrentHashMap is that it is safe for multiple threads to update it at once. To see why we need this, let's see what happens when we have two threads adding entries to a HashMap simultaneously (exception handling elided):

```
var map = new HashMap<String, String>();
var SIZE = 10_000;

Runnable r1 = () -> {
    for (int i = 0; i < SIZE; i = i + 1) {
        map.put("t1" + i, "0");
    }
    System.out.println("Thread 1 done");
};
Runnable r2 = () -> {
    for (int i = 0; i < SIZE; i = i + 1) {
        map.put("t2" + i, "0");
    }
    System.out.println("Thread 2 done");
};
Thread t1 = new Thread(r1);
Thread t2 = new Thread(r2);
t1.start();
```

```
t2.start();

t1.join();
t2.join();
System.out.println("Count: "+ map.size());
```

If we run this code, we will see a different manifestation of our old friend, the Lost Update antipattern—the output value for Count will be less than 2 * SIZE. However, in the case of concurrent access to a map, the situation is actually much, much worse.

The most dangerous behavior of HashMap under concurrent modification does not always manifest at small sizes. However, if we increase the value of SIZE it will, eventually, manifest itself.

If we increase SIZE to, say, 1_000_000, then we are likely to see the behavior. One of the threads making updates to map will fail to finish. That's right—one of the threads can (and will) get stuck in an actual infinite loop. This makes HashMap totally unsafe for use in multithreaded applications (and the same is true of our example Dictionary class).

On the other hand, if we replace HashMap with ConcurrentHashMap, then we can see that the concurrent version behaves properly—no infinite loops and no instances of Lost Update. It also has the nice property that, no matter what you do to it, map operations will never throw a ConcurrentModificationException.

Let's take a very brief look at how this is achieved. It turns out that figure 6.2, which shows the implementation of Dictionary, also points the way to a useful multi-threaded generalization of Map that is much better than either of our two previous attempts. It is based on the following insight: instead of needing to lock the whole structure when making a change, it's only necessary to lock the hash chain (aka bucket) that's being altered or read.

We can see how this works in figure 6.3. The implementation has moved the lock down onto the individual hash chains. This technique is known as *lock striping*, and it enables multiple threads to access the map, provided they are operating on different chains.

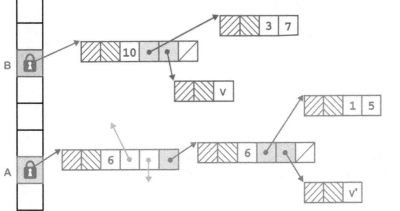

Figure 6.3
Lock striping

Of course, if two threads need to operate on the same chain, then they will still exclude each other, but in general, this provides better throughput than synchronizing the entire map.

> **NOTE** Recall that as the number of elements in the map increases, the table of buckets will resize, meaning that as more and more elements are added to a ConcurrentHashMap, it will become able to deal with more and more threads in an efficient manner.

The ConcurrentHashMap achieves this behavior, but some additional low-level details exist that most developers won't need to worry about too much. In fact, the implementation of ConcurrentHashMap changed substantially in Java 8, and it is now more complex than the design that we have described here.

Using ConcurrentHashMap can be almost too simple. In many cases, if you have a multithreaded program and need to share data, then just use a Map, and have the implementation be a ConcurrentHashMap. In fact, if there is ever a chance that a Map might need to be modified by more than one thread, then you should always use the concurrent implementation. It does use considerably more resources than a plain HashMap and will have worse throughput due to the synchronization of some operations. As we'll discuss in chapter 7, however, those inconveniences are nothing when compared to the possibility of a race condition leading to Lost Update or an infinite loop.

Finally, we should also note that ConcurrentHashMap actually implements the ConcurrentMap interface, which extends Map. It originally contained the following new methods to provide thread-safe modifications:

- putIfAbsent()—Adds the key-value pair to the HashMap if the key isn't already present.
- remove()—Safely removes the key-value pair if the key is present.
- replace()—The implementation provides two different forms of this method for safe replacement in the HashMap.

However, with Java 8, some of these methods were retrofitted to the Map interface as default methods, for example:

```
default V putIfAbsent(K key, V value) {
      V v = get(key);
      if (v == null) {
          v = put(key, value);
      }

      return v;
  }
```

The gap between ConcurrentHashMap and Map has narrowed somewhat in recent versions of Java, but don't forget that despite this, HashMap remains thread-unsafe. If you want to share data safely between threads, you should use ConcurrentHashMap.

Overall, the `ConcurrentHashMap` is one of the most useful classes in `java.util.concurrent`. It provides additional multithreaded safety and higher performance than synchronization, and it has no serious drawbacks in normal usage. The counterpart to it for `List` is the `CopyOnWriteArrayList`, which we'll discuss next.

6.6   *CopyOnWriteArrayList*

We can, of course, apply the two unsatisfactory concurrency patterns that we saw in the previous section to `List` as well. Fully synchronized and immutable (but with mutating methods that throw runtime exception) lists are as easy to write down as they are for maps, and they work no better than they do for maps.

Can we do better? Unfortunately, the linear nature of the list is not helpful here. Even in the case of a linked list, multiple threads attempting to modify the list raise the possibility of contention, for example, in workloads that have a large percentage of append operations.

One alternative that does exist is the `CopyOnWriteArrayList` class. As the name suggests, this type is a replacement for the standard `ArrayList` class that has been made thread-safe by the addition of *copy-on-write semantics*. This means that any operations that mutate the list will create a new copy of the array backing the list (as shown in figure 6.4). This also means that any iterators created don't have to worry about any modifications that they didn't expect.

The iterators are guaranteed not to throw `ConcurrentModificationException` and will not reflect any additions, removals, or changes to the list since the iterator was created—except, of course, that (as usual in Java) the list elements can still mutate. It is only the list that cannot.

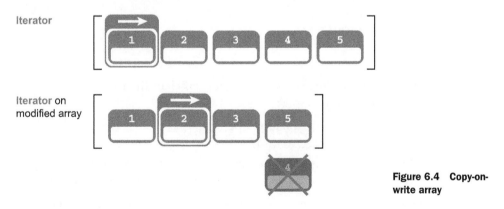

Figure 6.4   Copy-on-write array

This implementation is usually too expensive for general use but may be a good option when traversal operations vastly outnumber mutations, and when the programmer does not want the headache of synchronization, yet wants to rule out the possibility of threads interfering with each other.

Let's take a quick look at how the core idea is implemented. The key methods are iterator(), which always returns a new COWIterator object:

```
public Iterator<E> iterator() {
    return new COWIterator<E>(getArray(), 0);
}
```

and add(), remove(), and other mutation methods. The mutation methods always replace the delegate array with a new, cloned, and modified copy of the array. Protecting the array must be done within a synchronized block, so the CopyOnWriteArray-List class has an internal lock that is just used as a monitor (and note the comment on it), as shown here:

```
/**
 * The lock protecting all mutators.  (We have a mild preference
 * for builtin monitors over ReentrantLock when either will do.)
 */
final transient Object lock = new Object();

private transient volatile Object[] array;
```

Then, operations such as add() can be protected as follows:

```
public boolean add(E e) {
    synchronized (lock) {
        Object[] es = getArray();
        int len = es.length;
        es = Arrays.copyOf(es, len + 1);
        es[len] = e;
        setArray(es);
        return true;
    }
}
```

This makes the CopyOnWriteArrayList less efficient than the ArrayList for general operations, for several reasons:

- Synchronization of mutation operations.
- Volatile storage (i.e., array).
- ArrayList will only allocate memory when a resize of the underlying array is required; CopyOnWriteArrayList allocates and copies on every mutation.

Creating the iterator stores a reference to the array as it exists at that point in time. Further modifications to the list cause a new copy to be created, so the iterator will then be pointing at a past version of the array, as shown next:

```
static final class COWIterator<E> implements ListIterator<E> {
    /** Snapshot of the array */
    private final Object[] snapshot;
    /** Index of element to be returned by subsequent call to next */
```

```
        private int cursor;

        COWIterator(Object[] es, int initialCursor) {
            cursor = initialCursor;
            snapshot = es;
        }
        // ...
    }
```

Note that `COWIterator` implements `ListIterator` and so, according to the interface contract, is required to support list mutation methods, but for simplicity's sake, the mutators all throw `UnsupportedOperationException`.

The approach taken by `CopyOnWriteArrayList` to shared data may be useful when a quick, consistent snapshot of data (which may occasionally be different between readers) is more important than perfect synchronization. This is seen reasonably often in scenarios that involve non-mission-critical data, and the copy-on-write approach avoids the performance hit associated with synchronization.

Let's look at an example of copy-on-write in action in the next listing.

Listing 6.3   Copy-on-write example

```
        var ls = new CopyOnWriteArrayList(List.of(1, 2, 3));
        var it = ls.iterator();
        ls.add(4);
        var modifiedIt = ls.iterator();
        while (it.hasNext()) {
            System.out.println("Original: "+ it.next());
        }
        while (modifiedIt.hasNext()) {
            System.out.println("Modified: "+ modifiedIt.next());
        }
```

This code is specifically designed to illustrate the behavior of an `Iterator` under copy-on-write semantics. It produces output like this:

```
Original: 1
Original: 2
Original: 3
Modified: 1
Modified: 2
Modified: 3
Modified: 4
```

In general, the use of the `CopyOnWriteArrayList` class does require a bit more thought than using `ConcurrentHashMap`, which is basically a drop-in concurrent replacement for `HashMap` because of performance issues—the copy-on-write property means that if the list is altered, the entire array must be copied. If changes to the list are common, compared to read accesses, this approach won't necessarily yield high performance.

In general, the CopyOnWriteArrayList makes different trade-offs than synchronizedList(). The latter synchronizes on all operations, so reads from different threads can block each other, which is not true for a COW data structure. On the other hand, CopyOnWriteArrayList copies the backing array on every mutation, whereas the synchronized version does so only when the backing array is full (the same behavior as ArrayList). However, as we'll say repeatedly in chapter 7, reasoning about code from first principles is extremely difficult—the only way to reliably get well-performing code is to test, retest, and measure the results.

Later, in chapter 15, we'll meet the concept of a *persistent data structure*, which is another way of approaching concurrent data handling. The Clojure programming language makes very heavy use of persistent data structures, and the CopyOnWriteArrayList (and CopyOnWriteArraySet) is one example implementation of them.

Let's move on. The next major common building block of concurrent code in java.util.concurrent is the Queue. This is used to hand off work elements between threads, and it is used as the basis for many flexible and reliable multithreaded designs.

6.7   *Blocking queues*

The queue is a wonderful abstraction for concurrent programming. The queue provides a simple and reliable way to distribute processing resources to work units (or to assign work units to processing resources, depending on how you want to look at it).

A number of patterns in multithreaded Java programming rely heavily on the thread-safe implementations of Queue, so it's important that you fully understand it. The basic Queue interface is in java.util, because it can be an important pattern, even in single-threaded programming, but we'll focus on the multithreaded use cases.

One very common use case, and the one we'll focus on, is the use of a queue to transfer work units between threads. This pattern is often ideally suited for the simplest concurrent extension of Queue—the BlockingQueue.

The BlockingQueue is a queue that has the following two additional special properties:

- When trying to put() to the queue, it will cause the putting thread to wait for space to become available if the queue is full.
- When trying to take() from the queue, it will cause the taking thread to block if the queue is empty.

These two properties are very useful because if one thread (or pool of threads) is outstripping the ability of the other to keep up, the faster thread is forced to wait, thus regulating the overall system. This is illustrated in figure 6.5.

Java ships with two basic implementations of the BlockingQueue interface: the LinkedBlockingQueue and the ArrayBlockingQueue. They offer slightly different properties; for example, the array implementation is very efficient when an exact

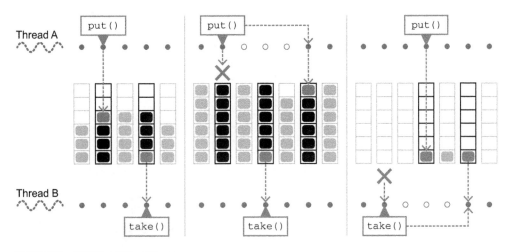

Figure 6.5   The BlockingQueue

bound is known for the size of the queue, whereas the linked implementation may be slightly faster under some circumstances.

However, the real difference between the implementations is in the implied semantics. Although the linked variant can be constructed with a size limit, it is usually created without one, which leads to an object with a queue size of Integer.MAX_VALUE. This is effectively infinite—a real application would never be able to recover from a backlog of over two billion items in one of its queues.

So, although in theory the put() method on LinkedBlockingQueue can block, in practice, it never does. This means that the threads that are writing to the queue can effectively proceed at an unlimited rate.

In contrast, the ArrayBlockingQueue has a fixed size for the queue—the size of the array that backs it. If the producer threads are putting objects into the queue faster than they are being processed by receivers, at some point the queue will fill completely, further attempts to call put() will block, and the producer threads will be forced to slow their rate of task production.

This property of the ArrayBlockingQueue is one form of what is known as *back pressure*, which is an important aspect of engineering concurrent and distributed systems.

Let's see the BlockingQueue in action in an example: altering the account example to use queues and threads. The aim of the example will be to get rid of the need to lock both account objects. The basic architecture of the application is shown in figure 6.6.

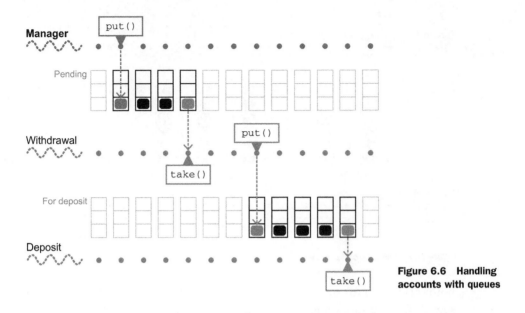

Figure 6.6 Handling accounts with queues

We start by introducing a `AccountManager` class with these fields, as shown in the next listing.

Listing 6.4 The `AccountManager` class

```java
public class AccountManager {
    private ConcurrentHashMap<Integer, Account> accounts =
        new ConcurrentHashMap<>();
    private volatile boolean shutdown = false;

    private BlockingQueue<TransferTask> pending =
        new LinkedBlockingQueue<>();
    private BlockingQueue<TransferTask> forDeposit =
        new LinkedBlockingQueue<>();
    private BlockingQueue<TransferTask> failed =
        new LinkedBlockingQueue<>();

    private Thread withdrawals;
    private Thread deposits;
```

The blocking queues contain `TransferTask` objects, which are simple data carriers that denote the transfer to be made, as shown next:

```java
public class TransferTask {
    private final Account sender;
    private final Account receiver;
    private final int amount;

    public TransferTask(Account sender, Account receiver, int amount) {
        this.sender = sender;
```

```
        this.receiver = receiver;
        this.amount = amount;
    }

    public Account sender() {
        return sender;
    }

    public int amount() {
        return amount;
    }

    public Account receiver() {
        return receiver;
    }

    // Other methods elided
}
```

There is no additional semantics for the transfer—the class is just a dumb *data carrier* type.

NOTE   The `TransferTask` type is very simple and, in Java 17, could be written as a record type (which we met in chapter 3)

The `AccountManager` class provides functionality for accounts to be created and for transfer tasks to be submitted, as illustrated here:

```
    public Account createAccount(int balance) {
        var out = new Account(balance);
        accounts.put(out.getAccountId(), out);
        return out;
    }

    public void submit(TransferTask transfer) {
        if (shutdown) {
            return false;
        }
        return pending.add(transfer);
    }
```

The real work of the `AccountManager` is handled by the two threads that manage the transfer tasks between the queues. Let's look at the withdraw operation first:

```
    public void init() {
        Runnable withdraw = () -> {
            boolean interrupted = false;
            while (!interrupted || !pending.isEmpty()) {
                try {
                    var task = pending.take();
                    var sender = task.sender();
                    if (sender.withdraw(task.amount())) {
                        forDeposit.add(task);
```

```
                    } else {
                        failed.add(task);
                    }
                } catch (InterruptedException e) {
                    interrupted = true;
                }
            }
        deposits.interrupt();
    };
```

The deposit operation is defined similarly, and then we initialize the account manager with the tasks:

```
Runnable deposit = () -> {
        boolean interrupted = false;
        while (!interrupted || !forDeposit.isEmpty()) {
            try {
                var task = forDeposit.take();
                var receiver = task.receiver();
                receiver.deposit(task.amount());
            } catch (InterruptedException e) {
                interrupted = true;
            }
        }
    };

    init(withdraw, deposit);
}
```

The package-private overload of the init() method is used to start the background threads. It exists as a separate method to allow for easier testing, as follows:

```
void init(Runnable withdraw, Runnable deposit) {
    withdrawals = new Thread(withdraw);
    deposits = new Thread(deposit);
    withdrawals.start();
    deposits.start();
}
```

We need some code to drive this:

```
            var manager = new AccountManager();
            manager.init();
            var acc1 = manager.createAccount(1000);
            var acc2 = manager.createAccount(20_000);

            var transfer = new TransferTask(acc1, acc2, 100);
            manager.submit(transfer);
            Thread.sleep(5000);
            System.out.println(acc1);
            System.out.println(acc2);
            manager.shutdown();
            manager.await();
```

Submits the transfer from acc1 to acc2 → (points to `manager.submit(transfer);`)

Sleeps to allow time for the transfer to execute (points to `Thread.sleep(5000);`)

This produces output like this:

```
Account{accountId=1, balance=900.0,
    lock=java.util.concurrent.locks.ReentrantLock@58372a00[Unlocked]}
Account{accountId=2, balance=20100.0,
    lock=java.util.concurrent.locks.ReentrantLock@4dd8dc3[Unlocked]}
```

However, the code as written does not execute cleanly, despite the calls to shutdown() and await() because of the blocking nature of the calls used. Let's look at figure 6.7 to see why.

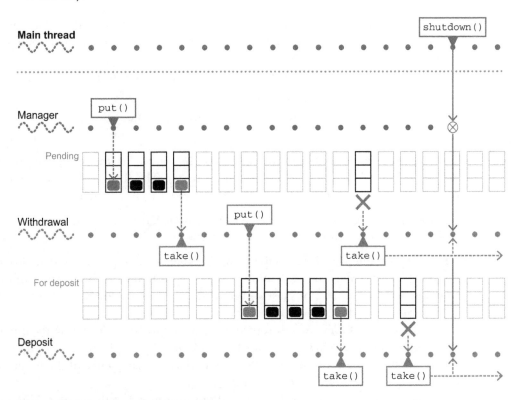

Figure 6.7 An incorrect shutdown sequence

When the main code calls shutdown(), the volatile boolean flag is flipped to true, so every subsequent read of the boolean will see the value as true. Unfortunately, both the withdrawal and depositing threads are blocked in calls to take() because the queues are empty. If an object was somehow placed into the pending queue, then the withdrawal thread would process it and then place the object into the forDeposit queue (assuming the withdrawal succeeds). The withdrawal thread would at this point exit the while loop, and the thread would terminate normally.

In turn, the depositing thread will now see the object in the forDeposit queue and will wake up, take it, process it, and then exit its own while loop and also terminate normally. However, this clean termination process depends on there still being tasks in the queue. In the edge case of an empty queue, the threads will sit in their blocking take() calls forever. To solve this issue, let's explore the full range of methods that are provided by the blocking queue implementations.

6.7.1   Using BlockingQueue APIs

The interface BlockingQueue actually provides three separate strategies for interacting with it. To understand the differences between the strategies, consider the possible behaviors that an API could display in the following scenario: a thread attempts to insert an item in a capacity-restricted queue that is currently unable to accommodate the item (i.e., the queue is full).

Logically, we have the following three possibilities. The insertion call could

- Block until space in the queue frees up
- Return a value (perhaps Boolean false) indicating failure
- Throw an exception

The same three possibilities would, of course, occur in the converse situation (attempting to take an item from an empty queue). The first of these possibilities is realized by the take() and put() methods that we have already met.

NOTE   The second and third are the options provided by the Queue interface, which is the super interface of BlockingQueue.

The second option provides a nonblocking API that returns special values and is manifested in the methods offer() and poll(). If insertion into the queue cannot be completed, then offer() fails fast and returns false. The programmer must examine the return code and take appropriate action.

Similarly, poll() immediately returns null on failure to retrieve from the queue. It might seem a bit odd to have a nonblocking API on a class explicitly named Blocking-Queue, but it is actually useful (and also required as a consequence of the inheritance relationship between BlockingQueue and Queue).

In fact, BlockingQueue provides an additional overload of the nonblocking methods. These methods provide the capability of polling or offering with a timeout, to allow the thread encountering issues to back out from its interaction with the queue and do something else instead.

We can modify the AccountManager in listing 6.4 to use the nonblocking APIs with a timeout, like so:

```
Runnable withdraw = () -> {
  LOOP:
  while (!shutdown) {
      try {
          var task = pending.poll(5,
```

If the timer expires, poll() returns null.

```
                             TimeUnit.SECONDS);
            if (task == null) {
                continue LOOP;                    ⟵──────────   Explicit use of a
            }                                                     Java loop label
            var sender = task.sender();                           to make it clear
            if (sender.withdraw(task.amount())) {                 what is being
                forDeposit.put(task);                             continued.
            } else {
                failed.put(task);
            }
        } catch (InterruptedException e) {
            // Log at critical and proceed to next item
        }
    }
    // Drain pending queue to failed or log
};
```

Similar modifications should be made for the deposit thread as well.

This solves the shutdown problem that we outlined in the previous subsection, because now the threads cannot block forever in the retrieval methods. Instead, if no object arrives before the timeout, then the poll will still return and provide the value null. The test then continues the loop, but the visibility guarantees of the volatile Boolean ensure that the while loop condition is now met and the loop is exited and the thread shuts down cleanly. This means that overall, once the shutdown() method has been called, the AccountManager will shut down in bounded time, which is the behavior we want.

To conclude the discussion of the APIs of BlockingQueue, we should look at the third approach we mentioned earlier: methods that throw exceptions if the queue operation cannot immediately complete. These methods, add() and remove(), are, frankly, problematic for several reasons, not least of which is that the exceptions they throw on failure (IllegalStateException and NoSuchElementException respectively) are runtime exceptions and so do not need to be explicitly handled.

The problems with the exception-throwing API are deeper than just this, though. A general principle in Java states that exceptions are to be used to deal with exceptional circumstances, that is, those that a program does not normally consider to be part of normal operation. The situation of an empty queue is, however, an entirely possible circumstance. So throwing an exception in response to it is a violation of the principle that is sometimes expressed as "Don't use exceptions for flow control."

Exceptions are, in general, quite expensive to use, due to stack trace construction when the exception is instantiated and stack unwinding during the throw. It is good practice not to create an exception unless it is going to immediately be thrown. For these reasons, we do recommend against using the exception-throwing form of the BlockingQueue APIs.

6.7.2   *Using WorkUnit*

The Queue interfaces are all generic: they're Queue<E>, BlockingQueue<E>, and so on. Although it may seem strange, it's sometimes wise to exploit this and introduce an artificial container class to wrap the items of work.

For example, if you have a class called MyAwesomeClass that represents the units of work that you want to process in a multithreaded application, then rather than having this:

```
BlockingQueue<MyAwesomeClass>
```

it can be better to have this:

```
BlockingQueue<WorkUnit<MyAwesomeClass>>
```

where WorkUnit (or QueueObject, or whatever you want to call the container class) is a packaging class that may look something like this:

```
public class WorkUnit<T> {
    private final T workUnit;

    public T getWork() {
        return workUnit;
    }

    public WorkUnit(T workUnit) {
        this.workUnit = workUnit;
    }

    // ... other methods elided
}
```

The reason for doing this is that this level of indirection provides a place to add additional metadata without compromising the conceptual integrity of the contained type (MyAwesomeClass, in this example). In figure 6.8, we can see how the external metadata wrapper works.

This is surprisingly useful. Use cases where additional metadata is helpful are abundant. Here are a few examples:

Figure 6.8   Use of a work unit as a metadata wrapper

- Testing (such as showing the change history for an object)
- Performance indicators (such as time of arrival or quality of service)
- Runtime system information (such as how this instance of MyAwesomeClass has been routed)

It can be much harder to add in this indirection after the fact. If you later discover that more metadata is needed in certain circumstances, it can be a major refactoring job to add in what would have been a simple change in the `WorkUnit` class. Let's move on to discuss futures, which are a way of representing a placeholder for an in-progress (usually on another thread) task in Java.

6.8 Futures

The interface `Future` in `java.util.concurrent` is a simple representation of an asynchronous task: it is a type that holds the result from a task that may not have finished yet but may at some point in the future. The primary methods on a `Future` follow:

- `get()`—Gets the result. If the result isn't yet available, will block until it is.
- `isDone()`—Allows the caller to determine whether the computation has finished. It is nonblocking.
- `cancel()`—Allows the computation to be canceled before completion.

There's also a version of `get()` that takes a timeout, which won't block forever, in a similar manner to the `BlockingQueue` methods with timeouts that we met earlier. The next listing shows a sample use of a `Future` in a prime number finder.

Listing 6.5 Finding prime numbers using a `Future`

```
Future<Long> fut = getNthPrime(1_000_000_000);
try {
    long result = fut.get(1, TimeUnit.MINUTES);
    System.out.println("Found it: " + result);
} catch (TimeoutException tox) {
    // Timed out - better cancel the task
    System.err.println("Task timed out, cancelling");
    fut.cancel(true);
} catch (InterruptedException e) {
    fut.cancel(true);
    throw e;
} catch (ExecutionException e) {
    fut.cancel(true);
    e.getCause().printStackTrace();
}
```

In this snippet, you should imagine that `getNthPrime()` returns a `Future` that is executing on some background thread (or even on multiple threads)—perhaps on one of the executor frameworks we'll discuss later in the chapter.

The thread running the snippet enters a get-with-timeout and blocks for up to 60 seconds for a response. If no response is received, then the thread loops and enters another blocking wait. Even on modern hardware, this calculation may be running for a long time, so you may need to use the `cancel()` method after all (although the code as written does not provide any mechanism to cancel our request).

As a second example, let's consider nonblocking I/O. Figure 6.9 shows the `Future` in action to allow us to use a background thread for I/O.

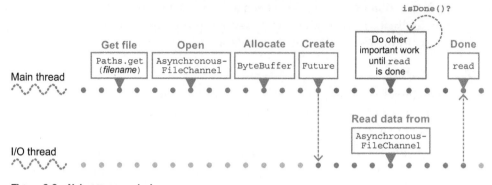

Figure 6.9   Using Future in Java

This API has been around for a while—it was introduced in Java 7 —and it allows the user to do nonblocking concurrency like this:

```
try {
    Path file = Paths.get("/Users/karianna/foobar.txt");

    var channel = AsynchronousFileChannel.open(file);      ⟵  Opens the file
                                                               asynchronously

    var buffer = ByteBuffer.allocate(1_000_000);           Requests a read of up
    Future<Integer> result = channel.read(buffer, 0);      to one million bytes

    BusinessProcess.doSomethingElse();      ⟵  Does something else

    var bytesRead = result.get();
    System.out.println("Bytes read [" + bytesRead + "]");
} catch (IOException | ExecutionException | InterruptedException e) {
    e.printStackTrace();
}
```

Gets the result when ready → `var bytesRead = result.get();`

This structure allows the main thread to doSomethingElse() while the I/O operation is proceeding on another thread—one that is managed by the Java runtime. This is a useful approach, but it requires support in the library that provides the capability. This can be somewhat limited—and what if we want to create our own asynchronous workflows?

6.8.1   *CompletableFuture*

The Java Future type is defined as an interface, rather than a concrete class. Any API that wants to use a Future-based style has to supply a concrete implementation of Future.

These can be challenging for some developers to write and represents an obvious gap in the toolkit, so from Java 8 onward, a new approach to futures was included in the JDK—a concrete implementation of Future that enhances capabilities and in some ways is more similar to futures in other languages (e.g., Kotlin and Scala).

The class is called `CompletableFuture`—it is a concrete type that implements the `Future` interface and provides additional functionality and is intended as a simple building block for building asynchronous applications. The central idea is that we can create instances of the `CompletableFuture<T>` type (it is generic in the type of the value that will be returned), and the object that is created represents the `Future` in an *uncompleted* (or "unfulfilled") state.

Later, any thread that has a reference to the completable `Future` can call `complete()` on it and provide a value—this completes (or "fulfills") the future. The completed value is immediately visible to all threads that are blocked on a `get()` call. After completion, any further calls to `complete()` are ignored.

The `CompletableFuture` cannot cause different threads to see different values. The `Future` is either uncompleted or completed, and if it is completed, the value it holds is the value provided by the first thread to call `complete()`.

This is obviously not immutability—the state of the `CompletableFuture` does change over time. However, it changes only *once*—from uncompleted to completed. There is no possibility of an inconsistent state being seen by different threads.

NOTE Java's `CompletableFuture` is similar to a *promise*, as seen in other languages (such as JavaScript), which is why we call out the alternative terminology of "fulfilling a promise" as well as "completing a future."

Let's look at an example and implement `getNthPrime()`, which we met earlier:

```
public static Future<Long> getNthPrime(int n) {        ┌ Creates the completable Future
    var numF = new CompletableFuture<Long>();    ◁─┘   in an uncompleted state

    new Thread( () -> {                      ◁─
        long num = NumberService.findPrime(n);    ◁─┐   Creates and starts a
        numF.complete(num);                             new thread that will
    } ).start();          The actual calculation       complete the Future
                          of the prime number
    return numF;
}
```

The method `getNthPrime()` creates an "empty" `CompletableFuture` and returns this container object to its caller. To drive this, we do need some code to call `getNthPrime()`—for example, the code shown in listing 6.5.

One way to think about `CompletableFuture` is by analogy with client/server systems. The `Future` interface provides only a query method— `isDone()` and a blocking `get()`. This is playing the role of the client. An instance of `CompletableFuture` plays the role of the server side—it provides full control over the execution and completion of the code that is fulfilling the future and providing the value.

In the example, `getNthPrime()` evaluates the call to the number service in a separate thread. When this call returns, we complete the future explicitly.

A slightly more concise way to achieve the same effect is to use the `CompletableFuture` `.supplyAsync()` method, passing a `Callable<T>` object representing the task to be executed. This call makes use of an application wide thread pool that is managed by the concurrency library, as follows:

```
public static Future<Long> getNthPrime(int n) {
    return CompletableFuture.supplyAsync(
        () -> NumberService.findPrime(n));
}
```

This concludes our initial tour of the concurrent data structures that are some of the main building blocks that provide the raw materials for developing solid multi-threaded applications.

> **NOTE** We will have more to say about the `CompletableFuture` later in the book, specifically in the chapters that discuss advanced concurrency and the interplay with functional programming.

Next, we'll introduce the *executors* and threadpools that provide a higher-level and more convenient way to handle execution than the raw API based on `Thread`.

6.9   *Tasks and execution*

The class `java.lang.Thread` has existed since Java 1.0—one of the original talking points of the Java language was built-in, language-level support for multithreading. It is powerful and expresses concurrency in a form that is close to the underlying operating system support. However, it is a fundamentally low-level API for handling concurrency.

This low-level nature makes it hard for many programmers to work with correctly or efficiently. Other languages that were released after Java learned from Java's experience with threads and built upon them to provide alternative approaches. Some of those approaches have, in turn, influenced the design of `java.util.concurrent` and later innovations in Java concurrency.

In this case, our immediate goal is to have tasks (or work units) that can be executed without spinning up a new thread for each one. Ultimately, this means that the tasks have to be modeled as code that can be called rather than directly represented as a thread.

Then, these tasks can be scheduled on a shared resource—a pool of threads—that executes a task to completion and then moves on to the next task. Let's take a look at how we model these tasks.

6.9.1   *Modeling tasks*

In this section, we'll look at two different ways of modeling tasks: the `Callable` interface and the `FutureTask` class. We could also consider `Runnable`, but it is not always that useful, because the `run()` method does not return a value, and, therefore, it can perform work only via side effects.

One other aspect of the task modeling is important but may not be obvious— the notion that if we assume that our thread capacity is finite, tasks must definitely complete in bounded time.

If we have the possibility of an infinite loop, some tasks could "steal" an executor thread from the pool, and this would reduce the overall capacity for all tasks from then on. Over time, this could eventually lead to exhaustion of the thread pool resource and no further work being possible. As a result, we must be careful that any tasks we construct do actually obey the "terminate in finite time" principle.

CALLABLE INTERFACE

The Callable interface represents a very common abstraction. It represents a piece of code that can be called and returns a result. Despite being a straightforward idea, this is actually a subtle and powerful concept that can lead to some extremely useful patterns.

One typical use of a Callable is the lambda expression (or an anonymous implementation). The last line of this snippet sets s to be the value of out.toString():

```
var out = getSampleObject();
Callable<String> cb = () -> out.toString();

String s = cb.call();
```

Think of a Callable as being a deferred invocation of the single method, call(), which the lambda provides.

FUTURETASK CLASS

The FutureTask class is one commonly used implementation of the Future interface, which also implements Runnable. As we'll see, this means that a FutureTask can be fed to executors. The API of FutureTask is basically that of Future and Runnable combined: get(), cancel(), isDone(), isCancelled(), and run(), although the last of these—the one that does the actual work—would be called by the executor, rather than directly by client code.

Two convenience constructors for FutureTask are provided: one that takes a Callable and one that takes a Runnable (which uses Executors.callable() to convert the Runnable to a Callable). This suggests a flexible approach to tasks, allowing a job to be written as a Callable then wrapped into a FutureTask that can then be scheduled (and cancelled, if necessary) on an executor, due to the Runnable nature of FutureTask.

The class provides a simple state model for tasks and management of a task through that model. The possible state transitions are shown in figure 6.10

This is sufficient for a wide range of ordinary execution possibilities. Let's meet the standard executors that are provided by the JDK.

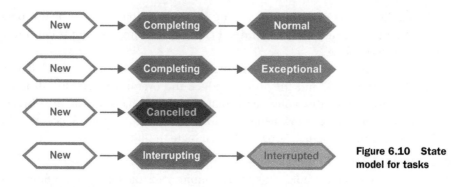

Figure 6.10　State model for tasks

6.9.2　*Executors*

A couple of standard interfaces are used to describe the threadpools present in the JDK. The first is Executor, which is very simple and defined like this:

```
public interface Executor {

    /**
     * Executes the given command at some time in the future. The command
     * may execute in a new thread, in a pooled thread, or in the calling
     * thread, at the discretion of the {@code Executor} implementation.
     *
     * @param command the runnable task
     * @throws RejectedExecutionException if this task cannot be
     * accepted for execution
     * @throws NullPointerException if command is null
     */
    void execute(Runnable command);
}
```

You should note that although this interface has only a single abstract method (i.e., it is a so-called SAM type), it is *not* tagged with the annotation @FunctionalInterface. It can still be used as the target type for a lambda expression, but it is not intended for use in functional programming.

In fact, the Executor is not widely used—far more common is the ExecutorService interface that extends Executor and adds submit() as well as several *life cycle* methods, such as shutdown().

To help the developer instantiate and work with some standard threadpools, the JDK provides the Executors class, which is a collection of static helper methods (mostly factories). Four of the most commonly used methods follow:

```
newSingleThreadExecutor()
newFixedThreadPool(int nThreads)
newCachedThreadPool()
newScheduledThreadPool(int corePoolSize)
```

Let's look at each of these in turn. Later in the book, we will dive into some of the other, more complex, possibilities that are also provided.

6.9.3 Single-threaded executor

The simplest of the executors is the single-threaded executor. This is essentially an encapsulated combination of a single thread and a task queue (which is a blocking queue).

Client code places an executable task onto the queue via `submit()`. The single execution thread then takes the tasks one at a time and runs each to completion before taking the next task.

> **NOTE** The executors are not implemented as distinct types but instead represent different parameter choices when constructing an underlying threadpool.

Any tasks that are submitted while the execution thread is busy are queued until the thread is available. Because this executor is backed by a single thread, if the previously mentioned "terminate in finite time" condition is violated, it means that no subsequently submitted job will ever run.

> **NOTE** This version of the executor is often useful for testing because it can be made more deterministic that other forms.

Here is a very simple example of how to use the single-threaded executor:

```
var pool = Executors.newSingleThreadExecutor();
Runnable hello = () -> System.out.println("Hello world");
pool.submit(hello);
```

The `submit()` call hands off the runnable task by placing it on the executor's job queue. That job submission is nonblocking (unless the job queue is full).

However, care must still be taken—for example, if the main thread exits immediately, the submitted job may not have had time to be collected by the pool thread and may not run. Instead of exiting straightaway, it is wise to call the `shutdown()` method on the executor first.

The details can be found in the `ThreadPoolExecutor` class, but basically this method starts an *orderly shutdown* in which previously submitted tasks are executed but no new tasks will be accepted. This effectively solves the issues we saw in listing 6.4 about draining the queues of pending transactions.

> **NOTE** The combination of a task that loops infinitely and an orderly shutdown request will interact badly, resulting in a threadpool that never shuts down.

Of course, if the single-threaded executor was all that was needed, there wouldn't be a need to develop a deep understanding of concurrent programming and its challenges. So, we should also look at the alternatives that utilize multiple-executor threads.

6.9.4   *Fixed-thread pool*

The fixed-thread pool, obtained via one of the variants of `Executors.newFixed-`
`ThreadPool()`, is essentially the multiple-thread generalization of the single-threaded
executor. At creation time, the user supplies an explicit thread count, and the pool is
created with that many threads.

These threads will be reused to run multiple tasks, one after another. The design
prevents users having to pay the cost of thread creation. As with the single-threaded
variant, if all threads are in use, new tasks are stored in a blocking queue until a thread
becomes free.

This version of the threadpool is particularly useful if task flow is stable and known
and if all submitted jobs are roughly the same size, in terms of computation duration.
It is, once again, most easily created from the appropriate factory method, as shown
here:

```
var pool = Executors.newFixedThreadPool(2);
```

This will create an explicit thread pool backed by two executor threads. The two
threads will take turns accepting tasks from the queue in a nondeterministic manner.
Even if there is a strict temporal (time-based) ordering of when tasks are submitted,
there is no guarantee of which thread will handle a given task.

One consequence of this is that in a situation like that shown in figure 6.11, the
tasks in the downstream queue cannot be relied upon to be accurately temporally
ordered, even if the tasks in the upstream queue are.

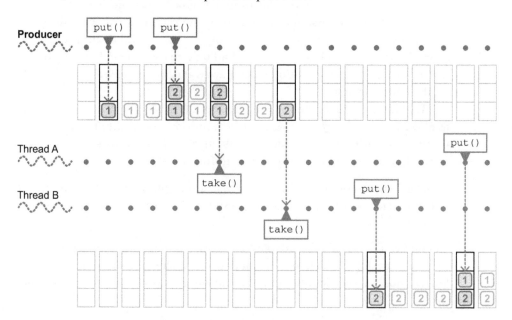

Figure 6.11   A threadpool and two queues

The fixed threadpool has its uses, but it is not the only game in town. For one thing, if the executor threads in it die, they are not replaced. If the possibility exists of the submitted jobs throwing a runtime exception, this can lead to the threadpool starving. Let's look at another alternative, which makes different trade-offs but which can avoid this possibility.

6.9.5 Cached thread pool

The fixed threadpool is often used when the activity pattern of the workload is known and fairly stable. However, if the incoming work is more uneven or bursty, then a pool with a fixed number of threads is likely to be suboptimal.

The `CachedThreadPool` is an unbounded pool, that will reuse threads if they are available but otherwise will create new threads as required to handle incoming tasks, as shown here:

```
var pool = Executors.newCachedThreadPool();
```

Threads are kept in the idle cache for 60 seconds, and if they are still present at the end of that period, they will be removed from the cache and destroyed.

It is, of course, still very important that the tasks do actually terminate. If not, then the threadpool will, over time, create more and more threads and consume more and more of the machine's resources and eventually crash or become unresponsive.

In general, the trade-off between fixed-size thread pools and cached thread pools is largely about reusing threads versus creating and destroying threads to achieve different effects. The design of the `CachedThreadPool` should give better performance with small asynchronous tasks as compared to the performance achieved from fixed-size pools. However, as always, if the effect is thought to be significant, proper performance testing much be undertaken.

6.9.6 ScheduledThreadPoolExecutor

The final example of an executor that we'll look at is a little bit different. This is the `ScheduledThreadPoolExecutor`, sometimes referred to as an STPE, as shown here:

```
ScheduledExecutorService pool = Executors.newScheduledThreadPool(4);
```

Note that the return type, which we've explicitly called out here, is `ScheduledExecutorService`. This is different from the other factory methods, which return `ExecutorService`.

> **NOTE** The `ScheduledThreadPoolExecutor` is a surprisingly capable choice of executor and can be used across a wide range of circumstances.

The scheduled service extends the usual executor service and adds a small amount of new capabilities: `schedule()`, which runs a one-off task after a specified delay, and two methods for scheduling periodic (i.e., repeating tasks)—`scheduleAtFixedRate()` and `scheduleWithFixedDelay()`.

The behavior of these two methods is slightly different. scheduleAtFixedRate() will activate a new copy of the task on a fixed timetable (and it will do so whether or not previous copies have completed), whereas scheduleWithFixedDelay() will activate a new copy of the task only after the previous instance has completed and the specified delay has elapsed.

Apart from the ScheduledThreadPoolExecutor, all the other pools we've met are obtained by choosing slightly different parameter choices for the quite general Thread-PoolExecutor class. For example, let's look at the following definition of Executors .newFixedThreadPool():

```
public static ExecutorService newFixedThreadPool(int nThreads) {
    return new ThreadPoolExecutor(nThreads, nThreads,
                                  0L, TimeUnit.MILLISECONDS,
                                  new LinkedBlockingQueue<Runnable>());
}
```

This is the purpose of the helper methods, of course: to provide a convenient way of accessing some standard choices for a threadpool without needing to engage with the full complexity of ThreadPoolExecutor. Beyond the JDK, many other examples of executors and related threadpools exist, such as the org.apache.catalina.Executor class from the Tomcat web server.

Summary

- java.util.concurrent classes should be your preferred toolkit for all new multithreaded Java code:
  - Atomic integers
  - Concurrent data structures, especially ConcurrentHashMap
  - Blocking queues and latches
  - Threadpools and executors
- These classes can be used to implement safe concurrent programming techniques including:
  - Addressing inflexibility of synchronized locks
  - Use of blocking queues for task handoff
  - Using latches for consensus among a group of threads
  - Partitioning execution into work units
  - Job control, including safe shutdown

7
Understanding Java performance

This chapter covers

- Why performance matters
- The G1 garbage collector
- Just-in-time (JIT) compilation
- JFR—the JDK Flight Recorder

Poor performance kills applications—it's bad for your customers and your application's reputation. Unless you have a totally captive market, your customers will vote with their feet—they'll already be out the door, heading to a competitor. To stop poor performance from harming your project, you need to understand performance analysis and how to make it work for you.

Performance analysis and tuning is a huge subject, and too many treatments focus on the wrong things. So, we're going to start by telling you the big secret of performance tuning. Here it is—the single biggest secret of performance tuning: *You have to measure. You can't tune properly without measuring.*

And here's why: the human brain is pretty much always wrong when it comes to guessing what the slow parts of systems are. Everyone's is. Yours, mine, James

207

Gosling's—we're all subject to our subconscious biases and tend to see patterns that may not be there. In fact, the answer to the question, "Which part of my Java code needs optimizing?" is quite often, "None of it."

Consider a typical (if rather conservative) ecommerce web application, providing services to a pool of registered customers. It has an SQL database, web servers fronting Java services, and a fairly standard network configuration connecting all of it. Very often, the non-Java parts of the system (database, filesystem, network) are the real bottleneck, but without measurement, the Java developer would never know that. Instead of finding and fixing the real problem, the developer may waste time on micro-optimization of code aspects that aren't really contributing to the issue.

The kinds of fundamental questions that you want to be able to answer are these:

- If you have a sales drive and suddenly have 10 times as many customers, will the system have enough memory to cope?
- What is the average response time your customers see from your application?
- How does that compare to your competitors?

Notice that all of these example questions are about aspects of your system that are directly relevant to your customers—the users of your system. There is nothing here about topics such as

- Are lambdas and streams faster than `for` loops?
- Are regular methods (virtual methods) faster than interface methods?
- What's the fastest implementation of `hashcode()`?

The inexperienced performance engineer will often make the mistake of assuming that user-visible performance is strongly dependent upon, or closely correlated with, the microperformance aspects that the second set of questions addresses.

This assumption—essentially a reductionist viewpoint—is actually not true in practice. Instead, the complexity of modern software systems causes overall performance to be an *emergent* property of the system and all of its layers. Specific microeffects are almost impossible to isolate, and microbenchmarking is of very limited utility to most application programmers.

Instead, to do performance tuning, you have to get out of the realm of guessing about what's making the system slow—and *slow* means "impacting the experience of customers." You have to start knowing, and the only way to know for sure is to measure.

You also need to understand what else performance tuning *isn't*. It isn't the following:

- A collection of tips and tricks
- Secret sauce
- Fairy dust that you sprinkle on at the end of a project

Be especially careful of the "tips and tricks" approaches. The truth is that the JVM is a very sophisticated and highly tuned environment, and without proper context, most of these tips are useless (and may actually be harmful). They also go out of date very quickly as the JVM gets smarter and smarter at optimizing code.

Performance analysis is really a type of experimental science. You can think of your code as a type of science experiment that has inputs and produces "outputs"— performance metrics that indicate how efficiently the system is performing the work asked of it. The job of the performance engineer is to study these outputs and look for patterns. This makes performance tuning a branch of applied statistics, rather than a collection of old wives' tales and applied folklore.

This chapter is here to help you get started. It's an introduction to the practice of Java performance tuning. But this is a big subject, and we have space to give you only a primer on some essential theory and some signposts. We'll try to answer the following most fundamental questions:

- Why does performance matter?
- Why is performance analysis hard?
- What aspects of the JVM make it potentially complex to tune?
- How should performance tuning be thought about and approached?
- What are the most common underlying causes of slowness?

We'll also give you an introduction to the following two subsystems in the JVM that are the most important when it comes to performance-related matters:

- The garbage collection subsystem
- The JIT compiler

This should be enough to get you started and help you apply this (admittedly somewhat theory-heavy) knowledge to the real problems you face in your code. Let's get going by taking a quick look at some fundamental vocabulary that will enable you to express and frame your performance problems and goals.

7.1   Performance terminology: Some basic definitions

To get the most out of our discussions in this chapter, we need to formalize some notions of performance that you may be aware of. We'll begin by defining some of the following important terms in the performance engineer's lexicon:

- Latency
- Throughput
- Utilization
- Efficiency
- Capacity
- Scalability
- Degradation

A number of these terms are discussed by Doug Lea in the context of multithreaded code, but we're considering a much wider context here. When we speak of performance, we could mean anything from a single multithreaded process all the way up to an entire cluster of services hosted in the cloud.

7.1.1   Latency

Latency is the end-to-end time taken to process a single work unit at a given workload. Quite often, latency is quoted just for "normal" workloads, but an often-useful performance measure is the graph showing latency as a function of increasing workload.

The graph in figure 7.1 shows a sudden, nonlinear degradation of a performance metric (e.g., latency) as the workload increases. This is usually called a performance elbow (or "hockey stick").

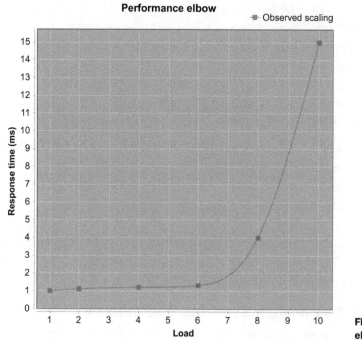

Figure 7.1   A performance elbow

7.1.2   Throughput

Throughput is the number of units of work that a system can perform in some time period with given resources. One commonly quoted number is transactions per second on some reference platform (e.g., a specific brand of server with specified hardware, OS, and software stack).

7.1.3   Utilization

Utilization represents the percentage of available resources that are being used to handle work units, instead of housekeeping tasks (or just being idle). People will commonly quote a server as being, for example, 10% utilized. This refers to the percentage of CPU processing work units during normal processing time. Note that the difference can be very large between the utilization levels of different resources, such as CPU and memory.

7.1.4   Efficiency

The *efficiency* of a system is equal to the throughput divided by the resources used. A system that requires more resources to produce the same throughput is less efficient.

For example, consider comparing two clustering solutions. If solution A requires twice as many servers as solution B for the same throughput, it's half as efficient.

Remember that resources can also be considered in cost terms—if solution A costs twice as much (or requires twice as many staff to run the production environment) as solution B, then it's only half as efficient.

7.1.5   Capacity

Capacity is the number of work units (such as transactions) that can be in flight through the system at any time. That is, it's the amount of simultaneous processing available at a specified latency or throughput.

7.1.6   Scalability

As resources are added to a system, the throughput (or latency) will change. This change in throughput or latency is the *scalability* of the system.

If solution A doubles its throughput when the available servers in a pool are doubled, it's scaling in a perfectly linear fashion. Perfect linear scaling is very, very difficult to achieve under most circumstances—remember Amdahl's law.

You should also note that the scalability of a system depends on a number of factors, and it isn't constant. A system can scale close to linearly up until some point and then begin to degrade badly. That's a different kind of performance elbow.

7.1.7   Degradation

If you add more work units, or clients for network systems, without adding more resources, you'll typically see a change in the observed latency or throughput. This change is the *degradation* of the system under additional load.

The degradation will, under normal circumstances, be negative. That is, adding work units to a system will cause a negative effect on performance (such as causing the latency of processing to increase). But some circumstances exist under which degradation could be positive. For example, if the additional load causes some part of the system to cross a threshold and switch to a high-performance mode, this can cause the system to work more efficiently and reduce processing times, even though there is actually more work to be done. The JVM is a very dynamic runtime system, and several parts of it could contribute to this sort of effect.

The preceding terms are the most frequently used indicators of performance. Others are occasionally important, but these are the basic system statistics that will normally be used to guide performance tuning. In the next section, we'll lay out an approach that is grounded in close attention to these numbers and that is as quantitative as possible.

7.2 *A pragmatic approach to performance analysis*

Many developers, when they approach the task of performance analysis, don't start with a clear picture of what they want to achieve by doing the analysis. A vague sense that the code "ought to run faster" is often all that developers or managers have when the work begins.

But this is completely backward. To do really effective performance tuning, you should have think about some key areas before beginning any kind of technical work. You should know the following things:

- What observable aspects of your code you're measuring
- How to measure those observables
- What the goals are for the observables
- How you'll recognize when you're done with performance tuning
- What the maximum acceptable cost is (in terms of developer time invested and additional complexity in the code) for the performance tuning
- What not to sacrifice as you optimize

Most important, as we'll say many times in this chapter, you *have* to measure. Without measurement of at least one observable, you aren't doing performance analysis.

It's also very common when you start measuring your code to discover that time isn't being spent where you think it is. A missing database index or contended filesystem locks can be the root of a lot of performance problems. When thinking about optimizing your code, you should always remember that it's possible that the code isn't the issue. To quantify where the problem is, the first thing you need to know is what you're measuring.

7.2.1 *Know what you're measuring*

In performance tuning, you always have to be measuring something. If you aren't measuring an observable, you're not doing performance tuning. Sitting and staring at your code, hoping that a faster way to solve the problem will strike you, isn't performance analysis.

> **TIP** To be a good performance engineer, you should understand terms such as *mean, median, mode, variance, percentile, standard deviation, sample size,* and *normal distribution.* If you aren't familiar with these concepts, you should start with a quick web search and do further reading if needed. Chapter 5 of Leonard Apeltsin's *Data Science Bookcamp* (Manning, 2021. http://mng.bz/e7Oq) is a good place to start.

When undertaking performance analysis, it's important to know exactly which of the observables we described in the last section are important to you. You should always tie your measurements, objectives, and conclusions to one or more of the basic observables we introduced. Some typical observables that are good targets for performance tuning follow:

- Average time taken for the `handleRequest()` method to run (after warmup)
- The 90th percentile of the system's end-to-end latency with 10 concurrent clients
- The degradation of the response time as you increase from 1 to 1,000 concurrent users

All of these represent quantities that the engineer might want to measure and potentially tune. To obtain accurate and useful numbers, a basic knowledge of statistics is essential.

Knowing what you're measuring and having confidence that your numbers are accurate is the first step. But vague or open-ended objectives don't often produce good results, and performance tuning is no exception. Instead, your performance goals should be what are sometimes referred to as SMART objectives (for *specific, measurable, agreed, relevant,* and *time-boxed*).

7.2.2 Know how to take measurements

We have really only the following two ways to determine precisely how long a method or other piece of Java code takes to run:

- Measure it directly, by inserting measurement code into the source class.
- Transform the class that is to be measured at class loading time.

These two approaches are referred to as *manual* and *automatic* instrumentation, respectively. All commonly used performance measuring techniques will rely on one (or both) of these techniques.

> **NOTE** There is also the JVM Tool Interface (JVMTI), which can be used to create very sophisticated performance tools, but it has drawbacks, notably that it requires the use of native code, which impacts both the complexity and safety of tools written using it.

DIRECT MEASUREMENT

Direct measurement is the easiest technique to understand, but it's also intrusive. In its simplest form, it looks like this:

```
long t0 = System.currentTimeMillis();
methodToBeMeasured();
long t1 = System.currentTimeMillis();

long elapsed = t1 - t0;
System.out.println("methodToBeMeasured took "+ elapsed +" millis");
```

This will produce an output line that should give a millisecond-accurate view of how long `methodToBeMeasured()` took to run. The inconvenient part is that code like this has to be added throughout the codebase, and as the number of measurements grows, it becomes difficult to avoid being swamped with data.

There are other problems too—for example, what happens if `methodToBe-Measured()` takes under a millisecond to run? As we'll see later in this chapter, there are also cold-start effects to worry about: JIT compilation means that later runs of the method may well be quicker than earlier runs.

There are also more subtle problems: the call to `currentTimeMillis()` requires a call to a native method and a system call to read the system clock. This is not only time-consuming but can also flush code from the execution pipelines, leading to additional performance degradation that would not occur if the measurement code was not there.

AUTOMATIC INSTRUMENTATION VIA CLASS LOADING

In chapters 1 and 4, we discussed how classes are assembled into an executing program. One of the key steps that is often overlooked is the transformation of bytecode as it's loaded. This is incredibly powerful, and it lies at the heart of many modern techniques in the Java platform.

One example of it is the automatic instrumentation of methods. In this approach, `methodToBeMeasured()` is loaded by a special class loader that adds in bytecode at the start and end of the method to record the times at which the method was entered and exited. These timings are typically written to a shared data structure, which is accessed by other threads. These threads act on the data, typically either writing output to log files or contacting a network-based server that processes the raw data.

This technique lies at the heart of many professional-grade Java performance-monitoring tools (such as New Relic), but actively maintained open source tools that fill the same niche have been scarce. This situation may now be changing with the rise of the OpenTelemetry OSS libraries and standards and their Java auto-instrumentation subproject.

> **NOTE**   As we'll discuss later, Java methods start off interpreted, then switch to compiled mode. For true performance numbers, you have to discard the timings generated when in interpreted mode, because they can badly skew the results. Later we'll discuss in more detail how you can know when a method has switched to compiled mode.

Using one or both of these techniques will allow you to produce numbers for how quickly a given method executes. The next question is, what do you want the numbers to look like when you've finished tuning?

7.2.3   *Know what your performance goals are*

Nothing focuses the mind like a clear target, so just as important as knowing what to measure is knowing and communicating the end goal of tuning. In most cases, this should be a simple and precisely stated goal, such as the following:

- Reduce the 90th percentile end-to-end latency by 20% at 10 concurrent users
- Reduce the mean latency of `handleRequest()` by 40%

In more complex cases, the goal may be to reach several related performance targets at once. You should be aware that the more separate observables that you measure and try to tune, the more complex the performance exercise can become. Optimizing for one performance goal can negatively impact on another.

Sometimes it's necessary to do some initial analysis, such as determining what the important methods are, before setting goals, such as making them run faster. This is fine, but after the initial exploration, it's almost always better to stop and state your goals before trying to achieve them. Too often developers will plow on with the analysis without stopping to elucidate their goals.

7.2.4 *Know when to stop*

In theory, knowing when it's time to stop optimizing is easy—you're done when you've achieved your goals. In practice, however, it's easy to get sucked into performance tuning. If things go well, the temptation to keep pushing and do even better can be very strong. Alternatively, if you're struggling to reach your goal, it's hard to keep from trying out different strategies in an attempt to hit the target.

Knowing when to stop involves having an awareness of your goals but also a sense of what they're worth. Getting 90% of the way to a performance goal can often be enough, and the engineer's time may well be spent better elsewhere.

Another important consideration is how much effort is being spent on rarely used code paths. Optimizing code that accounts for 1% or less of the program's runtime is almost always a waste of time, yet a surprising number of developers will engage in this behavior.

Here's a set of very simple guidelines for knowing what to optimize. You may need to adapt these for your particular circumstances, but they work well for a wide range of situations:

- Optimize what matters, not what is easy to optimize.
- Hit the most important (usually the most often called) methods first.
- Take low-hanging fruit as you come across it, but be aware of how often the code that it represents is called.

At the end, do another round of measurement. If you haven't hit your performance goals, take stock. Look and see how close you are to hitting those goals, and whether the gains you've made have had the desired impact on overall performance.

7.2.5 *Know the cost of achieving higher performance*

All performance tweaks have a price tag attached, such as the following:

- There's the time taken to do the analysis and develop an improvement (and it's worth remembering that the cost of developer time is almost always the greatest expense on any software project).

- There's the additional technical complexity that the fix will probably have introduced. (There are performance improvements that also simplify the code, but they're not the majority of cases.)
- Additional threads may have been introduced to perform auxiliary tasks to allow the main processing threads to go faster, and these threads may have unforeseen effects on the overall system at higher loads.

Whatever the price tag, pay attention to it, and try to identify it before you finish a round of optimization.

It often helps to have some idea of what the maximum acceptable cost for higher performance is. This can be set as a time constraint on the developers doing the tuning, or as numbers of additional classes or lines of code. For example, a developer could decide that no more than a week should be spent optimizing, or that the optimized classes should not grow by more than 100% (double their original size).

7.2.6   *Know the dangers of premature optimization*

One of the most famous quotes on optimization is from Donald Knuth ("Structured Programming with go to Statements," *Computing Surveys*, 6, no. 4 [December 1974].):

> *Programmers waste enormous amounts of time thinking about, or worrying about, the speed of noncritical parts of their programs, and these attempts at efficiency actually have a strong negative impact … premature optimization is the root of all evil.*

This statement has been widely debated in the community, and in many cases, only the second part is remembered. This is unfortunate for several reasons:

- In the first part of the quote, Knuth is reminding us implicitly of the need to measure, without which we can't determine the critical parts of programs.
- We need to remember yet again that it might not be the code that's causing the latency—it could be something else in the environment.
- In the full quote, it's easy to see that Knuth is talking about optimization that forms a conscious, concerted effort.
- The shorter form of the quote leads to the quote being used as a fairly pat excuse for poor design or execution choices.

Some optimizations, in particular, the following, are really a part of good style:

- Don't allocate an object you don't need to.
- Remove a debug log message if you'll never need it.

In the following snippet, we've added a check to see if the logging object will do anything with a debug log message. This kind of check is called a *loggability guard*. If the logging subsystem isn't set up for debug logs, this code will never construct the log message, saving the cost of the call to `currentTimeMillis()` and the construction of the `StringBuilder` object used for the log message:

```
if (log.isDebugEnabled()) {
  log.debug("Useless log at: "+ System.currentTimeMillis());
}
```

But if the debug log message is truly useless, we can save a couple of processor cycles (the cost of the loggability guard) by removing the code altogether. This cost is trivial and will get lost in the noise of the rest of the performance profile, but if it genuinely isn't needed, take it out.

One aspect of performance tuning is to write good, well-performing code in the first place. Gaining a better awareness of the platform and how it behaves under the hood (e.g., understanding the implicit object allocations that come from the concatenation of two strings) and thinking about aspects of performance as you go lead to better code.

We now have some basic vocabulary we can use to frame our performance problems and goals and an outline approach for how to tackle problems. But we still haven't explained why this is a software engineer's problem and where this need came from. To understand this, we need to delve briefly into the world of hardware.

7.3   What went wrong? Why do we have to care?

For a few halcyon years up until the mid-2000s, it seemed as though performance was not really a concern. Clock speeds were going up and up, and it seemed that all software engineers had to do was to wait a few months, and the improved CPU speeds would give an uptick to even badly written code.

How, then, did things go so wrong? Why are clock speeds not improving that much anymore? More worryingly, why does a computer with a 3 GHz chip not seem much faster than one with a 2 GHz chip? Where has this trend for software engineers across the industry to be concerned about performance come from?

In this section, we'll talk about the forces driving this trend, and why even the purest of software developers needs to care a bit about hardware. We'll set the stage for the topics in the rest of the chapter and give you the concepts you'll need to really understand JIT compilation and some of our in-depth examples.

You may have heard the term "Moore's law" bandied about. Many developers are aware that it has something to do with the rate at which computers get faster but are vague on the details. Let's get under way by explaining exactly what it means and what the consequences are of it possibly coming to an end in the near future.

7.3.1   Moore's law

Moore's law is named for Gordon Moore, one of the founders of Intel. Here is one of the most common formulations of his law: *The maximum number of transistors on a chip that is economic to produce roughly doubles every two years.*

The law, which is really an observation about trends in computer processors (CPUs), is based on a paper he wrote in 1965, in which he originally forecast for 10 years—that is, up until 1975. That it has lasted so well is truly remarkable.

In figure 7.2 we've plotted a number of real CPUs from various families (primarily Intel x86 family) all the way from 1980 through to the latest (2021) Apple Silicon (graph data is from Wikipedia, lightly edited for clarity). The graph shows the transistor counts of the chips against their release dates.

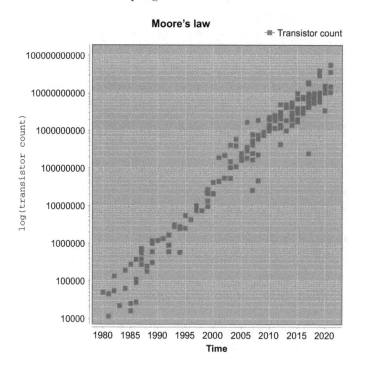

Figure 7.2   Log-linear plot of transistor count over time

This is a log-linear graph, so each increment on the *y*-axis is 10 times the previous one. As you can see, the line is essentially straight and takes about six or seven years to cross each vertical level. This demonstrates Moore's law, because taking six or seven years to increase tenfold is the same as roughly doubling every two years.

Keep in mind that the *y*-axis on the graph is a log scale—this means that a mainstream Intel chip produced in 2005 had around 100 million transistors. This is *100 times* as many as a chip produced in 1990.

It's important to notice that Moore's law specifically talks about transistor counts. This is the basic point that must be understood to grasp why Moore's law alone isn't enough for the software engineer to continue to obtain a free lunch from the hardware engineers (see Herb Sutter, "The Free Lunch Is Over: A Fundamental Turn Toward Concurrency in Software," *Dr. Dobb's Journal* 30 (2005): 202–210).

Moore's law has been a good guide to the past, but it is formulated in terms of transistor counts, which is not really a good guide to the performance that developers should expect from their code. Reality, as we'll see, is more complicated.

NOTE Transistor counts aren't the same thing as clock speed, and even the still-common idea that a higher clock speed means better performance is a gross oversimplification.

The truth is that real-world performance depends on a number of factors, all of which are important. If we had to pick just one, however, it would be this: how fast can data relevant to the next instructions be located? This is such an important concept to performance that we should take an in-depth look at it.

7.3.2 *Understanding the memory latency hierarchy*

Computer processors require data to work on. If the data to process isn't available, then it doesn't matter how fast the CPU cycles—it just has to wait, performing no-operation (NOP) and basically stalling until the data is available.

This means that two of the most fundamental questions when addressing latency are, "Where is the nearest copy of the data that the CPU core needs to work on?" and "How long will it take to get to where the core can use it?" The main possibilities follow (in the so-called *Von-Neumann architecture*, which is the most commonly used form):

- *Registers*—A memory location that's on the CPU and ready for immediate use. This is the part of memory that instructions operate on directly.
- *Main memory*—Usually DRAM. The access time for this is around 50 ns (but see later on for details about how processor caches are used to avoid this latency).
- *Solid-state drive (SSD)*—It takes 0.1 ms or less to access these disks, but they're still typically more expensive compared to traditional hard disks.
- *Hard disk*—It takes around 5 ms to access the disk and load the required data into main memory.

Moore's law has described an exponential increase in transistor count, and this has benefited memory as well—memory access speed has also increased exponentially. But the exponents for these two have not been the same. Memory speed has improved more slowly than CPUs have added transistors, which means there's a risk that the processing cores will fall idle due to not having the relevant data on hand to process.

To solve this problem, caches—small amounts of faster memory (SRAM, rather than DRAM)—have been introduced between the registers and main memory. This faster memory costs a lot more than DRAM, both in terms of money and transistor budget, which is why computers don't simply use SRAM for their entire memory.

Caches are referred to as L1 and L2 (some machines also have L3), with the numbers indicating how physically close to the core the cache is (closer caches will be faster). We'll talk more about caches in section 7.6 (on JIT compilation) and show an example of how important the L1 cache effects are to running code. Figure 7.3 shows just how much faster L1 and L2 cache are than main memory.

Figure 7.3   Relative access times (in clock cycles) for registers, processor caches, and main memory

As well as adding caches, another technique that was used extensively in the 1990s and early 2000s was to add increasingly complex processor features to try to work around the latency of memory. Sophisticated hardware techniques, such as instruction-level parallelism (ILP) and chip multithreading (CMT), were used to try to keep the CPU operating on data, even in the face of the widening gap between CPU capability and memory latency.

These techniques came to consume a large percentage of the transistor budget of the CPU, and the impact they had on real performance was subject to diminishing returns. This trend led to the viewpoint that the future of CPU design lay in chips with multiple (or many) cores. Modern processors are essentially all multicore—in fact, this is one of the second-order consequences of Moore's law: core counts have gone up as a way to utilize available transistors.

The future of performance is intimately tied to concurrency—one of the main ways that a system can be made more performant overall is by utilizing more cores. That way, even if one core is waiting for data, the other cores may still be able to progress (but remember the impact of Amdahl's law, which we introduced in chapter 5). This connection is so important that we're going to say it again:

- Essentially all modern CPUs are multicore.
- Performance and concurrency are tied together as concerns.

We've only scratched the surface of the world of computer architecture as it relates to software and Java programming. The interested reader who wants to know more should consult a specialist text, such as *Computer Architecture: A Quantitative Approach,* 6th edition, by Hennessy et al. (Morgan Kaufmann, December 2017).

These hardware concerns aren't specific to Java programmers, but the managed nature of the JVM brings in some additional complexities. Let's move on to take a look at these in the next section.

7.4   *Why is Java performance tuning hard?*

Tuning for performance on the JVM (or, indeed, any other managed runtime) is inherently more difficult than for code that runs unmanaged. In a managed system, the entire point is to allow the runtime to take some control of the environment, so that the developer doesn't have to cope with every detail. This makes programmers much more productive overall, but it does mean that some control has to be given up.

This shift in emphasis makes the system as a whole harder to reason about because the managed runtime is an opaque box to the developer. The alternative is to give up all the advantages that a managed runtime brings, forcing programmers of, say, C/C++, to do almost everything for themselves. In this case, the OS supplies only minimal services, such as rudimentary thread scheduling, which is almost always a much higher overall time commitment than the additional effort required to performance tune.

Some of the most important aspects of the Java platform that contribute to making tuning hard follow:

- Thread scheduling
- Garbage collection (GC)
- Just-in-time (JIT) compilation

These aspects can interact in subtle ways. For example, the compilation subsystem uses timers to decide which methods to compile. The set of methods that are candidates for compilation can be affected by concerns such as scheduling and GC. The methods that are compiled could be different from run to run.

As you've seen throughout this section, accurate measurement is key to the decision-making processes of performance analysis. An understanding of the details (and limitations) of how time is handled in the Java platform is, therefore, very useful if you want to get serious about performance tuning.

7.4.1   The role of time in performance tuning

Performance tuning requires you to understand how to interpret the measurements recorded during code execution, which means you also need to understand the limitations inherent in any measurement of time on the platform.

PRECISION

Quantities of time are usually quoted to the nearest unit on some scale. This is referred to as the *precision* of the measurement. For example, times are often measured to millisecond precision. A timing is precise if repeated measurements give a narrow spread around the same value.

Precision is a measure of the amount of random noise contained in a given measurement. We'll assume that the measurements made of a particular piece of code are normally distributed. In that case, a common way of quoting the precision is to quote the width of the 95% confidence interval.

ACCURACY

The *accuracy* of a measurement (in our case, of time) is the ability to obtain a value close to the true value. In reality, you won't normally know the true value, so the accuracy may be harder to determine than the precision.

Accuracy measures the systematic error in a measurement. It's possible to have accurate measurements that aren't very precise (so the basic reading is sound, but random environmental noise exists). It's also possible to have precise results that aren't accurate.

UNDERSTANDING MEASUREMENTS

An interval quoted at nanosecond precision as 5945 ns that came from a timer accurate to 1 μs is really somewhere between 3945–7945 ns (with 95% probability). Beware of performance numbers that seem overly precise; always check the precision and accuracy of the measurements.

GRANULARITY

The true *granularity* of the system is that of the frequency of the fastest timer—likely the interrupt timer, in the 10 ns range. This is sometimes called the *distinguishability*, the shortest interval between which two events can be definitely said to have occurred "close together but at different times."

As we progress through layers of OS, JVM, and library code, the resolution of these extremely short times becomes basically impossible. Under most circumstances, these very short times aren't available to the application developer.

NETWORK-DISTRIBUTED TIMING

Most of our discussion of performance tuning centers on systems where all the processing takes places on a single host. But you should be aware that a number of special problems can arise when doing performance tuning of systems spread over a network. Synchronization and timing over networks is far from easy, and not only over the internet—even Ethernet networks will show these issues.

A full discussion of network-distributed timing is outside the scope of this book, but you should be aware that in general, it's difficult to obtain accurate timings for workflows that extend over several boxes. In addition, even standard protocols such as NTP can be too inaccurate for high-precision work.

Let's recap the most important points about Java's timing systems:

- Most systems have several different clocks inside them.
- Millisecond timings are safe and reliable.
- Higher-precision time needs careful handling to avoid drift.
- You need to be aware of the precision and accuracy of timing measurements.

Before we move on to discuss garbage collection, let's look at an example we referred to earlier—the effects of memory caches on code performance.

7.4.2   Understanding cache misses

For many high-throughput pieces of code, one of the main factors reducing performance is the number of L1 cache misses that are involved in executing application code. Listing 7.1 runs over a 2 MiB array and prints the time taken to execute one of two loops. The first loop increments 1 in every 16 entries of an `int[]`. Almost always 64 bytes are in an L1 cache line (and a Java int is 4 bytes wide), so this means touching each cache line once.

Note that before you can get accurate results, we need to warm up the code, so that the JVM will compile the methods you're interested in. We'll talk about JIT warmup in more detail later in the chapter.

Listing 7.1   Understanding cache misses

```java
public class Caching {
    private final int ARR_SIZE = 2 * 1024 * 1024;
    private final int[] testData = new int[ARR_SIZE];

    private void touchEveryItem() {
        for (int i = 0; i < testData.length; i = i + 1) {
            testData[i] = testData[i] + 1;       ◁──────┐ Touches every item
        }                                               │
    }

    private void touchEveryLine() {
        for (int i = 0; i < testData.length; i = i + 16) {
            testData[i] = testData[i] + 1;       ◁──────┐ Touches each cache line
        }                                               │
    }

    private void run() {
        for (int i = 0; i < 10_000; i = i + 1) {   ◁────── Warms up the code
            touchEveryLine();
            touchEveryItem();
        }
        System.out.println("Line       Item");
        for (int i = 0; i < 100; i = i + 1) {
            long t0 = System.nanoTime();
            touchEveryLine();
            long t1 = System.nanoTime();
            touchEveryItem();
            long t2 = System.nanoTime();
            long el1 = t1 - t0;
            long el2 = t2 - t1;
            System.out.println("Line: "+ el1 +" ns ; Item: "+ el2);
        }
    }

    public static void main(String[] args) {
        Caching c = new Caching();
        c.run();
    }
}
```

The second function, touchEveryItem(), increments every byte in the array, so it does 16 times as much work as touchEveryLine(). But here are some sample results from a typical laptop:

```
Line: 487481 ns ; Item: 452421
Line: 425039 ns ; Item: 428397
Line: 415447 ns ; Item: 395332
Line: 372815 ns ; Item: 397519
Line: 366305 ns ; Item: 375376
Line: 332249 ns ; Item: 330512
```

The results of this code show that `touchEveryItem()` doesn't take 16 times as long to run as `touchEveryLine()`. It's the memory transfer time—loading from main memory to CPU cache—that dominates the overall performance profile. `touchEveryLine()` and `touchEveryItem()` have the same number of cache line reads, and the data transfer time vastly outweighs the cycles spent on actually modifying the data.

NOTE This demonstrates a key point: we need to develop at least a working understanding (or mental model) of how the CPU actually spends its time.

Our next topic is a discussion of the garbage collection subsystem of the platform. This is one of the most important pieces of the performance picture, and it has tunable parts that can be very important tools for the developer doing performance analysis.

7.5   *Garbage collection*

Automatic memory management is one of the most important parts of the Java platform. Before managed platforms such as Java and .NET, developers could expect to spend a noticeable percentage of their careers hunting down bugs caused by imperfect memory handling.

In recent years, however, automatic allocation techniques have become so advanced and reliable that they have become part of the furniture—a large number of Java developers are unaware of how the memory management capabilities of the platform work, what options are available to the developer, and how to optimize within the constraints of the framework.

This is a sign of how successful Java's approach has been. Most developers don't know about the details of the memory and GC systems because they usually just don't *need* to know. The JVM can do a pretty good job of handling memory for most applications without the need for any special tuning.

So, what can do when you're in a situation where you do need to do some tuning? Well, first you'll need to understand what the JVM actually does to manage memory for you. So, in this section we'll cover basic theory, including

- How memory is handled for a running Java process
- Basics of mark-and-sweep collection
- The Garbage First (G1) collector, which has been Java's default collector since Java 9

Let's start with the basics.

7.5.1   Basics

The standard Java process has both a stack and a heap. The *stack* is where local variables are stored. Local variables that hold primitives directly store the primitive value in the stack.

> **NOTE** Primitives hold bit patterns that will be interpreted according to their type, so the two bytes 00000000 01100001 will be interpreted as a if the type is char or 97 if the type is short.

On the other hand, local variables of reference type will point at a location in Java's *heap*, which is where the objects will actually be created. Figure 7.4 shows where storage for variables of various types is located.

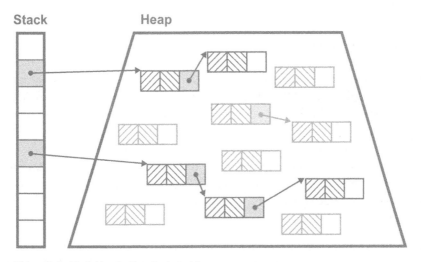

Figure 7.4   Variables in the stack and heap

Note that the primitive fields of an object are still allocated at addresses within the heap. As a Java program runs, new objects are created in the heap, and the relationships between the objects changes (as fields are updated). Eventually, the heap will run out of space for new objects to be created. However, many of the objects that have been created will no longer be needed (e.g., temporary objects that were created in one method and not passed to any other method, or returned to the caller).

Space in the heap can therefore be reclaimed, and the program can continue to run. The mechanism by which the platform recovers and reuses heap memory that is no longer in use by application code is called *garbage collection*.

7.5.2   Mark and sweep

A great example of a simple garbage collection algorithm is *mark and sweep*, and, in fact, it was the first to be developed (in LISP 1.5, released in 1965).

NOTE   Other automatic memory management techniques exist, such as the reference-counting approach used by languages like Perl, which are arguably simpler (at least superficially), but they aren't really garbage collection (as per Guy L. Steele "Multiprocessing Compactifying Garbage Collection," *Communications of the ACM* 18, no. 9 [September 1975]).

In its simplest form, the mark-and-sweep algorithm pauses all running program threads and starts from the set of objects that are known to be "live"—objects that have a reference in any stack frame (whether that reference is the content of a local variable, method parameter, temporary variable, or some rarer possibility) of any user thread. It then walks through the tree of references from the live objects, marking as live any object found en route. When this has completed, everything left is garbage and can be collected (swept). Note that the swept memory is returned to the JVM, not necessarily to the OS.

WHAT ABOUT THE NONDETERMINISTIC PAUSE?

One of the criticisms often leveled at Java (and other environments such as .NET) is that the mark-and-sweep form of garbage collection inevitably leads to Stop-the-World (usually referred to as STW). These are states in which all user threads must be stopped briefly, and this causes pauses that go on for some nondeterministic amount of time.

This issue is frequently overstated. For server software, very few applications have to care about the pause times displayed by the garbage collectors of modern versions of Java. For example, in Java 11 and upward, the default garbage collector is a concurrent collector that does most of its work alongside application threads and minimizes pause time.

NOTE   Developers sometimes dream up elaborate schemes to avoid a pause, or a full collection of memory. In almost all cases, these should be avoided because they usually do more harm than good.

The Java platform provides a number of enhancements to the basic mark-and-sweep approach. One of the simplest is the addition of *generational GC*. In this approach, the heap isn't a uniform area of memory—a number of different areas of heap memory participate in the life cycle of a Java object.

Depending on how long an object lives, it can be moved from area to area during collections. References to it can point to several different areas of memory during the lifespan of the object (as illustrated in figure 7.5).

The reason for this arrangement (and the movement of objects) is that analysis of running systems shows that objects tend to either have brief lives or be very long-lived. The different areas of heap memory are designed to allow the platform to exploit this property, by segregating the long-lived objects from the rest.

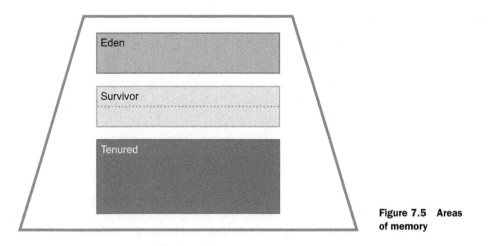

Figure 7.5   Areas of memory

Please note that figure 7.5 is a simple schematic of a heap designed to illustrate the concept of generational areas. The reality of a real Java heap is a little more complicated and depends upon the collector in use, as we'll explain later in this chapter.

7.5.3   Areas of memory

The JVM has the following different areas of memory that are used to store objects during their natural life cycle:

- *Eden*—Eden is the area of the heap where all objects are initially allocated, and for many objects, this will be the only part of memory in which they ever reside.
- *Survivor*—These spaces are where objects that survive a garbage collection cycle (hence the name) are moved. Initially they are moved from Eden, but they may also move between survivor spaces during subsequent GCs.
- *Tenured*—The tenured space (aka old generation) is where surviving objects deemed to be "old enough" are moved to (escaping from the survivor spaces). Tenured memory isn't collected during young collections.

As noted, these areas of memory also participate in collections in different ways. For example, the survivor spaces are really there as a catch-all mechanism, so that short-lived objects created immediately before a collection are handled properly.

If the survivor spaces were not present, then very recently created (but short-lived) objects would be marked as "live" by the GC and would be promoted into Tenured. They would then immediately die but continue to take up space in Tenured until the next time it was collected. This next collection would also happen sooner than necessary due to the improper promotion of what are actually short-lived objects. From a theoretical standpoint, the generational hypothesis also leads us to the idea that there are two types of collections: young and full.

7.5.4   Young collections

A *young collection* attempts to clear the "young" spaces (Eden and survivor). The process is relatively simple, as described next:

- All live young objects found during the marking phase are moved.
- Objects that are sufficiently old (those that have survived enough previous GC runs) go into Tenured.
- All other young, live objects go into an empty survivor space.
- At the end, Eden and any recently vacated survivor spaces are ready to be overwritten and reused, because they contain nothing but garbage.

A young collection is triggered when Eden is full. Note that the marking phase must traverse the entire live object graph. If a young object has a reference to a Tenured object, the references held by the Tenured object must still be scanned and marked. Otherwise, the situation could arise where a Tenured object holds a reference to an object in Eden, but nothing else does. If the mark phase doesn't fully traverse, this Eden object would never been seen and would not be correctly handled. In practice, some performance hacks (e.g. *card tables*) are used to reduce the potentially high cost of a full marking traversal.

7.5.5   Full collections

When a young collection can't promote an object to Tenured (due to lack of space), a full collection is triggered. Depending on the collector used, this may involve moving around objects within the old generation. This is done to ensure that the old generation has enough space to allocate a large object if necessary. This is called *compacting*.

7.5.6   Safepoints

Garbage collection can't take place without at least a short pause of all application threads. However, threads can't be stopped at any arbitrary time for GC, because application code can modify the contents of the heap. Instead, certain special times occur where the JVM can be sure that the heap is in a consistent state and GC can take place—these are called *safepoints*.

One of the simplest examples of a safepoint is "in between bytecode instructions." The JVM interpreter executes one bytecode at a time, and then loops to take the next bytecode from the stream. Just before looping, that interpreter thread must be finished with any modifications to the heap (e.g., from a `putfield`), so if the thread stops there, it is "safe." Once all of the application threads reach a safepoint, then garbage collection can take place.

This is a simple example of a safepoint, but there are others. A more complete discussion of safepoints, and how they impact certain JIT compiler techniques, can be found here: http://mng.bz/Oo8a. Let's move on from the theoretical discussion and meet some of the garbage collection algorithms in the JVM.

7.5.7   *G1: Java's default collector*

G1 is a relatively new collector for the Java platform. It became production-quality at Java 8u40 and was made the default collector with Java 9 (in 2017). It was originally intended as a *low-pause* collector but in practice has evolved into a general-purpose collector (hence its default status).

It is not only a generational garbage collector, but it is also *regionalized,* which means that the G1 Java heap divides the heap into equal-sized regions (such as 1, 2, or 4 MB each). Generations still exist, but they are now no longer necessarily contiguous in memory. The new arrangement of equal-sized regions in the heap is illustrated in figure 7.6.

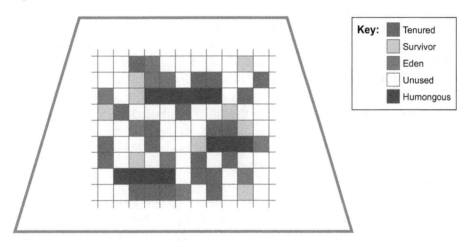

Figure 7.6   How G1 divides up the heap

Regionalization has been introduced to support the idea of predictability of GC pauses. Older collectors (such as Parallel) suffered from the problem that once a GC cycle had begun, it needed to run to completion, regardless of how long that took (i.e., they were *all-or-nothing*).

G1 provides a collection strategy that should not result in longer pause times for larger heaps. It was designed to avoid all-or-nothing behavior, and a key concept for this is the *pause goal.* This is how long the program can pause for GC before resuming execution. G1 will do everything it can to hit your pause goals, within reason. During a pause, surviving objects are evacuated to another region (like Eden objects being moved to survivor spaces), and the region is placed back on the *free list* of empty regions.

Young collections in G1 are fully STW and will run to completion. This avoids race conditions between collection and allocation threads (which could occur if young collections ran concurrently with application threads).

NOTE The generational hypothesis is that only a small fraction of objects encountered during a young collection are still alive. So, the time taken for a young collection should be very small, and much less than the pause goal.

The collection of old objects has a different character from young collections—first, because once objects have reached the old generation, they tend to live for a considerable length of time. Second, the space provided for the old generation tends to be much larger than the young generation.

G1 keeps track of the objects that are moved to the old generation, and when enough old space has been filled (controlled by the `InitiatingHeapOccupancyPercent` or IHOP, which defaults to 45%), an old collection is started. This is a *concurrent* collection, because it runs (as far as possible) concurrently with the application threads.

The first piece of this old collection is a concurrent marking phase. This is based on an algorithm that was first described by Dijkstra and Lamport in 1978 (see https://dl.acm.org/doi/10.1145/359642.359655). Once this completes, then a young collection is immediately triggered. This is followed by a *mixed collection*, which collects old regions based on how much garbage they have in them (which can be deduced from the statistics gathered during the concurrent mark). Surviving objects from the old regions are evacuated into fresh old regions (and compacted).

The nature of the G1 collection strategy also allows the platform to collect statistics on how long (on average) a single region takes to collect. This is how pause goals are implemented—G1 will collect only as many regions as it has time for (although there may be overruns if the last region takes longer to collect than expected).

It is possible that the collection of the entire old generation cannot be completed in a single GC cycle. In this case, G1 just collects a set of regions and then completes the collection, releasing the CPU cores that were being used for GC. Provided that, over a sustained period, the creation of long-lived objects does not outstrip the ability of the GC to reclaim them, all should be well.

In the case that allocation outstrips reclamation for a sustained amount of time, then, as a last-ditch effort, the GC will perform a STW full collection and fully clean and compact the old generation. In practice, this behavior is not seen unless the application is badly struggling.

One other point is worth mentioning: it is possible to allocate objects that are larger than a single region. In practice, this means a large array (often of bytes or other primitives).

NOTE It would be possible to artificially construct a class that had so many fields that a single object instance was larger than 1 MB, but this would never be done in a practical, real system.

Such objects require a special type of region—a *humongous region*. These require special treatment by the GC because the space allocated for large arrays must be contiguous in memory. If sufficient free regions are adjacent to each other, they can be converted to a single humongous region and the array can be allocated.

If there isn't anywhere in memory where the array can be allocated (even after a young collection), then memory is said to be *fragmented*. The GC must perform a fully STW and compacting collection to try to free up sufficient space for the allocation.

G1 is established as a very effective collector across a wide variety of workloads and application types. However, for some workloads (e.g., those that need pure throughput or are still running on Java 8), then another collector, such as Parallel, may be of use.

7.5.8   *The Parallel collector*

The Parallel collector was the default until Java 8, and it can still be used as an alternative choice to G1 today. The name Parallel needs a bit of explanation, because *concurrent* and *parallel* are both used to describe properties of GC algorithms. They sound as though they should mean the same thing, but in fact they have two totally different meanings, as described here:

- *Concurrent*—GC threads can run at the same time as application threads.
- *Parallel*—The GC algorithm is multithreaded and can use multiple cores.

The terms are in no way equivalent. Instead, it's better to think of them as the opposites to two other GC terms—*concurrent* is the opposite of STW, and *parallel* is the opposite of *single-threaded*.

In some collectors (including Parallel), the heap is not regionalized. Instead, the generations are contiguous areas of memory, which have headroom to grow and shrink as needed. In this heap configuration there are two survivor spaces. They are sometimes referred to as *From* and *To*, and one of the survivor spaces is always empty unless a collection is under way.

> **NOTE**   Very old versions of Java also had a space called *PermGen* (or Permanent Generation). This is where memory was allocated for the JVM's internal structures, such as the definitions of classes and methods. PermGen was removed in Java 8, so if you find any resources that refer to it, then they are old and likely to be outdated.

Parallel is a very efficient collector—the most efficient one available in mainstream Java—but it comes with a drawback: it has no real pause goal capability and old collections (that are STW) must run to completion, regardless of how long it takes.

Some developers sometimes ask questions about the complexity (aka "big-O") behavior of GC algorithms. However, this is not really a useful question to ask. GC algorithms are very general, and they are required to behave acceptably across an entire range of possible workloads. Focusing only on their asymptotic behavior is not all that useful, and it is definitely not a suitable proxy for their general-case performance.

Garbage collection is always about trade-offs, and the trade-offs that G1 makes are very good for most workloads (so much so that many developers can just ignore them). However, the trade-offs always exist, whether or not the developer is aware of them. Some applications cannot ignore the trade-offs and must choose to care about the details of the GC subsystem, either by changing collection algorithm or by tuning using GC parameters.

7.5.9   *GC configuration parameters*

The JVM ships with a huge number of useful parameters (at least a hundred) that can be used to customize many aspects of the runtime behavior of the JVM. In this section, we'll discuss some of the basic switches that pertain to garbage collection.

If a switch starts with `-X:`, it's nonstandard and may not be portable across JVM implementations (such as HotSpot or Eclipse OpenJ9). If it starts with `-XX:`, it's an extended switch and isn't recommended for casual use. Many performance-relevant switches are extended switches.

Some switches are Boolean in effect and take a + or - in front of them to turn it on or off. Other switches take a parameter, such as `-XX:CompileThreshold=20000` (which would set the number of times a method needs to be called before being considered for JIT compilation to 20000). Table 7.1 lists the basic GC switches and displays the default value (if any) of the switch.

Table 7.1   Basic garbage collection switches

Switch	Effect
-Xms<size in MB>m	Initial size of the heap (default 1/64 physical memory)
-Xmx<size in MB>m	Maximum size of the heap (default 1/4 physical memory)
-Xmn<size in MB>m	Size of the young generation in the heap
-XX: -DisableExplicitGC	Prevents calls to `System.gc()` from having any effect

One unfortunately common technique is to set the size of `-Xms` to the same as `-Xmx`. This then means that the process will run with exactly that heap size and will not resize during execution. Superficially, this makes sense, and it gives the illusion of control to the developer. However, in practice, this approach is an antipattern. Modern GCs have good dynamic sizing algorithms, and artificially constraining them almost always does more harm than good.

> **NOTE**   In 2022, best practice for most workloads, in the absence of any other evidence, is to set `Xmx` and not to set `Xms` at all.

It's also worth noting the behavior of the JVM in a container. For Java 11 and 17, "physical memory" means the container limit, so the heap max size must fit within any container limit and with space for the non-Java heap memory and any other processes other than the JVM. Early versions of Java 8 do not necessarily respect container limits, so the advice is always to upgrade to Java 11 if you are running your application in containers. For the G1 collector, two other settings may be useful during tuning exercises—they're shown in table 7.2.

Table 7.2 Flags for the G1 collector

Switch	Effect
-XX:MaxGCPauseMillis=50	Indicates to G1 that it should try to pause for no more than 50 ms during one collection
-XX:GCPauseIntervalMillis=200	Indicates to G1 that it should try to run for at least 200 ms between collections

The switches can be combined, such as to set a maximum pause goal of 50 ms with pauses occurring no closer together than 200 ms. Of course, there's a limit on how hard the GC system can be pushed. There has to be enough pause time to take out the trash. A pause goal of 1 ms per 100 years is certainly not going to be attainable or honored.

In the next section, we'll take a look at JIT compilation. For many programs, this is a major contributing factor to producing performant code. We'll look at some of the basics of JIT compilation, and at the end of the section, we'll explain how to switch on logging of JIT compilation to enable you to tell which of your methods are being compiled.

7.6 *JIT compilation with HotSpot*

As we discussed in chapter 1, the Java platform is perhaps best thought of as "dynamically compiled." Some application and framework classes undergo further compilation at runtime to transform them into machine code that can be directly executed.

This process is called *just-in-time (JIT) compilation*, or just JITing, and it usually occurs on one method at a time. Understanding this process is often key to identifying the important parts of any sizable codebase.

Let's look at some good basic facts about JIT compilation:

- Virtually all modern JVMs will have a JIT compiler of some sort.
- Purely interpreted JVMs are very slow by comparison.
- Compiled methods run much, much faster than interpreted code.
- It makes sense to compile the most heavily used methods first.
- When doing JIT compilation, it's always important to take the low-hanging fruit first.

This last point means that we should look at the compiled code first, because under normal circumstances, any method that is still in an interpreted state hasn't been run as often as one that has been compiled. (Occasionally a method will fail compilation, but this is quite rare.)

Methods start off being interpreted from their bytecode representation, with the JVM keeping track of how many times a method has been called (and some other statistics). When a threshold value is reached, if the method is eligible, a JVM thread will compile the bytecode to machine code in the background. If compilation succeeds, all further calls to the method will use the compiled form, unless something happens to invalidate it or otherwise cause deoptimization.

Depending on the exact nature of the code in a method, a compiled method can be vastly faster than the same method in interpreted mode. The figure of "up to 100 times faster" is sometimes given, but this is an extremely rough rule of thumb. The nature of JIT compilation changes the executed code so much that any kind of single number is misleading. Understanding which methods are important in a program, and which important methods are being compiled, is quite often a major technique in improving performance.

7.6.1   *Why have dynamic compilation?*

A question that is sometimes asked is, why does the Java platform bother with dynamic compilation? Why isn't all compilation done up front (like C++)? The first answer is usually that having platform-independent artifacts (.jar and .class files) as the basic unit of deployment is much less of a headache than trying to deal with a different compiled binary for each platform being targeted.

An alternative, and more ambitious, answer is that languages that use dynamic compilation have more information available to their compiler. Specifically, ahead-of-time (AOT) compiled languages don't have access to any runtime information, such as the availability of certain instructions or other hardware details, or any statistics on how the code is running. This opens the intriguing possibility that a dynamically compiled language like Java could actually run faster than AOT-compiled languages.

> **NOTE** Direct, AOT compilation of Java bytecode to machine code (aka "static Java") is a live area of research in the Java community but, unfortunately, is outside the scope of this book.

For the rest of this discussion of the mechanics of JITing, we'll be speaking specifically about the JVM called HotSpot. A lot of the general discussion will apply to other VMs, but the specifics could vary a lot.

We'll start by introducing the different JIT compilers that ship with HotSpot and then explain two of the most powerful optimizations available from HotSpot—*inlining* and *monomorphic dispatch*. We'll conclude this section by showing how to turn on logging of method compilation, so that you can see exactly which methods are being compiled. Let's get started by introducing HotSpot.

7.6.2 Introduction to HotSpot

HotSpot is the JVM that Oracle acquired when it bought Sun Microsystems (it already owned a JVM called JRockit, which was originally developed by BEA Systems). HotSpot is the JVM that forms the basis of OpenJDK. It's capable of running in two separate modes: client and server.

In the old days, the mode could be chosen by specifying the -client or -server switch to the JVM on startup. Each of these modes has different applications that they can be preferred for.

C1 (AKA CLIENT COMPILER)

The C1 compiler was originally intended for use in GUI applications. This is an area where consistency of operation is prized, so C1 (sometimes called the *client compiler*) tends to make more conservative decisions when compiling. It can't pause unexpectedly while it backs out an optimization decision that turned out to be incorrect or based on a faulty assumption. It has a fairly low compilation threshold—a method must be executed 1500 times before being eligible for compilation—so it has a relative short warmup period.

C2 (AKA SERVER COMPILER)

By contrast, the *server compiler* (C2) makes aggressive assumptions when compiling. To ensure that the code that's run is always correct, C2 adds a quick runtime check (usually called a *guard condition*) that the assumption it made is valid. If not, it backs out the aggressive compilation and often tries something else. This aggressive approach can yield far better performance than the rather risk-averse client compiler.

C2 has a much higher inlining threshold than C1. By default, a method is not eligible for C2 compilation until it hits 10,000 invocations, which implies a much longer warmup time.

REAL-TIME JAVA

Historically, a form of Java was developed called real-time Java, and some developers wonder why code that has a need for high performance doesn't simply use this platform (which is a separate JVM, not a HotSpot option). The answer is that a real-time system is not, despite common myth, necessarily the fastest system.

Real-time programming is really about the guarantees that can be made. In statistical terms, a real-time system seeks to reduce the variance of the time taken to perform certain operations and is prepared to sacrifice a certain amount of mean latency to do so. Overall performance may be slightly sacrificed to attain more consistent running. Teams in search of higher performance are usually in search of lower mean latency, even at the cost of higher variance, so the aggressive optimizations of the server compiler are especially suitable.

In modern JVMs, the client and server compilers are both used—the client compiler is used early on, and the advanced server-class optimizations are used after the application has warmed up. This dual use is known as *tiered compilation*. Our next topic is one that is extensively used by all of the JIT compilers.

7.6.3   *Inlining methods*

Inlining is one of the most powerful techniques that HotSpot has at its disposal. It works by eliminating the call to the inlined method and instead places the code of the called method inside the caller.

One of the advantages of the platform is that the compiler can make the decision to inline based on decent runtime statistics about how often the method is called and other factors (e.g., will it make the caller method too large and potentially affect code caches). HotSpot's compiler can make much smarter decisions about inlining than ahead-of-time compilers.

WHAT ABOUT ACCESSOR METHODS?

Some developers incorrectly assume that an accessor method (a public getter accessing a private member variable) can't be inlined by HotSpot. Their reasoning is that because the variable is private, the method call can't be optimized away, because access to it is prohibited outside the class. This is incorrect.

HotSpot can and will ignore access control when compiling methods to machine code and will replace an accessor method with a direct access to the private field. This doesn't compromise Java's security model, because all of the access control was checked when the class was loaded or linked.

Inlining of methods is entirely automatic, and under almost all circumstances, the default parameter values are fine. Switches are available to control what size of methods will be inlined and how often a method needs to be called before becoming a candidate.

These switches are mostly useful for the curious programmer to get a better understanding of how the inlining part of the internals works. They aren't often useful for production code and should be considered something of a last resort as a performance technique, because they may well have other unpredictable effects on the performance of the runtime system.

7.6.4   *Dynamic compilation and monomorphic calls*

One example of this type of aggressive optimization is that of the *monomorphic call.* This is an optimization that's based on the observation that, in most circumstances, a method call on an object, like this:

```
MyActualClassNotInterface obj = getInstance();

obj.callMyMethod();
```

will only ever be called by one type of object. Another way of saying this is that the call site obj.callMyMethod() will almost never encounter both a class and its subclass. In this case, the Java method lookup can be replaced with a direct call to the compiled code corresponding to `callMyMethod()`.

> **NOTE** Monomorphic dispatch provides an example of the JVM runtime profiling, allowing the platform to perform optimizations that an AOT language like C++ simply can't.

There's no technical reason why the `getInstance()` method can't return an object of type `MyActualClassNotInterface` under some circumstances and an object of some subclass under others. To guard against the possibility that this happens, `getInstance()` will not be put forward for monomorphic optimization unless the exact same type has been seen at the call site every single time, until the compilation threshold is reached. A runtime test to check the type of `obj` is also inserted into the compiled code for future calls. If this expectation is ever violated, the runtime backs out the optimization without the program ever noticing or ever doing anything incorrect.

This is a fairly aggressive optimization that is only ever performed by the server compiler. The client compiler does not do this.

7.6.5 *Reading the compilation logs*

Let's take a look at an example to illustrate how you can use the log messages output by the JIT compiler. The Hipparcos star catalog lists details about stars that can be observed from Earth. Our example application processes the catalog to generate star maps of the stars that can be seen on a given night, in a given location.

Let's look at some example output that shows which methods are being compiled when we run our star map application. The key JVM flag we're using is `-XX:+PrintCompilation`. This is one of the extended switches we briefly discussed earlier. Adding this switch to the command line used to start the JVM tells the JIT compilation threads to add messages to the standard log. These messages indicate when methods have passed the compilation threshold and been turned into machine code as follows:

```
1 java.lang.String::hashCode (64 bytes)
2 java.math.BigInteger::mulAdd (81 bytes)
3 java.math.BigInteger::multiplyToLen (219 bytes)
4 java.math.BigInteger::addOne (77 bytes)
5 java.math.BigInteger::squareToLen (172 bytes)
6 java.math.BigInteger::primitiveLeftShift (79 bytes)
7 java.math.BigInteger::montReduce (99 bytes)
8 sun.security.provider.SHA::implCompress (491 bytes)
9 java.lang.String::charAt (33 bytes)
1% ! sun.nio.cs.SingleByteDecoder::decodeArrayLoop @ 129 (308 bytes)
...
39 sun.misc.FloatingDecimal::doubleValue (1289 bytes)
40 org.camelot.hipparcos.DelimitedLine::getNextString (5 bytes)
41 ! org.camelot.hipparcos.Star::parseStar (301 bytes)
...
2% ! org.camelot.CamelotStarter::populateStarStore @ 25 (106 bytes)
65 s java.lang.StringBuffer::append (8 bytes)
```

This is pretty typical output from `PrintCompilation`. These lines indicate which methods have been deemed sufficiently "hot" to be compiled. As you might expect, the first methods to be compiled will likely be platform methods (such as `String ::hashCode()`). Over time, application methods (such as the `org.camelot.hipparcos .Star::parseStar()` method, which is used in the example to parse a record from the astronomical catalog) will also be compiled.

The output lines have a number, which indicates in which order the methods are compiled on this run. Note that this order may change slightly between runs due to the dynamic nature of the platform. Some of the other fields follow:

- `s`—Indicates the method is synchronized
- `!`—Indicates the method has exception handlers
- `%`—On-stack replacement (OSR)

OSR means that the method was compiled and replaced the interpreted version in running code. Note that OSR methods have their own numbering scheme, starting at 1.

BEWARE OF THE ZOMBIE

When looking at sample output logs on code that is run using the server compiler (C2), you'll occasionally see lines like "made not entrant" and "made zombie." These lines mean that a particular method, which had been compiled, has now been invalidated, usually because of a class loading operation.

7.6.6 Deoptimization

HotSpot is capable of deoptimizing code that's based on an assumption that turned out not to be true. In many cases, it then reconsiders and tries an alternative optimization. Thus, the same method may be deoptimized and recompiled several times.

Over time, you'll see that the number of compiled methods stabilizes. Code reaches a steady, compiled state and largely remains there. The exact details of which methods get compiled can depend on the exact JVM version and OS platform in use. It's a mistake to assume that all platforms will produce the same set of compiled methods and that the compiled code for a given method will be roughly the same size across platforms. As with so much else in the performance space, this should be measured, and the results may surprise. Even a fairly innocent-looking Java method has proved to have a factor-of-five difference between Mac and Linux in terms of the machine code generated by JIT compilation.

Measurement is always necessary. Fortunately, modern JVMs ship some great tools to facilitate deep-dive performance analysis. Let's take a look at them.

7.7 JDK Flight Recorder

Historically, the Flight Recorder and Mission Control tools (usually referred to as JFR and JMC) were obtained by Oracle as part of the acquisition of BEA Systems back in 2008. The two components work together—JFR is a low-overhead, event-based profiling engine with a high-performance backend for writing events in a binary format, whereas JMC is a GUI tool for examining a data file created by JFR from the telemetry of a single JVM.

The tools were originally part of the tooling offering for BEA's JRockit JVM and were moved to the commercial version of Oracle JDK as part of the process of merging JRockit with HotSpot. After the release of JDK 9, Oracle changed the release model of Java and announced that JFR and JMC would become open source tools. JFR was contributed to OpenJDK and was delivered in JDK 11 as JEP 328. JMC was spun out into a standalone open-source project and exists today as a separate download.

> **NOTE** Java 14 introduced a new feature to JFR: the ability for JFR to produce a continuous stream of events. This change provides a callback API to enable events to be handled immediately, rather than by parsing a file after the fact.

One issue, however, is that because JFR and JMC only recently became open source tools, many Java developers are not aware of their considerable capabilities. Let's take this opportunity to introduce JMC and JFR from the beginning.

7.7.1 Flight Recorder

JFR first became available as open source as part of OpenJDK 11, so to make use of it, you need to be running that version (or a more recent one). The technology was also back-ported to OpenJDK 8 and is available for versions 8u262 and upward.

There are various ways to create a JFR recording, but we're going to look at two in particular: the use of command-line arguments when starting up a JVM and the use of jcmd.

First, let's see what command-line switches we need to start JFR up at process start time. The key switch follows:

```
-XX:StartFlightRecording:<options>
```

This can either be done as a one-off dump file or a continuous ring buffer, and a large number of individual command-line options control what data is being captured.

In addition, JFR can capture more than a hundred different possible metrics. Most of these are very low-impact, but some do incur some overhead. Managing the configuration of all of these metrics individually would be a huge task.

Instead, to simplify the process, JFR uses profiling configuration files. These are simple XML files that contain configurations for each metric and whether or not it should be captured. The standard JDK download contains two basic files: default.jfc and profile.jfc.

The default level of recording is designed to be extremely low overhead and to be useable by basically every production Java process. The profile.jfc configuration contains more detailed information, but this, of course, comes at a higher runtime cost.

NOTE As well as the two supplied files, it is possible to create a custom configuration file that contains just the data points that are wanted. The JMC tool has a template manager that enables easy creation of these files.

As well as the settings file, other options that can be passed include the filename in which to store the recorded data and how much data to keep (in terms of the age of the data points). For example, an overall JFR command line might look like this (given on a single line):

```
-XX:StartFlightRecording:disk=true,filename=svc/sandbox/service.jfr,
                      maxage=12h,settings=profile
```

NOTE When JFR was a part of the commercial build, it was unlocked with the -XX:+UnlockCommercialFeatures switch. However, Oracle JDK 11+ emits a warning when the -XX:+UnlockCommercialFeatures option is used. This is because all the commercial features have been open sourced, and because the flag was never part of OpenJDK, it does not make sense to continue to use it. In OpenJDK builds, using the commercial features flag results in an error.

One of the great features of JFR is that it does not need to be configured at the process start. Instead, it can be controlled from the command line using the jcmd command, as shown here:

```
$ jcmd <pid> JFR.start name=Recording1 settings=default
$ jcmd <pid> JFR.dump filename=recording.jfr
$ jcmd <pid> JFR.stop
```

JFR also provides a JMX API for controlling JFR recordings as well. However, no matter how JFR is activated, the end result is the same—a single file per profiling run per JVM. The file contains a lot of binary data and is not human-readable, so we need some sort of tool to extract and visualize the data.

7.7.2   Mission Control

JDK Mission Control (JMC) is a graphical tool used to display the data contained in JFR output files. It is started up from the jmc command. This program used to be bundled with the Oracle JDK download but is now available separately from https://jdk.java.net/jmc/.

The startup screen for Mission Control can be seen in figure 7.7. After loading the file, JMC performs some automated analysis on it to identify any obvious problems present in the recorded run.

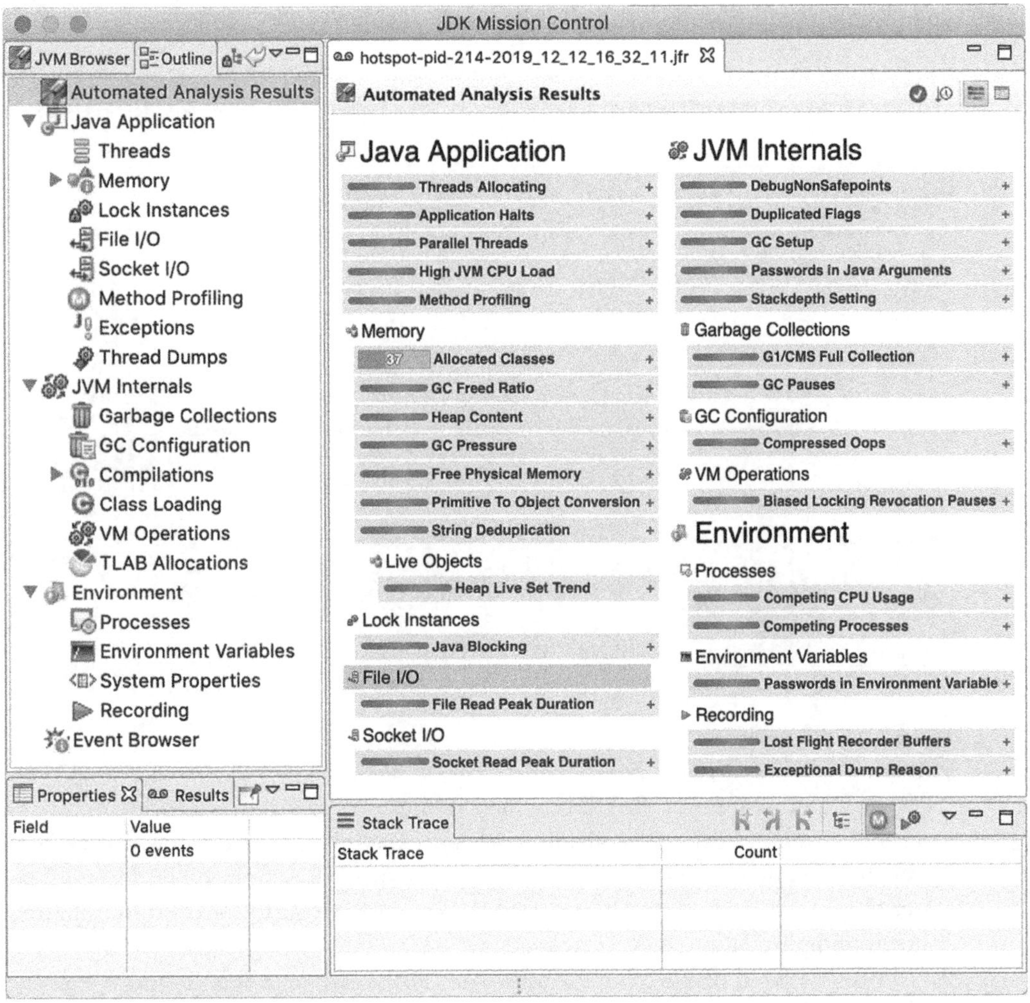

Figure 7.7 JMC startup screen

NOTE To profile, Flight Recorder must, of course, be enabled on the target application. As well as using a previously created file, it is also possible to dynamically attach it after the application has already started. For the latter option, JMC provides a tab on the left of the top-left panel labeled JVM Browser for attaching it dynamically to local applications.

One of the first screens encountered in JMC is the overview telemetry screen that shows a high-level dashboard of the overall health of the JVM. This can be seen in figure 7.8

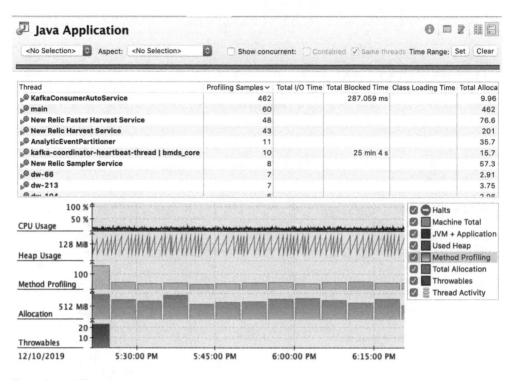

Figure 7.8   JMC dashboard

The major subsystems of the JVM all have dedicated screens to enable deep-dive analysis. For example, garbage collection has an overview screen to show the GC events over the lifetime of the JFR file. The "Longest Pause" display at the bottom allows the user to see where any anomalously long GC events have occurred over the timeline, as shown in figure 7.9

In the detailed profile configuration, it is also possible to see the individual events where new allocation buffers (TLABs) are handed out to application threads. We can see a much more accurate view of allocation within the process. The view looks like that shown in figure 7.10. This view allows developers to easily see which threads are allocating the most memory—in this example, it's a thread that is consuming data from Apache Kafka topics.

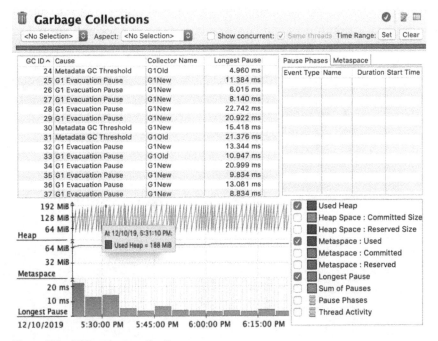

Figure 7.9   JMC garbage collection

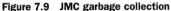

Figure 7.10   JMC TLAB allocation

The other major subsystem of the JVM is the JIT compiler, and JMC allows us to dig into the details of how the compiler is working, as we can see in figure 7.11.

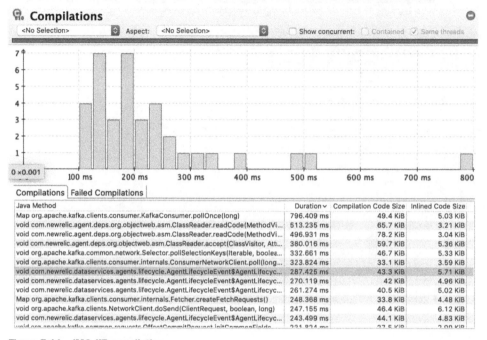

Figure 7.11 JMC JIT compilation

A key resource is the available memory in the JIT compiler's code cache. This is the area of memory where the compiled version of methods are stored. The usage of the code cache can be visualized in JMC— an example is shown in figure 7.12.

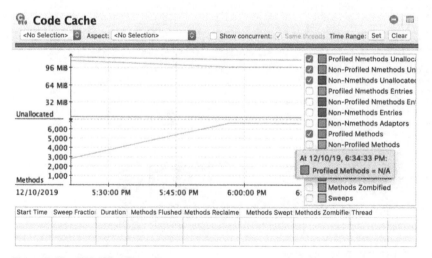

Figure 7.12 JMC JIT code cache

For processes that have a lot of compiled methods, this area of memory can be exhausted, causing the process to not reach peak performance.

JMC also includes a method-level profiler, which works in a very similar way to the one found in VisualVM or commercial tools such as JProfiler or YourKit. Figure 7.13 shows a typical result.

Ⓜ Method Profiling

<No Selection> ◇	Aspect:	<No Selection> ◇

Top Package	Count ∨
java.util	176
java.lang	83
org.apache.kafka.clients.consumer.internals	49
java.util.concurrent	29
org.apache.kafka.clients	25
org.apache.kafka.common.requests	24
org.apache.kafka.common.metrics	23
com.newrelic.agent.deps.org.objectweb.asm	19
org.apache.kafka.common.protocol.types	17
sun.security.provider	15
com.newrelic.agent	14
sun.nio.ch	14
org.eclipse.jetty.server	12
java.nio	10

Top Class	Count ∨
Ⓖ org.apache.kafka.clients.consumer.internals.SubscriptionState	9
Ⓒ org.apache.kafka.clients.consumer.internals.ConsumerNetworkClient	9
Ⓖ org.apache.kafka.clients.consumer.internals.Fetcher$1	7
Ⓖ org.apache.kafka.clients.consumer.internals.Fetcher	6
Ⓖ org.apache.kafka.clients.consumer.internals.AbstractCoordinator$HeartbeatThread	5
Ⓖ org.apache.kafka.clients.consumer.internals.ConsumerNetworkClient$RequestFut...	4
Ⓖ org.apache.kafka.clients.consumer.internals.RequestFuture	4
Ⓖ org.apache.kafka.clients.consumer.internals.Fetcher$FetchManagerMetrics	2
Ⓖ org.apache.kafka.clients.consumer.internals.ConsumerCoordinator	2
Ⓖ org.apache.kafka.clients.consumer.internals.Fetcher$PartitionRecords	1

Figure 7.13   JMC method profiling

One of the more advanced screens within JMC is the VM Operations view, which shows some of the internal operations the JVM performs and how long they take. This is not a view that we would expect to need for every analysis, but it would be potentially useful for detecting certain types of less-common problem. We can see a typical usage in figure 7.14.

JMC can be used to diagnose a single JVM, and this is a great capability to have. However, this use case does not scale to examining an entire cluster (or full application). In addition, modern systems frequently need a monitoring, or *observability*, solution as well as the deep-dive capability.

⚙ VM Operations

              ✔ ▦

| <No Selection> | Aspect: | <No Selection> | □ Show concurrent: ✓ Same threads | Time Range: | Set | Clear |

VM Operation	Longest Duration ⌄	Total Duration	StdDev (P) Duration	Count
G1CollectForAllocation	22.807 ms	472.188 ms	4.608 ms	83
CGC_Operation	21.440 ms	38.006 ms	7.805 ms	6
CollectForMetadataAllocation	15.527 ms	15.589 ms	7.733 ms	2
Deoptimize	4.729 ms	17.123 ms	1.057 ms	20
ClassLoaderStatsOperation	3.734 ms	13.393 ms	1.323 ms	6
JFRCheckpoint	3.095 ms	4.806 ms	691.869 µs	2
PrintThreads	1.470 ms	79.501 ms	136.471 µs	73
BulkRevokeBias	1.008 ms	48.574 ms	177.152 µs	106
GC_HeapInspection	835.576 µs	837.327 µs	416.912 µs	2
EnableBiasedLocking	696.242 µs	696.242 µs	0 s	1
RevokeBias	430.178 µs	33.189 ms	21.763 µs	1,366
FindDeadlocks	122.021 µs	11.414 ms	4.982 µs	1,826
PrintJNI	6.795 µs	129.516 µs	718 ns	73
ICBufferFull	595 ns	1.577 us	56 ns	3

Timeline | Durations | Event Log

Figure 7.14   JMC JVM operations

The classic JFR model of a recording file (and one-file JVM) does not make this easy. It is not a good fit for the stream of telemetry data delivered over the network to a SaaS provider or internal tool. Some vendors (e.g., New Relic and DataDog) do provide a JFR capability, but the use of these techniques is still somewhat niche.

Fortunately, the JFR Streaming API that was introduced with Java 14 provides an excellent building block for the observability use case as well as a deep dive. The community as a whole has tended not to adopt the non-LTS releases of Java, however. This means that it is likely that only with the arrival of Java 17 (which is LTS) will we see widespread adoption of a Java version that supports the streaming form of JFR.

Performance tuning isn't about staring at your code and praying for enlightenment or applying canned quick fixes. Instead, it's about meticulous measurement, attention to detail, and patience. It's about persistent reduction of sources of error in your tests, so that the true sources of performance problems emerge.

In this chapter, we've been able to give only a brief introduction to a rich and varied topic. There is so much more to explore, and the interested reader should consult a dedicated text, such as *Optimizing Java* by Ben Evans, James Gough, and Chris Newland (O'Reilly Media, May 2018).

Summary

- The JVM is an incredibly powerful and sophisticated runtime environment.
- The JVM's nature can make it sometimes challenging to optimize the code within.
- You have to measure to get an accurate idea of where the problems really are.
- Pay particular attention to the garbage collection subsystem and the JIT compiler.
- Monitoring and other tools can really help.
- Learn to read the logs and other indicators of the platform—tools aren't always available.

Part 3

Non-Java
languages on the JVM

This part of the book is all about exploring new language paradigms on the JVM. The JVM is an amazing runtime environment: it provides not only performance and power but also a surprising amount of flexibility to the programmer. In fact, the JVM is the gateway to exploring other languages beyond Java, and it allows you to try out different approaches to programming.

If you've programmed only in Java, you may be wondering what you'll gain from learning different languages. As we said in chapter 1, the essence of being a well-grounded Java developer is to have a growing mastery of all aspects of the Java language, platform, and ecosystem. That includes an appreciation of topics that are on the horizon now but that will be an integral part of the landscape in the near future.

The future is already here—it's just not evenly distributed.

—William Gibson

It turns out that many of the new ideas that will be needed in the future are present in other JVM languages today, such as functional programming. By learning a new JVM language, you can steal a glimpse into another world—one that may resemble some of your future projects. Exploring an unfamiliar point of view can also help you put your existing knowledge into a fresh light. This opens the possibility that by learning a new language you'll discover new talents you didn't know you had and add new skills that will prove useful going forward.

In chapter 9, we'll look at Kotlin, a relatively young language that addresses many of the criticisms of Java without radically altering the fundamentals. It aims for conciseness and safety, while also unlocking use cases that in the past leaned more toward dynamic scripting languages.

Functional programming has continued in recent years to draw attention as an alternative to the typical object-oriented viewpoint expressed by Java. To get a taste for this different world, you'll see Clojure, one of the functional languages on the JVM that departs the furthest from the Java mindset.

Parts 4 and 5 will frequently circle back to these languages, showing how they apply throughout your projects—from building and testing, through to deeper issues of concurrency and program structure. So let's step away from the comforts of Java for a bit to see the alternatives available to use.

Alternative
JVM languages

8

This chapter covers

- Language zoology
- Why you should use alternative JVM languages
- Selection criteria for alternative languages
- How the JVM handles alternative languages

If you've used Java for any sizable amount of work, you've probably noticed that it can tend toward being a bit verbose and clumsy at times. You may even have found yourself wishing that things were different—easier somehow.

Fortunately, as you've seen in the last few chapters, the JVM is awesome—so awesome, in fact, that it provides a natural home for programming languages other than Java. In this chapter, we'll show you why and how you might want to start mixing another JVM programming language into your project.

In this chapter, we'll cover ways of describing the different language types (such as static versus dynamic typing), why you might want to use alternative languages, and what criteria to look for in choosing them. You'll also be introduced to the two languages (Kotlin and Clojure) that we'll cover in more depth throughout the remainder of this book.

8.1 Language zoology

Programming languages come in many different flavors and classifications. Another way of saying this is that a wide range of styles and approaches to programming are embodied in different languages. Mastering these different styles is often easier when you understand how to classify the differences between languages.

> **NOTE** These classifications are an aid to thinking about the diversity of languages. Some of these divisions are more clear-cut than others, but none of the classifying schemes is perfect. Different people have different ideas about how the classification should be laid out.

In recent years, a trend has existed for languages to add features from across the spectrum of possibilities. It's often helpful to think of a given language as being "less functional" than another language, or "dynamically typed but with optional static typing when needed."

The classifications we'll cover are "interpreted versus compiled," "dynamic versus static," "imperative versus functional," and reimplementations of a language versus the original. In general, these classifications are tools for thinking about the space, rather than complete and precise academic schemes.

For example, we can say Java is a runtime-compiled, statically typed, imperative language with some functional features. It emphasizes safety, code clarity, backward compatibility, and performance, and it's happy to accept a certain amount of verbosity and *ceremony* (such as in deployment) to achieve those goals.

> **NOTE** Different languages may have different priorities; for example, dynamically typed languages may emphasize deployment speed.

Let's get started with the interpreted versus compiled classification.

8.1.1 Interpreted vs. compiled languages

An *interpreted language* is one in which each step of the source code is executed as is, rather than the entire program being transformed to machine code before execution begins. This contrasts with a *compiled language*, which is one that uses a compiler to convert the human-readable source code into a binary form as an initial task.

This distinction has become less clear recently. In the early '90s, the divide was fairly clear: C/C++, FORTRAN, and their friends were compiled languages, and Perl and Python were interpreted languages. But as we alluded to in chapter 1, Java has features of both compiled and interpreted languages. The use of bytecode further muddies the issue. Bytecode is certainly not human readable, but neither is it machine code.

For the JVM languages we'll study in this part of the book, the distinction we'll make is whether the language produces a class file from the source code and executes that—or not. In the latter case, an interpreter (probably written in Java) is used to execute the source code, line by line. Some languages provide both a compiler and an interpreter, and some provide an interpreter and a just-in-time (JIT) compiler that will emit JVM bytecode.

8.1.2 Dynamic vs. static typing

In languages with dynamic typing, a variable can contain different types at different times during a program's execution. As an example, let's look at a simple bit of code in a well-known dynamic language, JavaScript. This example should hopefully be comprehensible, even if you don't know the language in detail:

```
var answer = 40;
answer = answer + 2;
answer = "What is the answer? " + answer;
```

The var keyword used here creates a new variable. In JavaScript's dynamic type system, this variable can contain a value of any type. This variable starts off set to 40, which is, of course, a numeric value. We then add 2 to it, giving 42. Then we change track slightly and make answer hold a string value. This is a common technique in a dynamic language, and it causes no syntax errors.

The JavaScript interpreter is also able to distinguish between the two uses of the + operator. The first use of + is numeric addition— adding 2 to 40—whereas in the following line, the interpreter figures out from context that the developer meant string concatenation.

Let's try this trick again in Java using JShell:

```
jshell> var answer = 40;
answer ==> 40

jshell> answer = answer + 2;
answer ==> 42

jshell> answer = "What is the answer? " + answer;
|  Error:
|  incompatible types: java.lang.String cannot be converted to int
|  answer = "What is the answer? " + answer;
|              ^---------------------------^
|
```

Boom. Even though the exact same source code looked legal in both languages, Java's *static type system* prevented the final line from working. Java's var keyword does more than simply create the variable answer. As we learned in section 1.3, Java's var also inferred the type of this new variable from the right-hand side of the expression. We didn't have to specify the type of answer explicitly, but Java's static type system assigns a type that never subsequently changes.

NOTE The key point here is that dynamic typing tracks type information with the *value* a variable contains (e.g., a number or a string), where static typing tracks the type with the *variable* definition instead.

Static typing can be a good fit for a compiled language because the type information is all about the variables, not the values in them. This allows reasoning about potential type system violations at compile time, before the code even has a chance to run.

Dynamically typed languages carry type information on the values held in variables. This provides a lot of flexibility but means type violations (e.g., "I thought this was a number, but it's a string") happen during execution. This can lead to more runtime errors, which can be harder and more expensive to debug than compile-time errors.

8.1.3 *Imperative vs. functional languages*

Java is a classic example of an imperative language. *Imperative languages* can be thought of as languages that model the running state of a program as mutable data and issue a list of instructions that transform that running state. Program state is thus the concept that has center stage in imperative languages.

Two main subtypes of imperative languages exist. *Procedural languages*, such as BASIC and FORTRAN, treat code and data as completely separate and have a simple code-operates-on-data paradigm. The other subtype is *object-oriented (OO) languages*, where data and code (in the form of methods) are bundled together into objects. The program state in an object-oriented system is the state of all the objects in the program. In OO languages, additional structure is imposed to a greater or lesser degree by metadata (such as class information). The differences between these subtypes, though, may not always be clear. C++, for instance, is explicitly intended to support both OO and procedural coding, and some later varieties of BASIC sport object-oriented features.

Functional languages take the view that computation itself is the most important concept. Functions operate on values, as in procedural languages, but instead of altering their inputs, functions are seen as acting like mathematical functions and return new values. Composing separate functions together in new and novel ways is also fundamental in this model.

As illustrated in figure 8.1, functions are seen as "little processing machines" that take in values and output new values. They don't have any state of their own, and it doesn't really make sense to bundle them up with any external state. The object-centered view of the world is somewhat at odds with the natural viewpoint of functional languages.

A key feature of functional languages is *first-class functions*—the ability to treat a function as a value, assigning it to variables, passing it to other functions, and even returning functions from other functions.

This is a great example of the feature spectrum we discussed earlier, because Java 8 added the lambda expression syntax, which enables Java programmers to treat functions as value. However, as a recent addition, the feature isn't used everywhere it could

Object-oriented approach

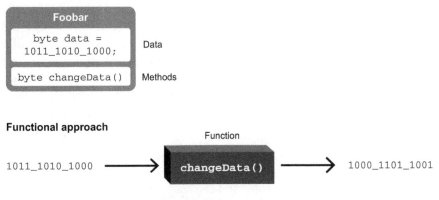

Figure 8.1 **Imperative and functional languages**

be in the platform, and older techniques for getting similar behavior, such as the Run-nable and Callable interfaces, remain in use.

In the next two chapters we'll learn about different languages, and a key focus will be on how they support functional programming approaches. With Kotlin, we'll see how even an imperative language can be designed to smoothly support functional ideas. Then we'll look at Clojure, a much purer functional language that no longer centers on object orientation at all.

8.1.4 Reimplementation vs. original

Another important distinction between JVM languages is the division into those that are reimplementations of existing languages versus those that were specifically written to target the JVM. In general, languages that were specifically written to target the JVM provide a much tighter binding between their type systems and the native types of the JVM.

The following three languages are JVM reimplementations of existing languages:

- *JRuby* is a JVM reimplementation of the Ruby programming language. Ruby is a dynamically typed OO language with some functional features. It's basically interpreted on the JVM, but recent versions have included a runtime JIT compiler to produce JVM bytecode under favorable conditions.
- *Jython* was started in 1997 by Jim Hugunin as a way to use high-performance Java libraries from Python. It's a reimplementation of Python on the JVM, so it's a dynamic, mostly OO language. It operates by generating internal Python bytecode, then translating that to JVM bytecode. Sadly, the project has seen little activity since 2015 and supports only Python 2.7, not the current Python 3.
- *Rhino* was originally developed by Netscape and later the Mozilla project. It provided an implementation of JavaScript on the JVM and shipped up through JDK.

– JDK 8 included a new JavaScript engine, *Nashorn* (The name "Nashorn" is a bit of a pun—it's the German word for "Rhino"), but the increasing pace of JavaScript language changes forced its deprecation with JDK 11 and removal in JDK 15. Although no JavaScript implementation will ship directly with future JDKs, both may still be found independently. (Rhino from Mozilla (https://github.com/mozilla/rhino) and Nashorn (https://openjdk.java .net/projects/nashorn/) as an independent OpenJDK project, which intends to live on and should be supported on future JDKs.

> **NOTE** The earliest JVM language? The earliest non-Java JVM language is hard to pin down. Certainly, Kawa, an implementation of Lisp, dates to 1997 or so. In the years since then, we've seen an explosion of languages, to the point that it's almost impossible to keep track of them.

A reasonable guess at the time of writing is that at least 200 languages target the JVM. Not all can be considered to be active or widely used (and some are really very niche), but the large number indicates that the JVM is a very active platform for language development and implementation.

> **NOTE** In the versions of the language and VM spec that debuted with Java 7, all direct references to the Java language have been removed from the VM spec. Java is now simply one language among many that run on the JVM—it no longer enjoys a privileged status.

The key piece of technology that enables so many different languages to target the JVM is the class file format, as we discussed in chapter 4. Any language that can produce a class file is considered a compiled language on the JVM.

Let's move on to discuss how polyglot programming came to be an area of interest for Java programmers. We'll explain the basic concepts and why and how to choose an alternative JVM language for your project.

8.2 Polyglot programming on the JVM

The phrase *polyglot programming on the JVM* was coined to describe projects using one or more non-Java JVM languages alongside a core of Java code. One common way to think about polyglot programming is as a form of separation of concerns. As you can see in figure 8.2, potentially three layers exist where non-Java technologies can play a useful role. This diagram is sometimes called the polyglot pro-

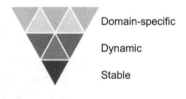

Domain-specific

Dynamic

Stable

Figure 8.2 The polyglot programming pyramid

gramming pyramid, and it's originally due to the work of Ola Bini (https://olabini .com/blog/tag/polyglot/).

Within the pyramid, dependencies run in one direction—the stable layer is relatively independent, the dynamic layer uses the stable, and domain-specific code can pull in from both layers below it.

Defining these layers in a given system isn't always easy; gray areas exist, and not all systems fit perfectly. However, it's a useful tool to identify the seams where different parts of the system have different needs and could benefit from different languages.

The stable layer contains core APIs and abstractions for your system. Type safety, thorough testing, and performance are all critical.

The dynamic layer uses the stable layer's abstractions to create a working system. This may include code such as how a system exposes itself over HTTP or interacts with other backend systems. Issues like compilation time and flexibility may make it worth considering a different language at the dynamic layer.

The domain-specific layer handles application-specific concerns such as presentation, customization of rules and processing, or CI/CD. This code is all about specific aspects of the application domain and may benefit from language choices that would be constraining in other layers.

> **NOTE** Polyglot programming makes sense because different pieces of code have different lifetimes. A risk calculation engine in a bank may last for five or more years. JSP pages for a website could last for a few months. The most short-lived code for a startup could be live for just a few days. The longer the code lives, the closer to the stable layer of the pyramid it is. See table 8.1.

Table 8.1   Three layers of the polyglot programming pyramid

Name	Description	Examples
Domain-specific	Domain-specific language. Tightly coupled to a specific part of the application domain	Apache Camel, DSLs, Drools, web templating
Dynamic	Rapid, productive, flexible development of functionality	Clojure, Groovy, JRuby
Stable	Core functionality, stable, well-tested, performant	Java, Kotlin, Scala

As you can see, patterns occur in the layers—the statically typed languages tend to gravitate toward tasks in the stable layer. Conversely, the technologies intended for more of a specific purpose tend to be well-suited to roles at the top of the pyramid.

Let's dig a little deeper to look at why Java isn't the best choice for everything in the pyramid. We'll begin by discussing why you should consider a non-Java language, and then we'll cover some of the major criteria to look at in choosing a non-Java language for your project.

8.2.1   Why use a non-Java language?

Java's nature as a general-purpose, statically typed, compiled language provides many advantages. These qualities make it a great choice for implementing functionality in the stable layer. But these same attributes become a burden in the upper tiers of the pyramid, as described here:

- Recompilation is laborious.
- Static typing can be inflexible.
- Deployment is a heavyweight process.
- Java's syntax can be rigid and isn't a natural fit for producing DSLs.

The recompilation and rebuild time of a Java project often reaches the 90 seconds to two-minute mark. This is a long enough to seriously break a developers' flow, and it's a bad fit for developing code that may live in production for only a few weeks.

JAVA'S RIGID SYNTAX

The Java language has a very rigid grammar. The fundamental language components are the keywords that are supplied. You cannot "make up new syntax" or create any new form that could be mistaken for a keyword.

The programmer can create new classes, and the capabilities of those classes consist of storing state in fields and calling methods on classes or objects. However, this is as far as it goes—the programmer cannot create anything that resembles a control structure. In other words, a field access will always look like the following:

```
anObject.someField
AClass.someStaticField
```

And a method call will always look like this:

```
anObject.someMethod(params)
AClass.someStaticMethod(params)
```

In Java, the method parameters are never optional (unlike in some other languages, such as Kotlin), so even the distinction between field access and methods calls cannot be blurred. For example, we cannot create constructs that look like keywords. For instance, we'd like to be able to create a when that looks like this:

```
when(value) {
  // action to be taken
}
```

But the best we can do is something like this:

```
import static when.When.when;

...

when(value, () -> {
  // action to be taken
});
```

This lack of redefinable syntax also shows up when trying to use Java to make DSLs. We'll see how our non-Java languages handle this issue in the next two chapters.

Overall, one pragmatic solution is to play to Java's strengths. Take advantage of its rich API and library support to do the heavy lifting for the application down in the stable layer.

Even within the stable layer you may find there are reasons a language other than Java may be desirable, such as the following:

- Java's verbosity can be off-putting for some developers, and it can hide certain classes of bugs.
- Although Java increasingly supports functional programming, limits in the ease of applying some patterns remain.
- Other languages present alternatives for concurrency that are not present in Java (coroutines in Kotlin, agents in Clojure).

NOTE Even if you choose another language to use in your stable layer for features it supports, you shouldn't throw out working code just to rewrite it so the languages match. Consider using the new language for new features or for low-risk areas we'll talk about identifying later in this chapter.

At this point, you may be asking yourself, What type of programming challenges fit inside these layers? Which languages should I choose? A well-grounded Java developer knows that there is no silver bullet, but we do have criteria to consider when evaluating your choices.

8.2.2 Up-and-coming languages

For the rest of the book, we've picked two languages that we see having great potential longevity and influence. These are two of the languages on the JVM (Kotlin and Clojure) that already have well-established mind share among polyglot programmers. Why are these languages gaining traction? Let's look at each in turn.

KOTLIN

Kotlin is an imperative, static-typed, OO language from JetBrains (makers of IntelliJ IDEA). It aims to address the most common complaints about Java, while keeping a familiar development environment. Kotlin is a compiled language and has a high degree of compatibility beyond the basics that just running on the JVM provides.

Key features in Kotlin include concise syntax, `null` safety, extremely strong interoperability with Java code, and coroutines—an alternate concurrency mechanism to Java's traditional threading model. A number of features from Kotlin have found their way back into Java in recent releases, confirming the value those changes presented to developers.

Although it has established itself as a key JVM language option in multiple areas, Kotlin has shown particular success in mobile, with the Android platform adopting it as the recommended language in 2019. Kotlin is also supported for Gradle build scripting at the same level as Groovy. It's also been embraced by many other frameworks, such as Spring. The wide range of convenience and safety improvements for developers are worth considering regardless of where your JVM is running. Chapter 9 gives an introduction to Kotlin.

Kotlin will be used in chapter 11 as the primary scripting language for Gradle builds. We will also revisit it to demonstrate some unique approaches to functional programming in chapter 15 and concurrent programming (coroutines) in chapter 16.

CLOJURE

Clojure, designed by Rich Hickey, is a language from the Lisp family. It inherits many syntactic features (and lots of parentheses) from that heritage. It's a dynamically typed, functional language, as is usual for Lisps. It's a compiled language but usually distributes code in source form for reasons we'll see later. It also adds a significant number of new features (especially in the arena of concurrency) to its Lisp core.

Lisps are usually seen as experts-only languages. Clojure is somewhat easier to learn than other Lisps, yet it still provides the developer with formidable power (and also lends itself very nicely to the test-driven development style). But it's likely to remain outside the mainstream, being primarily used by enthusiasts and for specialized jobs (e.g., some financial applications find its combination of features very appealing).

Clojure is best thought of as sitting in the dynamic layer but, due to its concurrency support and other features, can be seen as capable of performing many of the roles of a stable layer language. Chapter 10 provides an introduction to Clojure.

We will use Clojure extensively in learning more about functional programming beyond what Java can do in chapter 15. It will also feature in introducing the actor model, a powerful alternative in concurrent programming in chapter 16.

8.2.3   *Languages we could have picked but didn't*

As noted earlier, a huge variety of languages exist that we could look at. Here's a little more about a few other contenders that may be practical for you to look at more deeply yourself.

GROOVY

The Groovy language was invented by James Strachan in 2003. It's a dynamic, compiled language with syntax very similar to Java's but more flexible. It's widely used for scripting and testing. It was the original language used by the Gradle build tool and is used for configuring Jenkins, an extremely common CI/CD tool. It's often the first non-Java language that developers or teams investigate on the JVM. Groovy can be seen as sitting in the dynamic layer and is also known for being great for building DSLs.

We've chosen not to cover Groovy in more detail because it has seen declining mindshare in the prototyping and application use cases in the face of improving frameworks and other languages.

SCALA

Scala is an OO language that also supports many aspects of functional programming. It traces its origins to 2003, when Martin Odersky began work on it in an academic setting, following his earlier projects related to generics in Java. It's a statically typed, compiled language like Java, and it performs a large amount of type inference, so it often has the feel of a dynamic language.

Scala learned a great deal from Java, and its language design "fixes" several common annoyances with Java. However, Scala has ended up with a very large set of features, though, and a much more advanced type system compared to Java's.

It can be complicated to program and is not easy to learn thoroughly. As such we've chosen to focus on Kotlin for developers who just want improvements to the state of the Java language.

GRAALVM

Oracle Labs have produced GraalVM (https://www.graalvm.org/), which they describe as a polyglot virtual machine and platform that is partly derived from Java and JVM codebases. The current release includes the capability to run Java and other JVM languages (as bytecode) as well as support for JavaScript and LLVM bitcode (the intermediate representation from the popular LLVM compiler), with beta support for Ruby, Python, R, and WASM.

The overall platform comprises the following components:

- Java HotSpot VM
- A Node.js JavaScript runtime environment
- LLVM runtime to execute LLVM bitcode
- Graal—a JIT compiler written in Java
- Truffle—a toolkit and API for building language interpreters
- SubstrateVM—a lightweight execution container for native images

Within a GraalVM project, languages can be very freely bridged to each other, and the aim is to allow components implemented in different technologies to be combined and used in a single application process. This is a very different approach to polyglot programming, but it is close enough to the subject of interest that we wanted to at least mention it.

NON-JVM LANGUAGES

This chapter focuses on alternative languages that run on the JVM. It's worth admitting, though, that sometimes the polyglot programmer may have a reason that part of their system needs to leave the JVM behind entirely.

Examples of technologies which have broader support outside the JVM follow:

- Native system code (C, Go, or Rust)
- Machine learning (Python)
- Run in a user's web browser (JavaScript)

Although JVM-based approaches exist for many of these, it's worth taking stock of the maturity of alternatives and the composition of our team before trying to keep every line of code entirely on the JVM.

Now that we've outlined some possible choices, let's discuss the issues that should drive your decision of which language to choose.

8.3 How to choose a non-Java language for your project

Once you've decided to experiment with non-Java languages in your project, you need to identify which parts of your project naturally fit into the stable, dynamic, or domain-specific layers. Table 8.2 highlights tasks that might be suitable for each layer.

Table 8.2 Project areas suited for domain-specific, dynamic, and stable layers

Name	Example problem domains
Domain-specific	
Domain-specific areas often benefit from readability by experts who may not know Java. Software life cycle tooling also frequently has domain-specific languages and configuration.	Build, continuous integration, continuous deployment Dev-ops Business rules modeling
Dynamic	
Dynamic layers of the system may benefit from greater flexibility and speed of development available in other languages. This may be especially true for tooling that is internally facing (testing and administrative).	Rapid web development Prototyping Interactive administrative and user consoles Scripting Testing
Stable	
Stable layer code expresses a system's core abstractions. More rigorous type safety and testing are worth the additional developer overhead.	Concurrent code Application containers Core business functionality

As you can see, a wide range of use cases for alternative languages exists. But identifying a task that could be resolved with an alternative language is just the beginning. You next need to evaluate whether using an alternative language is appropriate. Here are some useful criteria that we take into account when considering technology stacks:

- Is the project area low-risk?
- How easily does the language interoperate with Java?
- What tooling support (e.g., IDE support) is there for the language?
- How steep is the learning curve for this language?
- How easy is it to hire developers with experience in this language?

Let's dive into each of these areas so you get an idea of the sorts of questions you need to be asking.

8.3.1 Is the project area low-risk?

Let's say you have a core payment-processing rules engine that handles millions of transactions a day. This is a stable piece of Java software that has been around for over seven years, but there aren't a lot of tests and plenty of dark corners are present in the code. The core of the payment-processing engine is clearly a high-risk area to bring a new language into, especially when it's running successfully and there's a lack of test coverage and of developers who fully understand it.

But there's more to a system than its core processing. For example, this is a situation where better tests would clearly help. Kotlin has a number of good options, including the Spek framework (https://www.spekframework.org/) and Kotest (https://kotest.io), which leverage the language to enable clear, readable specifications without the typical JUnit boilerplate. Or perhaps your rules engine would benefit from *property testing*, where tests are written to validate conditions against generated inputs and Clojure's `test.check` (https://clojure.org/guides/test_check_beginner) would be a valuable tool in the mix.

Or suppose you need to build a web console so that the operations users can administer some of the noncritical static data behind the payment-processing system. The development team members already know Struts and JSF but don't feel any enthusiasm for either technology. This is another low-risk area to try out a new language and technology stack. Spring Boot with Kotlin would be one obvious choice.

By focusing on a limited pilot in an area that is low-risk, there's always the option of terminating the project and porting to a different delivery technology without too much disruption if the new technology stack isn't a good fit.

8.3.2   *Does the language interoperate well with Java?*

You don't want to lose the value of all of that great Java code you've already written! This is one of the main reasons organizations are hesitant to introduce a new programming language into their technology stack. But with alternative languages that run on the JVM, you can turn this on its head, so it becomes about maximizing your existing value in the codebase and not throwing away working code.

Alternative languages on the JVM are able to cleanly interoperate with Java and can, of course, be deployed on a preexisting environment. This is especially important to avoid impacting whoever owns deployment, whether a production management team or DevOps folks in your own team. By using a non-Java JVM language as part of your system, you retain your organization's operational expertise, which can help alleviate worries and reduce risk around supporting the new solution.

> **NOTE** DSLs are typically built using a dynamic (or, in some cases, stable) layer language, so many of them run on the JVM via the languages that they were built in.

Some languages interoperate with Java more easily than others. We've found that most popular JVM alternatives (such as Kotlin, Clojure, JRuby, Groovy, and Scala) all have good interoperability with Java (and for some of the languages, the integration is excellent, almost completely seamless). If you're a really cautious shop, it's quick and easy to run a few experiments first and make certain that you understand how the integration can work for you.

Let's take Kotlin, for example. You can import Java packages directly into its code via the familiar import statement. From here you could easily write a small Kotlin script, or even use the interactive Kotlin shell, to poke at your Java model objects and see what the interoperation surfaces will look like. We'll talk specifically about Java interoperability in the language chapters coming up next.

8.3.3   *Is there good tooling and test support for the language?*

Most developers underestimate the amount of time they save once they've become comfortable in their environment. Their powerful IDEs and build and test tools help them to rapidly produce high quality software. Java developers have benefited from great tooling support for years, so it's important to remember that other languages may not be at quite the same level of maturity.

Some languages (such as Kotlin) have had longstanding IDE support for compiling, testing, and deploying the end result. Other languages may have tooling that hasn't matured as fully.

A related issue is that when an alternative language has developed a powerful tool for its own use (such as Clojure's awesome Leiningen build tool), the tool may not be well adapted to handle other languages. Therefore, the team will need to think carefully about how to divide up a project, especially for deployment of separate but related components.

8.3.4   *How hard is the language to learn?*

It always takes time to learn a new language, and that time only increases if the paradigm of the language isn't one that your development team is familiar with. Most Java development teams will be comfortable picking up a new language if it's object-oriented with a C-like syntax (such as Kotlin).

It gets harder for Java developers as they move further away from this paradigm. At the extreme of the popular alternative languages, a language such as Clojure can bring incredibly powerful benefits, but it can also represent a significant retraining requirement for development teams as they learn Clojure's functional nature and Lisp syntax.

One alternative is to look at the JVM languages that are reimplementations of existing languages. Ruby and Python are well-established languages, with plenty of material available for developers to use to educate themselves. The JVM incarnations of these languages could provide a sweet spot for your teams to begin working with an easy-to-learn non-Java language.

8.3.5   *Are there lots of developers using this language?*

Organizations have to be pragmatic; they can't always hire the top 2% (despite what their advertising might say), and their development teams will change throughout the course of a year. Some languages, such as Kotlin or Scala, are becoming well-established enough that there is a pool of developers to hire from. But a language such as Clojure may present more difficulties. Managers may push back against using something out of the ordinary from concern for creating an unmaintainable codebase they'll have difficulty hiring for.

> **NOTE** A warning about the reimplemented languages: many existing packages and applications written in Ruby, for example, are tested only against the original C-based implementation. There may be problems when trying to use them on top of the JVM. When making platform decisions, you should factor in extra testing time if you're planning to leverage an entire stack written in a reimplemented language.

Again, the reimplemented languages (JRuby, Jython, and so on) can potentially help here. Few developers may have JRuby on their CV, but because it's just Ruby on the JVM, there's actually a large pool of developers to hire from—a Ruby developer familiar with the C version can learn the differences induced by running on the JVM very easily.

  We now have a set of questions to ask when choosing an alternative language and an overview of some available options. At this point, it's worth a deeper understanding of how the JVM supports multiple languages. This peek reveals the roots of some design choices and limitations in alternative languages on the JVM.

8.4 How the JVM supports alternative languages

A language can run on the JVM in two possible ways:

- Have a source code compiler that emits class files. Kotlin and Clojure both function in this way.
- Have an interpreter that is implemented in JVM bytecode. JRuby is implemented in this way.

In both cases, it's usual to have a runtime environment that provides language-specific support for executing programs. Figure 8.3 shows the runtime environment stack for Java and for a typical non-Java language.

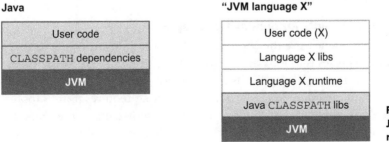

Figure 8.3 Non-Java language runtime support

These runtime support systems vary in complexity, depending on the amount of handholding that a given non-Java language requires at runtime. In almost all cases, the runtime will be implemented as a set of JARs or modules that an executing program needs to have on its classpath. In the interpreted case, the interpreter will bootstrap as program execution starts and then read in the source file to be executed.

8.4.1   *Performance*

One question developers often ask about different languages is, How do they perform relative to each other? Although superficially attractive, this question is not simple to answer and, in fact, is not actually all that meaningful.

As we saw in chapter 7, the well-grounded developer knows that performance is driven by measurement. Measurement is done on individual programs, not on the abstract notion of a programming language. Treat any claim that language X "performs better" than Y without accompanying, reliable data as suspect.

However, in practice, some overall performance characteristics of a JVM language can broadly be determined by how the language is implemented. A compiled language is just bytecode at runtime and will be JIT-compiled in the same way as Java is. An interpreted language will have very different performance behavior because the code that gets JIT-compiled is the interpreter, and not the program itself.

> **NOTE** Some languages (e.g., JRuby) have a hybrid strategy—they have an interpreter for scripts but can also dynamically compile individual source methods to JVM bytecode, which can then be compiled to machine code by the JVM's JIT compilers.

In this book, our focus is on compiled languages. The interpreted languages—such as Rhino—are mentioned for completeness, but we won't spend too much time on them. We, therefore, expect that performance will be broadly similar between the languages that we're considering. For a more detailed answer, you should undertake a detailed analysis of a specific program or workload.

In the rest of this section, we'll discuss the need for runtime support for alternative languages (even for compiled languages) and then talk about compiler fictions—language-specific features that are synthesized by the compiler and that may not appear in the low-level bytecode.

8.4.2   *Runtime environments for non-Java languages*

One simple way to measure the complexity of the runtime environment that a particular language requires is to look at the size of the JAR files that provide the implementation of the runtime. Using this as a metric, we can see that Clojure is a relatively lightweight runtime, whereas JRuby is a language that requires more support.

This isn't a completely fair test, because some languages bundle much larger standard libraries and additional functionality into their standard distributions than others. However, it can be a useful (if rough) rule of thumb.

In general, the purpose of the runtime environment is to help the type system and other aspects of the non-Java language achieve the desired semantics. Alternative languages don't always have exactly the same view as Java about basic programming concepts.

For example, Java's approach to OO isn't universally shared by other languages. In Java, all objects that are instances of a particular class all have exactly the same set of methods on them, and that set is fixed at compile time. In Ruby, on the other hand, an individual object instance can have additional methods attached to it at runtime that were not known when the class was defined and that aren't necessarily defined on other instances of the same class.

NOTE The invokedynamic bytecode was, in fact, originally added to the JVM to facilitate the efficient implementation of these types of language features.

This ability to dynamically add methods (which is somewhat confusingly called "open classes") needs to be replicated by the JRuby implementation. This is possible only with some advanced support from the JRuby runtime.

8.4.3 Compiler fictions

Certain language features are synthesized by the programming environment and high-level language and aren't present in the underlying JVM implementation. These are referred to as *compiler fictions*.

NOTE It helps to have some knowledge of how these features are implemented; otherwise, you can find your code running slowly or, in some cases, even crashing the process. Sometimes the environment has to do a lot of work to synthesize a particular feature.

Other examples in Java include checked exceptions and inner classes (which are always converted to top-level classes with specially synthesized access methods if necessary, as shown in figure 8.4). If you've ever looked inside a JAR file (using jar tvf) and seen a load of classes with $ in their names, these are the inner classes unpacked and converted to "regular" classes.

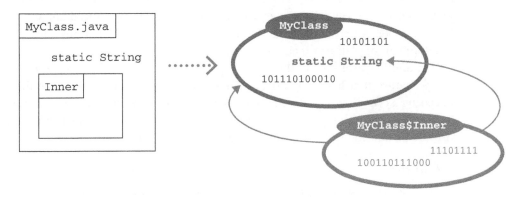

Figure 8.4 Inner classes as a compiler fiction

Alternative languages also have compiler fictions. In some cases, these compiler fictions even form a core part of the language's functionality.

In section 8.2, we introduced the key concept of *first-class functions* in functional programming—that functions should be values that can be put into variables. All the non-Java languages in part 3 of this book supported this feature long before Java added lambda expressions. How did they accomplish this when the JVM handles only classes as the smallest unit of code and functionality?

The original solution to this discrepancy between source code and JVM bytecode is to remember that objects are just bundles of data along with methods to act on that data. Imagine an object with no state and just one method—for example, a simple anonymous implementation of Java's `Callable`. It wouldn't be at all unusual to put such an object in a variable, pass it around, and then invoke its `call()` method later, like this:

```
Callable<String> myFn = new Callable<String>() {
    @Override
    public String call() {
        return "The result";
    }
};

System.out.println(myFn.call());
```

> **NOTE** The `myFn` variable in this example is an anonymous type, so it will show up after compilation as something like `NameOfEnclosingClass$1.class`. The class numbers start at 1 and go up for each anonymous type the compiler encounters. If they're dynamically created, and there are a lot of them (as sometimes happens in languages like JRuby), this can place pressure in the off-heap memory where the definitions of classes are stored.

Java lambda expressions don't actually use this anonymous type approach but instead are built on a general JVM feature called `invokedynamic`, which we'll discuss in detail in chapter 17. Alternate languages are moving from their specialized implementations to use `invokedynamic`, too. It's an interesting case of compiler fictions influencing the development of platform realities.

For another example, in the next chapter we will meet Kotlin's *data classes*— a language feature that helps to lower the amount of typing and *ceremony* required when declaring a class that is "just a dumb bunch of fields." In Kotlin as it exists today, this is a compiler fiction, but Java 17 has added a feature called *records*, which may eventually provide an alternative basis for Kotlin to build data classes upon.

Summary

- Alternative languages on the JVM have come a long way to offer better solutions than Java for certain problems.
- Languages can be classified in different ways (static versus dynamic, imperative versus functional, and compiled versus interpreted), which can assist in picking the right language for the right task.

- Polyglot programming is often separated into three layers: stable, dynamic, and domain-specific. Java and Kotlin are best for the stable layer of software development. Clojure may be more suited to tasks in the dynamic or domain-specific realms.
- Core business functionality of an existing production application is almost never the correct place to introduce a new language. Choose a low-risk area for your first deployment of an alternative language.
- Teams and projects have unique characteristics that will impact language choice. There are no universal right answers here.

Kotlin

Kotlin is a language created by JetBrains (https://jetbrains.com), makers of the popular IntelliJ IDEA. Announced publicly in 2011, Kotlin aims to fill language gaps they felt developing in Java, without the friction they saw with other existing JVM languages.

Kotlin was open sourced the following year and reached 1.0—with guaranteed levels of support and maintenance from JetBrains—in 2016. Since then, it has gone on to become the recommended language for the Android platform and has gathered a solid following in other JVM coding circles. The Kotlin Foundation, announced in 2018, brings the support of both JetBrains and Google to the language for the long term. Kotlin is even reaching beyond the JVM to support JavaScript and native backends.

9.1 Why use Kotlin?

As alternate languages go, Kotlin provides many quality of life improvements over Java, while not radically changing the entire world. Its focus on convenience, safety, and solid interoperability has given it a great story for incremental usage in existing Java projects. With first-class support in IntelliJ IDEA, turning a file from Java to Kotlin is often just a click away.

It's worth noting that some features originally available only in Kotlin have made their way back into Java. A great example of this is Kotlin script—Kotlin can run a source file directly, typically with the `kts` extension, without the developer asking to compile it. If this sounds like Java 11's single-file feature that we showed off in chapter 1, you're not wrong!

Following this chapter, we will use our new familiarity with Kotlin in chapter 11 as the main scripting language for our builds with Gradle. It will also be revisited in chapter 15 where we examine functional programming on the JVM, and in chapter 16 where Kotlin's built-in coroutine mechanism provides a compelling alternative to classical multithreading in Java. Let's start seeing what Kotlin can provide for us.

9.1.1 Installing

If you use IntelliJ IDEA, Kotlin is provided via a plugin. With that installed, you can start writing code in Kotlin straight away, just like any other supported language in the IDE.

For those who are more inclined to bare-bones setups, Kotlin also provides a command-line compiler (`kotlinc`) (see http://mng.bz/YGoa) and interactive shell (`kotlin`).

Adding Kotlin to an existing project requires updating your build scripts. Chapter 11 will get you more familiar with these systems, but for now, you can refer to Kotlin's excellent documentation to get you started with either Maven (http://mng.bz/GEYJ) or Gradle (http://mng.bz/z4vA). With Kotlin ready to run, a good place to start exploring is in how its basic features work and improve on Java.

9.2 Convenience and conciseness

Java has a reputation for being verbose. Although it retains a lot of visual similarity with Java, Kotlin relentlessly streamlines the code you have to write.

9.2.1 Starting with less

One example of its streamlined nature is the simple character, the semicolon. Kotlin doesn't require semicolons for line ending, allowing the typical newlines to stand in their place. Semicolons are allowed—and, in fact, required if you want to put multiple statements on a single line, for instance—but most often, they aren't needed.

Kotlin took advantage of its blank slate to alter other defaults that would be diffi-cult to change in Java. Although Java imports only `java.lang` by default, Kotlin pro-vides the following packages everywhere:

- `java.lang.*`
- `kotlin.*`
- `kotlin.annotation.*`
- `kotlin.collections.*`
- `kotlin.comparisons.*`
- `kotlin.io.*`
- `kotlin.ranges.*`
- `kotlin.sequences.*`
- `kotlin.text.*`
- `kotlin.jvm.*`

It's the rare program that doesn't need Collections, text, or IO, so these inclusions save a lot of needless importing.

A spot where Java's verbosity often shows up is with types—and we saw in chapter 1 how the var keyword cuts down on repetition of type information. Kotlin has had this style of type inference since the beginning, although it is far from the only source for the idea.

9.2.2 *Variables*

When introducing a variable, Kotlin even uses the same keyword as newer Java releases: var. It will infer from the expression on the right-hand side what type to use for the variable, as shown here:

```
var i = 1              ⟵————— i is of type kotlin.Int.
var s = "String"       ⟵————— s is of type kotlin.String.
```

Unlike Java, though, in Kotlin var is not just a shortcut. If you want to explicitly call out the type of the variable, var remains, but the type is added after the variable name, as shown in the next code snippet. This is sometimes referred to as a *type hint*:

```
var i: Int = 1                This assignment will fail with a compile
var s: String = "String"      error, error: type mismatch: inferred
var n: Int = "error"   ⟵——┘   type is String but Int was expected.
```

In Kotlin, var has a friend in the val keyword. Variables declared with val are immutable and cannot be written after assignment. It's the equivalent of final var in Java—a highly recommended default for any variable that isn't expected to be reas-signed. Kotlin nicely makes this safer setting just as concise as the mutable alternative, as illustrated here:

```
var i = 1
i = 2      ◁────── Reassignment is allowed to var variables.

val s = "String"
s = "boom"      ◁────── Compile error, error: val cannot be reassigned.
```

var and val are used consistently through Kotlin for variables and arguments. The theme of favoring immutability by default is also a key design factor in Kotlin that we'll see time and again throughout the language.

Once we have variables it's natural to want to compare them. Kotlin has some fresh help to give us on equality that's worth knowing about.

9.2.3 Equality

A common mistake in many Java programs is shown in the following code:

```
// Java                              Receives a string from somewhere. Note that string literals
String s = retrieveString();  ◁───   may actually be interned to the same object, giving a false
if (s == "A value") {                sense of security in the incorrect comparison.
    // ...      ◁─────── Not reached, even when same value
}                                    but separate references are used
```

We quickly learn that == in Java compares *references*, not *values*, so this doesn't do what you'd expect from many other languages.

Kotlin eliminates this quirk and treats == as value equality on common types such as String. Effectively, calls to == are equivalent to a null-safe call to equals. This optimizes for the more common programming case and avoids a huge cause of errors in Java programming, as shown next:

```
// Kotlin
var s: String = retrieveString()
if (s == "A value") {             Will be reached if the
    // ...      ◁─────────────    value of s is "A value"
}
```

On rare occasions, you may still have reason to compare references. When those cases arise, Kotlin's === (and its pair !==) gives you the behavior Java used for == and !=. Comparing variables is important, but you won't get far without needing to call other code or define your own subroutines.

9.2.4 Functions

Sometimes when speaking, we use the terms "function" and "method" interchangeably, but, in fact, Java only has methods—you can't define a reusable block of code outside of the context of a class. Although Kotlin supports all the object-oriented goodness of Java—we'll see it in an upcoming section—it also recognizes that sometimes you just want a function by itself.

Keeping to Kotlin's principle of conciseness, a minimal function definition looks like this:

```
fun doTheThing() {          fun defines a function in Kotlin. We'll
  println("Done!")          see it again when we get to defining
}                           methods attached to classes.
```

This looks a little different than the Java way of doing things, but it is still fairly recognizable. Apart from the `fun` keyword to start the declaration, the biggest difference is the lack of return type. In Kotlin if your function doesn't return anything, rather than stating `void` explicitly, you can say nothing, and the return type is treated as `Unit` (Kotlin's way of saying "no return value").

If we do want to return a value, we must state that directly, as follows:

```
fun doTheThing(): Boolean {     Declares that our function returns type Boolean
  println("Done!")
  return true         Returns our success
}
```

Functions aren't much use without taking arguments. Kotlin's syntax for that looks much like variable declaration, shown next:

```
                                 Our function now takes a
                                 single argument of type Int.
fun doTheThing(value: Int): Boolean {
  println("Done $value!")
  return true          Arguments appear within the function like
}                      locally defined variables. Here we use one
                       in Kotlin's handy string interpolation.
```

Even the simple function definition in Kotlin has a few tricks up its sleeve, though. Sometimes the order of arguments to a function can be unclear, particularly when types match between arguments, as in the following example:

```
fun coordinates(x: Int, y: Int) {
  // ...
}
```

When we call this function, we have to remember the order of the arguments—x comes before y—or risk a bug. Kotlin solves this with *named arguments*, shown next:

```
fun coordinates(x: Int, y: Int) {
  // ...
}                    Normal positional
                     call to the function      This call has the same result
coordinates(10, 20)                            despite reordering because
coordinates(y = 20, x = 10)                    we name the arguments.
```

NOTE Named arguments can't be used when calling Java functions or, conversely, when calling a Kotlin function from Java. The names of arguments aren't preserved in the bytecode to allow this. Also, altering argument names can be considered a breaking API change in Kotlin code, where in Java, only changes to type, number, or ordering of arguments will cause trouble.

Sometimes it's not necessary to pass all arguments to a function— reasonable defaults exist. In Java we accommodate this with multiple method overloads taking varying sets of arguments. Although this is supported in Kotlin too, we can use a more direct approach for default values, as shown here:

```
fun callOtherServices(value: Int, retry: Boolean = false) {
  // ...
}

callOtherServices(10)
```

| retry in the function is false,
thanks to the default value.

Instead of needing to provide two definitions of callOtherServices—one with a single argument, another with the two—we can keep all the related bits in one function without boilerplate.

Another common case that Kotlin provides syntax for is single-line functions, as shown in the following code. These provide encapsulation and a name to a particular calculation or check. Kotlin supports this as part of its trend toward conciseness via an alternate declaration for such short functions:

```
fun checkCondition(n: Int) = n == 42
```

This format is shorter not only for the lack of curly braces in favor of the single = but also because of type inference. Return types may be excluded, and Kotlin will infer the type of the expression automatically.

This feature hints at a deeper part of Kotlin's design, which is its support for *first-class functions*. Functions in Kotlin may be passed as arguments, stored in variables and properties, and returned from other functions. Although Kotlin isn't considered a functional programming language, support for first-class functions allows Kotlin to benefit from many common patterns in functional programming.

Assigning a function to a variable can take a few different forms, depending on the source of your function. If we've previously declared the function, we can use the :: operator to reference it by name:

```
fun checkCondition(n: Int) = n == 42
val check = ::checkCondition
```

Kotlin also has *lambda expression* syntax to create an anonymous function on the fly:

```
val anotherCheck = { n: Int -> n > 100 }
```

Regardless of how it was assigned, references to functions can be invoked as if the variable name were the function's own name. Alternatively, an invoke function is available, as illustrated here, if that's clearer:

```
   println(check(42))                      ◄────────┐
┌─▷ println(anotherCheck.invoke(42))                │
```

Runs our lambda to see if we're greater than 100 and prints false

Runs our previously fun declared checkCondition captured in the check variable and prints true

We're not limited to assigning functions to local variables. We can pass them to other functions as arguments like any other value. This is one of the key properties of languages with first-class functions.

As we've seen previously, Kotlin requires arguments to declare their type. Functions are no exception, and there's a specific syntax for expressing the type of functions, shown here:

callsAnother takes an argument that is a function taking an Int and returning nothing.

```
fun callsAnother(funky: (Int) -> Unit) { ◄─┘
    funky(42)  ◄──────┐
}                     │
```

callsAnother invokes the function it is passed.

We can invoke callsAnother, passing a lambda whose function type matches.

```
callsAnother({ n: Int -> println("Got $n") })  ◄──────┘
```

A function type is composed of two parts separated by an ->—its list of arguments in () and the return type. The list of argument types can be empty, but the return type cannot be excluded. If the function you are passing doesn't return anything, its type must be specified as Unit.

> **NOTE** When a lambda takes a single argument and the type can be inferred, the identifier it can be used, excluding the need both for a specific name and for the -> at the start of the lambda.

Function arguments must specify the types they expect callers to pass, but Kotlin does save some typing for the caller by applying type inference to lambdas. The following are all allowed forms of our earlier invocation of callsAnother with progressively less and less explicit typing:

The original invocation of callsAnother with our lambda types fully specified

```
   callsAnother({ n: Int -> println("Got $n") })  ◄──┘
   callsAnother({ n -> println("Got $n") })  ◄──────┐
┌─▷ callsAnother({ println("Got $it") })            │
```

The pattern of passing a single parameter to lambda is so common that Kotlin provides special support with an implicit it parameter.

Kotlin can infer that n must be an Int because that's what callsAnother needs.

Kotlin has one more trick when passing lambdas as arguments. If a function call's last argument is a lambda, that lambda may appear after the parentheses. If the only argument to a function is a lambda, you don't even have to use parentheses at all! The following three calls are all identical:

```
callsAnother({ println("Got $it") })
callsAnother() { println("Got $it") }
callsAnother { println("Got $it") }
```

We'll dig into more details of functional programming with Kotlin in chapter 15, but let's now look at how Kotlin puts all this functional goodness to use in improving a point of frequent discontent in Java—Collections.

9.2.5 *Collections*

Collections are one of the most common data structures in programs. Java's standard Collection library, from the earliest versions, has provided a lot of power and flexibility. But constraints of both the language and backward compatibility often end up with more verbose, ceremony-laden code, especially when compared to scripting languages like Python or functional languages like Haskell. Recent Java releases have improved the situation dramatically—see chapter 1's coverage of Collections factories and appendix B for streams—but difficulties from Java's original collection design remain with us today.

Naturally, Kotlin learned from these mistakes and from day one had a seamless collection experience. Standard functions, shown next, have always existed in Kotlin for creating the most common types of Collections—a feature that arrived in Java only with version 9:

Create lists with the inferred types kotlin.collections.List<String> and kotlin.collections.MutableList<String>

Create maps with the inferred types kotlin.collections.Map<String, Int> and kotlin.collections.MutableMap<String, Int>. Note the built-in syntax for defining maps with the to keyword.

```
val readOnlyList = listOf("a", "b", "c")
val mutableList  = mutableListOf("a", "b", "c")

val readOnlyMap = mapOf("a" to 1, "b" to 2, "c" to 3)
val mutMap = mutableMapOf("a" to 1, "b" to 2, "c" to 3)

val readOnlySet = setOf(0, 1, 2)
val mutableMap  = mutableSetOf(1, 2, 3)
```

Create sets with the inferred types kotlin.collections.Set<String> and kotlin.collections.MutableSet<String>

The default functions return read-only copies of their Collections—a great default choice for performance and correctness. You have to explicitly ask for the `mutable` flavor to get a Collection with the interfaces for modification. Kotlin again aims to protect you from whole classes of bugs by nudging your code toward immutability as the easier, shorter option.

You may have noted that the inferred types for these Collections differ from the standard Java counterparts—though similarly named, they live in the `kotlin.collections` package. Kotlin defines its own hierarchy of collection interfaces, as shown in figure 9.1, but, under the covers, reuses the implementations from the JDK. This allows for cleaner APIs with the `kotlin.collections` interfaces, while preserving the ability to pass our Collections across to Java code, because the implementations also support the `java.util` collection interfaces.

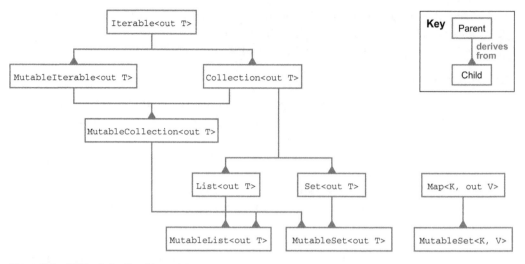

Figure 9.1   Kotlin Collection hierarchy

These Collections participate in all the standard Java interfaces and patterns. You can iterate over them with `for ... in` as follows:

```
val l = listOf("a", "b", "c")

for (s in l) {
  println(s)
}
```

However, the `for` loop to iterate over a Collection is the only operation directly in the language. A lot of other work on Collections happens over and over, and Kotlin's Collections have a ton of features using the first-class functions we saw in the previous section. These features almost always return a new Collection rather than mutating the Collection they are called against. You may have encountered this style of Collection code in Java since the release of lambdas and streams, which share many common ideas.

Often we take a value in one Collection and transform each element to a different value based on some calculation. `map` does exactly this using the function we pass in, as follows:

```
val l = listOf("a", "b", "c")
val result = l.map { it.toUpperCase() }   ⟵──┐  result contains a list
                                              of "A", "B", "C".
```

Another common operation is to remove certain values from a Collection before doing further processing. `filter` expects a lambda that returns a `Boolean`. This lambda is called a *predicate*, and `filter` calls the predicate repeatedly to decide which elements to return in a new Collection, as shown next:

```
val l = listOf("a", "b", "c")
val result = l.filter { it != "b" }   ⟵────  result contains a list of "a", "c".
```

If you care only whether a Collection fulfills certain conditions but you don't need the elements, the `all`, `any`, and `none` functions are just what you need. These avoid copying data and will return early where possible (i.e., after the first `false` for `all()`), as shown here:

```
val l = listOf("a", "b", "c")
val all  = l.all  { it.length == 1 }        all == true
val any  = l.any  { it.length == 2 }        any == false
val none = l.none { it == "a" }
                                            none == false
```

You can build a map from a list with the functions `associateWith` and `associateBy`. `associateWith` expects the Collection element to be the key in the resulting map. `associateBy` assumes instead the Collection element is the value in the map. If duplicates are encountered with either of these functions, the last calculated value wins, as illustrated in the next code snippet:

```
val l = listOf("!", "-", "--", "---")

val resultWith = l.associateWith { it.length }
val resultBy   = l.associateBy   { it.length }
```

resultWith contains mapOf("!" to 1, "-" to 1, "--" to 2, "---" to 3).

resultBy contains mapOf(1 to "-", 2 to "--", 3 to "---").

This just scratches the surface of the rich set of functions in Kotlin for working with Collections. These functions can be chained together to allow expressive, concise descriptions of operations over a Collection. The documentation is excellent with examples that walk through other topics like grouping, sorting, aggregating, and copying. See https://kotlinlang.org/docs/collections-overview.html.

Kotlin's focus on maintaining a tight flow between bits of code carries to other fundamental features, too. A preference for expressions over statements is another way Kotlin smooths the edges in your code.

9.2.6 *Express yourself*

Among the first structures we encounter when learning to program is `if`. In Java, `if` is a statement used to control the flow of execution through your program. Kotlin also uses `if` for this purpose, but rather than a *statement* that is just executed, `if` is an *expression* that returns a value, as shown here:

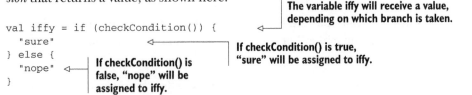

```
val iffy = if (checkCondition()) {
    "sure"
} else {
    "nope"
}
```

The variable iffy will receive a value, depending on which branch is taken.

If checkCondition() is true, "sure" will be assigned to iffy.

If checkCondition() is false, "nope" will be assigned to iffy.

Like with any other variable assignment, Kotlin allows us to infer the type. In this case, the final line of each branch is accounted for in determining the type.

`if` expressions are powerful enough that Kotlin actually dropped a feature that Java inherited from C—the ternary `condition ? "sure" : "nope"` operator. The ternary shortens code, but it also has a reputation for compressing to the point of losing readability. Although it has slightly more characters, Kotlin's version is more readable in many cases, as shown in the next code sample, and naturally converts to a multiline if should the logic grow further:

```
val myTurn = if (condition) "sure" else "nope"
```

In chapter 1, we discussed the introduction of *switch expressions* to Java. This is another case where Kotlin's design preceded similar enhancements in Java. Kotlin doesn't use the traditional C-style switch syntax at all but supports a powerful alternative with the keyword when, as follows:

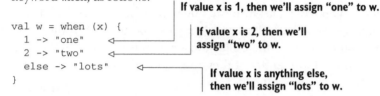

```
val w = when (x) {
  1 -> "one"      ◁————   If value x is 1, then we'll assign "one" to w.
  2 -> "two"      ◁————   If value x is 2, then we'll assign "two" to w.
  else -> "lots"  ◁————   If value x is anything else,
}                         then we'll assign "lots" to w.
```

when supports a number of other very useful forms. With the in keyword, you can check for membership in a Collection, as follows:

```
val valid = listOf(1, 2, 3)
val invalid = listOf(4, 5, 6)

val w = when (x) {             Checks whether x is in each
  in valid   -> "valid"        Collection—the equivalent of calling
  in invalid -> "invalid"      valid.contains(x) and invalid.contains(x)
  else       -> "unknown"
}
```

Kotlin also has language-level support for numeric ranges, which plays nicely with when and in, too, as shown next:

```
val w = when (x) {           The .. syntax defines an inclusive range,
  in 1..3 -> "valid"         so this code is equivalent to the prior
  in 4..6 -> "invalid"       list-based example.
  else    -> "unknown"
}
```

It's worth noting that the left-hand condition of when can be any valid expression as long the type matches what's required. For example, function calls can be used, a nice trick for clarifying complex conditions, as follows:

```
fun theBest() = 1              Because the return value from theBest is used
fun okValues() = listOf(2, 3)  directly, it must return an Int to be compared
                               to incoming.
val message = when (incoming) {
  theBest()     -> "best!"  ◁————   Because the return value from okValues is
  in okValues() -> "ok!"    ◁————   used with an in, it must be a Collection.
  else          -> "nope"
}
```

A final point on when, if you aren't already convinced of its superpowers, is safety. All of our examples provide an else case. Removing any of those causes a compilation error complaining we haven't handled all the cases, shown here:

```
error: 'when' expression must be exhaustive, add necessary 'else' branch
```

Kotlin has one other trick for replacing a statement construct in Java with an expression—error handling with try catch, as shown in the following code:

A function call that might fail
```
val message = try {
    dangerousCall()
    "fine"
} catch (e: Exception) {
    "oops"
}
```
message will be assigned "fine" if we get past the dangerous call.

message will be assigned "oops" if our dangerous call throws an exception.

This avoids the awkward construct of declaring a variable outside the try catch which all paths inside must remember to set properly. Not only is this shorter to write, but it's safer, too, because the compiler can guarantee the assignment is valid.

Although both Kotlin and Java have adopted aspects of functional programming, they are at heart object-oriented languages. Next we'll examine defining classes and objects in Kotlin.

9.3 A different view of classes and objects

Kotlin's classes provide very similar functionality to Java, starting with the keyword class. But, just as we've seen elsewhere, the code is different, with an emphasis on conciseness and convenience.

For starters, Kotlin doesn't use the new keyword for creating instances of a class. Instead, its syntax is more akin to invoking a function using the class name, as shown here:

```
val person = Person()
```

Kotlin doesn't really have fields in the same way that Java does. Instead, our friends val and var show up when declaring *properties* within the class. These can be initialized inline in the same fashion as Java fields, as follows:

```
import java.time.LocalDate

class Person {
    val birthdate = LocalDate.of(1996, 1, 23)
    var name = "Name Here"
}
```
The read-only property birthdate

The mutable property name

> **NOTE** As we saw in chapter 4, fields are present at JVM level, so Kotlin's properties are actually converted into field access in the bytecode. However, at the language level, it is better to think in terms of properties.

A major source of boilerplate in Java classes is getter and setter methods for fields. Kotlin addresses this by providing accessors for properties automatically by default. To take it a step further, Kotlin also allows us to use those accessor methods as if we were accessing a field in Java, as shown next:

```
println("Hi ${person.name}. " +
        "You were born on ${person.birthdate}")
person.name = "Somebody Else"
// person.birthdate = LocalDate.of(2000, 1, 1)
```

Prints Hi Name here. You were born on 1996-01-23.

val properties cannot be set.

var properties also get setters, which can be used with =.

A big topic in class designing is visibility of state data, especially as it relates to *encapsulation*. Kotlin takes a slightly controversial move of defaulting visibility to `public`, which differs from Java's *package-protected* default. Freely exposing all properties isn't considered good practice, but Kotlin's designers found that `public` had to be stated far more often in real code, so choosing it as the default has a major slimming effect.

Kotlin supports the following four levels of visibility, most of which align with their Java counterparts:

- *private*—Visible only within the current class or file for top-level functions
- *protected*—Visible within the class and child classes
- *internal*—Visible to the set of code you compile together
- *public*—Visible to everyone

For example, if we wanted to make `birthdate` private, it would look like this:

```
class Person {
  private val birthdate = LocalDate.of(1996, 1, 23)
  var name = "Name Here"
}
```

Because Kotlin exposes only properties, not fields, to the programmer, it opens the possibility for *delegated properties*. When followed with the `by` keyword, a property can provide a custom implementation of its getting and setting behavior. This practice will show up in a number of advanced techniques in later chapters.

Several useful delegates come with the standard library. For instance, it's not uncommon when debugging to want to know when a value was changed. `Delegates.observable` provides just such a hook, as shown here:

```
import kotlin.properties.Delegates

class Person {
  var name: String by Delegates.observable("Name Here") {
      prop, old, new -> println("Name changed from $old to $new")
  }
}
```

The value passed when calling `Delegates.observable` is treated as the initial value of the property. The lambda we pass to `Delegates.observable` will be invoked after the backing property value has been changed. A handle to the property itself, along with the old and new values, is passed into the lambda for us to work with. Here we simply print out what changed.

Like Java, Kotlin supports constructors for creating instances of our classes, and, in fact, Kotlin actually has a few different forms for construction. The first of these is declaring a *primary constructor* at the very top with your class name, as shown next. Kotlin uses this as an alternative location where you can specify your properties as well:

```
class Person(
  val birthdate: LocalDate,
  var name: String) {

}

val person = Person(LocalDate.of(1996, 1, 23),
                    "Somebody Else")
```

val and var in the primary constructor create properties so we don't need to declare them later.

Because we didn't provide defaults, parameters must be passed at construction.

If you need visibility modifiers or annotations on a constructor, you can use a longer syntax using the `constructor` keyword. For instance, if we wanted to hide our constructor from the world, we can do it like this:

```
class Person private constructor(
  val birthdate: LocalDate,
  var name: String) {
}
```

If we want to run other logic during all object construction, Kotlin uses the `init` keyword like so:

```
class Person(
  val birthdate: LocalDate,
  var name: String) {

  init {
    if (birthdate.year < 2000) {
      println("So last century")
    }
  }
}
```

init runs after we've assigned the properties from the constructor so we can access them in our code.

A class may have multiple `init` blocks, and they are run in the order in which they're defined in the class, as shown here. Properties defined in the class body are accessible to `init` blocks only after the definition:

```
class Person(
  val birthdate: LocalDate,
  var name: String) {
```

```
init {
  // println(nameParts)     ◁────┐  Fails to compile with error: variable
}                                   'nameParts' must be initialized

val nameParts: List<String> = name.split(" ")

init {
  println(nameParts)   ◁────── Works as expected, and prints out a list
}
}
```

If we need additional constructors, we define them in the class body with the constructor keyword, as follows. These are referred to as *secondary constructors*:

```
class Person(
  val birthdate: LocalDate,
  var name: String) {                          When a class has a primary
                                               constructor, secondary constructors
  constructor(name: String)                    must call it (directly or through other
    : this(LocalDate.of(0, 1, 1), name) {  ◁──┘  secondary constructors) via this.
  }
}
```

> **NOTE** Many cases in Java where multiple constructor overrides exist for supplying defaults can be handled in Kotlin with default argument values instead.

Although a class with only properties can be of use, most of the time, our classes have other functionality, too. The next code sample uses the familiar function syntax we've already seen earlier in the chapter to add a method to the class:

```
class Person(
  val birthdate: LocalDate,
  var name: String) {

  fun isBirthday(): Boolean {
    val today = LocalDateTime.now().toLocalDate()
    return today == birthdate
  }
}
```

As mentioned before, functions in Kotlin default to public visibility. If we want to hide a function, precede it with the desired access modifier like this:

```
class Person(
  val birthdate: LocalDate,
  var name: String) {
                                     isBirthday is available for anyone
  fun isBirthday(): Boolean {  ◁──┘  who can see the Person class.
    return today() == birthdate
  }
```

```
private fun today(): LocalDate {
  return LocalDateTime.now().toLocalDate()
}
}
```

today is available only
within the Person class.

Another key part of object-oriented programming is *inheritance*. Kotlin doesn't have the extends keyword but instead expresses inheritance via the familiar : syntax we've seen in type declarations previously and shown next:

```
class Child(birthdate: LocalDate, name: String)
  : Person(birthdate, name) {
}
```

Calling to the superclass constructor

Parameters to the Child constructor. Note these are not marked val and var, so they don't collide with the parent properties but are available as local variables to pass to the superclass constructor.

Inheritance requires one other change to the Parent class. To encourage subclassing only where we intend and plan for it, Kotlin classes are *closed* by default. If a class may be subclassed, it must use the open keyword, as shown in the next code sample. This is the inverse of the situation in Java, where classes are open by default and use final to indicate that they may *not* be subclassed:

```
open class Person(
  val birthdate: LocalDate,
  var name: String) {
  //...
}
```

open precedes the class keyword along with visibility modifiers.

The same closed-by-default principle applies to methods. The parent class must declare a method to be overridden open, and overrides must be marked with override in the child, as follows:

```
open class Person(
  val birthdate: LocalDate,
  var name: String) {

  open fun isBirthday(): Boolean {
    return today() == birthdate
  }

  private fun today() : LocalDate {
    return LocalDateTime.now().toLocalDate()
  }
}

class Child(birthdate: LocalDate, name: String)
  : Person(birthdate, name) {

  override fun isBirthday(): Boolean {
    val itsToday = super.isBirthday()
    if (itsToday) {
      println("YIPPY!!")
    }
```

The Person class declares that the isBirthday function can be overridden in subclasses.

The Child class must explicitly mark its method as an override.

Child can call the parent implementation of the isBirthday with super.

```
        return itsToday
    }
}
```

Like Java, Kotlin allows only a single base class, but classes may inherit multiple inter-faces, as shown in the next code. Kotlin's interfaces allow the default implementations of functions, much like Java has since version 8:

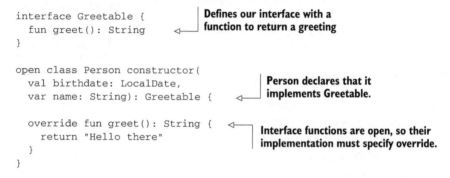

```
interface Greetable {          Defines our interface with a
    fun greet(): String        function to return a greeting
}

open class Person constructor(
    val birthdate: LocalDate,       Person declares that it
    var name: String): Greetable {  implements Greetable.

    override fun greet(): String {    Interface functions are open, so their
        return "Hello there"          implementation must specify override.
    }
}
```

In typical Kotlin style, implementing an interface uses a concise form that looks a lot like what we already use for extending a base class—no more remembering whether to use extends or implements like in Java.

9.3.1 *Data classes*

Although these basic constructs allow us to make rich object models in Kotlin, some-times you just want a container to pass data around. Kotlin provides support for this with *data classes.*

> **NOTE** We met Java's new record capability in chapter 3, and Kotlin data classes are very similar to Java records in some ways.

Kotlin already makes the property side of this seamless, but the equality issues remain with standard classes—the default equals and hashCode implementations are based on object references, rather than the values of its properties.

When we declare a type as a data class, though, Kotlin will create the equality functions we'd want (unless we provide an implementation ourselves explicitly), as follows:

```
class PlainPoint(val x: Int, val y: Int)

val pl1 = PlainPoint(1, 1)
val pl2 = PlainPoint(1, 1)
                                 The default equals compares reference
                                 equality, so this prints false.
println(pl1 == pl2)

data class DataPoint(val x: Int, val y: Int)
```

```
val pd1 = DataPoint(1, 1)
val pd2 = DataPoint(1, 1)                    With Kotlin's data class
                                             implementation, this prints true.
println(pd1 == pd2)     ◁──────────┘
```

Data classes must have a primary constructor with a least one val or var. They can't be open, because it's impossible at compile time for Kotlin to correctly generate the equality functions if child classes might exist for the type. Data classes also aren't allowed as inner classes. Apart from these and a handful of more exotic constraints, though, they are normal classes on which you can implementation functions or interfaces to your heart's content.

A last feature that folks coming from Java might look for in classes is declaring a function that belongs not to instances but to the class as a whole. Kotlin chose not to support static, though—functions are either free-floating or are members of a type.

However, the convenience of associating functions with a class can't be denied, and Kotlin provides similar functionality via its companion object. This syntax declares a singleton object that lives within the class. object declarations in Kotlin are full objects with typical properties and functions. This avoids weird edges that static methods suffer from in Java (i.e., testing difficulties), while retaining the convenience of keeping functionality associated with the class.

A common use case for these functions is factory methods, where you want to keep the constructors of your objects private but allow controlled creation by more specifically named methods, as shown here:

```
class ShyObject private constructor(val name: String) {   ◁──┐   ShyObject declares its
                                                                constructor private so
  companion object {                                            no one outside the class
    fun create(name: String): ShyObject {   ◁──┐               can use it.
      return ShyObject(name)
    }                                            Our factory method inside the companion
  }                                              object is part of the ShyObject class, so it
}                                                can access the private constructor.
```

```
┌─▷ ShyObject.create("The Thing")
│
│ Outside of our class, functions on ShyObject's
│ companion are available directly via its class name.
```

As a pragmatic alternative to Java, Kotlin brings a lot of convenience and boilerplate reduction to the table. But it doesn't stop there, as we'll see in the next section.

9.4   *Safety*

Kotlin is built on top of the JVM, and so it has no choice but to live within some design constraints that really come from the design of the virtual machine. For example, the JVM specification defines null as a value that can be assigned to any variable of reference type.

Despite these issues, the Kotlin language seeks to address some common code safety concerns to try to minimize the inherited pain and suffering. This manifests itself by elevating a number of Java code patterns to language features to make your code safer by default.

9.4.1 *Null safety*

Among the most common Java exceptions is the `NullPointerException`. This happens when we try to access a variable or field that should have contained an object but instead was `null`. Nulls have been referred to by Tony Hoare, the original creator of the Quicksort algorithm, as his "billion dollar mistake" (see https://qconlondon.com/london-2009/qconlondon.com/london-2009/speaker/Tony+Hoare.html), given his role in introducing the `null` reference in ALGOL.

Over its history, Java has developed several different approaches to provide protection against `null`s. The `Optional` type lets you always have a concrete object, while still indicating a "missing" value without resorting to `null`. The `@NotNull` and `@Nullable` annotations, supported by many different validation and serialization frameworks, can ensure that values aren't unexpectedly `null` at key points in our applications.

As you might expect, Kotlin has taken these common patterns and baked them right into the language itself. Let's revisit our earlier example of assigning variables. How do they behave when combined with `null`s?

```
val i: Int = null          Trying to assign null to these
val s: String = null       types will fail to compile.
```

Both assignments give a compilation error, `error: null can not be a value of a non-null type Int`. Although those `Int` and `String` type declarations look like Java's, they, in fact, disallow `null` values.

> **NOTE** Kotlin has made nullability part of its type system. The Kotlin type `String` is *not* actually the same as the Java type `String` that allows `null`.

For a Kotlin variable to allow `null`, we must state it explicitly by adding a suffix of ? to the type as follows:

```
val i: Int? = null          Changing our types to Int? and
val s: String? = null       String? will tell Kotlin to allow nulls.
```

> **NOTE** Whenever possible, declare your variables and arguments with non-null types. You can rest assured that Kotlin is protecting you from those `Null-PointerException` headaches.

We can't always avoid `null`s, though. Perhaps we're interacting with Java code, or our classes weren't designed with `null` safety in mind. Even once we've dipped our toes into the dangers of nullability, Kotlin still does its best to inform us of the risks, like this:

```
val s: String? = null      ⟵  Creates a nullable variable
println(s.length)          ⟵  Attempts to access a property on that variable
```

Kotlin recognizes the dereference in calling `s.length` is potentially unsafe and refuses to compile with `error: only safe (?.) or non-null asserted (!!.) calls are allowed` on a nullable receiver of type `String?`.

The first option Kotlin suggests is to correct this to the safe operator `?.`. This operator examines the object its being applied to. If the object is `null`, it returns `null` instead of making the further function call, like so:

```
val s: String? = null
println(s?.length)         ⟵——— ?. results in printing the value null.
```

The safe operator returns early, so it works fine, even with a nested chain of calls. Any point along the way in our following example can safely return a `null` and the whole expression will just turn to `null`, as shown here:

```
                                              A data class that allows for
data class Node(val parent: Node?, val value: String) ⟵—┘ an optional parent node

                              Retrieves a Node from somewhere
val node = getNode()    ⟵——┘
node.parent?.parent?.parent  ⟵——— Sees whether node has a great-grandparent node
```

This may be convenient, but `?.` potentially hides data issues. If we got a `null` back on our previous great-grandparent check, we can't assure which level of our hierarchy it came from without further inspection.

The second option for our compilation failure, (`error: only safe (?.) or non-null asserted (!!.) calls are allowed on a nullable receiver of type String?.`) is using `!!` on the variable. This operator forces Kotlin to see whether the object is `null` and will raise the familiar `NullPointerException` if the value is `null`, as shown here:

```
val s: String? = null
println(s!!.length)      ⟵——— Throws a NullPointerException
```

Although it should be needed less often, we can still check whether a variable is `null`. In fact, Kotlin can often notice such checks and let us avoid further `?.` or `!!`, like this:

```
Checks
for null   val s: String? = null
in all                          Because we know that s
cases  ⤷ if (s != null) {       isn't null, it can be safely
            println(s.length)  ⟵——┘ referenced.
         }
```

What we've seen here is actually a deeper feature of Kotlin called *smart casting*, which is worth looking at more closely in its own right.

9.4.2 Smart casting

Although good object-oriented design tries to avoid directly checking the type of objects, sometimes it's necessary. Data formats at the edges of our system may be loose about types (i.e., JSON) and often outside our control. At other times, we have plugin systems that must dynamically probe for capabilities of an object.

Kotlin embraces this need and takes it a step further in how the compiler supports the common patterns. To start, Kotlin uses the `is` operator to check an object's type as follows:

```
val s: Any = "Hello"
if (s is String) {
    println(s.toUpperCase())
}
```

Any is the equivalent of Java's Object type—the base type for all objects.

Checks whether s contains a String instance

Uses the variable s as a String. toUpperCase wouldn't be available if the compiler treated it as type Any still within the branch.

If you're familiar with Java's `instanceof` construct, this code appears to miss a crucial step—we look to see whether s is a `String`, but then we don't cast it before treating it as a `String`. Fortunately, Kotlin has us covered. Within the `if` block where the compiler can ensure we have a `String`, we may use s as a `String` without explicitly casting. This is known as *smart casting*.

> **NOTE** Java has a new feature called *pattern matching* that is being slowly rolled out as part of Project Amber. The first piece of it applies to `instanceof` and provides some of the same benefits as smart casting. We will discuss pattern matching in more detail in chapter 18.

Kotlin's smart casting functionality is allowed within an `if` conditional as well, as shown next:

```
val s: Any = "Hello"
if (s is String && s.toUpperCase() == "HELLO") {
    println("Got something")
}
```

Kotlin can ensure the type from our check on the left-hand side of the && so it can safely uppercase without casting.

Constraints exist around where smart casting can kick in. In particular, it won't work with `var` properties on a class. This protects us against the property being mutated concurrently to a different compatible subtype after the smart cast check has been performed but before the following block executes.

Even if Kotlin can't do it directly, we may still cast to the type we expect—it's just a little less convenient, as shown here:

```
class Example(var s: Any) {
    fun checkIt() {
        if (s is String) {
            val cast = s as String
            println(cast.toUpperCase())
        }
    }
}
```

Assumes s is defined in a way that we can't smart cast

as casts to the expected type.

When we use `as`, we're back to the same spot as in Java when we cast. We'll see `ClassCastException` if the types aren't actually compatible. Kotlin does provide the following alternative if we would prefer allowing nullability into the picture instead of exceptions:

```
val cast: String? = s as? String
if (cast != null) {
  println(cast.toUpperCase())
}
```

as? attempts the cast but won't throw. Note also that the resulting type is String? *not* String.

If s couldn't be cast, the variable will be null instead.

A lot of Kotlin's power comes from taking a fresh look at the common, practical coding that Java developers have been doing for years. One area where the language provides more than just polish and protection, though, is in concurrency. Kotlin provides a technique called coroutines, which can be thought of as an alternative to the classical threading approaches that are most widely used in Java.

9.5 Concurrency

As we discussed in chapter 5, since its very first versions the JVM has supported the `Thread` class as a model of operating-system-managed threads. The thread model is well understood, but it comes with many problems.

> **NOTE** Although threads are so deeply embedded in the Java language and ecosystem that it would be almost impossible to remove them, moving to a new, non-Java language allows us to potentially reimagine the concurrency primitives that the language might use.

Although Kotlin as a JVM language still exposes threads, it also introduces another construct called *coroutines*. At the simplest level, a coroutine can be thought of as a lighter-weight thread. These are implemented and scheduled within the runtime instead of at the operating system level, making them much less resource intensive. Spinning up thousands of coroutines isn't a problem at all, where similar counts of threads would grind a system to a halt.

> **NOTE** We'll meet Java's take on coroutines in chapter 18 when we discuss Project Loom.

Part of Kotlin's support for coroutines is directly in the language (`suspend` functions), but to use coroutines practically requires an additional library, `kotlin-coroutine-core`. We'll see a lot more about introducing these sorts of dependencies in chapter 11, but for now the addition would look like this in Maven:

```
<dependency>
    <groupId>org.jetbrains.kotlinx</groupId>
    <artifactId>kotlinx-coroutines-core</artifactId>
    <version>1.6.0</version>
</dependency>
```

The equivalent in Kotlin-flavored Gradle follows:

```
dependencies {
    implementation("org.jetbrains.kotlinx:kotlinx-coroutines-core:1.6.0")
}
```

In Java a thread is started by handing it an object that implements the Runnable interface. Coroutines in Kotlin also need a way to receive the code to run, but instead they use the language's lambda syntax.

A coroutine is always started in a *scope*, which controls how the coroutine will be scheduled and run. We'll start with the simplest option, which is GlobalScope, a scope that exists for the entire duration of your application. GlobalScope has a launch function we call with a lambda to get ourselves started, as shown next:

```
import kotlinx.coroutines.GlobalScope        Imports for the coroutine
import kotlinx.coroutines.launch             function and object we'll use

fun main() {                                 Starts a new coroutine in the GlobalScope,
    GlobalScope.launch {   ⭠───              which lives as long as our program does
        println("Inside!")
    }                                         Back outside of our coroutine, we'll
    println("Outside")    ⭠───               print to see that main still runs.
}
```

When we run this example, most often you'll simply see it output the following:

```
Outside
```

Why isn't our coroutine working? We expect at some point to see Inside printed as well. Looking closer, though, we can spot the problem if we think about the sequence of events. main starts up our program. We then launch our coroutine to run asynchronously. Following that, we print our Outside message, and then the program is finished. When main is done, the program exits, regardless what coroutines may be waiting to run.

To get the result we wanted, we need to introduce a pause before the program finishes. This could be done with a loop or asking for user input at the console. We'll just use a Thread.sleep(1000) to give enough time for everything to settle, like this:

```
import kotlinx.coroutines.GlobalScope
import kotlinx.coroutines.launch

fun main() {
    GlobalScope.launch {   ⭠──── Starts our coroutine again
        println("Inside!")
    }
    println("Outside")
    Thread.sleep(1000)     ⭠──── Gives the coroutine time to run
}
```

Now we'll see output with both messages, although the order is potentially nondeterministic, depending on how fast the coroutine starts up and what the main thread is doing.

At a high level, this doesn't look much different from using threads to get similar concurrent execution of code. But the underlying implementation requires fewer operating system resources (each coroutine doesn't have its own execution stack and local storage) and allows safety for operations like cancelling a coroutine.

To see this in action, we can capture a handle to the coroutine with the return value of `launch`. This coroutine object presents a `cancel` function, which we can call immediately if we want, as shown here:

```
import kotlinx.coroutines.GlobalScope
import kotlinx.coroutines.delay
import kotlinx.coroutines.launch                    Captures the coroutine
                                                    object returned by launch

fun main() {
    val co = GlobalScope.launch {        ◁───      Inside of coroutines, we can call
        delay(1000)                      ◁─────    delay to wait a period of time.
        println("Inside!")
    }
    co.cancel()
    println("Outside")
    Thread.sleep(2000)  ◁───   Wait as long as you like here—you'll
                               never see the coroutine output.
}
```

Cancels the coroutine immediately →

This code will safely stop the coroutine and print only `Outside`. This is a marked contrast to the `stop()` method on `java.lang.Thread` which was deprecated long ago due to being hopelessly unsafe, as we discussed in chapter 5.

Why can coroutines accomplish this safely when threads can't? The key is the `delay` function. Its declaration is marked with a special modifier: `suspend`. Kotlin knows to treat `suspend` functions as safe spots in coroutine execution for operations like switching to another task or looking for cancellations. This is known as *cooperative multitasking,* and it's only because the code inside our coroutine "cooperates" in its calls to suspend functions that it can be cancelled.

This cooperation gives benefits beyond just the ability to safely cancel. For example, Kotlin understands when one coroutine (parent) starts another coroutine (child). Cancelling the parent automatically cancels the child coroutines without additional management on our part, as shown next:

```
import kotlinx.coroutines.GlobalScope
import kotlinx.coroutines.coroutineScope
import kotlinx.coroutines.delay
import kotlinx.coroutines.launch                    Starts our parent coroutine as before

fun main() {                                        Starts two child coroutines. coroutineScope
    val co = GlobalScope.launch {    ◁───           associates those to the enclosing scope—in
        coroutineScope {             ◁─────         this case, our global coroutine.
            delay(1000)
```

```
        println("First")
    }
    coroutineScope {
        delay(1000)
        println("Second")
    }
}
⌐> co.cancel()
    Thread.sleep(2000)
}
```

Starts two child coroutines. coroutineScope associates those to the enclosing scope—in this case, our global coroutine.

Cancels the parent coroutine

Again, we can wait here, but we won't see any output.

If you've seen the implementation necessary in Java to accomplish this sort of coordination, the value Kotlin brings here is pretty apparent.

Coroutines are a great example of how Kotlin uses its strength as a separate language with its own compiler to work with libraries to accomplish a lot of complex behavior cleanly. In fact, there's enough to coroutines that we'll be back for a deeper investigation in chapter 16.

But no language lives in a vacuum, especially on the JVM. Kotlin has seen great success and uptake because of its strong focus on interoperating with the vast world of Java code out there.

9.6   Java interoperability

As we learned in chapter 4, the class file is the center of the JVM's execution model. It should come as no surprise that the Kotlin compiler (`kotlinc`) produces class files much like `javac` does for Java, as illustrated in figure 9.2.

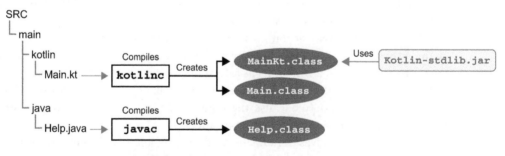

Figure 9.2   Kotlin and Java working side by side to generate class files

Basic class definitions end up looking similar between the languages, but when Kotlin provides a feature that isn't available in Java, we see more interesting differences in the generated class files. These are evidence of compiler fictions, which we discussed in chapter 8.

An example is Kotlin's top-level functions outside of classes. This isn't even directly supported in the JVM class file format. Kotlin bridges this gap by generating a class with the Kt suffix, named after its compilation file. Any top-level functions from within that file will appear in the Kt class.

NOTE You can alter the name of the generated class with the @file:Jvm-Name("AlternateClassName") annotation in your .kt file.

For example:

The filename by default influences the wrapping class name generated.

```
// Main.kt
package com.wellgrounded.kotlin

fun shout() {
  println("No classes in sight!")
}
```

Users of the function will need to import from our package as usual.

When compiled, this will produce a class file MainKt.class with our function in it. Because Java doesn't provide top-level functions itself, using the function from Java must go through that intermediate class as follows:

```
// Help.java
import com.wellgrounded.kotlin.MainKt;

public class Help {
  public static void main(String[] args) {
    MainKt.shout();
  }
}
```

Imports the class Kotlin created to wrap the function

Invokes the function through Java's static method syntax

Another key convenience in Kotlin is its built-in treatment of properties. By using a little val and var, we never end up writing screens full of boilerplate getters and setters. Using Kotlin classes from Java reveals that at the lower level, those methods have been there all along—Kotlin just wraps them up for our convenience, as shown here:

```
// Person.kt
class Person(var name: String)
```

Our property is var, so it is mutable.

```
// App.java
public class App {
  public static void main(String[] args) {
    Person p = new Person("Some Body");
    System.out.println(p.getName());

    p.setName("Somebody Else");
    System.out.println(p.getName());
  }
}
```

The Kotlin class is still instantiated with new when used from Java.

Accessing Person.name in Kotlin, is Person.getName() in Java.

Accessing Person.name = "…" in Kotlin is Person.setName("…") in Java. Note that this accessor is available only because the Person class declares the name property a var, or mutable. If name was instead declared val, only the getName() accessor would be generated.

NOTE This example reveals that under the covers, Kotlin has been doing the standard pattern of creating a private field and wrapping access to the field. Kotlin lets us use the more natural property access form without the risks of exposing fields directly.

A number of other convenient features in Kotlin don't manifest in the resulting code when used from another JVM language. Named arguments are one example— Java just doesn't have a way to address an argument by name, so that nicety remains only in Kotlin code.

At the surface level, it might seem as though default values would suffer the same fate—after all, calling from Java requires that you explicitly pass in all arguments to the function as follows:

```
// Person.kt
class Person(var name: String) {
  fun greet(words: String = "Hi there") {          The standard Kotlin default
    println(words)                                  value for the argument words
  }
}
```

```
// App.java
public class App {                                      We can't invoke with default or we
  public static void main(String[] args) {              get a compile error, reason: actual
    Person p = new Person("Some Body");                 and formal argument lists differ in
    // p.greet();                                        length.
    p.greet("Howdy");
  }
}
```

We can pass our own value.

However, an escape hatch exists, which means we don't have to abandon Kotlin's tidiness. The @JvmOverloads annotation tells Kotlin to explicitly generate the necessary variations of a function, so calling it from other JVM languages looks the same:

```
// Person.kt
class Person(var name: String) {
  @JvmOverloads                                    Annotates our Kotlin function and
  fun greet(words: String = "Hi there") {          provides the default as before
    println(words)
  }
}
```

```
// App.java
public class App {
  public static void main(String[] args) {         Works fine and prints
    Person p = new Person("Some Body");             the default "Hi there"
    p.greet();
    p.greet("Howdy");
  }                                                 Works as before and prints our
}                                                   passed alternate greeting
```

Several other annotations allow for controlling how our Kotlin code manifests at the JVM level. One we've already seen in another context is @JvmName. This applies to functions as well as files to control the eventual naming outside Kotlin. @JvmField lets us avoid property wrappers and expose a bare field to the world if required.

Last, but certainly not least, is @JvmStatic. As we've seen earlier, Kotlin will wrap top-level functions in specially named classes, which can be accessed as static methods in Java. There's one prominent static method in all Java applications, even if you avoid statics otherwise: the main method that starts an application.

If we wanted to create an application in Kotlin, you can define its `main` method with `@JvmStatic` to avoid any weird naming needs on startup like this:

```
class App {              <───── The App class we'd specify as our main class to start up.
  companion object {
    @JvmStatic fun main(args: Array<String>) {   <───┐  @JvmStatic means this function
      println("Hello from Kotlin")                    │  will present as a static method on
    }                                                 │  the containing class, not just on
  }                                                   │  the companion.
}
```

Making a change of language on a project is usually a huge step. Kotlin eases this burden, though, by leaning on standard patterns for multilanguage projects on the JVM. Unsurprisingly, there's additional tooling as well if you're using IntelliJ IDEA. We'll look at the standard project layout in chapter 11, but for now it's enough to know that projects typically embed the languages used into the directory layout like this:

```
└─  src
     └─  main
          └─  java
          │    └─  JavaCode.java
          └─  kotlin
               └─  KotlinCode.kt
```

This separation makes it easy for build tools to find what they need for all your code to coexist.

If you're using IntelliJ IDEA, the good folks at JetBrains have taken this a step further. By right-clicking on a Java file, you'll find an item convert that single file directly to Kotlin. Pasting Java code into a Kotlin file will also offer this same conversion. This makes it possible to start conversion on a system from whatever point makes the most sense—perhaps with tests or a module that isn't deeply entangled in the remainder of an app.

The IDE will walk you through additional steps as necessary, but converting does take a little more than just switching some source files. Your build tools need to know about Kotlin to compile it alongside your existing code. Also, the Kotlin standard library `kotlin-stdlib` needs to be included in your project as a dependency. We'll see more about how to manage these sorts of dependencies in chapter 11.

> **NOTE** Although IntelliJ IDEA provides a Java-to-Kotlin translation, it does not go the other direction. Its translations may also not be the ideal way to write your code in Kotlin. Keep that source control handy as always when starting a big conversion.

The fact that Kotlin compiles to class files and provides much of its additional functionality through libraries means that even including this new language in your project doesn't change that you're just running on the good old JVM.

Summary

- Kotlin is a pragmatic, attractive alternative language on the JVM.
- Kotlin draws on years of production Java use and, as a new language, made changes that Java can likely never duplicate due to backward compatibility.
- Kotlin prizes its conciseness. Familiar constructs in Java can almost always be written with less code in Kotlin.
- Safety is key for Kotlin, with `null` safety baked directly into the language to reduce `NullPointerExceptions` in production.
- Coroutines provide a compelling concurrency alternative to Java's classic threading model.
- Kotlin script (`kts`) enables scripting that previously would have been the domain of dynamic languages or shell.
- Even build scripts can be written using Kotlin, as we'll see in detail in chapter 11 when we discuss Gradle.

Clojure: A different view of programming

10

This chapter covers

- Clojure's concept of identity and state
- The Clojure REPL
- Clojure syntax, data structures, and sequences
- Clojure interoperability with Java
- Clojure macros

Clojure is a very different style of language from Java and the other languages we've studied so far. Clojure is a JVM reboot of one of the oldest programming languages—Lisp. If you're not familiar with Lisp, don't worry. We'll teach you everything you need to know about the Lisp family of languages to get you started with Clojure.

> **NOTE** Because Clojure is such a different language, it might help to have an additional, Clojure-specific resource to consult while reading this chapter. A couple of excellent books are *Clojure in Action* (Manning, 2011; https://livebook.manning.com/book/clojure-in-action) and *The Joy of Clojure* (Manning, 2014; https://livebook.manning.com/book/the-joy-of-clojure-second-edition).

In addition to its heritage of powerful programming techniques from classic Lisp, Clojure adds amazing cutting-edge technology that's very relevant to the modern Java developer. This combination makes Clojure a standout language on the JVM and an attractive choice for application development. Particular examples of Clojure's new tech are its concurrency toolkits (which we will meet in chapter 16) and data structures (which we will introduce here and expand on in chapter 15).

For the avid reader who can't wait until later, let us just say this: the concurrency abstractions enable programmers to write much safer multithreaded code than when working in Java. These abstractions can be combined with Clojure's seq concept (a different take on collections and data structures) to provide a powerful developer toolbox.

To access all of this power, some important language concepts are approached in a fundamentally different way from Java. This difference in approach makes Clojure interesting to learn, and it will probably also change the way you think about programming.

> **NOTE** Learning Clojure will help make you a better programmer in any language. Functional programming matters.

We'll kick off with a discussion of Clojure's approach to state and variables. After some simple examples, we'll introduce the basic vocabulary of the language—the *special forms* that are equivalent to keywords in languages like Java. A small number of these are used to build up the rest of the language.

We'll also delve into Clojure's syntax for data structures, loops, and functions. This will allow us to introduce sequences, which are one of Clojure's most powerful abstractions.

We'll conclude the chapter by looking at two very compelling features: tight Java integration and Clojure's amazing macro support (which is the key to Lisp's very flexible syntax). Later in the book, we'll meet more Clojure goodness (as well as Kotlin and Java examples) when we talk about advanced functional programming (chapter 15) and advanced concurrency (chapter 16).

10.1 Introducing Clojure

The basic unit of Lisp syntax consists of an expression to be evaluated. These expressions are typically represented as zero or more symbols surrounded by brackets. If the evaluation succeeds without errors, the expression is called a *form*.

> **NOTE** Clojure is compiled, not interpreted, but the compiler is very simple. Also remember that Clojure is dynamically typed, so there won't be many type-checking errors to help you—they will show up as runtime exceptions instead.

Simple examples of forms include:

```
0
(+ 3 4)
(list 42)
(quote (a b c))
```

The true core of the language has very few built-in forms (the special forms). They are the Clojure equivalent of Java keywords, but be aware of the following:

1 Clojure has a different meaning for the term *keyword*, which we'll encounter later.

2 Clojure (like all Lisps) allows the creation of constructs that are indistinguishable from built-in syntax.

When working with Clojure code, it almost never matters whether the forms you're using are special forms or library functions that are built up from them.

Let's get started with forms by looking at one of Clojure's most important conceptual differences from Java. This is the treatment of state, variables, and storage. As you can see in figure 10.1, Java (like Kotlin) has a model of memory and state that involves a variable being a "box" (really, a memory location) with contents that can change over time.

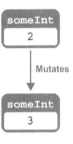

Programming languages like Java are *mutable by default*, because we are trying to alter the program state, which in Java is made up of objects. Languages that follow this model are often called *imperative languages*, as we discussed in chapter 8.

Figure 10.1 Imperative language memory use

Clojure is a little bit different. The important concept is that of a *value*. Values can be numbers, strings, vectors, maps, sets, or a number of other things. Once created, values never alter. This is really important, so we'll say it again: *once created, Clojure values can't be altered*—they're *immutable*.

> **NOTE** Immutability is a common property of languages that are used for functional programming, because it allows mathematical reasoning techniques about the properties of functions (such as the same input always giving the same output) to be used.

The imperative language model of a box that has contents that change isn't the way Clojure works. Figure 10.2 shows how Clojure deals with state and memory. It creates an association between a name and a value.

Figure 10.2   Clojure memory use

This is called *binding*, and it's done using the def special form. Let's meet the syntax for (def) here:

```
(def <name> <value>)
```

Don't worry that the syntax looks a little weird—this is entirely normal for Lisp syntax, and you'll get used to it really quickly. For now you can pretend that the brackets are arranged slightly differently and that you're calling a method like this:

```
def(<name>, <value>)
```

Let's demonstrate (def) with a time-honored example that uses the Clojure interactive environment.

10.1.1 Hello World in Clojure

If you haven't already installed Clojure, you can do so on a Mac by running this command:

```
brew install clojure/tools/clojure
```

This will install the command-line tools with brew from the clojure/tools tap. For other operating systems, instructions can be found on the clojure.org website.

> **NOTE** Windows support isn't so great for Clojure. For example, clj is still in an alpha state. Follow the instructions on the website carefully.

Once installed, you can use the clj command to start the Clojure interactive session. Or, if you built Clojure from source, change into the directory where you installed Clojure and run this command:

```
java -cp clojure.jar clojure.main
```

Either way, this brings up the user prompt for the Clojure read-evaluate-print loop (REPL). This is the interactive session, which is where you'll typically spend quite a lot of time when developing Clojure code. It looks like this:

```
$ clj
Clojure 1.10.1
user=>
```

The user=> part is the Clojure prompt for the session, which can be thought of as a bit like an advanced debugger or a command line. To exit the session (which will cause all the accumulated state in the session to be lost), use the traditional Unix sequence Ctrl-D. Let's write a "Hello World" program in Clojure:

```
user=> (def hello (fn [] "Hello world"))
#'user/hello

user=> (hello)
"Hello world"
user=>
```

In this code, you start off by binding the *identifier* hello to a value. (def) always binds identifiers (which Clojure calls *symbols*) to *values*. Behind the scenes, it will also create an object, called a *var*, that represents the binding (and the name of the symbol), as shown next:

```
(def hello (fn [] "Hello world"))
 ---  -----  --------------------
  |     |             |
  |     |            value
  |   symbol
  |
special form
```

What is the value you're binding `hello` to? It's the value

```
(fn [] "Hello world")
```

This is a function, which is a genuine value (so, therefore, immutable) in Clojure. It's a function that takes no arguments and returns the string "Hello world". The empty argument list is represented by the `[]`.

> **NOTE**   In Clojure (but not in other Lisps), square brackets indicate a linear data structure called a vector—in this case, a vector of function arguments.

After binding it, you execute it via `(hello)`. This causes the Clojure runtime to print the results of evaluating the function, which is "Hello world".

Remember that the round brackets mean "function evaluation" in Lisps, so the example basically consists of the following:

- Create a function, and bind it to the symbol `hello`.
- Call the function bound to the symbol `hello`.

At this point, you should enter the Hello World example (if you haven't already) and see that it behaves as described. Once you've done that, we can explore a little further.

10.1.2   Getting started with the REPL

The REPL allows you to enter Clojure code and execute Clojure functions. It's an interactive environment, and the results of earlier evaluations are still around. This enables a type of programming called *exploratory programming*, which basically means that you can experiment with code. In many cases the right thing to do is to play around in the REPL, building up larger and larger functions once the building blocks are correct.

> **NOTE**   Subdivision is a key technique in functional programming—breaking down a problem into smaller parts until it becomes either soluble or amenable to a reusable pattern (which may already be in the standard library).

Let's look at a bit more Clojure syntax. One of the first things to point out is that the binding of a symbol to a value can be changed by another call to `(def)`, so let's see that in action in the REPL. We'll actually use a slight variant of `(def)` called `(defn)`, as follows:

```
user=> (hello)
"Hello world"

user=> (defn hello [] "Goodnight Moon")
#'user/hello

user=> (hello)
"Goodnight Moon"
```

Notice that the original binding for hello is still in play until you change it—this is a key feature of the REPL. There is still state, in terms of which symbols are bound to which values, and that state persists between lines the user enters.

The ability to change which value a symbol is bound to is Clojure's alternative to mutating state. Rather than allowing the contents of a storage location (or "memory box") to change over time, Clojure allows a symbol to be bound to different immutable values at different points in time. Another way of saying this is that the var can point to different values during the lifetime of a program. An example can be seen in figure 10.3.

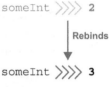

Figure 10.3   Clojure bindings changing over time

> **NOTE** This distinction between mutable state and different bindings at different times is subtle, but it's an important concept to grasp. Remember, *mutable state* means the contents of the box change, whereas *rebinding* means pointing at different boxes at different points in time.

This is in some ways similar to the Java concept of `final` references. In Java, if we say `final int`, the contents of the storage location cannot change. As ints are stored as bit patterns, which means that the value of the `int` cannot change.

However, if we say `final AtomicInteger`, the contents of the storage location once again cannot change. This case is different, though, because a variable containing an atomic integer actually holds an object reference. The atomic integer object stored in the heap can change the value it stores (whereas an `Integer` cannot), and this is true whether or not the reference to the object is final.

We've also slipped in another Clojure concept in the last code snippet—the `(defn)` "define function" *macro*. Macros are one of the key concepts of Lisp-like languages. The central idea is that there should be as little distinction between built-in constructs and ordinary code as possible.

> **NOTE** Macros allow you to create forms that behave like built-in syntax. The creation of macros is an advanced topic, but mastering their creation will allow you to produce incredibly powerful tools.

The true language primitives of the system (the special forms) can be used to build up the core of the language in such a way that you don't really notice the difference between the two.

NOTE The (defn) macro is an example of this. It's just a slightly easier way to bind a function value to a symbol (and create a suitable var, of course). It's not a special form but instead is a macro built up from the special forms (def) and (fn).

We will introduce macros properly at the end of this chapter.

10.1.3   Making a mistake

What happens if you make a mistake? Suppose you're trying to declare a function but accidentally just def a value instead, like this:

```
user=> (def hello "Goodnight Moon")
#'user/hello

user=> (hello)
Execution error (ClassCastException) at user/eval137 (REPL:1).
class java.lang.String cannot be cast to class clojure.lang.IFn
(java.lang.String is in module java.base of loader 'bootstrap';
clojure.lang.IFn is in unnamed module of loader 'app')
```

There's a couple of things to notice here. First is that the error is a runtime exception. This means that the form (hello) compiled fine; it just failed at runtime. In terms of the equivalent code in Java, it looks a bit like this (we've simplified things somewhat to make it easier to understand for folks who are new to Clojure or language implementation):

```
// (def hello "Goodnight Moon")
var helloSym = Symbol.of("user", "hello");
var hello = Var.of(helloSym, "Goodnight Moon");

// Or just
// var hello = Var.of(Symbol.of("user", "hello"), "Goodnight Moon");

// #'user/hello

// (hello)
hello.invoke();

// ClassCastException
```

where Symbol and Var are classes in the package clojure.lang that provides the core of the Clojure runtime. They look similar to these basic implementations, which we have simplified here:

```
public class Symbol {
    private final String ns;
    private final String name;

    private Symbol(String ns, String name) {
        this.ns = ns;
```

```
            this.name = name;
        }
        // toString() etc
    }

    public class Var implements IFn {
        private volatile Object root;

        public final Symbol sym;
        public final Namespace ns;

        private Var(Symbol sym, Namespace ns, Object root) {
            this.sym = sym;
            this.ns = ns;
            this.root = root;
        }

        public static Var of(Symbol sym, Object root){
            return new Var(sym, Namespace.of(sym), root);
        }

        static public class Unbound implements IFn {
            final public Var v;
            public Unbound(Var v){
                this.v = v;
            }

            @Override
            public String toString(){
                return "Unbound: " + v;
            }
        }

        public synchronized void bindRoot(Object root) {
            this.root = root;
        }

        public synchronized void unBindRoot(Object root) {
            this.root = new Unbound(this);
        }

        @Override
        public Object invoke() {
            return ((IFn)root).invoke();
        }

        @Override
        public Object invoke(Object o1) {
            return ((IFn)root).invoke(o1);
        }

        @Override
        public Object invoke(Object o1, Object o2) {
            return ((IFn)root).invoke(o1, o2);
        }
```

```
    @Override
    public Object invoke(Object o1, Object o2, Object o3) {
        return ((IFn)root).invoke(o1, o2, o3);
    }
    // ...
}
```

The all-important interface `IFn` looks a bit like this:

```
public interface IFn {
    default Object invoke() {
        return throwArity();
    }
    default Object invoke(Object o1) {
        return throwArity();
    }
    default Object invoke(Object o1, Object o2) {
        return throwArity();
    }
    default Object invoke(Object o1, Object o2, Object o3) {
        return throwArity();
    }

    // ... many others including eventually a variadic form

    default Object throwArity(){
        throw new IllegalArgumentException("Wrong number of args passed: "
                + toString());
    }
}
```

`IFn` is the key to how Clojure forms work—the first element in a form is taken to be a function, or the name of a function, to be invoked. The remaining elements are the arguments to the function, and the `invoke()` method with the appropriate number of arguments (arity) is called.

If a Clojure var is not bound to a value that implements `IFn`, a `ClassCastException` is thrown at runtime. If the value is an `IFn` but the form tries to invoke it with the wrong number of arguments, an `IllegalArgumentException` is thrown (it's actually a subtype called an `ArityException`).

NOTE Remember that Clojure is dynamically typed, as you can see in several places, for example, all the arguments and return types of the methods in `IFn` are `Object` and `IFn` is *not* a Java-style `@FunctionalInterface` but instead has multiple methods defined on it to handle many different arities.

This peek under the hood should help clarify both a little of Clojure's syntax and how it all fits together. However, we still have some broken code to fix—but fortunately it's not too hard!

All that's happened is that you've got your `hello` identifier bound to something that isn't a function so it can't be called. In the REPL, you can fix this by simply rebinding it like so:

```
user=> (defn hello [] (println "Dydh da an Nor")) ; "Hello World" in Cornish
#'user/hello

user=> (hello)
Dydh da an Nor
nil
```

As you might guess from the preceding snippet, the semicolon (`;`) character means that everything to the end of the line is a comment, and (`println`) is the function that prints a string. Notice that (`println`), like all functions, returns a value, which is echoed back to the REPL at the end of the function's execution.

Clojure does not have statements like Java, only expressions, so all functions must return a value. If there is no value to return, then `nil` is used, which is basically the Clojure equivalent of Java's `null`. Functions that would be `void` in Java will return `nil` in Clojure.

10.1.4 *Learning to love the brackets*

The culture of programmers has always had a large element of whimsy and humor. One of the oldest jokes is that Lisp is an acronym for *Lots of Irritating Silly Parentheses* (instead of the more prosaic truth—that it's an abbreviation for *list processing*). This rather self-deprecating joke is popular with some Lisp coders, partly because it points out the unfortunate truth that Lisp syntax has a reputation for being difficult to learn.

In reality, this hurdle is rather exaggerated. Lisp syntax is different from what most programmers are used to, but it isn't the obstacle that it's sometimes presented as. In addition, Clojure has several innovations that reduce the barrier to entry even further.

Let's take another look at the Hello World example. To call the function that returns the value "Hello World", we wrote this:

```
(hello)
```

If we want functions with arguments, rather than having expressions such as `myFunction(someObj)`, in Clojure we write (`myFunction someObj`). This syntax is called *Polish notation*, because it was developed by Polish mathematicians in the early 20th century (it is also called *prefix notation*).

If you've studied compiler theory, you might wonder whether there's a connection here to concepts like the abstract syntax tree (AST). The short answer is yes, there is. A Clojure (or other Lisp) program that is written in Polish notation (usually called an s-*expression* by Lisp programmers) can be shown to be a very simple and direct representation of the AST of that program.

NOTE This relates back, once again, to the simple nature of the Clojure compiler. Compilation of Lisp code is a very cheap operation, because the structure is so close to the AST.

You can think of a Lisp program as being written in terms of its AST directly. There's no real distinction between a data structure representing a Lisp program and the code, so code and data are very interchangeable. This is the reason for the slightly strange notation: it's used by Lisp-like languages to blur the distinction between built-in primitives and user and library code. This power is so great that it far outweighs the slight oddity of the syntax to the eyes of a newly arrived Java programmer. Let's dive into some more of the syntax and start using Clojure to build real programs.

10.2 Looking for Clojure: Syntax and semantics

In the previous section, you met the (def) and (fn) special forms (we also met (defn), but it's a macro, not a special form). You need to know a small number of other special forms immediately to provide a basic vocabulary for the language. In addition, Clojure offers a large number of useful forms and macros, of which a greater awareness will develop with practice.

Clojure is blessed with multiple useful functions for doing a wide range of conceivable tasks. Don't be daunted by this— embrace it. Be happy that for many practical programming tasks you may face in Clojure, somebody else has already done the heavy lifting for you.

In this section, we'll cover the basic working set of special forms, then progress to Clojure's native data types (the equivalent of Java's collections). After that, we'll progress to a natural style for writing Clojure—one in which functions rather than variables have center stage. The object-oriented nature of the JVM will still be present beneath the surface, but Clojure's emphasis on functions has a power that is not as obviously present in purely OO languages and which goes far beyond the basics of map(), filter(), and reduce().

10.2.1 Special forms bootcamp

Table 10.1 covers the definitions of some of Clojure's most commonly used special forms. To get best use of the table, skim through it now and refer back to it as necessary when you reach some of the examples in sections 10.3 onward. The table uses the traditional regular expression syntax notation where ? represents a single optional value and * represents zero or more values.

This isn't an exhaustive list of special forms, and a high percentage of them have multiple ways of being used. Table 10.1 is a starter collection of basic use cases and not anything comprehensive.

A couple of points deserve further explanation, because the structure of Clojure code can seem very different to Java code at first glance. First, the (do) form is one of the simplest ways to construct what would be a block of statements in Java.

Table 10.1   Some of Clojure's basic special forms

Special form	Meaning
`(def <symbol> <value?>)`	Binds a symbol to a value (if provided); creates a var corresponding to the symbol if necessary
`(fn <name>? [<arg>*] <expr>*)`	Returns a function value that takes the specified args and applies them to the exprs; often combined with `(def)` into forms like `(defn)`
`(if <test> <then> <else>?)`	If test evaluates to logical-true, evaluate and yield then; otherwise, evaluate and yield else, if present
`(do <expr>*)`	Evaluates the exprs in left-to-right order and yields the value of the last
`(let [<binding>*] <expr>*)`	Aliases values to a local name and implicitly defines a scope; makes the alias available inside all exprs within the scope of let
`(quote <form>)`	Returns form as is without evaluating anything; takes a single form and ignores all other arguments
`(var <symbol>)`	Returns the var corresponding to symbol (returns a Clojure JVM object, not a value)

Second, we need to dig a bit deeper into the distinction between a var, a value, and the symbol that a value is (temporarily) bound to. This simple code creates a Clojure var called hi. This is a JVM object (an instance of the type `clojure.lang.Var`) that lives in the heap—as all objects do—and binds it to a `java.lang.String` object containing "hello":

```
user=> (def hi "Hello")
#'user/hi
```

The var has a *symbol* hi, and it also has a *namespace* user that Clojure uses to organize programs—a bit like a Java package. If we use the symbol unadorned in the REPL, it evaluates to the value it is currently bound to, as shown here:

```
user=> hi
"Hello"
```

In the `(def)` form, we bind a new symbol to a value, so in this code

```
user=> (def bye hi)
#'user/bye
```

the symbol bye is bound to the *value* currently bound to hi, as shown next:

```
user=> bye
"Hello"
```

Effectively, in this simple form, hi is evaluated and the symbol is replaced with the value that results.

However, Clojure offers us more possibilities than just this. For example, the value that a symbol is bound to is just any JVM value. So, we can bind a symbol to the var we have created because the var is itself a JVM object. This is achieved using the (var) special form as shown here:

```
user=> (def bye (var hi))
#'user/bye

user=> bye
#'user/hi
```

This effectively uses the fact that Java/JVM objects are always handled by reference, as we can see in figure 10.4.

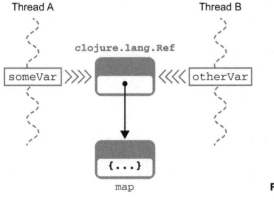

Figure 10.4   Clojure var acting by reference

To get back the value contained in a var, we can use the (deref) form (short for "dereference"), like this:

```
user=> (deref bye)
"Hello"
```

There is also a (ref) form that is used for safe concurrent programming in Clojure—we will meet it in chapter 16.

From this distinction between a var and the value it is currently bound to, the (quote) form should be easier to understand. Instead of evaluating the form it is passed, it simply returns a form comprising the unevaluated symbols.

Now that you have an appreciation of the syntax for some basic special forms, let's turn to Clojure's data structures and start to see how the forms can operate on data.

10.2.2 *Lists, vectors, maps, and sets*

Clojure has several native data structures. The most familiar is the *list*, which in Clojure is a singly linked list.

> **NOTE** In some respects, a Clojure list is similar to a `LinkedList` in Java, except that `LinkedList` is a doubly-linked list where each element has a reference to both the next element and the previous one.

Lists are typically surrounded with parentheses, which seemingly presents a slight syntactic hurdle because round brackets are also used for general forms. In particular, parentheses are used for evaluation of function calls. This leads to the following common beginner's syntax error:

```
user=> (1 2 3)
Execution error (ClassCastException) at user/eval1 (REPL:1).
class java.lang.Long cannot be cast to class clojure.lang.IFn
(java.lang.Long is in module java.base of loader 'bootstrap';
clojure.lang.IFn is in unnamed module of loader 'app')
```

The problem here is that, because Clojure is very flexible about its values, it's expecting a function value (or a symbol that resolves to one) as the first argument, so it can call that function and pass 2 and 3 as arguments; 1 isn't a value that is a function, so Clojure can't evaluate this form. We say that this *s*-expression is invalid, and recall that only valid *s*-expressions are Clojure forms.

The solution is to use the `(quote)` form that we met in the previous section. This has a handy short form, which is `'`. This gives us these two equivalent ways of writing this list, which consists of the immutable list of three elements that are the numbers 1, 2 and 3, as follows:

```
user=> '(1 2 3)
(1 2 3)

user=> (quote (1 2 3))
(1 2 3)
```

Note that `(quote)` handles its arguments in a special way. In particular, there is no attempt made to evaluate the argument, so there's no error arising from a lack of a function value in the first slot.

Clojure has vectors, which are like arrays (in fact, it's not too far from the truth to think of lists as being basically like Java's `LinkedList` and vectors as like `ArrayList`). They have a convenient literal form that makes use of square brackets, so all of the following are equivalent:

```
user=> (vector 1 2 3)
[1 2 3]

user=> (vec '(1 2 3))
```

```
[1 2 3]

user=> [1 2 3]
[1 2 3]
```

We've already met vectors. When we declared the Hello World function and others, we used a vector to indicate the parameters that the declared function takes. Note that the form (vec) accepts a list and creates a vector from it, whereas (vector) is a form that accepts multiple individual symbols and returns a vector of them.

The function (nth) for collections takes two parameters: a collection and an index. It can be thought of as similar to the get() method from Java's List interface. It can be used on vectors and lists, and also on Java collections and even strings, which are treated as collections of characters. Here's an example:

```
user=> (nth '(1 2 3) 1)
2
```

Clojure also supports maps (which you can think of as being very similar to Java's HashMap—and they do in fact implement the Map interface) with this simple literal syntax:

```
{key1 value1 key2 value2}
```

To get a value back out of a map, the syntax, shown next, is very simple:

```
user=> (def foo {"aaa" "111" "bbb" "2222"})
#'user/foo

user=> foo
{"aaa" "111", "bbb" "2222"}         This syntax is equivalent to
                                    the use of a get() method in
user=> (foo "aaa")      ←─────────┘ Java.
"111"
```

In addition to the Map interface, Clojure maps also implement the IFn interface, which is why they can be used in a form like (foo "aaa") without a runtime exception.

One very useful stylistic point is the use of keys that have a colon in front of them. Clojure refers to these as *keywords*.

> **NOTE** The Clojure usage of "keyword" is, of course, very different from the meaning of that term in other languages (including Java) where the term means the parts of the language grammar that are reserved and not able to be used as identifiers.

Here are some useful points about keywords and maps to keep in mind:

- A keyword in Clojure is a function that takes one argument, which must be a map.

- Calling a keyword function on a map returns the value that corresponds to the keyword function in the map.
- When using keywords, there's a useful symmetry in the syntax, as `(my-map :key)` and `(:key my-map)` are both legal.
- As a value, a keyword returns itself.
- Keywords don't need to be declared or `def`'d before use.
- Remember that Clojure functions are values and, therefore, are eligible to be used as keys in maps.
- Commas can be used (but aren't necessary) to separate key-value pairs, because Clojure considers them whitespace.
- Symbols other than keywords can be used as keys in Clojure maps, but the keyword syntax is extremely useful and is worth emphasizing as a style in your own code.

Let's see some of these points in action here:

```
user=> (def martijn {:name "Martijn Verburg", :city "London",
:area "Finsbury Park"})
#'user/martijn

user=> (:name martijn)        ◁──┐ Calls the keyword
"Martijn Verburg"                 │ function on the map

user=> (martijn :area)        ◁──┐ Looks up the value associated
"Finsbury Park"                   │ to the keyword in the map

user=> :area   ◁──┐
:area             │ Shows that when
                  │ evaluated as a value, a
user=> :foo   ◁──┘ keyword returns itself
:foo
```

In addition to map literals, Clojure also has a `(map)` function. But don't be caught out. Unlike `(list)`, the `(map)` function doesn't produce a map. Instead, `(map)` applies a supplied function to each element in a collection in turn and builds a new collection (actually a Clojure sequence, which you'll meet in detail in section 10.4) from the new values returned. This is, of course, the Clojure equivalent to the `map()` method that you have already met from Java's Streams API, shown here:

```
user=> (def ben {:name "Ben Evans", :city "Barcelona", :area
"El Born"})
#'user/ben
                                        ┐ Creates a vector of
user=> (def authors [ben martijn])  ◁──┘ maps of author data
#'user/authors

user=> (defn get-name [y] (:name y))
#'user/get-name
```

```
user=> (map get-name authors)      <──┐  Maps the get-name
("Ben Evans" "Martijn Verburg")       │  function over the data
```

```
user=> (map (fn [y] (:name y)) authors)   <──┐  Alternates form using an
("Ben Evans" "Martijn Verburg")              │  inline function literal
```

There are additional forms of (map) that are able to handle multiple collections at once, but the form that takes a single collection as input is the most common.

Clojure also supports sets, which are very similar to Java's HashSet. They have a short form for data structure literals that do not support repeated keys (unlike HashSet), shown here:

```
user=> #{"a" "b" "c"}
#{"a" "b" "c"}
```

```
user=> #{"a" "b" "a"}
Syntax error reading source at (REPL:15:15).
Duplicate key: a
```

These data structures provide the fundamentals for building up Clojure programs.

One thing that may surprise the Java native is the lack of any immediate mention of objects as first-class citizens. This isn't to say that Clojure isn't object-oriented, but it doesn't see OO in quite the same way as Java. Java chooses to see the world in terms of statically typed bundles of data and code in explicit class definitions of user-defined data types. Clojure emphasizes the functions and forms instead, although these are implemented as objects on the JVM behind the scenes.

This philosophical distinction between Clojure and Java manifests itself in how code is written in the two languages, and to fully understand the Clojure viewpoint, it's necessary to write programs in Clojure and understand some of the advantages that deemphasizing Java's OO constructs brings.

10.2.3 Arithmetic, equality, and other operations

Clojure has no operators in the sense that you might expect them in Java. So, how would you, for example, add two numbers? In Java it's easy:

```
3 + 4
```

But Clojure has no operators. We'll have to use a function instead, as follows:

```
(add 3 4)   <──── This code won't work as it stands, unless we supply an add function.
```

That's all well and good, but we can do better. Because there aren't any operators in Clojure, we don't need to reserve any of the keyboard's characters to represent them. That means our function names can be more outlandish than in Java, so we can write this:

```
(+ 3 4)     <──── This is literally Polish notation, as discussed earlier.
```

Clojure's functions are in many cases *variadic* (they take a variable number of inputs), so you can, for example, write this:

```
(+ 1 2 3)
```

This will give the value 6.

For the equality forms (the equivalent of `equals()` and `==` in Java), the situation is a little more complex. Clojure has two main forms that relate to equality: `(=)` and `(identical?)`. Note that these are both examples of how the lack of operators in Clojure means that more characters can be used in function names. Also, `(=)` is a single equals sign, because there's not the same notion of assignment as in Java-like languages.

This bit of REPL code sets up a list, `list-int`, and a vector, `vect-int`, and applies equality logic to them like so:

```
user=> (def list-int '(1 2 3 4))
#'user/list-int

user=> (def vect-int (vec list-int))
#'user/vect-int

user=> (= vect-int list-int)
true

user=> (identical? vect-int list-int)
false
```

The key point is that the `(=)` form on collections checks to see whether the collections comprise the same objects in the same order (which is true for `list-int` and `vect-int`), whereas `(identical?)` checks to see whether they're really the same object.

You might also notice that our symbol names don't use camel case. This is usual for Clojure. Symbols are usually all in lowercase, with hyphens between words (sometimes called *kebab case*).

TRUE AND FALSE IN CLOJURE

Clojure provides two values for logical false: `false` and `nil`. Anything else is logical true (including the literal `true`). This parallels the situation in many dynamic languages (e.g., JavaScript), but it's a bit strange for Java programmers encountering it for the first time.

With basic data structures and operators under our belts, let's put together some of the special forms and functions we've seen and write slightly longer example Clojure functions.

10.2.4 *Working with functions in Clojure*

In this section, we'll start dealing with some of the meat of Clojure programming. We'll start writing functions to act on data and bring Clojure's focus on functions to the fore. Next up are Clojure's looping constructs, then reader macros and dispatch forms. We'll round out the section by discussing Clojure's approach to functional programming and its take on closures.

The best way to start doing all of this is by example, so let's get going with a few simple examples and build up toward some of the powerful functional programming techniques that Clojure provides.

SOME SIMPLE CLOJURE FUNCTIONS

The next listing defines three functions, two of which are very simple functions of one argument; the third is a little more complex.

Listing 10.1 Defining simple Clojure functions

```
(defn const-fun1 [y] 1)

(defn ident-fun [y] y)                The list maker takes two arguments,
                                      the second of which is a function.
(defn list-maker-fun [x f]
    (map (fn [z] (let [w z]           An inline, anonymous function
        (list w (f w))
    )) x))                            Makes a list of two elements: the value
                                      and the result of applying f to the value
```

In this listing, (const-fun1) takes in a value and returns 1, and (ident-fun) takes in a value and returns the very same value. Mathematicians would call these a *constant function* and the *identity function.* You can also see that the definition of a function uses vector literals to denote the arguments to a function and for the (let) form.

The third function is more complex. The function (list-maker-fun) takes two arguments: first a vector of values to operate on, which is called x, and second, a function (called f). If we were to write it in Java, it might look a bit like this:

```
public List<Object> listMakerFun(List<Object> x,
                                  Function<Object, Object> f) {
    return x.stream()
            .map(o -> List.of(o, f.apply(o)))
            .collect(toList());
}
```

The role of the inline anonymous function in Clojure is played by the lambda expression in the Java code. However, it is important not to overstate the equivalence of these two code listings—Clojure and Java are *very* different languages.

> **NOTE** Functions that take other functions as arguments are called higher-order functions. We'll meet them properly in chapter 15.

Let's take a look at how (list-maker-fun) works.

Listing 10.2   Working with functions

```
user=> (list-maker-fun ["a"] const-fun1)
(("a" 1))

user=> (list-maker-fun ["a" "b"] const-fun1)
(("a" 1) ("b" 1))

user=> (list-maker-fun [2 1 3] ident-fun)
((2 2) (1 1) (3 3))

user=> (list-maker-fun [2 1 3] "a")
java.lang.ClassCastException: java.lang.String cannot be cast to
  clojure.lang.IFn
```

Note that when you're typing these expressions into the REPL, you're interacting with the Clojure compiler. The expression (list-maker-fun [2 1 3] "a") fails to run (although it does compile) because (list-maker-fun) expects its second argument to be a function, which a string isn't. So although the Clojure compiler outputs byte-code for the form, it fails with a runtime exception.

> **NOTE**   In Java, we can write valid code like Integer.parseInt("foo"), which will compile fine but will always fail at runtime. The Clojure situation is similar.

This example shows that when interacting with the REPL, you still have a certain amount of static typing in play because Clojure isn't an interpreted language. Even in the REPL, every Clojure form that is typed is compiled to JVM bytecode and linked into the running system. The Clojure function is compiled to JVM bytecode when it's defined, so the ClassCastException occurs because of a static typing violation in the JVM.

Listing 10.3 shows a longer piece of Clojure code, the *Schwartzian transform*. This is a piece of programming history, made popular by the Perl programming language in the 1990s. The idea is to do a sort operation on a vector, based not on the provided vector but on some property of the elements of the vector. The property values to sort on are found by calling a *keying function* on the elements.

The definition of the Schwartzian transform in listing 10.3 calls the keying function key-fn. When you actually want to call the (schwartz) function, you need to supply a function to use for keying. In this code sample, we use our old friend, (ident-fun), from listing 10.1.

Listing 10.3   Schwartzian transform

```
user=> (defn schwartz [x key-fn]        ◁── Makes a list consisting of pairs using the keying function
  (map (fn [y] (nth y 0))        ◁──
    (sort-by (fn [t] (nth t 1))        ◁── Sorts the pairs based on the values of the keying function
      (map (fn [z] (let [w z]        ◁──
        (list w (key-fn w))        │  Constructs a new list by reducing—taking
      )) x))))        │  only the original value from each pair
```

```
#'user/schwartz

user=> (schwartz [2 3 1 5 4] ident-fun)
(1 2 3 4 5)

user=> (apply schwartz [[2 3 1 5 4] ident-fun])
(1 2 3 4 5)
```

This code is performing three separate steps, which may seem a little inside out at first glance. The steps are shown in figure 10.5.

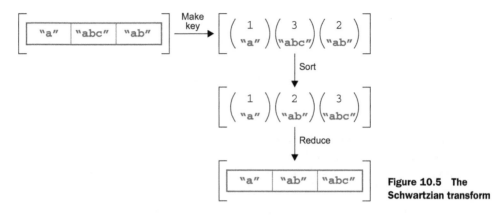

Figure 10.5 The Schwartzian transform

Note that in listing 10.3 we introduced a new form: (sort-by). This is a function that takes two arguments: a function to do the sorting and a vector to be sorted. We've also showcased the (apply) form, which takes two arguments: a function to call and a vector of arguments to pass to it.

One amusing aspect of the Schwartzian transform is that the person for whom it was named was deliberately aping Lisp when he came up with the Perl version. Representing it in the Clojure code here means we've come full circle—back to a Lisp again!

The Schwartzian transform is a useful example that we'll refer back to later. It contains just enough complexity to demonstrate quite a few useful concepts. Now let's move on to discuss loops in Clojure, which work a bit differently from what you may be used to.

10.2.5 *Loops in Clojure*

Loops in Java are a fairly straightforward proposition: the developer can choose from a for, a while, and a couple of other loop types. Usually central is the concept of repeating a group of statements until a condition (often expressed in terms of a mutable variable) is met.

This presents us with a slight conundrum in Clojure: how can we express a for loop when there are no mutable variables to act as the loop index? In more traditional

Lisps, this situation is often solved by rewriting iterative loops into a form that uses recursion.

However, the JVM doesn't guarantee optimizing tail recursion (as is required by Scheme and other Lisps), so naïvely using recursion can cause the stack to blow up. We will have more to say about this issue in chapter 15.

Instead, Clojure provides some useful constructions to allow looping without increasing the size of the stack. One of the most common is loop-recur. The next snippet shows how loop-recur can be used to build up a simple construction similar to a Java for loop:

```clojure
(defn like-for [counter]
  (loop [ctr counter]      ◁——— The loop entry point
    (println ctr)
    (if (< ctr 10)
      (recur (inc ctr))    ◁——— The recur point where we jump backward
    ctr
)))
```

The (loop) form takes a vector of arguments of local names for symbols—effectively aliases as (let) does. Then, when execution reaches the (recur) form (which it will do in this example only if the ctr alias is less than 10), the (recur) causes control to branch back to the (loop) form but with the new value specified. This is similar to a rather primitive form of Java loop construction, shown here:

```java
public int likeFor(int ctr) {
        LOOP: while (true) {
            System.out.println(ctr);
            if (ctr < 10) {
                ctr = ctr + 1;
                continue LOOP;
            } else {
                return ctr;
            }
        }
    }
```

However, for a functional programmer, the only common reason to return early is if some condition is met. However, functions return the result of the last form evaluated, and (if) basically already does this for us.

In our example, we put the (recur) in the body of the if and the countervalue in the else position. This allows us to build up iteration-style constructs (such as the equivalent of Java's for and while loops) but still have a functional flavor to the implementation. We'll now turn to our next topic, which is a look at useful shorthand in Clojure syntax to help make your programs even shorter and less verbose.

10.2.6 *Reader macros and dispatch*

Clojure has syntax features that surprise many Java programmers. One of them is the lack of operators. This has the side effect of relaxing Java's restrictions on which characters can be used in function names. You've already met functions such as (identical?), which would be illegal in Java, but we haven't addressed the issue of exactly which characters are and aren't allowed in symbols.

Table 10.2 lists the characters that aren't allowed in Clojure symbols. These are all characters that are reserved by the Clojure parser for its own use. They're usually referred to as *reader macros*, and they are effectively a special character sequence, which, when seen by the reader (the first part of the Clojure compiler), modifies the reader's behavior.

For example, the ; reader macro is how Clojure implements single-line comments. When the reader sees ;, it immediately ignores all remaining characters on this line, then resets to take the next line of input.

> **NOTE** Later we will meet Clojure's general (or regular) macros. It is important not to confuse a reader macro with a regular macro.

Reader macros exist only for syntactical concision and convenience, not to provide a full general-purpose metaprogramming capability.

Table 10.2   Reader macros

Character	Name	Meaning
'	Quote	Expands to (quote); yields the unevaluated form
;	Comment	Marks a comment to end of line; like // in Java
\	Character	Produces a literal character, for example, \n for newline
@	Deref	Expands to (deref), which takes in a var object and returns the value in that object (the opposite action of the (var) form); has additional meaning in a transactional memory context (see chapter 15)
^	Metadata	Attaches a map of metadata to an object; see the Clojure documentation for details
`	Syntax-quote	Form of quote often used in macro definitions; see the macros section for details
#	Dispatch	Has several different subforms; see table 10.3

The dispatch reader macro has several different subforms, depending on what follows the # character. Table 10.3 shows the different possible forms.

Table 10.3   The subforms of the dispatch reader macro

Dispatch form	Meaning
`#'`	Expands to (var)
`#{}`	Creates a set literal, as discussed in section 10.2.2
`#()`	Creates an anonymous function literal; useful for single uses where (fn) is too wordy
`#_`	Skips the next form; can be used to produce a multiline comment, via #_(... multiline ...)
`#"<pattern>"`	Creates a regular expression literal (as a `java.util.regex.Pattern` object)

A couple of additional points follow from the dispatch forms. The var-quote (`#'`) form, shown next, explains why the REPL behaves as it does after a `(def)`:

```
user=> (def someSymbol)

#'user/someSymbol
```

The `(def)` form returns the newly created var object named `someSymbol`, which lives in the current namespace (which is `user` in the REPL), so `#'user/someSymbol` is the full value of what's returned from `(def)`.

The anonymous function literal `#()` also has a major innovation to reduce verboseness—it omits the vector of arguments and instead uses a special syntax to allow the Clojure reader to infer how many arguments are required for the function literal. The syntax is `%N`, where N is the number of the argument to the function.

Let's return to an earlier example and see how to use it with anonymous functions. Recall the `(list-maker-fun)` that takes two arguments (a list and a function) and creates a new list by applying the function to each element in turn:

```
(defn list-maker-fun [x f]
   (map (fn [z] (let [w z]
      (list w (f w))
   )) x))
```

Rather than going to all the bother of defining a separate symbol, we can call this function with an inline function as follows:

```
user=> (list-maker-fun ["a" "b"] (fn [x] x))
(("a" "a") ("b" "b"))
```

But we can go one step further and use the move compact `#()` syntax like this:

```
user=> (list-maker-fun ["a" "b"] #(do %1))
(("a" "a") ("b" "b"))
```

This example is a little unusual, because we're using the (do) form we met back in the table of basic special forms, but it works. Now, let's simplify (list-maker-fun) itself using the #() form:

```
(defn list-maker-fun [x f]
   (map #(list %1 (f %1)) x))
```

The Schwartzian transform also makes an excellent use case to see how to use this syntax in a more complex example, as shown in the next code sample.

Listing 10.4 Rewritten Schwartzian transform

```
(defn schwartz [x key-fn]
   (map #(nth %1 0)                      Anonymous function literals
     (sort-by #(nth %1 1)                corresponding to the three steps
       (map #(let [w %1]
         (list w (key-fn w))
       ) x))))
```

The use of %1 as a placeholder for a function literal's argument (and %2, %3, and so on for subsequent arguments) makes the usage really stand out and makes the code a lot easier to read. This visual clue can be a real help for the programmer, similar to the arrow symbol used in lambda expressions in Java.

As you've seen, Clojure relies heavily on the concept of functions as the basic unit of computation, rather than on objects, which are the staple of languages like Java. The natural setting for this approach is functional programming, which is our next topic.

10.3 *Functional programming and closures*

We're now going to turn to the scary world of functional programming in Clojure. Or rather, we're *not*, because it's just not that scary. In fact, we've been doing functional programming for this entire chapter; we just didn't tell you to not put you off.

As we mentioned in section 8.1.3, functional programming is a somewhat nebulous concept—all it can be relied upon to mean is that a function is a value. A function can be passed around, placed in variables and manipulated, just like 2 or "hello." But so what? We did that back in our very first example: (def hello (fn [] "Hello world")). We created a function (one that takes no arguments and returns the string "Hello world") and bound it to the symbol hello. The function was just a value, not fundamentally different for a value like 2.

In listing 10.3, we introduced the Schwartzian transform as an example of a function that takes another function as an input value. Again, this is just a function taking a particular type as one of its input arguments. The only thing that's slightly different about it is that the type it's taking is a function.

It's probably also a good time to introduce the (filter) form, shown next, which should remind you of the similarly named method in Java Streams:

```
user=> (defn gt4 [x] (> x 4))
#'user/gt4
user=> (filter gt4 [1 2 3 4 5 6])
(5 6)
```

There is also the (reduce) form, to complete the set of filter-map-reduce operations. It is most commonly seen in two variants, one that takes an initial starting value (sometimes called a "zero") and one that doesn't:

```
user=> (reduce + 1 [2 3 4 5])
15
user=> (reduce + [1 2 3 4 5])
15
```

What about closures? Surely they're really scary, right? Well, not so much. Let's take a look at a simple example that should hopefully remind you of some of the examples we did for Kotlin in chapter 9:

```
user=> (defn adder [constToAdd] #(+ constToAdd %1))
#'user/adder

user=> (def plus2 (adder 2))
#'user/plus2

user=> (plus2 3)
5

user=> 1:9 user=> (plus2 5)
7
```

You first set up a function called (adder). This is a function that makes other functions. If you're familiar with the Factory Method pattern in Java, you can think of this as kind of a Clojure equivalent. There's nothing strange about functions that have other functions as their return values—this is a key part of the concept that functions are just ordinary values.

Notice that this example uses the shorthand form #() for an anonymous function literal. The function (adder) takes in a number and returns a function, and the function returned from (adder) takes one argument.

You then use (adder) to define a new form: (plus2). This is a function that takes one numeric argument and adds 2 to it. The value that was bound to constToAdd inside (adder) was 2. Now let's make a new function:

```
user=> (def plus3 (adder 3))
#'user/plus3

user=> (plus3 4)
7

user=> (plus2 4)
6
```

This shows that you can make a different function, (plus3), that has a different value bound to constToAdd. We say that the functions (plus3) and (plus2) have *captured*, or *closed over* a value from their environment. Note that the values that were captured by (plus3) and (plus2) were different and that defining (plus3) had no effect on the value captured by (plus2).

Functions that close over some values in their environment are called *closures*; (plus2) and (plus3) are examples of closures. The pattern whereby a function-making function returns another, simpler function that has closed over something is a very common one in languages that have closures.

> **NOTE** Remember that although Clojure will compile any syntactically valid form, the program will throw a runtime exception if a function is called with the wrong number of arguments. A two-argument function could not be used in a place where a one-argument function was expected.

We will have a lot more to say about functional programming in context in chapter 15. Now let's turn to a powerful Clojure feature— sequences.

10.4 Introducing Clojure sequences

Clojure has a powerful core abstraction called the *sequence* or, more usually, *seq*.

> **NOTE** Sequences are a major part of writing Clojure code that utilizes the strengths of the language, and they'll provide an interesting contrast to how Java handles similar concepts.

The seq type roughly corresponds to collections and iterators in Java, but seqs have somewhat different properties. The fundamental idea is that seqs essentially merge some of the features of both Java types into one concept. This is motivated by wanting the three following things:

- Immutability, allowing the seqs to be passed around between functions (and threads) without problems
- A more robust iterator-like abstraction, especially for multipass algorithms
- The possibility of *lazy sequences* (more on these later)

Of these three things, the one that Java programmers sometimes struggle with the most is the immutability. The Java concept of an iterator is inherently mutable, partly because it does not provide a cleanly separable interface. In fact, Java's Iterator violates the Single Responsibility Principle because next() does the following *two* things logically distinct things when called:

- It returns the currently pointed-at element.
- It mutates the iterator by advancing the element pointer.

The seq is based on functional ideas and avoids the mutation by dividing up the capabilities of hasNext() and next() in a different way. Let's meet a slightly simplified version of another of Clojure's most important interfaces, clojure.lang.ISeq:

```
interface ISeq {                          Returns the object that is first in the seq
    Object first();
    ISeq rest();
}                                         Returns a new seq that contains all the
                                          elements of the old seq, except the first
```

Now, the seq is never mutated. Instead a new seq value is created every time we call rest(), which is when we would have stepped the iterator to the next value. Let's look at some code to show how we might implement this in Java:

```
public class ArraySeq implements ISeq {
    private final int index;
    private final Object[] values;        Final fields

    private ArraySeq(int index, Object[] values) {
        this.index = index;
        this.values = values;
    }
                                                          Factory method
    public static ArraySeq of(List<Object> objects) {     that takes a List
        if (objects == null || objects.size() == 0) {
            return Empty.of();
        }
        return new ArraySeq(0, objects.toArray());
    }

    @Override
    public Object first() {
        return values[index];
    }

    @Override
    public ISeq rest() {
        if (index >= values.length - 1) {     Needs an empty
            return Empty.of();                 implementation as well
        }
        return new ArraySeq(index + 1, values);
    }

    public int count() {
        return values.length - index;
    }
}
```

As you can see, we need a special-case seq for the end of the sequence. Let's represent it as an inner class within ArraySeq like this:

```
public static class Empty extends ArraySeq {
    private static Empty EMPTY = new Empty(-1, null);

    private Empty(int index, Object[] values) {
        super(index, values);
    }
```

```
        public static Empty of() {
            return EMPTY;
        }

        @Override
        public Object first() {
            return null;
        }

        @Override
        public ISeq rest() {
            return of();
        }

        public int count() {
            return 0;
        }
    }
```

Let's see this in action:

```
ISeq seq = ArraySeq.of(List.of(10000,20000,30000));
var o1 = seq.first();
var o2 = seq.first();
System.out.println(o1 == o2);
```

As expected, calls to `first()` are *idempotent*—they do not change the seq and will repeatedly return the same value.

Let's look at how we'd write a loop in Java using `ISeq`:

```
while (seq.first() != null) {
    System.out.println(seq.first());
    seq = seq.rest();
}
```

This example shows how we deal with one objection that some Java programmers sometimes have with the immutable seq approach: "What about all the garbage?"

It's true that each call to `rest()` will create a new seq, which is an object. However, if you look closely at the implementing code you can see that we're careful not to duplicate `values`—the array storage. Copying that would be expensive, so we don't do that.

All we're really creating at each step is a tiny object that contains an int and a reference to an object. If these temporaries aren't stored anywhere, they'll fall out of scope as we walk down the seq and very quickly become eligible for garbage collection.

NOTE The method bodies for `Empty` do not refer to either `index` or `values`, so we are free to use special values (–1 and `null`), which would not be able to be reached by any other instance of `ArraySeq`—this is a debugging aid.

Let's switch back into Clojure now that we've explained some of the theory of seqs using Java.

> **NOTE** The real `ISeq` interface that all Clojure sequences implement is a little more complex than the version we've met so far, but the basic intent is the same.

Some core functions that relate to sequences are shown in table 10.4. Note that none of these functions will mutate their input arguments; if they need to return a different value, it will be a different seq.

Table 10.4   Basic sequence functions

Function	Effect
`(seq <coll>)`	Returns a seq that acts as a "view" onto the collection acted upon
`(first <coll>)`	Returns the first element of the collection, calling `(seq)` on it first if necessary; returns nil if the collection is nil
`(rest <coll>)`	Returns a new seq, made from the collection, minus the first element
`(seq? <o>)`	Returns true if o is a seq (meaning, if it implements `ISeq`)
`(cons <elt> <coll>)`	Returns a seq made from the collection, with the additional element prepended
`(conj <coll> <elt>)`	Returns a new collection with the new element added to the appropriate end—the end for vectors and the head for lists
`(every? <pred-fn> <coll>)`	Returns true if `(pred-fn)` returns logical-true for every item in the collection

Clojure differs from other Lisps because `(cons)` requires the second argument to be a collection (or, really an `ISeq`). In general, a lot of Clojure programmers favor `(conj)` over `(cons)`. Here are a few examples:

```
user=> (rest '(1 2 3))
(2 3)

user=> (first '(1 2 3))
1

user=> (rest [1 2 3])
(2 3)

user=> (seq ())
nil

user=> (seq [])
nil
```

```
user=> (cons 1 [2 3])
(1 2 3)

user=> (every? is-prime [2 3 5 7 11])
true
```

One important point to note is that Clojure lists are their own seqs, but vectors aren't. In theory, you shouldn't be able to call (rest) on a vector. The reason you're able to is that (rest) acts by calling (seq) on the vector before operating on it.

> **NOTE** Many of the sequence functions take more general objects than seqs and will call (seq) on them before they begin.

In the next section, we're going to explore some of the basic properties and uses of the seq abstraction, paying special attention to variadic functions. Later, in chapter 15, we'll meet lazy sequences—a very important functional technique.

10.4.1 Sequences and variable-arity functions

We've delayed discussing fully one powerful feature of Clojure's approach to functions until now. This is the natural ability to easily have variable numbers of arguments to functions, sometimes called the *arity* of functions. Functions that accept variable numbers of parameters are called *variadic*, and they are frequently used when operating on seqs.

> **NOTE** Java supports variadic methods, with a syntax in which the final parameter of a method is shown with ... on the type, to indicate that any number of parameters of that type are allowed at the end of the parameter list.

As a trivial example, consider the constant function (const-fun1) that we discussed in listing 10.1. This function takes in a single argument and discards it, always returning the value 1. But consider what happens when you pass more than one argument to (const-fun1) like this:

```
user=> (const-fun1 2 3)
java.lang.IllegalArgumentException:
  Wrong number of args (2) passed to: user$const-fun1 (repl-1:32)
```

The Clojure compiler cannot enforce compile-time static checks on the number (and types) of arguments passed to (const-fun1), and instead we have to risk runtime exceptions.

This seems overly restrictive, especially for a function that simply discards all of its arguments and returns a constant value. What would a function that could take any number of arguments look like in Clojure?

The following listing shows how to do this for a version of the (const-fun1) constant function from earlier in the chapter. We've called it (const-fun-arity1), for *constant function 1* with variable *arity*.

NOTE   This is, in fact, a homebrew version of the (constantly) function provided in the Clojure standard function library.

Listing 10.5   Variable arity function

```
user=> (defn const-fun-arity1
  ([] 1)                          Multiple function definitions
  ([x] 1)                         with different signatures
  ([x & more] 1)
)
#'user/const-fun-arity1

user=> (const-fun-arity1)
1

user=> (const-fun-arity1 2)
1

user=> (const-fun-arity1 2 3 4)
1
```

The key is that the function definition is followed not by a vector of function parameters and then a form defining the behavior of the function. Instead, there is a list of pairs, with each pair consisting of a vector of parameters (effectively the signature of this version of the function) and the implementation for this version of the function.

This can be thought of as a similar concept to method overloading in Java. Alternatively, it could also be seen as related to pattern matching (which we met in chapter 3). However, because Clojure is a dynamically typed language, there is no equivalent of type patterns, and so the connection is not as strong as it might be.

The usual convention is to define a few special-case forms (that take none, one, or two parameters) and an additional form that has as its last parameter a seq. In listing 10.5, this is the form that has the parameter vector of [x & more]. The & sign indicates that this is the variadic version of the function.

Sequences are a powerful Clojure innovation. In fact, a large part of learning to think in Clojure is to start thinking about how the seq abstraction can be put to use to solve your specific coding problems. Another important innovation in Clojure is the integration between Clojure and Java, which is the subject of the next section.

10.5   *Interoperating between Clojure and Java*

Clojure was designed from the ground up to be a JVM language and to not attempt to completely hide the JVM character from the programmer. These specific design choices are apparent in a number of places. For example, at the type-system level, Clojure's lists and vectors both implement List—the standard interface from the Java collections library. In addition, it's very easy to use Java libraries from Clojure and vice versa. These properties are extremely useful, because Clojure programmers can make

use of the rich variety of Java libraries and tooling, as well as the performance and
other features of the JVM.

In this section, we'll cover a number of aspects of this interoperability decision,
specifically:

- Calling Java from Clojure
- How Java sees the type of Clojure functions
- Clojure proxies
- Exploratory programming with the REPL
- Calling Clojure from Java

Let's start exploring this integration by looking at how to access Java methods from
Clojure.

10.5.1 *Calling Java from Clojure*

Consider this piece of Clojure code being evaluated in the REPL:

```
user=> (defn lenStr [y] (.length (.toString y)))
#'user/lenStr

user=> (schwartz ["bab" "aa" "dgfwg" "droopy"] lenStr)
("aa" "bab" "dgfwg" "droopy")
```

In this snippet, we've used the Schwartzian transform to sort a vector of strings by
their lengths. To do that, we've used the forms (.toString) and (.length), which
are Java methods. They're being called on the Clojure objects. The period at the start
of the symbol means that the runtime should invoke the named method on the next
argument. This is achieved by the behind-the-scenes use of another macro that we
haven't met yet—(.).

Recall that all Clojure values defined by (def) or a variant of it are placed into
instances of clojure.lang.Var, which can house any java.lang.Object, so any
method that can be called on java.lang.Object can be called on a Clojure value.
Some of the other forms for interacting with the Java world are

```
(System/getProperty "java.vm.version")
```

for calling static methods (in this case the System.getProperty() method) and

```
Boolean/TRUE
```

for accessing static public variables (such as constants).

The familiar "Hello World" example looks like this:

```
user=> (.println System/out "Hello World")
Hello World
nil
```

Note that the final `nil` is because, of course, all Clojure forms must return a value, even if they are a call to a `void` Java method.

In these three examples, we've implicitly used Clojure's namespaces concept, which is similar to Java packages and has mappings from shorthand forms to Java package names for common cases, such as the preceding ones.

10.5.2 *The nature of Clojure calls*

A function call in Clojure is compiled to a JVM method call. The JVM does not guarantee optimizing away tail recursion, which Lisps (especially Scheme implementations) usually do. Some other Lisp dialects on the JVM take the viewpoint that they want true tail recursion, so they are prepared to have a Lisp function call not be exactly equivalent to a JVM method call under all circumstances. Clojure, however, fully embraces the JVM as a platform, even at the expense of full compliance with usual Lisp practice.

If you want to create a new instance of a Java object and manipulate it in Clojure, you can easily do so by using the `(new)` form. This has an alternative short form, which is the class name followed by the full stop, which boils down to another use of the `(.)` macro, as shown next:

```
(import '(java.util.concurrent CountDownLatch LinkedBlockingQueue))

(def cdl (new CountDownLatch 2))

(def lbq (LinkedBlockingQueue.))
```

Here we're also using the `(import)` form, which allows multiple Java classes from a single package to be imported in just one line.

We mentioned earlier that there's a certain amount of alignment between Clojure's type system and that of Java. Let's take a look at this concept in a bit more detail.

10.5.3 *The Java type of Clojure values*

From the REPL, it's very easy to take a look at the Java types of some Clojure values as follows:

```
user=> (.getClass "foo")
java.lang.String

user=> (.getClass 2.3)
java.lang.Double

user=> (.getClass [1 2 3])
clojure.lang.PersistentVector

user=> (.getClass '(1 2 3))
clojure.lang.PersistentList

user=> (.getClass (fn [] "Hello world!"))
user$eval110$fn__111
```

The first thing to notice is that all Clojure values are objects; the primitive types of the JVM aren't exposed by default (although there are ways of getting at the primitive types for the performance-conscious). As you might expect, the string and numeric values map directly onto the corresponding Java reference types (java.lang.String, java.lang.Double, and so on).

The anonymous "Hello world!" function has a name that indicates that it's an instance of a dynamically generated class. This class will implement the interface IFn, which is the very important interface that Clojure uses to indicate that a value is a function.

As we discussed a bit earlier, seqs implement the ISeq interface. They will typically be one of the concrete subclasses of the abstract ASeq or the lazy implementation, LazySeq (we'll meet laziness in chapter 15 when we talk about advanced functional programming).

We've looked at the types of various values, but what about the storage for those values? As we mentioned at the start of this chapter, (def) binds a symbol to a value and, in doing so, creates a var. These vars are objects of type clojure.lang.Var (which implements IFn, among other interfaces).

10.5.4 Using Clojure proxies

Clojure has a powerful macro called (proxy) that enables you to create a bona fide Clojure object that extends a Java class (or implements an interface). For example, the next listing revisits an earlier example (using the ScheduledThreadPoolExecutor from chapter 6), but the heart of the execution example is now done in a fraction of the code, due to Clojure's more compact syntax.

Listing 10.6 Revisiting scheduled executors

```
(import '(java.util.concurrent Executors LinkedBlockingQueue TimeUnit))

(def stpe (Executors/newScheduledThreadPool 2))      ◁─┐  Factory method to
                                                         create an executor
(def lbq (LinkedBlockingQueue.))

(def msgRdr (proxy [Runnable] []                      ◁──┐  Defines an anonymous
  (run [] (.println System/out (.toString (.poll lbq))))      implementation of
))                                                           Runnable

(def rdrHndl
  (.scheduleAtFixedRate stpe msgRdr 10 10 TimeUnit/MILLISECONDS))
```

The general form of (proxy) follows:

```
(proxy [<superclass/interfaces>] [<args>] <impls of named functions>+)
```

The first vector argument holds the interfaces that this proxy class should implement. If the proxy should also extend a Java class (and it can, of course, extend only one Java class), that class name must be the first element of the vector.

The second vector argument comprises the parameters to be passed to a superclass constructor. This is quite often the empty vector, and it will certainly be empty for all cases where the (proxy) form is just implementing Java interfaces.

After these two arguments come the forms that represent the implementations of individual methods, as required by the interfaces or superclasses specified. In our example, the proxy needs to implement only Runnable, so that is the only symbol in the first vector of arguments. No superclass parameters are needed, so the second vector is empty (as it very often is).

Following the two vectors, comes a list of forms that define the methods that the proxy will implement. In our case, that is just run(), and we give it the definition (run [] (.println System/out (.toString (.poll lbq)))). This is, of course, just the Clojure way of writing this bit of Java:

```
public void run() {
    System.out.println(lbq.poll().toString());
}
```

The (proxy) form allows for the simple implementation of any Java interface. This leads to an intriguing possibility—that of using the Clojure REPL as an extended playpen for experimenting with Java and JVM code.

10.5.5 *Exploratory programming with the REPL*

The key concept of exploratory programming is that with less code to write, due to Clojure's syntax, and the live, interactive environment that the REPL provides, the REPL can be a great environment for not only exploring Clojure programming but for learning about Java libraries as well.

Let's consider the Java list implementations. They have an iterator() method that returns an object of type Iterator. But Iterator is an interface, so you might be curious about what the real implementing type is. Using the REPL, it's easy to find out as shown here:

```
user=> (import '(java.util ArrayList LinkedList))
java.util.LinkedList

user=> (.getClass (.iterator (ArrayList.)))
java.util.ArrayList$Itr

user=> (.getClass (.iterator (LinkedList.)))
java.util.LinkedList$ListItr
```

The (import) form brings in two different classes from the java.util package. Then you can use the getClass() Java method from within the REPL just as you did in section 10.5.3. As you can see, the iterators are actually provided by inner classes. This perhaps shouldn't be surprising; as we discussed in section 10.4, iterators are tightly bound up with the collections they come from, so they may need to see internal implementation details of those collections.

Notice that in the preceding example, we didn't use a single Clojure construct—just a little bit of syntax. Everything we were manipulating was a true Java construct. Let's suppose, though, that you wanted to use a different approach and use the powerful abstractions that Clojure brings within a Java program. The next subsection will show you just how to accomplish this.

10.5.6 *Using Clojure from Java*

Recall that Clojure's type system is closely aligned with Java's. The Clojure data structures are all true Java collections that implement the whole of the mandatory part of the Java interfaces. The optional parts aren't usually implemented, because they're often about mutation of the data structures, which Clojure doesn't support.

This alignment of type systems opens the possibility of using Clojure data structures in a Java program. This is made even more viable by the nature of Clojure itself—it's a compiled language with a calling mechanism that matches that of the JVM. This minimizes the runtime aspects and means a class obtained from Clojure can be treated almost like any other Java class. Interpreted languages would find it a lot harder to interoperate and would typically require a minimal non-Java language runtime for support.

The next example shows how Clojure's seq construct can be used on an ordinary Java string. For this code to run, `clojure.jar` will need to be on the classpath:

```
ISeq seq = StringSeq.create("foobar");

while (seq != null) {
  Object first = seq.first();
  System.out.println("Seq: "+ seq +" ; first: "+ first);
  seq = seq.next();
}
```

The preceding code snippet uses the factory method `create()` from the `StringSeq` class. This provides a seq view on the character sequence of the string. The `first()` and `next()` methods return new values, as opposed to mutating the existing seq, just as we discussed in section 10.4.

In the next section, we'll move on to talk Clojure's macros. This is a powerful technique that allows the experienced programmer to effectively modify the Clojure language itself. This capability is common in languages like Lisp but rather alien to Java programmers, so it warrants an entire section to itself.

10.6 *Macros*

In chapter 8, we discussed the rigidity of the language grammar of Java. By contrast, Clojure provides and actively encourages macros as a mechanism to provide a much more flexible approach, allowing the programmer to write more or less ordinary program code that behaves in the same way as built-in language syntax.

NOTE Many languages have macros (including C++), and they mostly all operate in a roughly similar way—by providing a special phase of source code compilation, often the very first phase.

For example, in the C language, the first step is *preprocessing*, which removes comments, inlines included files, and expands macros, which are the different types of *preprocessor directives* such as #include and #define.

However, although C macros were very powerful, they also make it possible for engineers to produce some very subtly confusing code that is hard to understand and debug. To avoid this complexity, the Java language never implemented a macro system or a preprocessor.

C macros work by providing very simple text-replacement capabilities during the preprocessing phase. Clojure macros are safer, because they work within the syntax of Clojure itself. Effectively, they allow the programmer to create a special kind of function that is evaluated (in a special way) at compile time. The macro can transform source code during compilation during what is referred to as *macro expansion time.*

NOTE The key to the power of macros is the fact that Clojure code is written down as a valid Clojure data structure—specifically as a list of forms.

We say that Clojure, like other Lisps (and a few other languages), is *homoiconic*, which means that programs are represented in the same way as data. Other programming languages, like Java, write their source code as a string, and without parsing that string in a Java compiler, the structure of the program cannot be determined.

Recall that Clojure compiles source code as it is encountered. Many Lisps are interpreted languages, but Clojure is not. Instead, when Clojure source code is loaded, it is compiled on the fly into JVM bytecode. This can give the superficial impression that Clojure is interpreted, but the (very simple) Clojure compiler is hiding just below the surface.

NOTE A Clojure form is a list, and a macro is essentially a function that does not evaluate its arguments but instead manipulates them to return another list, which will then be compiled as a Clojure form.

To demonstrate this, let's try to write a macro form that acts like the opposite of (if). In some languages, this would be represented with the unless keyword, so in Clojure it will be an (unless) form. What we want is a form that looks like (if) but behaves as the logical opposite, like this:

```
user=> (def test-me false)
#'user/test-me

user=> (unless test-me "yes")
"yes"

user=> (def test-me true)
```

```
#'user/test-me

user=> (unless test-me "yes")
nil
```

Note that we don't provide the equivalent of an else condition. This somewhat simplifies the example and "unless ... else" sounds weird anyway. In our examples, if the unless logical test fails, the form evaluates to nil.

   If we try to write this using (defn), we can write a simple first attempt like this (spoiler: it won't actually work properly):

```
user=> (defn unless [p t]
  (if (not p) t))
#'user/unless

user=> (def test-me false)
#'user/test-me

user=> (unless test-me "yes")
"yes"

user=> (def test-me true)
#'user/test-me

user=> (unless test-me "yes")
nil
```

This seems fine. However, consider that we want (unless) to work the same way as (if)—in particular, the then form should evaluated only if the Boolean predicate condition is true. In other words, for (if) we see this behavior:

```
user=> (def test-me true)
#'user/test-me

user=> (if test-me (do (println "Test passed") true))
Test passed
true

user=> (def test-me false)
#'user/test-me

user=> (if test-me (do (println "Test passed") true))
nil
```

When we try to use our (unless) function in the same way, the problem becomes clear, as illustrated here:

```
user=> (def test-me false)
#'user/test-me

user=> (unless test-me (do (println "Test passed") true))
```

```
Test passed
true

user=> (def test-me true)
#'user/test-me

user=> (unless test-me (do (println "Test passed") true))
Test passed
nil
```

Regardless of whether the predicate is true or false, the then form is still evaluated, and as it is (println) in our example, it produces output, which provides the clue that lets us know that the evaluation is taking place. To solve this problem, we need to handle the forms that we are passed *without evaluating them.* This is essentially a (slightly different) kind of the laziness concept that is so important in functional programming (and which we will describe in detail in chapter 15). The special form (defmacro) is used to declare a new macro, like this:

```
(defmacro unless [p t]
  (list 'if (list 'not p) t))
```

Let's see if it does the right thing:

```
user=> (def test-me true)
#'user/test-me

user=> (unless test-me (do (println "Test passed") true))
nil

user=> (def test-me false)
#'user/test-me

user=> (unless test-me (do (println "Test passed") true))
Test passed
true
```

This now behaves as we want it to: essentially, the (unless) form now looks and behaves just like the built-in (if) special form.

As you can see, one of the drawbacks of writing macros is that a lot of quoting is involved. The macro transforms its arguments to a new Clojure form at compile time, so it is natural that the output should be a (list).

The list contains Clojure symbols that will be evaluated at runtime, so anything that we do not explicitly need to evaluate during macro expansion must be quoted. This relies upon the fact that macros receive their arguments at compile time, so they are available as unevaluated data.

In our example, we need to quote everything that is *not* one of our arguments—these will be string-replaced as symbols during expansion. This gets pretty cumbersome fairly quickly. Can we do better?

Let's meet a helpful tool that might point us in the right direction. When writing or debugging macros, the (macroexpand-1) form can be very useful. If this form is passed a macro form, it expands the macro and returns the expansion. If the passed form is not a macro, it just returns the form, for example:

```
user=> (macroexpand-1 '(unless test-me (do (println "Test passed") true)))
(if (not test-me) (do (println "Test passed") true))
```

What we would really like is the ability to write macros that look like their macro-expanded form without the huge amount of quoting that we've seen in examples so far.

> **NOTE** Full macro expansion, using the form (macroexpand), is then constructed by just repeatedly calling the former, simpler form. When applying (macroexpand-1) is a no-op, macro expansion is over. The key to this capability is the special reader macro `` ` ``, which is pronounced "syntax-quote" and which we previewed earlier in the chapter as part of the section about reader macros. The syntax quoting reader macro works by basically quoting everything in the following form. If you want something to *not* be quoted, you have to use the syntax-unquote (~) operator to exempt a value from syntax quoting. This means our example macro (unless) can be written as follows:

```
(defmacro unless [p t]
  `(if (not ~p) ~t))
```

This form is now much clearer and closer to the form we see when macro expanding. The ~ character provides a nice visual clue to let us know that those symbols will be replaced when the macro is expanded. This fits nicely with the idea of a macro as a compile-time code template.

Along with syntax-quote and -unquote, some important special variables are sometimes used in macro definitions. Of these, two of the most common follow:

- &form—the expression that is being invoked
- &env—a map of local bindings at the point of macro expansion

Full details of the information that can be obtained from each special variable can be found in the Clojure documentation.

We should also note that care needs to be taken when writing Clojure macros. For example, it is possible to create macros that create recursive expansions that do not terminate and instead *diverge*, such as the following example:

```
(defmacro diverge [t]
  `((diverge ~t) (diverge ~t)))
#'user/diverge

user=> (diverge true)
Syntax error (StackOverflowError) compiling at (REPL:1:1).
null
```

As a final example, let's confirm that macros do in fact operate at compile time by constructing a macro that essentially acts as a closure that bridges from compile to runtime, shown next:

```
user=> (defmacro print-msg-with-compile []
  (let [num (System/currentTimeMillis)]
    `(fn [t#] (println t# " " ~num))))
#'user/print-msg-with-compile

user=> (def p1 (print-msg-with-compile))
#'user/p1

user=> (p1 "aaa")
aaa    1603437421852
nil

user=> (p1 "bbb")
bbb    1603437421852
nil
```

Notice how the (let) form is evaluated at compile time, so the value of (System/currentTimeMillis) is captured when the macro is evaluated, bound to the symbol num, and then replaced in the expanded form with the value that was bound—effectively a constant determined at compile time.

Even though we have introduced macros at the very end of this chapter, macros are actually all around us in Clojure. In fact, much of the Clojure standard library is implemented as macros. The well-grounded developer can learn a lot by spending some time reading the source of the standard library and observing how key parts of it have been written.

At this point, a word of warning is also timely: macros are a powerful technique, and there is a temptation (just as there is with other techniques that "level up" a programmer's thinking) that some developers can fall prey to—the tendency to overuse the technique by including when it is not strictly necessary.

To guard against this, we highly recommend that you keep in mind the following simple general rules for the use of Clojure macros:

- Never write a macro when the goal can be accomplished with a function.
- Write a macro to implement a feature, capability, or pattern that is not already present in the language or standard library.

The first of these is, of course, merely the old adage that "just because you *can* do something doesn't mean that you *should*" in a different guise.

The second is a reminder that macros exist for a reason: there are things that you can do with them that cannot really be done in any other way. A proficient Clojure programmer will be able to use macros to great effect where appropriate.

Beyond macros, there is still more to learn about Clojure, such as the language's approach to dynamic runtime behavior. In Java this is usually handled using class and interface inheritance and virtual dispatch, but these are fundamentally object-oriented concepts and are not a particularly good fit for Clojure.

Instead, Clojure uses *protocols* and *datatypes*—along with the proxies that we have already met—to provide much of this flexibility. There are even more possibilities, such as custom dispatch schemes that use *multimethods*. These are also very powerful techniques but, unfortunately, are a little far outside of this introductory treatment of Clojure.

As a language, Clojure is arguably the most different from Java of the languages we've looked at. Its Lisp heritage, emphasis on immutability, and different approaches seem to make it into an entirely separate language. But its tight integration with the JVM, alignment of its type system (even when it provides alternatives, such as seqs), and the power of exploratory programming make it a very complementary language to Java.

The differences between the languages we've studied in this part clearly show the power of the Java platform to evolve and to continue to be a viable destination for application development. This is also a testament to the flexibility and capability of the JVM.

Summary

- Clojure is dynamically typed, and Java programmers need to be careful of runtime exceptions.
- Exploratory and REPL-based development is a different feel from a Java IDE.
- Clojure provides and promotes a very immutable style of programming.
- Functional programming pervades Clojure—far more so than Java or Kotlin.
- Seqs are a functional equivalent to Java's iterators and collections.
- Macros define a compile-time transformation of Clojure source.

Part 4

Build and deployment

This part of the book is all about working effectively with the tooling to build, test, and deploy our Java applications. Although build tools have existed since long before Java entered the scene, the field continues advancing. In chapter 11, you'll look at the two most popular Java build tools—Maven and Gradle—and learn about their similarities and differences. Beyond the basic commands, you'll see how they model the world and where those models are open for the well-grounded developer to extend and customize.

Over the past years, containerization has taken the industry by storm. From its roots as a somewhat niche set of Linux primitives, Docker and Kubernetes have turned these techniques mainstream. You'll take a look at the specifics of integrating our Java application environments with the norms in containers, what needs to change, and what stays the same.

Before you deploy your applications, though, you need to test them. What precisely that testing means can vary widely, depending who you talk to and what a project needs. A well-grounded developer knows that one size does not fit all, so we'll grapple with a number of different testing approaches and their pros and cons, and get a vocabulary for being more precise about our tests. You'll also see the big changes to JUnit's most recent major version, using many of the newer JDK features you've learned about along the way.

The variety of ways to test code stretches out in every direction, and, in particular, other languages and technologies beyond Java have valuable insights to bring. You'll see how containers, Kotlin, and Clojure all bring their own special spin to your testing toolbox in chapter 14. By the end of part 4, you'll be ready to get your JVM application out in the real world, confident that it's built and tested properly.

Building with
Gradle and Maven

The JDK ships with a compiler to turn Java source code into class files, as we saw in chapter 4. Despite that fact, few projects of any size rely just on `javac`. Let's start by looking at why a well-grounded developer should invest in familiarity with this layer of tooling.

11.1 Why build tools matter for a well-grounded developer

Build tools are the norm for the following reasons:

- Automating tedious operations
- Managing dependencies
- Ensuring consistency between developers

Although many options exist, two choices dominate the landscape today: Maven and Gradle. Understanding what these tools aim to solve, digging below the surface of how they get their job done, and understanding the differences between them—and how to extend them—will pay off for the well-grounded developer.

11.1.1 Automating tedious operations

`javac` can turn any Java source file into a class file, but there's more to building a typical Java project than that. Just getting all the files properly listed to the compiler could be tedious in a large project if done by hand. Build tools provide defaults for finding code and let you easily configure if you have a nonstandard layout instead.

The conventional layout popularized by Maven, and used by default by Gradle as well, looks like this:

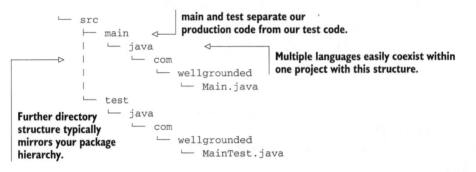

As you can see, testing is baked all the way into the layout of our code. Java's come a long way since the time when folks used to ask whether they really needed to write tests for their code. The build tools have been a key part in making testing available in a consistent manner everywhere.

> **NOTE** You probably already know about how to unit test in Java with JUnit or another library. We will discuss other forms of testing in chapter 14.

Although compiling to class files is the start of a Java program's existence, generally, it isn't the end of the line. Fortunately, build tools also provide support for packaging your class files into a JAR or other format for easier distribution.

11.1.2 Managing dependencies

In the early days of Java, if you wanted to use a library, you had to find its JAR somewhere, download the file, and put it into the classpath for your application. This caused several problems—in particular, the lack of a central, authoritative source for all libraries meant that a treasure hunt was sometimes necessary to find the JARs for less-common dependencies.

That obviously wasn't ideal, and so Maven (among other projects) gave the Java ecosystem repositories where tools could find and install dependencies for us. Maven Central remains to this day one of the most commonly used registries for Java dependencies on the internet. Others also exist—public registries such as those hosted by Google or those shared on GitHub, and private installations via products such as Artifactory.

Downloading all that code can be time-consuming, too, so build tools have standardized on a few ways of reducing the pain by sharing artifacts between projects. With a local repository to cache, if a second project needs the same library, you don't need to download it again, as shown in figure 11.1. This approach also saves disk space, of course, but the single source of artifacts is the real win here.

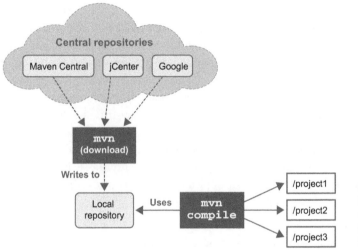

Figure 11.1 Maven's local repository helping not only to find dependencies online but to manage them efficiently locally

NOTE You might be wondering where modules fit in this dependency landscape. Modularized libraries are shipped as JAR files with the addition of the `module-info.class` file, as we saw in chapter 2. A modularized JAR can be downloaded from the standard repositories. The real differences come into play when you start compiling and running with modules, not in the packaging and distribution.

More than just providing a central place to find and download dependencies, though, registries opened the door for better management of *transitive dependencies*. In Java, we commonly see this situation when a library that our project uses itself depends on *another* library. We actually already met transitive dependency of modules in chapter 2, but the problem existed long before Java modules. In fact, before modules, the problem was significantly worse.

Recall that JAR files are just a zipped file—they don't have any metadata that describes the dependencies of the JAR. This means that the dependencies of a JAR are just the union of all of the dependencies of all the classes in the JAR.

To make matters worse, the class file format does not describe which version of a class is needed to satisfy the dependency—all we have is a symbolic descriptor of the class or method name that the class requires to link (as we saw in chapter 4). This implies the following two things:

1 An external source of dependency information is required.

2 As projects get larger, the transitive dependency graph will get increasingly complex.

With the explosion of open source libraries and frameworks to support developers, the typical tree of transitive dependencies in a real project has only gotten larger and larger.

One potential bit of good news is that the situation for the JVM ecosystem is somewhat better than it is for, say, JavaScript. JavaScript lacks a rich, central runtime library that is guaranteed to be always present, so a lot of basic capabilities have to be managed as external dependencies. This introduces problems such as multiple incompatible libraries that each provide a version of a common feature and a fragile ecosystem where mistakes and hostile attacks can have a disproportionate impact on the commons (e.g., the "left-pad" incident from 2016 [see http://mng.bz/5Q64]).

Java, on the other hand, has a runtime library (the JRE) that contains a lot of commonly needed classes, and this is available in every Java environment. However, a real production application will require capabilities beyond those in the JRE and will almost always have too many layers of dependencies to comfortably manage manually. The only solution is to automate.

A CONFLICT EMERGES

This automation is a boon for developers building on the rich ecosystem of open source code available, but upgrading dependencies often reveals problems as well. For instance, figure 11.2 shows a dependency tree that might set us up for trouble.

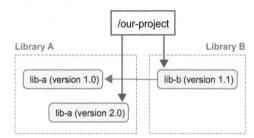

Figure 11.2   **Conflicting transitive dependencies**

We've asked explicitly for version 2.0 of lib-a, but our dependency lib-b has asked for the older version 1.0. This is known as a *dependency conflict*, and depending on how it is resolved, it can cause a variety of other problems.

What types of breakage can result from mismatched library versions? This depends on the nature of the changes between the versions. Changes fall into a few categories, shown here:

a   Stable APIs where only the behavior changes between versions

b   Added APIs where new classes or methods appear between versions

c   Changed APIs where method signatures or interfaces extended changes between versions

d   Removed APIs where classes or methods are removed between versions

In the case of a) or b), you may not even notice which version of the dependency your build tool has chosen. The most common case of c) is a change to the signature of a method between library versions. In our previous example, if `lib-a` 2.0 altered the signature of a method that `lib-b` relied upon, when `lib-b` tried to call that method, it would receive a `NoSuchMethodError` exception.

Removed methods in case d) would result in the same sorts of `NoSuchMethodError`. This includes "renaming" a method, which at the bytecode level isn't any different from removing a method and adding a new one that just happens to have the same implementation.

Classes are also prone to d) on deletion or renaming and will cause a `NoClassDef-FoundError`. It's also possible that removal of interfaces from a class could land you with an ugly `ClassCastException`.

This list of issues with conflicting transitive dependencies is by no means exhaustive. It all boils down to *what* actually changes between two versions of the same package.

In fact, communicating about the nature of changes between versions is a common problem across languages. One of the most broadly adopted approaches to handling the problem is *semantic versioning* (see https://semver.org/). Semantic versioning gives us a vocabulary for stating the requirements of our transitive dependencies, which in turn allows the machines to help us sort them out.

When using semantic versioning, keep in mind the following:

- *MAJOR* version increments (1.x -> 2.x) on breaking changes to your API, like cases c) and d) above.
- *MINOR* version increments (1.1 -> 1.2) on backward-compatible additions like case b).
- *PATCH* increments on bug fixes (1.1.0 -> 1.1.1).

Though not foolproof, it at least gives an expectation as to what level of changes come with a version update and is broadly used in open source.

Having gotten a taste of why dependency management isn't easy, rest assured that both Maven and Gradle provide tooling to help. Later in the chapter, we'll look in detail at what each tool provides to unravel problems when you hit dependency conflicts.

11.1.3   *Ensuring consistency between developers*

As projects grow in volume of code and developers involved, they often get more complex and harder to work with. Your build tooling can lessen this pain, though. Built-in features like ensuring everyone is compiling and running the same tests are a start. But we should consider many additions beyond the basics as well.

Tests are good, but how certain are you that *all* your code is tested? Code coverage tools are key for detecting what code is hit by your tests and what isn't. Although arguments swirl on the internet about the right target for code coverage, the line-level output coverage tools provide can save you from missing a test for that one extra special conditional.

Java as a language also lends itself well to a variety of static analysis tools. From detecting common patterns (i.e., overriding `equals` without overriding `hashCode`) to sniffing out unused variables, static analysis lets a computer validate aspects of the code that are legal but will bite you in production.

Beyond the realms of correctness, though, are style and formatting tools. Ever fought with someone about where the curly braces should go in a statement? How to indent your code? Agreeing once to a set of rules, even if they aren't all perfectly to your taste, lets you focus forever after in the project on the actual work instead of nit-picking details about how the code looks.

Last and certainly not least, your build tool is a pivotal central point for providing custom functionality. Are there special setup or operational commands folks need to run periodically for your project? Validations your project should run after a build but before you deploy? All of these are excellent to consider wiring into the build tooling so they're available to everyone working with the code. Both Maven and Gradle provide many ways to extend them for your own logic and needs.

Hopefully you're now convinced that build tools aren't just something to set up once on a project but are worth the investment in understanding. Let's start by taking a look at one of the most common: Maven.

11.2   Maven

Early in Java history, the Ant framework was the default build tool. With tasks described in XML, it allowed a more Java-centric way to script builds than tools like Make. But Ant lacked structure around how to configure your build—what the steps were, how they related, how dependencies were managed. Maven addressed many of these gaps with its concept of a standardized *build lifecycle* and a consistent approach to handling dependencies.

11.2.1   The build lifecycle

Maven is an opinionated tool. One of the biggest areas where these opinions show is in its build lifecycles. Rather than users defining their own tasks and determining their order, Maven has a *default lifecycle* encompassing the usual steps, known as *phases*, that you'd expect in a build. Though not comprehensive, the following phases capture the high points in the default lifecycle:

- *Validate*—Check project configuration is correct and can build
- *Compile*—Compile the source code
- *Test*—Run unit tests
- *Package*—Generate artifacts such as JAR files

- *Verify*—Run integration tests
- *Install*—Install package to the local repository
- *Deploy*—Make package result available to others, typically run from a CI environment

Chances are that these map to most of the steps you'll take from source code to a deployed application or library. This is a major bonus to Maven's opinionated approach—any Maven project will share this same lifecycle. Your knowledge of how to run builds is more transportable than it used to be.

The phases are well-defined in Maven, but every project needs something special in the details. In Maven's model, various *plugins* attach *goals* to these phases. A goal is a concrete task, with the implementation of how to execute it.

Beyond the default lifecycle, Maven also includes the *clean* and *site* lifecycles. The *clean* lifecycle is intended for cleanup (e.g., removing intermediate build results), whereas the *site* lifecycle is meant for documentation generation.

We'll look closer at hooking into a lifecycle later when we discuss extending Maven, but if you truly need to redefine the universe, Maven does support authoring fully custom lifecycles. This is a very advanced topic, however, and beyond the scope of this book.

11.2.2 Commands/POM intro

Maven is a project of the Apache Software Foundation and is open source. Installation instructions can be found on the project website at https://maven.apache.org/install.html.

Typically, Maven is installed globally on a developer's workstation, and it works on any not-ancient JVM (JDK 7 or higher). Once installed, invoking it gets us this output:

```
~: mvn

   [INFO] Scanning for projects...
   [INFO] ------------------------------------------------------------------
   [INFO] BUILD FAILURE
   [INFO] ------------------------------------------------------------------
   [INFO] Total time:  0.066 s
   [INFO] Finished at: 2020-07-05T21:28:22+02:00
   [INFO] ------------------------------------------------------------------
   [ERROR] No goals have been specified for this build. You must specify a
   valid lifecycle phase or a goal in the format <plugin-prefix>:<goal> or
   <plugin-group-id>:<plugin-artifact-id>[:<plugin-version>]:<goal>.
   Available lifecycle phases are: validate, initialize, ....
```

Of particular interest is the message that No goals have been specified for this build. This indicates that Maven doesn't know anything about our project. We provide that information in the pom.xml file, which is the center of the universe for a Maven project.

NOTE POM stands for Project Object Model.

Although a full-blown `pom.xml` file can be intimidatingly long and complex, you can get started with much less. For example, a more-or-less minimal `pom.xml` file looks like this:

```
<project>
  <modelVersion>4.0.0</modelVersion>
  <groupId>com.wellgrounded</groupId>        Identifying
  <artifactId>example</artifactId>           our project
  <version>1.0-SNAPSHOT</version>
  <name>example</name>
                                             The Maven plugins default
                                             to Java 1.6. We obviously
  <properties>                               want a newer version.
    <maven.compiler.source>11</maven.compiler.source> ⊲
    <maven.compiler.target>11</maven.compiler.target>
  </properties>
</project>
```

Our `pom.xml` file declares two particularly important fields: the `groupId` and the `artifactId`. These fields combine with a version to form the *GAV coordinates* (group, artifact, version), which uniquely, globally identifies a specific release of your package. `groupId` typically specifies the company, organization, or open source project responsible for the library, whereas `artifactId` is the name for the specific library. GAV coordinates are often expressed with each part separated by a colon (`:`), such as `org.apache.commons:collections4:4.4` or `com.google.guava:guava:30.1-jre`.

These coordinates are important not just for configuring your project locally. Coordinates act as the address for dependencies, so our build tooling can find them. The following sections will dig into the mechanics of how we express those dependencies in more detail.

Much like Maven standardized the build lifecycle, it also popularized the standard layout we saw earlier in section 11.1.1 and shown next. If you follow these conventions, you don't have to tell Maven anything about your project for it to be able to compile:

```
.
├── pom.xml
└── src
    ├── main
    |   └── java
    |       └── com
    |           └── wellgrounded
    |               └── Main.java
    └── test
        └── java
            └── com
                └── wellgrounded
                    └── MainTest.java
```

Notice the parallel structures—`src/main/java` and `src/test/java`— with the same directories mapping to our package hierarchy. This convention keeps the test code separate from the main app code, which simplifies the process of packaging our main code for deployment, excluding the test code, which users of a package won't typically want or use.

Other standard directories exist beyond these two. For instance, src/main/ resources is the typical location for additional non-code files to include in a JAR. See the documentation at http://mng.bz/6XoG for a full listing of the Maven standard layout.

While you're getting used to Maven, it's a good idea to stick to the conventions, standard layouts, and other defaults that Maven provides. As we mentioned, it's an opinionated tool, so it's better to stay within the guardrails it provides while you're learning. Experienced Maven developers can (and do) stray outside the conventions and break the rules, but let's not try to run before we walk.

11.2.3 *Building*

We saw previously that just running mvn on the command line warns us that we need to choose a lifecycle phase or goal to actually take action. Most often we'll want to run a phase, which may include many goals.

The simplest place to get started is compiling our code by requesting the compile phase like this:

Although we don't have resources in our project, the maven-resources-plugin from the default lifecycle checks for us.

```
~: mvn compile

[INFO] Scanning for projects...
[INFO]
[INFO] ------------------< com.wellgrounded:example >---------------
[INFO] Building example 1.0-SNAPSHOT
[INFO] --------------------------[ jar ]---------------------------
[INFO]
[INFO] -- maven-resources-plugin:2.6:resources (default-resources) --
[INFO] Using 'UTF-8' to copy filtered resources.          ◁───────
[INFO] Copying 0 resource
[INFO]
[INFO] ----- maven-compiler-plugin:3.1:compile (default-compile) ----
[INFO] Changes detected - recompiling the module!         ◁────────
[INFO] Compiling 1 source file to ./maven-example/target/classes
[INFO] ------------------------------------------------------------
[INFO] BUILD SUCCESS
[INFO] ------------------------------------------------------------
[INFO] Total time:  0.940 s
[INFO] Finished at: 2020-07-05T21:46:25+02:00
[INFO] ------------------------------------------------------------
```

Our actual compilation is provided by maven-compiler-plugin.

Maven defaults our output to the target directory. After our mvn compile, we can find the class files under target/classes. Close inspection will reveal we only built the code under our main directory. If we want to compile our tests, you can use the test-compile phase.

The default lifecycle includes more than just compilation. For instance, `mvn` package for the previous project will result in a JAR file at `target/example-1.0-SNAPSHOT.jar`.

Although we can use this JAR as a library, if we try to run it via `java -jar target/example-1.0-SNAPSHOT.jar`, we'll find that Java complains it can't find a main class. To see how we start growing our Maven build, let's change it so the produced JAR is a runnable application.

11.2.4 *Controlling the manifest*

The JAR Maven produced from `mvn package` was missing a *manifest* to tell the JVM where to look for a `main` method on startup. Fortunately, Maven ships with a plugin for constructing JARs that knows how to write the manifest. The plugin exposes configuration via our `pom.xml` after the `properties` element and still inside the `project` element as follows:

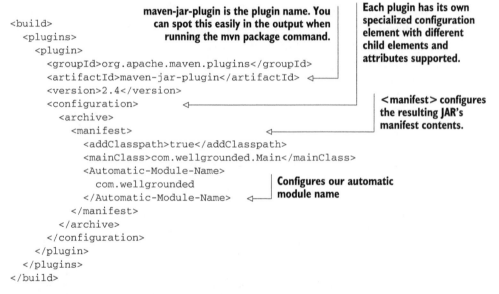

Adding this section sets up the main class so the `java` launcher knows how to directly execute the JAR. We have also added an automatic module name—this is to be good citizens in the modular world. As we discussed back in chapter 2, even if the code we're writing is not modular (as in this case), it still makes sense to provide an explicit automatic module name so modular applications can more easily use our code.

This pattern of setting configuration under a `plugin` element is very standard in Maven. To simplify things, most default plugins will kindly warn if you use an unsupported or unexpected configuration property, although the details may vary by plugin.

11.2.5 *Adding another language*

As we discussed in chapter 8, an advantage of the JVM as a platform is the ability to use multiple languages within the same project. This may be useful when a specific language has better facilities for a given part of your application, or even to allow gradual conversion of an application from one language to another.

Let's take a look at how we would configure our simple Maven project to build some classes from Kotlin instead of Java. Our standard layout is fortunately already set to allow for easy adding languages, as shown next:

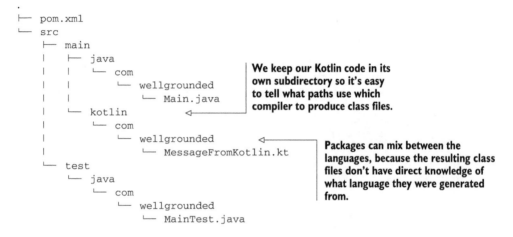

```
.
├── pom.xml
└── src
    ├── main
    |   ├── java
    |   |   └── com
    |   |       └── wellgrounded
    |   |           └── Main.java
    |   └── kotlin
    |       └── com
    |           └── wellgrounded
    |               └── MessageFromKotlin.kt
    └── test
        └── java
            └── com
                └── wellgrounded
                    └── MainTest.java
```

We keep our Kotlin code in its own subdirectory so it's easy to tell what paths use which compiler to produce class files.

Packages can mix between the languages, because the resulting class files don't have direct knowledge of what language they were generated from.

Unlike Java, Maven by default doesn't know how to compile Kotlin so we need to add `kotlin-maven-plugin` in our `pom.xml`. We recommend consulting the Kotlin documentation at https://kotlinlang.org/docs/maven.html for the most up-to-date usage, but we'll demonstrate here so you can know what to expect.

If a project is fully written in Kotlin, compilation only needs the plugin added and attached to the `compile` goal as follows:

```xml
<build>
  <plugins>
    <plugin>
      <groupId>org.jetbrains.kotlin</groupId>
      <artifactId>kotlin-maven-plugin</artifactId>
      <version>1.6.10</version>
      <executions>
        <execution>
          <id>compile</id>
          <goals>
            <goal>compile</goal>
          </goals>
        </execution>
        <execution>
          <id>test-compile</id>
          <goals>
```

Current version of Kotlin, as of when this chapter was written.

Adds this plugin to the goals for compiling main and test code.

```
        <goal>test-compile</goal>
      </goals>
    </execution>
  </executions>
</plugin>
</plugins>
</build>
```

The situation gets more complex when mixing Kotlin and Java. Maven's default maven-compiler-plugin, which compiles Java for us, needs to be overridden to let Kotlin compile first, as shown next, or our Java code will be unable to use the Kotlin classes:

```
<build>
  <plugins>
    <plugin>
      <groupId>org.jetbrains.kotlin</groupId>
      <artifactId>kotlin-maven-plugin</artifactId>  ◄── Adds the kotlin-maven-plugin
      <version>1.6.10</version>                          mostly as before, making
      <executions>                                       sure now it's aware of both
        <execution>                                      Java and Kotlin paths
          <id>compile</id>
          <goals>
            <goal>compile</goal>
          </goals>
          <configuration>
            <sourceDirs>                                                    ◄──
              <sourceDir>${project.basedir}/src/main/kotlin</sourceDir>
              <sourceDir>${project.basedir}/src/main/java</sourceDir>
            </sourceDirs>
          </configuration>
        </execution>                              The Kotlin compiler
        <execution>                               needs to know about
          <id>test-compile</id>                   both our Kotlin and
          <goals>                                  Java code locations.
            <goal>test-compile</goal>
          </goals>
          <configuration>
            <sourceDirs>                                                    ◄──
              <sourceDir>${project.basedir}/src/test/kotlin</sourceDir>
              <sourceDir>${project.basedir}/src/test/java</sourceDir>
            </sourceDirs>
          </configuration>
        </execution>
      </executions>
    </plugin>
    <plugin>
      <groupId>org.apache.maven.plugins</groupId>
      <artifactId>maven-compiler-plugin</artifactId>
      <version>3.8.1</version>
      <executions>
        <execution>
```

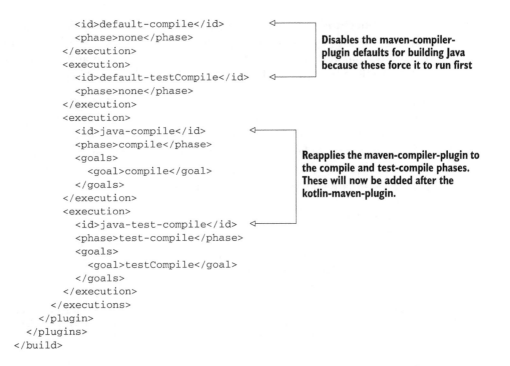

```
        <id>default-compile</id>
        <phase>none</phase>
    </execution>
    <execution>
        <id>default-testCompile</id>
        <phase>none</phase>
    </execution>
    <execution>
        <id>java-compile</id>
        <phase>compile</phase>
        <goals>
            <goal>compile</goal>
        </goals>
    </execution>
    <execution>
        <id>java-test-compile</id>
        <phase>test-compile</phase>
        <goals>
            <goal>testCompile</goal>
        </goals>
    </execution>
    </executions>
  </plugin>
 </plugins>
</build>
```

Disables the maven-compiler-plugin defaults for building Java because these force it to run first

Reapplies the maven-compiler-plugin to the compile and test-compile phases. These will now be added after the kotlin-maven-plugin.

NOTE The above overrides may get complicated when using Maven features like parent projects, where additional POM definitions might come into conflict. We'll see some tactics soon for debugging when these issues arise.

Your project will need a dependency on at least the Kotlin standard library, so we add that explicitly like so:

```
<dependencies>
    <dependency>
        <groupId>org.jetbrains.kotlin</groupId>
        <artifactId>kotlin-stdlib</artifactId>
        <version>1.6.10</version>
    </dependency>
</dependencies>
```

With this in place, our multilingual project builds and runs as before.

11.2.6 *Testing*

Once your code builds, a smart next step is to test it. Maven integrates testing deeply into its lifecycle. In fact, where compilation of your main code is only a single phase, Maven supports two separate phases of testing out of the box: test and integration-test. test is used for typical unit testing, whereas the integration-test phase runs after construction of artifacts such as JARs, with the intent of performing end-to-end validation on your final outputs.

NOTE Integration tests may also be run with JUnit because, despite the name, JUnit is a very capable test runner for more than just unit testing. Do not fall into the trap of thinking that any test executed by JUnit is automatically a unit test! We'll examine the different types of tests in detail in chapter 13.

Almost any project will benefit from some testing. As you might expect from Maven's opinionated stance, testing happens (by default) using the near ubiquitous framework JUnit. Other frameworks are just a plugin away.

Although the standard plugins know about running JUnit, we still must declare the library as a dependency so Maven knows how to compile our tests. You can add a library with a snippet like the following under the `<project>` element:

```
<dependencies>
  <dependency>
    <groupId>org.junit.jupiter</groupId>
    <artifactId>junit-jupiter-api</artifactId>
    <version>5.8.1</version>
    <scope>test</scope>
  </dependency>
  <dependency>
    <groupId>org.junit.jupiter</groupId>
    <artifactId>junit-jupiter-engine</artifactId>
    <version>5.8.1</version>
    <scope>test</scope>
  </dependency>
</dependencies>
```

`<scope>` indicates this library is needed only for the test-compile phase.

With that in place, we can try to run our unit tests. Depending on your version of Maven, even the most recent versions may give us this odd result:

```
~:mvn test

  [INFO] Scanning for projects...
  [INFO]
  [INFO] ------------------< com.wellgrounded:example >----------------
  [INFO] Building example 1.0-SNAPSHOT
  [INFO] --------------------------------[ jar ]-----------------------
  [INFO]
  [INFO] .....
  [INFO]
  [INFO] -- maven-surefire-plugin:2.12.4:test (default-test) @ example -
  [INFO] Surefire report dir: ./target/surefire-reports

  -------------------------------------------------------
   T E S T S
  -------------------------------------------------------
  Running com.wellgrounded.MainTest
  Tests run: 0, Failures: 0, Errors: 0, Skipped: 0, Time elapsed: 0.001 sec

  Results :

  Tests run: 0, Failures: 0, Errors: 0, Skipped: 0
```

Maven's default for running JUnit tests is the maven-surefire-plugin.

No tests were run? That's not right!

```
[INFO] -------------------------------------------------
[INFO] BUILD SUCCESS
[INFO] -------------------------------------------------
[INFO] Total time:  5.605 s
[INFO] Finished at: 2021-11-29T09:41:06+01:00
[INFO] -------------------------------------------------
```

For compatibility reasons, the plugin `maven-surefire-plugin` that is installed by default, even as late as Maven 3.8.4, isn't aware of JUnit 5. We'll dig more into these conversion issues in chapter 13, but in the meantime, let's just bump our version of the plugin to something more recent, as shown here:

```
<plugin>
  <groupId>org.apache.maven.plugins</groupId>
  <artifactId>maven-surefire-plugin</artifactId>
  <version>3.0.0-M5</version>              ⟵
</plugin>
```

Moving later than 2.12, the plugins understand JUnit 5 directly.

With that in place we see the following more reassuring outcome:

```
~:mvn test

  [INFO] .....

  ---------------------------------------------------------
   T E S T S
  ---------------------------------------------------------
  Running com.wellgrounded.MainTest
  Tests run: 1, Failures: 0, Errors: 0, Skipped: 0, Time elapsed: 0.04 sec

  Results :

  Tests run: 1, Failures: 0, Errors: 0, Skipped: 0

  [INFO] -------------------------------------------------
  [INFO] BUILD SUCCESS
  [INFO] -------------------------------------------------
  [INFO] Total time:  1.010 s
  [INFO] Finished at: 2020-07-06T15:45:22+02:00
  [INFO] ---------------------------------------------------------
```

By default, the Surefire plugin runs all unit tests in the standard location, `src/test/*`, during the `test` phase. If we want to take advantage of the `integration-test` phase, it's recommended to use a separate plugin, such as `maven-failsafe-plugin`. Failsafe is maintained by the same folks who make `maven-surefire-plugin` and specifically targets the integration testing case. We add the plugin in our `<build><plugins>` section we previously used for configuring our manifest as follows:

```
<plugin>
  <groupId>org.apache.maven.plugins</groupId>
  <artifactId>maven-failsafe-plugin</artifactId>
```

```
  <version>3.0.0-M5</version>
  <executions>
    <execution>
      <goals>
        <goal>integration-test</goal>
        <goal>verify</goal>
      </goals>
    </execution>
  </executions>
</plugin>
```

Failsafe treats the following filename patterns as integration tests, although it can be reconfigured:

- `**/IT*.java`
- `**/*IT.java`
- `**/*ITCase.java`

Because it's part of the same suite of plugins, Surefire is also aware of this convention and excludes these tests from the `test` phase.

It's recommended to run integration tests via `mvn verify`, as shown next, rather than `mvn integration-test`. `verify` includes `post-integration-test`, which is the typical location for plugins to attach any post-test cleanup work if any is needed:

```
~: mvn verify

  [INFO] ... compilation output omitted for length ...

  [INFO] --- maven-failsafe-plugin:3.0.0-M5:integration-test @ example ---
  [INFO]
  [INFO] -------------------------------------------------------
  [INFO]  T E S T S
  [INFO] -------------------------------------------------------
  [INFO] Running com.wellgrounded.LongRunningIT
  [INFO] Tests run: 1, Failures: 0, Errors: 0, Skipped: 0,
  [INFO] Time elapsed: 0.032 s - in com.wellgrounded.LongRunningIT
  [INFO]
  [INFO] Results:
  [INFO]
  [INFO] Tests run: 1, Failures: 0, Errors: 0, Skipped: 0
  [INFO]
  [INFO]
  [INFO] --- maven-failsafe-plugin:3.0.0-M5:verify (default) @ example ---
  [INFO] -------------------------------------------------------------------
  [INFO] BUILD SUCCESS
  [INFO] -------------------------------------------------------------------
```

11.2.7 *Dependency management*

A key feature Maven brought to the ecosystem was a standard format for expressing dependency management information via the `pom.xml` file. Maven also established a central repository for libraries. Maven can walk your `pom.xml` and the `pom.xml` files from your dependencies to determine the entire set of *transitive dependencies* your application requires.

The process of walking the tree and finding all the necessary libraries is called *dependency resolution*. Though critical for managing modern applications, the process does have its sharp edges.

To see where the problems arise, let's revisit the project setup we saw earlier in section 11.1.2. Recall that the project's dependencies have resulted in a tree that looks like that shown in figure 11.3.

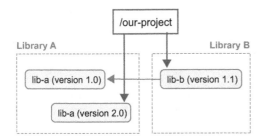

Figure 11.3 Conflicting transitive dependencies where a dependency requests an older version

Here we've asked explicitly for version 2.0 of `lib-a`, but our dependency `lib-b` has asked for the older version 1.0. Maven's dependency resolution algorithm favors the version of a library closest to the root. The end result of the configuration shown in figure 11.3 is that we will use `lib-a` 2.0 in our application. As we outlined in section 11.1.2, this may work fine or be disastrously broken.

Another common scenario that can also cause problems is when the reverse occurs and the dependency that is closest to the root is *older* than the one expected as a transitive dependency, as depicted in figure 11.4.

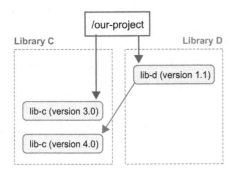
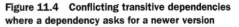

Figure 11.4 Conflicting transitive dependencies where a dependency asks for a newer version

In this case, it's entirely possible that `lib-d` is relying on an API in `lib-c` that didn't exist in version 3.0, so adding a dependency on `lib-d` to a project that is already using `lib-c` will result in runtime exceptions.

NOTE Given those possibilities, we recommended any package your code directly interacts with should be declared explicitly in your pom.xml. If you don't, and instead rely upon transitive dependency, updating your direct dependency could result in unexpected build breakage.

Before we can solve our dependency problems, it's important to know what our dependencies are. Maven has us covered with the mvn dependency:tree command, shown here:

```
~:mvn dependency:tree
   [INFO] Scanning for projects...
   [INFO]
   [INFO] -------------------< com.wellgrounded:example >---------------
   [INFO] Building example 1.0-SNAPSHOT
   [INFO] --------------------------[ jar ]--------------------------
   [INFO]
   [INFO] -- maven-dependency-plugin:2.8:tree (default-cli) @ example --
   [INFO] com.wellgrounded:example:jar:1.0-SNAPSHOT
   [INFO] +- org.junit.jupiter:junit-jupiter-api:jar:5.8.1:test
   [INFO] |  +- org.opentest4j:opentest4j:jar:1.2.0:test
   [INFO] |  +- org.junit.platform:junit-platform-commons:jar:1.8.1:test
   [INFO] |  \- org.apiguardian:apiguardian-api:jar:1.1.2:test
   [INFO] \- org.junit.jupiter:junit-jupiter-engine:jar:5.8.1:test
   [INFO]    \- org.junit.platform:junit-platform-engine:jar:1.8.1:test
   [INFO] -------------------------------------------------------------
   [INFO] BUILD SUCCESS
   [INFO] -------------------------------------------------------------
   [INFO] Total time:  0.790 s
   [INFO] Finished at: 2020-08-13T23:02:10+02:00
   [INFO] -------------------------------------------------------------
```

The tree from this command shows us our direct dependencies on JUnit from the pom .xml file at the first level of nesting, followed by JUnit's own transitive dependencies.

JUnit comes with a slim set of dependencies, so to explore transitive dependency issues further, let's imagine that our team wants to use two internal libraries at our company to get support for doing custom assertions. These are both built using the assertj library, but unfortunately different versions, as shown next:

```
[INFO] com.wellgrounded:example:jar:1.0-SNAPSHOT
[INFO] +- org.junit.jupiter:junit-jupiter-api:jar:5.8.1:test
[INFO] |  +- org.opentest4j:opentest4j:jar:1.2.0:test
[INFO] |  +- org.junit.platform:junit-platform-commons:jar:1.8.1:test
[INFO] |  \- org.apiguardian:apiguardian-api:jar:1.1.2:test
[INFO] +- org.junit.jupiter:junit-jupiter-engine:jar:5.8.1:test
[INFO] |  \- org.junit.platform:junit-platform-engine:jar:1.8.1:test
[INFO] +- com.wellgrounded:first-test-helper:1.0.0:test
[INFO] |  \- org.assertj:assertj-core:3.21.0:test         ◁
[INFO] \- com.wellgrounded:second-test-helper:2.0.0:test
[INFO]    \- org.assertj:assertj-core:2.9.1:test  ◁
```

Our first helper library brings assertj-core with version 3.21.0.

Our second helper library wants assertj-core with version 2.9.1.

The best possible approach is finding newer versions of our dependencies that can all agree on their dependencies. As internal libraries, this is obviously a possibility. Even in the broader world of open source, it's often possible. Having said that, sometimes libraries lose their maintainers and fall out of date, so it is entirely possible to get stuck in a situation where it's difficult to get the update we desire.

This leaves us looking for other ways to deal with the conflict. Two main approaches come into play if we can't find a natural resolution. Be aware that both of these solutions require finding *some* compatible version that will satisfy your dependencies.

If one of your dependencies specifies a version that everyone could agree on, but it isn't being chosen by Maven's resolution algorithm, you can tell Maven to exclude parts of the tree when resolving. If both of our helper libraries can work fine with the newer `assertj-core`, we can just ignore the older one brought by the second library, as shown here:

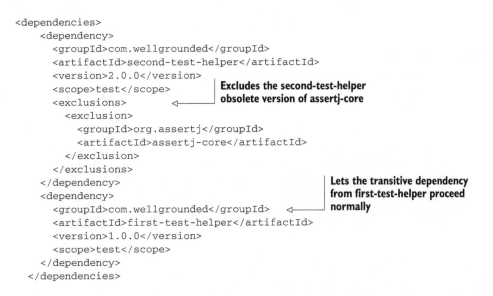

```
<dependencies>
    <dependency>
      <groupId>com.wellgrounded</groupId>
      <artifactId>second-test-helper</artifactId>
      <version>2.0.0</version>
      <scope>test</scope>                    Excludes the second-test-helper
      <exclusions>                           obsolete version of assertj-core
        <exclusion>
          <groupId>org.assertj</groupId>
          <artifactId>assertj-core</artifactId>
        </exclusion>
      </exclusions>
    </dependency>                            Lets the transitive dependency
    <dependency>                            from first-test-helper proceed
      <groupId>com.wellgrounded</groupId>   normally
      <artifactId>first-test-helper</artifactId>
      <version>1.0.0</version>
      <scope>test</scope>
    </dependency>
  </dependencies>
```

In the worst case, perhaps neither library expresses the compatible version. To handle this, we specify the precise version as a direct dependency in our project, as shown in the following code sample. By its resolution rules, Maven will choose that version because it is closer to the project root. Although this convinces the tool to do what we want, we are taking on the risk of runtime errors from mixing libraries versions, so it is important to test the interactions thoroughly:

```
<dependencies>
    <dependency>                                    Our dependencies will
      <groupId>com.wellgrounded</groupId>           ask for assertj-core at
      <artifactId>second-test-helper</artifactId>   a different version.
      <version>2.0.0</version>
      <scope>test</scope>
    </dependency>
```

```
<dependency>
  <groupId>com.wellgrounded</groupId>
  <artifactId>first-test-helper</artifactId>          ◁——
  <version>1.0.0</version>
  <scope>test</scope>
</dependency>
<dependency>
  <groupId>org.assertj</groupId>
  <artifactId>org.assertj</artifactId>
  <version>3.1.0</version>                              ◁——
  <scope>test</scope>
</dependency>
</dependencies>
```

Our dependencies will ask for assertj-core at a different version.

But we force resolution on assertj-core to the precise version we want.

Finally, it's worth noting that the `maven-enforcer-plugin` can be configured to fail the build if any mismatched dependencies are found so we can avoid relying on bad runtime behavior to surface problems. (See http://mng.bz/o2WN.) These build failures can then be addressed using the techniques we've discussed earlier.

11.2.8 Reviewing

Our build process is an excellent spot to hook in additional tooling and checks. One key bit of information is code coverage, which informs us what parts of our code our tests execute.

A leading option for code coverage in the Java ecosystem is JaCoCo (http://mng.bz/nNjv). JaCoCo can be configured to enforce certain coverage levels during testing and will output reports that tell you what is and isn't covered.

Enabling JaCoCo requires only adding a plugin to the `<build><plugins>` section of your `pom.xml` file. It doesn't enable itself by default, so you have to tell it when it should execute. In this example we've bound it to the `test` phase like this:

```
<build>
  <plugins>
    <plugin>
      <groupId>org.jacoco</groupId>
      <artifactId>jacoco-maven-plugin</artifactId>
      <version>0.8.5</version>
      <executions>
        <execution>                          ◁——
          <goals>
            <goal>prepare-agent</goal>
          </goals>
        </execution>
        <execution>                          ◁——
          <id>report</id>
          <phase>test</phase>
          <goals>
            <goal>report</goal>
          </goals>
        </execution>
      </executions>
```

JaCoCo needs to start running early in the process. This adds it to the initialize phase.

Tells JaCoCo to report during the test phase

```
      </plugin>
    </plugins>
  </build>
```

This produces reports on all of your classes in `target/site/jacoco` by default, as shown in figure 11.5, with a full HTML version at `index.html` to be explored.

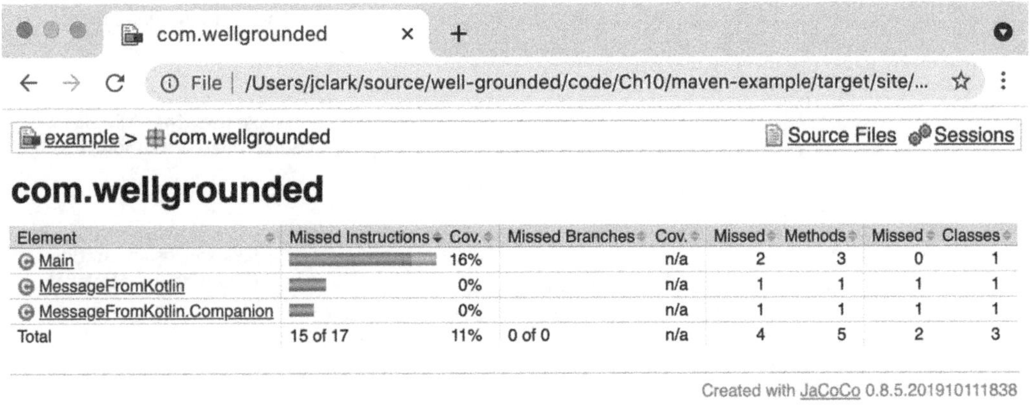

Figure 11.5   JaCoCo coverage report page

11.2.9   *Moving beyond Java 8*

In chapter 1, we noted the following series of modules that belonged with Java Enterprise Edition but were present in the core JDK. These were deprecated with JDK 9 and removed with JDK 11 but remain available as external libraries:

- `java.activation` (JAF)
- `java.corba` (CORBA)
- `java.transaction` (JTA)
- `java.xml.bind` (JAXB)
- `java.xml.ws` (JAX-WS, plus some related technologies)
- `java.xml.ws.annotation` (Common Annotations)

If your project relies on any of these modules, your build might break when you move to a more recent JDK. Fortunately a few simple dependency additions in your `pom.xml`, shown here, address the issue:

```
<dependencies>
  <dependency>
    <groupId>com.sun.activation</groupId>      ⟵─── java.activation (JAF)
    <artifactId>jakarta.activation</artifactId>
    <version>1.2.2</version>
  </dependency>
  <dependency>
    <groupId>org.glassfish.corba</groupId>      ⟵─── java.corba (CORBA)
    <artifactId>glassfish-corba-omgapi</artifactId>
```

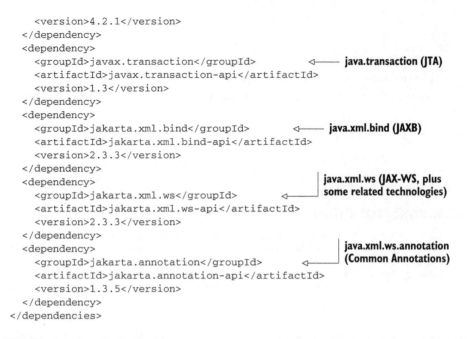

```
        <version>4.2.1</version>
    </dependency>
    <dependency>
        <groupId>javax.transaction</groupId>          ⟵——— java.transaction (JTA)
        <artifactId>javax.transaction-api</artifactId>
        <version>1.3</version>
    </dependency>
    <dependency>
        <groupId>jakarta.xml.bind</groupId>           ⟵——— java.xml.bind (JAXB)
        <artifactId>jakarta.xml.bind-api</artifactId>
        <version>2.3.3</version>
    </dependency>
    <dependency>                                           java.xml.ws (JAX-WS, plus
        <groupId>jakarta.xml.ws</groupId>            ⟵——  some related technologies)
        <artifactId>jakarta.xml.ws-api</artifactId>
        <version>2.3.3</version>
    </dependency>
    <dependency>                                          java.xml.ws.annotation
        <groupId>jakarta.annotation</groupId>        ⟵——  (Common Annotations)
        <artifactId>jakarta.annotation-api</artifactId>
        <version>1.3.5</version>
    </dependency>
</dependencies>
```

11.2.10 *Multirelease JARs in Maven*

A feature that arrived in JDK 9 was the ability to package JARs that target different code for different JDKs. This allows us to take advantage of new features in the platform, while still supporting clients of our code on older versions.

In chapter 2, we examined the feature and hand-crafted the specific JAR format necessary to enable this capability. The layout places versioned directories under META-INF/versions within the JAR where the JVM from 9 onward will check for newer versions of a given class during loading, as shown next:

```
.
├── META-INF
│   ├── MANIFEST.MF
│   └── versions
│       └── 11
│           └── wgjd2ed
│               └── GetPID.class
└── wgjd2ed
    ├── GetPID.class
    └── Main.class
```

Within this structure, the classes in wgjd2ed will have a class file version representing the oldest JVM the JAR may be used with. (In our later example, this will be JDK 8.) Classes under META-INF/versions/11, though, may be compiled with a newer JDK and have a newer class file version. Because older JDKs ignore the META-INF/versions directory (and those from 9 onward understand what versions they're allowed to use), we can mix newer code in a JAR while still having everything work on an older JVM. This is exactly the sort of tedious process that Maven was built to automate.

Although the output format in our JAR is all that really matters to enable the multirelease feature, we'll mimic the structure in our code layout for clarity. As shown here, the code in `src` is the baseline functionality that will be seen by any JDK by default. The code under `versions` optionally replaces specific classes with an alternate implementation:

```
.
├── pom.xml
├── src
│   └── main
│       └── java
│           └── wgjd2ed
│               ├── GetPID.java
│               └── Main.java
└── versions
    └── 11
        └── src
            └── wgjd2ed
                └── GetPID.java
```

Maven's defaults will find and compile our code in `src/main`, but we have two complications we need to sort out:

- Maven needs to *also* find our code in the `versions` directory.
- Further, Maven needs to compile that source targeted to a different JDK than the main project.

Both of these goals can be accomplished by configuring the `maven-compiler-plugin` that builds our Java class files. We introduce two separate `<execution>` steps in the next code snippet—one to compile the base code targeting JDK 8, and then a second pass to compile the versioned code targeting JDK 11.

> **NOTE** We must compile using a JDK version at least as new as the latest version you're targeting. However, we'll explicitly instruct some build steps to target a lower version than the compiler is capable of.

```xml
<plugins>
  <plugin>
    <groupId>org.apache.maven.plugins</groupId>
    <artifactId>maven-compiler-plugin</artifactId>
    <version>3.8.1</version>
    <executions>
      <execution>
        <id>compile-java-8</id>        ◁──┐ Execution step to
        <goals>                            compile for JDK 8
          <goal>compile</goal>
        </goals>
        <configuration>                    We'll compile with JDK 11,
          <source>1.8</source>         ◁──┘ so we target this step's
                                           output to JDK 8.
```

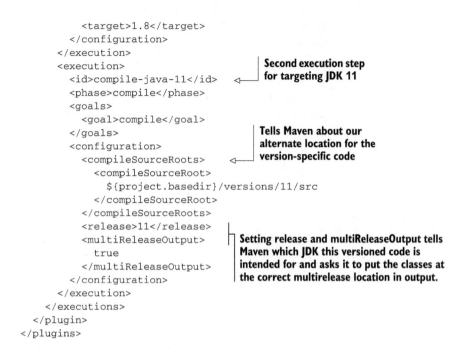

```
        <target>1.8</target>
      </configuration>
    </execution>
    <execution>
      <id>compile-java-11</id>          Second execution step
      <phase>compile</phase>            for targeting JDK 11
      <goals>
        <goal>compile</goal>
      </goals>                          Tells Maven about our
      <configuration>                   alternate location for the
        <compileSourceRoots>            version-specific code
          <compileSourceRoot>
            ${project.basedir}/versions/11/src
          </compileSourceRoot>
        </compileSourceRoots>
        <release>11</release>
        <multiReleaseOutput>            Setting release and multiReleaseOutput tells
          true                          Maven which JDK this versioned code is
        </multiReleaseOutput>           intended for and asks it to put the classes at
      </configuration>                  the correct multirelease location in output.
    </execution>
  </executions>
</plugin>
</plugins>
```

This gets our JAR built and packaged with the right layout. There's one more step, and that's marking the manifest as multirelease. This is configured in the maven-jar-plugin, as shown here, close to where we made our application JAR executable in section 11.2.4:

```
<plugin>
  <groupId>org.apache.maven.plugins</groupId>
  <artifactId>maven-jar-plugin</artifactId>
  <version>3.2.0</version>
  <configuration>
    <archive>
      <manifest>
        <addClasspath>true</addClasspath>
        <mainClass>wgjd2ed.Main</mainClass>
      </manifest>                                 Attribute to mark the
      <manifestEntries>                           JAR as multirelease
        <Multi-Release>true</Multi-Release>
      </manifestEntries>
    </archive>
  </configuration>
</plugin>
```

With that we can execute our code against different JDKs and see it behave as expected. In the case of our sample app, the base implementation for JDK 8 will output an additional version message, as illustrated here, so we can see it's working:

```
~:mvn clean compile package
[INFO] Scanning for projects...
[INFO]
[INFO] ----------------< wgjd2ed:maven-multi-release >-------------------
[INFO] Building maven-multi-release 1.0-SNAPSHOT
[INFO] -------------------------[ jar ]-----------------------------
[INFO]
[INFO] .... Lots of additional steps
[INFO]
[INFO] - maven-jar-plugin:3.2.0:jar (default-jar) @ maven-multi-release -
[INFO] Building jar: ~/target/maven-multi-release-1.0-SNAPSHOT.jar
[INFO] ------------------------------------------------------------
[INFO] BUILD SUCCESS
[INFO] ------------------------------------------------------------
[INFO] Total time:  1.813 s
[INFO] Finished at: 2021-03-05T09:39:16+01:00
[INFO] ------------------------------------------------------------

~:java -version
openjdk version "11.0.6" 2020-01-14
OpenJDK Runtime Environment AdoptOpenJDK (build 11.0.6+10)
OpenJDK 64-Bit Server VM AdoptOpenJDK (build 11.0.6+10, mixed mode)

~:java -jar target/maven-multi-release-1.0-SNAPSHOT.jar
75891

# Change JDK versions by your favorite means....

~:java -version
openjdk version "1.8.0_265"
OpenJDK Runtime Environment (AdoptOpenJDK)(build 1.8.0_265-b01)
OpenJDK 64-Bit Server VM (AdoptOpenJDK)(build 25.265-b01, mixed mode)

~:java -jar target/maven-multi-release-1.0-SNAPSHOT.jar
Java 8 version...
76087
```

The path to using new features in the JDK without abandoning older clients is all set!

11.2.11 Maven and modules

In chapter 2, we examined the JDK's new module system in detail. Let's look at how it influences our build scripting. We'll start looking at a simple library that exposes one of its packages publicly while hiding the other.

A MODULAR LIBRARY

Modular projects vary slightly in their code layout from the strict Maven standard. The main directory instead reflects the name of the module, as shown here:

```
.
├── pom.xml
└── src
    └── com.wellgrounded.modlib  ◁──── Our modular code directory
        └── java
```

```
            └── com
                └── wellgrounded
                    ├── hidden
A class we intend   │    └── CantTouchThis.java  ◄──── A class we intend to keep private
to share publicly   └── visible
through our module ──►   └── UseThis.java
```

Having made that change, we have to inform Maven of this new location to look for source code to compile as follows:

```
<build>
  <sourceDirectory>src/com.wellgrounded.modlib/java</sourceDirectory>
</build>
```

The final piece to making our library modular is the addition of a `module-info.java` at the root of our code (alongside the `com` directory). This will name our module, and declare what we allow access to, as shown here:

```
module com.wellgrounded.modlib {
    exports com.wellgrounded.modlib.visible;
}
```

Everything else about this simple library remains the same, and if we `mvn package`, we'll get a JAR file in `target`. Before we proceed further, we can also put this library into the local Maven cache via `mvn install`.

> **NOTE** The JDK's module system is about access control at build and runtime, *not* packaging. A modular library can be shared as a plain old JAR file, just with the additional `module-info.class` included to tell modular applications how to interact with it.

Now that we have a modular library, let's build a modular application to consume it.

A MODULAR APPLICATION
Our modular application gets a similar layout to what we used for the library, as shown next:

```
.
├── pom.xml
└── src
    └── com.wellgrounded.modapp
        └── java
            ├── com
            │    └── wellgrounded
            │         └── Main.java
            └── module-info.java
```

Our `module-info.java` for the application declares our name, and states that we require the package exported by our library as follows:

```
module com.wellgrounded.modapp {
    requires com.wellgrounded.modlib;
}
```

This by itself doesn't tell Maven where to find our library JAR, though, so we include it as a normal <dependency> like this:

```
<dependencies>
    <dependency>
        <groupId>com.wellgrounded</groupId>      ◁──┐  Our library from the prior
        <artifactId>modlib</artifactId>                section, installed into the
        <version>2.0</version>                         local Maven repository
    </dependency>
</dependencies>
```

When we're compiling and subsequently running, it's important that this dependency be placed on the module path instead of the classpath. How does Maven accomplish this? Fortunately, recent versions of the maven-compiler-plugin are smart enough to notice that 1) our application has a module-info.java, so it's modular; and 2) the dependency includes module-info.class, so it, too, is a module. As long as you are on a recent version of maven-compiler-plugin (3.8 worked great at the time of writing), Maven figures it out for you.

Our application code is perfectly normal Java, and we can use the modular library's functionality as intended, as follows:

```
package com.wellgrounded.modapp;
                                                       import from the module,
import com.wellgrounded.modlib.visible.UseThis;  ◁──┘  just like any other package.

public class Main {
  public static void main(String[] args) {           Uses the class from our
    System.out.println(UseThis.getMessage());  ◁──┘   module to get a message
  }
}
```

You may remember that we had another package in our library that we didn't provide access to. What happens if we modify our application to try and pull that in, like so:

```
package com.wellgrounded.modapp;
                                                              com.wellgrounded.modlib
                                                              .hidden was not listed in
import com.wellgrounded.modlib.visible.UseThis;               the library's exports.
import com.wellgrounded.modlib.hidden.CantTouchThis;  ◁──┘

public class Main {
  public static void main(String[] args) {
    System.out.println(UseThis.getMessage());
  }
}
```

Compiling this will give us the following error straight away:

```
[INFO] - maven-compiler-plugin:3.8.1:compile @ modapp ---
  [INFO] Changes detected - recompiling the module!
  [INFO] Compiling 2 source files to /mod-app/target/classes
  [INFO] ------------------------------------------------------------
  [ERROR] COMPILATION ERROR :
  [INFO] ------------------------------------------------------------
  [ERROR]
    src/com.wellgrounded.modapp/java/com/wellgrounded/Main.java:[4,31]
       package com.wellgrounded.modlib.hidden is not visible (package
       com.wellgrounded.modlib.hidden is declared in module
       com.wellgrounded.modlib, which does not export it)

  [INFO] 1 error
  [INFO] ------------------------------------------------------------
  [INFO] BUILD FAILURE
  [INFO] ------------------------------------------------------------
```

> javac and the module system won't even let us try to touch things that aren't exported!

Maven's tooling has come a long way since the release of modules in JDK 9. All the standard scenarios are well covered with a minimum of additional configuration required.

Before we go, though, let's take one brief tangent. Throughout this section, `module-info.class` was frequently the signal to Maven that it should start applying modular rules. But modules are an *opt-in* feature in the JDK to preserve compatibility with the vast quantities of premodular code out there.

What happens if we build the same application using our modular library, but the application doesn't mark itself to use modules by including the `module-info.java` file? In that case, the library—although it is modular—will be included via the classpath. This places it in the unnamed module along with the application's own code, and all those access restrictions we defined in the library are effectively ignored. A sample application is included in the supplement alongside the modular one that uses our library by classpath so you can see more clearly how opting into or out of modules works.

With that, our tour of Maven's default features is done. But what do we do if we need to extend the system beyond the admittedly vast array of plugins we can find online?

11.2.12 *Authoring Maven plugins*

Even the most basic defaults in Maven are supplied as plugins, and there's no reason you can't write one, too, when we need to do more. As we've seen, referencing a plugin is a lot like pulling in a dependent library. It isn't surprising, then, that we implement our Maven plugins as separate JAR files.

For our example, we start with a `pom.xml` file. Much of the boilerplate is similar to before with a couple small additions, shown here:

Lets
Maven
know we
intend to
build a
plugin
package

```
<project>
  <modelVersion>4.0.0</modelVersion>

  <name>A Well-Grounded Maven Plugin</name>
  <groupId>com.wellgrounded</groupId>
  <artifactId>wellgrounded-maven-plugin</artifactId>
  <packaging>maven-plugin</packaging>
  <version>1.0-SNAPSHOT</version>

  <properties>
    <project.build.sourceEncoding>UTF-8</project.build.sourceEncoding>
    <maven.compiler.source>11</maven.compiler.source>
    <maven.compiler.target>11</maven.compiler.target>
  </properties>

  <dependencies>
    <dependency>
      <groupId>org.apache.maven</groupId>
      <artifactId>maven-plugin-api</artifactId>
      <version>3.0</version>
    </dependency>

    <dependency>
      <groupId>org.apache.maven.plugin-tools</groupId>
      <artifactId>maven-plugin-annotations</artifactId>
      <version>3.4</version>
      <scope>provided</scope>
    </dependency>
  </dependencies>
</project>
```

-SNAPSHOT is a typical suffix added to not-yet-released versions of a library. This shows up when pulling in the library because you must specify the full string 1.0-SNAPSHOT, for example, when asking for the dependency.

Maven API dependencies our implementation will need

That gets us set to start adding code. Placing a Java file in the standard layout location, we implement what is called a `Mojo`—effectively a Maven *goal*, as follows:

```
package com.wellgrounded;

import org.apache.maven.plugin.AbstractMojo;
import org.apache.maven.plugin.MojoExecutionException;
import org.apache.maven.plugins.annotations.Mojo;

@Mojo(name = "wellgrounded")
public class WellGroundedMojo extends AbstractMojo
{
    public void execute() throws MojoExecutionException
    {
        getLog().info("Extending Maven for fun and profit.");
    }
}
```

Our class extends `AbstractMojo` and tells Maven via the `@Mojo` annotation what our goal name is. The body of the method takes care of whatever job we want. In this case, we simply log some text, but you have the full Java language and ecosystem available at this point to implement your goal.

To test the plugin in another project, we need to `mvn install` it, which will place our JAR into the local caching repository. Once there, we can pull our plugin into another project just like all the other "real" plugins we've seen already in this chapter, as follows:

```
<build>
  <plugins>
    <plugin>
      <groupId>com.wellgrounded</groupId>     ◁
      <artifactId>wellgrounded-maven-plugin</artifactId>
      <version>1.0-SNAPSHOT</version>
      <executions>
        <execution>          ◁────  Binds our goal to the compile phase
          <phase>compile</phase>
          <goals>
            <goal>wellgrounded</goal>
          </goals>
        </execution>
      </executions>
    </plugin>
  </plugins>
</build>
```

References to our plugin coordinates by groupId and artifactId

With this in place, we can see our plugin in action when we compile, as shown here:

```
~: mvn compile
  [INFO] Scanning for projects...
  [INFO]
  [INFO] -----------------< com.wellgrounded:example >--------------
  [INFO] Building example 1.0-SNAPSHOT
  [INFO] --------------------------[ jar ]------------------------
  [INFO]
  [INFO] - maven-resources-plugin:2.6:resources (default-resources) -
  [INFO] Using 'UTF-8' encoding to copy filtered resources.
  [INFO] skip non existing resourceDirectory /src/main/resources
  [INFO]
  [INFO] --- maven-compiler-plugin:3.1:compile (default-compile)   ---
  [INFO] Nothing to compile - all classes are up to date
  [INFO]
  [INFO] --- wellgrounded-maven-plugin:1.0-SNAPSHOT:wellgrounded   ---
  [INFO] Extending Maven for fun and profit.     ◁───────
  [INFO] ------------------------------------------------------------
  [INFO] BUILD SUCCESS
  [INFO] ------------------------------------------------------------
  [INFO] Total time:  0.872 s
  [INFO] Finished at: 2020-08-16T22:26:20+02:00
  [INFO] ------------------------------------------------------------
```

Our plugin running as part of the compile phase

It's worth noting that if we simply include the plugin without the `<executions>` element, we won't see our plugin show up anywhere in our project. Custom plugins must declare their desired phase in the lifecycle via the `pom.xml` file.

Visibility into the lifecycle and what goals are bound to what phases can be difficult, but fortunately there's a plugin to help with that. `buildplan-maven-plugin` brings clarity to your current tasks.

Although it can be included in a `pom.xml` like any other plugin, a useful alternative to avoid repetition is putting it in your user's ~/.m2/settings.xml file, as shown next. `settings.xml` files are similar to `pom.xml` files in Maven, but they are not associated to any specific project:

```
<settings xmlns="http://maven.apache.org/SETTINGS/1.0.0"
  xmlns:xsi="http://www.w3.org/2001/XMLSchema-instance"
  xsi:schemaLocation="http://maven.apache.org/SETTINGS/1.0.0
                      https://maven.apache.org/xsd/settings-1.0.0.xsd">
  <pluginGroups>
    <pluginGroup>fr.jcgay.maven.plugins</pluginGroup>
  </pluginGroups>
</settings>
```

Once there, you can invoke it in any project building with Maven like this:

```
~: mvn buildplan:list

  [INFO] Scanning for projects...
  [INFO]
  [INFO] --------------------< com.wellgrounded:example >-----------------
  [INFO] Building example 1.0-SNAPSHOT
  [INFO] ---------------------------[ jar ]---------------------------
  [INFO]
  [INFO] ---- buildplan-maven-plugin:1.3:list (default-cli) @ example ----
  [INFO] Build Plan for example:
  ----------------------------------------------------------------
  PLUGIN                  | PHASE            | ID                  | GOAL
  ----------------------------------------------------------------
  jacoco-maven-plugin     | initialize       | default             | prep-agent
  maven-compiler-plugin   | compile          | default-compile     | compile
  maven-compiler-plugin   | test-compile     | default-testCompile | testCompile
  maven-surefire-plugin   | test             | default-test        | test
  jacoco-maven-plugin     | test             | report              | report
  maven-jar-plugin        | package          | default-jar         | jar
  maven-failsafe-plugin   | integration-test | default             | int-test
  maven-failsafe-plugin   | verify           | default             | verify
  maven-install-plugin    | install          | default-install     | install
  maven-deploy-plugin     | deploy           | default-deploy      | deploy
  [INFO] ----------------------------------------------------------------
  [INFO] BUILD SUCCESS
  [INFO] ----------------------------------------------------------------
  [INFO] Total time:  0.461 s
  [INFO] Finished at: 2020-08-30T15:54:30+02:00
  [INFO] ----------------------------------------------------------------
```

NOTE If you don't want to add a plugin to your `pom.xml` *or* your `settings.xml`, you can just ask Maven to a run a command using the fully qualified plugin name! In our previous example, we can just say `mvn fr.jcgay.maven .plugins:buildplan-maven-plugin:list` and Maven will download the plugin and run it once. This is great for uncommon tasks or experimentation. Maven's documentation for authoring plugins (see http://mng.bz/v6dx) is thorough and well maintained, so do take a look when starting to implement your own plugins.

Maven remains among the most common build tools for Java and has been hugely influential. However, not everyone loves its strongly opinionated stance. Gradle is the most popular alternative, so let's see how it tackles the same problem space.

11.3   Gradle

Gradle came onto the scene after Maven and is compatible with much of the dependency management infrastructure Maven pioneered. It supports the familiar standard directory layout and provides a default build lifecycle for JVM projects, but unlike Maven, all of these features are fully customizable.

Instead of XML, Gradle uses a declarative domain-specific language (DSL) on top of an actual programming language (either Kotlin or Groovy). This typically results in concise build logic for simple cases and a lot of flexibility when things get more complex.

Gradle also includes a number of performance features for avoiding unnecessary work and processing tasks incrementally. This often provides faster builds and higher scalability. Let's get our feet wet by seeing how to run Gradle commands.

11.3.1   Installing Gradle

Gradle can be installed from its website (https://gradle.org/install). Recent versions rely on having only JVM version 8 or greater. Once installed, you can run it at the command line, and it will default to displaying help, as shown here:

```
~: gradle

  > Task :help

  Welcome to Gradle 7.3.3.

  To run a build, run gradlew <task> ...

  To see a list of available tasks, run gradlew tasks

  To see more detail about a task, run gradlew help --task <task>

  To see a list of command-line options, run gradlew --help

  For more detail on using Gradle, see
    https://docs.gradle.org/7.3.3/userguide/command_line_interface.html

  For troubleshooting, visit https://help.gradle.org

  BUILD SUCCESSFUL in 606ms
  1 actionable task: 1 executed
```

This makes it easy to get started, but having a single global Gradle version isn't ideal. It is common for a developer to build multiple different projects that could each have different versions of Gradle.

To handle this, Gradle introduces the idea of a *wrapper*. The `gradle wrapper` task will capture a specific version of Gradle locally into your project. This is then accessed via the `./gradlew` or `gradlew.bat` commands. It's considered good practice to use the `gradlew` wrappers to avoid version incompatibilities so you may find yourself rarely actually running `gradle` itself directly.

> **NOTE**   It's recommended that you include the `gradle` and `gradlew*` results of the wrapper in source control but exclude the local caching of `.gradle`.

With the wrappers committed, anyone downloading your project gets the properly versioned build tooling without any additional installs.

11.3.2 Tasks

Gradle's key concept is the *task*. A task defines a piece of work that can be invoked. Tasks can depend on other tasks, be configured via scripting, and added through Gradle's plugin system. These resemble Maven's goals but are conceptually more like functions. They have well-defined inputs and outputs and can be composed and chained. Whereas Maven goals must be associated to a given phase of the build lifecycle, Gradle tasks may be invoked and used in whatever fashion is convenient for you.

Gradle provides excellent introspection features. Key among these is the `./gradlew tasks` meta-task, which lists currently available tasks in your project. Before you've even declared anything, running `tasks` will present the following task list:

```
~: ./gradlew tasks

  > Task :tasks

  ------------------------------------------------------------
  Tasks runnable from root project
  ------------------------------------------------------------

  Build Setup tasks
  -----------------
  init - Initializes a new Gradle build.
  wrapper - Generates Gradle wrapper files.

  Help tasks
   ----------
  buildEnvironment - Displays all buildscript dependencies in root project
  components - Displays the components produced by root project.
  dependencies - Displays all dependencies declared in root project.
  dependencyInsight - Displays insight for dependency in root project
  dependentComponents - Displays dependent components in root project
  help - Displays a help message.
  model - Displays the configuration model of root project. [incubating]
  outgoingVariants - Displays the outgoing variants of root project.
```

```
projects - Displays the sub-projects of root project.
properties - Displays the properties of root project.
tasks - Displays the tasks runnable from root project.
```

Providing the `--dry-run` flag to any task will display the tasks Gradle would have run, without performing the actions. This is useful for understanding the flow of your build system or debugging misbehaving plugins or custom tasks.

11.3.3 *What's in a script?*

The heart of a Gradle build is its *buildscript*. This is a key difference between Gradle and Maven—not only is the format different but the entire philosophy is different, too. Maven POM files are XML-based, whereas in Gradle, the buildscript is an executable script written in a programming language—what's often referred to as a *domain-specific language* or DSL. Modern versions of Gradle support both Groovy and Kotlin.

GROOVY VS. KOTLIN

Gradle's DSL approach started out with Groovy. As we learned when we met it briefly in chapter 8, Groovy is a dynamic language on the JVM, and it fits nicely with the goal of flexibility and concise build scripting. Since Gradle 5.0, however, another option has been available: Kotlin, which we covered in detail in chapter 9.

> **NOTE** Kotlin buildscripts use the extension `.gradle.kts` instead of `.gradle`.

This makes a lot of sense because Kotlin is now the dominant language for Android development, where Gradle is the platform's official build tool. Sharing the same language across all parts of your project can be a great simplifying factor.

For our purposes, Kotlin is also more like Java than Groovy. Narrowing this language gap means that if you're new to the Gradle ecosystem, it might make sense to write your buildscript with Kotlin if you are coding in Java.

Groovy remains a prominent and very viable option, but we're going to double down on our Kotlin experience and use it for all of our following examples. Anything we show in this chapter can be expressed similarly in a Groovy buildscript with identical Gradle behavior. The Gradle documentation shows both DSL for all its examples.

11.3.4 *Using plugins*

Gradle uses plugins to define everything about the tasks we use. As we saw earlier, listing tasks in a blank Gradle project doesn't say anything about building, testing, or deploying. All of that comes from plugins.

Numerous plugins ship with Gradle itself, so using them requires only a declaration in your `build.gradle.kts`. A key one is the `base` plugin, shown here:

```
plugins {
  base
}
```

A look at our tasks after including the `base` plugin reveals some common build life-cycle tasks that we might expect, as shown next:

```
~:./gradlew tasks

 > Task :tasks

 ------------------------------------------------------------
 Tasks runnable from root project
 ------------------------------------------------------------

 Build tasks
 -----------
 assemble - Assembles the outputs of this project.
 build - Assembles and tests this project.
 clean - Deletes the build directory.

 ... Other tasks omitted for length

 Verification tasks
 ------------------
 check - Runs all checks.

 ...

 BUILD SUCCESSFUL in 640ms
 1 actionable task: 1 executed
```

With that in place, let's get building a Gradle project for our code.

11.3.5 *Building*

Although Gradle allows for customization to your heart's content, it defaults to expecting the same code layout that Maven established and popularized. For many (perhaps even most) projects, it doesn't make sense to change this layout, although it is possible to do so.

Let's start with a basic Java library. To do this, we create the following source tree:

```
.
├── build.gradle.kts
├── gradle
│   └── wrapper
│       ├── gradle-wrapper.jar
│       └── gradle-wrapper.properties
├── gradlew
├── gradlew.bat
├── settings.gradle.kts
└── src
    └── main
        └── java
            └── com
                └── wellgrounded
                    └── AwesomeLib.java
```

These files were automatically created by the Gradle wrapper command.

The `base` plugin doesn't know anything about Java, so we need a plugin with more awareness. For our use case of a plain Java JAR, we'll use Gradle's `java-library` plugin, shown next. This plugin builds on all the necessary parts from `base`—in practice, you'll rarely see the `base` plugin alone in a Gradle build. That's because plugins can apply other plugins to build off of them, like composition in object-oriented programming:

```
plugins {
  `java-library`
}
```

Backticks (not apostrophes) are used around plugin names when they include special characters such as - here.

This yields a growing set of tasks in our build section, as shown here:

```
Build tasks
-----------
    assemble - Assembles the outputs of this project.
    build - Assembles and tests this project.
    buildDependents - Assembles and tests this project and dependent projects.
    buildNeeded - Assembles and tests this project and dependent projects.
    classes - Assembles main classes.
    clean - Deletes the build directory.
    jar - Assembles a jar archive containing the main classes.
    testClasses - Assembles test classes.
```

In Gradle's terminology, `assemble` is the task that will compile and package up a JAR file. A dry run shows all of the steps, some of which the default tasks list doesn't show:

```
./gradlew assemble --dry-run
  :compileJava SKIPPED
  :processResources SKIPPED
  :classes SKIPPED
  :jar SKIPPED
  :assemble SKIPPED
```

Running `./gradlew assemble` generates output in the `build` directory as follows:

```
.
└── build
    ├── classes
    │   └── java
    │       └── main
    │           └── com
    │               └── wellgrounded
    │                   └── Main.class
    └── libs
        └── wellgrounded.jar
```

MAKING AN APPLICATION
A plain JAR is a good start, but eventually you want to run an application. This takes more configuration, but again the pieces are available by default.

We'll change up our plugins and tell Gradle what the main class is for our application. We also can see several of the nice features that Kotlin brings in just this brief snippet:

```
plugins {         ◁─────┐  Kotlin's optional parentheses when
  application  ◁─┐      │  the final argument is a lambda
}                │
                 └──  Plugin that knows how to
                      compile and run a Java app

application {
  mainClass.set("wgjd.Main")
}
tasks.jar {  ◁─────┐  Task for assembling a JAR
  manifest {       │  with a modified manifest              Kotlin uses to syntax to
    attributes("Main-Class" to application.mainClass)  ◁─┐ declare a hash map in
  }                                                       │ place (aka a hash literal).
}
```

Building with `./gradlew build` gets us the same JAR output as before, but if we execute `java -jar build/libs/wellgrounded.jar`, our test program will run. Alternatively, the `application` plugin also supports `./gradlew run` to directly load and execute your main class for you.

> **NOTE** The `application` plugin requires only that `mainClass` be set, but excluding the `tasks.jar` configuration will yield a JAR that `./gradlew run` knows how to start but `java -jar` doesn't. Definitely not recommended!

We now have the pieces we need to examine another key feature of Gradle: its ability to avoid work and reduce our build times.

11.3.6 Work avoidance

To run builds as fast as possible, Gradle tries to avoid repeating unnecessary work. One strategy for this is incremental build. Every task in Gradle declares its inputs and outputs. Gradle uses this information to check whether anything has changed since the last time the build ran. If there is no change, Gradle skips the task and reuses its outputs from the previous build.

> **NOTE** You shouldn't regularly run `clean` when using Gradle, because Gradle will ensure that the necessary—and only the necessary—work is done to produce the build results.

We can see this with our application build by taking a look at the build times after one full run (forced clean) and a second run, shown here:

```
~: ./gradlew clean build

  BUILD SUCCESSFUL in 2s
  13 actionable tasks: 13 executed
```

```
~: ./gradlew build

BUILD SUCCESSFUL in 804ms
12 actionable tasks: 12 up-to-date
```

Incremental build can only reuse outputs from the last execution of a task in the same location on this computer. Gradle does even better: the Build Cache allows reusing task outputs from any earlier build—or even a build run elsewhere.

This feature can be enabled in your project via a property with the `--build-cache` command-line flag. We can see that even the following `clean` build is faster because it can reuse cached outputs from the prior execution:

```
~: ./gradlew clean build --build-cache

BUILD SUCCESSFUL in 2s
13 actionable tasks: 13 executed

~: ./gradlew clean build --build-cache

BUILD SUCCESSFUL in 1s
13 actionable tasks: 6 executed, 7 from cache
```

Performance is a key feature of Gradle in keeping your project build times down even as the size of your code grows. Other abilities exist that we won't have time to cover, such as incremental Java compilation, the Gradle Daemon, and parallel task and test execution.

No person is an island. Similarly, few applications get far without pulling in other library dependencies. This is a major subject in Gradle and a point of considerable difference from Maven.

11.3.7   *Dependencies in Gradle*

To start introducing dependencies, we must first tell Gradle which repositories it can download from. There are built-in functions for `mavenCentral` (shown next) and `google`. You can use more detailed APIs to configure other repositories, including your own private instances:

```
repositories {
  mavenCentral()
}
```

We can then introduce our dependencies via the standard coordinate format popularized by Maven. Much like Maven had the `<scope>` element to control where a given dependency was used, Gradle expresses this through *dependency configurations*. Each configuration tracks a particular set of dependencies. Your plugins define which configurations are available, and you add to a configuration's list with a function call. For example, to pull the SLF4J library (http://www.slf4j.org/) to help with logging, we'd use the following configurations:

```
dependencies {
    implementation("org.slf4j:slf4j-api:1.7.30")
    runtimeOnly("org.slf4j:slf4j-simple:1.7.30")
}
```

In this example, our code directly calls classes and methods in slf4j-api, so it is included via the implementation configuration. This makes it available during compilation and running the application. Our application should never directly call methods in slf4j-simple, though—that's done strictly through the slf4j-api—so requesting slf4j-simple as runtimeOnly ensures that code isn't available during compilation, preventing us from misusing the library. This achieves the same purpose as the <scope> element with dependencies in Maven.

The distinction between dependencies we use directly and those just needed in our classpath at runtime isn't the only way to distinguish differences between dependencies. For library authors in particular, there is also a distinction between libraries that we use and those that are part of our public API. If a dependency is part of the public API of a project, we can mark it with api. In the following example, we're declaring that Guava is part of the public API of our project:

```
dependencies {
    api("com.google.guava:guava:31.0.1-jre")
}
```

Configurations can extend one another, much like deriving from a base class. Gradle applies this feature in many areas. For example when creating classpaths, Gradle uses a compileClasspath and runtimeClassPath, which extends implementation and runtimeOnly. You aren't meant to directly add to the *Classpath configurations—the dependencies we add to their base configurations build up the resulting classpath configuration, as shown in figure 11.6.

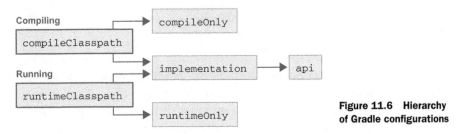

Figure 11.6   Hierarchy of Gradle configurations

Table 11.1 shows some primary configurations available when using the Java plugin that ships with Gradle, along with an indication of what other configurations each extends from. A full list is available in the Java plugin documentation at http://mng.bz/445B.

NOTE Version 7 of Gradle removed a number of long-standing deprecated configurations, for instance, `compile` and `runtime`. If you're reading around the internet, you may still find reference to these but should move to the newer options, `implementation` (or `api`) and `runtimeOnly`.

Table 11.1 Typical Gradle dependency configurations

Name	Purpose	Extends
`api`	Primary dependencies that are part of the project's external, public API	
`implementation`	Primary dependencies used during compiling and running	
`compileOnly`	Dependencies needed only during compilation	
`compileClasspath`	Configuration Gradle uses to look up compilation classpath	`compileOnly,` `implementation`
`runtimeOnly`	Dependencies needed only during runtime	
`runtimeClasspath`	Configuration Gradle uses to look up runtime classpath	`runtimeOnly,` `implementation`
`testImplementation`	Dependencies used during compiling and running tests	`implementation`
`testCompileOnly`	Dependencies needed only during compilation of tests	
`testCompileClasspath`	Configuration Gradle uses to look up test compilation classpath	`testCompileOnly,` `testImplementation`
`testRuntimeOnly`	Dependencies needed only during runtime	`runtimeOnly`
`testRuntimeClasspath`	Configuration Gradle uses to look up test runtime classpath	`testRuntimeOnly,` `testImplementation`
`archives`	List of output JARs from our project	

Like Maven, Gradle uses the package information to create a transitive dependency tree. However, Gradle's default algorithm for handling version conflicts differs from Maven's "closest-to-the-root-wins" approach. When resolving, Gradle walks the full dependency tree to determine all the requested versions for any given package. From the full set of requested versions, Gradle will then default to the *highest* available version.

This approach avoids some unexpected behavior in Maven's approach—for instance, changes in the ordering/depth of packages could result in different resolution. Gradle can also use additional information such as rich version constraints to customize the resolution process. Even further, if Gradle can't satisfy the defined constraints, it will fail the build with a clear message rather than choose a version that may be problematic.

Given this, Gradle provides rich APIs to override and control its resolution behavior. It also has solid introspecting tools built in to pull back the curtains when something goes wrong. A key command when transitive dependency problems rear their ugly head is `./gradlew dependencies`, shown here:

```
~: ./gradlew dependencies

testImplementation - Implementation only dependencies for compilation 'test'
\--- org.junit.jupiter:junit-jupiter-api:5.8.1 (n)

... Other configurations skipped for length

testRuntimeClasspath - Runtime classpath of compilation 'test'
+--- org.junit.jupiter:junit-jupiter-api:5.8.1
|    +--- org.junit:junit-bom:5.8.1
|    |    +--- org.junit.jupiter:junit-jupiter-api:5.8.1 (c)
|    |    +--- org.junit.jupiter:junit-jupiter-engine:5.8.1 (c)
|    |    +--- org.junit.platform:junit-platform-commons:1.8.1 (c)
|    |    \--- org.junit.platform:junit-platform-engine:1.8.1 (c)
|    +--- org.opentest4j:opentest4j:1.2.0
|    \--- org.junit.platform:junit-platform-commons:1.8.1
|         \--- org.junit:junit-bom:5.8.1 (*)
\--- org.junit.jupiter:junit-jupiter-engine:5.8.1
     +--- org.junit:junit-bom:5.8.1 (*)
     +--- org.junit.platform:junit-platform-engine:1.8.1
     |    +--- org.junit:junit-bom:5.8.1 (*)
     |    +--- org.opentest4j:opentest4j:1.2.0
     |    \--- org.junit.platform:junit-platform-commons:1.8.1 (*)
     \--- org.junit.jupiter:junit-jupiter-api:5.8.1 (*)

testRuntimeOnly - Runtime only dependencies for compilation 'test'
\--- org.junit.jupiter:junit-jupiter-engine:5.8.1 (n)
```

In a large project, this output can be overwhelming, so `dependencyInsight` lets you focus on the specific dependency you care about like this:

```
~: ./gradlew dependencyInsight \
       --configuration testRuntimeClasspath \
       --dependency junit-jupiter-api

> Task :dependencyInsight
org.junit.jupiter:junit-jupiter-api:5.8.1 (by constraint)
   variant "runtimeElements" [
      org.gradle.category              = library
      org.gradle.dependency.bundling   = external
      org.gradle.jvm.version           = 8 (compatible with: 11)
      org.gradle.libraryelements       = jar
      org.gradle.usage                 = java-runtime
      org.jetbrains.kotlin.localToProject = public (not requested)
      org.jetbrains.kotlin.platform.type  = jvm
      org.gradle.status                = release (not requested)
   ]
```

```
org.junit.jupiter:junit-jupiter-api:5.8.1
+--- testRuntimeClasspath
+--- org.junit:junit-bom:5.8.1
|     +--- org.junit.platform:junit-platform-engine:1.8.1
|     |     +--- org.junit:junit-bom:5.8.1 (*)
|     |     \--- org.junit.jupiter:junit-jupiter-engine:5.8.1
|     |           +--- testRuntimeClasspath
|     |           \--- org.junit:junit-bom:5.8.1 (*)
|     +--- org.junit.platform:junit-platform-commons:1.8.1
|     |     +--- org.junit.platform:junit-platform-engine:1.8.1 (*)
|     |     +--- org.junit:junit-bom:5.8.1 (*)
|     |     \--- org.junit.jupiter:junit-jupiter-api:5.8.1 (*)
|     +--- org.junit.jupiter:junit-jupiter-engine:5.8.1 (*)
|     \--- org.junit.jupiter:junit-jupiter-api:5.8.1 (*)
\--- org.junit.jupiter:junit-jupiter-engine:5.8.1 (*)

(*) - dependencies omitted (listed previously)
```

Dependency conflicts can be hard to resolve. The best approach, if possible, is to use the dependency tools in Gradle to find mismatches and upgrade to mutually compatible versions. Ah, to live in a world where that were always possible!

Let's revisit the example we had previously where two versions of an internal helper library were bringing in assertj at incompatible major versions. In that case, first-test-helper was dependent on assertj-core 3.21.0, whereas second-test-helper wanted 2.9.1.

Gradle's constraints provides a mechanism to inform the resolution process how we'd like it to choose versions, as shown here:

```
dependencies {
  testImplementation("org.junit.jupiter:junit-jupiter-api:5.8.1")
  testRuntimeOnly("org.junit.jupiter:junit-jupiter-engine:5.8.1")

  testImplementation(
      "com.wellgrounded:first-test-helper:1.0.0")    ◁──┐ All dependencies just ask for
  testImplementation(                                    │ what they want as before.
      "com.wellgrounded:second-test-helper:2.0.0") ◁──┘

  constraints {
    testImplementation(                           ┐ Gradle will respect this constraint
      "org.assertj:assertj-core:3.1.0") {  ◁──┘ or fail the resolution.
        because("Newer incompatible because...")      ◁─────────────────────┐
    }                     It's good practice to use because for documenting why we're │
  }                       intervening because Gradle's tooling can use that text, versus │
}                         comments in the script, which are useful only to human readers. │
```

If you really need to get precise, you can set a version using strictly, which will override any other resolution, as follows:

```
dependencies {
  testImplementation("org.junit.jupiter:junit-jupiter-api:5.8.1")
  testRuntimeOnly("org.junit.jupiter:junit-jupiter-engine:5.8.1")
```

```
testImplementation(
  "com.wellgrounded:first-test-helper:1.0.0")     ◁——┐   All dependencies just ask for
testImplementation(                                    │   what they want as before.
  "com.wellgrounded:second-test-helper:2.0.0")    ◁——┘

testImplementation("org.assertj:assertj-core") {
  version {
    strictly("3.1.0")    ◁——┐   Forces version 3.1.0. This won't match
  }                          │   3.1 or any other related version.
}
}
```

If these mechanisms aren't enough or a library simply has an error in its listed dependencies, you can also ask Gradle to just ignore a given group or artifact via `exclude` as follows:

```
dependencies {
  testImplementation("org.junit.jupiter:junit-jupiter-api:5.8.1")
  testRuntimeOnly("org.junit.jupiter:junit-jupiter-engine:5.8.1")

  testImplementation(                                          Dependency from first-test-
    "com.wellgrounded:first-test-helper:1.0.0")     ◁——┘      helper will be chosen.
  testImplementation(
    "com.wellgrounded:second-test-helper:2.0.0") {  ◁——┐
    exclude(group = "org.assertj")                      │   Gradle will ignore the
  }                                                     │   org.assertj dependencies
}                                                           from the second helper.
```

This is a more drastic option, though, and as written here applies only to the dependency that we apply the `exclude` to. If we can find a solution using `constraints`, we'll be better off in the long run.

As we've mentioned in prior sections, manually forcing dependency versions is a last resort and deserves special attention to ensure you aren't getting runtime exceptions. A robust test suite can be critical to save time when ensuring your mix of libraries works together smoothly.

11.3.8 *Adding Kotlin*

As we've discussed in both chapter 8 and the Maven section of this chapter, the ability to add another language to a project is a huge benefit of running on the JVM.

Adding Kotlin shows off the benefits of Gradle's scripted approach over Maven's more static XML-based configuration. Following the standard multilingual layout from our original code yields this:

```
.
├── build.gradle.kts
├── gradle
│   └── wrapper
│       ├── gradle-wrapper.jar
```

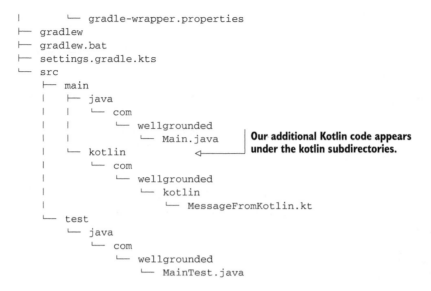

```
|           └── gradle-wrapper.properties
├── gradlew
├── gradlew.bat
├── settings.gradle.kts
└── src
    ├── main
    │   ├── java
    │   │   └── com
    │   │       └── wellgrounded
    │   │           └── Main.java
    │   └── kotlin
    │       └── com
    │           └── wellgrounded
    │               └── kotlin
    │                   └── MessageFromKotlin.kt
    └── test
        └── java
            └── com
                └── wellgrounded
                    └── MainTest.java
```

Our additional Kotlin code appears under the kotlin subdirectories.

We enable Kotlin support via a Gradle plugin in our `build.gradle.kts` like this:

```
plugins {
    application
    id("org.jetbrains.kotlin.jvm") version "1.6.10"
}
```

And that's it. Because of Gradle's flexibility, the plugin is able to alter the build order and add the necessary `kotlin-stdlib` dependencies without us having to take additional steps.

11.3.9   Testing

The `assemble` task we first discussed will compile and package your main code, but we need to compile and run our tests as well. The `build` task is configured by default for just that, as shown here:

```
./gradlew build --dry-run
  :compileJava SKIPPED
  :processResources SKIPPED
  :classes SKIPPED
  :jar SKIPPED
  :assemble SKIPPED
  :compileTestJava SKIPPED
  :processTestResources SKIPPED
  :testClasses SKIPPED
  :test SKIPPED
  :check SKIPPED
  :build SKIPPED
```

We'll add a test case using the standard locations as follows:

```
src
  └─ test
      └─ java
          └─ com
              └─ wellgrounded
                  └─ MainTest.java
```

Next up, we need to add our test framework to the right dependency configuration to make it available to our code. We also let Gradle know that it should use JUnit when running the test tasks, as shown next:

```
dependencies {
  ....
  testImplementation("org.junit.jupiter:junit-jupiter-api:5.8.1")
  testRuntimeOnly("org.junit.jupiter:junit-jupiter-engine:5.8.1")
}

tasks.named<Test>("test") {
  useJUnitPlatform()
}
```

The `testImplementation` configuration makes `org.junit.jupiter` available when building and executing test—but not main—code. When we next run the `./gradlew build`, you'll see that it's downloading the library into our local cache if it wasn't already there.

Full listings with stack traces, including an HTML-based report, are generated under `build/reports/test`.

11.3.10 Automating static analysis

The build is a great place to add functionality to protect your project. One type of check beyond unit testing is static analysis. There are several tools in this category, but SpotBugs (https://spotbugs.github.io/) (the successor to FindBugs) is an easy one to get started with. Note that most of these tools have plugins for Maven as well as Gradle, so the treatment shown here is just to give you a taste of the possibilities:

```
plugins {
  application
  id("com.github.spotbugs") version "4.3.0"
}
```

If we deliberately introduce a problem in our code (e.g., implementing `equals` on a class without also overriding `hashCode`), a typical `./gradlew check` will let us know there's a problem, as illustrated here:

```
~:./gradlew check

> Task :spotbugsTest FAILED
```

```
FAILURE: Build failed with an exception.

* What went wrong:
Execution failed for task ':spotbugsTest'.
> A failure occurred while executing SpotBugsRunnerForWorker
  > Verification failed: SpotBugs violation found:
    2. SpotBugs report can be found in build/reports/spotbugs/test.xml

* Try:
Run with --stacktrace option to get the stack trace.
Run with --info or --debug option to get more log output.
Run with --scan to get full insights.

* Get more help at https://help.gradle.org

BUILD FAILED in 1s
5 actionable tasks: 3 executed, 2 up-to-date
```

As with unit testing failures, report files are under build/reports/spotbugs. Out of the box, SpotBugs may generate only an XML file, which, although nice for computers, is less useful to most people. We can configure the plugin to emit HTML for us as follows:

```
tasks.withType<com.github.spotbugs.snom.SpotBugsTask>()      ⟵  tasks.withType looks
  .configureEach {        ⟵                                      up tasks for us in a
    reports.create("html") {   ⟵                                 typesafe manner.
      isEnabled = true
      setStylesheet("fancy-hist.xsl")
    }
  }
}
```

tasks.withType looks up tasks for us in a typesafe manner.

configureEach runs the block as if we had written tasks.spotbugsMain { } and then tasks.spotbugsTest { } with the same code.

The remaining configuration is taken from the project's README on GitHub (http://mng.bz/Qvdm).

11.3.11 Moving beyond Java 8

In chapter 1, we noted the following series of modules that belonged with Java Enterprise Edition but were present in the core JDK. These were deprecated with JDK 9 and removed with JDK 11 but remain available as external libraries:

- java.activation (JAF)
- java.corba (CORBA)
- java.transaction (JTA)
- java.xml.bind (JAXB)
- java.xml.ws (JAX-WS, plus some related technologies)
- java.xml.ws.annotation (Common Annotations)

If your project relies on any of these modules, your build might break when you move to a more recent JDK. Fortunately, you can add the following simple dependencies in your build.gradle.kts to address the issue:

```
dependencies {
  implementation("com.sun.activation:jakarta.activation:1.2.2")
  implementation("org.glassfish.corba:glassfish-corba-omgapi:4.2.1")
  implementation("javax.transaction:javax.transaction-api:1.3")
  implementation("jakarta.xml.bind:jakarta.xml.bind-api:2.3.3")
  implementation("jakarta.xml.ws:jakarta.xml.ws-api:2.3.3")
  implementation("jakarta.annotation:jakarta.annotation-api:1.3.5")
}
```

11.3.12 Using Gradle with modules

Like Maven, Gradle supports the JDK module system fully. Let's break down what we need to alter to use our modular projects with Gradle.

A MODULAR LIBRARY

A modular library typically has two major structural differences: the change from using main to the module name in the directory under src, and the addition of a module-info.java file at the root of our module, as shown next:

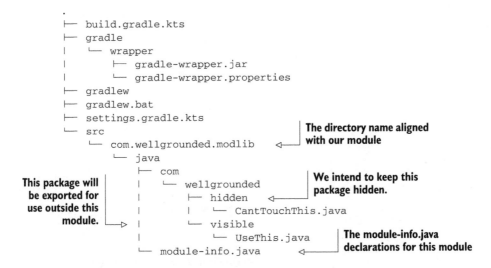

Gradle doesn't automatically find our altered source location, so we need to give it a hint in build.gradle.kts where to look as follows:

```
sourceSets {
  main {
    java {
      setSrcDirs(listOf("src/com.wellgrounded.modlib/java"))
    }
  }
}
```

The `module-info.java` file contains the typical declarations that we saw demonstrated earlier in this chapter and in chapter 2. We'll name our module and select one, but not both, of our packages to export like this:

```
module com.wellgrounded.modlib {
    exports com.wellgrounded.modlib.visible;
}
```

That's all that's required to make our library consumable as a module. Next we'll use the library from a modular app.

A MODULAR APPLICATION

When we set out to test our modular application under Maven, the simplest way to share the library we'd created with our app was to install it to the local Maven repository. This is also supported from Gradle via the `maven-publish` plugin, but we have another option that is worth understanding the mechanics of.

Our modular application has a standard layout as shown next. For ease of testing, we'll make sure the top-level directories live next to each other:

```
mod-lib        ◄─────┐  The mod-lib library source is at
  └── ...             │  the same level as our mod-app
                      │  application.
mod-app
├── build.gradle.kts
├── gradle
│   └── wrapper
│       ├── gradle-wrapper.jar
│       └── gradle-wrapper.properties
├── gradlew
├── gradlew.bat
├── settings.gradle.kts
└── src                       ┌──  The directory name is aligned
    └── com.wellgrounded.modapp  ◄─┘  with the module name.
        └── java
            ├── com
            │   └── wellgrounded
            │       └── Main.java
            └── module-info.java  ◄──┐  We use module-info.java to declare
                                      │  this a modularized application.
```

Our `module-info.java` file tells our name and module requirements, as shown here:

```
module com.wellgrounded.modapp {      ◄──── Our module name
    requires com.wellgrounded.modlib; ◄─┐
}                                         │
                            Our requirement on our library's exported packages
```

For testing our local library, rather than installing it, we'll refer to it locally for the moment, as shown in the next code snippet. This can be accomplished using the `files` function in the spot where we'd previously have given the GAV coordinates for our dependency. This obviously won't work once we're ready to start sharing and deploying, but it's a quick move to get our local testing started:

```
dependencies {
  implementation(files("../mod-lib/build/libs/gradle-mod-lib.jar"))
}
```

Next up, current versions of Gradle require a hint that we want it to sniff out which dependencies are modular to properly put them on the module path instead of the classpath as follows. This may become a default eventually, but at the time of this writing (Gradle 7.3) it remains an opt-in:

```
java {
  modularity.inferModulePath.set(true)
}
```

Last and most mundanely, like our library, we need to let Gradle know about our non-Maven standard file location as follows:

```
sourceSets {
  main {
    java {
      setSrcDirs(listOf("src/com.wellgrounded.modapp/java"))
    }
  }
}
```

With all this in place, `./gradlew` build run has the expected result. If we attempt to use a package from the library that isn't exported, we confront the error at compilation time as shown here:

```
> Task :compileJava FAILED
/mod-app/src/com.wellgrounded.modapp/java/com/wellgrounded/Main.java:4:
error: package com.wellgrounded.modlib.hidden is not visible

import com.wellgrounded.modlib.hidden.CantTouchThis;
                              ^
  (package com.wellgrounded.modlib.hidden is declared in module
   com.wellgrounded.modlib, which does not export it)
1 error
```

JLINK

A capability we saw in chapter 2 that modules unlock is the ability to create a streamlined environment for an application to work in, with only the dependencies it requires. This is possible because the module system gives us concrete guarantees about which modules our code uses, so tooling can construct the necessary, minimal set of modules.

> **NOTE** JLink can work only with fully modularized applications. If an application is still loading some code via the classpath, JLink can't succeed in making a safe, complete image.

This feature is most evident through the `jlink` tool. For a modular application, JLink can produce a fully functioning JVM image that can be run without depending on a system-installed JVM.

Let's revisit the application from chapter 2 that we demonstrated JLink with to see how Gradle plugins streamline the management. The sample application, available in the supplement, uses JDK classes to attach to all the running JVM processes on a machine and display various information about them.

In the modular application we're going to package, an important bit to review is the application's own `module-info.java` declarations. As shown next, these tell us what JLink will need to pull into it's custom image for our build to work:

```
module wgjd.discovery {
  exports wgjd.discovery;

  requires java.instrument;
  requires java.logging;
  requires jdk.attach;
  requires jdk.internal.jvmstat;    ◁───  Red flag: note the
}                                          jdk.internal package that
                                           we're reaching into!
```

Before we even get started with JLink, moving from hand-compiling to our Gradle build takes a little extra configuration. We need to apply the same modularization changes explained in the preceding section as a start as follows. But even once those are in place, we can't compile successfully:

```
~:./gradlew build

> Task :compileJava FAILED
/gradle-jlink/src/wgjd.discovery/wgjd/discovery/VMIntrospector.java:4:
error: package sun.jvmstat.monitor is not visible
  import sun.jvmstat.monitor.MonitorException;
                    ^
  (package sun.jvmstat.monitor is declared in module jdk.internal.jvmstat,
   which does not export it to module wgjd.discovery)

/gradle-jlink/src/wgjd.discovery/wgjd/discovery/VMIntrospector.java:5:
error: package sun.jvmstat.monitor is not visible
  import sun.jvmstat.monitor.MonitoredHost;
                    ^
  (package sun.jvmstat.monitor is declared in module jdk.internal.jvmstat,
   which does not export it to module wgjd.discovery)

/gradle-jlink/src/wgjd.discovery/wgjd/discovery/VMIntrospector.java:6:
error: package sun.jvmstat.monitor is not visible
  import sun.jvmstat.monitor.MonitoredVmUtil;
                    ^
  (package sun.jvmstat.monitor is declared in module jdk.internal.jvmstat,
   which does not export it to module wgjd.discovery)

/gradle-jlink/src/wgjd.discovery/wgjd/discovery/VMIntrospector.java:7:
error: package sun.jvmstat.monitor is not visible
```

```
import sun.jvmstat.monitor.VmIdentifier;
                      ^
(package sun.jvmstat.monitor is declared in module jdk.internal.jvmstat,
 which does not export it to module wgjd.discovery)
```

```
4 errors
```

```
FAILURE: Build failed with an exception.
```

The module system is letting us know that we're breaking the rules by trying to use classes that are in jdk.internal.jvmstat. Our module, wgjd.discovery is not included in the jdk.internal.jvmstat list of allowed modules. Understanding the rules and the risks we're taking, we can use --add-exports to force our module into the list. This is done via a compiler flag, and looks like this in our Gradle configuration:

```
tasks.withType<JavaCompile> {
  options.compilerArgs = listOf(
      "--add-exports",
      "jdk.internal.jvmstat/sun.jvmstat.monitor=wgjd.discovery")
}
```

With that we get a clean compile and we can turn to using JLink to package it up. The plugin with the most mindshare today is org.beryx.jlink, known in the documentation as "The Badass JLink Plugin" (https://badass-jlink-plugin.beryx.org). We add it to our Gradle project with a plugin line.

```
plugins {
  id("org.beryx.jlink") version("2.23.3")  ⟵┐ This plugin automatically applies
}                                             │ application for us, so we don't need
                                              ┘ to repeat that declaration.
```

After adding that, we'll see a jlink task in our list, which we can run straight away. The result will show up in the build/image directory like this:

```
build/image/
├── bin
│    ├── gradle-jlink
│    ├── gradle-jlink.bat
│    ├── java
│    └── keytool
├── conf
│    └── ... various configuration files
├── include
│    └── ... require headers
├── legal
│    └── ... license and legal information for all included modules
├── lib
│    └── ... library files and dependencies for our image
└── release
```

The `build/image/bin/java` is our custom JVM with only our application's module dependencies available to it. You can run it just like you would your normal `java` command from the terminal as follows:

```
~:build/image/bin/java -version
openjdk version "11.0.6" 2020-01-14
OpenJDK Runtime Environment AdoptOpenJDK (build 11.0.6+10)
OpenJDK 64-Bit Server VM AdoptOpenJDK (build 11.0.6+10, mixed mode)
```

We can pass `build/image/bin/java` our module to start up, but the plugin has neatly generated a startup script at `build/image/bin/gradle-jlink` (named after our project and shown next) that we can use instead. But not all is well with our newly minted image:

```
~:build/image/bin/gradle-jlink

Java processes:
PID     Display Name    VM Version    Attachable
Exception in thread "main" java.lang.IllegalAccessError:
 class wgjd.discovery.VMIntrospector (in module wgjd.discovery) cannot
   access class sun.jvmstat.monitor.MonitorException (in module
   jdk.internal.jvmstat) because module jdk.internal.jvmstat does not
   export sun.jvmstat.monitor to module wgjd.discovery
 wgjd.discovery/wgjd.discovery.VMIntrospector.accept(VMIntrospector.java:19)
 wgjd.discovery/wgjd.discovery.Discovery.main(Discovery.java:26)
```

This isn't an entirely unfamiliar error message—it's another flavor of the same access issue we solved with the compiler options earlier. Apparently we need to inform the application startup of our module-cheating needs as well. Fortunately, the plugin has extensive configuration for the parameters both to run `jlink` and for the resulting scripts created for us, as shown here:

```
jlink {
  launcher{
    jvmArgs = listOf(
                "--add-exports",
                "jdk.internal.jvmstat/sun.jvmstat.monitor=wgjd.discovery")
  }
}
```

With that addition, the startup script gets everything running as follows:

```
~:build/image/bin/gradle-jlink
Java processes:
PID     Display Name    VM Version    Attachable
833 wgjd.discovery/wgjd.discovery.Discovery    11.0.6+10    true
276 org.jetbrains.jps.cmdline.Launcher /Applications/IntelliJ IDEA CE.app...
```

It's worth noting that the image we generated here defaults to targeting the same operating system that JLink is running on, as illustrated in the next code sample.

However, that isn't required—cross-platform support is available. The primary requirement is that you have the files from the target platform's JDK installation available. These are easily available from sources such as the Eclipse Adoptium website at https://adoptium.net/:

```
jlink {
  targetPlatform("local",
                System.getProperty("java.home"))
  targetPlatform("linux-x64",
                "/linux_jdk-11.0.10+9")
  launcher{
    jvmArgs = listOf(
                "--add-exports",
                "jdk.internal.jvmstat/sun.jvmstat.monitor=wgjd.discovery")
  }
}
```

Builds an image based on whatever the local JDK is

Builds an image pointed to a Linux JDK we've downloaded

Once you start targeting specific platforms, the plugin will put additional directories in the `build/image` results. Obviously, you'll have to take those results to a matching system to test them.

A final roadblock that may come up in trying to use JLink is its restrictions around automatically named modules. Although the feature to just add a name into the JAR manifest and get some basic ability to participate in the modular world is great for migrations, JLink sadly doesn't support it.

The Badass JLink Plugin, though, has you covered. It will repackage any automatically named modules into a proper module that JLink can consume. The documentation (found at http://mng.bz/XZ2Y) gives full coverage to this feature, which may be the difference between JLink working or not, depending on your application's dependencies.

11.3.13 *Customizing*

One of Gradle's biggest strengths is its open-ended flexibility. Without pulling in plugins, it doesn't even have a concept of a build lifecycle. You can add tasks and reconfigure existing tasks with few restrictions. There's no need to keep a `scripts` directory around in your project with random tooling—your custom needs can be integrated right into your day-to-day build and testing tool.

CUSTOM TASKS

Defining a custom task can be done directly in your `build.gradle.kts` file like this:

```
tasks.register("wellgrounded") {
  println("configuring")
  doLast {
    println("Hello from Gradle")
  }
}
```

Running this will produce the following output:

```
~: ./gradlew wellgrounded
  configuring...

  > Task :wellgrounded
  Hello from Gradle
```

The `println("configuring")` line is run during setup of the task, but the contents of the `doLast` block happens when the task actually ran. We can confirm this by doing a dry-run on our task as follows:

```
~: ./gradlew wellgrounded --dry-run
  configuring...
  :wellgrounded SKIPPED
```

Tasks can be configured to depend on other tasks, as shown next:

```
tasks.register("wellgrounded") {
  println("configuring...")
  dependsOn("assemble")
  doLast {
    println("Hello from Gradle")
  }
}
```

This technique applies equally well to tasks you didn't author—you can look them up and add your task as a dependency like so:

```
tasks {
  named<Task>("help") {
    dependsOn("wellgrounded")
  }
}
```

```
~: ./gradlew help
  configuring...

  > Task :wellgrounded
  Hello from Gradle

  > Task :help

  Welcome to Gradle 7.3.3.

  To run a build, run gradlew <task> ...

  To see a list of available tasks, run gradlew tasks

  To see more detail about a task, run gradlew help --task <task>

  To see a list of command-line options, run gradlew --help
```

```
For more detail on using Gradle, see
  https://docs.gradle.org/7.3.3/userguide/command_line_interface.html
```

```
For troubleshooting, visit https://help.gradle.org
```

It's extremely powerful to be able to write custom tasks directly in your build file. However, putting them in `build.gradle.kts` has a few rather severe limitations: they cannot be easily shared between projects, and they aren't easy to write automated tests against. Gradle plugins are built to address just those issues.

CREATING CUSTOM PLUGINS

Gradle plugins are implemented as JVM code. They can be provided directly in your project as source files, or they can be pulled in through libraries. Many plugins have been written in Groovy, the original scripting language supported by Gradle, but you can do it in any JVM language. For the largest compatibility and to minimize issues with specific language idioms, if you plan to share your plugin, writing it in Java is a good idea.

Plugins can be coded directly in your buildscript, and we'll demonstrate the main APIs using that technique. When you're ready to share, you can pull the code into its own separate project. Here is an equivalent to our earlier `wellgrounded` task:

```
class WellgroundedPlugin : Plugin<Project> {      ◁──── Derives from Plugin
    override fun apply(project: Project) {
        project.task("wellgrounded") {      ◁
            doLast {                              Uses familiar project-level API
                println("Hello from Gradle")       and task implementation
            }
        }
    }
}
                                           Use apply to actually use the plugin—
                                           it isn't automatically invoked like our
apply<WellgroundedPlugin>()      ◁───┘     earlier task definition.
```

Apart from sharing, authoring tasks as plugins allows us more ability to customize configuration. The standard Gradle object representing our `Project` has a specific place where plugin configurations live under an `extensions` property. We can add to these extensions with our own `Extension` objects as follows:

```
open class WellgroundedExtensions {
  var count: Int = 1
}

class WellgroundedPlugin : Plugin<Project> {
    override fun apply(proj: Project) {
      val extensions = proj.extensions
      val ext = extensions.create<WellgroundedExtensions>("wellgrounded")
      proj.task("wellgrounded") {
        doLast {
          repeat(ext.count) {
            println("Hello from Gradle")
          }
```

```
        }
      }
    }
  }
}

apply<WellgroundedPlugin>()

configure<WellgroundedExtensions> {
  count = 4
}
```

All the power of our programming language is available within our plugins.

If you extract a plugin to another library, you can include it in your build through the same mechanism we saw earlier for including the SpotBugs plugin, as shown here:

```
plugins {
  id("com.wellgrounded.gradle") version "1000.0"
}

apply<WellgroundedPlugin>()

configure<WellgroundedExtensions> {
  count = 4
}
```

Summary

- Build tools are central to how Java software is constructed in the real world. They automate tedious operations, help with dependency management, ensure that developers are doing their work consistently, and, critically, ensure that the same project built on different machines gets the same results.
- Maven and Gradle are the two most common build tools in the Java ecosystem, and most tasks can be accomplished in either.
  - Maven takes an approach of configuration via XML combined with plugins written in JVM code.
  - Gradle provides a declarative build language using an actual programming language (Kotlin or Groovy), resulting in concise build logic for simple cases and flexibility for complex use cases.
- Dealing with conflicting dependencies is a major topic whatever your build tool. Both Maven and Gradle give you ways to handle conflicting library versions. Gradle provides a number of more advanced features for dealing with common dependency management issues.
- Gradle offers features for work avoidance such as incremental builds, resulting in faster builds.
- Modules, as seen in chapter 2, require some changes to our build scripting and source code layout, but these are well supported by the tooling.

12

Running Java in containers

This chapter covers

- Why container-driven development is important for the well-grounded Java developer
- The difference between an OS, a VM, a container, and orchestration
- Docker
- Kubernetes
- Practical guidance on running Java workloads in containers
- Performance and observability in containers

Docker (https://www.docker.com/) containers have become the de facto standard for packaging Java applications for deployment, and Kubernetes (https://kubernetes .io/) (k8s) is the most popular option for orchestrating those containers. Especially if you are deploying to any of the major cloud providers, you will need to know about these technologies and, more importantly, how Java behaves with them.

> **NOTE** Although other container and container orchestration technologies exist, Docker and Kubernetes dominate the container and orchestration markets, respectively.

12.1 Why containers matter for a well-grounded developer

To better understand what containers are and why they are important for a well-grounded Java developer, we will look at the following:

- Host operating system versus virtual machines versus containers
- The benefits of containers
- The drawbacks of containers

12.1.1 Host operating systems vs. virtual machines vs. containers

Since the early days of computing, we've been introducing layers of abstraction between our software and the hardware that it runs on. Containers are another natural step in this progression. Let's take a brief tour through these layers to see how containers fix in.

BARE METAL

Let us start by going right back to basics—a *bare metal machine* that has no host operating system installed. This bare metal machine represents a set of finite resources to whatever software might be installed on it, including CPU, RAM, hard disk, networking and so forth.

> **NOTE** This concept of finite resources is a critical one to keep in your head. Far too often, developers are fooled into thinking that containers somehow give them magical infinite resources!

Always remember that underneath the host operating system, virtual machines, or containers is a piece of bare metal with *finite resources*.

HOST OPERATING SYSTEM OR TYPE 1 HYPERVISOR

In modern data centers, the bare metal machines have either a host operating system (e.g., Linux) or a Type 1 hypervisor (e.g., VMWare ESXi, Microsoft Hyper-V) installed on them. *Hypervisor* is the term for software that enables the creation and management of virtual machines. Hypervisors can exist at multiple layers of the stack. A Type 1 hypervisor is installed on bare metal and serves as a lightweight operating system, dedicating most of the machine's resources to the virtual machines it runs.

Whether running a traditional operating system or a hypervisor, this first layer is typically lightweight and doesn't do much more than look after security guarantees and allow for higher-level abstractions to be installed on top. That said, the host operating system does require some CPU, RAM, and networking to run.

TYPE 2 HYPERVISORS

If our bare metal has a traditional operating system such as Linux installed, then the next layer up is usually a Type 2 hypervisor. Whether Type 1 or Type 2, hypervisors are responsible for managing the resources of the underlying hardware for the virtual machines (VMs) with guest operating systems.

For example, a bare metal machine with 32 GB of RAM and a 16 core CPU with a Linux host operating system could run a Type 2 hypervisor, which in turn hosts four VMs, each running a Linux guest operating system with what appears to be 8 GB of RAM and 4 CPU cores each. Modern hypervisors normally don't take up much of the underlying resources to run themselves. If a Type 1 hypervisor is used directly on our bare metal, it's ready to run the next layer, virtual machines, without additional intervention.

VIRTUAL MACHINES

Each VM is fully self-contained. As far as the user is concerned, it has its own CPU, RAM, network, and disk resources. When you log on to a server in a production environment, chances are that you are logging on to a VM and not a bare metal server.

The self-contained VM also has its own operating system, referred to as the guest operating system. In the past, VMs paid a performance penalty to provide this isolated environment, but advances in the technology have removed many of those issues over the years.

Remember what we said about finite resources? Each virtual machine is just that—*virtual.* When the hypervisor isn't configured correctly, or virtual machines are given more resources than what physically exists, or are not dedicated to you (very common in cloud environments), you can have unpredictable performance.

CONTAINER ENGINES

Prior to modern container engine technology, it was common to run a container engine on top of the guest operating system. This container engine could itself then run multiple containers.

This layer demonstrates one of the main differences between VMs and containers, because one of the container engine's key responsibilities is sharing access to a single operating system kernel across the containers it runs. This setup is much lighter than the VM model, where each instance has a full copy of its own operating system. This advantage, though, requires a lot of support from many different parts of the Linux kernel itself.

CONTAINERS

Finally we arrive at the container. You can think of a container as a custom-built, isolated environment in which to run an application. A container has a filesystem and runs at least one process. Although the processes in that container can all communicate with a kernel, many limits are imposed to keep the container separate from the rest of the world, including limits on memory, CPU, network (usage and visibility), and disk.

Inside containers, you run your Java application, data store, or other services that you require. Let's look at all of those layers of abstraction.

In Figure 12.1, the host operating system is the bottom layer of abstraction. The hypervisor is the next layer, followed by the container engine, the container, and the Java application. That seems a little over the top, doesn't it? In more pure container environments, it is, so in the past few years, you'll see dedicated container host machines, shown in figure 12.2, which remove the hypervisor and guest operating system layers.

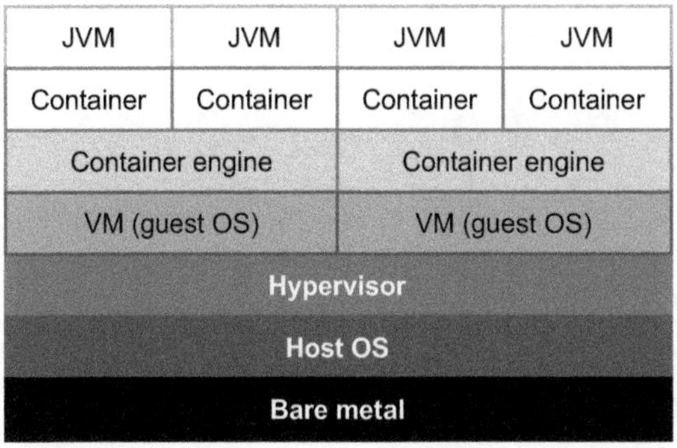

JVM	JVM	JVM	JVM
Container	Container	Container	Container
Container engine		Container engine	
VM (guest OS)		VM (guest OS)	
Hypervisor			
Host OS			
Bare metal			

Figure 12.1   Target environment for Java applications

JVM	JVM	JVM	JVM
Container	Container	Container	Container
Container engine		Container engine	
Host OS			
Bare metal			

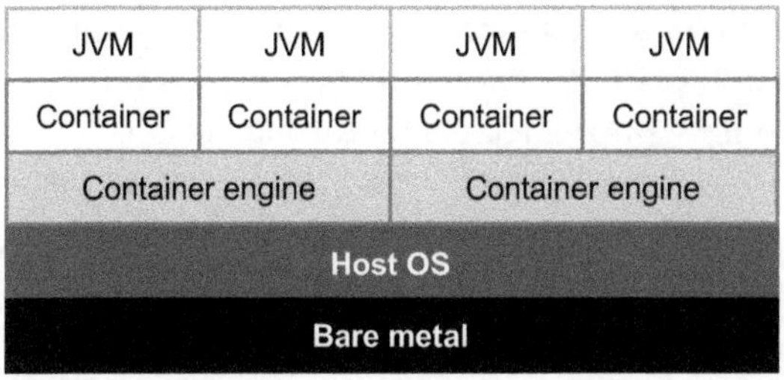

Figure 12.2   Target environment for Java applications on dedicated container engines

That's much better! That said, most developers aren't sure what their target environment looks like. The takeaway here is to make sure you check with your system administrators to understand exactly what your target environment looks like and how much of that bare metal finite resource is being allocated at each layer.

Despite all of the complexity within these layers of abstraction, as a Java developer, you will be focused mainly on the container as a deployment target, and this way of doing things has some important benefits.

12.1.2 Benefits of containers

With all the additional moving parts needed to run containers, why have they become the new standard for deployment? One of the key benefits is the ability of containers to apply limits, isolating individual running processes from each other. In the past, if you deployed two Java applications on the same host, there was a high probability that they could interfere with each other's performance—stealing too much CPU time or gobbling up more than their fair share of memory. Mitigations existed, but these ideas are baked into the fundamental layers of containers. In fact, having limits we can trust, in practice, allows us to more thoroughly use our computing resources, running more software on a host than would have felt safe before containers.

This isolation is so key that for the remainder of the chapter we'll illustrate the relationship between containers, hosts, and processes by showing nested rather than stacked images. Both ways of visualizing the relationship are valid, so don't be surprised to find both in the wild, depending on the context.

Containers have also ushered in a world of more consistent packaging for deployment. How you copied the bits for your application to the deployment environment, how you managed the operating system dependencies, and even how you managed process startup used to be all up for grabs. Containers provide an answer to all of that, making a gigantic pile of tooling and custom scripts unnecessary. They also provide insulation between our deployment environment and the container's contents. Our container engine doesn't have to care how we lay out the internals of our container—it just has to know how to start itself when asked. Packaging of container images is a key example of Infrastructure as a Service (IaaS), with a declarative, source-controlled description of layers in our system, which used to require careful, imperative construction.

A final benefit builds on that consistent packaging—the ecosystem that's developed around containers. Today almost any significant piece of software that you want to run has likely been packaged in a container already on Docker Hub or elsewhere. Vast READMEs of installation instructions or custom install scripts are now unnecessary.

But it can't all be upsides, right? What are the drawbacks to running in containers?

12.1.3 *Drawbacks of containers*

As it turns out, the first point that we listed as a benefit for containers—their built-in isolation—is actually one of the difficulties in using them. The job of containers is keeping the world inside the container separate from the outside world, and that outside world includes you, the developer. Many of the techniques and tools that you commonly use outside of containers may require special handling and configuration with a move to containers.

This can be especially true when trying to factor containers into your local development processes. Longer builds and time spent shuffling huge container images around may not always feel worth it.

And although containers introduce a consistent interface for how we package and start our application, real-world deployment isn't always simple. For example, an application that expects full access to the disk on its host may require configuration to make the required files visible to the container. If a set of processes communicate with each other, separating them into containers will need explicit configuration for how they can access each other. Capturing and applying this sort of configuration is a key task for orchestrators such as Kubernetes. Be aware, however, that Kubernetes, which we'll examine briefly in this chapter, is a topic fit to fill books, and the ecosystem continues to develop rapidly.

Although containers are becoming entirely mainstream, the well-grounded developer knows how to examine the trade-offs to find the right balance for their system. Let's start to see how to use these tools, so we can get a feel for where they fit.

12.2 Docker fundamentals

Though many of the constituent technologies that make up containers existed earlier, Docker introduced convenient tooling and abstractions that catapulted containerization to the mainstream. Let's take a look at two central pieces of functionality that Docker gives us—building images and running containers—and see how we interact with those as Java developers in practice.

12.2.1 Building Docker images

A Docker container is launched from an *image*. An image is essentially a snapshot that captures all the filesystem dependencies needed to run a piece of software. An image includes native libraries, languages runtimes, tools, and, most importantly, a specific version of your software to run.

The `Dockerfile` is typical format for capturing the set of steps to build an image. The simplest image possible, one which is entirely empty, looks like this:

```
FROM scratch
```

We build the image using the `docker build` command as follows:

```
$ docker build .
```

```
[+] Building 0.1s (3/3) FINISHED
 => [internal] load build definition Dockerfile    0.0s
 => => transferring dockerfile: 55B                0.0s
 => [internal] load .dockerignore                  0.0s
 => => transferring context: 2B                    0.0s
 => exporting to image                             0.0s
 => writing image sha256:71de1148337f4d1845be0...  0.0s   ◁
```

> The sha256 ID 71de114... uniquely identifies the resulting image. We'll see how to give things a more friendly name in a moment.

```
Use 'docker scan' to run Snyk tests against images to find vulnerabilities
and learn how to fix them
```

Of course, an empty image isn't much use. In practice, many base images exist with useful software already installed. The default source of these base images is Docker Hub (https://hub.docker.com/). We'll talk more later about selecting the right Java base image, but for now, let's start building an image off an Eclipse Temurin version of OpenJDK provided by Adoptium. We'll specifically choose the `eclipse-temurin:11` image as show here, which contains the latest version of Java 11:

```
FROM eclipse-temurin:11
RUN java -version
```

By default, recent versions of Docker will dynamically hide output when building in an interactive terminal. We'll use --progress plain here to get a clearer picture of what's happening:

```
$ docker build --progress plain .

=1 [internal] load build definition from Dockerfile
=1 sha256:261a2389333859f063c39502b306e984de49700a9...
=1 transferring dockerfile: 36B done
=1 DONE 0.0s

=2 [internal] load .dockerignore
=2 sha256:909e36a5a9cd7cc4e95e7926f84f982542233925d...
=2 transferring context: 2B done
=2 DONE 0.0s

=3 [internal] load docker.io/library/eclipse-temurin:11
=3 sha256:6a73b62137bbf64760945abf21baf23bf909644cf...
=3 DONE 0.5s

=4 [1/2] FROM docker.io/library/eclipse-temurin:11...
=4 sha256:f225b618d7ad96bd25e0182d6e89aa8e77643f42f...
=4 CACHED

=5 [2/2] RUN java -version
=5 sha256:556476b43b8626a27892422f8688979c4ba1e6029...
=5 0.38 openjdk version "11.0.13" 2021-10-19
=5 0.38 OpenJDK Runtime Environment Temurin-11.0.13+8 (build 11.0.13+8)
=5 0.38 OpenJDK 64-Bit Server VM Temurin-11.0.13+8 (build 11.0.13+8)
=5 DONE 0.4s

=6 exporting to image
=6 sha256:e8c613e07b0b7ff33893b694f7759a10d42e180f2...
=6 exporting layers 0.0s done
=6 writing image sha256:9796a789e295989cec550f... done
=6 DONE 0.0s
```

Internal steps Docker takes when preparing to build our images

Retrieving our requested base image

Our RUN command is executed during the build, and we can see its output.

Use 'docker scan' to run Snyk tests against images to find vulnerabilities and learn how to fix them

You may note that this code takes longer to run, at least the first time, because Docker has to download the relevant base image from Docker Hub. The RUN command we've added introduces our own new step on top of that base image. RUN can execute any valid command in the container environment. If the command alters the filesystem, those changes are captured as part of our final image. This example doesn't actually alter the filesystem, but RUN is frequently used to download files (e.g., via curl), install operating system packages with standard package managers, or make other local modifications.

We can see another important part of building Docker images if we run the same build command again without touching the Dockerfile like this:

```
$ docker build --progress plain .

=1-4 excluded for length...

=5 [2/2] RUN java -version
=5 sha256:556476b43b8626a27892422f8688979c4ba1e602907a09d62a39a2
=5 CACHED

=6 exporting to image
=6 sha256:e8c613e07b0b7ff33893b694f7759a10d42e180f2b4dc349fb57dc
=6 exporting layers done
=6 writing image sha256:9796a789e295989cec5550fb3c17bc6c1d9c0867  done
=6 DONE 0.0s
```

> **Docker informs us when it skipped a step because the result was cached.**

Each of the leading commands (like FROM and RUN) in the Dockerfile creates what is called a *layer*. Because these commands can often be time-consuming, those layers are cached, and Docker does its best to avoid unnecessary work.

Now that our container has a Java environment, we can run our own code there. We'll create a simple Java file alongside our Dockerfile in HelloDocker.java. To keep things easy to start, we'll use the Java single-file execution to run this instead of putting a full build together yet. The basic code looks like this:

```java
public class HelloDocker {
  public static void main(String[] args) {
    System.out.println("Hello Docker!");
  }
}
```

We can then instruct the Docker build to include this file in our image and set the default command for containers running this image as follows:

```
FROM eclipse-temurin:11
RUN java -version

COPY HelloDocker.java .

CMD ["java", "HelloDocker.java"]
```

> **Copies our file to whatever that current working directory Docker has set**

> **Sets the default command for the image. Note each command-line argument is in its own separate string.**

COPY (and the more complex ADD command) take files from our local build environment and puts them in our container. ADD, in particular, has a lot of options, including fetching from remote source and auto-extracting TAR files, but generally, you'll be better off with a simple COPY where you can.

CMD points us to the next stage in an image's lifecycle. We aren't just building these images for fun—we want to run the software we're configuring in them. As mentioned earlier, each image has a unique SHA256 identity, but those are cumbersome to work with and change every time you build. Before we get to running our image, let's tag our image with an easier name, as shown next:

```
$ docker build -t hello .

... Previous build steps excluded for length

=8 exporting to image
=8 sha256:e8c613e07b0b7ff33893b694f7759a10d42e...
=8 exporting layers done
=8 writing image sha256:666fdc7613189865b9a5f2... done
=8 naming to docker.io/library/hello done
=8 DONE 0.0s
```

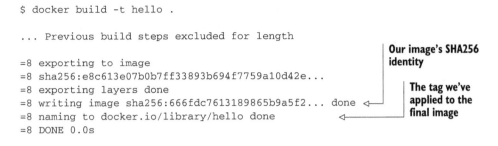

Our image's SHA256 identity

The tag we've applied to the final image

Our `hello` image is available only locally at this point, but we've already seen via the `FROM` line that images can be shared. This is accomplished through what's known as a *container registry*. When we asked for the `eclipse-temurin:11` base image, Docker defaulted to looking for that image on Docker Hub (https://hub.docker.com/). Other container registries exist, and, in fact, they can be run internally for hosting your application images.

You can push and pull images via the `docker push` and `docker pull` commands, respectively, as shown in the following code. If working with a non-default registry, that name is given before the image and tag name:

```
$ docker pull k8s.gcr.io/echoserver:1.4
1.4: Pulling from echoserver
6d9e6e7d968b: Pull complete
...
7abee76f69c0: Pull complete
Digest: sha256:5d99aa1120524c801bc8c1a7077e8f5ec122ba16b6ddala...
Status: Image is up to date for k8s.gcr.io/echoserver:1.4
k8s.gcr.io/echoserver:1.4
```

k8s.gcr.io is the registry domain, echoserver is the image name, and 1.4 is the tag.

If the registry requires authentication, you may have to use `docker login` before proceeding. Publicly available images on Docker Hub don't require that step, though.

There's a lot more to building good Docker images, and we'll cycle back to some of those topics later. But first, let's see how to turn these images into running containers.

12.2.2 *Running Docker containers*

For all the hype and discussion you hear around Docker and containers, the central idea is simply being able to execute a well-defined process in a strictly controlled environment. The environment is largely defined by the image that we construct. Docker allows us to run a container with the `docker run` command, as shown here:

```
$ docker run hello
Hello Docker!
```

In this command, Docker created a new filesystem based on our image, applied limits and controls (such as CPU and memory), and then started the default process defined by `CMD`. Our program outputs a message and exits, but it could as easily have started a a server and kept running indefinitely.

In figure 12.3, we can see the `java` process we listed in the `CMD` for the image. Remember that the host shown here may in fact hide many additional layers before you reach the bare metal machine.

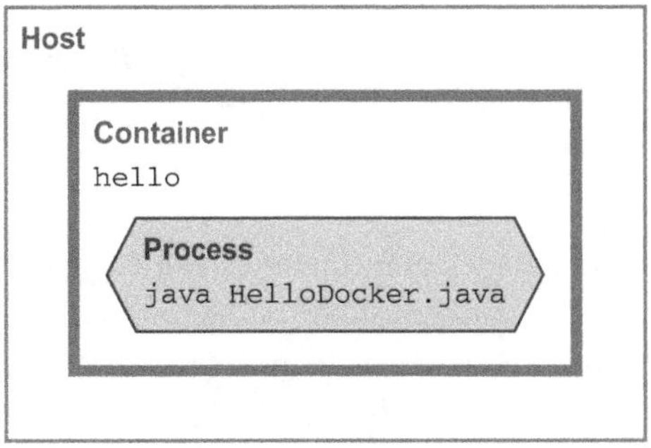

Figure 12.3   **Running a basic container**

Our `CMD` defines only the default command for starting the container. We can ask Docker to run the image with any alternative command we wish. We mentioned earlier that the container has a working directory, much like your interactive terminals do. We can ask the container what that path is with the `pwd` command as follows:

```
$ docker run hello pwd
/
```

As Figure 12.4 shows, when we run an alternative command to start the container, the default `CMD` process is nowhere to be seen.

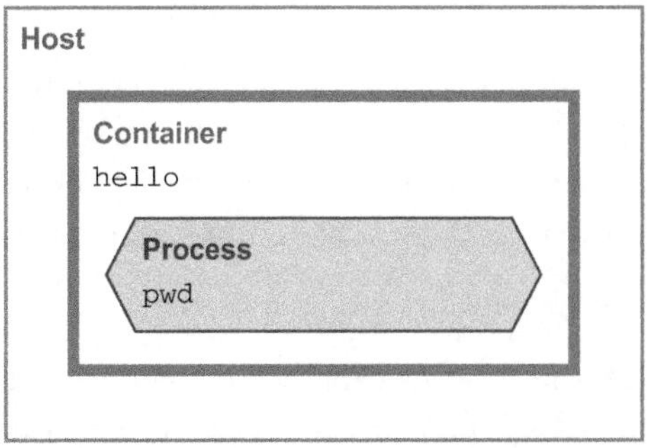

Figure 12.4   **Running an alternative command in a container**

We can write configuration into our image via files, but it's often desirable to allow defining them at runtime. One of the principles from the Twelve-Factor App (https://12factor.net/), an influential set of ideas about running software such as containers, is defining configuration via the *environment* so the same built resource (in our case, the image) can be deployed to new destinations without changing code.

As shown in the following code snippet, we can alter the environment variables within our container when we start it using the -e flag, which may be passed multiple times. In our application code, these variables may be read via standard means such as the `System.getenv()` method:

```
$ docker run -e MY_VAR=here -e OTHER_VAR=there hello env
PATH=/opt/java/openjdk/bin:/usr/local/sbin:/usr/local/bin:...
HOSTNAME=f25762652561
MY_VAR=here
OTHER_VAR=there
LANG=en_US.UTF-8
LANGUAGE=en_US:en
LC_ALL=en_US.UTF-8
JAVA_VERSION=jdk-11.0.13+8
JAVA_HOME=/opt/java/openjdk
HOME=/root
```

Runs the standard env command to see our container's environment

Our full environment variable list

Let's discuss one last technique before we look at more realistic approaches to building our Java applications in containers: interactively running an image. We've seen changing the default command to run in the container. We can use that same ability to start a shell such as `bash` in the container for additional debugging. This requires extra flags to `docker run`—specifically `-i`, so `STDIN` is attached for our input to reach the container, and `-t`, so the container starts an interactive TTY for us, as shown here:

```
$ docker run -it hello bash
root@b770c2ac829c: ls *.java
HelloDocker.java
root@b770c2ac829c:
```

Interactively enters shell commands to inspect the container

This lets us see the world precisely as our deployed applications will within the container.

It's all well and good to copy a hello world single-file app into a container, but let's look now at more realistic approaches to using Docker and Java together.

12.3 Developing Java applications with Docker

In this section, we'll tackle a variety of practical considerations for developing Java applications with Docker. We'll start with looking a bit deeper at our JVM base images and how to build our images. From there, we'll dig into various considerations about configuring, running, and debugging our containers. Our container has to get a JVM from somewhere, which brings us to the topic of choosing a base image.

12.3.1 Selecting your base image

There isn't a single answer to what the "right" base image is for running your JVM application. Determining what image works for you requires considering the following:

- What vendor do I want?
- What operating system do I want inside my container?
- What system architectures do I need to run on?

The choice of vendor also includes a number of factors that may influence your choice (we discussed this briefly back in chapter 1), including the following:

- Support availability and contracts
- Security update policies and timeliness
- Special considerations for cloud deployment—Microsoft Build of OpenJDK for Azure, Amazon Corretto for AWS

The cloud vendor–specific builds, while based on OpenJDK, may include performance and other enhancements that are beneficial in that vendor's cloud. They also may have additional support and release-frequency benefits.

Most vendors provide support on more than one operating system in their containers. It's common to see Debian, Ubuntu, or Alpine, along with some other Linux variants. The choice of operating system largely dictates what package manager is used to install native dependencies and what additional tooling is available within the container. If your requirements don't dictate a specific operating system, keeping to the more mainstream options like Debian/Ubuntu often avoids difficulties in finding and updating packages.

> **NOTE** Take particular care with Alpine Linux. Until very recently, no official images for Java on Alpine existed. You should check with your Java vendor and make sure that they provide images for Alpine.

If you need to run on an operating system that isn't directly shipped by the vendor, don't despair. In these cases, you can build an image yourself that will use the system's typical package management to install the JDK manually. Remember, base images and our Docker builds are just about getting the right bits in the container's filesystem. There's often more than one way to get to that end result you're after.

A final note is on system architecture for images. It is becoming increasingly common to run on ARM-based chips, especially in the cloud. Although this has performance advantages, be aware that you'll need images that are built specifically for that architecture. If you need to run across architectures, you may end up having to build and publish multiple images, but the Docker tooling supports this well already.

12.3.2 *Building an image with Gradle*

As we saw in chapter 11, any sizeable Java project will benefit from using a consistent build tool. For demonstration purposes, we'll walk through how to construct an image based on a Gradle build, but a similar Maven version is available in the resources.

At a minimum, our image needs to contain all our application's JARs (or class files) and all the dependencies for our classpath. For our sample, our application takes a dependency on `org.apache.commons:commons-lang3`, as shown next:

```
plugins {
  application
  java
```

```
}

application {
  mainClass.set("com.wellgrounded.Main")
}

tasks.jar {
  manifest {
    attributes("Main-Class" to application.mainClass)
  }
}

repositories {
  mavenCentral()
}

dependencies {
  implementation("org.apache.commons:commons-lang3:3.12.0")
}
```

We need a slightly different command from our usual `build` or `assemble`, but Gradle's defaults have what we need wrapped up via `installDist`, as shown here:

```
$ ./gradlew installDist
```

The simplified build result from this command follows:

```
build
└── install
    └── docker-gradle
        ├── bin
        │   ├── docker-gradle
        │   └── docker-gradle.bat
        └── lib
            ├── commons-lang3-3.12.0.jar
            └── docker-gradle.jar
```

We could just take the JAR files and run from them in the container, but Gradle has created some helper scripts for starting our application. Let's take advantage of those next:

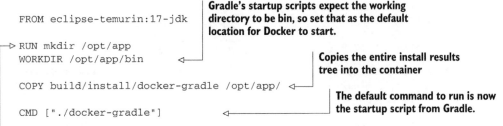

FROM eclipse-temurin:17-jdk

RUN mkdir /opt/app
WORKDIR /opt/app/bin

COPY build/install/docker-gradle /opt/app/

CMD ["./docker-gradle"]

Gradle's startup scripts expect the working directory to be bin, so set that as the default location for Docker to start.

Copies the entire install results tree into the container

The default command to run is now the startup script from Gradle.

Ensures the directory exists for us to copy results into

You can find out more about Gradle's start scripts in the documentation for the Application plugin (see http://mng.bz/yvxJ).

This approach assumes that we have an appropriate JDK installed locally to build with Gradle before copying the results into our image. Up next, we'll see how we can wrap that up entirely in Docker.

12.3.3 Running the build in Docker

A key promise of containers is the ability to create an isolated, repeatable environment for our software to run in. This is a huge advantage for deploying our services, but it doesn't stop there. A classic problem for many projects is setting up a local environment for development. If you've ever plowed through a README with step after step of installs, making sure you got the right versions of everything, you know this pain. Containers can help us escape this. Let's examine how we can alter our build to leverage that isolation.

Our `Dockerfile` to date has involved only the one resulting image that we're trying to construct. But Docker allows us to define multiple images in the same file and, most important, copy between them. With this ability, we can construct an image in which to build our application—fully removed from whatever JDKs our local system has—and then copy the results into our deployment image. This has advantages for both security and image sizes.

This process is referred to as a *multistage build*, and you can see it in action when a `Dockerfile` has multiple `FROM` statements. `FROM` lines that are just intermediate stages of the build also include an `AS` keyword to name them for later use in the `Dockerfile`, whereas our main resulting image is left as before, as shown here:

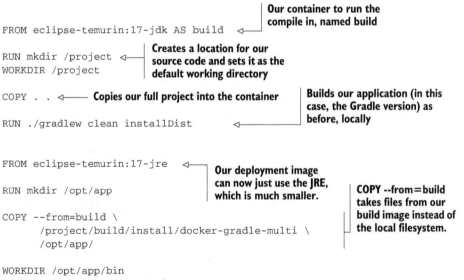

Now our continuous integration environment needs only Docker, not a JDK installed, to be able to build our application for deployment. As figure 12.5 shows, all the necessary components for the build remain fully within the containers.

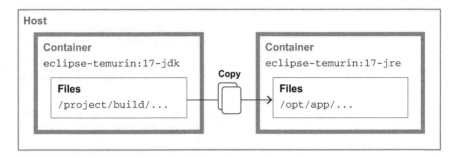

Figure 12.5 Multistage builds in Docker

It's worth calling out that this is close to the minimal setup for this type of build, but it has some downsides around build times. As we mentioned, each Docker command creates a layer that is cached, but those caches can be invalidated unnecessarily if we're not careful.

One source of such cache breaking in our current Dockerfile is where we copy the full project directory into the container. Any file change, no matter how small, will invalidate the COPY . . line, and we have to run everything after that fresh. It's possible that some local files don't matter to our build, though—for instance, our git history, IDE files, and local build output really don't need to end up in our build container image. Fortunately, we can exclude such files from Docker's consideration by placing a .dockerignore file alongside our Dockerfile. The format is simple and may be familiar if you've worked with .gitignore files before. As shown in the next code snippet, each line expresses a pattern (standard shell wildcarding allowed) that Docker should ignore when finding files to copy:

```
.git
.idea/
*.iml
*.class

# Ignore build folders
out/
build/
target/
.gradle/
```

A second more subtle issue is with our Gradle wrapper. If we watch the output when running the build, we'll see that it spends a while on startup downloading the proper distribution. Because our containers start without any of Gradle's local caching, this download repeats each time we run.

Avoiding this repetition requires breaking out a first execution of Gradle into a separate set of layers which happen before copying our full project into the container, as shown next. We want to copy only the minimum required for Gradle to run its download, so this layer's cache breaks only if we alter our Gradle wrapper (e.g., updating the version):

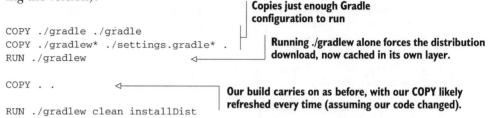

Copies just enough Gradle configuration to run

```
COPY ./gradle ./gradle
COPY ./gradlew* ./settings.gradle* .
RUN ./gradlew
```

Running ./gradlew alone forces the distribution download, now cached in its own layer.

```
COPY . .

RUN ./gradlew clean installDist
```

Our build carries on as before, with our COPY likely refreshed every time (assuming our code changed).

This is just the beginning of the sorts of optimizations that can be applied in the construction of your container images. The key to take away is carefully considering what belongs in each layer. If parts of your system will change at different paces, giving them separate layers may be beneficial.

We've shown a fairly raw approach to building Docker images. As you might expect, a ton of plugins for both Maven and Gradle exist if you want to wrap up this functionality and not hand-code your Dockerfiles. There are even options like Jib (https://github.com/GoogleContainerTools/jib), which avoid using the Docker tools at all. All of these are useful, but a well-grounded developer is aided by understanding more deeply how containers are built, even if they get help doing it day to day.

12.3.4 *Ports and hosts*

Along with providing our application with its own isolated filesystem, containers also do the same for the network. With our sample application, let's imagine that we added code to run a standard HTTP server, for example, the basic one provided in the JDK at com.sun.net.httpserver.HttpServer. If we docker run our container, we'll find that there's no way to call that HTTP endpoint.

To address this, we need to ask Docker to make a port available to us. We can do this directly by adding to our run command as follows:

```
$ docker run -p 8080:8080 hello
```

-p takes a pair of ports separated by a :. The first value is the port that we want available *outside* the container. The second value is the port that our software *inside* the container is listening on. If we go to another terminal (or a web browser) we can see it working, as shown here and in figure 12.6:

```
$ curl http://localhost:8080/hello
Hello from HttpServer
```

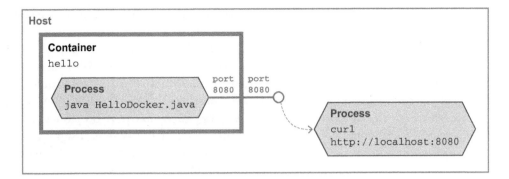

Figure 12.6 Exposing a port in Docker

As you might expect from the format and Figure 12.6, these two port values don't have to match. If we instead run with this command-line:

```
$ docker run -p 9000:8080 hello
```

Port 9000 will be visible outside the container, connected to port 8080 on the process inside the container.

we'll now see a good response on port 9000, whereas 8080 is no longer accessible, as shown here:

```
$ curl http://localhost:9000/hello
Hello from HttpServer

$ curl http://localhost:8080/hello
curl: (7) Failed to connect to localhost port 8080: Connection refused
```

Exposing ports is such a fundamental part of how containers are deployed that the `Dockerfile` allows us to note the ports our image is expected to provide, like this:

```
EXPOSE 8080
```

If we set this, `docker build` again, and run without the port switches, you might be surprised to find that Docker doesn't default to making the `EXPOSE` ports available. However, if you provide the `-P` switch by itself (note the uppercase and lack of arguments), Docker will bind each `EXPOSE` port in our image to a random, or *ephemeral*, port. Because we can't guess what port will be assigned, we need a new command to peek and find our ephemeral port. This is done with `docker ps` as follows:

```
$ docker run -P hello

... In another terminal, some columns trimmed...
$ docker ps
CONTAINER ID    IMAGE    COMMAND           PORTS
94d7f125caad    hello    "./docker-gradle"  0.0.0.0:55031->8080/tcp
```

The value `0.0.0.0:55031->8080/tcp` tells us that port 55031 outside the container is bound to port 8080 inside.

This ephemeral port business may seem like an annoyance at first, particularly when testing, because the port shifts around. But it's actually a critical feature when running containers in production. Imagine that you have a host that you want to fully utilize running many different Java containers. Each of those applications may want to run using the same port, but the host can assign that port only once. Although it requires additional coordination in other parts of the system, assigning ephemeral ports allows the containers to keep their simpler view of the world—"I run on 8080"— while still coexisting in a broader, more complex environment.

That gets us set to talk to our application when running it in a container locally. But what about the other direction—when our container needs to reach out to another services such as a database?

When we're running in production, it's a good practice to explicitly configure locations of services and use normal load balancing and DNS to reach them. These can be injected into containers via environment variables or other service discovery systems, but the key is that you don't assume where resources are located in relation to your container.

But this gets much harder when working locally, because a normal developer setup isn't going to have that same sort of infrastructure available. If you're using Docker for Mac or Docker for Windows, you can use the name `host.docker.internal` inside your containers, which automatically points to your host machine. Docker for Linux can have the same set on container startup with the `--add-host host.docker.internal :host-gateway` flag. In these cases, if your application is set up to receive such locations via environment variables, you can point your container to that hostname.

If this doesn't work for your given environment, an IP address for your host exists inside the container. Commands such as `sudo ip addr show` may give you hints on the location, but this gets tedious in a hurry.

Containers have a lot of networking options that are beyond the scope of this book, but some of them that can help us with this exact issue are used by a tool called Docker Compose. Let's see how containers can help us locally solve our external resource access problems.

12.3.5 *Local development with Docker Compose*

Much like the dreaded install list for a new project, it's common for applications to also require multiple other services at runtime as well. Maybe you've got a database, a cache, a NoSQL store, or even other custom applications, which all have to be up and running for your application to work locally.

Docker Compose is a tool for declaring and running sets of containers. It lets us capture the precise set of services and start them together. It also manages saving state for these containers so we can stop and restart without having to do everything from scratch.

If this sounds similar to orchestration tools like Kubernetes, you're not wrong. There is overlap in the container management aspects of both tools. However, Docker Compose is aimed at running on a single machine, which excludes it as a reasonable choice for many production environments.

> **NOTE** Docker Compose was originally a separate tool, but it has been integrated as another command within `docker` itself. If you see information on the internet suggesting running `docker-compose`, you can just replace the - with a space these days.

By default we describe our configuration in a file called `docker-compose.yml`. For a start, let's tell Docker Compose about our application as follows:

```
version: "3.9"      ◁—— The Docker Compose file version
services:
    app:            Instructs Docker Compose to run a typical docker build in
        build: .  ◁— the current directory to generate the image for this service
Declares a  ports:
service to run  - "8080:8080"     ◁
called app                        Port declarations, like on our manual docker run before
```

We run this at the command line with `docker compose up`. This will show our familiar build output as it starts, and then some new output as it starts our container, as shown next:

```
[+] Running 2/2
 - Network docker-gradle_default  Created                    0.1s
 - Container docker-gradle-app-1  Created                    0.1s
Attaching to docker-gradle-app-1
docker-gradle-app-1  | (Howdy,Docker)
```

Our `docker-compose.yml` can contain multiple services, as we'll see in a moment. The output from each gets prefixed with a name to distinguish them, by default based on our current directory and the service name, so ours is `docker-gradle-app-1`.

Let's say that our application needs a Redis instance. We add that as a new key we'll call `redis` under the `services` key like this:

```
version: "3.9"
services:
  app:
    build: .
    ports:
      - "8080:8080"
  redis:
    image: "redis:alpine"   ◁—— The redis:alpine image from Docker Hub
```

Now when we run, Docker Compose will pull the `redis:alpine` image and start it with our application container. Figure 12.7 and the next code sample illustrate these containers running in relation to each other:

```
[+] Running 7/7
 - redis Pulled                                        5.0s
   - 59bf1c3509f3 Pull complete                        1.2s
   - 719adce26c52 Pull complete                        1.2s
[+] Running 2/2
 - Container docker-gradle-redis-1   Created           0.2s
 - Container docker-gradle-app-1     Created           0.0s
Attaching to docker-gradle-app-1, docker-gradle-redis-1
docker-gradle-redis-1  | # oO0Oo Redis is starting...
docker-gradle-redis-1  | # Redis version=6.2.6, ...
docker-gradle-redis-1  | * monotonic clock: POSIX ...
docker-gradle-redis-1  | # Warning: no config file...
docker-gradle-redis-1  | * Running mode=standalone, ...
docker-gradle-redis-1  | # Server initialized
docker-gradle-redis-1  | * Ready to accept connections
docker-gradle-app-1    | (Howdy,Docker)
```

Redis container output

Our application container output

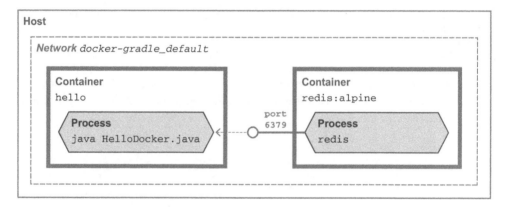

Figure 12.7 Docker Compose containers running

This is already convenient—we can get the precise right version of our databases and other external services locally without manual installation. But Docker Compose brings another helpful feature to avoid many of the networking struggles we saw before. During initial startup, there was a message reading `Network docker-gradle_default Created`. This informed us that Docker Compose had created a new, separate network namespace `docker-gradle_default`. This network is shared between all the services that Docker Compose has started for us. Even better, each service name we spelled out in our `docker-compose.yml`—app and redis—shows up like a real host name inside all of the containers.

If we've designed our application with the Twelve-factor principles and pass in the location of Redis via an environment variable, we can configure this entirely in the `docker-compose.yml`, as shown here:

```
version: "3.9"
services:
  app:
```

```
    build: .
    ports:
      - "8080:8080"
    environment:
      REDIS_URL: redis://redis:6379
  redis:
    image: "redis:alpine"
```

> The first redis is the URL scheme, and the second redis is the hostname.

This just scratches the surface of Docker Compose. All the common options for controlling `docker run` can be set in `docker-compose.yml`, and it's a great way to smooth ramp-up on local development.

12.3.6 Debugging in Docker

When our software isn't behaving, sometimes we need to peek inside the boundaries that our containers set up for us. Earlier we met `docker ps` for determining the port that our container was exposing. `docker ps` provides us more information than just that, though. In particular, by default, a container is given a handy, randomly generated name that it can be referred to by, as shown next:

```
$ docker ps
CONTAINER ID    IMAGE     COMMAND            ...  PORTS       NAMES
c103de6e6634    hello     "./docker-gradle" ...  8080/tcp    vigilant_austin
```

This container can be referred to as `vigilant_austin`. If you want to avoid having the name change every time your container runs, you can control this with the `--name container-name` parameter on `docker run`. You'll want to couple that with `--rm` to remove the container when it exits; otherwise, the name won't be available for reuse the second time you run.

Having the name of the container allows us to take other debugging steps. With `docker exec`, we can execute commands in the running container. As we saw with `docker run -it` before, we can even get an interactive shell inside the container, as shown here, assuming it has `bash` or something similar installed:

```
$ docker run --name hello-container --rm hello

# In another terminal start a shell in the container
$ docker exec -it hello-container bash

root@18a5f04bb4c8: ps aux
USER PID %CPU %MEM COMMAND
root   1  1.6  1.9 /opt/java/openjdk/bin/java -cp /opt/app/lib/docker-gradle
root  37  0.1  0.1 bash
root  47  0.0  0.1 ps aux
```

It's important to remember that `exec` doesn't start a new container—it attaches to an existing one. Figure 12.8 shows how the processes coexist within the single container.

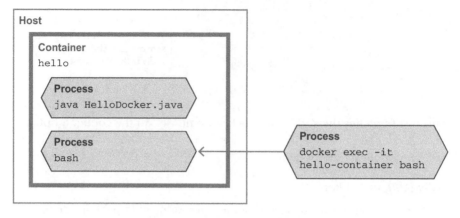

Figure 12.8   `docker exec` into a container

We aren't limited to just basic Unix commands, though. For instance, we can use `jps` and `jcmd` to inspect the running JVMs in our container as follows:

```
root@18a5f04bb4c8: jps
1 Main
148 Jps

root@18a5f04bb4c8: jcmd 1 VM.version
1:
OpenJDK 64-Bit Server VM version 17.0.1+12
JDK 17.0.1
```

In chapter 7, we explored the deep visibility we can gain with the JFR (JDK Flight Recorder) tools. With a shell into the running container, we can gather JFR data with a few simple commands. If it's not already running, we tell JFR to start recording like this:

```
root@4f146639fcfc: jcmd 1 JFR.start
1:
Started recording 1. No limit specified, using maxsize=250MB as default.
```

After we've let the application gather data for a while, we save the current recording to a file inside the container as follows:

```
root@4f146639fcfc: jcmd 1 JFR.dump name=1 filename=./capture.jfr
1:
Dumped recording "1", 293.3 kB written to:
```

To inspect the file offline, we'll need to copy it out of the container. Back on our host system, we can do this with the `docker cp` command, as shown in the next code sample. Again, our container name comes in handy to specify where to grab the file from:

```
$ docker cp hello-container:/opt/app/bin/capture.jfr .
```

The first parameter to cp is the file source, and the second, its destination. It's specified with the format container-name:path. The second parameter is local, so we don't need a container name and just use the path.

`capture.jfr` is now available on your local system to open via JDK Mission Control (JMC).

Because Docker exposes an API, your `docker` commands can be pointed at a remote host instead of your local environment. See the Docker documentation at https://docs.docker.com/ for details on how to configure that.

All of these shells and command-line options are good for getting at the low level of what's happening in our containers. But what if we just want a breakpoint in our IDE for the Java application in a local container? Fortunately the JDK's remote debugging facilities have all the pieces we need to configure this, as shown next:

```
docker run --rm \
  -p 8090:8090 \
  -e JAVA_TOOL_OPTIONS=\
  '-agentlib:jdwp=transport=dt_socket,server=y,suspend=n,address=*:8090' \
  --name hello-container \
  hello
```

In addition to the normal output of our application starting up, you should see a message like this indicating the remote debugging port is available:

```
Listening for transport dt_socket at address: 8090
```

From here you can use your IDE features to debug a Remote JVM, pointed at port 8090. Everything should behave much like debugging the application on your local environment, but all from the cozy, bounded world of the container.

12.3.7 Logging with Docker

As we've seen repeatedly, the separation that containers introduce from their host environment requires a change of mind-set. One common stumbling block is logging. Whether you use one of the popular logging frameworks or simply write to `System.out`, it's common for a service to produce output when running. We don't want to lose access to this information just because we've moved into a container.

You can take a manual approach with techniques we've already seen in this chapter. Simply write your logs to disk as before. When you need to examine them, you can use `docker exec` or `docker cp` to access to the files like this:

```
// Start our container
$ docker run --rm --name hello-container hello

// In another shell, copy the file locally
// Assumes log is at /log/application.log
$ docker cp hello-container:/log/application.log .

// Or alternatively, tail the file continually
$ docker exec hello-container tail -f /log/application.log
```

However, this introduces some friction in retrieving this information—and the potential for data loss if the container is fully removed prematurely.

A common practice—with or without containers—is to forward logs from the application to a central location. The destination of this forwarding could be just centralized storage, an indexing service such as Elasticsearch, or even a fully external logging provider.

If we try to keep the simple practice of writing to a local file in our containers, though, we must answer the question of where our log-forwarding application runs. Putting it inside the containers consumes additional memory and resources we need to account for, and generally it's recommended to avoid having multiple things within a single container. Containers allow for mounting a volume so log files could be shared between the containers and host, but this requires configuration and isn't always performant.

A better alternative is to lean on the fact that Docker captures anything our containers write to the typical output streams, STDOUT and STDERR. On the host, these streams are saved to well-known file locations for every container being run. This simplifies configuration because we can install log forwarding once on the host and just tell our individual containers to write to STDOUT instead of files. It's also compatible with existing logging libraries such as log4j2, which has appenders to write to CONSOLE for exactly this purpose.

This type of infrastructure setup around how to run your containers and capture their logs is an example of issues that come with scaling containers beyond a single host. Providing a systematic way to address such questions is one of the key benefits of our next topic: Kubernetes.

12.4   *Kubernetes*

This introduction to Docker really only scratches the surface of configuring and customizing our containers. In a real production environment, you may need many instances of your containers. Managing large fleets of containers with just docker commands quickly gets out of control, and it's not uncommon for a production environment to have hundreds of separate containers. You need to automate these tasks. The general term for such automation is an *orchestrator*, and although there are many options in the field, Kubernetes is the dominant solution.

Kubernetes (often referred to as K8s) is an open source project originally derived out of Google's internal work on container orchestration. At its heart, it provides standard, API-driven tools to describe the desired state for a system and then ensure that state is maintained over time.

Kubernetes models your system as a set of *objects* of different types. A set of *controllers* run continually, watching the actual state of the system and applying changes (such as creating a new container if an old one dies) so the desired and actual state of the system match.

A full treatment of Kubernetes is far beyond the scope of this book, but to get a taste of how it works, let's look at the most basic object types and how we'd use them with the container skills we've gotten so far.

- *Cluster*—A single installation of Kubernetes on anything from a single machine to many hundreds of nodes
- *Node*—A single machine (virtual or physical) in the cluster
- *Pod*—A deployable unit of one (or more) containers
- *Deployment*—A declarative way to deploy a pod
- *Service*—An object exposing containers in the cluster to callers

To step through these ideas and demonstrate we'll use `minikube`, a local development environment from the Kubernetes project itself. See the linked instructions for current installation instructions on your OS (https://minikube.sigs.k8s.io/docs/start/).

Once installed we can start a local cluster with the command `minikube start`, as shown next. Note this may take several minutes the first time to download all the required images:

```
$ minikube start

  minikube v1.25.2 on Darwin 11.6.2
  Using the docker driver based on existing profile
  Starting control plane node minikube in cluster minikube
  Pulling base image ...
  Downloading Kubernetes v1.23.1 preload ...
  > preloaded-images-k8s-v17-v1...: 504.44 MiB / 504.44 MiB  100.00%
  Restarting existing docker container for "minikube" ...
  Preparing Kubernetes v1.23.1 on Docker 20.10.12 ...
  * kubelet.housekeeping-interval=5m
  Verifying Kubernetes components...
  * Using image kubernetesui/dashboard:v2.3.1
  * Using image kubernetesui/metrics-scraper:v1.0.7
  * Using image gcr.io/k8s-minikube/storage-provisioner:v5
  Enabled addons: storage-provisioner, default-storageclass, dashboard

  Done! kubectl is now configured to use "minikube" cluster and "default"
  namespace by default
```

Our Kubernetes cluster is now running locally. We can stop the cluster with the `minikube stop` command or, if we're entirely finished experimenting, remove it with `minikube delete`.

Although Kubernetes provides a REST API for systems to interact with, there's a convenient wrapper more suitable for human consumption via the `kubectl` command. We can use this to view, create, and edit the objects in our cluster. For instance, `minikube` takes care of creating our node objects by default, but we can `kubectl describe node` to see what it set up on our behalf. This listing highlights only a few portions of the output as it provides a lot of detail:

```
$ kubectl describe node

Name:          minikube
Roles:         control-plane,master
Labels:        kubernetes.io/arch=amd64
               kubernetes.io/hostname=minikube
```

```
                          kubernetes.io/os=linux
Addresses:
  InternalIP:  192.168.49.2
  Hostname:    minikube
```

Kubernetes itself runs in pods on the node, listed here.

```
Non-terminated Pods:              (12 in total)
  Namespace                       Name
  ---------                       ----
  kube-system                     coredns-64897985d-n8fzv
  kube-system                     etcd-minikube
  kube-system                     kube-apiserver-minikube
  kube-system                     kube-controller-manager-minikube
  kube-system                     kube-proxy-4zvll
  kube-system                     kube-scheduler-minikube
  kube-system                     storage-provisioner
  kubernetes-dashboard            dashboard-metrics-scraper-58549894f-bcjh4
  kubernetes-dashboard            kubernetes-dashboard-ccd587f44-mq8zv
```

Events can be helpful when debugging if unexpected problems occur in a node.

```
Events:
  Type    Reason                  Message
  ----    ------                  -------
  Normal  Starting                Starting kubelet.
  Normal  NodeHasSufficientMemory Node status is: NodeHasSufficientMemory
  Normal  NodeHasNoDiskPressure   Node status is: NodeHasNoDiskPressure
  Normal  NodeHasSufficientPID    Node status is: NodeHasSufficientPID
```

With `minikube` providing our cluster and node, we're ready to run some software. To keep things simple we'll use the `k8s.gcr.io/echoserver:1.4` image, which as the name suggests just echoes back information about HTTP requests sent to it.

NOTE `minikube` supports working with local images, but it runs a separate Docker daemon, so the image management gets a little more complex. Consult the README at https://github.com/kubernetes/minikube if you are looking to do more local development using `minikube`. We'll stick to published images in our examples to keep it simple.

Our first goal is to get a pod on the cluster running the `echoserver` container. We do that by asking `kubectl` to create a deployment, as shown in the next code snippet. The deployment object tells the Kubernetes cluster the desired state of having our pod running. Kubernetes's control loop notices the desired state doesn't match reality and start our pods for us to address that:

```
$ kubectl create deployment echoes --image=k8s.gcr.io/echoserver:1.4
deployment.apps/echoes created
```

We can inspect the cluster to see that our deployment exists using the standard `kubectl get` command, as follows. This command works across any type of object in the system:

```
$ kubectl get deployments
NAME      READY  UP-TO-DATE  AVAILABLE  AGE
echoes    1/1    1           1          55s
```

If we look for pods, we'll also see shortly that the cluster has aligned its actual state with what our deployment requested, as shown here. Figure 12.9 gives a visual of the single pod state we've reached.

```
$ kubectl get pods
NAME                        READY   STATUS    RESTARTS   AGE
echoes-7989cff4bc-7m4df     1/1     Running   0          78s
```

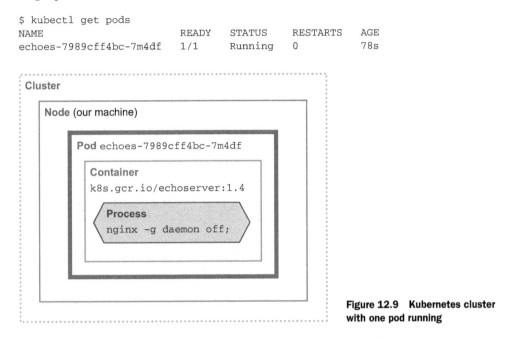

Figure 12.9 Kubernetes cluster with one pod running

The `kubectl create deployment` command is an easy way to get started, but its arguments only scratch the surface of what Kubernetes can configure. The natural representation of a Kubernetes object is given in YAML, and we can access the full picture via `kubectl edit deployment echoes`, as shown in the next code sample. This will open your default editor with the object's current YAML. If you make changes to the file, they are applied when the editor exits. We won't discuss all of these options, so refer to the documentation at http://mng.bz/M5m2 for further information:

```
# Please edit the object below. Lines beginning with a '#' will be ignored,
# and an empty file will abort the edit. If an error occurs while saving
# this file will be reopened with the relevant failures.
#
apiVersion: apps/v1
kind: Deployment
metadata:
  annotations:
    deployment.kubernetes.io/revision: "1"
  creationTimestamp: "2022-02-01T08:26:32Z"
  generation: 1
  labels:
    app: echoes              The echoes name we
  name: echoes      ◄─────┘  gave our deployment
  namespace: default
  resourceVersion: "1310"
```

```
   uid: e8b775f6-243e-46c1-9275-dadaecf2db3b
spec:
  progressDeadlineSeconds: 600
  replicas: 1
  revisionHistoryLimit: 10
  selector:
    matchLabels:
      app: echoes
  strategy:
    rollingUpdate:
      maxSurge: 25%
      maxUnavailable: 25%
    type: RollingUpdate
  template:
    metadata:
      creationTimestamp: null
      labels:
        app: echoes
    spec:
      containers:
      - image: k8s.gcr.io/echoserver:1.4
        imagePullPolicy: IfNotPresent
        name: echoserver
        resources: {}
        terminationMessagePath: /dev/termination-log
        terminationMessagePolicy: File
      dnsPolicy: ClusterFirst
      restartPolicy: Always
      schedulerName: default-scheduler
      securityContext: {}
      terminationGracePeriodSeconds: 30
status:
  availableReplicas: 1
  conditions:
  - lastTransitionTime: "2022-02-01T08:26:33Z"
    lastUpdateTime: "2022-02-01T08:26:33Z"
    message: Deployment has minimum availability.
    reason: MinimumReplicasAvailable
    status: "True"
    type: Available
  - lastTransitionTime: "2022-02-01T08:26:32Z"
    lastUpdateTime: "2022-02-01T08:26:33Z"
    message: ReplicaSet "echoes-7989cff4bc" has successfully progressed.
    reason: NewReplicaSetAvailable
    status: "True"
    type: Progressing
  observedGeneration: 1
  readyReplicas: 1
  replicas: 1
  updatedReplicas: 1
```

spec describes the desired state of our deployment.

An important value we'll discuss in a moment that determines the number of pods we want running

The image we requested for our pods to run

status tells us what's currently observed about the state of the deployment. Note that it also has replicas, telling us how many are seen running now.

What happens if we change the spec value of replicas: 1 to 3? Kubernetes will see the mismatch between the deployment state and what's actually on the cluster and start new containers on our behalf, as shown next. Figure 12.10 shows the result after the containers have had a chance to start up.

```
$ kubectl get pods
NAME                        READY   STATUS    RESTARTS   AGE
echoes-7989cff4bc-7m4df     1/1     Running   0          7m38s
echoes-7989cff4bc-7qn47     1/1     Running   0          8s
echoes-7989cff4bc-cmngm     1/1     Running   0          8s
```

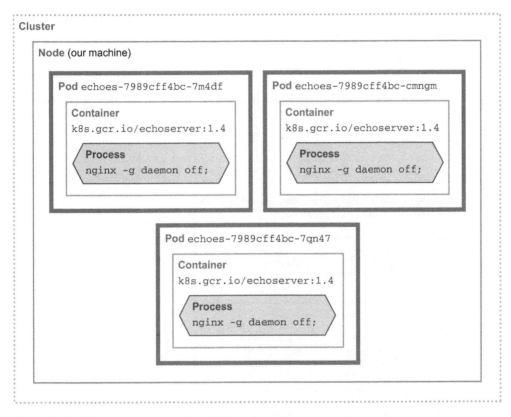

Figure 12.10   Kubernetes cluster with multiple pods running

In practice, you likely won't be hand-editing YAML files on a production Kubernetes cluster, but all the tooling builds on this—CI/CD systems, generated or source-controlled Kubernetes manifests—are just helpers creating the right YAML and API calls for us.

On our local system, the same tricks we played before with docker ps and docker exec will work to let us take a closer look at the running containers. Once we know the container name, kubectl has a slightly cleaner command for letting us start a shell inside the pod, as shown here:

```
$ kubectl exec echoes-7989cff4bc-7m4df -- bash
root@echoes-7989cff4bc-7m4df: uname -a
Linux echoes-7989cff4bc-7m4df 5.10.76-linuxkit #1 SMP \
  Mon Nov 8 10:21:19 2021 x86_64 x86_64 x86_64 GNU/Linux
```

One last step is needed to make this deployment more useful. By default we can't talk to the pods in the cluster at all. If we look at the docker ps for the containers, you'll see that no ports are exposed.

Kubernetes addresses this via its *service* abstraction, which is a general interface for working with various load balancing and traffic routing into the cluster. The details here quickly get beyond the scope of this introduction, but we'll set up the simplest of them, called a NodePort with kubectl expose, as follows:

```
$ kubectl expose deployment echoes --type=NodePort --port=8080
service/echoes exposed
```

As seen in figure 12.11, this creates a new object in the cluster representing our NodePort.

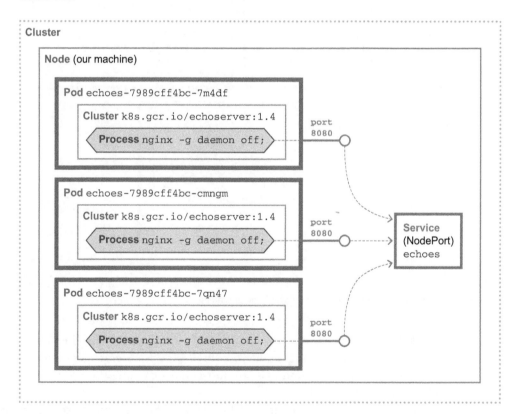

Figure 12.11 NodePort and services in the Kubernetes cluster

Viewing the services, we can see a NodePort configured in the cluster, as shown next:

```
$ kubectl get services
NAME          TYPE         CLUSTER-IP       EXTERNAL-IP   PORT(S)          AGE
echoes        NodePort     10.108.182.100   <none>        8080:31980/TCP   12s
kubernetes    ClusterIP    10.96.0.1        <none>        443/TCP          35m
```

Internally, this means that port 8080 is available on every node in the cluster and will forward traffic to our pods. Now that we have a way for traffic to reach our pods, we still need to reveal this outside the cluster to be able to call it. kubectl supports this with its port-forwarding feature like this:

```
$ kubectl port-forward service/echoes 7080:8080
Forwarding from 127.0.0.1:7080 -> 8080
Forwarding from [::1]:7080 -> 8080
Handling connection for 7080
```

With this forwarding running in a terminal, we can visit 127.0.0.1:7080 in the browser, and we'll see our request echoed back. Figure 12.12 shows the flow of traffic through the various components to the pods.

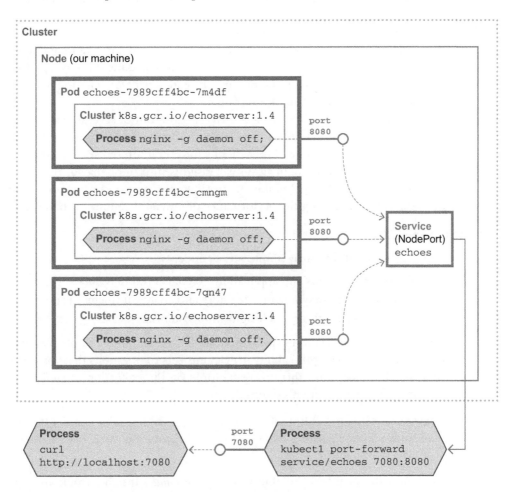

Figure 12.12 Port-forwarding into our Kubernetes cluster

Kubernetes is a large step up in complexity from just running our Docker containers locally, but it also provides a solution to the difficulties of running containers at scale. Whether or not we're running on Kubernetes, though, we almost always care about the performance of our services. Let's examine how to manage how well our containers are running in production.

12.5 *Observability and performance*

Java technology was originally designed for a world where JVMs ran on bare metal in data centers, and where the developer could remain relatively isolated from (or even ignorant of) the details of the deployment environment. The world is changing at a fundamental level, however. Cloud native deployments—especially containers—are here and are being adopted quickly (but at varying rates across different parts of the industry).

Containers present some particular challenges for understanding the details of what is happening in a modern application. For example, it is not common practice for containers to run services such as an ssh daemon, making it impossible to log in to a container to observe what is happening. Instead, any data about the health of applications must be exported out of the container.

The DevOps practice known as *observability* grew out of several separate strands of modern development practice, including both the application performance monitoring (APM) space and the need for visibility into orchestrated systems, such as Kubernetes. It aims to provide highly granular insights into the behavior of systems along with rich context. The techniques it provides are very useful, if not essential, for understanding and tuning the performance of Java applications in containers.

12.5.1 *Observability*

Overall, observability is fairly simple set of concepts:

1 Instrument systems and applications to collect relevant data
2 Send this data to a system that can store and analyze it (including query capability)
3 Provide visualizations and insights into systems as a whole

The query and visualization capability is the key to the power of observability. It has been described as being the ability to "Get answers to questions that you didn't know you'd need to ask"—and this is possible only via the collection of sufficient data to accurately model the system's internal state.

> **NOTE** The theory behind Observability comes from system control theory—essentially the question: "How well can the internal state of a system be inferred from outside?"

Ultimately, the goal is to be able to obtain *actionable* insights from, and about, the entire system. This should replace fragmentary views that are based on just one or two pieces of the overall system.

So, while incident resolution is an obvious use case that is a good fit for observability—it is where the practice originated after all—it is also true that the potential domain of applicability is much larger. If the right data is being collected, the stakeholders for observability are much broader than just software reliability engineers (SREs), production support, and DevOps folks.

Observability is particularly relevant to containerized applications, because these deployments tend to be more complex than traditional on-premises applications. There are typically more services and components in cloud-deployed application, with more complex topology as well as a much faster pace of change (driven by practices such as continuous deployment).

This is also combined with the increasing popularity of new Cloud native technologies that have new operational behaviors. This includes Kubernetes, as well as Function as a Service deployments, such as AWS Lambda. This new world makes root cause analysis and incident resolution potentially a lot harder.

Observability data is often conceptualized in terms of "three pillars." This is a simple mental model (some would argue *too* simple) but is useful for developers who are new to observability. The pillars follow:

- *Distributed traces*—Records of a single service invocation, corresponding to a single request from a user
- *Metrics*—Values measuring specific activity over a time interval
- *Logs*—Immutable records of discrete events that happen over time (can be plain text, structured, or binary)

The core libraries and instrumentation components are all open source, and most of them are managed through industry bodies such as the Cloud Native Compute Foundation (CNCF).

OPENTELEMETRY

The OpenTelemetry project (https://opentelemetry.io/), a major project within CNCF, is a set of standards, formats, client libraries, and associated software components for providing observability. The standards are explicitly cross-platform and not tied to any particular technology stack.

This provides a framework that integrates with OSs and commercial products and can collect observability data from apps written in many languages. Because the implementations are open source, they are of varying levels of technical maturity, depending on the interest that OpenTelemetry has attracted in the particular language community.

OpenTelemetry came from the merger of two prior open source projects, OpenTracing and OpenCensus projects. Although OpenTelemetry is still maturing, it is gaining momentum and an increasing number of applications and teams are investigating and implementing it. This number seems set to grow significantly during 2022 and 2023.

From our perspective, the Java/JVM implementation is one of the most mature available and has a number of advantages over traditional APM/monitoring. In particular, the use of an open standard provides the following:

- Vastly reduced vendor lock-in
- Open specification wire protocols
- Open source client components
- Standardized architecture patterns
- Increasing quantity and quality of open source backend components

OpenTelemetry has several subprojects that make up the standard as a whole, and they are not all at the same level of maturity in terms of their overall lifecycle.

The Distributed Tracing specification is at v1.0 and is being actively deployed into production systems. It replaces OpenTracing completely, and the OpenTracing project has been officially archived. The Jaeger project, one of the most popular distributing tracing backends, has also discontinued its client libraries and will default to OpenTelemetry protocols going forward.

The OpenTelemetry Metrics project is not quite as advanced but has reached v1.0 and general availability (GA). At time of writing, the protocol is stable, and the API is at feature-freeze.

Finally, the Logging specification is still in draft and is not expected to reach v1.0 until late 2022. There is still acknowledged to be a certain amount of work to do on the spec.

Overall, OpenTelemetry as a whole will be considered to be v1.0/GA when the Metrics standard reaches v1.0 alongside Tracing.

The Java libraries for OpenTelemetry can be deployed into your application using either manual methods (where the developer must consciously choose which parts of the application need to be instrumented) or the use of automatic instrumentation (using a Java agent). Java components for OpenTelemetry can be found on GitHub and live in several projects, including http://mng.bz/aJyJ.

A full discussion of how to implement a full observability solution (whether based on OpenTelemetry or another stack) is outside the scope of this book, but the well-grounded Java developer would be well advised to explore this area thoroughly.

Related to observability are some performance subtleties that engineers who are not Java/VM specialists may not be aware of. Let's take a closer look.

12.5.2 *Performance in containers*

Many developers, when migrating their Java applications into containers, will try to use the smallest possible containers. This seems to make sense, because cloud-based applications are typically charged by the amount of RAM and CPU that they use.

However, the JVM is a very dynamic platform, and certain important parameters are automatically determined by the JVM at startup time, based on the observed properties of the machine the JVM is running on.

These properties include the type and count of the CPUs and the physical memory. The behavior of the running application can and will be different when running on differently sized machines—and this includes containers. Some of these dynamic properties follow:

- JVM Intrinsics, a JIT technique that can make use of very specific CPU features (e.g. vector support)
- Sizing of internal threadpools (such as the "common pool")
- Number of threads used for GC

Just from this list, we can see that incorrectly choosing the size of the container image can cause problems related to GC or common thread operations. However, the problem is fundamentally deeper than this.

Current versions of Java, including Java 17, perform some dynamic checks and decide the GC to use *ergonomically* (automatically), if a GC is not explicitly specified on the command line. If you didn't specify a collector, then the logic is as follows:

- If the machine is "server class," choose G1 (Parallel for Java 8).
- If the machine is not "server class," then choose Serial.

The working definition of a server class machine is: >= two physical CPUs and >=2 GB of memory

This means that if a Java application is run on a machine that appears to have less than two CPUs and 2 GB of memory, then unless a specific collector algorithm is explicitly chosen, the Serial algorithm will be used. This is usually not what teams want—and leads to the following best practice:

TIP Always run Java applications in containers with at least two CPUs and 2 GB of memory.

It is also important to recognize that the traditional Java application lifecycle consists of a number of phases: bootstrap, intense class loading, warmup (with JIT compilation), and then a long-lived steady state (lasting for days or weeks) with relatively little class loading and JIT. This model is challenged by cloud deployments where containers may live for much shorter time periods and cluster sizes may be dynamically readjusted.

In this new world, Java has to ensure that it remains competitive along several key axes, including the following:

- Footprint
- Density
- Startup time

Fortunately, there is ongoing work and research into making sure that the platform continues to optimize for these characteristics—we'll hear more about it in chapter 18.

Summary

- Containers have radically changed how we package and deploy applications and require some new techniques and ideas.
- Containers represent another layer of abstraction on top of the classic operating systems, hypervisors, and VMs that we've seen in the past.
- Docker is the most common tool for building, publishing, and running container images.
- We specify a container image via a `Dockerfile`. The resulting image contains our application and a complete environment in which it can run, including the JVM, native dependencies, and additional tooling.
- Containers introduce an additional layer to networking in particular. In its most basic form, we have to manage the ports that our containers expose for them to be accessible to the outside world.
- Running fleets of containers at scale is a lot to keep track of, so orchestrators are used to do that systematically. The most popular choice for this is Kubernetes.
- Kubernetes provides a rich, extensible API for declaring the desired state of your system and bringing that to life at runtime. It is accessible via the command line and a REST API with an enormous ecosystem of supporting tools around it.
- A key feature of containers is enforcing constraints around resources. These limits on memory and CPU can have performance implications for your application running in a container.

Testing fundamentals

Recent years in programming have seen a growing acceptance of automated testing as an expected part of the development process. Tests are run both locally by developers and in build and continuous integration environments to ensure our systems are behaving. Along with that has come an explosion of different tools, approaches, and philosophies.

As with any technology, there are no silver bullets—no approach to testing will cover every possible situation. Given this, it's important to understand *why* you are testing so that you can determine best *how* to test.

13.1 Why we test

In fact, that word *test* hides a multitude of possible reasons we're examining our code's behavior. A non-exhaustive (and occasionally overlapping) list to consider follows:

- Confirming the logic of an individual method is correct
- Confirming the interaction between two objects within your code
- Confirming a library or other external dependency behaves as expected
- Confirming data produced or consumed by a part of the system is valid
- Confirming a system works correctly with an external component (such as a database)
- Confirming a system's end-to-end behavior fulfills important business scenarios
- Documenting assumptions for later maintainers (because tests don't get out of sync the same way comments and documentation can)
- Influencing your system design by exposing tight coupling and object responsibilities
- Automating post release checklists that a human would otherwise execute
- Finding unexpected corner cases in code via randomized inputs

Even this short list of testing motivations shows that the simple idea of "testing your code" isn't necessarily so simple. So, when we approach testing, we need to ask ourselves the following questions:

- What is my motivation in testing this piece of code?
- Which techniques let me fulfill that goal most accurately and cleanly?

13.2 How we test

One of the most common tools in discussing different types of testing is the Testing Pyramid, shown in figure 13.1. Originally from Mike Cohn's book *Succeeding with Agile* (Addison-Wesley Professional, 2009), the pyramid expresses one way of balancing the costs of different types of testing to maximize the aid they give us.

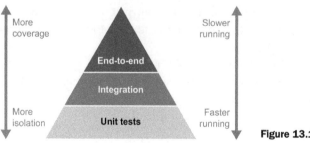

Figure 13.1   The Testing Pyramid

Although arguments rage on the internet about the exact boundaries between these types of testing, the central ideas are quite useful.

NOTE These types of tests are *not* defined by the tool you use—you aren't writing a unit test just because you are using JUnit, and using a specification library doesn't guarantee you're actually creating usable acceptance tests your stakeholders will benefit from. These types of tests are about what we want to exercise and prove.

Unit tests form the base of the pyramid. These are focused tests that exercise one aspect of a system. What do we mean, though, by "one aspect?" The easiest part is how the code under test relates to external dependencies. If your test calls the database before doing some logic on the result, that's no longer "one" thing you're testing— you're now testing the database retrieval *and* that your logic works. Such external dependencies may also commonly include network services or files.

A common approach to avoid violating that single focus is to use *test doubles*—for example, having our unit test talk to a fake object instead of the real database. We'll discuss this in detail in the next section, but the basic idea is that this fakery has many flavors and we need to consider many necessary things if it is to be done well.

Unit tests are attractive for a number of reasons, hence their traditional placement as the largest segment in the testing pyramid. These reasons include the following:

- *Fast*—If a test has no external dependencies, it shouldn't take long to execute.
- *Focused*—By talking only about one "unit" of code, it's often clearer what the test is expressing than in larger, more setup-laden tests.
- *Reliable failure*—Minimizing external dependencies, especially dependencies on external state, helps make unit tests more deterministic.

This all sounds great, so why don't we write only unit tests all the time? The truth is that unit tests have limitations that prevent them from being useful at every scale that we need to test at. The issues include the following:

- *Tight coupling*—Because unit tests are by definition closely related to their implementation, they are also prone to binding too tightly to those implementation choices. It's not uncommon for a whole suite of unit tests to be invalidated when the underlying implementation changes.
- *Missing meaningful interactions*—Although it's attractive to think about our code as a fleet of objects all just minding their own business, the reality is that the real work of a program includes interaction between those dependent pieces, which unit tests will miss.
- *Inwardly focused*—Often the goal of testing is showing that the end users of our software get the right results. Rarely does a single method's correctness actually translate to happy users.

Integration tests, the next step up the pyramid, break free from the constraint of unit tests about talking to dependencies. Integration tests cross those boundaries and may in fact focus on ensuring different pieces of the system integrate seamlessly.

As with unit tests, integration tests may also pick and choose only parts of the system to exercise. Some dependencies, such as external services, may still be replaced by test doubles, whereas others, such as databases, are in bounds for testing. What's key is that the tests reach out beyond a single "unit" of code in their scope.

The exact line between unit and integration tests can be blurry. Here are some examples, though, which clearly step over the line into integration testing territory:

- You need a database instance and make calls to your data access code.
- You spin up a special in-process HTTP server and test requests against it.
- You make actual calls against another service (whether or not a testing environment).

Integration tests come with a lot of nice properties, such as the following:

- *Broader coverage*—An integration test necessarily works more of your code and the code of the libraries you depend on.
- *More validation*—Certain types of errors may be detectable only when using real dependencies. For instance, a syntax error in a SQL statement will be difficult to find without calling an actual database.

Of course, no choice is without its trade-offs. Integration tests can be a source of significant pain if not managed correctly for reasons such as the following:

- *Slow tests*—Going to a real database instead of reading a value from memory is drastically slower. Multiply that by hundreds or thousands of tests, and you may find yourself waiting… a lot.
- *Nondeterministic results*—External dependencies increase the chances that important state may change between test runs. For instance, records left over in a database might alter what comes back from a SQL statement.
- *False confidence*—Integration tests sometimes use dependencies that differ subtly from those of the main system. For instance, if the test database is a different version than production, the integration test may incorrectly suggest everything is good when it isn't.

For all those difficulties, integration testing is a critical part of the testing landscape.

End-to-end tests push beyond integration tests with the aim of duplicating the full user experience of a system. This may mean programmatically driving a web browser or other application, or exercising a fully deployed instance of a service in a testing environment. End-to-end testing brings the following advantages that are difficult to duplicate at lower levels of our systems:

- *The "real" user experience*—A good end-to-end test is close to what users see. This lets us validate the users' high-level expectations directly.
- *A "real" environment*—Many end-to-end tests run against test, staging, or even production environments. This validates that our code works outside of our comfortable, carefully managed build environment.

- *UI available*—Many end-to-end testing approaches, such as those that drive web browsers, can see aspects of the system (e.g., was the button rendered, so it can be clicked) that may be difficult to validate anywhere else.

But this greater reality in our end-to-end tests comes with the next stark list of difficulties:

- *Even slower testing*—Where many unit tests run almost instantly and even integration tests can often be sub-second, an end-to-end test controlling a web browser to walk through a site will necessarily take much longer to run.
- *Flaky tests*—Historically, the tools for end-to-end testing, particularly of UIs, have been prone to flakiness, requiring retries and long timeouts to avoid unnecessary failures.
- *Brittle tests*—Because end-to-end tests live at the top of the pyramid, changes at any level below can cause failure. Seemingly innocuous text changes can unintentionally break these sprawling tests.
- *Harder debugging*—Because end-to-end testing often introduces another layer that drives the tests, figuring out what went wrong is often a chore.

With this pyramid in hand, you may be tempted to ask, "What's the right ratio of tests between the layers?" The truth is that there is no single answer. The needs of every project and system are different. But the pyramid can help guide you in the pluses and minuses of how you choose to exercise each bit of functionality in your system.

Although certainly not the only way, the well-grounded developer may find that test-driven development helps in keeping these different levels of testing clear as systems evolve.

13.3   Test-driven development

Test-driven development (TDD) has been part of the software development industry for quite some time. Its basic premise is that you write tests during your implementation rather than afterward, and those tests influence the design of your code. A commonly recommended approach to TDD, known as *test first*, is to actually write a failing test before providing an implementation, then refactoring as needed. For example, to write an implementation of concatenating two string objects (`"foo"` and `"bar"`), you'd write the test first (testing the result must equal `"foobar"`) to ensure that you know your implementation is correct. Though many developers write tests, more often than not, they're writing them after the implementation and losing some major benefits of TDD.

Despite its seeming pervasiveness, many developers don't understand why they should be doing TDD. The question for many developers remains, "Why write test-driven code? What's the benefit?"

We believe that *eliminating fear and uncertainty* is the overriding reason you should write test-driven code. Kent Beck (co-inventor of the JUnit testing framework) also sums this up nicely in his book, *Test-Driven Development: By Example* (Addison-Wesley Professional, 2002):

- Fear makes you tentative.
- Fear makes you want to communicate less.
- Fear makes you shy away from feedback.
- Fear makes you grumpy.

TDD takes away the fear, making the well-grounded Java developer a more confident, communicative, receptive, and happier developer. In other words, TDD helps you break free from the mind-set that leads to statements like these:

- When starting a new piece of work, "I don't know where to start, so I'll just start hacking."
- When changing existing code, "I don't know how the existing code is going to behave, so I'm secretly too scared to change it."

TDD brings many other benefits that aren't always immediately obvious, such as the following:

- *Cleaner code*—You write only the code you need.
- *Better design*—Some developers call TDD *test-driven design*.
- *Better APIs*—Your tests serve as an additional client to the implementation, revealing rough spots early.
- *Greater flexibility*—TDD encourages coding to interfaces.
- *Documentation through tests*—Because you don't write code without a test, everything has example usage in the tests.
- *Fast feedback*—You learn about bugs *now*, not in production.

One barrier for developers who are just getting started is that TDD can sometimes be viewed as a technique that isn't used by "ordinary" developers. The perception can be that only practitioners of some imaginary "Church of Agile" or other esoteric movement use TDD, and that every TDD principle must be followed strictly to gain the benefits. This perception is completely false, as we'll demonstrate. TDD is a technique for every developer.

13.3.1 TDD in a nutshell

TDD is easiest at the unit-testing level, and if you're unfamiliar with TDD, this is a good place to start. We'll start there, but proceed to show how TDD works, in particular on the boundary of unit and integration testing.

> **NOTE** Dealing with existing code that has very few or no tests can be a daunting task. It's almost impossible to retroactively fill in all of the tests. Instead, you should simply add tests for each new bit of functionality that you add. See Michael Feathers's excellent book *Working Effectively with Legacy Code* (Prentice Hall, 2004) for further help.

We'll start with brief coverage of the red-green-refactor premise behind TDD, using JUnit to test-drive code for calculating sales revenue for selling theater tickets. If the

JUnit framework is unfamiliar, we recommend the online user guides (see https://junit.org/junit5/docs/current/user-guide) or, for more detail, *JUnit in Action* by Cătălin Tudose (Manning, 2020; http://mng.bz/gwOR). Let's start with a working example of the three basic steps of TDD—the red-green-refactor loop—by calculating the revenue when selling theater tickets.

13.3.2 *A TDD example with a single use case*

If you're an experienced TDD practitioner, you may want to skip this small example, although we'll offer insights that may be new. Suppose you've been asked to write a rock-solid method to calculate the revenue generated by selling a number of theater tickets. The initial business rules from the theater company's accountant are simple, as shown here:

- The baseline price of a ticket is $30.
- Total revenue = number of tickets sold * price.
- The theater seats = 100 people.

Because the theater doesn't have very good point-of-sale software, the user currently has to manually enter the number of tickets sold.

If you have practiced TDD, you'll be familiar with the three basic steps of TDD: red, green, refactor. If you're new to TDD or are looking for a little refresher, let's take a look at Kent Beck's definition of those steps, from *Test-Driven Development: By Example*:

- *Red*—Write a little test that doesn't work (*failing test*).
- *Green*—Make that test pass as quickly as possible (*passing test*).
- *Refactor*—Eliminate the duplication (*refined passing test*).

To give you an idea of the `TicketRevenue` implementation that we're trying to achieve, here is some pseudocode you might have in your head:

```
estimateRevenue(int numberOfTicketsSold)
  if (numberOfTicketsSold is less than 0 OR greater than 100)
    Deal with error and exit
  else
    revenue = 30 * numberOfTicketsSold;
    return revenue;
  endif
```

Note that it's important that you don't think too deeply about this. The tests will end up driving your design and partly your implementation, too.

WRITING A FAILING TEST (RED)

The point in this step is to start with a test that fails. In fact, the test won't even compile, because you haven't even written a `TicketRevenue` class yet!

After a brief whiteboard session with the accountant, you realize that you'll want to write tests for five cases: ticket sales that are negative, 0, 1, 2–100, and > 100.

NOTE A good rule of thumb when writing tests (especially involving numbers) is to think of the zero/null case, the one case, and the many (*N*) case. A step beyond that is to think about other constraints on *N*, such as a negative amount or an amount beyond a maximum limit.

To begin, you decide to write a test that covers the revenue received from one ticket sale. Your JUnit test would look similar to the following code (remember we're not writing a perfect, passing test at this stage):

```
import org.junit.jupiter.api.BeforeEach;
import org.junit.jupiter.api.Test;

import java.math.BigDecimal;

import static org.junit.jupiter.api.Assertions.*;

public class TicketRevenueTest {
  private TicketRevenue venueRevenue;

  @BeforeEach
  public void setUp() {
    venueRevenue = new TicketRevenue();
  }

  @Test
  public void oneTicketSoldIsThirtyInRevenue() {     ◁——— One sold case
    var expectedRevenue = new BigDecimal("30");
    assertEquals(expectedRevenue, venueRevenue.estimateTotalRevenue(1));
  }
}
```

As you can see from the code, the test quite clearly expects the revenue from one ticket sale to equal 30 in revenue.

But as it stands, this test won't compile, because you haven't written a `TicketRevenue` class with the `estimateTotalRevenue(int numberOfTicketsSold)` method. To make the compilation error go away so that you can run the test, you can add a random implementation so that the test will compile, as follows:

```
public class TicketRevenue {
  public BigDecimal estimateTotalRevenue(int i) {
    return BigDecimal.ZERO;
  }
}
```

You may also find it a bit odd that the test extracts a mutable `venueRevenue` field when our general advice has been to favor immutability. The reasoning behind this is that the shared field allows us to express a common setup between our (soon-to-arrive) different test cases. Our tests don't need the same protections as our production code, and the increased clarity of highlighting which bits are the same between all the test cases is a win overall.

Now that the test compiles, you can run it from your favorite IDE or the command line. For the command-line test, our typical options of Gradle and Maven both provide easy ways to run tests (`gradle test` or `mvn test`).

NOTE IDEs also have their own individual ways of running JUnit tests, but generally speaking, they all allow you to right-click on the test class for a Run Test option. Once you do that, the IDE will display a window or section that informs you that your test has failed, because the expected value of 30 was not returned by the call to `estimateTotalRevenue(1)`; instead, 0 was returned.

Now that you have a failing test, the next step is to make the test pass (go green).

WRITING A PASSING TEST (GREEN)

The point in this step is to make the test pass, but the implementation doesn't have to be perfect. By providing the `TicketRevenue` class with a better implementation of `estimateTotalRevenue()` (an implementation that doesn't just return 0), you'll make the test pass (go green).

Remember, at this stage, you're trying to make the test pass without necessarily writing perfect code. Your initial solution might look something like the following code:

```
import java.math.BigDecimal;

public class TicketRevenue {
  public BigDecimal estimateTotalRevenue(int numberOfTicketsSold) {
    BigDecimal totalRevenue = BigDecimal.ZERO;
    if (numberOfTicketsSold == 1) {
      totalRevenue = new BigDecimal("30");      ◁─── An implementation
    }                                                that passes the test

    return totalRevenue;
  }
}
```

When you now run the test, it will pass, and in most IDEs, that will be indicated with a green bar or tick. Even our command lines give us a friendly green message to let us know all is well with the code.

The next question is, should you then say "I'm done!" and move on to the next bit of work? The resounding answer here should be "No!" Like us, you'll be itching to tidy up the previous code listing, so let's get into that right now.

REFACTORING THE TEST

The point of this step is to look at the quick implementation you wrote to pass the test and make sure that you're following accepted practice. Clearly the code isn't as clean and tidy as it could be. You can certainly refactor it and improve life for yourself and others in the future.

Remember, now that you have a passing test, you can *refactor without fear*. There's no chance of losing sight of the business logic that you've implemented so far.

TIP Another benefit that you've given yourself and the broader team by writing the initial passing test is a faster overall development process. The rest of the team can immediately take this first version of the code and begin to test it alongside the larger codebase (for integration tests and beyond).

In this example, you don't want to be using magic numbers—you want to make sure that the ticket price of 30 is a named concept in the code—so we write the following code:

```java
import java.math.BigDecimal;

public class TicketRevenue {

  private final static int TICKET_PRICE = 30;    ◁—— No magic number

  public BigDecimal estimateTotalRevenue(int numberOfTicketsSold) {
    BigDecimal totalRevenue = BigDecimal.ZERO;

    if (numberOfTicketsSold == 1) {
      totalRevenue = new BigDecimal(TICKET_PRICE *    ◁—— Refactored calculation
                                    numberOfTicketsSold);
    }

    return totalRevenue;
  }
}
```

The refactoring has improved the code, but clearly it doesn't cover all potential use cases (e.g., negative, 0, 2–100, and > 100 ticket sales).

Instead of trying to guess what the implementation should look like for the other use cases, you should have further tests drive the design and the implementation. The next section follows test-driven design by taking you through more use cases in this ticket revenue example.

A TDD EXAMPLE WITH MULTIPLE USE CASES

One particular style of TDD would continue to add one test at a time for the negative, 0, 2–100, and > 100 ticket sale test cases we presented before. But it's entirely valid to write a set of test cases up front, especially if they're related to the original test.

Note that it's still very important to follow the red-green-refactor lifecycle here. After adding all of these use cases, you might end up with a test class with failing tests (red) as follows:

```java
import org.junit.jupiter.api.BeforeEach;
import org.junit.jupiter.api.Test;

import java.math.BigDecimal;

import static org.junit.jupiter.api.Assertions.*;

public class TicketRevenueTest {
```

```java
  private TicketRevenue venueRevenue;
  private BigDecimal expectedRevenue;

  @BeforeEach
  public void setUp() {
    venueRevenue = new TicketRevenue();
  }

  @Test
  public void failIfLessThanZeroTicketsAreSold() {       // <──── Negative sold case
    assertThrows(IllegalArgumentException.class,
               () -> venueRevenue.estimateTotalRevenue(-1));
  }

  @Test                                                  // ┐ 0 sold case
  public void zeroSalesEqualsZeroRevenue() {       // <────┘
    assertEquals(BigDecimal.ZERO, venueRevenue.estimateTotalRevenue(0));
  }

  @Test
  public void oneTicketSoldIsThirtyInRevenue() {       // <──── 1 sold case
    expectedRevenue = new BigDecimal("30");
    assertEquals(expectedRevenue, venueRevenue.estimateTotalRevenue(1));
  }

  @Test
  public void tenTicketsSoldIsThreeHundredInRevenue() {       // <──── N sold case
    expectedRevenue = new BigDecimal("300");
    assertEquals(expectedRevenue, venueRevenue.estimateTotalRevenue(10));
  }

  @Test
  public void failIfMoreThanOneHundredTicketsAreSold() {       // <──── > 100 sold case
    assertThrows(IllegalArgumentException.class,
               () -> venueRevenue.estimateTotalRevenue(101));
  }
}
```

The initial basic implementation to pass all of those tests (green) would then look something like the following:

```java
import java.math.BigDecimal;

public class TicketRevenue {
  public BigDecimal estimateTotalRevenue(int numberOfTicketsSold)
    throws IllegalArgumentException {

    if (numberOfTicketsSold < 0) {
      throw new IllegalArgumentException(       // <──── Exceptional cases
              "Must be > -1");
    }

    if (numberOfTicketsSold == 0) {
```

```
        return BigDecimal.ZERO;
    }

    if (numberOfTicketsSold == 1) {
      return new BigDecimal("30");
    }

    if (numberOfTicketsSold == 101) {
      throw new IllegalArgumentException(        ◁──── Exceptional cases
              "Must be < 101");
    }

    return new BigDecimal(30 * numberOfTicketsSold);  ◁──── N sold case
  }
}
```

With the implementation just completed, you now have passing tests.

Again, by following the TDD lifecycle, you'll now refactor that implementation. For example, you could combine the illegal numberOfTicketsSold cases (< 0 or > 100) into one if statement and use a formula (TICKET_PRICE * numberOfTicketsSold) to return the revenue for all other legal values of numberOfTicketsSold. The following code should be similar to what you would come up with:

```
import java.math.BigDecimal;

public class TicketRevenue {

  private final static int TICKET_PRICE = 30;

  public BigDecimal estimateTotalRevenue(int numberOfTicketsSold)
    throws IllegalArgumentException {

    if (numberOfTicketsSold < 0 || numberOfTicketsSold > 100) {
      throw new IllegalArgumentException(        ◁──┐
              "# Tix sold must == 1..100");          │ Exceptional case
    }

    return new BigDecimal(TICKET_PRICE *        ◁──── All other cases
                    numberOfTicketsSold);
  }
}
```

The TicketRevenue class is now far more compact and yet still passes all of the tests! You've completed the full red-green-refactor cycle and can confidently move on to your next piece of business logic. Alternatively, you can start the cycle again, should you (or the accountant) spot any edge cases you've missed, such as having a variable ticket price.

13.4   Test doubles

As you continue to write code in a TDD style, you'll quickly run into the situation where your code references some (often third-party) dependency or subsystem. In this situation, you'll typically want to ensure that the code under test is isolated from that dependency to ensure that you're writing test code only against what you're actually building. You'll also want the tests to run as quickly as possible, especially if you're aiming to write unit rather than integration tests. Invoking a third-party dependency or subsystem, such as a database, can take a lot of time, which means you lose the fast feedback benefit of TDD. *Test doubles* are the solution to this problem.

In this section, you'll learn how a test double can help you to effectively isolate dependencies and subsystems. You'll work through examples that use the four types of test double (dummy, stub, fake, and mock). We'll also look at some of the perils and difficulties test doubles bring alongside their benefits.

We like Gerard Meszaros's simple explanation of a test double in his *xUnit Test Patterns* book (Addison-Wesley Professional, 2007), so we'll gladly quote him here: "A *Test Double* (think Stunt Double) is the generic term for any kind of pretend object used in place of a real object for testing purposes."

Meszaros defines four kinds of test doubles, which are outlined in table 13.1.

Table 13.1   The four types of test doubles

Type	Description
Dummy	An object that is passed around but never used; typically used to fulfill the parameter list of a method
Stub	An object that always returns the same canned response; may also hold some dummy state
Fake	An actual working implementation (not of production quality or configuration) that can replace the real implementation
Mock	An object that represents a series of expectations and provides canned responses

The four types of test doubles are far easier to understand when you work through code examples that use them. Let's go do that now, starting with the dummy object.

13.4.1   Dummy object

A *dummy* object is the easiest of the four test double types to use. Remember, it's designed to help fill parameter lists or fulfill some mandatory field requirements where you know the object will never get used. In many cases, you can even pass in an empty object (or even `null`, although this is not guaranteed to be safe).

Let's go back to the theater tickets scenario. It's all very good having an estimate of the revenue coming in from your single kiosk, but the owners of the theater have started to think a bit bigger. Better modeling of the tickets sold and the revenue expected is needed, and you hear murmurings of more requirements and complexity coming down the pipe.

You've been asked to keep track of the tickets sold, and to allow for a 10% discounted price on some tickets. It looks like you're going to need a `Ticket` class that provides a discounted price method. You start the familiar TDD cycle with a failing test, focusing on a new `getDiscountPrice()` method. You also know that there will need to be a couple of constructors: one for a regular-priced ticket, and one where the face value of the ticket may vary. The `Ticket` object will ultimately expect the following two arguments:

- *The client name*—A `String` that won't be referenced at all for this test
- *The normal price*—A `BigDecimal` that will get used for this test

You're pretty sure that the client name won't be referenced in the `getDiscount-Price()` method. This means you can pass the constructor a dummy object (in this case, the arbitrary string `"Riley"`), as shown in the following code:

```java
import org.junit.jupiter.api.Test;

import java.math.BigDecimal;

import static org.junit.jupiter.api.Assertions.*;

public class TicketTest {

    private static String dummyName = "Riley";    ⟵──── Creates a dummy object

    @Test
    public void tenPercentDiscount() {                        Passes in a dummy object
        Ticket ticket = new Ticket(dummyName,    ⟵────┘
                                   new BigDecimal("10"));

        assertEquals(new BigDecimal("9.0"), ticket.getDiscountPrice());
    }
}
```

As you can see, the concept of a dummy object is trivial.

To make the concept extremely clear, the code in the following snippet has a partial implementation of the `Ticket` class:

```java
import java.math.BigDecimal;

public class Ticket {

    public static final int BASIC_TICKET_PRICE = 30;    ⟵──── The default price
    private static final BigDecimal DISCOUNT_RATE =    ⟵────┐
                                    new BigDecimal("0.9");  │  The default discount

    private final BigDecimal price;
    private final String clientName;

    public Ticket(String clientName) {
        this.clientName = clientName;
```

```
    price = new BigDecimal(BASIC_TICKET_PRICE);
  }

  public Ticket(String clientName, BigDecimal price) {
    this.clientName = clientName;
    this.price = price;
  }

  public BigDecimal getPrice() {
    return price;
  }

  public BigDecimal getDiscountPrice() {
    return price.multiply(DISCOUNT_RATE);
  }
}
```

Some developers become confused by dummy objects—they look for complexity that doesn't exist. Dummy objects are very straightforward: they're any old object used to avoid `NullPointerException` and to get the code to run.

Let's move on to the next type of test double. The next step up (in terms of complexity) is the stub object.

13.4.2 *Stub object*

You typically use a *stub* object when you want to replace a real implementation with an object that will return the same response every time. Let's return to our theater ticket pricing example to see this in action.

You've come back from a well-deserved holiday after implementing the `Ticket` class, and the first thing in your inbox is a bug report stating that your `tenPercent-Discount()` test is now failing intermittently. When you look into the codebase, you see that the `Ticket` class is now using a concrete `HttpPrice` class that implements a newly introduced `Price` interface. As the name suggests, `HttpPrice` contacts an external website and can return different values—or fail—at any point.

This is making the test fail, but further has polluted the purpose of our test. Remember, all you wanted was to unit-test calculating the 10% discount!

> **NOTE** Calling a third-party pricing site is certainly not part of this test's responsibility. Separate integration tests should cover the `HttpPrice` class and its third-party `HttpPricingService`.

To get our test back to a consistent, stable point, we will replace the `HttpPrice` class with a stub instead. First, let's take a look at the current state of the code, as shown in the three following code snippets:

```
import org.junit.jupiter.api.Test;

import java.math.BigDecimal;

import static org.junit.jupiter.api.Assertions.*;
```

```
public class TicketTest {

  private static String dummyName = "Riley";

  @Test
  public void tenPercentDiscount() {            HttpPrice implements Price.
    Price price = new HttpPrice();     ←──────┘
    Ticket ticket = new Ticket(dummyName, price);   ←──── Creates Ticket
    assertEquals(new BigDecimal("9.0"),    ←──────┐
                ticket.getDiscountPrice());    │ The test can fail.
  }
}
```

The next snippet shows the new implementation of `Ticket`:

```
import java.math.BigDecimal;

public class Ticket {
  private final String clientName;
  private final Price priceSource;
  private final BigDecimal discountRate;

  private BigDecimal faceValue = null;

  public Ticket(String clientName,
                Price price,
                BigDecimal discountRate) {   ←──── The altered constructor
    this.clientName = clientName;
    this.priceSource = price;
    this.discountRate = discountRate;
  }

  public BigDecimal getPrice() {
    if (faceValue == null) {
      faceValue = priceSource.getInitialPrice();   ←──── The new getInitialPrice call
    }

    return faceValue;
  }

  public BigDecimal getDiscountPrice() {
    return faceValue.multiply(discountRate);   ←──── The unchanged calculation
  }
}
```

Providing a full implementation of the `HttpPrice` class would take us too far afield, so let's just suppose that it calls out to another class, `HttpPricingService`, as shown here:

```
import java.math.BigDecimal;

public interface Price {
  BigDecimal getInitialPrice();
}
```

```
public class HttpPrice implements Price {
  @Override
  public BigDecimal getInitialPrice() {
    return HttpPricingService.getInitialPrice();    <──── Returns random results
  }
}
```

Now that we've surveyed the damage, let's think about what we intended to test. Our goal was to show the multiplication in the `Ticket` class's `getDiscountPrice()` method works as expected. No external websites are required for proving that.

The `Price` interfaces gives us the seam we need to replace our touchy `HttpPrice` instance with a consistent `StubPrice` implementation, as follows:

```
import org.junit.jupiter.api.Test;

import java.math.BigDecimal;

import static org.junit.jupiter.api.Assertions.*;

public class TicketTest {
  @Test
  public void tenPercentDiscount() {                  │ The StubPrice stub
    Price price = new StubPrice();       <───────
    Ticket ticket = new Ticket(price);   <────── Creates a Ticket
    assertEquals(new BigDecimal("9.0"),        <─────
                 ticket.getDiscountPrice());          │ Checks the price
  }
}
```

The `StubPrice` class is a simple little class that consistently returns the initial price of 10, as shown here:

```
import java.math.BigDecimal;

public class StubPrice implements Price {
  @Override
  public BigDecimal getInitialPrice() {
    return new BigDecimal("10");        <────── Returns a consistent price
  }
}
```

Phew! Now the test passes again, and, equally important, you can look at refactoring the rest of the implementation details without fear.

Stubs are a useful type of test double, but sometimes it's desirable to have the stub perform some real work that's closer to the production system. For that, you use a fake object as your test double.

13.4.3 *Fake object*

A *fake* object can be seen as an enhanced stub that almost does the same work as your production code, but that takes a few shortcuts to fulfill your testing requirements. Fakes are especially useful when you'd like your code to run against something that's very close to the real third-party subsystem or dependency that you'll use in the live implementation.

For our ticketing application, let's imagine that our database layer provides us with a simple interface for working with tickets, shown next:

```
package com.wellgrounded;

public interface TicketDatabase {
    Ticket findById(int id);
    Ticket findByName(String name);
    int count();

    void insert(Ticket ticket);
    void delete(int id);
}
```

Our class for managing an individual show needs to work with this database interface and manage features such as checking we haven't oversold like this:

```
package com.wellgrounded;

import java.math.BigDecimal;

public class Show {
    private TicketDatabase db;
    private int capacity;

    public Show(TicketDatabase db, int capacity) {
        this.db = db;
        this.capacity = capacity;
    }

    public void addTicket(String name, BigDecimal amount) {
        if (db.count() < capacity) {
            var ticket = new Ticket(name, amount);
            db.insert(ticket);
        } else {
            throw new RuntimeException("Oversold");
        }
    }
}
```

We'd like to unit test `addTicket` without relying on a fully instance of our relational database. Such a test might look like this:

```
package com.wellgrounded;

import org.junit.jupiter.api.Test;
import java.math.BigDecimal;
import static org.junit.jupiter.api.Assertions.*;

public class ShowTest {
    @Test
    public void plentyOfSpace() {
        var db = new FakeTicketDatabase();        ◁─┐  FakeTicketDatabase doesn't exist,
        var show = new Show(db, 5);                     but in the spirit of TDD, we'll write
                                                        the code we want to pass.
        var name = "New One";
        show.addTicket(name, BigDecimal.ONE);

        var mine = db.findByName(name);
        assertEquals(name, mine.getName());
        assertEquals(BigDecimal.ONE, mine.getAmount());
    }
}
```

Although we could accomplish this via stubbing, it would have major drawbacks. We'd have to stub out the methods count and insert on the database, which aren't even visible in the test, cluttering it up with lower-level details and distracting from its actual purpose. But the difficulties go deeper still—each test must ensure the relationship between count and the number of calls to insert are aligned. Even worse, our final call to findByName, which is meant to ensure our data was saved, would also need to be stubbed. But that very stubbing means the assertion is useless—it would pass whether or not our implementation code was correct! Stubs fall short of letting us accurately validate this set of tightly related actions.

A fake object provides an alternative by having a real but simplified, implementation. The provided interface, shown next, is easy to serve with a wrapper around a simple HashMap:

```
package com.wellgrounded;

import java.util.HashMap;
                                                            Our map takes the place of a
                                                            database for the lifetime of
class FakeTicketDatabase implements TicketDatabase {        our unit test.
    private HashMap<Integer, Ticket> tickets =      ◁─┘
                                new HashMap<>();
    private Integer nextId = 1;         ◁─┐
                                            We have to replicate features such
    @Override                               as databases autoincrementing IDs.
    public Ticket findByName(String name) {
        var found = tickets.values()
                .stream()
                .filter(ticket -> ticket.getName().equals(name))
                .findFirst();
        return found.orElse(null);
    }
```

```
@Override
public int count() {
    return tickets.size();
}

@Override
public void insert(Ticket ticket) {
    tickets.put(nextId, ticket);
    nextId++;
}

// Remaining methods available in resources
}
```

Fake objects, especially when shared throughout a project with strong interfaces, can be a nice solution for supporting unit tests. They aren't appropriate everywhere—if our database interface allowed us to pass SQL clauses for additional filtering, this would quickly get beyond our fake's ability to handle—but they're a useful tool to have. Just keep an eye out that the implementation doesn't get too large or complex, because every line of code we write is a possible source of bugs.

13.4.4 Mock object

Mock objects are related to the stub test doubles that you've already met, but stub objects are usually pretty dumb beasts. For example, stubs typically fake out methods to always give the same result. This doesn't provide any way to model state-dependent behavior.

As an example: you're trying to follow TDD, and you're writing a text analysis system. One of your unit tests instructs the text analysis classes to count the number of occurrences of the phrase "Java11" for a particular blog post. But because the blog post is a third-party resource, a number of possible failure scenarios exist that have very little to do with the counting algorithm you're writing. In other words, the code under test isn't isolated, and calling the third-party resource could be time-consuming. Here are some common failure scenarios:

- Your code might not be able to go out to the internet to query the blog post, due to firewall restrictions in your organization.
- The blog post may have been moved with no redirect.
- The blog post might be edited to increase or decrease the number of times "Java11" appears.

Using stubs, this test would be almost impossible to write, and it would be incredibly verbose for each test case. Enter the *mock object*. This is a special kind of test double, which you can think of as a programmable stub. Using the mock object is very simple: when you're preparing the mock for use, you tell it the sequence of calls to expect and how it should respond to each one.

Let's see this in action by looking at a simple example for the theater tickets use case. We'll be using the popular mocking library, Mockito (https://site.mockito.org). The following snippet shows how to use it:

```
import org.junit.jupiter.api.Test;
import java.math.BigDecimal;
import static org.junit.jupiter.api.Assertions.*;
import static org.mockito.Mockito.*;

public class TicketTest {
  @Test
  public void tenPercentDiscount() {
    Price price = mock(Price.class);      <──── Creates a mock

    when(price.getInitialPrice())
      .thenReturn(new BigDecimal("10"));   <──── Programs the mock for testing

    Ticket ticket = new Ticket(price, new BigDecimal("0.9"));
    assertEquals(new BigDecimal("9.0"), ticket.getDiscountPrice());

    verify(price).getInitialPrice();
  }
}
```

To create a mock object, you call the static `mock()` method with the class object of the type you want to mock up. Then you "record" the behavior that you want your mock to display by calling the `when()` method to indicate which method to record, and `thenReturn()` to specify the expected result. Last, you verify that you've called the expected methods on the mocked object. This ensures that you didn't get to the correct result via an incorrect path.

This verification captures the big difference between a stub and a mock. With a stub, your primary focus is returning canned values. With a mock, the intent is *verifying behavior*, such as the exact calls actually made. In practice, Mockito's richly featured `mock()` method can be used easily to create stubs if we ignore verification, but it's important that you as the programmer be aware of what you're intending to test.

You can use the mock just like a regular object and pass it to your call to the `Ticket` constructor without any further ceremony. This makes mock objects a very powerful tool for TDD. Some practitioners don't really use the other types of test doubles, preferring to do almost everything with mocks. But as with many powerful tools, mocking comes with sharp edges to be aware of.

13.4.5 *Problems with mocking*

One of the largest difficulties with test doubles is precisely that they are fake, so their behavior can diverge from the actual production system. Unfortunately, this can happen while still leaving you with the warm, comforting sense that your tests have you fully covered—until reality bites.

These behavior differences can come in a number of flavors. Common ones include the following:

- Differences in returned payloads, particularly with complex nested objects
- Serialization/deserialization differences from testing data
- Ordering of items in collections
- Responses to error conditions—either failing to throw, or throwing different exception types

Although there's no blanket solution, these problems can often be spotted when we step up a level to integration tests. Again, if we keep firmly in mind *what* we're testing in each set of tests, we can focus our unit tests on localized logic and use integration testing elsewhere to cover interactions with our dependencies.

Solid design of our interfaces also helps our test doubles. Rather than a service class returning a raw contents string from an HTTP call, returning a specific object gives our test doubles less room to vary. Having precise subclasses for the exceptions your class raises, wrapping more primitive exception types, not only makes your code more expressive but also easier to mock accurately.

Mocking, if used everywhere, can also lead to our tests too closely mimicking our production code. When this happens, each line in your actual code has a mirroring line in test configuration, restating the precise expected call. Such tests are extremely brittle, often leading to huge swathes of seemingly unrelated changes when altering code.

This brittleness when mocking extends down to the level of individual arguments. Although the frameworks make it easy to be extremely precise about the values being passed, consider whether your test truly needs to verify that argument. As we saw with dummy objects, for some test cases, a given value might not matter. Mocking frameworks provide mechanisms for effectively allowing statements like "any integer," and if the value doesn't matter, such statements both clarify what your test cares about and allows room for the production code to evolve more easily. Give your tests room to breathe!

Tests can also surface issues when they require large amounts of intricate setup before running. Mocking, particularly when paired with dependency injection, can make it easy to pile up dependencies in a class without taking much notice. If your test setup is longer than the code needed to execute and verify your results, that's a hint your classes may be overly complex and ripe for refactoring. Test setup is also a great way to watch for violations of the Law of Demeter, which suggests objects should have knowledge only of their direct neighbors. If your test setup needs to muck about with objects many levels removed from itself, your objects might be reaching too far outside themselves.

Test doubles are a valuable tool for the well-grounded developer. We've demonstrated a little bit of JUnit in our discussion so far, but we have not explored it in depth yet. Let's look a little closer at it and take the opportunity to see what's new with JUnit 5, the most recent major version.

13.5   From JUnit 4 to 5

JUnit is a JVM-based implementation of the xUnit style of test framework, developed initially by Kent Beck and Erich Gamma. This flavor of unit testing has proven versatile and easy to use, placing JUnit among the most commonly used libraries in the JVM ecosystem.

This long history and broad usage brings many constraints as well. JUnit 4, initially released in 2006, couldn't use features like lambda expressions without breaking compatibility. In 2017, JUnit 5 was released, using the opportunity afforded by the major version change to introduce significant changes.

> **NOTE** The next chapter will focus plenty of time on other tools and techniques, but the well-grounded Java developer will almost certainly encounter JUnit code that's worth moving to the most modern versions.

One of the biggest changes with JUnit 5 is its packaging. Where prior versions were monolithic, containing both the API for authoring tests and the support for running and reporting on those tests, JUnit 5 breaks things down into more focused packages. JUnit 5 also steps away from the external dependency on Hamcrest that came with JUnit 4.

JUnit 5 lives in an entirely new package—`org.junit.jupiter`—which means both version can coexist during migration. We'll look more at the mechanics of that in a moment.

JUnit 5's primary two dependencies follow:

- `org.junit.jupiter.junit-jupiter-api`—This is referenced from your testing code to provide all the necessary annotations and helpers to author tests.
- `org.junit.jupiter.junit-jupiter-engine`—This is the default engine for running JUnit 5 tests. It is only needed as a runtime, not compile-time, dependency and can be augmented or swapped out for other test runners.

In Gradle, that would look like this, along with a hint to tell Gradle to use the new JUnit bits when running tests:

```
dependencies {
  testImplementation("org.junit.jupiter:junit-jupiter-api:5.7.1")
  testRuntimeOnly("org.junit.jupiter:junit-jupiter-engine:5.7.1")
}

tasks.named<Test>("test") {
  useJUnitPlatform()
}
```

The equivalent for Maven would be as follows. The Maven `surefire` and `failsafe` plugins know how to work automatically with JUnit 5, as long as you have a new-enough version (2.22 or greater is recommended):

```
<project>
  <dependencies>
    <dependency>
      <groupId>org.junit.jupiter</groupId>
      <artifactId>junit-jupiter-api</artifactId>
      <version>5.7.1</version>
      <scope>test</scope>
    </dependency>
    <dependency>
      <groupId>org.junit.jupiter</groupId>
      <artifactId>junit-jupiter-engine</artifactId>
      <version>5.7.1</version>
      <scope>test</scope>
    </dependency>
  </dependencies>
</project>
```

If you add these to a JUnit 4 project and simply run the tests, you'll find an odd out-come—the suite will likely pass—but if you look more closely at the reports, *no tests actually ran!* This is because the actual annotation to mark test cases changed with JUnit 5.

> **NOTE** JUnit 5 brings its own `@Test` annotation in the package `org.junit`
> `.jupiter.api`. It won't recognize existing tests marked with the older `org`
> `.junit` version of `@Test` by default!

There are two paths to take from this point. The first is to change over each place where you're importing the old annotations to use the new version. Class by class, your test suite will start running under JUnit 5. These conversions may require other work we'll discuss shortly.

An alternative is to pull in an additional runtime dependency on the `junit-vintage-engine`. This package uses JUnit 5's richer ability to plug in different runners and support classes to allow for backward compatibility with JUnit 4 (and even 3) tests.

In Gradle:

```
dependencies {
  testImplementation("org.junit.jupiter:junit-jupiter-api:5.7.1")
  testRuntimeOnly("org.junit.jupiter:junit-jupiter-engine:5.7.1")

  testRuntimeOnly("org.junit.vintage:junit-vintage-engine:5.7.1")
}
```

In Maven:

```
<project>
  <dependencies>
    <dependency>                   ⟵── Support for running JUnit 4
      <groupId>junit</groupId>           tests alongside JUnit 5
      <artifactId>junit</artifactId>
      <version>4.13</version>
      <scope>test</scope>
    </dependency>
```

```
    <dependency>
      <groupId>org.junit.vintage</groupId>
      <artifactId>junit-vintage-engine</artifactId>
      <version>5.7.1</version>
      <scope>test</scope>              Our main JUnit 5 dependencies,
    </dependency>                      api and engine
    <dependency>               ◄─────
      <groupId>org.junit.jupiter</groupId>
      <artifactId>junit-jupiter-api</artifactId>
      <version>5.7.1</version>
      <scope>test</scope>
    </dependency>
    <dependency>
      <groupId>org.junit.jupiter</groupId>
      <artifactId>junit-jupiter-engine</artifactId>
      <version>5.7.1</version>
      <scope>test</scope>
    </dependency>
  </dependencies>
</project>
```

This support can allow for an easier transition as you can enable JUnit 5, then convert test by test over time, rather than requiring everything to move at once. It's worth noting, though, that the vintage support does have some limitations, which are well documented in the JUnit users guide at http://mng.bz/5Q61.

Along with the new packaging, a variety of classes have been renamed to make them clearer and more accurate about their usage, shown here:

- `@Before` changed to `@BeforeEach`.
- `@After` changed to `@AfterEach`.
- `@BeforeClass` changed to `@BeforeAll`.
- `@AfterClass` changed to `@AfterAll`.
- `@Category` changed to `@Tag`.
- `@Ignored` changed to `@Disabled` (or may be handled with `ExecutionCondition` in the new extension model).
- `@RunWith`, `@Rule` and `@ClassRule` are replaced by the new extension model.

As the final couple of points allude to, a big feature of JUnit 5 is a new extension model that covers a variety of separate features in earlier versions of JUnit. These features let you share behavior between classes—steps like test setup, teardown, and expectation setting—but didn't all fit together cohesively.

As an example, here's a basic JUnit 4 test that needs to start up a server before tests can run. It uses the `ExternalResource` class, along with a `@Rule` annotation to ask that it be called at the right points in the lifecycle:

```
package com.wellgrounded;

import org.junit.Rule;
import org.junit.Test;
```

```
import org.junit.rules.ExpectedException;
import org.junit.rules.ExternalResource;

import static org.junit.Assert.*;

public class PasswordCheckerTest {
    private PasswordChecker checker = new PasswordChecker();

    @Rule
    public ExternalResource passwordServer =
                        new ExternalResource() {
        @Override
        protected void before() throws Throwable {
            super.before();
            checker.reset();
            checker.start();
        }

        @Override
        protected void after() {
            super.after();
            checker.stop();
        }
    };

    @Test
    public void ok() {
        assertTrue(checker.isOk("abcd1234!"));
    }
}
```

@Rule requests that this be applied before/after each test.

ExternalResource is provided by JUnit specifically for such custom setup/teardown scenarios.

Our overrides on `ExternalResource` could easily be pulled into another location and shared between our tests.

JUnit 5 instead breaks down the testing lifecycle into smaller interfaces that you implement. These extensions can then be applied at the class or test-method level, as shown next:

We implement AfterEachCallback and BeforeEachCallback to get called as we did before for each test method. AfterAllCallback and BeforeAllCallback exist as well to replace @ClassRule functionality.

```
package com.wellgrounded;

import org.junit.jupiter.api.extension.AfterEachCallback;
import org.junit.jupiter.api.extension.BeforeEachCallback;
import org.junit.jupiter.api.extension.ExtensionContext;

public class PasswordCheckerExtension
    implements AfterEachCallback, BeforeEachCallback {

    private PasswordChecker checker;

    PasswordCheckerExtension(PasswordChecker checker) {
        this.checker = checker;
    }
```

Because our extension worked with a field on the test class, we need to have that passed on construction.

```
    @Override
    public void beforeEach(ExtensionContext context) {
        checker.reset();
        checker.start();
    }

    @Override
    public void afterEach(ExtensionContext context) {
        checker.stop();
    }
}
```

Callbacks proceed
as before to do the
setup/teardown work.

With this class in hand, we can apply it in our test as follows:

```
package com.wellgrounded;

import org.junit.jupiter.api.Test;
import org.junit.jupiter.api.extension.RegisterExtension;

import static org.junit.Assert.*;

public class PasswordCheckerTest {
    private static PasswordChecker checker = new PasswordChecker();

    @RegisterExtension
    static PasswordCheckerExtension ext =
            new PasswordCheckerExtension(checker);

    @Test
    public void ok() {
        assertTrue(checker.isOk("abcd1234!"));
    }
}
```

@RegisterExtension
allows us to instantiate
our extension for the test.

The field on the test
class must be public
to work with
@RegisterExtension.

If an extension doesn't require parameters on construction, it can also be applied to the class or method definition using @ExtendWith, as shown here:

```
@ExtendWith(CustomConfigurationExtension.class)
public class PasswordCheckerTest {
    // ....
}
```

JUnit 5's move to require more recent JDK versions also tidied up some corners where rules used to be a standard approach. Checking whether a test method raised an exception could take the following two forms in JUnit 4 and earlier:

```
package com.wellgrounded;

import org.junit.Rule;
import org.junit.Test;
import org.junit.rules.ExpectedException;

import static org.junit.Assert.*;
```

```
public class PasswordCheckerTest {
    private PasswordChecker checker = new PasswordChecker();

    @Rule
    public ExpectedException ex = ExpectedException.none();

    @Test
    public void nullThrows() {
        ex.expect(IllegalArgumentException.class);
        checker.isOk(null);
    }

    @Test(expected = IllegalArgumentException.class)
    public void alsoThrows() {
        checker.isOk(null);
    }
}
```

A rule-based exception checking on a test method

The @Test annotation configuration of the excepted exception

Lambda expressions open up a new way of expressing this that looks more like our typical assertions, like this:

```
package com.wellgrounded;

import org.junit.jupiter.api.Test;

import static org.junit.Assert.*;

public class PasswordCheckerTest {
    private static PasswordChecker checker = new PasswordChecker();

    @Test
    public void nullThrows() {
        assertThrows(IllegalArgumentException.class, () -> {
            checker.isOk(null);
        });
    }
}
```

assertThrows is preferable to the old expected argument on our test annotations or the ExpectedException rule for a couple of reasons. First, the assertion is more direct, located right where the code we're actually testing is found instead of earlier in the method. Also, assertThrows returns the exception without us needing to scaffold a try/catch in place, so we can more easily do typical assertions about what happened without special plumbing. Although JUnit 4's legacy across the ecosystem means it'll still be around—and maintained—for a long while, if you're using JUnit, it's worth looking at what the new version offers.

Our test libraries are only part of the picture, though, especially once we're writing integration tests. The next chapter will delve into some helpful tools in approaching the long-standing hassles of testing with external dependencies.

Summary

- We've discussed the motivations and types of testing, and how it's critical to know the answers to what we're testing for to decide on an approach.
- We took a walk through test-driven development, seeing how it allows us to evolve a design with confidence in a step-by-step fashion.
- We've examined the wide variety of test doubles, what they're useful for, and, more important, where they'll cause trouble if misused.
- After many years, a new version of JUnit is out that addresses long-standing design problems, often constraints from long-deprecated JDKs. We looked briefly at moving to this latest version for the basics of our testing.

Testing beyond JUnit

This chapter covers

- Integration testing with Testcontainers
- Specification-style testing with Spek and Kotlin
- Property-based testing with Clojure

In the previous chapter, we looked at the general principles that guide our testing. Now we're going to dive deeper into specific approaches to improve our testing for different situations. Whether our goal is cleaner testing of dependencies, better communication in our testing code, or even discovery of edge cases we hadn't considered, the JVM ecosystem provides many tools to help out, and we will highlight only a few. Let's start with that ever-present struggle: how to deal with external dependencies effectively when writing integration tests.

14.1 Integration testing with Testcontainers

As we move up the pyramid from our isolated unit tests, we encounter a variety of obstacles. To integration test against a real database requires that we have a real database available to use! Getting the benefits of that realistic testing implies a huge increase in setup complexity. The statefulness of these external systems also increases the chances of our tests failing, not because of problems with our code but because of unexpected state lingering between tests.

Over the years, this has been tackled in many ways, from in-memory databases to frameworks for running tests fully within transactions that clean up after themselves. But these solutions often bring their own edge cases and difficulties.

Containerization technology, as discussed in chapter 12, provides an interesting new approach to the problem. Because containers are ephemeral, they are well suited to spinning up for a given test run. Because they encapsulate the real databases and other services we want to interact with, they avoid the subtle mismatches substitutes that in-memory databases are prone to.

14.1.1   *Installing testcontainers*

One of the simplest ways to leverage containers in our testing is through the `test-containers` library (see https://www.testcontainers.org/). This provides an API to control containers directly from our test code, with a wide variety of supported modules for common dependencies. The core functionality is provided through the `org .testcontainers.testcontainers` JAR in Maven:

```
<dependency>
  <groupId>org.testcontainers</groupId>
  <artifactId>testcontainers</artifactId>
  <version>1.15.3</version>
  <scope>test</scope>
</dependency>
```

or Gradle:

```
testImplementation "org.testcontainers:testcontainers:1.15.3"
```

14.1.2   *An example with Redis*

If you recall, we left our theater application downloading prices from an HTTP service. We'd like to introduce a cache for those values. Although proper caching is a whole topic of its own, imagine we decided to externalize the cache rather than just putting the values in memory. A typical datastore for this is Redis (https://redis.io/). Redis exposes blazing fast access to get, set, and delete key-value pairs, along with other more complex data structures.

The `Price` interface that we already introduced for data lookups from an HTTP service, shown next, allows us the flexibility to add the caching as a separate concern:

```
package com.wellgrounded;

import redis.clients.jedis.Jedis;

import java.math.BigDecimal;

public class CachedPrice implements Price {
```

```
    private final Price priceLookup;
    private final Jedis cacheClient;

    private static final String priceKey = "price";
```
The name of the key we will cache the price in Redis

```
    CachedPrice(Price priceLookup, Jedis cacheClient) {
        this.priceLookup = priceLookup;
        this.cacheClient = cacheClient;
    }
```
We use the Jedis (https://github.com/redis/jedis) library for access to Redis.

```
    @Override
    public BigDecimal getInitialPrice() {
        String cachedPrice = cacheClient.get(priceKey);
        if (cachedPrice != null) {
            return new BigDecimal(cachedPrice);
        }
```
Checks whether the cache has this price already

```
        BigDecimal price =
            priceLookup.getInitialPrice();
        cacheClient.set(priceKey,
                        price.toPlainString());
        return price;
    }
}
```
If we don't have the price, uses the lookup provided

Caches the value we just retrieved

At this point it's worth pausing to consider what aspect of the system we want to test. The main point of the `CachedPrice` class is the interaction between Redis and our underlying price lookup. How we work with Redis is key, and Testcontainers lets us test against the real thing as follows:

```
package com.wellgrounded;

import org.junit.jupiter.api.Test;
import org.testcontainers.containers.GenericContainer;
import org.testcontainers.junit.jupiter.*;
import org.testcontainers.utility.DockerImageName;
import redis.clients.jedis.*;

import java.math.BigDecimal;

import static org.junit.jupiter.api.Assertions.assertEquals;

@Testcontainers
public class CachedPriceTest {
    private static final DockerImageName imageName =
            DockerImageName.parse("redis:6.2.3-alpine");

    @Container
    public static GenericContainer redis = new GenericContainer(imageName)
            .withExposedPorts(6379);

    // Tests to follow...
}
```

In this beginning section of the test, we see the most basic form of wiring up with Test-containers. We apply the `@Testcontainers` annotation to the test class as a whole, let-ting the library know that it should watch for containers we require during the test execution. The field marked with `@Container` then requests our specific container image `"redis:6.2.3-alpine"` to start, using the standard Redis port, 6379.

When this test class executes, as shown in figure 14.1, Testcontainers starts up the container we've asked for. Testcontainers will wait for a default timeout (60 seconds) for the first mapped port to be available, so we can be confident the container is ready to talk to. The `redis` field then allows us to get information like the hostname and ports for use later in our test.

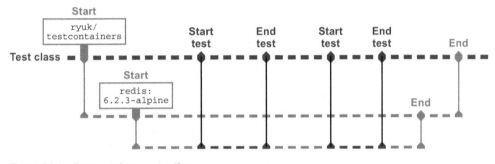

Figure 14.1   Testcontainers execution

With our containerized Redis running, we can get down to the actual tests. Because the key point is our interaction between Redis and the lookup—not how the underly-ing price lookup is actually implemented—we can reuse our prior `StubPrice`, which always returns 10 to simplify the testing, as shown here:

```
@Test
    public void cached() {                          Sets a price that differs from
        var jedis = getJedisConnection();           our stubbed price in Redis
        jedis.set("price", "20");   ◄───────┘

                                                        Passes StubPrice as our
        CachedPrice price =                             lookup, which will return
            new CachedPrice(new StubPrice(), jedis);  ◄─┘ 10, not 20
        BigDecimal result = price.getInitialPrice();
                                                        Asserts that we received
        assertEquals(new BigDecimal("20"), result);  ◄─┘ the cached value
    }

    @Test
    public void noCache() {                         Removes any previously
        var jedis = getJedisConnection();           cached value in Redis
        jedis.del("price");         ◄───────┘       with the del call

        CachedPrice price = new CachedPrice(new StubPrice(), jedis);
        BigDecimal result = price.getInitialPrice();
```

```
        assertEquals(new BigDecimal("10"), result);
    }
    private Jedis getJedisConnection() {              Helper method for setting
        HostAndPort hostAndPort = new HostAndPort(    up our Jedis instance.
                                    redis.getHost(),
                                    redis.getFirstMappedPort());
        return new Jedis(hostAndPort);
    }
```

It's important to note how the getJedisConnection method uses the configuration from Testcontainers to connect to Redis. Although you may observe that redis .getHost() is a common value, such as localhost, this isn't necessarily guaranteed in every environment. It's better to ask Testcontainers for such values and protect ourselves from unexpected changes to those values in the future.

Although the automated spinup of containers here is quite convenient, it's worth understanding how to control it more directly. This is especially true if your containers require time to start up, as we'll see with later examples like relational databases with required schemas.

The @Container annotation recognizes when it's being applied on a static field versus an instance field, as shown in figure 14.2. When applied to a static field, the container will be spun up once for the duration of the test class's execution. If you instead left the field at an instance level, then each individual test will start and stop the container instead.

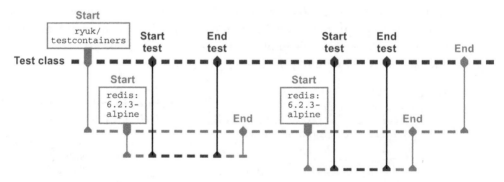

Figure 14.2   Fields and @Container

This points to another potential way to manage our container life time: what if we wanted to run the container only once for our entire test suite? To accomplish this, we have to leave the @Container annotation behind and use the API directly exposed by the GenericContainer object itself as follows:

```
private static final DockerImageName imageName =
        DockerImageName.parse("redis:6.2.3-alpine");

public static GenericContainer redis = new GenericContainer(imageName)
```

```
        .withExposedPorts(6379);

@BeforeAll
public void setUp() {
    redis.start();    ◄────────┐
}
```
> **start may be safely called multiple times on an instance—it will begin the container only once for each object.**

We aren't required to provide a `tearDown` to explicitly stop the container, because the `testcontainers` library takes care of that automatically for us.

Although the previous example calls `start` for each test, the `redis` object could move to a location where it could be shared between multiple test classes safely.

14.1.3 Gathering container logs

If you run these tests at the command line or in your IDE, you may notice that by default there is no output from the containers. For our simple Redis case, this isn't a problem, but more complex setups or debugging may have you wishing for more visibility into those containers. To assist here, Testcontainers allows accessing `STDOUT` and `STDERR` from the containers it spins up.

This support is based on the JDK's `Consumer<>` interface, and several implementations ship with the library. You can connect to standard logging providers or, as we'll demonstrate, get at the raw logging directly.

You may find it inconvenient to have the container logs spewed into your main output, but it's also a pain having to do something custom when you do want them. One solution is to plumb in support to always capture them to a separate location, such as a file in your build output, like this:

```
@Container                      ◄──────────┐
public static GenericContainer redis =
    new GenericContainer(imageName)
        .withExposedPorts(6379);

public static ToStringConsumer consumer =   ◄──┐
                      new ToStringConsumer();


@BeforeAll
public static void setUp() {
    redis.followOutput(consumer,
               OutputType.STDOUT,
               OutputType.STDERR);    ◄──┘
}


@AfterAll
public static void tearDown() throws IOException {
    Path log = Path.of("./build/tc.log");    ◄──────┐
    byte[] bytes = consumer.toUtf8String().getBytes();
    Files.write(log, bytes,
               StandardOpenOption.CREATE);    ◄──┐
}
```
> **We're using the @Container annotation for spinup again because it's so easy.**

> **Our consumer instance will gather the logs during the course of our test run.**

> **Attaches the consumer to our container, asking for both STDOUT and STDERR**

> **Writes to convenient location**

> **Uses java.nio.Files for easy writing of the file contents**

14.1.4 *An example with Postgres*

Redis makes an easy example given its lack of dependencies, the temporary nature of data normally stored there, and the fast startup time on the container. But what about that sticking point in traditional integration testing: the relational database? Often the data we put in a relational store is the most critical to our application's true functionality, but testing it is fraught with stale data, awkward mocking, and false positives.

Testcontainers supports a wide variety of different datastores. These are packaged in separate modules, which must be pulled in. We'll demonstrate using Postgres, but on the Testcontainers website (https://www.testcontainers.org/modules/databases/), you'll find a long list of other options.

We include the Postgres module as a test dependency and the main Postgres driver as well to be able to connect to our new database in Maven:

```
<dependency>
  <groupId>org.postgresql</groupId>
  <artifactId>postgresql</artifactId>
  <version>42.2.1</version>
</dependency>
<dependency>
  <groupId>org.testcontainers</groupId>
  <artifactId>postgresql</artifactId>
  <version>1.15.3</version>
  <scope>test</scope>
</dependency>
```

or Gradle:

```
implementation("org.postgresql:postgresql:42.2.1")
testImplementation("org.testcontainers:postgresql:1.15.3")
```

It's important that this version match the base `org.testcontainers:testcontainers` library you're using.

A specific class wraps our access to Postgres container. This has helpers for configuring information such as the database name and credentials, as shown here:

```
public static DockerImageName imageName =
          DockerImageName.parse("postgres:9.6.12"));

    @Container
    public static PostgreSQLContainer postgres =
        new PostgreSQLContainer<>(imageName)
            .withDatabaseName("theater_db")
            .withUsername("theater")
            .withPassword("password");
```

All the same lifecycle management considerations apply here, with the added wrinkle that a relational database needs schema applied before it's usable. Many common database migration projects can be run from code, but we'll demonstrate just using JDBC directly to show that nothing magic is going on.

First off, we need a connection to our container instance. Using the JDBC classes, we set it up with parameters from our `postgres` Testcontainer object like this:

```
private static Connection getConnection() throws SQLException {
    String url = String.format(
            "jdbc:postgresql://%s:%s/%s",
            postgres.getHost(),
            postgres.getFirstMappedPort(),
            postgres.getDatabaseName());

    return DriverManager.getConnection(url,
                                       postgres.getUsername(),
                                       postgres.getPassword());
}
```

NOTE Testcontainers includes a feature where you can modify your connection strings, and it will automatically start containers for your databases. Although convenient, it's less direct to demonstrate. This may be especially valuable, though, when integrating Testcontainers into an existing test suite.

With our connection, we want to ensure our schema is in place before any of our tests run. Within the scope of one test class, we'd accomplish this with a `@BeforeAll` as follows:

```
@BeforeAll
public static void setup() throws SQLException, IOException {
    var path = Path.of("src/main/resources/init.sql");    ◁──────── For our example, a SQL file has our schema definitions.
    var sql = Files.readString(path);
    try (Connection conn = getConnection()) {
        conn.createStatement().execute(sql);    ◁──────── Applies the SQL
    }
}
```

With the schema in place, our tests can now run against this full-fledged, empty Postgres database as shown next:

```
@Test
public void emptyDatabase() throws SQLException {
    try (Connection conn = getConnection()) {
        Statement st = conn.createStatement();
        ResultSet result = st.executeQuery("SELECT * FROM prices");
        assertEquals(0, result.getFetchSize());
    }
}
```

If you have other abstractions such as DAO (data access objects), repositories, or other ways of reading from the database, they should all work fine with the connection to the container.

14.1.5 *An example for end-to-end testing with Selenium*

The move to using external resources in containers is a natural fit for integration testing. Similar techniques apply with end-to-end testing as well. Though it depends on your precise system, often an end-to-end test will want to exercise a browser to ensure that a web application is running as expected.

Historically, driving a web browser from code was a touchy proposition. The techniques remain fragile and slow, but Testcontainers takes away the installation and configuration pain by letting you spin up a browser inside a container and control it there remotely.

As with our Postgres example, we'll need to pull in dependencies. In this case, there's a module for Testcontainers support alongside the libraries required for our tests to remote-control the browser instance in Maven:

```
<dependency>
  <groupId>org.testcontainers</groupId>
  <artifactId>selenium</artifactId>
  <version>1.15.3</version>
  <scope>test</scope>
</dependency>
<dependency>
  <groupId>org.seleniumhq.selenium</groupId>
  <artifactId>selenium-remote-driver</artifactId>
  <version>3.141.59</version>
  <scope>test</scope>
</dependency>
<dependency>
  <groupId>org.seleniumhq.selenium</groupId>
  <artifactId>selenium-chrome-driver</artifactId>
  <version>3.141.59</version>
  <scope>test</scope>
</dependency>
```

or Gradle:

> Support for other web browsers also exists in similarly named packages.

```
testImplementation("org.testcontainers:selenium:1.15.3")
testImplementation(
  "org.seleniumhq.selenium:selenium-remote-driver:3.141.59")
testImplementation(
  "org.seleniumhq.selenium:selenium-chrome-driver:3.141.59")
```

Specific classes configure the browser instances. We'll pass in `ChromeOptions` here to indicate that we're starting that particular browser:

```
@Container
public static BrowserWebDriverContainer<?> chrome =
    new BrowserWebDriverContainer<>()
        .withCapabilities(new ChromeOptions());
```

With this instance, we can now write tests that visit web pages and inspect the results as follows:

```
@Test
public void checkTheSiteOut() {
    var url = "https://github.com/well-grounded-java";
    RemoteWebDriver driver = chrome.getWebDriver();
    driver.get(url);

    WebElement title =
                driver.findElementByTagName("h1");
    assertEquals("well-grounded-java", title.getText());
}
```

Once the page loads, checks the first `<h1>` contents

Navigates to the GitHub organization for well-grounded-java

This simple example already shows the sort of fragility that end-to-end testing is prone to. What if GitHub redesigns and decides to add another `<h1>` in the page? What if they alter the title text in some subtle way? If you're testing your own applications, this may be less of a problem, but the tight coupling to the presentation remains an issue.

Running inside a container, if things aren't what we expect, it can be difficult to understand why. Fortunately, we can get visual feedback in a couple of ways.

First off, we can screenshot at specific points in time like this:

```
@Test
public void checkTheSiteOut() {
    RemoteWebDriver driver = chrome.getWebDriver();
    driver.get("https://github.com/well-grounded-java");

    File screen = driver.getScreenshotAs(OutputType.FILE);
}
```

The file returned is temporary and will be removed at the end of the test, but you can copy it elsewhere in the code after it's been created.

Seeing more than just a point in time is common enough. You can also just request a video of the session to be recorded automatically as follows:

```
private static final File tmpDirectory = new File("build");

@Container
public static BrowserWebDriverContainer<?> chrome =
    new BrowserWebDriverContainer<>()
        .withCapabilities(new ChromeOptions())
        .withRecordingMode(RECORD_ALL,
                           tmpDirectory,
                           VncRecordingFormat.MP4);
```

As we did with container logs, this will make recordings in our build output any time the tests are run. Everything we need to debug is ready, right there already, should trouble arise.

This just scratches the surface of what Testcontainers will allow you to accomplish. Now let's take a look at leaving JUnit behind to write our tests in a different, potentially more readable form.

14.2 Specification-style testing with Spek and Kotlin

The way JUnit uses methods, classes, and annotations is very natural to a Java developer. But whether or not we're aware of it, it shapes how we express and group our tests. Although not required, we often end up with one test class mapping to our production class and loose clusters of test methods for each implementation method.

An alternative idea is what's known as writing *specifications*. This grew out of frameworks such as RSpec and Cucumber, and rather than focusing on how our code is shaped, it aims to support specifying how the system works at a higher level, more aligned to how humans would discuss requirements.

An example of this sort of testing is available in Kotlin via the Spek framework (see https://www.spekframework.org/). As we'll see, many of Kotlin's built-in features allow for a very different organization and feel in our specs.

Installing Spek follows the typical process for dependencies. Spek focuses entirely on how we structure our specifications and leans on the ecosystem for functionality such as assertions and test running. For simplicity here, we'll demonstrate with the assertions and test runner from JUnit 5, but you are not required to use these if you have other libraries you prefer.

In Maven, the `maven-surefire-plugin` from section 11.2.6 just needs to be informed about our specification files, which we'll mark by including Spek in the filenames, as shown next. We'll also need the Kotlin support described in section 11.2.5 (not repeated here for length):

```
<build>
  <plugins>
    <plugin>
      <artifactId>maven-surefire-plugin</artifactId>
      <version>2.22.2</version>
      <configuration>
        <includes>
          <include>**/*Spek*.*</include>      ◁─┐ Because of our custom file
        </includes>                             │ convention, we have to tell
      </configuration>                          │ Maven what to run.
    </plugin>
  </plugins>
</build>


<dependencies>
  <dependency>
    <groupId>org.junit.jupiter</groupId>
    <artifactId>junit-jupiter-api</artifactId>     ◁─┐ Uses JUnit's
    <version>5.7.1</version>                         │ assertion API
    <scope>test</scope>
  </dependency>
```

```
<dependency>
  <groupId>org.spekframework.spek2</groupId>
  <artifactId>spek-dsl-jvm</artifactId>
  <version>2.0.15</version>
  <scope>test</scope>
</dependency>
<dependency>
  <groupId>org.spekframework.spek2</groupId>
  <artifactId>spek-runner-junit5</artifactId>
  <version>2.0.15</version>
  <scope>test</scope>
</dependency>
</dependencies>
```

Uses Spek's integration
with JUnit test runners

In Gradle, we plug into the standard `test` task and notify the JUnit platform of Spek's engine, as shown in the next code snippet. You may find that command-line tests will see our specifications without the engine line, but other systems like our IDE may miss them:

```
dependencies {
    testImplementation(                        Uses JUnit's assertion API
        "org.junit.jupiter:junit-jupiter-api:5.7.1")

    testImplementation("org.spekframework.spek2:spek-dsl-jvm:2.0.15")
    testRuntimeOnly(
        "org.spekframework.spek2:spek-runner-junit5:2.0.15")
}

tasks.named<Test>("test") {
    useJUnitPlatform() {
        includeEngines("spek2")
    }
}
```

Uses Spek's
integration with
JUnit test runners

Looks up the test task, informing that
it's of type Test so we can access the
useJUnitPlatform and following methods

Notifies JUnit of our engine
for better IDE integration

Now we can get down to writing our first specification. To examine this, we'll take the prior testing we've done against the `InMemoryCachedPrice` class and see how Spek alters the structure and flow of our testing as follows:

```
import org.spekframework.spek2.Spek
import org.junit.jupiter.api.Assertions.assertEquals
import java.math.BigDecimal

object InMemoryCachedPriceSpek : Spek({
    group("empty cache") {
        test("gets default value") {
            val stubbedPrice = StubPrice()
            val cachedPrice = InMemoryCachedPrice(stubbedPrice)

            assertEquals(BigDecimal(10), cachedPrice.initialPrice)
        }

        test("gets same value when called again") {
```

```
        val stubbedPrice = StubPrice()
        val cachedPrice = InMemoryCachedPrice(stubbedPrice)

        val first = cachedPrice.initialPrice
        val second = cachedPrice.initialPrice
        assertTrue(first === second)    ◁
    }
  }
})
```

=== is Kotlin's operator for reference equality, so this checks that we get the exact same object between calls, not just an identical value.

Our first specification spells out behavior around an empty cache. We can see a number of Kotlin features at work. First off, our specification is declared as a singleton object instead of a class. This helps to clarify test lifetime issues that occasionally happen in JUnit, depending on whether the test runner constructs a single instance of the test per class or per individual test method.

The main specification is declared within a lambda expression, passed as a parameter to the Spek class. In this lambda, two important functions are available: group and test. Each of these is given a full String description. No camel-casing, underscores, or other tricks are required to make the description readable. group is intended for you to put together various related test calls. The group constructs can also be nested, if desired.

If this reformatting was all that specification-style testing brought to the table, it wouldn't be very compelling. However, the grouping is more than just naming because we can declare *fixtures* that share the setup across multiple tests as follows:

```
object InMemoryCachedPriceSpek : Spek({
    group("empty cache") {
        lateinit var stubbedPrice : Price
        lateinit var cachedPrice : InMemoryCachedPrice

        beforeEachTest {
          stubbedPrice = StubPrice()
          cachedPrice = InMemoryCachedPrice(stubbedPrice)
        }

        test("gets default value") {
            assertEquals(BigDecimal(10), cachedPrice.initialPrice)
        }

        test("gets same value when called again") {
            val first = cachedPrice.initialPrice
            val second = cachedPrice.initialPrice
            assertTrue(first === second)
        }
    }
})
```

In our "empty cache" group, we declare two fixtures: a stubbedPrice for use in setting up the cache and the cachedPrice instance we'll test. Any test call that's a member of this group gets an identical view of these fixtures.

The recommended pattern for fixtures is to use `lateinit` and initialize them in `beforeEachTest`. This need for late initialization actually reflects that Spek runs our specification in two phases: discovery and then execution.

During the discovery phase, the top-level lambda for our specification is run. `group` lambdas are eagerly evaluated, but `test` calls aren't made yet; instead, they are noticed for later execution. After all of the specification's groups have been evaluated, the `test` lambdas are executed. This separation, shown next, allows for tighter control over the context of each `group` before each individual `test` runs:

```
object InMemoryCachedPriceSpek : Spek({
    group("empty cache") {                                  Runs during the
        lateinit var stubPrice : Price                      discovery phase
        lateinit var cachedPrice : InMemoryCachedPrice

        beforeEachTest {
            stubPrice = StubPrice()
            cachedPrice = InMemoryCachedPrice(stubPrice)
        }

        test("gets default value") {
            assertEquals(BigDecimal(10),                     Runs during the
                        cachedPrice.initialPrice)            execution phase
        }

        test("gets same value when called again") {
            val first = cachedPrice.initialPrice
            val second = cachedPrice.initialPrice
            assertTrue(first === second)
        }
    }
})
```

The use of `lateinit` is a little clunky, so Spek wraps that up using Kotlin's *delegated properties*. Each fixture can be followed with a `by memoized` call and a lambda to provide the value.

> **NOTE** *memoized* (not memorized!) is a term for a value that's calculated once and cached for later use.

Don't use these for the result of actions you're testing—those should be done within the `test` lambdas themselves, like this:

```
object InMemoryCachedPriceSpek : Spek({
    val stubbedPrice : Price by memoized { StubPrice() }

    group("empty cache") {
        val cachedPrice by memoized { InMemoryCachedPrice(stubbedPrice) }

        test("gets default value") {
            assertEquals(BigDecimal(10), cachedPrice.initialPrice)
        }
```

```
test("gets same value when called again") {
    val first = cachedPrice.initialPrice
    val second = cachedPrice.initialPrice
    assertTrue(first === second)
    }
  }
})
```

The test discovery phase happening via plain execution of our Kotlin code allows for much simpler parameterization than is available in JUnit. Rather than needing additional annotations and reflection-based lookups, we can just loop and repeat calls to test as follows:

```
object InMemoryCachedPriceSpek : Spek({
    group("parameterized example") {                    Use of it on each time through
        listOf(1, 2, 3).forEach {                       loop gives us the tests testing
            test("testing $it") {   ⟵──────────         1, testing 2, and testing 3.
                assertNotEquals(it, 0)
                }
            }
        }
})
```

For those who may have encountered specification-style testing in other ecosystems, such as RSpec in Ruby or Jasmine in JavaScript, you can substitute the group and test methods with describe and it instead for an even more natural narrative flow, like this:

```
object InMemoryCachedPriceSpek : Spek({
    val stubbedPrice : Price by memoized { StubPrice() }

    describe("empty cache") {
        val cachedPrice by memoized { InMemoryCachedPrice(stubbedPrice) }

        it("gets default value") {
            assertEquals(BigDecimal(10), cachedPrice.initialPrice)
        }

        it("gets same value when called again") {
            val first = cachedPrice.initialPrice
            val second = cachedPrice.initialPrice
            assertEquals(true, first === second)
        }
    }
})
```

Another common format for writing specifications is *Gherkin syntax* (https://cucumber .io/docs/gherkin/reference/), popularized by the Cucumber testing tool. This syntax declares our specification in a series of given-when-then statements: *given* this setup, *when* this action happens, *then* we see these consequences. Enforcing this structure often makes specifications more readable as natural language, not just code.

Restating a prior test in Gherkin style could look like this: *Given* an empty cache, *when* calculating the price, *then* we look up the default value. Here's how that translates to Spek's Gherkin support:

```
object InMemoryCachedPriceSpekGherkin : Spek({
    Feature("caching") {
        val stubbedPrice by memoized { StubPrice() }

        lateinit var cachedPrice : Price
        lateinit var result : BigDecimal

        Scenario("empty cache") {
            Given("an empty cache") {
                cachedPrice = InMemoryCachedPrice(stubbedPrice)
            }

            When("calculating") {
                result = cachedPrice.initialPrice
            }

            Then("it looks up the default value") {
                assertEquals(BigDecimal(10), result)
            }
        }
    }
})
```

You'll notice this also brings additional grouping from Cucumber by dividing our specification by `Feature` and `Scenario` before we apply given-when-then organization.

Specifications give us a different way to order our testing code to better communicate to later readers. But they still require that we write all of our cases out by hand. Clojure presents some different possibilities to explore how we choose our testing data.

14.3   Property-based testing with Clojure

Unlike Java and Kotlin, Clojure comes with a testing framework in its standard library, `clojure.test`. Although we won't cover this library in depth, let's get familiar with the basics before visiting other, more exotic parts of Clojure's testing ecosystem.

14.3.1   clojure.test

We'll exercise our tests via the Clojure REPL, much like we did throughout chapter 10. If you skipped that chapter or it's been a while, now's a good time to review the basics of Clojure if any of these tests are hard to follow.

Although it ships directly with Clojure, `clojure.test` isn't automatically bundled with our code. We need to request the library via `require`. Entering the following in our REPL makes all of the functions in `clojure.test` available with the prefix `test` that we declare via `:as`:

```
user=> (require '[clojure.test :as test])
nil
user=> (test/is (= 1 1))
true
```

Alternatively, we can pick specific functions via `:refer` to use without prefix like this:

```
user=> (require '[clojure.test :refer [is]])
nil
user=> (is (= 1 1))
true
```

The `is` function represents the base of assertions in `clojure.test`. When the assertion passes, we see the function returns `true`. How about when it fails?

```
user=> (is (= 1 2))

FAIL in () (NO_SOURCE_FILE:1)
expected: (= 1 2)
  actual: (not (= 1 2))
false
```

Any predicate can be used with `is`. For example, here's how we can confirm that a function will throw an exception we expect:

```
user=> (defn oops [] (throw (RuntimeException. "Oops")))   ◁──────  A function to
#'user/oops                                                         always throw a
                                                                    RuntimeException
user=> (is (thrown? RuntimeException (oops)))              We receive an #error value, not
#error {                                          ◁────── a FAIL message. This indicates
 :cause "Oops"                                            that the assertion passed.
 :via
 [{:type java.lang.RuntimeException
   :message "Oops"                                       The error also contains a full
   :at [user$oops invokeStatic "NO_SOURCE_FILE" 1]}]     stack trace, excluded here for
   ...                                         ◁──────── space.
```

With our assertions, we're now ready to start constructing tests. A primary method for this is the `deftest` function, shown next:

```
user=> (require '[clojure.test :refer [deftest]])
nil
user=> (deftest one-is-one (is (= 1 1)))
#'user/one-is-one
```

Having defined our test, we now need to execute it. We can do this via the `run-tests` function, which will find all defined tests in our current namespace. For the REPL, a default namespace called `user` exists automatically, and that's where our `deftest` put our test, as shown here:

```
user=> (require '[clojure.test :refer [run-tests]])
nil
user=> (run-tests)

Testing user

Ran 1 tests containing 1 assertions.
0 failures, 0 errors.
{:test 1, :pass 1, :fail 0, :error 0, :type :summary}
```

Obviously writing and running tests in a REPL is good for learning but not supportable for any long-term use in a project. Eventually it's worth setting up a test runner, although unlike the Java world where JUnit is the standout leader, a few competing options exist in Clojure. A few to consider follow:

- Leiningen (https://leiningen.org/) is a popular Clojure build tool that includes support for testing, much like Maven and Gradle.
- Cognitect Labs `test-runner` (https://github.com/cognitect-labs/test-runner) is a simple test runner built purely on Clojure's native dependency support.
- Kaocha (https://github.com/lambdaisland/kaocha) is a full-featured test runner with a focus on modular design to the testing process.

Having said that, we'll continue in our REPL and look now at an interesting ability that comes along with Clojure: data specifications.

14.3.2 clojure.spec

Although Clojure's integration with the JVM means you can naturally work with classes and objects, functional programming doesn't couple behavior as tightly to data. It's common to have functions that operate against data structures composed of basic primitives, particularly with maps fulfilling the data-carrying behavior we associate with classes in object-oriented programming.

This makes it attractive to have better facilities to test the shape and contents of built-in data structures. That's provided in the standard library with `clojure.spec`. As with `clojure.test`, we need to require the library to get access to it, as follows:

```
user=> (require '[clojure.spec.alpha :as spec])
nil
```

> **NOTE** Although `clojure.spec` uses the term "specification," this is an entirely different use of the term from specifications we saw with Spek in Kotlin. `clojure.spec` defines specifications for *data* rather than for *behavior*.

With that library available, we can start making statements about different values with the function `valid?`. This executes the predicate function we pass it against the value and gives us a Boolean in return, as shown next:

```
user=> (spec/valid? even? 10)
true
user=> (spec/valid? even? 13)
false
```

The `conform` function provides us with the next level of checking, shown in the next code sample. If the value passes the predicate, we receive back that value. Otherwise, the return is a keyword `:clojure.spec.alpha/invalid`:

```
user=> (spec/conform even? 10)
10
user=> (spec/conform even? 13)
:clojure.spec.alpha/invalid
```

We can combine different checks together using the `and` function. It's possible to do this directly via writing our own predicate functions, but using the version from `clojure.spec`, illustrated in the next code snippet, means the library understands the combination we're creating. We'll see in a moment how that can give us more information:

```
user=> (spec/conform (spec/and int? even?) 10)
10
user=> (spec/conform (spec/and int? even?) 13)
:clojure.spec.alpha/invalid
user=> (spec/conform (spec/and int? even?) "not int")
:clojure.spec.alpha/invalid
```

After seeing `and`, it may come as no surprise that there's an `or` function. But the plot thickens if we try to use `or` just like we did with `and`, as shown here:

```
user=> (spec/conform (spec/or int? string?) 10)
Unexpected error (AssertionError) macroexpanding spec/or at (REPL:1:15).
Assert failed: spec/or expects k1 p1 k2 p2..., where ks are keywords
(c/and (even? (count key-pred-forms)) (every? keyword? keys))
```

This error message tells us that `or` expects to include keywords between the predicates we pass it. This may seem like a strange requirement for a simple Boolean function. However, the reason becomes clearer when we look closer at the results from `conform` when given `or` conditions here:

```
user=> (spec/conform (spec/or :a-number int? :a-string string?) "hello")
[:a-string "hello"]
user=> (spec/conform (spec/or :a-number int? :a-string string?) 10)
[:a-number 10]
user=> (spec/conform (spec/or :a-number int? :a-string string?) nil)
:clojure.spec.alpha/invalid
```

The library tells us not just that the value matches our specification—it tells us which branch of our `or` condition fulfilled the spec. Our specification is bringing more than simple yes/no validity. We're finding out *why* the value passed at the same time.

Repeating our specifications is getting tedious, and in a real application, such repetition is an obvious code smell. `clojure.spec` allows registering specifications against a namespaced keyword. Then we just call `conform` with the keyword like this:

```
user=> (spec/def :well/even (spec/and int? even?))
:well/even
user=> (spec/conform :well/even 10)
10
user=> (spec/conform :well/even 11)
:clojure.spec.alpha/invalid
```

The Clojure REPL comes with a handy `doc` function, which integrates nicely with our specifications. When handed a registered keyword, we get a neatly formatted version of the spec as follows:

```
user=> (doc :well/even)
-------------------------
 :well/even
Spec
  (and int? even?)
```

Although `conform` provides feedback on how a successful match happened, the `:clojure.spec.alpha/invalid` keyword is rather opaque about failure. The `explain` function leans on the deeper knowledge our specs already have to tell us why a given value fails, shown next:

```
user=> (spec/explain :well/even 10)
Success!
nil
user=> (spec/explain :well/even 11)
11 - failed: even? spec: :well/even
nil
user=> (spec/explain :well/even "")
"" - failed: int? spec: :well/even
nil
```

Now that we've defined reusable specifications for values, we can apply them in our unit tests directly like this:

```
(deftest its-even
    (is (spec/valid? :well/even 4)))

(deftest its-not-even
    (is (not (spec/valid? :well/even 5))))
```

To this point our specifications have focused on checking individual values. When we work with maps, though, there's an additional question: does the shape of the provided data match our expectations? We validate this with the `keys` function.

Let's imagine part of our theater ticketing system is being written in Clojure. We want to confirm any ticket we're passed has an `id` and `amount`. Optionally, we allow notes. We can define a specification for this like so:

```
user=> (spec/def :well/ticket (spec/keys
                                :req [:ticket/id :ticket/amount]
                                :opt [:ticket/notes]))
:well/ticket
```

Note that the keys here are all namespaced with `:ticket`. This is considered good form for Clojure map keys, because it allows us to maintain a distinction between, say, the `amount` a ticket costs and the `amount` of seats available in a given venue. Should you need to use non-namespaced keys, the various functions like `req` provide alternate versions by appending `-un`, such as, `req-un`.

Calling `conform` on a map will validate the presence of the keys we've spelled out. It also allows unspecified keys alongside the required keys, as illustrated next:

```
user=> (spec/conform :well/ticket
                      {:ticket/id 1
                       :ticket/amount 100
                       :ticket/notes "Noted"})
#:ticket{:id 1, :amount 100, :notes "Noted"}

user=> (spec/conform :well/ticket
                      {:ticket/id 1
                       :ticket/amount 100
                       :ticket/other-stuff true})
#:ticket{:id 1, :amount 100, :other-stuff true}

user=> (spec/conform :well/ticket {:ticket/id 1})
:clojure.spec.alpha/invalid
```

Namespacing keys clearly shows its value, though, in how seamlessly it works with our prior value checking. If a key name has a registered spec, then that value will be validated when we `conform`, as follows:

```
user=> (spec/def :ticket/amount int?)
:ticket/amount

user=> (spec/conform :well/ticket
                      {:ticket/id 1 :ticket/amount 100})
#:ticket{:id 1, :amount 100]}

user=> (spec/conform :well/ticket {:ticket/id 1 :ticket/amount "100"})
:clojure.spec.alpha/invalid
```

`clojure.spec` provides a rich set of abilities for validating our data. But Clojure's focus on how we interact with data doesn't end there.

14.3.3 *test.check*

When we're writing tests, a lot of our time is spent picking good data to exercise our code. Whether it's building out representative objects or finding the values at the edges of our validation, much energy goes into this search for what to test.

Property-based testing turns this relationship on its head. Instead of constructing examples to execute, we instead define *properties* that should hold true for our functions and then feed in randomized data to ensure those properties are true.

> **NOTE** Much of the recent buzz around property-based testing is credited to the Haskell library, QuickCheck (https://hackage.haskell.org/package/QuickCheck). Other languages have equivalents, such as Hypothesis (https://hypothesis.readthedocs.io/en/latest/) in Python. In Clojure, this is provided by the test.check library.

This paradigm of testing is a significant change from the traditional unit testing most folks have experienced. In the sort of testing we've seen so far, you expect 100% deterministic results. Any flakiness in running the tests is a sign of a poorly written test and should be eradicated.

Why is property-based testing different—not only allowing but relying on randomized data? For one, although the inputs are randomized, failure doesn't indicate a faulty test—it reveals that our understanding of the system, as expressed by the properties we've defined, is wrong. In effect, property-based tests find edge cases our manually selected data might have missed.

This isn't an argument for entirely abandoning more traditional unit tests, either. It's reasonable to supplement our typical testing with property-based tests, especially in areas where incoming data presents a lot of variety that could trip us up.

Unlike clojure.test and clojure.spec, test.check is a separate package, not in Clojure's standard library. To use it in our REPL, we'll have to tell Clojure about this dependency. The simplest way to do this is to put a file called deps.edn in the same directory where we run clj. That file instructs Clojure to download the library from the Maven repository as follows:

```
{
  :deps { org.clojure/test.check {:mvn/version "1.1.0"}}
}
```

You'll need to restart the clj REPL after creating the deps.edn file. You should see messages the first time you start the REPL indicating it's downloading the necessary JARs.

Property-based testing has two big parts: how you define properties to check about your code, and how you generate the randomized data to test those. Let's start off by configuring generators for our data, which may help inspire us for properties we could check.

`test.check` provides its main support for creating randomized data in the `gener-ators` package. We'll pull in the whole package and alias it to `gen` for a little less typing like this:

```
user=> (require '[clojure.test.check.generators :as gen])
nil
```

Two main functions serve as our entry point into generating random data: `generate` and `sample`. `generate` get a single value, and `sample` gets a set of values instead. Each of these functions requires a generator, of which many are built-in. For instance, here we can simulate flipping a coin by generating randomized Boolean values:

```
user=> (gen/generate gen/boolean)
false

user=> (gen/sample gen/boolean)
(true false true false false false true true false false)

user=> (gen/sample gen/boolean 5)
(true true true true true)
```

The basic generators provided by `test.check` cover much of what you need for primitive types in Clojure. Here's a sampling of their usage. You can see the docs at http://mng.bz/6XoD for further details and additional, optional parameters that some of these generators take:

```
user=> (gen/sample gen/nat)        ◄──── Small, natural (non-negative) integers
(0 1 0 2 3 5 5 7 4 5)

user=> (gen/sample gen/small-integer)    ◄──── Small integers, including negatives
(0 -1 1 1 2 4 0 5 -7 -8)

user=> (gen/sample gen/large-integer)    ◄──── Larger integers, including negatives
(-1 0 -1 -3 3 -1 -8 9 26 -249)

user=> (gen/sample (gen/choose 10 20))   ◄──── Choose from the provided integer range
(11 20 17 16 11 16 14 19 14 13)
                                         ┌ Any Clojure value
user=> (gen/sample gen/any)        ◄────┘
(#{} (true) (-3.0) () (Xs/B 553N -4460N) {} #{-3 W_/R? :? \} () #{} [])
                                         ┌ Any valid Clojure string
user=> (gen/sample gen/string)     ◄────┘
("" "" "" "ØI_" "" "rý" "?HODÄ" "?fÿí'ß" "ü<Ò29eXÔ" "?ÅÆk0®<")
                                            ┌ Any string of alphanumeric characters
user=> (gen/sample gen/string-alphanumeric)  ◄────┘
("" "" "3" "G" "pB9" "e2" "oRt98" "18" "T61T75k4" "b8505NXt")

user=> (gen/sample (gen/elements [:a :b :c]))   ◄──── Choose from a list of elements
(:b :c :b :a :c :b :a :c :a :b)
                                         ┌ Create a list based on the provided generator
user=> (gen/sample (gen/list gen/nat))  ◄────┘
(() (1) (1) (0 2 1) (0 3) (3 3) (1) (1 6 5 1 2 4 4) (4 7 3 4 7 0) (3 2))
```

These generators can be useful for a type of testing referred to as *fuzzing*. The practice of fuzzing, frequently used in the security field, throws varied, and particularly invalid, data at a system to see where it breaks down. Often the examples we test against aren't imaginative enough, particularly when it comes to input from the outside world. Generators allow us an easy way to strengthen our testing with data we wouldn't have thought up.

Imagine our ticketing application allows open text input for notes but would like to try to extract keywords. If our application is internet facing, we never want that function to throw unexpected exceptions. We could fuzz it like so:

```
user=> (defn validate-input [s]
; imagine implementation here that should never throw
)
#'user/validate-input
```

```
user=> (deftest never-throws
         (doall (map (gen/sample gen/string)   ◁─┐  doall ensures Clojure doesn't
                     validate-input)))              lazily ignore our map because
                                                    its return value is unused.
```

```
user=> (run-tests)
```

```
Testing user
```

```
Ran 1 tests containing 0 assertions.
0 failures, 0 errors.
{:test 1, :pass 0, :fail 0, :error 0, :type :summary}
```

Fuzzing can be a useful first step, but there are obviously more interesting properties for our functions than "doesn't crash unexpectedly."

Revisiting our theater ticketing system, the owners are now interested in a new feature where people can bid on tickets. A complex algorithm has been purchased from a machine learning consultancy to maximize the number of people who will purchase in a given set of bid prices. The algorithm guarantees that it won't offer a price outside of the ranges of the bids provided.

We haven't received the code yet, but we want to be prepared to check their claims when it does arrive. Until then, we've provided a stub implementation, shown next, which, given a list of bid prices, will randomly pick one:

```
user=> (defn bid-price [prices] (rand-nth prices))
#'user/bid-price
user=> user=> (bid-price [1 2 3])
1
user=> (bid-price [1 2 3])
3
```

Let's examine how we can use test.check to define the properties about our bidding function. In addition to the generators that we pulled in earlier, we'll need to require the functions in both `clojure.test.check` and `clojure.test.check.properties`, as shown here:

```
user=>(require '[clojure.test.check :as tc])
nil

user=>(require '[clojure.test.check.properties :as prop])
nil
```

The first property we'll look to check—and most important to theater owners!—is that we'll never return a bid smaller than what someone has offered:

```
user=>(def bigger-than-minimum
  (prop/for-all [prices (gen/not-empty (gen/list gen/nat))]
    (<= (apply min prices) (bid-price prices))))
#'user/bigger-than-minimum
```

There's a lot going on in this small snippet, so let's break it down. First off, our `def` `bigger-than-minimum` is giving our property a name for referencing later. It's important to remember that this is only defining the property, not actually checking it yet.

The next line declares `prop/for-all`, which is how we state a property we want to check. It's followed by a list that determines how we'll generate data and what to bind those values to. `[prices (gen/not-empty (gen/list gen/nat))]`. `prices` gets each generated value in turn from the generator statement following it. In this case we're asking for a list of natural (non-negative) integers that is not empty.

The final line finally expresses the actual logic of our property. `(<= (apply min prices) (bid-price prices))` finds the minimum value in our generated list, calls our bid function on that same list, and assures the bid isn't smaller than the minimum.

With that, we can now ask `test.check` to run a set of generated values against the property as follows. The `quick-check` function requires a number of iterations to try and a property to check:

```
user=> (tc/quick-check 100 bigger-than-minimum)
{:result true, :pass? true, :num-tests 100,
 :time-elapsed-ms 13, :seed 1631172881794}
```

Our property passed! The other condition that was requested—that we don't offer a price larger than anyone bid—is an easy extension to make from what we've already written, shown next:

```
user=>(def smaller-than-maximum
  (prop/for-all [prices (gen/not-empty (gen/list gen/nat))]
    (>= (apply max prices) (bid-price prices))))
#'user/smaller-than-maximum

user=>(tc/quick-check 100 smaller-than-maximum)
{:result true, :pass? true, :num-tests 100,
 :time-elapsed-ms 13, :seed 1631173295156}
```

Although it's nice that our properties are passing, let's break them and see what happens then. An easy way to do that is to sneak in a little increase to the bidding function and recheck our property, like so:

```
user=>(defn bid-price [prices] (+ (rand-nth prices) 2))
#'user/bid-price

user=>(tc/quick-check 100 smaller-than-maximum)
{:shrunk {:total-nodes-visited 3, :depth 1, :pass? false, :result false,
:result-data nil, :time-shrinking-ms 1, :smallest [(0)]},
:failed-after-ms 5, :num-tests 1, :seed 1631173486892, :fail [(2)] }
```

Now, this looks different! Our check failed as we hoped that it would, and we've got all the information we need to know about the failing case here. In particular, the :smallest [(0)] key indicates the precise failing value seen during the run. We've seen the :seed in our prior results. If we want to run the property again with identical values generated, we can pass that seed into the call like this:

```
user=>(tc/quick-check 100 smaller-than-maximum
        :seed 1631173486892)                          ◁────
{:shrunk {:total-nodes-visited 3, :depth 1, :pass? false, :result false,
:result-data nil, :time-shrinking-ms 1, :smallest [(0)]},
:failed-after-ms 5, :num-tests 1, :seed 1631173486892, :fail [(2)] }
```

> Passing in the same seed
> value as before to get the
> same failure

A point of interest in the response is the key :shrunk. When test.check finds a failure, it doesn't just stop and report that. It goes through a process of *shrinking*—creating smaller permutations from the failing generated data to find a minimal case. This is incredibly useful, especially with more complex randomized data. Having the smallest, simplest input that will fail is a huge help for debugging.

test.check integrates with the base clojure.test library. The defspec function both defines a test (as in deftest) and a property simultaneously, as shown next:

```
user=> (require '[clojure.test.check.clojure-test :refer [defspec]])
nil

user=> (defspec smaller-than-maximum
  (prop/for-all [prices (gen/not-empty (gen/list gen/nat))]
    (>= (apply max prices) (bid-price prices))))
#'user/smaller-than-maximum

user=> (run-tests)
Testing user
{:result true, :num-tests 100, :seed 1631516389835,
 :time-elapsed-ms 36, :test-var "smaller-than-maximum"}

Ran 1 tests containing 1 assertions.
0 failures, 0 errors.
{:test 1, :pass 1, :fail 0, :error 0, :type :summary}
```

The most difficult aspect of property-based testing often isn't the coding but determining the properties themselves. Although our ticketing example and many basic algorithms, like sorting, lend themselves to obvious properties, many real-world scenarios aren't as clear cut.

Here are some ideas where to look for properties in your systems:

- *Validation and boundaries*—If a function has a condition that you'd validate at runtime, such as the limits of a value, the length of a list, or the contents of a string, this is a ripe location for defining a property.
- *Round-tripping data*—A common operation in many systems is transforming data between various formats. Maybe we receive one type of data on our web request and need to convert it to a different shape before storing it in the database. For these cases, we can define properties showing that a value will round-trip successfully through our conversions and back to its original form without loss.
- *Oracles*—Sometimes we end up writing replacements for existing functionality. This may be for performance, better readability, or any number of other reasons. If we have an alternative path that we consider to be the "right" answer, this can serve as a rich source of properties to compare, even if only during development of the replacements.

14.3.4 *clojure.spec and test.check*

test.check provides a rich set of generators for the primitives in Clojure, but we almost always end up working with richer structures. Writing out accurate generators for those more complex shapes can be tedious and difficult.

Fortunately, clojure.spec helps close this gap. clojure.spec lets us describe our higher-level data structures generically, and it can automatically turn those into test.check-compatible generators that would be messy to define by hand.

To refresh, here are the definitions for our ticketing structure—both the map requirements and the constraints on values:

```
user=> (spec/def :well/ticket (spec/keys
                                   :req [:ticket/id :ticket/amount]
                                   :opt [:ticket/notes]))
:well/ticket

user=> (spec/def :ticket/amount int?)
:ticket/amount

user=> (spec/def :ticket/id int?)
:ticket/id

user=> (spec/def :ticket/notes string?)
:ticket/notes
```

The gen function in clojure.spec.alpha will convert a spec into a generator. We can then pass that generator to the same test.check functions methods we've used previously to create randomized data like this:

```
user=> (gen/generate (spec/gen :well/ticket))
#:ticket{:notes "fZBvSkOAWERawpNz", :id -3, :amount 233194633}
```

This random ticket already reveals corners we may not have considered in our spec: Do we really want negative IDs? Should we enforce a range on the amount for our tickets? Looks like we've got more specification and testing to do!

Summary

- Testing isn't one-size-fits-all. Different techniques have different strengths. Test code is an excellent spot to mix and match libraries and languages to enhance those strengths.
- Other languages, like Kotlin and Clojure, can open up styles of testing that are harder to accomplish in Java.
- Integration testing—interacting with datastores and other services—can be finicky and error prone. Testcontainers provides smooth integration for approaching these external dependencies, leveraging the knowledge we have of containers from chapter 12.
- How we write our specification influences how we think about our systems. Spek in Kotlin, and similar specification-style testing frameworks elsewhere, provide an alternative to the code-focused JUnit type of tests. We saw how it can level up the communication in our testing.
- Last, we took an entirely different approach to testing from "write an example and check the result" with property-based testing in Clojure. From generating random data, defining global properties of our system, all the way to shrinking failures to the smallest possible input, property-based testing opens new avenues to ensuring the quality of our systems.

Part 5

Java frontiers

This part of the book brings together many of the techniques and concepts you've seen throughout the other parts.

Continuing on from the introduction to Clojure in chapter 10, you'll dig into functional programming beyond the basics of map-filter-reduce. You'll see in detail why Java's design and history present some barriers to the functional style. Then you'll get a further taste of how more advanced techniques in functional languages appear in Kotlin and Clojure to simplify and empower your code.

Building on the concurrency topics from part 2, you'll also see other possibilities for building safe, performant applications. From recently introduced capabilities in Java like Fork/Join, to Kotlin's coroutines, and Clojure's agents, you'll come away with more options managing the multicore, multithreaded world of modern computing.

From there, you'll finish out by looking into the internals of the JVM. If you've ever wondered why reflection is slow or how dynamic languages can target the JVM, chapter 17 will fill in the gaps.

Finally, you'll get an introduction to the major OpenJDK projects currently in flight, what their goals are, and what to expect from each of them in coming releases.

Advanced functional programming

This chapter covers

- Functional programming concepts
- Limits of functional programming in Java
- Kotlin advanced functional programming
- Clojure advanced functional programming

We have already met functional programming concepts earlier in the book, but in this chapter we want to draw together the threads and step it up. There is a lot of talk about *functional programming* in the industry, but it remains a rather ill-defined concept. The sole point that is agreed upon is that in a functional programming (FP) language, code is representable as a first-class data item, that is, that it should be possible to represent a piece of deferred computation as a value that can be assigned to a variable.

This definition is, of course, ludicrously broad—for all practical purposes, every mainstream language (with very few exceptions) in the last 30 years meets this definition. So, when different groups of programmers discuss FP, they are talking about different things. Each tribe has a different, tacit understanding of what other language properties are implicitly understood to *also* be included under the term "FP."

In other words—just as with OO—there is no fundamentally agreed-upon definition of what a "functional programming language" is. Alternatively, if everything is a FP language, then nothing is.

The well-grounded developer is well advised to visualize programming languages upon an axis (or, better yet, as a point in a multidimensional space of possible language characteristics). Languages are simply more or less functional than other languages—there is not some absolute scale that they are weighed against. Let's meet some of the concepts of the common toolbox of functional programming languages that go beyond the somewhat facile "code is data" notion.

15.1 Introduction to functional programming concepts

In what follows, we will frequently speak of *functions*, but neither the Java language nor the JVM has any such thing—all executable code must be expressed as a *method*, which is defined, linked, and loaded within a *class*. Other, non-JVM languages, however, have a different conception of executable code, so when we refer to a function in this chapter, it should be understood that we mean a piece of executable code that roughly corresponds to a Java method.

15.1.1 Pure functions

A *pure function* is a function that does not alter the state of any other entity. It is sometimes said to be *side-effect free*, which is intended to mean that the function behaves like an ideation of a mathematical function: it takes in arguments, does not affect them in any way, and returns a result that is dependent only on the values that have been passed.

Related to the concept of purity is the idea of *referential transparency*. This is somewhat unfortunately named—it has nothing to do with references as a Java programmer would understand them. Instead, it means that a function call can be replaced with the result of any previous call to the same function with the same arguments.

It is obvious that all pure functions are referentially transparent, but there may also exist functions that are not pure and yet are also referentially transparent. To allow a non-pure function to be considered in this way would require a formal proof based on code analysis. Purity is about code, but immutability is about data, and that's the next FP concept we will look at.

15.1.2 Immutability

Immutability means that after an object has been created, its state cannot be altered. The default in Java is for objects to be mutable. The keyword `final` is used in various ways in Java, but the one that concerns us here is to prevent modification of fields after creation. Other languages may favor immutability and indicate that preference in various ways—such as Rust, which requires programmers to explicitly make variables mutable with the `mut` modifier.

Immutability makes code easier to reason about: objects have a trivial state model, simply because they are constructed in the only state they will ever exist in. Among other benefits, this means that they can be copied and shared safely, even between threads.

> **NOTE** We might ask whether any "almost immutable" approaches to data exist that still maintain some (or most) of the attractive properties of immutability. In fact, the Java `CompletableFuture` class that we have already met is one such example. We'll have more to say about this in the next chapter.

One consequence is that, because immutable objects cannot be altered, the only way that state change can be expressed in a system is by starting from an immutable value and constructing a completely new immutable value that is more or less the same but with some fields altered—possibly by the use of *withers* (aka `with*()` methods).

For example, the `java.time` API makes very extensive use of immutable data, and new instances can be created by the use of withers like this:

```
LocalDate ld = LocalDate.of(1984, Month.APRIL, 13);
LocalDate dec = ld.withMonth(12);
System.out.println(dec);
```

The immutable approach has consequences—specifically a potentially large impact on the memory subsystem, because the components of the old value have to be copied as part of the creation of the modified value. This means that in-place mutation is often much cheaper from a performance perspective.

15.1.3 Higher-order functions

Higher-order functions are actually a very simple concept, described by the following insight: if a function can be represented as a data item, then it should be able to be treated as though it was any other value.

We can define a *higher-order function* as a function value that does one or both of the following:

- Takes a function value as a parameter
- Returns a function value

Consider, for example, a static method that takes in a Java `String` and generates a function object from it, as shown here:

```
public static Function<String, String> makePrefixer(String prefix) {
    return s -> prefix +": "+ s;
}
```

This provides a straightforward way to make function objects. Let's now combine it with another static method, shown next, that this time accepts a function object as input:

```
public static String doubleApplier(String input,
                                   Function<String, String> f) {
    return f.apply(f.apply(input));
}
```

This provides us with the following simple example:

```
var f = makePrefixer("NaNa");  ⟵──┘ Creates a function object
System.out.println(doubleApplier("Batman", f));  ⟵─────┘
```

Passes the function object as a parameter to another method

However, this is not quite the whole story for Java, as we will see in the next section.

15.1.4 *Recursion*

A *recursive* function is one that calls itself on at least some of the code paths through the function. This leads to one of the oldest jokes in programming: "in order to understand recursion, one must first understand recursion."

However, to be more strictly accurate, we might write it as follows: in order to understand recursion, one must first understand

1 recursion, and
2 that in a physically realizable system, every chain of recursive calls must eventually terminate and return a value.

The second point is important: programming languages use call stacks to allow functions to call other functions, and this occupies space in memory. Recursion, therefore, has the problem that deep recursive calls may potentially use up too much memory and crash.

In terms of theoretical computer science, recursion is interesting and important for many different reasons. One of the most important is that recursion can be used as a basis to explore theories of computation and ideas such as *Turing completeness*, which is loosely the idea that all nontrivial computation systems have the same theoretical capability to perform calculations.

15.1.5 *Closures*

A *closure* is usually defined as a lambda expression that "captures" some state from the surrounding context. However, for this definition to make sense, we need to explain the meaning of the capturing concept.

When we create a value and assign (or bind) it to a local variable, the variable will exist and can be used until some later point in the code. This later point may well be the end of the function or block where the variable was declared. The area of code where the variable exists and can be used is the *scope* of the variable.

When we create a function value, the local variables declared within the function body will still be in scope during the invocation of the function value, which will occur later than the point where the function value is declared. If, in the declaration of the function value, we mention a variable (or other state, such as a field) that is declared outside the scope of the function body, then the function value is said to have *closed over* the state, and the function value is known as a closure.

When the closure is later invoked, it has full access to the captured variables, even if the invocation happens in a different scope to that in which the capture was declared.

For example, in Java:

```
public static Function<Integer, Integer> closure() {
    var atomic = new AtomicInteger(0);
    return i -> atomic.addAndGet(i);
}
```

This static method is a higher-order function that returns a Java closure because it returns a lambda expression that references `atomic`, which was declared as a local variable inside the method, that is, in the scope where the lambda was itself declared. The closure returned from `closure()` can be called repeatedly, and it will aggregate state on each call.

15.1.6 *Laziness*

We briefly mentioned the concept of *laziness* in chapter 10. Essentially, *lazy evaluation* allows the computation of the value of an expression to be deferred until the value is actually required. By contrast, the immediate evaluation of an expression is known as *eager evaluation* (or *strict evaluation*).

The idea of laziness is simple: if you don't need to do work, don't do it! It sounds simple but has deep ramifications for how you write your programs and how they perform. A key part of this additional complexity is that your program needs to track what work has and hasn't been completed already.

Not every language supports lazy evaluation, and many programmers may have encountered only eager evaluation at this point in their journey—and that's completely OK.

For example, there is no general language-level support for laziness in Java, so it's difficult to give a clear example of the feature. We'll have to wait until we talk about Kotlin to make it concrete.

However, although laziness is not necessarily a natural concept for a Java programmer, laziness is an extremely useful and powerful technique in FP. In fact, for some FP languages, such as Haskell, lazy evaluation is the default.

15.1.7   *Currying and partial application*

Currying, unfortunately, has nothing to do with food. Instead, it is a programming technique named after Haskell Curry (who also gave his name to the Haskell programming language). To explain it, let's start with a concrete example.

Consider an eagerly-evaluated, pure function that takes two arguments. If we supply both arguments, we will get a value, and the function call can be replaced everywhere by the resulting value (this is referential transparency). But what happens if we supply not both but only one of the two arguments?

Intuitively, we can think of this as creating a new function, but one that needs only a single argument to calculate a result. This new function is called a *curried function* (or *partially-applied function*). Java does not have direct support for currying, so we will again defer making a concrete example until later in the chapter.

Looking farther afield, some programming languages support the notion of functions with multiple argument lists (or have syntax that allows the programmer to fake them). In this case, another way to think about currying is as a transformation of functions. In mathematical notation, we are translating a multiple-argument function that is called as `f(a, b)` into one callable as `(g(a))(b)`, where `g(a)` is the partially applied function.

As should be obvious now, the different languages we've met so far have different levels of support for functional programming—for example, Clojure has very good support for many of the concepts that we have discussed in this section. Java, on the other hand, is a very different story, as we'll see in the next section.

15.2   *Limitations of Java as a FP language*

Let's start with the good news, such as it is: Java definitely clears the rather low bar of "represent code as data" via the types in `java.util.function` and also via the extensive introspective support the runtime provides (such as Reflection and Method Handles).

> **NOTE**   The use of inner classes to simulate function objects as a technique predates Java 8 and was present in libraries like Google Guava, so strictly speaking, Java's ability to represent code as data is not tied to that version.

Since version 8, the Java language goes somewhat further than the bare minimum with the introduction of streams and, with them, a heavily restricted domain of lazy operations. However, despite the arrival of streams, Java is not a naturally functional environment. Some of this is due to the history of the platform and what are—by now—decades-old design decisions.

> **NOTE**   It is worth remembering that Java is a 25-year-old imperative language that has been iterated upon extensively. Some of its APIs are amenable to FP, immutable data, and so on, and some are not. This is the reality of working in a language that has survived, and thrived, yet still remains backward compatible.

So, overall, Java is perhaps best described as a "slightly functional programming language." It has the basic features needed to support FP and provides developers with access to basic patterns like filter-map-reduce via the Streams API, but most advanced functional features are either incomplete or missing entirely. Let's take a detailed look.

15.2.1 *Pure functions*

As we saw in chapter 4, Java's bytecodes do many different sorts of things, including arithmetic, stack manipulation, flow control, and especially invocation and data storage and retrieval. For well-grounded developers who already understand JVM bytecode, this means that we can express purity of methods by thinking about the effect of bytecodes. Specifically, a pure method in a JVM language is one that does the following:

- Does not modify object or static state (does not contain `putfield` or `putstatic`)
- Does not depend upon external mutable object or static state
- Does not call any non pure method

This is a pretty restrictive set of conditions and underlines the difficulty of using the JVM as a basis for pure functional programming.

There is also a question about the semantics—that is, the intent—of the different interfaces present in the JDK. For example, `Callable` (in `java.util.concurrent`) and `Supplier` (in `java.util.function`) both do basically the same thing: they perform some calculation and return a value, as shown here:

```
@FunctionalInterface
public interface Callable<V> {
    V call() throws Exception;
}

@FunctionalInterface
public interface Supplier<T> {
    T get();
}
```

They are both `@FunctionalInterface` and are both routinely used as the target type for a lambda. The signatures of the interfaces are the same, apart from different approaches to handling exceptions.

However, they can be seen as having different roles: a `Callable` implies potentially nontrivial amounts of work in the called code to create the value that will be returned. On the other hand, the name `Supplier` seems to imply less work—perhaps just returning a cached value.

15.2.2 *Mutability*

Java is a mutable language—mutability is baked into its design from the earliest days. Partly this is an accident of history—the machines of the late 1990s (from when Java hails) were very restricted (by modern standards) in terms of memory. An immutable data model would have greatly increased stress on the memory management subsystem, and caused much more frequent GC events, leading to far worse throughput.

Java's design, therefore, favors mutation over the creation of modified copies. So in-place mutation can be seen as a design choice caused by performance trade-offs from 25 years ago.

The situation, however, is even worse than that. Java refers to all composite data by reference, and the final keyword applies to the reference, *not* to the data. For instance, when applied to fields, the field can be assigned to only once.

This means that even if a object has all final fields, the composite state can still be mutable because the object can hold a final reference to another object that has some nonfinal fields. This leads to the problem of shallow immutability, as we discussed in chapter 5.

> **NOTE** For C++ programmers: Java has no concept of const, although it does have it as an (unused) keyword.

For example, here is a slightly enhanced version of the immutable Deposit class that we met in chapter 5:

```java
public final class Deposit implements Comparable<Deposit> {
    private final double amount;
    private final LocalDate date;
    private final Account payee;

    private Deposit(double amount, LocalDate date, Account payee) {
        this.amount = amount;
        this.date = date;
        this.payee = payee;
    }

    @Override
    public int compareTo(Deposit other) {
        return Comparator.nullsFirst(LocalDate::compareTo)
                        .compare(this.date, other.date);
    }

    // methods elided
}
```

The immutability of this class rests upon the assumption that Account and all of its transitive dependencies are also immutable. This means there are limits to what can be done—fundamentally the data model of Java and the JVM is not naturally friendly to immutability.

In the bytecode, we can see that finality fields shows up as a piece of field metadata as follows:

```
$ javap -c -p out/production/resources/ch13/Deposit.class
Compiled from "Deposit.java"
public final class ch13.Deposit
    implements java.lang.Comparable<ch13.Deposit> {

    private final double amount;

    private final java.time.LocalDate date;

    private final ch13.Account payee;

 // ...
 }
```

Trying to use immutable approaches to state in Java is bailing out a leaking boat. Every single reference has to be checked for mutability, and if even one is missed, then the entire object graph is mutable.

Worse still, the JVM's reflection and other subsystems also provide ways to circumvent immutability, as shown next:

```
var account = new Account(100);
var deposit = Deposit.of(42.0, LocalDate.now(), account);
try {
    Field f = Deposit.class.getDeclaredField("amount");
    f.setAccessible(true);
    f.setDouble(deposit, 21.0);
    System.out.println("Value: "+ deposit.amount());
} catch (NoSuchFieldException e) {
    e.printStackTrace();
} catch (IllegalAccessException e) {
    e.printStackTrace();
}
```

Taken together, all of this means that neither Java nor the JVM is an environment that provides any particular support for programming with immutable data. Languages like Clojure, which have stronger requirements, end up having to do a lot of the work in their language-specific runtime.

15.2.3 *Higher-order functions*

The concept of a higher-order function should not be surprising to a Java programmer. We have already seen an example of a static method, makePrefixer(), that takes in a prefix string and returns a function object. Let's rewrite the code and change the static factory into another function object like this:

```
Function<String, Function<String, String>> prefixer =
                                 prefix -> s -> prefix +": "+ s;
```

This can be a little hard to read at first glance, so let's include some extra bits of syntax that we don't actually need, to make what's going on clearer:

```
Function<String, Function<String, String>> prefixer = prefix -> {
    return s -> prefix +": "+ s;
};
```

In this expanded view, we can see that `prefix` is the argument to the function and the returned value is a lambda (actually a Java closure) that implements `Function<String, String>`.

Notice the appearance of the function type `Function<String, Function<String, String>>`—it has two type parameters that define the input and output types. The second (output) type parameter is just another type—in this case, it is another function type. This is one way to recognize a higher-order function type in Java: a `Function` (or other functional type) that has `Function` as one of its type parameters.

Finally, we should point out that language syntax does matter—after all, function objects can be created as anonymous implementations, like this:

```
public class PrefixerOld
    implements Function<String, Function<String, String>> {

    @Override
    public Function<String, String> apply(String prefix) {
        return new Function<String, String>() {
            @Override
            public String apply(String s) {
                return prefix +": "+ s;
            }
        };
    }
}
```

This code would even have been legal as far back as Java 5, if the `Function` type had existed back then (and as far back as Java 1.1, if we remove the annotations and generics). But it's a total eyesore. It's very hard to see the structure, which is why many programmers think of functional programming as arriving only with Java 8.

15.2.4 Recursion

The `javac` compiler provides a straightforward translation of Java source code into bytecode. As we can see here, this applies to recursive calls:

```
    public static long simpleFactorial(long n) {
        if (n <= 0) {
            return 1;
        } else {
            return n * simpleFactorial(n - 1);
        }
    }
```

which compiles to the following bytecode:

```
public static long simpleFactorial(long);
    Code:
        0: lload_0
        1: lconst_0
        2: lcmp
        3: ifgt          8
        6: lconst_1
        7: lreturn
        8: lload_0
        9: lload_0
       10: lconst_1
       11: lsub
       12: invokestatic  #37                // Method simpleFactorial:(J)J
       15: lmul
       16: lreturn
```

This, of course, has some major limitations. In this case, making a call like simple-
Factorial(100000) will result in a StackOverflowError because of the invokestatic
call at byte 12, which will cause an additional interpreter frame to be placed on the
stack for each recursive call.

NOTE   A *recursive* method is one that calls itself. A *tail-recursive* method is one
where the self-call is the last thing that the method does.

Let's try to find a way to see whether the recursive call could be avoided. One
approach is to rewrite the factorial code into a tail-recursive form, which in Java we
can do most easily with a private helper method, as follows:

```
public static long tailrecFactorial(long n) {
    if (n <= 0) {
        return 1;
    }
    return helpFact(n, 1);
}

private static long helpFact(long i, long j) {
    if (i == 0) {
        return j;
    }
    return helpFact(i - 1, i * j);
}
```

The entry method, tailrecFactorial(), does not do any recursion; it merely sets up
the tail-recursive call and hides the details of the more complex signature from the user.
The bytecode for the method is basically trivial, but let's include it for completeness:

```
public static long tailrecFactorial(long);
    Code:
        0: lload_0
```

```
 1: lconst_0
 2: lcmp
 3: ifgt           8
 6: lconst_1
 7: lreturn
 8: lload_0
 9: lconst_1
10: invokestatic   #49                    // Method helpFact:(JJ)J
13: lreturn
```

As you can see, there are no loops and only a single branching `if` at bytecode 3. The real action (and the recursion) happens in `helpFact()`. This is still compiled by `javac` into bytecode, which contains a recursive call, as we can see:

```
private static long helpFact(long, long);
    Code:
        0: lload_0
        1: lconst_0
        2: lcmp                          Longs are 8 bytes, so they need
        3: ifne            8             two local variable slots each
        6: lload_2         ◄─┐
        7: lreturn         ◄──── Returns from the i == 0 path
        8: lload_0
        9: lconst_1
       10: lsub
       11: lload_0
       12: lload_2
       13: lmul
       14: invokestatic  #49  // Method helpFact:(JJ)J   ◄─── Tail-recursive call
       17: lreturn
```

In this form, however, we can now see that there are two paths through this method. The simple `i == 0` path starts at bytecode 0, falls through the `if` condition at 3 and returns `j` at bytecode 7. The more general case is 0 to 3, then 8 to 14, which triggers a recursive call.

So, on the only path that has a method call on it, the call is recursive and always the last thing that happens before the `return`—that is, the call is in *tail position*. However, it *could* be compiled into the following bytecode instead, which avoids the call:

```
private static long helpFact(long, long);
    Code:
        0: lload_0
        1: lconst_0
        2: lcmp                          Longs are 8 bytes, so they need
        3: ifne            8             two local variable slots each
        6: lload_2         ◄─┐
        7: lreturn         ◄──── Returns from the i == 0 path
        8: lload_0
        9: lconst_1
       10: lsub
       11: lload_0
```

```
12: lload_2
13: lmul
14: lstore_2    Resets the local variables
15: lstore_0
16: goto        0    ⟵───── Jumps to the top of the method
```

Now for the bad news: `javac` does not perform this operation automatically, despite it being possible. This is yet another example of how the compiler tries to translate Java source into bytecode as exactly as possible.

> **NOTE** In the Resources project that accompanies this book is an example of how to use the ASM library to generate a class that implements the previous bytecode sequence because `javac` will not emit it from recursive code.

For completeness, we should say that, in practice, implementing a factorial function that handles longs with recursive calls rather than overwriting frames is not actually going to cause a problem, because the factorial increases so quickly that it will overflow the available space in a `long` well before any stack size limits are reached, as shown here:

```
$ java TailRecFactorial 20
2432902008176640000

$ jshell
jshell> 2432902008176640000L + 0.0
$1 ==> 2.43290200817664E18

jshell> Long.MAX_VALUE + 0.0
$2 ==> 9.223372036854776E18
```

So `factorial(21)` is already larger than the largest positive `long` that the JVM can express. However, although this specific trivial example is reasonably safe, it does not alter the difficult fact that all recursive algorithms in Java are potentially vulnerable to stack overflow.

This specific flaw is one of the Java language—and not of the JVM. Other languages on the JVM can, and do, handle this differently, for example, by use of an annotation or a keyword. We will see examples of this when we discuss how Kotlin and Clojure handle recursion later in the chapter.

15.2.5 Closures

As we've already seen, a closure is essentially a lambda expression that captures some visible state from the scope in which the lambda is declared, like this:

```
int i = 42;
Function<String, String> f = s -> s + i;
// i = 37;
System.out.println(f.apply("Hello "));
```

When this runs, it produces, as expected: `Hello 42`. However, if we uncomment the line that reassigns the value of `i`, then something different happens: the code stops compiling at all.

To understand why this happens, let's take a look at the bytecode that the code is compiled into. As we'll see in chapter 17, the bodies of lambda expressions in Java are turned into private static methods. In this case, the lambda body turns into this:

```
private static java.lang.String lambda$main$0(int, java.lang.String);
    Code:
        0: aload_1
        1: iload_0
        2: invokedynamic #32,  0 // InvokeDynamic #1:makeConcatWithConstants:
                                  // (Ljava/lang/String;I)Ljava/lang/String;
        7: areturn
```

The clue is in the signature of `lambda$main$0()`. It takes *two* parameters, not one. The first parameter is the value of `i` that is passed in—which is 42 at the time that the closure is created (the second is the `String` parameter that the lambda takes when executed). Java closures contain copies of *values*, which are bit patterns (whether of primitives or object references) and not *variables*.

> **NOTE** Java is strictly a *pass-by-value* language—there is no way in the core language to *pass-by-reference* or *pass-by-name*.

To see the effect of changes to captured state outside the scope of the closure body (or to effect things in other scopes), the captured state must be a mutable object, like this:

```
var i = new AtomicInteger(42);                    Reassigning a value to
Function<String, String> f = s -> s + i.get();    mutable object state works.
i.set(37);                          ◄
// i = new AtomicInteger(37);          ◄────── This would fail to compile.
System.out.println(f.apply("Hello "));
```

In fact, in earlier versions of Java, only variables that were explicitly marked as `final` could have their value captured by Java closures. However, from Java 8 onward, that restriction was changed to variables that are *effectively final*—variables that are used as though they were final, even if they don't actually have the keyword attached to their declaration.

This is actually symptomatic of a deeper problem. The JVM has a shared heap, method-private local variables, and a method-private evaluation stack, and that's it. As compared to other languages, neither the JVM nor the Java language has the concept of an *environment* or a symbol table, or the ability to pass a reference to an entry in one.

Non-Java languages on the JVM that do have those concepts are required to support them in their language runtime because the JVM does not provide any intrinsic support for them. Some programming language theorists, therefore, reach the conclusion that what Java provides are not actually true closures, because of the additional level of indirection required. A Java programmer must mutate the state of an object value, rather than being able to change the captured variable directly.

15.2.6 Laziness

Java does not provide first-class support for lazy evaluation in the core language for ordinary values. However, one interesting place where we can see lazy evaluation in use is within the Java Streams API. Appendix B has a refresher on aspects of streams, should you require one.

> **NOTE** Laziness does play a role in some parts of the JVM and its programming environment (e.g., aspects of class loading are lazy).

Calling `stream()` on a Java collection produces a `Stream` object, which is effectively a lazy representation of an ensemble of elements. Some streams can also be represented as a Java collection; however, streams are more general and not every stream can be represented as a collection.

Let's look again at a typical Java `filter()` and `map()` pipeline:

```
              stream()  filter()  map()      collect()
Collection -> Stream -> Stream -> Stream -> Collection
```

The `stream()` method returns a `Stream` object. The `map()` and `filter()` methods (like almost all of the operations on `Stream`) are lazy. At the other end of the pipeline, we have a `collect()` operation, which *materializes* the contents of the remaining `Stream` back into a `Collection`. This *terminal* method is eager, so the complete pipeline behaves like this:

```
              lazy      lazy      lazy       eager
Collection -> Stream -> Stream -> Stream -> Collection
```

Apart from the materialization back into the collection, the platform has complete control over how much of the stream to evaluate. This opens the door to a range of optimizations that are not available in purely eager approaches.

It can sometimes be helpful to think of the lazy, functional mode of Java streams as being analogous to hyperspace travel in a science-fiction movie. Calling `stream()` is the equivalent of jumping from "normal space" into a hyperspace realm where the rules are different (functional and lazy, rather than OO and eager).

At the end of the operational pipeline, a terminal stream operation jumps us back from the lazy functional world into "normal space," either by re-materializing the stream into a `Collection` (e.g., via `toList()`) or by aggregating the stream, via a `reduce()` or other operation.

Use of lazy evaluation does require more care from the programmer, but this burden largely falls upon library writers, such as the JDK developers. However, a Java developer should be aware of and respect the rules of some aspects of the lazy nature of streams. For example, implementations of some of the `java.util.function` interfaces (e.g., `Predicate`, `Function`) should not mutate internal state or cause side effects. Violating this assumption can cause major problems if developers write implementations or lambdas that do.

Another important aspect of streams is that the stream objects themselves (the instances of `Stream` that are seen as intermediate objects within a pipeline of stream calls) are single shot. Once they have been traversed, they should be considered invalid. In other words, developers should not attempt to store or reuse a stream object, because the results of doing so are almost certainly incorrect and attempts may throw an error.

> **NOTE** Placing a stream object into a temporary variable is almost always a code smell, although doing so during development when debugging a complex generics issue with a stream is acceptable, provided the use of stream temporaries is removed when the code is completed.

One other aspect of the laziness of streams is the ability to model more general data than collections. For example, it is possible to construct an infinite stream by use of `Stream.generate()` combined with a generating function. Let's take a look:

```
public class DaySupplier implements Supplier<LocalDate> {
    private LocalDate current = LocalDate.now().plusDays(1);

    @Override
    public LocalDate get() {
        var tmp = current;
        current = current.plusDays(1);
        return tmp;
    }
}

final var tomorrow = new DaySupplier();
Stream.generate(() -> tomorrow.get())
        .limit(10)
        .forEach(System.out::println);
```

This produces a stream of days that is infinite (or as large as is needed, if you prefer). This would be impossible to represent as a collection without running out of space, thus showing that streams are more general.

This example also shows that Java's restrictions, such as pass by value, restrict the design space somewhat. The `LocalDate` class is immutable, and so we are required to have a class containing a mutable field `current` and then to mutate `current` within the `get()` method to provide a stateful method that can generate a sequence of `LocalDate` objects.

In a language that supported pass by reference, the type `DaySupplier` would have been unnecessary, because `current` could have been a local variable declared in the same scope as `tomorrow`, which could then have been a lambda.

15.2.7 *Currying and partial application*

We already know that Java does not have any language-level support for currying, but we can take a quick look at how something could have been added. For example, here is the declaration for the BiFunction interface in java.util.function:

```
@FunctionalInterface
public interface BiFunction<T, U, R> {
    R apply(T t, U u);

    default <V> BiFunction<T, U, V> andThen(
                            Function<? super R, ? extends V> after) {

        Objects.requireNonNull(after);
        return (T t, U u) -> after.apply(apply(t, u));
    }
}
```

Notice how the default methods feature of interfaces is used to define andThen()—an additional method, beyond the standard apply() method for the BiFunction. This same technique could have been used to provide some support for currying, for example, by defining two new default methods as follows:

```
default Function<U, R> curryLeft(T t) {
        return u -> this.apply(t, u);
    }

    default Function<T, R> curryRight(U u) {
        return t -> this.apply(t, u);
    }
```

These define two ways to produce Java Function objects, that is, functions of one argument from our original BiFunction. Notice that they are implemented as closures. We're simply capturing the supplied value and storing it for later, when we actually apply the function. We could then use these additional default methods like this:

```
BiFunction<Integer, LocalDate, String> bif =
                            (i, d) -> "Count for "+ d + " = "+ i;

Function<LocalDate, String> withCount = bif.curryLeft(42);
Function<Integer, String> forToday = bif.curryRight(LocalDate.now());
```

However, the syntax is somewhat clunky: it requires two different methods for the two possible currys, and they must have different names due to type erasure. Even after all that, the resulting feature is arguably of only limited use, so this approach was never implemented, and, as discussed, Java does not support currying out of the box.

15.2.8 *Java's type system and collections*

To conclude our unfortunate tale about Java's less-than-great affinity to functional programming, let's talk about Java's type system and collections. The following three main issues with these parts of the Java language contribute to the somewhat poor fit to the functional programming style:

- Non-single-rooted type system
- `void`
- Design of the Java Collections

First of all, Java has a non-single-rooted type system (i.e., there is no common super-type of `Object` and `int`). This makes it impossible to write `List<int>` in Java and, as a result, leads to autoboxing and the attendant problems.

> **NOTE** Lots of developers complain about the erasure of type parameters of generic types during compilation, but in reality, it is more often the non-single-rooted type system that really causes problems with generics in the collections.

Java has another problem, connected to the non-single-rooted type system: `void`. This keyword indicates that a method does not return a value (or, looked at another way, that the evaluation stack of the method is empty when the method returns). The keyword therefore carries the semantics that whatever the method does, it is acting purely by side effect—it's the opposite of "pure" in some sense.

The existence of `void` means that Java has both statements and expressions and that it is impossible to implement the design principle, "everything is an expression," which some functional programming traditions are very keen on.

> **NOTE** In chapter 18, we will discuss Project Valhalla, which provides an opportunity for the Java language designers to potentially revisit the non-single-rooted nature of Java's type system (among other goals).

Another problem is related to the shape and nature of the Java Collections interfaces. They were added to the Java language with version 1.2 (aka Java 2), which was released in December 1998. They were not designed with functional programming in mind.

A major problem for doing FP with the Java Collections is that an assumption of mutability is built in everywhere. The Collections interfaces are large and explicitly contain methods like these from `List<E>`:

- `boolean add(E e)`
- `E remove(int index)`

These are mutation methods—the signature of them implies that the Collection object itself has been modified in place.

The corresponding methods on an immutable list would have signatures such as `List<E> add(E e)` that return a new, modified copy of the list. The case of `remove()`

would be difficult to implement, because Java doesn't have the ability to return multiple values from a method.

> **NOTE** The real problem is that `remove()` is incorrectly factored for FP, a very similar case to that of the `Iterator` that we discussed in section 10.4.

All of this therefore implies that *any* implementation of the Collections is implicitly expected to be mutable. There does exist the horrible hack of using `Unsupported-OperationException`, which we discussed in section 6.5.3, but this is not something that a well-grounded Java developer should use.

Other, non-Java languages separate out the concept of the collection type from mutability, for example, by representing them as different interfaces (or different *traits* in languages that support that concept). This enables implementations to specify whether or not they are mutable at type level, by choosing to implement—or not—the separate interfaces.

Lurking behind all of this is that one of Java's main virtues and most important design principles is backward compatibility. This makes it difficult, or impossible, to change some of these aspects to make the language more functional. For example, in the case of the Collections, rather than try to add additional, functional methods directly onto the Collections interfaces, a clean break was made and `Stream` was introduced, to act as a new container type that did not have the implicit semantics of the Collections.

Of course, just introducing a new container type and API does nothing to change the millions upon millions of lines of existing code that use the collections. Nor does it help in the slightest for the common case where an API is already expressed in terms of a collection type.

> **NOTE** This problem is not unique to the stream/collection divide. For example, Java Reflection was introduced in Java 1.1 and predates the arrival of the Collections. As a result, the API is annoyingly difficult to use, because it relies upon arrays as element containers.

This section has shown some rather depressing facts about the state of support for functional programming in Java. The takeaway message is that simple functional patterns (such as filter-map-reduce) are available. These are very useful for all sorts of applications as well as generalizing well to concurrent (and even distributed) applications, but they are about the limit of what Java is able to do. Let's move on to look at our non-Java languages and see if the news is any better.

15.3 *Kotlin FP*

We've already demonstrated how modern Java handles some basic, common patterns in the functional programming paradigm. It probably comes as no surprise that Kotlin brings conciseness and a few additional ideas to the table for the functionally inclined.

This section will hit the high points, but take a look at *Functional Programming in Kotlin* by Marco Vermeulen, Rúnar Bjarnason, and Paul Chiusano (Manning, 2021, http://mng.bz/o2Wr) if you want to go even deeper.

15.3.1 *Pure and higher-order functions*

Back in section 9.2.4, we introduced Kotlin's functions. In Kotlin, functions are part of the type system, expressed with syntax like `(Int) -> Int`, where the contents of the parenthesized list are the argument types and to the right of the arrow is the return type.

By using this notation, we can easily write signatures for functions that accept other functions as arguments or return a function—that is, *higher-order functions*. Kotlin naturally encourages the use of such higher-order functions. Much of the API around working with collections such as `map` and `filter` are in fact built off these higher-order functions, just as we see in the Java (and Clojure) APIs that provide the equivalent language feature.

But higher-order functions aren't restricted to collections and streams. For instance, here's a classic functional programming function called `compose`. `compose` will return a function that calls each of the functions passed as arguments to it:

```kotlin
fun compose(callFirst: (Int) -> Int,
            callSecond: (Int) -> Int): (Int) -> Int {
  return { callSecond(callFirst(it)) }
}
```
> **compose returns a function, so callFirst and callSecond aren't called when this line executes.**

```kotlin
val c = compose({ it * 2 }, { it + 10 })
c(10)
```
> **We pass two lambdas, using the it shorthand described in chapter 9 to avoid explicitly listing the single argument to the lambdas.**

> **We invoke and run the function returned by compose, which returns 30.**

Kotlin provides a number of ways to get a handle to a function, depending on your needs. You can declare lambda expressions as shown earlier (and with many other flavors and features discussed in chapter 9). Alternatively, we can refer to a named function via the `::` syntax as follows:

```kotlin
fun double(x: Int): Int {
  return x * 2
}

val c = compose(::double, { it + 10 })
c(10)
```
> **◁—— Same result as our prior example**

`::` knows more than just top-level functions. It can also refer to a function belonging to a specific object instance like this:

```kotlin
data class Multiply(var factor: Int) {
  fun apply(x: Int): Int = x * factor
}
```

```
val m = Multiply(2)
val c = compose(m::apply, { it + 10 })
c(10)
```
References the apply method on the Multiply class bound specifically to our instance m.

Sadly, much like Java, Kotlin provides no built-in way of guaranteeing the purity of a given function. Although defining functions at the top level (outside of any class) and using val to ensure immutable data can take you a long way, they don't ensure the referential transparency of your functions.

15.3.2   Closures

An aspect of lambda expressions that may not be obvious on the surface is how they interact with the surrounding code. For instance, the following code works, even though local isn't declared within our lambda:

```
var local = 0
val lambda = { println(local) }
lambda()                              ◁──── Prints 0
```

This is referred to as *closure* (as in, the lambda *closes over* the values it can see). Importantly, and unlike Java, it is not just the value of the variables the lambda can access—under the covers, it actually keeps a reference to the variables themselves, as shown here:

```
var local = 0
val lambda = { println(local) }
lambda()                              ◁──── Prints 0

local = 10        Prints 10, the updated value of
lambda()     ◁──┘ local at the time lambda is invoked
```

This closure over variables remains even if the variables themselves would otherwise have gone out of scope. Here we return a lambda from a function, keeping a reference to a variable that normally would be inaccessible:

```
fun makeLambda(): () -> Unit {
  val inFunction = "I'm from makeLambda"
  return { println(inFunction) }
}
```
inFunction would normally go out of scope when makeLambda is done.

```
val lambda = makeLambda()
lambda()                  ◁──────
```
Because our lambda expression closes over inFunction, it is still available here—but only inside our lambda.

> **NOTE** Lambdas carrying references outside their typical scope can be a source for unexpected object leaks!

The location of a lambda expression's declaration determines what it may capture in its closure. For instance, if declared within a class, then the lambda can close over properties in the object as follows:

```
class ClosedForBusiness {
    private val amount = 100
    val check = { println(amount) }
}
```

A lambda saved into check closes over the private property amount.

```
fun getTheCheck(): () -> Unit {
    val closed = ClosedForBusiness()
    return closed.check
}
```

This function returns that lambda, which keeps a reference to amount. This keeps the instance closed alive when normally it wouldn't exist after the function completes.

```
val check = getTheCheck()
check()
```

Prints 100 when called. When the check variable exits scope, the closed instance will also finally be eligible for garbage collection.

Closures with higher-order functions provide a rich basis for building new functions from old ones.

15.3.3 *Currying and partial application*

The currying story for Kotlin is very similar to that in Java. Let's look at an example:

```
fun add(x: Int, y: Int): Int {
    return x + y
}

fun partialAdd(x: Int): (Int) -> Int {
    return { add(x, it) }
}

val addOne = partialAdd(1)
println(addOne(1))
println(addOne(2))

val addTen = partialAdd(10)
println(addTen(1))
println(addTen(2))
```

This is really just a syntactic trick that works because the () operator desugars to a call to the apply() method. At bytecode level, this is really just the same as the Java example. We could imagine some helper syntax for automatically creating curries, perhaps something like

```
val addOne: (Int) -> Int = add(1, _)
println(addOne(10))
```

However, the core language does not directly support this. Various third-party libraries can provide similar, slightly more verbose abilities, often via an extension method.

15.3.4 *Immutability*

Section 15.1.2 framed immutability as a key technique for success in functional programming. If a pure function returns data that is meant to be identical for a given input, allowing an object to change after the fact breaks the guarantees that purity bought us.

A primary feature of Kotlin that aids in our quest for immutability is the `val` declaration. `val` ensures a property may be written only during object construction, much like Java's `final`. In fact, `val` is effectively the same as Java's `final var` combination, but is also applicable to properties and much less awkward to write.

Chapter 9 covers the many locations where Kotlin supports use of `val`/`var`, but to succeed in functional programming, it's recommended to embrace immutability and favor `val` over `var`. Kotlin's built-in support for properties also sweeps away the getter boilerplate required in Java, as shown next:

```
class Point(val x: Int, val y: Int)

val point = Point(10, 20)
println(point.x)
// point.x = 20   // Won't compile because x is immutable!
```

A major hangup with immutable objects, though, is the difficulty when you actually want to change something. To retain our immutability, we must create entirely new instances, but this can be tedious and error prone. In Java, this is often tackled with static factory methods, builder objects, or wither methods to cut down on the noise.

Kotlin's `data class` construct gives us a nice alternative to those approaches. In addition to the constructor and equality operations we covered in section 9.3.1, a data class also gets a `copy` method. Pairing `copy` with Kotlin's named arguments, you can generate the new instance we want, writing out only the changes you actually want, as follows:

```
data class Point(val x: Int, val y: Int)

val point = Point(10, 20)
val offsetPoint = point.copy(x = 100)
```

`copy` does come with a couple important caveats. First, it is a shallow copy. If one of our fields is an object, we copy the reference to that object, not the full object itself. Like in Java, if any of the chain of objects allows mutation, then our guarantees are broken. For true immutability, all the objects involved need to play along, but the language will not enforce it for you.

Another point of caution is that `copy` is generated from the constructor of the class alone. If we bend our rules and put `var` fields elsewhere on our objects, `copy` doesn't know about these additional fields, and they get default values only in any copy, as shown here:

```
data class Point(val x: Int, val y: Int) {
  var shown: Boolean = false
}

val point = Point(10, 20)
point.shown = true

val newPoint = point.copy(x = 100)
println(newPoint.shown)
```

> Outputs false, because the non constructor fields aren't touched by copy

But we'd never let a mutable field sneak into our nice immutable objects to begin with, right?

Controlling the mutability of our objects is an important first step, but most non-trivial code will involve collections of objects, not just individual instances. We saw in chapter 9 that Kotlin's functions for constructing collections (e.g., listOf, mapOf) return interfaces such as kotlin.collections.List and kotlin.collections.Map, which, unlike their counterparts in java.util, are read-only. Sadly, although this is a good start, it doesn't provide us the guarantees we want.

We can't trust the immutability of these objects because the mutable interfaces extend the read-only flavors. Anywhere you can pass a List, you can pass a Mutable-List as follows:

```
fun takesList(list: List<String>) {
  println(list.size)
}

val mutable = mutableListOf("Oh", "hi")
takesList(mutable)

mutable.add("there")
takesList(mutable)
```

takesList receives the same object in both invocations, but the result of the call is different. Our functionality purity is shattered!

> **NOTE** The read-only helpers like listOf use underlying JDK collections and return objects that are read-only. For instance, listOf defaults to an array-backed list implementation that cannot be added to. It's just the mix of Kotlin's mutable interfaces with the standard read-only interfaces that spoil the party.

Implementing these collections via JDK classes also leaves some sharp edges if you cast between interfaces. Kotlin's aim for clean interoperation with Java Collections means the result from listOf() can be cast to both Kotlin's mutable interfaces and the classic java.util.List<T> where we can attempt to modify the collection! The following code compiles without a complaint but fails at runtime:

```
fun takesMutableList(muted: MutableList<Int>) {
  muted.add(4)
}

val list = listOf(1,2,3)
takesMutableList(list as MutableList<Int>)
```

This call will throw a java.lang.UnsupportedOperationException.

This lack of real immutability becomes problematic especially when we're talking about concurrency. As we saw in chapter 6, making mutable collections safe between multiple threads takes quite an effort. If we had a collection instance that was truly immutable, though, that could be freely distributed among different threads of execution, assured that everyone is getting an identical picture of the world.

Although Kotlin doesn't have them in the standard library, the `kotlinx.collections.immutable` library (see http://mng.bz/nNjg) provides a variety of immutable and *persistent* data structures. Frequently seen libraries such as Guava and Apache Commons also have many similar options.

What does it mean for a collection to be persistent? As we've discussed multiple times, immutability means that when you need to "change" an object, you instead create a new instance of it. For large collections, this could be really inefficient. Persistent collections lean on immutability to lower that cost of modification—they are built to safely share immutable parts of their internal storage. Though you still create a new object to effect any change, those new objects can be much smaller than a full copy, as shown next:

```
import kotlinx.collections.immutable.persistentListOf

val pers = persistentListOf(1, 2, 3)
val added = pers.add(4)
println(pers)
println(added)
```

Prints [1, 2, 3]

Prints [1, 2, 3, 4]

The core of the library implements two groups of interfaces typified by `Immutable-List` and `PersistentList`. Matching pairs exist for maps, sets, and general collections as well. `ImmutableList` extends `List`, but unlike its base interface, it guarantees any instance is immutable. `ImmutableList` can then be used in any locations where you're passing lists and want to enforce immutability. `PersistentList` builds off of `ImmutableList` to provide us with the "modify and return" methods.

The library also includes the following familiar extensions for converting other collections into persistent versions:

```
val mutable = mutableListOf(1,2,3)
val immutable = mutable.toImmutableList()
val persistent = mutable.toPersistentList()
```

At this point, you might be wondering why we don't change every `listOf` to `persistentListOf` "just in case." But these aren't the default implementation for a reason. Although persistent data structures lower the cost of copies, they still can't touch the speed of classic mutable data structures. Less copying *does not* equal no copying! How much does this cost?

As chapter 7 has hopefully convinced you, the only way to know is to measure in your own use cases. But if you need concurrent access to a collection across threads, it's worth comparing how these persistent structures perform versus more standard copying with synchronization. Now that we have Kotlin's toolkit for making data immutable in hand, let's look at a feature it brings to the world of recursive functions.

15.3.5 *Tail recursion*

In section 15.2.4, we examined recursive functions in Java. They have a major limitation because each successive recursive function call adds a stack frame, which eventually exhausts the available space. Kotlin has the same limitation with basic recursion, as we can see from the translation of our `simpleFactorial` function to Kotlin (note the use of a Kotlin `if` expression as the return value):

```kotlin
fun simpleFactorial(n: Long): Long {
  return if (n <= 0) {
    1
  } else {
    n * simpleFactorial(n - 1)
  }
}
```

This yields the following bytecode, which is equivalent to what `javac` emitted for our Java function:

```
public final long simpleFactorial(long);
    Code:
        0: lload_1
        1: lconst_0
        2: lcmp
        3: ifgt          10
        6: lconst_1
        7: goto          22
       10: lload_1
       11: aload_0
       12: checkcast     #2                 // class Factorial
       15: lload_1
       16: lconst_1
       17: lsub
       18: invokevirtual #19                // Method simpleFactorial:(J)J
       21: lmul
       22: lreturn
```

Apart from a little additional validation (byte 12) and the use of a `goto` instead of multiple `lreturn` instructions, this is fundamentally the same. The recursive call at byte 18 where we `invokevirtual` on `simpleFactorial` will eventually blow the stack, as shown here:

```
java.lang.StackOverflowError
    at Factorial.simpleFactorial(factorial.kts:32)
    at Factorial.simpleFactorial(factorial.kts:32)
    at Factorial.simpleFactorial(factorial.kts:32)
 . . .
```

Although this problem is unavoidable in the general case, Kotlin can help us out if our function is tail-recursive. Remember that a tail-recursive function is one where the recursion is the last operation in the entire function. Earlier, we showed how at the bytecode level we could reset state and `goto` the top of the function instead of adding a stack frame. This transforms our recursive call into a loop, with no danger of overflowing the stack. Java didn't provide us any way to do this, but Kotlin does.

> **NOTE** Any recursive function can be rewritten to be tail-recursive. It may require additional parameters, variables, and tricks to do the transformation, but it is always possible. Given that tail-recursive functions can be transformed into simple looping, this shows that any recursive function can also be implemented iteratively using only loop constructs.

Getting our factorial recursive call into the final position takes a little shuffling. As in Java, we split the function to retain the nice single-argument form for users and put the more complicated recursive function—which now needs multiple arguments—into a separate function like this:

```
fun tailrecFactorial(n: Long): Long {
  return if (n <= 0) {
    1
  } else {
    helpFact(n, 1)
  }
}

tailrec fun helpFact(i: Long, j: Long): Long {    ⟵┐  Our helper is marked tailrec
  return if (i == 0L) {                              │  so Kotlin knows to look for
    j                                                └─ tail recursion.
  } else {
    helpFact(i - 1, i * j)
  }
}
```

The entry function `tailrecFactorial` doesn't hide any surprises in the bytecode. It does our beginning range check and then hands off to our tail-recursive helper as follows:

```
public final long tailrecFactorial(long);
    Code:
        0: lload_1
        1: lconst_0
        2: lcmp
        3: ifgt          10
        6: lconst_1
        7: goto          19
       10: aload_0
       11: checkcast     #2                    // class Factorial
       14: lload_1
       15: lconst_1
       16: invokevirtual #10                   // Method helpFact:(JJ)J
       19: lreturn
```

Bytes 0–3 check for an early return implemented by bytes 6–7. If we need to make the recursive call, then it loads up the values needed to invokevirtual for helpFact at byte 16.

The important difference the tailrec keyword introduces shows up in the bytecode for helpFact, shown here:

```
public final long helpFact(long, long);
    Code:
        0: lload_1
        1: lconst_0
        2: lcmp
        3: ifne          10
        6: lload_3
        7: goto          26
       10: aload_0
       11: checkcast     #2                    // class Factorial
       14: pop
       15: lload_1
       16: lconst_1
       17: lsub
       18: lload_1
       19: lload_3
       20: lmul
       21: lstore_3
       22: lstore_1
       23: goto          0
       26: lreturn
```

The majority of this method is doing the logical checks and arithmetic of our factorial, but the key is at byte 23. Instead of doing an invokevirtual for helpFact to recurse, instead we simply goto 0 and start the function again. With no invoke instructions present, we have no danger of stack overflows, which is great news. Who says goto is always hazardous?

Tail recursion is an elegant solution when your function can be rewritten in the proper form. But what if you ask for it on a function that isn't tail-recursive, as shown next:

```
tailrec fun simpleFactorial(n: Long): Long {
  return if (n <= 0) {
    1
  } else {
    n * simpleFactorial(n - 1)
  }
}
```

Inappropriately asking for tailrec when our final call isn't ourselves—in this case, the final operation is the * on the result of the recursive call.

Kotlin spots the problem and warns us that it can't transform the bytecode to take advantage of tail recursion, pointing us straight to our incorrect, not-at-the-end call like so:

```
factorial.kts:28:1: warning: a function is marked as tail-recursive
                    but no tail calls are found

tailrec fun simpleFactorial(n: Long): Long {
^
factorial.kts:32:9: warning: recursive call is not a tail call
    n * simpleFactorial(n - 1)
        ^
```

Issuing a warning is not an especially strong behavior for the compiler because it's possible that after a tail-recursive implementation has been created, it can be subsequently subtly modified to *not* be tail-recursive. Unless the build process flags the warning, this code can escape into production and cause a StackOverflowError at runtime. Arguably, it would be better if declaring a non-tail-recursive function as tailrec caused a compilation error, as is done in some other languages (e.g., Scala).

15.3.6 *Lazy evaluation*

As we mentioned earlier in the chapter, many functional languages (such as Haskell) rely heavily on *lazy evaluation*. As a language on the JVM, Kotlin doesn't center lazy evaluation in its core execution model. But it does bring first-class support for laziness where you want it via the Lazy<T> interface. This provides a standard structure for when you want to delay—or potentially skip entirely—a bit of processing.

Typically you don't implement Lazy<T> yourself, but instead use the lazy() function to construct instances. In the simplest form, lazy() takes a lambda, the return type of which determines the type T of the returned interface. The lambda is not executed until value is explicitly requested. We can also check whether we've calculated the value already as follows:

```
val lazing = lazy {
  42
}

println("init? ${lazing.isInitialized()}")
println("value = ${lazing.value}")
println("init? ${lazing.isInitialized()}")
```

Checks whether we're initialized; will report false

Access to value will force our lambda to execute and save the result.

Checks whether we're initialized; will report true

Our desire to put off unneeded computation may overlap with the need to execute across multiple threads. When that happens, lazy() takes a LazyThreadSafetyMode enumeration to help control how that happens. The enum values are SYNCHRONIZED (the default for lazy()), PUBLICATION, and NONE, described here:

- SYNCHRONIZED uses the Lazy<T> instance itself to synchronize execution of the initializing lambda.
- PUBLICATION instead allows multiple concurrent executions of the initialization lambda but saves only the first value seen.
- NONE skips synchronization, with undefined behavior if accessed concurrently.

NOTE LazyThreadSafetyMode.NONE should be used only if you've 1) measured that synchronization in your lazy instances is an actual performance problem and 2) can somehow guarantee you'll never access the object from multiple threads. The other options, SYNCHRONIZED and PUBLICATION, can be chosen between based on whether your use case is sensitive to the initialization lambda running multiple times concurrently.

The Lazy<T> interface is designed to work with another advanced Kotlin feature called *delegated properties*. When defining a property on a class, instead of providing the value or a custom getter/setter, you can instead provide an object with the by keyword. That object must have an implementation of getValue() and (for var properties) setValue(). Lazy<T> fits this specification, as shown next, so we can easily put off initializing properties in our classes without repeating boilerplate or veering away from natural Kotlin syntax:

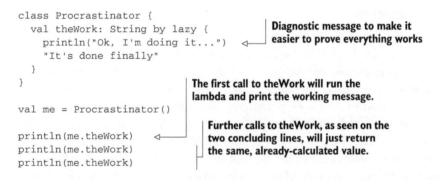

```
class Procrastinator {
  val theWork: String by lazy {          Diagnostic message to make it
    println("Ok, I'm doing it...")   ◁── easier to prove everything works
    "It's done finally"
  }
}
                                    The first call to theWork will run the
val me = Procrastinator()           lambda and print the working message.

println(me.theWork)   ◁──           Further calls to theWork, as seen on the
println(me.theWork)                 two concluding lines, will just return
println(me.theWork)                 the same, already-calculated value.
```

Much like immutability, laziness is excellent for our own objects but leaves us wondering about collections and iteration. Next we'll look at how Kotlin allows us to better control the flow of execution when streaming through collections with the Sequence<T> interface.

15.3.7 Sequences

Although Kotlin's collection functions are frequently convenient, they assume we will eagerly apply the function to the entire collection. An intermediate collection is created for each step in our chain of functions, as shown next—potentially a waste if we don't actually need the whole result:

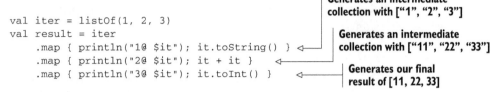

```
val iter = listOf(1, 2, 3)
val result = iter
    .map { println("1@ $it"); it.toString() }
    .map { println("2@ $it"); it + it }
    .map { println("3@ $it"); it.toInt() }
```

Generates an intermediate collection with ["1", "2", "3"]

Generates an intermediate collection with ["11", "22", "33"]

Generates our final result of [11, 22, 33]

If we follow the execution via figure 15.1, we can see each step of our chain of map calls happens on the full list before the next map runs.

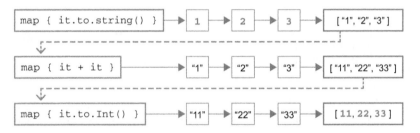

```
val iter = listOf(1, 2, 3)
val result = iter
    .map { it.toString() }
    .map { it + it }
    .map { it.toInt() }
```

Figure 15.1   Standard iteration through collections

This results in the following output:

```
1@ 1
1@ 2
1@ 3
2@ 1
2@ 2
2@ 3
3@ 11
3@ 22
3@ 33
```

Beyond the possibility for wasted resources, there are also use cases where our inputs are potentially infinite. What if we wanted to continue this mapping across as many numbers as we can until the user tells us to stop? We can't create the list ahead of time and process the full thing step by step.

To handle this, Kotlin has *sequences*. At the core of sequences is the interface Sequence<T>, which looks similar to Iterable<T> but under the covers gives us a whole new set of capabilities.

We can create a new sequence using the `sequenceOf()` function and then start applying functions just like the collections we're used to. In the following example, we've turned our list into a sequence and kept the diagnostic prints so we can see what's going on:

```
val seq = sequenceOf(1, 2, 3)
val result = seq
    .map { println("1@ $it"); it.toString() }
    .map { println("2@ $it"); it + it }
    .map { println("3@ $it"); it.toInt() }
```

Note that + here is string concatenation, not numeric addition.

When we run this short program we'll find that nothing prints. The primary feature of sequences is that they are lazy in their evaluation. Nothing in this program actually requires the return of our `map` calls, so Kotlin just doesn't run them! If we turn the sequence into a list using the following code, though, the program will be forced to evaluate everything and we can see how the control flow of the sequence runs:

```
val seq = sequenceOf(1, 2, 3)
val result = seq
    .map { println("1@ $it"); it.toString() }
    .map { println("2@ $it"); it + it }
    .map { println("3@ $it"); it.toInt() }
    .toList()
```

We can see in figure 15.2 that each element of the sequence goes through the `map` chain individually, first 1, then 2, and so on, before the next element is processed.

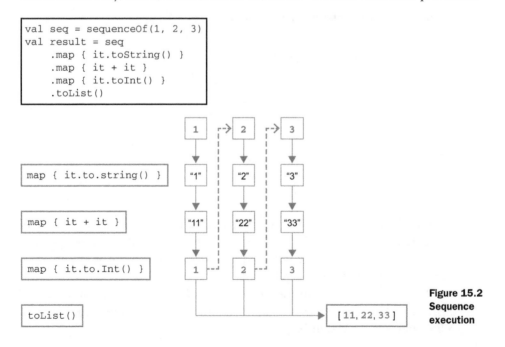

Figure 15.2 Sequence execution

This will have the following output:

```
1@ 1
2@ 1
3@ 11
1@ 2
2@ 2
3@ 22
1@ 3
2@ 3
3@ 33
```

This is interesting, but on relatively small, static lists, probably not that compelling—proper measurement is deserved, but the bookkeeping that sequences require may well drown out the wins for not allocating intermediate collections. The power of sequences becomes clearer with the alternative ways of creating sequences.

Our first stop is the asSequence() function. This will, unsurprisingly, turn things that are iterable into a sequence. The function works with more than just the lists and collections you might expect, though, and may be called on *ranges.*

We met Kotlin's numeric ranges back in section 9.2.6 where they were used to check inclusion with when expressions. But ranges may be iterated across, too. We can combine this with asSequence() to create long numeric lists without bothersome typing or over allocating, as shown next:

```
(0..1000000000)          ◄──┐  Range tracks only its begin and end,
  .asSequence()              │  so we don't create a billion elements.
  .map { it * 2 }
```

But what if even the large-but-still-bounded nature of ranges feels too restrictive? generateSequence() from kotlin.sequences in the standard library has you covered. This function creates a new general sequence object with an optional starting value. Each time it needs the next element, it runs the provided lambda, passing in the prior value, like this:

```
generateSequence(0) { it + 2 }    ◄──── An infinite sequence of even numbers
```

An infinite Iterable<T> would be impossible to chain methods with because the first call on it would never return. Sequence<T> will just get what it needs and leave the rest for later. This pairs nicely with the take() function, where we can ask for a specific number of elements to be retrieved as a new, bounded sequence like so:

```
generateSequence(0) { it + 2 }         Creates a sequence with the
  .take(3)                        ◄──── first three elements in it
  .forEach { println(it) }    ◄──┐
                                 │  Forces evaluation through the
                                 │  sequence and prints what we received
```

`forEach()` on sequences is what's referred to as *terminal*, because it ends the sequence's laziness and evaluates everything it has. We've seen another terminal already with `toList()`, which necessarily steps through every element to construct a list.

Kotlin offers another option for creating a sequence if, for some reason, it's difficult to work from just the prior element in the sequence. The pairing of `sequence()` with `yield()` lets us construct completely arbitrary sequences as follows:

```
val yielded = sequence {
  yield(1)
  yield(100)
  yieldAll(listOf(42, 3))    ⟵─── yieldAll() takes an iterable of the same
}                                   type we're yielding and will yield each
                                    element in turn when asked.
```

As we'd expect with sequences, the lambda is lazily executed to determine the next element. What's unique here, though, is that for each call for the next element, the lambda runs only until the next `yield` and then pauses. A subsequent request for another element will resume the lambda where it had paused and run until the next `yield` again, as shown in figure 15.3.

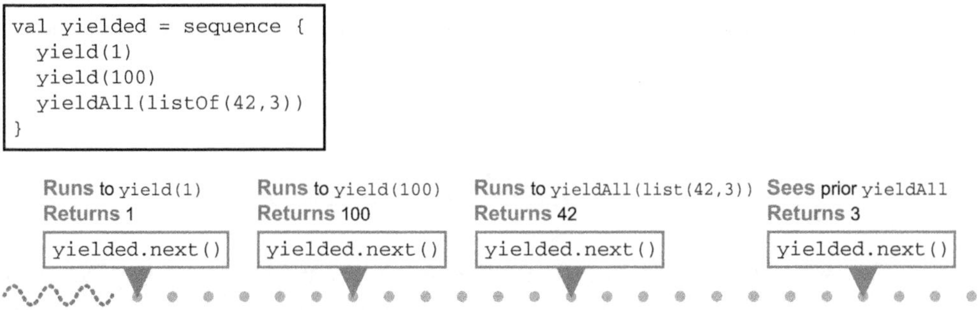

Figure 15.3   Timeline view of yield execution

`yield` uses a Kotlin feature known as *suspend* functions. As the name suggests, these are functions where Kotlin recognizes points in code execution that can stop and resume. In this case, Kotlin sees that each time we `yield` a value, execution of our sequence lambda should pause until the next value is requested. Though our code looks like a simple lambda, the Kotlin compiler is actually doing a lot of additional work for us behind the scenes.

Suspend functions are deeply related to Kotlin's alternative concurrency model, coroutines, which we introduced in section 9.4 and will discuss in more detail in chapter 16. It's an interesting point to note, though, that a feature that we often consider in light of concurrency also unlocks unique ways of functional programming as well.

15.4   *Clojure FP*

We met the basics of functional programming in Clojure in chapter 10 with forms like
(map). We also had early introductions to concepts like immutability and higher-order
functions because those ideas and capabilities are very close to the core of the Clojure
programming model.

So, in this section, rather than introducing the Clojure take on the features we
discussed for Java and Kotlin, we will go beyond those foundations and show how
some of Clojure's more advanced functional features work, starting with a note on list
comprehensions.

15.4.1   *Comprehensions*

An important idea in functional programming is the concept of a *comprehension*, where
the word means a "complete description" of a set or other data structure. This concept is derived from mathematics, where we often see set-theoretic notation used to
describe sets, like this:

```
{ x ∈ ℕ : (x / 2) ∈ ℕ }
```

In this notation, ∈ means "is a member of," ℕ is the infinite set of all *natural numbers*
(or counting numbers), which are the numbers we would use to count objects (so 1, 2,
3, and so on), and the : defines a condition or a *restriction*.

So this comprehension is describing a set of counting numbers that have a special
property: every number in the set, when divided by two, yields a number that is also a
counting number. Of course, we already know this set by another name—it is the set
of even numbers.

The key point is that we did not specify the set of even numbers by listing out the
elements (that would be impossible—there are an infinite number of them). Instead,
we defined "even numbers" by starting from the natural numbers and specifying an
additional condition that had to hold for each element to be included in the new set.

If that sounds a bit like the use of functional techniques, such as filter, then it
should—they are very closely related concepts. However, functional languages often
offer both comprehensions and filter-map because each approach turns out to be
conceptually easier to use in different circumstances.

Clojure implements *list comprehensions* using the (for) form to return either a list
(or an iterator, in some cases). This is why, when we met Clojure loops in chapter 10,
we didn't introduce (for)—it isn't really a loop. Let's see it in action:

```
user=> (for [x [1 2 3]] (* x x))
(1 4 9)
```

The (for) form takes two arguments: an argument vector, and a form that will represent the values to *yield* as part of the overall list that (for) will return.

The argument vector contains a pair (or multiple pairs) of elements: a temporary that will be used in the definition of the yielded values and a seq to provide the inputs. We can think of the temporary as being used to bind each of the values, in turn. This could, of course, easily be written as a map like this:

```
user=> (map #(* % %) [1 2 3])
(1 4 9)
```

So, where would we want to use (for)? It comes into its own when we have more complex structures to build up, for example:

```
(for [num [1 2 3]
      ch [:a :b :c]]
  (str num ch))
("1:a" "1:b" "1:c" "2:a" "2:b" "2:c" "3:a" "3:b" "3:c")
```

We could also do this with a map, but the construction would potentially be more complex and cumbersome, whereas with (for) it is clear and straightforward. To get the effect of a filter, we can also use an additional qualifier on the (for) that can act as a restriction, as follows:

```
user=> (for [x (range 8) :when (even? x)] x)
(0 2 4 6)
```

Let's move on to look at how Clojure implements laziness, especially as applied to sequences.

15.4.2 *Lazy sequences*

In Clojure, laziness is mostly commonly seen when working with sequences rather than lazy evaluation of a single value. For sequences, laziness means that instead of having a complete list of every value that's in a sequence, values can instead be obtained when they're required (such as by calling a function to generate them on demand).

In the Java Collections, such an idea would require something like a custom implementation of List, and there would be no convenient way to write it without large amounts of boilerplate code. Using an implementation of ISeq, on the other hand, would allow us to write something like this:

```
public class SquareSeq implements ISeq {
    private final int current;

    private SquareSeq(int current) {
        this.current = current;
    }

    public static SquareSeq of(int start) {
        if (start < 0) {
```

```
            return new SquareSeq(-start);
        }
        return new SquareSeq(start);
    }

    @Override
    public Object first() {
        return Integer.valueOf(current * current);
    }

    @Override
    public ISeq rest() {
        return new SquareSeq(current + 1);
    }
}
```

There is no storage of values, and instead, each new element of the sequence is generated on demand. This allows us to model infinite sequences. Or consider this example:

```
public class IntGeneratorSeq implements ISeq {
  private final int current;
  private final Function<Integer, Integer> generator;

  private IntGeneratorSeq(int seed,
                          Function<Integer, Integer> generator) {
      this.current = seed;
      this.generator = generator;
  }

  public static IntGeneratorSeq of(int seed,
                                   Function<Integer, Integer> generator) {
      return new IntGeneratorSeq(seed, generator);
  }

  @Override
  public Object first() {
      return generator.apply(current);
  }

  @Override
  public ISeq rest() {
      return new IntGeneratorSeq(generator.apply(current), generator);
  }
}
```

This code sample uses the result of applying the function to provide the seed of the next sequence. This is fine, provided that the generator function is pure, but, of course, nothing guarantees that in Java. Let's move on and take a look at some powerful Clojure macros designed to help you create lazy seqs with only a small amount of effort.

Consider how you could represent a lazy, potentially infinite sequence. One obvious choice would be to use a function to generate items in the sequence. The function should do two things:

- Return the next item in a sequence
- Take a fixed, finite number of arguments

Mathematicians would say that such a function defines a *recurrence relation,* and the theory of such relations immediately suggests that recursion is an appropriate way to proceed.

Imagine you have a machine in which stack space and other constraints aren't present, and suppose that you can set up two threads of execution: one will prepare the infinite sequence, and the other will use it. Then you could use recursion to define the lazy seq in the generation thread with something like the following snippet of pseudocode:

```
(defn infinite-seq <vec-args>
  (let [new-val (seq-fn <vec-args>)]
    (cons new-val (infinite-seq <new-vec-args>))
  ))
```

This doesn't actually work, because the recursive call to (infinite-seq) blows up the stack.

The solution is to add a construct that tells Clojure to optimize the recursion away and only proceed as needed: the (lazy-seq) macro. Let's look at a quick example in the next listing that defines the lazy sequence k, k+1, k+2, ... for some number *k.*

Listing 15.1   Lazy sequence example

```
(defn next-big-n [n] (let [new-val (+ 1 n)]
  (lazy-seq                                  <—— lazy-seq marker
    (cons new-val (next-big-n new-val))  <—┐
  )))                                        │ Infinite recursion

(defn natural-k [k]
  (concat [k] (next-big-n k)))   <—— concat constrains recursion.

1:57 user=> (take 10 (natural-k 3))
(3 4 5 6 7 8 9 10 11 12)
```

The key points are the form (lazy-seq), which marks a point where an infinite recursion could occur, and the (concat) form, which handles it safely. You can then use the (take) form to pull the required number of elements from the lazy sequence. Lazy sequences are an extremely powerful feature, and with practice, you'll find them a very useful tool in your Clojure arsenal.

15.4.3 *Currying in Clojure*

Currying functions in Clojure has an additional complexity compared to other languages. This is caused by the fact that many Clojure forms are variadic, as we discussed in chapter 10.

Variadic functions are a complication because they raise questions like: "Does the user mean to curry the two-argument form or evaluate the one-argument form?"—especially because Clojure uses eager evaluation of functions.

The solution is the (partial) form, which, by the way, is a genuine Clojure function, not a macro. Let's see it in action:

```
user=> (filter (partial = :b) [:a :b :c :b :d])
(:b :b)
```

The function = takes 1 or more arguments, and so (= :b) would eagerly evaluate to true, but the use of (partial) turns it into a curried function. Its use in a (filter) call causes it to be recognized as a function of one argument (effectively, the one-argument overload), and then it is used to test each element in the following vector.

> **NOTE** (partial) by itself will curry only the first parameter of a form. If we wanted to curry some other parameter, we would need to combine (partial) with another form—one that permuted the argument list before function application.

Clojure is by far the most functional of the three languages we have looked at, and if the treatment here has whetted your appetite, you have a great deal more that you can explore. What we have covered so far is only the beginning, but it does help to demonstrate that the JVM itself can be a good home for functional programming—it's more the Java language that encumbers programming in a functional style.

In this chapter, we have delved far deeper into functional programming than just the traditional filter-map-reduce paradigm of Java Streams. We have largely done so by moving outside of Java to other JVM languages.

It is, of course, possible to go even further than this. Two major schools of functional programming exist: the dynamically typed school, as represented by Clojure (and languages like Erlang outside of the JVM), and the statically typed school, which includes Kotlin but is perhaps better represented by Scala (and Haskell for non-JVM languages).

However, one of Java's major design virtues—backward compatibility—can also be seen as a potential weakness. Java code that was compiled for version 1.0 (more than 25 years ago) will still run without modification on modern JVMs. However, this remarkable achievement does not come without a price tag. Java's APIs and even the design of the bytecode and JVM have to live with design decisions that are difficult or impossible to change now and that are not especially friendly to FP. This is one major reason developers who want to use functional styles frequently find themselves moving to non-Java JVM languages.

Summary

- Filter-map-reduce is the starting point, not the end point, of functional programming.
- Java is not a language that is especially suited to a functional style, because it lacks built-in features like lazy evaluation, currying, and tail-recursion optimization.
- Other languages on the JVM can do a better job of supporting FP, with features such as Kotlin's `Lazy<T>` and Clojure's lazy sequences.
- Issues still exist at the JVM level, such as default mutability of data, that changing the choice of programming language cannot fundamentally fix.

Advanced concurrent programming

In this chapter, we will bring together several themes from earlier chapters. In particular, we will weave together the functional programming concepts from previous chapters with the Java concurrency libraries from chapter 6. Our non-Java languages get included as well, with some novel concurrency aspects of both Kotlin and Clojure appearing later in the chapter.

> **NOTE** The concepts in this chapter, such as coroutines and agents (aka actors), are also increasingly part of the landscape of Java concurrency.

We'll kick off with a slight oddity: the Java Fork/Join API. This framework allows a certain class of concurrent problems to be handled more efficiently than the executors we saw in chapter 6.

16.1 The Fork/Join framework

As we discussed in chapter 7, processor speeds (or, more properly, transistor counts on CPUs) have increased hugely in recent years. I/O performance has not had the same remarkable improvement, and so the end result is that waiting for I/O is now a common situation. This suggests that we could make better use of the processing capabilities inside our computers. The Fork/Join (F/J) framework is an attempt to do just that.

F/J is all about automatic scheduling of tasks on a thread pool that is invisible to the user. To do this, the tasks must be able to be broken up in a way that the user specifies. In many applications, F/J has a notion of "small" and "large" tasks that is very natural for the framework.

Let's take a quick look at some of the headline facts and fundamentals related to F/J:

- The framework introduces a new kind of executor service, called a `ForkJoinPool`.
- `ForkJoinPool` handles a unit of concurrency (the `ForkJoinTask`) that is "smaller" than a `Thread`.
- `ForkJoinTask` can be scheduled in a more lightweight manner by the `ForkJoinPool`.
- F/J makes use of the following two kinds of tasks (both represented as instances of `ForkJoinTask`):
  - "Small" tasks are those that can be performed straightaway without consuming too much processor time.
  - "Large" tasks are those that need to be split up (possibly more than once) before they can be directly performed.
- The framework provides basic methods to support the splitting up of large tasks.
- The framework has automatic scheduling and rescheduling.

One key feature of the framework is that it's expected that these lightweight tasks may well spawn other instances of `ForkJoinTask`, which will be scheduled on the same thread pool that executed their parent task. This pattern is sometimes called *divide and conquer.*

We'll start with a simple example of using the F/J framework, then briefly touch on the features of problems that are well suited to this type of parallel processing approach. We will then discuss the feature called "work-stealing" as used in F/J and its relevance in a wider context. The best way to get started with F/J is with an example.

16.1.1 A simple F/J example

As a simple example of what the F/J framework can do, consider the following case: we have a number of transaction objects created at various times. The class we'll use to represent them is `Transaction`, as shown here, which is an evolution of the `Transfer-Task` class we met in chapters 5 and 6:

```java
public class Transaction implements Comparable<Transaction> {
    private final Account sender;
    private final Account receiver;
    private final int amount;
    private final long id;
    private final LocalDateTime time;

    private static final AtomicLong counter = new AtomicLong(1);

    Transaction(Account sender, Account receiver,
                int amount, LocalDateTime time) {
        this.sender = sender;
        this.receiver = receiver;
        this.amount = amount;
        this.id = counter.getAndIncrement();
        this.time = time;
    }

    public static Transaction of(Account sender, Account receiver,
                                 int amount) {
        return new Transaction(sender, receiver,
                               amount, LocalDateTime.now());
    }

    @Override
    public int compareTo(Transaction other) {
        return Comparator.nullsFirst(LocalDateTime::compareTo)
                         .compare(this.time, other.time);
    }

    // Getter and other methods (equals, hashcode, etc) elided
}
```

We want to obtain a list of transactions, sorted by time. To achieve this, we'll use F/J as a multithreaded sort—in fact a variant of the *MergeSort* algorithm.

Our example uses `RecursiveAction`, which is a specialized subclass of `ForkJoinTask`. It is simpler than general `ForkJoinTask` because it's explicit about not having any overall result (the transactions will be reordered in place), and it emphasizes the recursive nature of the tasks.

The `TransactionSorter` class provides a way of ordering a list of updates using the `compareTo()` method on `Transaction` objects. The `compute()` method (which you have to implement because it's abstract in the RecursiveAction superclass) basically orders an array of transactions by their creation time, as shown in the next listing.

Listing 16.1   Sorting with a `RecursiveAction`

```
public class TransactionSorter extends RecursiveAction {
    private static final int SMALL_ENOUGH = 32;          ◁───────┐  32 or fewer
    private final Transaction[] transactions;                    │  sorted serially
    private final int start, end;
    private final Transaction[] result;

    public TransactionSorter(List<Transaction> transactions) {
        this(transactions.toArray(new Transaction[0]),
            0, transactions.size());
    }

    public TransactionSorter(Transaction[] transactions) {
        this(transactions, 0, transactions.length);
    }

    public TransactionSorter(Transaction[] txns, int start, int end) {
        this.start = start;
        this.end = end;
        this.transactions = txns;
        this.result = new Transaction[this.transactions.length];
    }

    /**
     * This method implements a simple Mergesort. Please consult a suitable
     * textbook if you are interested in the implementation details.
     *
     * @param left
     * @param right
     */
    private void merge(TransactionSorter left, TransactionSorter right) {
        int i = 0;
        int lCount = 0;
        int rCount = 0;

        while (lCount < left.size() && rCount < right.size()) {
            int comp = left.result[lCount].compareTo(right.result[rCount]);
            result[i++] = (comp < 0)
                    ? left.result[lCount++]
                    : right.result[rCount++];
        }

        while (lCount < left.size()) {
            result[i++] = left.result[lCount++];
        }

        while (rCount < right.size()) {
            result[i++] = right.result[rCount++];
        }
    }
```

```
    public int size() {
        return end - start;
    }

    public Transaction[] getResult() {
        return result;
    }

    @Override                              The method defined
    protected void compute() {        ◄─── in RecursiveAction
        if (size() < SMALL_ENOUGH) {
            System.arraycopy(transactions, start, result, 0, size());
            Arrays.sort(result, 0, size());
        } else {
            int mid = size() / 2;
            TransactionSorter left =
                new TransactionSorter(transactions, start, start + mid);
            TransactionSorter right =
                new TransactionSorter(transactions, start + mid, end);
            invokeAll(left, right);

            merge(left, right);
        }
    }
}
```

To use the sorter, you can drive it with some code like that shown next, which will generate some transactions and shuffle them, before passing them to the sorter. The output is the reordered updates:

```
var transactions = new ArrayList<Transaction>();
var accs = new Account[] {
            new Account(1000),
            new Account(1000)};

for (var i = 0; i < 256; i = i + 1) {
  transactions.add(Transaction.of(accs[i % 2], accs[(i + 1) % 2], 1));
  Thread.sleep(1);
}
Collections.shuffle(transactions);

var sorter = new TransactionSorter(transactions);
var pool = new ForkJoinPool(4);

pool.invoke(sorter);

for (var txn : sorter.getResult()) {
  System.out.println(txn);
}
```

The promise of F/J seems tantalizing, but in practice, not every problem is easily reduced to as simple a form as the multithreaded MergeSort we've just discussed.

This is an example of the antipattern *Easy Cases Are Easy*, in which developers can be seduced by a simple-seeming technology that allows an easy task to be achieved with very little effort but disguises the fact that the technology does not scale or generalize well to the less-easy cases. We should say something about the sorts of problems that are likely to be tractable by the use of F/J, and those problems for which another approach will likely be better.

16.1.2 *Parallelizing problems for F/J*

Here are some examples of problems well suited to the F/J approach:

- Simulating the motion of large numbers of simple objects (e.g., particle effects)
- Log file analysis
- Data operations where a quantity is calculated from aggregated inputs (e.g., map-reduce operations)

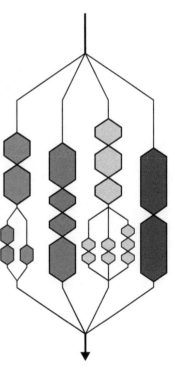

Another way of looking at this is to say that a good problem for F/J is one that can be broken up, as shown in figure 16.1.

One practical way of determining whether a problem is likely to reduce well is to apply the following checklist to the problem and its subtasks:

- Can the problem's subtasks work without explicit cooperation or synchronization between the subtasks?
- Do the subtasks calculate some value from their data without altering it (i.e., are they pure functions)?
- Is divide and conquer natural for the subtasks?

If the answer to the preceding questions is "Yes!" or "Mostly, but with edge cases," your problem may well be amenable to a F/J approach. If, on the other hand, the answer to those questions is "Maybe" or "Not really," you may well find that F/J performs poorly, and a different approach may work better.

Designing good multithreaded algorithms is hard, and F/J doesn't work in every circumstance. It's very useful within its own domain of applicability,

Figure 16.1 Fork and join

but in the end, you have to decide whether your problem fits within the framework. If not, you must be prepared to develop your own solution, which probably means building on top of the superb toolbox of `java.util.concurrent`.

16.1.3   *Work-stealing algorithms*

`ForkJoinTask` is the superclass of `RecursiveAction`. It's a generic class in the return type of an action (so `RecursiveAction` extends `ForkJoinTask<Void>`). This makes `ForkJoinTask` very suitable for map-reduce approaches that boil down a dataset and either return a result or act via side effect (as is the case for `RecursiveAction`).

Objects of type `ForkJoinTask` are scheduled on a `ForkJoinPool`, which is a new type of executor service designed specifically for these lightweight tasks. The service maintains a list of tasks for each thread, and if one task finishes, the service can reassign tasks from a fully loaded thread to an idle one. We can see this happening in figure 16.2

Without this *work-stealing algorithm*, scheduling problems could arise related to the two sizes of tasks. In general, the two sizes of tasks could take very different lengths of time to run.

For example, one thread may have a run queue consisting of only small tasks, whereas another may have only large tasks. If the small tasks run five times faster than large tasks, the thread with only small tasks may well find itself idle before the large-task thread finishes.

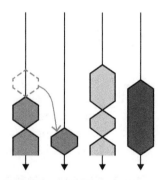

Figure 16.2   Work-stealing: When the second thread completes its task, the service reassigns a task from the still-busy first thread to the second.

> **WARNING** Work-stealing depends on the assumption that the tasks are independent of each other. If this assumption is not valid, the results of calculations could be different from run to run.

Work-stealing has been implemented precisely to work around this problem and allow all the pool threads to be used throughout the lifecycle of the F/J job. It's completely automatic, and you don't need to do anything specific to reap the benefits of work-stealing. It's another example of the runtime environment doing more to help developers manage concurrency, rather than making it a manual task. The documentation also makes it explicit: `ForkJoinPool` may also be appropriate for use with event-style tasks that are never joined.

> **NOTE** `ForkJoinPool` is also used in popular Java/JVM libraries, such as the Akka system of actor-based concurrency in Scala and Java.

To interact with a `ForkJoinPool`, the class exposes the following primary methods:

- `execute()`—Starts an asynchronous execution
- `invoke()`—Starts execution and awaits the result
- `submit()`—Starts execution and returns a future for the result

Since Java 8, the runtime has included a common pool, which is accessed via `ForkJoinPool.commonPool()`. This is provided primarily for its work-stealing capabilities—there is not a lot of expectation that many programs will use it for recursive decomposition.

The common pool has a number of configurable properties that can be set to control things like the parallelism level (i.e.. how many threads to use) and the thread factory class used to create new threads for the common pool.

16.2   *Concurrency and functional programming*

In chapter 5, we met the concept of immutable objects and showed that they are extremely useful for concurrent programming because they sidestep the problem of *shared mutable state*, which is at the heart of so many concurrency problems. So, we might guess that functional techniques that utilize immutability are an important tool for building concurrent applications. This is true, but a small extension to immutability is also relevant to concurrent programming.

16.2.1   *CompletableFuture revisited*

In chapter 6, we met the `CompletableFuture` class. This type is not immutable, but it has a very simple state model, described next:

- It starts in an uncompleted state.
- Any attempt to `get()` a value from it will block.
- At some later time, a publication event occurs.
- This sets the value and passes it to any threads blocking on `get()`.
- The published value is now immutable.

Figure 16.3 shows the future and the publication event.

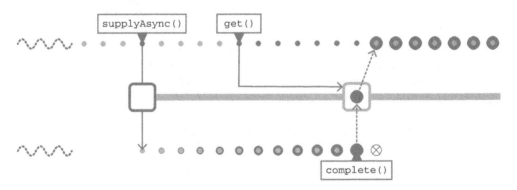

Figure 16.3   Event publication sets the value and passes it to any threads blocking on `get()`.

One big strength of `CompletableFuture` is that it is possible to compose functions with the result, and the result will be lazily evaluated, that is, the function will not be executed until the value has arrived.

This function composition can occur either synchronously or asynchronously. This is perhaps easiest to see by running a few examples. Let's reuse the idea of the Number-Service from chapter 6 and use a dummy implementation for it, for example:

```java
public class NumberService {
    public static long findPrime(int n) {
        try {
            Thread.sleep(5_000);
        } catch (InterruptedException e) {
            throw new CancellationException("interrupted");
        }
        return 42L;
    }
}
```

This obviously doesn't actually compute primes, but it is good enough to demonstrate the threading behavior, which is our goal. We need a bit of code to drive this, as shown next:

```java
var n = 1000;
var future =
  CompletableFuture.supplyAsync(() -> {          // Supplies the computation
                                                 // to run asynchronously
    System.out.println("Starting on: "+ Thread.currentThread().getName());
    return NumberService.findPrime(n);
});                                              // Supplies the function to apply to the result
var f2 = future.thenApply(l -> {                 // of the asynchronous computation
    System.out.println("Applying on: "+ Thread.currentThread().getName());
    return l * 2;
});                                              // Supplies another function to apply
var f3 = future.thenApplyAsync(l -> {            // asynchronously to the result
    System.out.println("Async on: "+ Thread.currentThread().getName());
    return l * 3;
});

try {
  System.out.println("F2: "+ f2.get());
  System.out.println("F3: "+ f3.get());
} catch (InterruptedException | ExecutionException e) {
  e.printStackTrace();
}
```

When we run this code, we get some output like this:

```
Starting up on thread: ForkJoinPool.commonPool-worker-19
Applying on thread: ForkJoinPool.commonPool-worker-19
Applying async on thread: ForkJoinPool.commonPool-worker-5
F2: 84
F3: 126
```

The future f2, which uses thenApply(), executes on the same thread as future, whereas f3 (which uses thenApplyAsync()) executes on a different thread in the pool.

You might notice that, by default, execution of `CompletableFuture` code all uses the common pool. This pool shows up with the name of `ForkJoinPool.commonPool`, as can be seen in the previous output.

Under some circumstances, developers may want to use an alternate thread pool. For example, the common pool isn't configurable in terms of the maximum number of threads that can be used, and this may not be acceptable for certain workloads. Fortunately, the factory methods of `CompletableFuture`, such as `supplyAsync()`, come with overloads that take an explicit `Executor` argument. This allows the future to run on a specific threadpool instead.

As well as the `thenApply()` method, `CompletableFuture` also provides `then-Compose()`. Some developers find the difference between the two confusing, so let's take a moment to explain.

Recall that `thenApply()` takes as its argument a `Function` that maps T -> U. This function is applied synchronously on whichever thread the `CompletableFuture` is running on after the original future completes.

On the other hand, `thenCompose()` takes a `Function` that maps T -> `Completable-Future<U>` (the actual return type is `CompletionStage<U>` rather than `Completable-Future<U>`, but let's gloss over that detail for now). This is, effectively, an asynchronous function (and it could run on a different thread). Let's look at a concrete example:

```
Function<Long, CompletableFuture<Long>> f = l ->
  CompletableFuture.supplyAsync(() -> {
    System.out.println("Applying on thread: " +
                        Thread.currentThread().getName());
    return l * 2;
  });
```

We *could* pass this function to `thenApply()`, but the result would be a `Completable-Future<CompletableFuture<Long>>`. Instead, `thenCompose()` flattens the result back to a `CompletableFuture<Long>`. This is similar to how the `flatMap()` method works in the Java Streams API—it applies a function that returns `Stream<T>` to a stream object, but instead of returning a `Stream<Stream<T>>`, the separate streams are flattened and joined together into a single stream.

`CompletableFuture` also supports `join()`, which essentially works like a thread join but returns a value. It is also possible to "join together" futures by having code that is intended to run after either (or both) of them have finished. For example:

```
var n = 1000;
var future = CompletableFuture.supplyAsync(() -> {
    System.out.println("Starting up: "+ Thread.currentThread().getName());
    return NumberService.findPrime(n);
});

var future2 = CompletableFuture.supplyAsync(() -> {
    System.out.println("Starting up: "+ Thread.currentThread().getName());
```

```
        return NumberService.findPrime(n);
});

Runnable dontKnow = () -> System.out.println("One of the futures finished");
future.runAfterEither(future2, dontKnow);
```

We now want to bring together the discussion of functional programming in the previous chapter with the ideas here.

If the functions that we want to apply to the result of a `CompletableFuture` are pure and do not depend upon anything but the input value, the action of applying a function to the future is the same as applying the function to the result. Put another way: if the future is thought of as a container type, which holds a value, then the container is "transparent" to the function that is applied to the value once it has arrived.

In particular, two of the major benefits of referential transparency (e.g., using pure functions) follow:

- Memoization
- Transportability

The first means that any pure function call can be replaced by an already-calculated value—we don't have to rerun the function call with the same arguments, because we already know what the answer is. Second, of course, if we're calculating a pure function, then it doesn't matter what thread it takes place on, so whether we've supplied a function to be applied synchronously or asynchronously won't affect the result.

> **NOTE** Java, as already discussed, is quite an impure language, so many of these benefits will apply only if the programmer is careful to use pure functions and immutable data throughout.

While we're discussing concurrent functional programming, it seems pertinent to say something about *parallel streams*, which are an area of the Streams API that many developers misunderstand.

16.2.2 Parallel streams

In chapter 5, we met Amdahl's law, which is one of the fundamental results about concurrency as it pertains to *data parallelism*. This is the approach to concurrency that we often want to use when we have a large amount of bulk data that is pretty similar and all has to be processed in more or less the same way. In general, the data parallelism approach is useful if all of the following are true:

- You have a lot of data to process in the same (or a very similar) way.
- Ordering doesn't matter.
- Items are independent of each other.
- You can show a particular processing step is the bottleneck.

Parallel streams are a type of data parallelism that a lot of Java developers got quite excited about when they were included in Java 8. However, as we'll see, the reality has turned out rather differently to the initial hope. The API, shown here, seems simple enough:

```
// Just replace stream() with parallelStream()
List<String> origins = musicians
      .parallelStream()
      .filter(artist -> artist.getName().startsWith("The"))
      .map(artist -> artist.getNationality())
      .collect(toList());
```

Under the hood, the work is distributed using F/J framework and uses the work-stealing algorithm to spread out the computation over multiple cores. The following seems too good to be true:

- The work is managed by the framework.
- API aims to be explicit but unobtrusive.
- Distributed by data.
- `parallelStream()` allows the programmer to flip between sequential and parallel.
- "Free speedup."

In fact, it *is* too good to be true. The first and most obvious problem is Amdahl's law. To split a sequential task into a set of chunks that can be executed in parallel requires work—that is, computation time. The more preparation and communication overhead, the less benefit multiple processors provide—this is the essence of Amdahl's law.

No general way exists to easily and reliably estimate the relative costs of splitting versus the linear operation cost. The framework passes the cognitive cost of deciding whether parallelism is actually worthwhile back up to the developer. This already sounds like "automatic parallelism" is not the nirvana that was promised. Instead, the end user must be acutely aware of many details that would ideally be abstracted away.

To take just one example: the splitting and recombining work must take place on a thread pool within the JVM. The more threads that the JVM creates, the more they compete for CPU time. The Streams API does not, a priori, know how many other instances of parallel streams exist within the current process. This leads to the following two possible, equally unpalatable strategies:

- Create a new, dedicated thread pool for each invocation of parallel streams.
- Create a single instance of a thread pool (private to the JVM), and make all invocations of parallel streams use it.

The first option leads to a potentially unbounded creation of threads, which will ultimately starve or crash a JVM. For this reason, in Java 8, there is a single shared thread pool underlying parallel streams: `ForkJoinPool.commonPool()`. This choice leads to potential contention on a shared resource (which, as we have seen in chapter 7, is the real root of a great many performance problems).

There is a workaround: if you execute a parallel stream as a task on a ForkJoin-Pool, it will execute there and not use the common pool, like this:

```
// Use a custom pool
var forkJoinPool = new ForkJoinPool(4);
List<String> origins2 = forkJoinPool.submit(() -> musicians
    .parallelStream()
    .filter(artist -> artist.getName().startsWith("The"))
    .map(artist -> artist.getNationality())
    .collect(toList())).get();
forkJoinPool.shutdown();
```

Note that the forkJoinPool must be explicitly shut down, or it will persist in memory waiting for new tasks and thus leak memory and threads.

In general, the best advice that can be given about parallel streams is not to apply the parallelism blindly. Instead, actually show you have a use case for it. As always, this is done by measuring and by showing that the stream operations are indeed the bottleneck first, before attempting to see whether parallel streams will help.

Unfortunately, there is no general class of problem where parallel streams might be expected to help. Each case must be examined and tested from first principles. Only then can you try to apply parallelism to the stream and prove with data that a worthwhile improvement can be achieved.

16.3   Under the hood with Kotlin coroutines

As we introduced in chapter 9, Kotlin provides an alternative to the Thread model for concurrency with *coroutines*. Coroutines can be thought of as "light-weight threads" without the resource penalties of full operating system threads. This bears some resemblance to Java's Fork/Join. How does Kotlin provide this alternate means of execution? A deeper understanding of what's going on under the surface is warranted.

16.3.1   How coroutines work

Let's start from the following modified example of what we saw in chapter 9:

```
package com.wgjd

import kotlinx.coroutines.GlobalScope
import kotlinx.coroutines.delay
import kotlinx.coroutines.launch

fun main() {
  GlobalScope.launch {
    delay(1000)
    sus()
  }

  Thread.sleep(2000)
```

```
}

suspend fun sus() {
  println("Totally sus...")
}
```

Here we use the `GlobalScope.launch` to start a new coroutine. *Scopes* are used to express how a coroutine should be run, and we'll look at them more carefully in the next section.

The coroutine we create here will wait for a second using the `delay` function, and then call our own function, `sus`. Lastly, we `Thread.sleep` for 2 seconds to make sure our coroutine has time to complete before our whole program exits.

Part of how coroutines differ from threads is that their execution may be paused at specific points. How does Kotlin know where it can pause? That comes from the `sus-pend` keyword we put on our `sus` function (and also on the library-provided `delay` function). The `suspend` function marks off the blocks of code that Kotlin treats as the units for execution.

With `suspend` functions marking the chunks of code in our coroutine between which we can pause, Kotlin can create a *state machine* to manage our coroutine's execution. Progress through that state machine is tracked by our generated code, with our suspend-defined blocks providing the steps to that machine.

Let's translate our coroutine into a state machine like this:

```
GlobalScope.launch {
  delay(1000)
  sus()
}
```

The steps in our coroutine follow and are illustrated in figure 16.4:

- Create our new coroutine instance by calling `launch`.
- Execute through `delay`.
- Control returns to Kotlin, which will wait the requested 1 second.
- Resume after `delay` and execute through `sus`.
- Hand control back to Kotlin, without requiring a pause this time.
- Resume after `sus`, and finish the coroutine.

Figure 16.4   Coroutine state machine

This breakdown into steps clarifies why coroutines are sometimes described as "cooperative multitasking." The code between our calls to suspend functions is executed synchronously, with the `suspend` points providing the only opportunity to pause and execute other coroutine steps. Imagine between `delay` and `sus` we entered an infinite loop. That loop would block whatever thread it's executing on forever.

This state machine isn't just an idea—Kotlin directly generates code that does this, and we can examine it. Let's look at the output from our previous function to see how it gets translated. (Note, some minor details are excluded for length and clarity.)

The compilation results from our basic app has more class files than we might expect. For example, here's the resulting output under Gradle's build directory:

```
build
└── classes
     └── kotlin
          └── main
               └── com
                    └── wgjd
                         ├── MainKt$main$1.class
                         └── MainKt.class
```

We encountered the `MainKt.class` in chapter 9. Kotlin transparently creates a holding class for top-level functions, because the JVM doesn't natively support free-floating functions and must place all method code in some class.

Alongside that, though, we have a new class: `MainKt$main$1.class`. Disassembling that class file reveals that Kotlin has done similar work creating "secret" classes for our coroutine, just like it did for our top-level functions. This generated class represents a single execution of our coroutine. As we can see next, this generated class is a mixture of our code and the plumbing to run what we've written as a coroutine:

```
final class com.wgjd.MainKt$main$1
    extends kotlin.coroutines.jvm.internal.SuspendLambda ◄──── Our generated class gets
    implements kotlin.jvm.functions.Function2< ◄──── functionality from Kotlin's
        kotlinx.coroutines.CoroutineScope,               SuspendLambda.
        kotlin.coroutines.Continuation<? super kotlin.Unit>,
        java.lang.Object> {                    Our generated class
                                               implements a specific
                                               interface that calling
                                               code will use to invoke
                                               our coroutine.
```

If we check out the code generated from our `main` function in `MainKt.class`, we see Kotlin created an instance of our coroutine and then invoked it:

```
Compiled from "Main.kt"
public final class com.wgjd.MainKt {

    public static final void main();
      Code:                                   Retrieves the GlobalScope instance
          0: getstatic      #41  // Field ◄──── to use starting our coroutine
                                  // kotlinx/coroutines/GlobalScope.INSTANCE:
                                  // Lkotlinx/coroutines/GlobalScope;
          3: checkcast      #43  // class kotlinx/coroutines/CoroutineScope
          6: aconst_null
```

```
 7: aconst_null
 8: new              #45   // class com/wgjd/        Creates and initializes a new instance
                           // MainKt$main$1          of our generated coroutine class
11: dup
12: aconst_null
13: invokespecial #49      // Method com/wgjd/MainKt$main$1."<init>":
                           // (Lkotlin/coroutines/Continuation;)V
16: checkcast       #51   // class kotlin/jvm/functions/Function2
19: iconst_3
20: aconst_null
21: invokestatic   #57   // Method kotlinx/coroutines/
                         // BuildersKt.launch$
                         // default:(Lkotlinx/coroutines/CoroutineScope;
                         // Lkotlin/coroutines/CoroutineContext;
                         // Lkotlinx/coroutines/CoroutineStart;
                         // Lkotlin/jvm/functions/Function2;
                         // ILjava/lang/Object;)Lkotlinx/coroutines/Job;
24: pop
25: ldc2_w          #58   // long 20001
28: invokestatic   #65   // Method java/lang/Thread.sleep:(J)V
31: return
```

Calls the launch method, providing it the scope and our coroutine instance. In particular, our coroutine instance is passed as the Function2 parameter.

The code in the `launch` method will then start calling methods on our generated coroutine instance, running our state machine. Let's look at the bytecode implementing that state machine. First up, the coroutine instance has two separate fields. These track the coroutine scope and the current location in our state machine:

```
final class com.wgjd.MainKt$main$1
    extends kotlin.coroutines.jvm.internal.SuspendLambda
    implements kotlin.jvm.functions.Function2<
        kotlinx.coroutines.CoroutineScope,
        kotlin.coroutines.Continuation<? super kotlin.Unit>,
        java.lang.Object> {
    java.lang.Object L$0;

    int label;
```

CoroutineScope for our current execution

The int value representing our state machine's current step

When our state machine runs, the heart of it is a method that decides our next step based on these fields. Kotlin generates a method called `invokeSuspend` for just that purpose. `invokeSuspend` ends up as a mixture of our code and the state machine tracking our progress. During the lifetime of our coroutine, Kotlin will repeatedly call `invokeSuspend` whenever the coroutine is ready for its next execution step.

The next code snippet shows us the beginning of `invokeSuspend`, along with our first step from the state machine (from the coroutine's start until we call `delay`):

```
public final java.lang.Object invokeSuspend(java.lang.Object);
    Code:
        0: invokestatic   #36   // Method kotlin/coroutines/intrinsics/
                                 // IntrinsicsKt.getCOROUTINE_SUSPENDED:
                                 // ()Ljava/lang/Object;
```

```
  3: astore_3
  4: aload_0
  5: getfield      #40   // Field label:I
  8: tableswitch   {     // 0 to 2
                0: 36
                1: 69
                2: 104
          default: 122
     }
 36: aload_1
 37: invokestatic  #46   // Method kotlin/ResultKt.throwOnFailure:
                         // (Ljava/lang/Object;)V
 40: aload_0
 41: getfield      #48   // Field p$:Lkotlinx/coroutines/CoroutineScope;
 44: astore_2
 45: ldc2_w        #49   // long 10001
 48: aload_0
 49: aload_0
 50: aload_2
 51: putfield      #52   // Field L$0:Ljava/lang/Object;
 54: aload_0
 55: iconst_1
 56: putfield      #40   // Field label:I
 59: invokestatic  #58   // Method kotlinx/coroutines/DelayKt.delay:
                         // (JLkotlin/coroutines/Continuation;)
                         // Ljava/lang/Object;
 62: dup
 63: aload_3
 64: if_acmpne     82
 67: aload_3
 68: areturn
 69: aload_0
 70: getfield      #52   // Field L$0:Ljava/lang/Object;
 73: checkcast     #60   // class kotlinx/coroutines/CoroutineScope
```

Determines our next step in the state machine (annotation pointing to byte 5)

The beginning of first step (up to the delay call) (annotation pointing to byte 36)

The beginning of second step (up to the sus call), which will happen when invokeSuspend is called again (annotation pointing to byte 69)

```
// Further steps excluded for length.
// See resources for full listing
```

After gathering information on the current coroutine, byte 5 loads up what step we're executing next from the `label` field. Then at byte 8, it uses an opcode we haven't seen before, `tableswitch`. This opcode looks at the value on the stack and jumps based on the values defined. Because this is our first time through `invokeSuspend`, our `label` has a value of 0, and we proceed to byte 36. We execute linearly from there. At bytes 55 and 56, we update our state `label` to 1 and advance to the next step. We call `delay` at byte 59 and then `areturn` from `invokeSuspend` at byte 68.

At this point Kotlin's code is given control, and it decides when to run the coroutine's next step. When it determines the time is right, it will call `invokeSuspend` on the same coroutine instance. Our state `label` will be set to 1, and we jump ahead to execute the code for our second step, after `delay` but before our sus call.

Although it's not truly necessary to get down to the bytecode level for day-to-day use of coroutines, understanding the mechanism is valuable. The well-grounded developer also shouldn't be satisfied when a feature seems too magical. At the end of the day, it's all just code executing one instruction at a time, and we have the tools to understand it.

This examination also may answer some questions from section 15.3.7 where we saw the `yield` function used in defining a Kotlin sequence. We hand-waved a little at that point about how our lambda to define the sequence could "pause" its execution. This is, in fact, using the same mechanism of a generated state machine based on `suspend` functions. Each successive calls to `invokeSuspend` gets the next item in the sequence.

16.3.2 *Coroutine scoping and dispatching*

Although coroutines provide a different abstraction to the standard operating system threading model, under the surface our code is still executing in a thread somewhere. How that work gets distributed and coordinated by Kotlin's coroutines is managed by coroutine scopes and *dispatchers*.

Let's revise our example to peek at where each step of our coroutine is actually executing:

```
package com.wgjd

import kotlinx.coroutines.GlobalScope
import kotlinx.coroutines.delay
import kotlinx.coroutines.launch

fun main() {
  GlobalScope.launch {
    println("On thread ${Thread.currentThread().name}")
    delay(500)

    println("On thread ${Thread.currentThread().name}")
    delay(500)

    println("On thread ${Thread.currentThread().name}")
  }

  Thread.sleep(2000)
}
```

The results aren't deterministic but will look something like this:

```
On thread DefaultDispatcher-worker-1
On thread DefaultDispatcher-worker-2
On thread DefaultDispatcher-worker-1
```

Our thread name provides two interesting pieces of information: a name for a dispatcher (`DefaultDispatcher`) and a number indicating which thread from an available pool we're using. When we asked for a particular scope—in our case, the

GlobalScope, which lasts the entire application lifetime—part of what we're choosing is the dispatcher, which determines how our work is actually scheduled.

   Let's say that we want greater control over how that work dispatching happens. Rather than using GlobalScope, we can create our own, separate CoroutineScope instance, as shown next. Typically, a scope is associated with a different object in our system with its own specific lifetime. Our custom scopes require a context at construction, and the standard functions factory methods are largely identified by how they configured dispatching:

```
val context: CoroutineContext = newFixedThreadPoolContext(3, "New-Pool")

CoroutineScope(context).launch {
  println("On thread ${Thread.currentThread().name}")
  delay(500)

  println("On thread ${Thread.currentThread().name}")
  delay(500)

  println("On thread ${Thread.currentThread().name}")
}
```

The not terribly surprising output shows we're executing on an entirely separate set of threads than we saw before:

```
On thread New-Pool-1
On thread New-Pool-2
On thread New-Pool-1
```

> **NOTE** It's worth paying attention because the newFixedThreadPoolContext and other related functions are marked as obsolete, but their replacements are not available as of this writing. Check out the Kotlin coroutine documentation at https://kotlin.github.io/kotlinx.coroutines for the most up-to-date practices.

Context classes wrap up more than just a dispatcher for coroutines. Examples of additional information we can provide are a name for our coroutine (which improves the debugging experience in IDEs, particularly when many coroutines share dispatchers) and a generalized error handler. Elements are added to an existing context object using the plus function, as shown here:

```
val context: CoroutineContext = newFixedThreadPoolContext(3, "New-Pool")
  .plus(CoroutineExceptionHandler { _, thrown ->
    println(thrown.message + "!!!!") })
  .plus(CoroutineName("Our Coroutine"))

CoroutineScope(context).launch {
  throw RuntimeException("Failed")
}
```

Alongside automatic cancellation of coroutines when the exception is raised, our CoroutineExceptionHandler will be run and print "Failed!!!!". You may wish to consider a more thorough error-handling strategy for your production applications, but coroutines provide the necessary hooks.

It's not unusual to want to execute various steps in parallel but then require the results from those stages before continuing. Within a coroutine this is supported by the async function, as shown next, which returns a Deferred<T>— effectively a coroutine Job that also allows for waiting and retrieving the value:

```
GlobalScope.launch {
    val result: Deferred<Int> = async {
      10;
    }

    println("Got ${result.await()}")     ⟵—— Unsurprisingly, prints Got 10
}
```

Back in section 9.5, we saw that by default, coroutines will cancel the entire coroutine hierarchy on errors as follows:

```
val failed = GlobalScope.launch {
  launch { throw RuntimeException("Failing...") }
}

Thread.sleep(2000)     ⟵—— Gives time to finish executing

println("Cancelled ${failed.isCancelled}")     ⟵—— Prints Cancelled true
```

When you want it, this behavior is extremely powerful. However, it may not always be desirable. If some child coroutines can safely fail, we can wrap them with the supervisorScope as follows. This behaves like a typical coroutine wrapper, but doesn't percolate up cancellations:

```
val supervised = GlobalScope.launch {
  supervisorScope {
    launch { throw RuntimeException("Failing...") }
  }
}

Thread.sleep(2000)     ⟵—— Again, needs time to finish

println("Cancelled ${supervised.isCancelled}")  ⟵┐
```
Prints Cancelled false, indicating our supervisor allowed the child coroutine to fail without cancelling the parent

Coroutines provide us with many options for how we handle concurrent execution. They are far from the only alternate way of thinking about the world, though. Let's see what Clojure brings to the table.

16.4   *Concurrent Clojure*

Java's model of state is based fundamentally around the idea of mutable objects. As we saw in chapter 5, this leads directly to problems with safety in concurrent code. We need to introduce quite complicated locking strategies to prevent other threads from seeing intermediate (aka *inconsistent*) object states while a given thread is working on mutating an object's state. These strategies are hard to come up with, hard to debug, and harder to test.

Clojure takes a different view, and its abstractions for concurrency aren't as low-level as Java's in some respects. For example, the use of thread pools that are managed by the Clojure runtime (and over which the developer has little or no control) may seem strange. But the power gained stems from allowing the platform (in this case, the Clojure runtime) to perform the bookkeeping for you, allowing you to free up your mind for much more important tasks, such as overall design.

Overall, the philosophy guiding Clojure is to isolate threads from each other by default, which goes a long way to making the language concurrently typesafe by default. By assuming a baseline of "nothing needs to be shared" and having immutable values, Clojure sidesteps a lot of Java's issues and instead can focus on ways to share state safely for concurrent programming.

> **NOTE**   To help promote safety, Clojure's runtime provides mechanisms for coordinating between threads, and it's very strongly recommended that you use these mechanisms rather than trying to use Java idioms or making your own concurrency constructs.

Let's look at the first of these building blocks: persistent data structures.

16.4.1   *Persistent data structures*

A *persistent data structure* is one that preserves previous versions when it is modified. As a result, they are thread safe, because operations on them do not mutate the structure as seen by existing readers and instead always yield a new updated object.

All of the Clojure collections are persistent and allow for the efficient creation of modified copies, by using *structural sharing*. The collections are inherently thread safe and designed to be efficient.

It's important to note that Clojure's persistent collections do not permit in-place mutation or deletion of elements. They will throw `UnsupportedOperationException` if your program calls those methods of the Java Collections interfaces (such as `List` or `Map`). Instead, the expectation is that the persistent collections will be built up using operations like `(cons)` and `(conj)`, in the Lisp tradition.

All the collections support the following basic methods:

- `count` gets the size of the collection.
- `cons` and `conj` add to the collection.
- `seq` gets a sequence that can walk the collection.

All of the sequence functions can therefore be used with any collection, via the support for seq. Let's look at an example—Clojure's PersistentVector—starting with some Java code to show how the vector is build up by repeatedly adding new elements with (cons):

```
var aList = new ArrayList<PersistentVector>();
var vector = PersistentVector.EMPTY;
for (int i=0; i < 32; i = i + 1) {
    vector = vector.cons(i);
    aList.add(vector);
}
System.out.println(aList);
```

This will output something like

```
[[0], [0 1], [0 1 2], [0 1 2 3],

...

[0 1 2 3 4 5 6 7 8 9 10 11 12 13 14 15 16 17 18 19 20 21 22 23 24 25 26 27
 28 29 30 31]]
```

which shows that it is possible to keep each earlier version of the persistent vector around, should you need to. This would also mean that it would be possible to pass the vector between threads and have each thread modify it without affecting the others.

Let's take a quick look at how this data structure is implemented. Recall that array-backed data structures (such as vectors) in other languages are usually implemented in terms of a single continuous chunk of memory. This implementation makes indexed operations, such as lookup, fast, but for operations such as making a mutated copy of the vector (while retaining the original), we must copy the entire backing array.

Clojure's PersistentVector is very different. Instead, Clojure stores elements for the vector in chunks of 32 elements. The general idea is that if an element is added, only the current *tail* of 32 elements needs to be copied. If a vector has more than 32 elements added to it, a structure called a *node* is created that contains an array of 32 elements, which are themselves references to nodes that contain full arrays of 32 elements.

> **NOTE** PersistentVector is one of Clojure's core abstractions, and it is so widely used that is actually implemented in Java (not Clojure), because it is needed to bootstrap the basic Clojure language runtime.

The class definition looks like this (slightly simplified for clarity):

```
public class PersistentVector extends APersistentVector
                        implements IObj, ... {

    // ...
```

```
    public final PersistentVector.Node root;
    public final Object[] tail;
    private final int cnt;

    // ...

    public static final PersistentVector EMPTY;
    public static final PersistentVector.Node EMPTY_NODE;

    // ...
}
```

with the inner class `PersistentVector.Node` defined as follows:

```
public static class Node implements Serializable {
        public final transient AtomicReference<Thread> edit;
        public final Object[] array;

        public Node(AtomicReference<Thread> edit, Object[] array) {
            this.edit = edit;
            this.array = array;
        }

        Node(AtomicReference<Thread> edit) {
            this.edit = edit;
            this.array = new Object[32];
        }
    }
```

Note that the `array` field is just an `Object[]`. This is an aspect of Clojure's dynamically typed nature—there are no generics here.

In addition, Clojure makes use of public final fields frequently in its core and does not always define accessor methods. We can therefore peek inside the data structure and see how the nodes work. For example:

```
var vector = PersistentVector.EMPTY;
for (int i = 0; i < 32; i = i + 1) {
    vector = vector.cons(i);
}
System.out.println(Arrays.toString(vector.tail));
System.out.println(Arrays.toString(vector.root.array));
System.out.println("----------------");
for (int i=32; i < 64; i = i + 1) {
    vector = vector.cons(i);
}
System.out.println(Arrays.toString(vector.tail));
System.out.println(Arrays.toString(vector.root.array));
var earlier = (PersistentVector.Node)(vector.root.array[0]);
System.out.println("Earlier: "+ Arrays.toString(earlier.array));
```

produces output like this:

```
[0, 1, 2, 3, ... 31]
[null, null, null, null, ... null]
----------------
[32, 33, 34, 35,  ...  63]
[clojure.lang.PersistentVector$Node@783e6358, null, null, null, ... null]
Full Tail: [0, 1, 2, 3, ... 31]
```

After 64 elements have been added, the tail is [32, … 63], and root.array contains a single PersistentVector.Node that contains the elements [0, … 31] as its array field. So, in pictorial form, for 0–32 elements, the vector looks like figure 16.5.

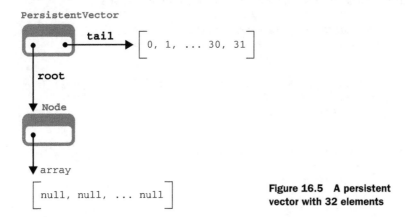

Figure 16.5   A persistent vector with 32 elements

For a number of elements more than 32 and less than 64, the structure will look like figure 16.6.

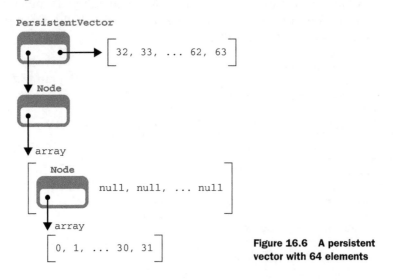

Figure 16.6   A persistent vector with 64 elements

And for 64 to 96 elements, it will look like it does in figure 16.7 and so on.

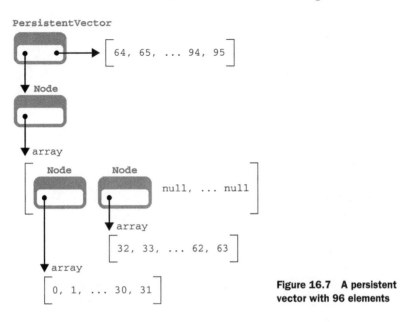

Figure 16.7 A persistent vector with 96 elements

You might, legitimately, ask what happens when all of the node's array slots are full. This occurs when the vector contains 32 + (32 * 32)—or 1,056—elements. The reader might be expecting this number to be 1,024, but we also have the *tail*, which contains 32 elements—effectively an "off-by-one effect." A full PersistentVector with one level of Node can be seen in figure 16.8.

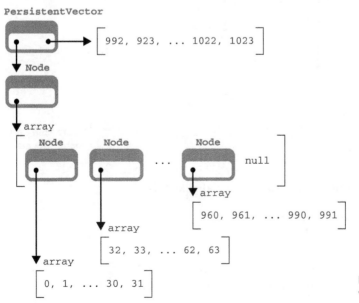

Figure 16.8 A persistent vector with 1,056 elements

If we continue to add elements, the tree structure grows another level, as shown in figure 16.9.

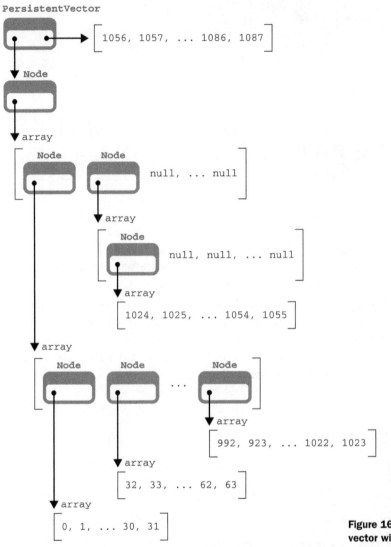

Figure 16.9   A persistent vector with many elements

To see this in code, we can run some code like this:

```
var vector = PersistentVector.EMPTY;
for (int i = 0; i < 1088; i = i + 1) {
    vector = vector.cons(i);
}
System.out.println(Arrays.toString(vector.tail));
System.out.println(Arrays.toString(vector.root.array));
```

```
System.out.println();

var v0 = (PersistentVector.Node) (vector.root.array[0]);
var v1 = (PersistentVector.Node) (vector.root.array[1]);
System.out.println("r.a[0] : " + Arrays.toString(v0.array));
System.out.println("r.a[1] : " + Arrays.toString(v1.array));
System.out.println();

var v0A0 = (PersistentVector.Node)(((PersistentVector.Node)v0).array[0]);
var v0A31 = (PersistentVector.Node)(((PersistentVector.Node)v0).array[31]);
var v1A0 = (PersistentVector.Node)(((PersistentVector.Node)v1).array[0]);
System.out.println("r.a[0].a[0] : " + Arrays.toString(v0A0.array));
System.out.println("r.a[0].a[31] : " + Arrays.toString(v0A31.array));
System.out.println("r.a[1].array[0] : " + Arrays.toString(v1A0.array));
```

This produces output like this:

```
[1056, 1057, 1058, 1059, ... 1087]
[clojure.lang.PersistentVector$Node@2344fc66,
clojure.lang.PersistentVector$Node@458ad742, null, null, ... null]

r.a[0] : [clojure.lang.PersistentVector$Node@735f7ae5,
          clojure.lang.PersistentVector$Node@180bc464, ... ,
          clojure.lang.PersistentVector$Node@617c74e5]
r.a[1] : [clojure.lang.PersistentVector$Node@6ea12c19, null, ... , null]

r.a[0].a[0] : [0, 1, ... , 31]
r.a[0].a[31] : [992, 993, ... , 1023]
r.a[1].a[0] : [1024, 1025, ... , 1055]
```

Notice how in this example, the array field of v0 and v1 no longer contains Integer elements but instead now contains Node objects. This is why the array field is typed as Object[], to allow for this sort of dynamic typing.

> **NOTE** If we continue adding elements, we will build a multilevel structure, and this allows PersistentVector to handle vectors of any size (albeit at an increasing cost of indirection for larger vectors).

However, data structures aren't the only things that Clojure needs to be a successful concurrent language. For example, a notion of concurrency models and execution is absolutely essential. Fortunately, Clojure has you covered!

In fact, Clojure uses several methods to provide different sorts of concurrency models: futures and pcalls, refs, and agents. Let's look at each in turn, starting with one of the simplest.

16.4.2 Futures and pcalls

We should start by making it clear that you can always start new threads by exploiting Clojure's tight binding to Java. Anything you can do in Java, you can also do in Clojure, and you can write concurrent Java code very easily in Clojure.

However, some of Java's abstractions have a cleaned-up form within Clojure. For example, Clojure provides a very clean approach to the Future concept that we encountered in Java in chapter 6. The following listing shows a simple example.

Listing 16.2   Futures in Clojure

```
user=> (def simple-future
  (future (do
        (println "Line 0")
        (Thread/sleep 10000)
        (println "Line 1")
        (Thread/sleep 10000)
        (println "Line 2"))))

#'user/simple-future      │ Starts executing at once
Line 0                   ←─┘
user=> (future-done? simple-future)
user=> false
Line 1
user=> @simple-future      ←──── Blocks when dereferencing
Line 2
nil
user=>
```

In this listing, you set up a Future with (future). As soon as this is created, it begins to run on a background thread, which is why you see the printout of line 0 (and later line 1) on the Clojure REPL—the code has started to run on another thread.

You can then test to see whether the code has completed using (future-done?), which is a nonblocking call (like isDone() in Java). The attempt to dereference the future, however, causes the calling thread to block until the function has completed.

This is effectively a thin Clojure wrapper over a Java Future, with some slightly cleaner syntax. Clojure also provides helper forms that can be very useful to the concurrent programmer. One simple function is (pcalls), which takes in a variable number of zero-argument functions and executes them in parallel.

NOTE (pcalls) is somewhat similar to Java's ExecutorService.invokeAll() helper method.

The calls are executed on a runtime-managed threadpool and will return a lazy seq of the results. Trying to access any elements of the seq that haven't yet completed will cause the accessing thread to block.

Listing 16.3 sets up a one-argument function called (wait-with-for). This uses a loop form similar to the one introduced in section 10.2.5. From this, you create a number of zero-argument functions—(wait-1), (wait-2), and so on—which you can feed to (pcalls).

```
 Listing 16.3   Parallel calls in Clojure
user=> (defn wait-with-for [limit]
  (let [counter 1]
    (loop [ctr counter]
      (Thread/sleep 500)
      (println (str "Ctr=" ctr))
    (if (< ctr limit)
      (recur (inc ctr))
    ctr))))
#'user/wait-with-for

user=> (defn wait-1 [] (wait-with-for 1))
#'user/wait-1

user=> (defn wait-2 [] (wait-with-for 2))
#'user/wait-2

user=> (defn wait-3 [] (wait-with-for 3))
#'user/wait-3

user=> (def wait-seq (pcalls wait-1 wait-2 wait-3))
#'user/wait-seq
Ctr=1
Ctr=1
Ctr=1
Ctr=2
Ctr=2
Ctr=3

user=> (first wait-seq)
1

user=> (first (next wait-seq))
2
```

With a thread sleep value of only 500 ms, the wait functions complete very quickly. By playing with the timeout (such as by extending it to 10 seconds), it's easy to verify that the lazy sequence called wait-seq that is returned by (pcalls) has the described blocking behavior.

This access to simple multithreaded constructs is fine for the case where you don't need to share state, but in many applications, different processing threads need to communicate in flight. Clojure has a couple of models for handling this, so let's look at one of these next: the shared state enabled by the (ref) form that is handled in a transaction.

16.4.3 *Software transactional memory*

The first, and most obvious, way to share state is not to. In fact, the Clojure construct that we've been using up until now, the var, isn't really able to be shared. If two different threads inherit the same name for a var and rebind it in-thread, then those rebindings are visible only within those individual threads and can never be shared by other threads.

This is by design, and Clojure provides an alternative way of sharing state between threads: the *ref*. This concept relies upon a model provided by the runtime for state changes that need to be seen by multiple threads. The model effectively introduces an additional level of indirection between a symbol and a value—that is, a symbol is bound to a reference to a value, rather than directly to a value.

The system is essentially transactional, and changes to the underlying value are coordinated by the Clojure runtime. This is illustrated in figure 16.10.

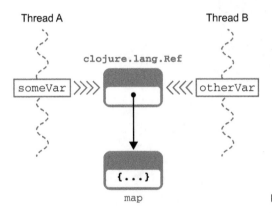

Figure 16.10   Software transactional memory

This indirection means that before a ref can be altered or updated, it has to be placed inside a transaction. When the transaction is completed, either all or none of the updates will take effect, and this has an obvious analogy to a transaction in a database.

This can seem a bit abstract, so let's return to an earlier example, the `Account` classes we discussed in chapters 5 and 6. Recall that, to avoid concurrency problems like lost update, in Java you're required to protect every sensitive bit of data with locks, as shown here:

```
// ...

private final Lock lock = new ReentrantLock();
private int balance;

public boolean withdraw(final int amount) {
    // Elided code - check to see amount > 0, throw if not

    lock.lock();
    try {
        if (balance >= amount) {
            balance = balance - amount;
            return true;
        }
    } finally {
        lock.unlock();
```

```
        }
        return false;
    }

    // ...
```

Let's see how you could try to write something similar to this in Clojure. However, it's here that we run into something of a conceptual problem.

In Java, the default is to use mutable state, and this is the case in the previous code. The `withdraw()` method takes in a single parameter, `amount`, and one of the following three things happens:

- `amount` *is less than or equal to zero*—An `IllegalArgumentException` is thrown, because this is not a valid withdrawal.
- *The withdrawal succeeds*—The balance is updated, and `true` is returned.
- *The withdrawal fails (not enough money available)*—The balance is *not* updated, and `false` is returned.

Leaving aside the invalid case, two separate aspects are happening here: updating mutable state and signaling via the return code whether or not the operation succeeded.

In functional programming, rather than updating mutable state, we would usually return a new value that contains the updated state. However, if the withdrawal fails, how will the user of the code know whether the balance has been updated? We could imagine changing the return code to be a pair of return codes and possibly an updated value, but this is somewhat clumsy.

Instead, let's start with a slightly different single-threaded version shown in the next listing. The semantics here are that the (debit) form operates on a map (representing an account) and returns a new map if the withdrawal succeeds—and throws if it fails.

Listing 16.4   Simple account model in Clojure

```
(defn make-new-acc [account-name opening-balance]
  {:name account-name :bal opening-balance})

(defn debit [account amount]
  (let [balance (:bal account) my-name (:name account)]
    (if (<= amount 0)
      (throw (AssertionError. "Withdrawal amount cannot be < 0")))
    (if (> balance amount)
      (make-new-acc my-name (- balance amount))
      (throw (AssertionError. "Withdrawal amount cannot exceed balance"))
    )))

(debit (make-new-acc "Ben" 5000) 1000)
```

Notice how compact this code is compared to the Java version. Admittedly, this is still single threaded, but it's a lot less code than was needed for Java. Running the code will give you the expected result: you end up with a map with a balance of 4000.

Despite the relative simplicity, this is not entirely satisfactory—we are actually solving a different problem with different semantics. Let's see if we can resolve some of the problems by generalizing to a concurrent version.

To make this code concurrent, we need to introduce Clojure's refs. These are created with the (ref) form and are JVM objects of type clojure.lang.Ref. Usually they're set up with a Clojure map to hold the state.

We'll also need the (dosync) form, which sets up a transaction. Within this transaction, we'll also use the (alter) form, which can be used to modify a ref's contents. Let's see how to use refs for this multithreaded approach to our account construct, as shown in the following.

Listing 16.5 Multithreaded account handling

```
user=> (defn safe-debit [ref-account amount]
  (dosync
    (alter ref-account debit amount)
    ref-account))
#'user/safe-debit

user=> (def my-acc (make-new-acc "Ben" 5000))
#'user/my-acc

user=> (def r-my-acc (ref my-acc))
#'user/r-my-acc

user=> (safe-debit r-my-acc 1000)
#object[clojure.lang.Ref 0x6b1e7ad3 {:status :ready,
                                     :val {:name "Ben", :bal 4000}}]
```

As noted, the (alter) form acts on a ref by applying a function with arguments. The value acted upon is the local value visible to this thread during the transaction. This is called the *in-transaction value*. The value returned is the new value of the ref after the alter function returns. This value isn't visible outside the altering thread until you exit the transaction block defined by (dosync).

Other transactions may be proceeding at the same time as this one. If so, the Clojure STM system will keep track of that and will allow a transaction to commit only if it's consistent with other transactions that have committed since it started. If it's inconsistent, it will be rolled back and may be retried with an updated view of the world.

This retry behavior can cause problems if the transaction does anything that produces side effects (such as a log file or other output). It's up to you to keep the transactional parts as simple and as pure in the functional programming sense (meaning as side-effect-free) as possible.

For some multithreaded approaches, this optimistic transactional behavior can seem to be a rather heavyweight approach. Some concurrent applications need to communicate between threads only occasionally and in a rather asymmetric fashion. Fortunately, Clojure provides another concurrency mechanism that is much more fire-and-forget, and it's the topic of our next section.

16.4.4   Agents

Agents are another of Clojure's concurrency primitives. Instead of using a shared state, a Clojure agent is an asynchronous, message-oriented execution object. They are similar to the *actor* concept in other languages (such as Scala and Erlang).

An agent is an execution context that can receive messages (in the form of functions) sent to it from another thread (or the same one). New agents are declared with the (agent) function and messages can be sent to them using (send).

> *"They must go by the carrier," she thought; "and how funny it'll seem, sending presents to one's own feet! And how odd the directions will look!"*
>
> —Lewis Carroll

The agents are not threads themselves but are instead executable objects that are "smaller" than a thread. They are scheduled on a threadpool that is managed by the Clojure runtime (the threadpool isn't usually accessible to the programmer directly).

NOTE Clojure agents are potentially long-lived, unlike task objects for Java threadpools, which typically have bounded lifetimes.

The runtime also ensures that the values of the agent that are seen from outside are isolated and atomic. This means that user code will only see the value of the agent in its before or after state.

NOTE We will meet another example of executable objects smaller than a thread in chapter 18.

The following listing shows a simple example of agents, similar to the example we used to discuss futures.

Listing 16.6   Agents in Clojure

```
user=> (defn wait-and-log [coll str-to-add]
  (do (Thread/sleep 10000)
    (let [my-coll (conj coll str-to-add)]
      (Thread/sleep 10000)
      (conj my-coll str-to-add))))
#'user/wait-and-log

user=> (def str-coll (agent []))
#'user/str-coll

user=> (send str-coll wait-and-log "foo")
```

```
#object[clojure.lang.Agent 0x38499e48 {:status :ready, :val []}]

user=> @str-coll
[]

// Wait to allow message to be handled

user=> @str-coll
["foo" "foo"]
```

The (send) call dispatches a (wait-and-log) call to the agent, and by using the REPL to dereference it, you can see that, as promised, you can never see an intermediate state of the agent—only the final state appears (where the "foo" string has been added twice).

It could seem odd that in the agent approach, we're sending a message to an agent that's scheduled on a thread in a Clojure-managed threadpool, when both threads already share an address space. But one of the themes in concurrency that you've now encountered several times is that additional abstraction can be a good thing if it enables a simpler and clearer usage.

Nowhere is this synergy clearer than in Clojure's delegation of many low-level aspects of threading and concurrency control to the runtime. This frees the programmer to focus on good multithreaded design and higher-level concerns. This is analogous to the way in which Java's garbage collection facilities allow you to free yourself from the details of memory management.

Summary

- Each language has extended the core concepts of execution in their own way.
- Java has introduced decomposable tasks and work-stealing through the Fork/Join library; Kotlin uses advanced compiler tricks to produce a version of coroutines; and Clojure builds in a form of the actor model using the agent concept.
- The treatment of state differs between our three languages and is key to concurrent programming
- In Java, mutability is the default, with some enhancements such as CompletableFuture.
- Kotlin places a greater emphasis on immutability but is still fundamentally drawing from the same worldview of shared, mutable state.
- Clojure centers immutability, via software transactional memory, but at the cost of a less-familiar programming model and a less-close integration with the Java Collections.

Modern internals

This chapter covers

- Introducing JVM internals
- Reflection internals
- Method handles
- Invokedynamic
- Recent internal changes
- Unsafe

Java's virtual machine (JVM) is an extremely sophisticated runtime environment that has, for decades, prioritized stability and production-grade engineering. For these reasons, many Java developers have never needed to poke about in the internals, because it is simply not necessary to do so most of the time.

This chapter, on the other hand, is for the curious—the people who would like to know more, who would like to draw back the curtain and see some of the details of how the JVM is implemented. Let's start with method invocation.

17.1 Introducing JVM internals: Method invocation

To get going, let's look at a simple example, defined by the classes Pet, Cat, and Bear and the interface Furry. This can be seen in figure 17.1

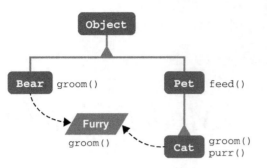

Figure 17.1   **Simple inheritance hierarchy**

We might also suppose that other subclasses of `Pet` exist (e.g., `Dog` and `Fish`) that aren't shown in the diagram to keep things clear. We'll use this example to explain in detail how the different invoke opcodes work, starting with `invokevirtual`.

17.1.1 *Invoking virtual methods*

The most common type of method invocation is calling an instance method on an object of a specific class (or a subclass) by use of an `invokevirtual` bytecode. This is known as a *dispatch* (i.e., call) of a *virtual method* (or just virtual dispatch), which means that the exact method to be invoked is determined at runtime, rather than compile time, by looking at the actual type of the object at runtime. When the JVM executes this bit of code:

```
Pet p = getPet();
p.feed();
```

the implementation of `feed()` that is actually called is determined at the point when the method needs to be executed.

The implementations can be different depending on whether p holds a `Cat` or a `Dog` (or a `Pet`, assuming the superclass is not abstract). It is also possible that `getPet()` returns an object of different subtypes of `Pet` at different times during the execution of the program. That doesn't matter—the implementation to be called is looked up each time the method is to be executed. Despite being a bit of a wall of text, this description is just how Java methods have always worked ever since you first learned the language.

Internally, to make this work, the JVM stores a table (per class), which holds the method definitions corresponding to that type, called the *vtable* (this is what C++ programmers call a virtual function table). This table is stored inside a special area of memory, called *metaspace*, inside the JVM that holds metadata that the VM needs.

> **NOTE** In Java 7 and earlier, this metadata lived in an area of the Java heap called *permgen*.

To see how the vtable is used, we need to look briefly at the JVM metadata for a class. In Java, all objects live within the Java heap and are handled by reference only.

HotSpot uses the general term *oop* (for "ordinary object pointer") to refer to the various internal data structures that live in the heap.

Every Java object must have an *object header*, which contains the following two types of metadata:

- Metadata that is specific to the particular instance of a class (the "mark word")
- Metadata that is shared by all instances of a class (the "klass word")

To save space, only one copy of the per-class metadata is stored, and each object that belongs to that class has a pointer to it—the klass word. In Figure 17.2 we can see a representation of a Java reference, held in a local variable, pointing at the start of a Java object header in the heap.

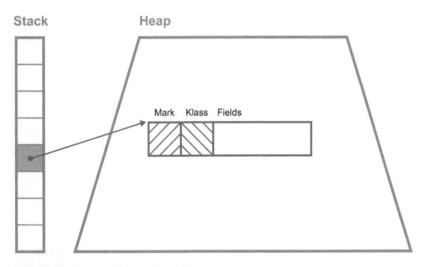

Figure 17.2 Java object header and layout

A *klass* is the JVM's internal representation of a Java class at runtime, stored in metaspace. It contains all of the information needed for the JVM to work with the class at runtime (e.g., method definitions and field layout).

Some of the information from the klass is available to the Java programmer via the Class<?> object corresponding to the type, but the klass and the Class are separate concepts. In particular, the klass contains information that is deliberately kept out of the reach of ordinary application code.

> **NOTE** The choice of the spelling "klass" is quite deliberate, because it disambiguates the internal data structure from the other uses of the word "class" in written documentation but, sadly, not in spoken English. You may also see the word "clazz" or "clz" used—these usually name a Java variable that contains a Class object.

We can now explain virtual dispatch (implemented by the `invokevirtual` bytecode) in terms of the internal JVM structures, such as the klass, and, in particular, its vtable. When the JVM encounters an `invokevirtual` instruction to execute, it pops the receiver object and any arguments for the method from the current method's evaluation stack.

NOTE A receiver object is the object upon which an instance method is being called.

The JVM object header layout starts with the mark word, with the klass word immediately following. So, to locate the method to be executed, the JVM follows the pointer into metaspace, where it consults the vtable of the klass to see exactly which code needs to be executed. This process can be seen in figure 17.3.

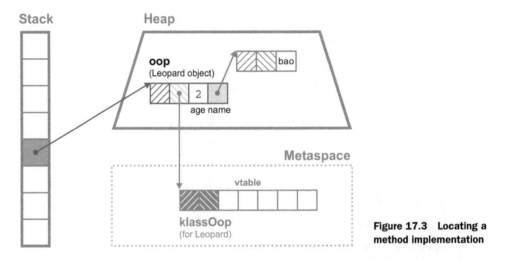

Figure 17.3 Locating a method implementation

If the klass does not have a definition for the method, the JVM follows a pointer to the klass corresponding to the direct superclass and tries again. This process is the basis of method overriding in the JVM.

To make it efficient, the vtables are laid out in a specific way. Each klass lays out its vtable so that the first methods to appear are those methods that the parent type defines. These methods are laid out in the exact order that the parent type used. The methods that are new to this type and are not declared by the parent type come at the end of the vtable.

When a subclass overrides a method, it will be at the same offset in the vtable as the implementation being overridden. This makes lookup of overridden methods completely trivial, because their offset in the vtable will be the same as their parent. In figure 17.4, we can see the vtable layout for some of the classes in our example.

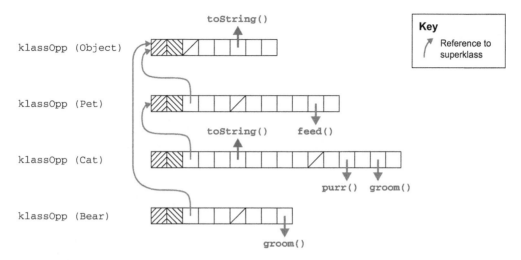

Figure 17.4   Vtable structure

So, if we call `Cat::feed`, the JVM will not find an override in the `Cat` class and will instead follow the superclass pointer to the klass of `Pet`. This does have an implementation for `feed()`, so this is the code that will be called.

> **NOTE** This vtable structure—and efficient implementation of overriding—works well because Java implements only single inheritance of classes. There is only one direct superclass of any type (except `Object`, which has no superclass).

17.1.2 *Invoking interface methods*

In the case of `invokeinterface`, the situation is a little more complicated. For example, note that the `groom()` method will not necessarily appear in the same place in the vtable for every implementation of `Furry`. The different offsets for `Cat::groom` and `Bear::groom` are caused by the fact that their class inheritance hierarchies differ. The end result of this is that some additional lookup is needed when a method is invoked on an object for which only the interface type is known at compile time.

> **NOTE** Even though slightly more work is done for the lookup of an interface call, you should not try to micro-optimize by avoiding interfaces. Remember that the JVM has a JIT compiler, and it will essentially eliminate the performance difference between the two cases.

Let's look at an example. Consider this bit of code:

```
Cat tom = new Cat();
Bear pooh = new Bear();
Furry f;

tom.groom();
pooh.groom();
```

```
f = tom;
f.groom();
f = pooh;
f.groom();
```

This produces the following bytecode:

```
0: new            #2                      // class ch15/Cat
      3: dup
      4: invokespecial #3                 // Method ch15/Cat."<init>":()V
      7: astore_1
      8: new            #4                 // class ch15/Bear
     11: dup
     12: invokespecial #5                 // Method ch15/Bear."<init>":()V
     15: astore_2
     16: aload_1
     17: invokevirtual #6                 // Method ch15/Cat.groom:()V
     20: aload_2
     21: invokevirtual #7                 // Method ch15/Bear.groom:()V
     24: aload_1
     25: astore_3
     26: aload_3
     27: invokeinterface #8,   1          // InterfaceMethod
                                          // ch15/Furry.groom:()V
     32: aload_2
     33: astore_3
     34: aload_3
     35: invokeinterface #8,   1          // InterfaceMethod
                                          // ch15/Furry.groom:()V
```

The two calls at 27 and 35 look like they are the same in the Java code but will actually invoke different methods, because the runtime contents of f is different. The call at 27 will actually invoke `Cat::groom`, whereas the call at 35 will invoke `Bear::groom`.

17.1.3 *Invoking "special" methods*

With this background of `invokevirtual` and `invokeinterface`, the behavior of `invokespecial` is now easy to understand. If a method is invoked by `invokespecial`, it does not undergo virtual lookup. Instead, the JVM will look only in the exact place in the exact vtable for the requested method.

An `invokespecial` is used for two cases: calls to a superclass method and calls to the constructor body (which is turned into a method called `<init>` in bytecode). In both of these cases, virtual lookup and the possibility of overriding are explicitly excluded.

We should mention two further corner cases that might seem to suggest the use of `invokespecial` (which is also called *exact dispatch*). The first is private methods—they cannot be overridden, and the exact method to be called is known when the class is compiled, so it might seem that they should be called via `invokespecial`. However, this situation is more complex than it appears. Let's look at an example to demonstrate:

```
public class ExamplePrivate {

  public void entry() {
    callThePrivate();
  }

  private void callThePrivate() {
    System.out.println("Private method");
  }
}
```

Let's compile this with Java 8 first. Decompiling it using `javap` gives this:

```
$ javap -c ch15/ExamplePrivate.class
Compiled from "ExamplePrivate.java"
public class ch15.ExamplePrivate {
  public ch15.ExamplePrivate();
    Code:
       0: aload_0
       1: invokespecial #1    // Method java/lang/Object."<init>":()V
       4: return

  public void entry();
    Code:
       0: aload_0
       1: invokespecial #2    // Method callThePrivate:()V
       4: return
}
```

Note that `javap` is being invoked without the -p switch, so the decompilation of the private method does not appear. So far, so good—the private method is indeed called via `invokespecial`. However, if we recompile with Java 11 and look closely, we will see a different result, shown here:

```
$ javap -c ch15/ExamplePrivate.class
Compiled from "ExamplePrivate.java"
public class ch15.ExamplePrivate {
  public ch15.ExamplePrivate();
    Code:
       0: aload_0
       1: invokespecial #1 // Method java/lang/Object."<init>":()V
       4: return

  public void entry();
    Code:
       0: aload_0
       1: invokevirtual #2 // Method callThePrivate:()V        This is now
       4: return                                               invokevirtual.
}
```

As we can see, calls to private methods are handled differently in modern Java, which we will explain in section 17.5.3, when we meet nestmates.

17.1.4 *Final methods*

The other corner case is the use of `final` methods. At first glance, it might appear that calls to `final` methods would also be turned into `invokespecial` instructions—after all, they can't be overridden and the implementation that is to be called is known at compile time. However, the Java Language Specification has something to say about this case:

> *Changing a method that is declared* `final` *to no longer be declared* `final` *does not break compatibility with pre-existing binaries.*

Suppose code in one class had a call to a `final` method in another class, which had been compiled into an `invokespecial`. Then, if the class with the `final` method was changed so that the method was made non-`final` (and recompiled), it could be over-ridden in a subclass.

Now suppose that an instance of the subclass was passed into the calling method in the first class. The `invokespecial` would be executed, and now the wrong implementation of the method would be called. This is a violation of the rules of Java's object orientation (strictly speaking, it violates the Liskov Substitution Principle). For this reason, calls to `final` methods must be compiled into `invokevirtual` instructions.

NOTE In practice, HotSpot contains optimizations that allow the case of final methods to be detected and executed extremely efficiently.

We've introduced the basics of HotSpot's internals through the lens of virtual method dispatch. At this point, it might be interesting to reread the JIT compilation section of chapter 7—especially the sections on monomorphic dispatch and inlining. You may be able to gain a deeper understanding of these techniques now that you've seen a few of the details of how they are implemented.

17.2 *Reflection internals*

We met reflection in chapter 4 as a way of handling objects and calling methods dynamically at runtime. Now that we know about vtables, we can dig a bit deeper and see how reflection is implemented by the JVM.

Recall that we can obtain a `java.lang.reflect.Method` object from a class object and then invoke it, like this (eliding the exception handling):

```
Class<?> clazz = // ... some class
Method m = clazz.getMethod("toString");
Object ret = m.invoke(this);
System.out.println(ret);
```

But what does this `Method` object represent? It is really "the capability of calling a specific method dynamically at runtime." The dynamic nature of the call means that in the compiled code, we see only an `invokevirtual` of the `invoke()` method on `Method`, as shown next:

```
 0: ldc             #7    // ... some class
 2: astore_1
 3: aload_1
 4: ldc             #24   // String toString
 6: iconst_0
 7: anewarray       #26   // class java/lang/Class
10: invokevirtual   #28   // Method java/lang/
                          // Class.getMethod:
                          // (Ljava/lang/String;[Ljava/lang/Class;)
                          // Ljava/lang/reflect/Method;
13: astore_2
14: aload_2
15: aload_0
16: iconst_0
17: anewarray       #2    // class java/lang/Object
20: invokevirtual   #32   // Method java/lang/reflect/
                          // Method.invoke:
                          // (Ljava/lang/Object;[Ljava/lang/Object;)
                          // Ljava/lang/Object;
23: astore_3
```

The call to getMethod() is variadic and is passed a size-0 array of Class objects.

The call to invoke() is passed a size-0 array of Object objects (the arguments).

Note that there is no bytecode that refers to toString() via a method descriptor (such as java/lang/Object.toString:()Ljava/lang/String;)—only as the string toString.

Now, let's recall that class objects (e.g., String.class) are just regular Java objects—they have the properties of regular Java objects and are represented by oops. A class object contains a Method object for each method on the class, and these method objects are, again, just regular Java objects.

NOTE The Method objects are created lazily after class loading. You can sometimes see traces of this effect in an IDE's code debugger.

So how does the JVM actually implement reflection? Let's take a look at a bit of source for the Method class and see some of its fields:

```
private Class<?>          clazz;      ◄──┐   The class this method belongs to
private int               slot;           ◄────┐
// This is guaranteed to be interned by the VM in the 1.4   The offset in
// reflection implementation                                the vtable
private String            name;                             where this
private Class<?>          returnType;                        methods
private Class<?>[]        parameterTypes;                    lives
private Class<?>[]        exceptionTypes;
private int               modifiers;
// Generics and annotations support
private transient String  signature;
// generic info repository; lazily initialized
private transient MethodRepository genericInfo;
private byte[]            annotations;
private byte[]            parameterAnnotations;
private byte[]            annotationDefault;           ◄──┐  The delegate that carries
private volatile MethodAccessor methodAccessor;   ◄───────┘  out the invocation
```

We already know that in Java, calling an instance method involves looking it up in a vtable. So, conceptually, we want to exploit the duality between the vtable and the array of `Method` objects held by the `Class` object. We can see this duality in figure 17.5 where the array of `Method` objects help by `Entry.class` is dual to the vtable on the klassOop for `Entry`.

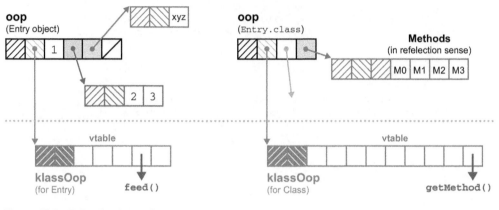

Figure 17.5   Reflection internals

Let's see how `Method` uses this duality to implement reflection. The key turns out to be the `MethodAccessor` object.

> **NOTE**   Some of the code that follows is simplified and based on an earlier version of Java, to aid understanding of the mechanism. The current shipping production code in Java 11 and later is more complex.

The `invoke()` method on `Method` looks a bit like this:

```
public Object invoke(Object obj, Object... args)
    throws IllegalAccessException, IllegalArgumentException,
           InvocationTargetException {
                                              Performs a security access
                                              check (if not setAccessible())
  if (!override) {
    if (!Reflection.quickCheckMemberAccess(clazz, modifiers)) {
      Class<?> caller = Reflection.getCallerClass();
      checkAccess(caller, clazz, obj, modifiers);
    }
  }
  MethodAccessor ma = methodAccessor;      ◄─── Volatile read of accessor
  if (ma == null) {
    ma = acquireMethodAccessor();
  }
  return ma.invoke(obj, args);             ◄─── Delegates to MethodAccessor
}
```

At the first reflective invocation of this method, `acquireMethodAccessor()` creates an instance of `DelegatingMethodAccessorImpl` that holds a reference to a `Native-MethodAccessorImpl`. These are classes defined in `sun.reflect` that both implement `MethodAccessor`. Note that they are not part of the API of the `java.base` module and cannot be called directly.

Here's `DelegatingMethodAccessorImpl` in full:

```
class DelegatingMethodAccessorImpl extends MethodAccessorImpl {
  private MethodAccessorImpl delegate;

  DelegatingMethodAccessorImpl(MethodAccessorImpl delegate) {
    setDelegate(delegate);
  }

  public Object invoke(Object obj, Object[] args)
      throws IllegalArgumentException, InvocationTargetException {
    return delegate.invoke(obj, args);
  }

  void setDelegate(MethodAccessorImpl delegate) {
    this.delegate = delegate;
  }
}
```

and here's `NativeMethodAccessorImpl`:

```
class NativeMethodAccessorImpl extends MethodAccessorImpl {
  private Method method;
  private DelegatingMethodAccessorImpl parent;
  private int numInvocations;

  // ...

  public Object invoke(Object obj, Object[] args)
      throws IllegalArgumentException, InvocationTargetException {

    if (++numInvocations >                                        ⟵──  Entered after an invocation
        ReflectionFactory.inflationThreshold()) {                      threshold is reached
      MethodAccessorImpl acc = (MethodAccessorImpl)
        new MethodAccessorGenerator()
          .generateMethod(method.getDeclaringClass(),
                          method.getName(),
                          method.getParameterTypes(),           Uses
                          method.getReturnType(),               MethodAccessorGenerator
                          method.getExceptionTypes(),           to create a custom class that
                          method.getModifiers());       ⟵──     implements the reflective call
      parent.setDelegate(acc);             ⟵────────┐
    }                                               │  Replaces the current object as a delegate
                                                       with an instance of the new custom class
    return invoke0(method, obj, args);
  }
```

If the threshold is not hit yet, proceeds with the native call

```
private static native Object invoke0(Method m, Object obj, Object[] args);

// ...
}
```

This technique—using a delegating accessor that can be patched with the new dynamically generated bytecode accessor—can be seen in figure 17.6. Note that the custom accessor class is a subclass of `MethodAccessorImpl` to allow the cast to succeed.

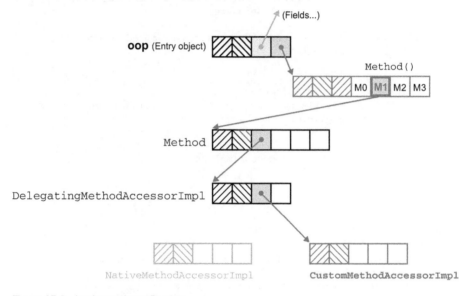

Figure 17.6   Implementing reflection

A word about performance: this mechanism involves trading off two different possible sources of slowness. On one hand, the native accessor uses a native call, which is slower than a Java method call and can't be JIT compiled. On the other, dynamically generating bytecode in `MethodAccessorGenerator` is potentially slow, and this can be a bad trade-off that we want to avoid for methods that are called by reflection only once. This trick, of lazily loading an accessor object and then dynamically patching the call site, is one that we will meet again, in a different guise, later in this chapter.

Also of note is that reflection also defeats inlining and the standard kinds of method dispatch that the JVM can optimize well. The call site for the method of `Delegating-MethodAccessorImpl` is said to be *megamorphic* (many possible implementations for the method) after patching because each instance of `Method` has a different, dynamically spun method accessor object. This means that some of the JVM's primary optimization mechanisms won't work well for reflective calls.

So the use of delegation and patching out of the native accessor is a compromise that aims to balance between acceptable performance for rarely called reflective methods while still preserving some of the benefits of JIT. This compromise, as well as the other problems of reflection, which we discussed back in chapter 4, led to a search for a better approach to the problems of dynamic invocation and lightweight method objects. In the next section, we introduce the first result of that research: the *Method Handles* API.

17.3   *Method handles*

The Method Handles API was added to Java with version 7. The core of this API is the package `java.lang.invoke`, and especially the class `MethodHandle`. Instances of this type represent the ability to call a method and are directly executable, in a similar way to `java.lang.reflect.Method` objects.

The API was produced as part of the project to bring `invokedynamic` (which we discuss in section 17.4) to the JVM. But method handle objects have applications in framework and regular user code that go far beyond the `invokedynamic` use cases.

We'll start by introducing the basic technology of method handles; then, we'll look at an extended example that compares them to some alternatives and summarizes the differences.

17.3.1   *MethodHandle*

What is a `MethodHandle`? The official answer is that it's a typed reference to a method that is directly executable. Another way of saying this is that a `MethodHandle` is an object that represents the ability to call a method safely.

> **NOTE** A `MethodHandle` is similar, in many ways, to a `Method` object from `java.lang.reflect`, but the API is generally better, less cumbersome, and with several significant design flaws corrected.

There are two aspects to using method handles: obtaining them and using them. The second, using them, is very easy. Let's see a very simple example of calling a method handle. For now, we'll just assume that we have some static helper method `get-TwoArgMH()` that returns a method handle that takes a receiver object `obj` and one call argument `arg0` and returns `String`.

Later, we'll explain how we'd get a method handle that matches that signature, but for now we just assume that we have a helper method that will create a method handle for us. The following usage should remind you of reflective calls:

```
MethodHandle mh = getTwoArgMH();    ◁─── Gets the method handle
                                         from a helper method
try {
  String result = mh.invokeExact(obj, arg0);    ◁─── Performs the call, passing a
} catch (Throwable e) {                               receiver and one argument
  e.printStackTrace();
}
```

This looks like a reflective call to a method, as we saw in section 4.5.1—we're using `invokeExact()` on `MethodHandle` rather than `invoke()` on `Method`, but other than that, it should look pretty similar. However, this is possible only once we actually have a method handle object in the first place—so, how do we get one?

To get a handle for a method, we need to look it up via a *lookup context*. The usual way to get a context is to call the static helper method `MethodHandles.lookup()`. This will return a lookup context based on the currently executing method. From the lookup, we can obtain method handles by calling one of the `find*()` methods such as `findVirtual()` or `findConstructor()`.

The lookup context object can provide a method handle on any method that's visible from the execution context where the lookup was created. However, as well as the lookup context for methods, we also need to consider how to represent the signature of the method we want a handle to.

Recall the `Callable` interface from chapter 6. It represents a block of code to be executed, which is similar to method handles. However, one problem with `Callable` is that it can model only methods that take no arguments.

If we want to model all types of methods, we would have to create other interfaces, with increasing numbers of type parameters. We'd end up with a set of interfaces like this:

```
Function0<R>
Function1<R, P>
Function2<R, P1, P2>
Function3<R, P1, P2, P3>
...
```

This would very quickly lead to a huge proliferation of interfaces. This approach is taken by some non-Java languages (e.g., Scala), but not in Java.

It's also insightful to consider the way that Clojure does it. The `IFn` interface has `invoke` methods that represent all the different arities of functions (including a variadic form for functions that take more than 20 args). We met a simplified version of `IFn` in chapter 10.

However, Clojure is dynamically typed, so all `invoke` methods take `Object` for every parameter and also return `Object`—this eliminates all the complexity from handling generics. Clojure forms can also be written variadically quite naturally—Clojure will throw a runtime exception if a form is called with the wrong arity. Java uses neither of these approaches.

Instead, Java's method handles implement an approach that can model any method signature, without needing to produce a vast number of small classes. This is done by means of the new `MethodType` class.

17.3.2 *MethodType*

A `MethodType` is an immutable object that represents the type signature of a method. Every method handle has a `MethodType` instance that includes the return type and the argument types. But it doesn't include the name of the method or the receiver type—the type that an instance method is called on.

As one simple way to get new `MethodType` instances, you can use factory methods in the `MethodType` class. Here are a few examples:

```
var mtToString = MethodType.methodType(String.class);
var mtSetter = MethodType.methodType(void.class, Object.class);
var mtStringComparator = MethodType.methodType(int.class,
                                        String.class, String.class);
```

These are the `MethodType` instances that represent the type signatures of `toString()`, a setter method (for a member of type `Object`), and the `compareTo()` method defined by a `Comparator<String>`. The general instance follows the same pattern, with the return type passed in first, followed by the types of the arguments (all as `Class` objects), like this:

```
MethodType.methodType(RetType.class, Arg0Type.class, Arg1Type.class, ...);
```

As you can see, different method signatures can now be represented as normal instance objects, without the need to define a new type for each signature that was required. This also provides a simple way to ensure as much type safety as possible. If you want to know whether a candidate method handle can be called with a certain set of arguments, you can examine the `MethodType` belonging to the handle.

NOTE Passing around a single `MethodType` object is much more convenient than the cumbersome `Class[]` that reflection forces you to use.

Now that you've seen how `MethodType` objects solve the interface-proliferation problem, let's see how we can create method handles that point at methods from our types.

17.3.3 Looking up method handles

Let's take a look at how to get a method handle that points at the `toString()` method on the current class. Notice that we want `mtToString` to exactly match the signature of `toString()`—it has a return type of `String` and takes no arguments. The corresponding `MethodType` instance should be `MethodType.methodType(String.class)`, as shown here:

```
public MethodHandle getToStringMH() {
  MethodHandle mh;
  var mt = MethodType.methodType(String.class);      Obtains the lookup context
  var lk = MethodHandles.lookup();           ◄──────┘

                                                        Looks up the handle
  try {                                                  from context
    mh = lk.findVirtual(getClass(), "toString", mt);  ◄──────┘
  } catch (NoSuchMethodException | IllegalAccessException mhx) {
    throw (AssertionError)new AssertionError().initCause(mhx);
  }

  return mh;
}
```

To get a method handle from a lookup object, you need to provide the class that holds the method you want, the name of the method, and a `MethodType` representing the appropriate signature. The method type is necessary to deal with overloaded methods.

It is very common to use a lookup context to find methods on the current class, but you can, in fact, use the context to get handles on methods belonging to *any* type, including JDK types. Of course, if you get handles from a class in a different package or module, the lookup context will be able to see only methods you have access to (e.g., public methods on public classes in exported packages). This is an important aspect of the method handles API: access control for a method handle is checked when the method is found, *not* when the handle is executed.

Once a method handle has been obtained, it's always safe to call it, because there are no further access control checks. A method handle can be created in one context, where access is allowed, and then passed to another context where access is *not* allowed, and it will still execute. This is an important difference from reflection.

> **NOTE** Access control for invoking method handles cannot be circumvented, unlike reflective calls. There is no equivalent of the reflection `setAccessible()` hack we met in chapter 4.

Now that we have a method handle, the natural thing to do with it is to execute it. The API provides two main ways to do this: the `invokeExact()` and `invoke()` methods.

The `invokeExact()` method requires the types of arguments to exactly match what the underlying method expects. The `invoke()` method performs some transformations to try to get the types to match if they're not quite right (e.g., boxing or unboxing, as required).

After this introduction, we'll now move on to show a longer example of how method handles can be used to replace other techniques, such as reflection and small inner classes used to proxy capabilities.

17.3.4 *Reflection vs. proxies vs. method handles*

If you've spent any time dealing with a codebase that contains a lot of reflection, you're probably all too familiar with some of the pain that comes from reflective code. In this subsection, we want to show you how method handles can be used to replace a lot of reflective boilerplate and make your coding life a little easier.

To show the differences between method handles and other techniques, we've provided three ways to access the private `callThePrivate()` method from outside the class. There are two standard techniques: reflection and the use of an inner class acting as a proxy. We can compare these to a modern approach based on `MethodHandle`. An example of the three alternatives appears in the next listing.

> **Listing 17.1 Providing access three ways**

```
public class ExamplePrivate {
    // Some state ...
```

```
    public void entry() {
        callThePrivate();
    }

    private void callThePrivate() {            The private method we
        System.out.println("Private method");  want to provide access to
    }

    public Method makeReflective() {
        Method meth = null;

        try {
            Class<?>[] argTypes = new Class[] { Void.class };
            meth = ExamplePrivate.class
                    .getDeclaredMethod("callThePrivate", argTypes);
            meth.setAccessible(true);
        } catch (IllegalArgumentException |
                    NoSuchMethodException |
                    SecurityException e) {
            throw (AssertionError)new AssertionError().initCause(e);
        }

        return meth;
    }

    public static class Proxy {
        private Proxy() {}

        public static void invoke(ExamplePrivate priv) {
            priv.callThePrivate();
        }
    }
                                                MethodType creation—
                                                we can use the exact
    public MethodHandle makeMh() {              type rather than
        MethodHandle mh;                        needing to box here.
        var desc = MethodType.methodType(void.class);

        try {
            mh = MethodHandles.lookup()              The MethodHandle
                    .findVirtual(ExamplePrivate.class, lookup
                        "callThePrivate", desc);
        } catch (NoSuchMethodException | IllegalAccessException e) {
            throw (AssertionError)new AssertionError().initCause(e);
        }

        return mh;
    }

}
```

The example class provides three different capabilities that can access the private
callThePrivate() method. In practice, only one of these capabilities would usually

be provided—we're only showing all three to discuss the distinctions between them. In practice, as a user of an API, you should not need to care which approach is used.

In table 17.1, you can see that the main advantage of reflection is familiarity. Proxies may be easier to understand for simple use cases, but we believe method handles represent the best of both worlds. We strongly recommend their use in all new applications.

Table 17.1   Comparing Java's indirect method access technologies

Feature	Reflection	Inner class/lambda	Method handle
Access control	Must use `setAccessible()`. Can be disallowed by an active security manager.	Inner classes can access restricted methods.	Full access to all methods allowed from current context. No issue with security managers.
Type discipline	None. Ugly exception on mismatch.	Static. Can be too strict. May need a lot of metaspace for all proxies.	Typesafe at runtime. Doesn't consume much (if any) metaspace.
Performance	Slow compared to alternatives.	As fast as any other method call.	Aims to be as fast as other method calls.

One additional feature that method handles provide is the ability to determine the current class from a static context. If you've ever written logging code (such as for log4j) that looked like this:

```
Logger lgr = LoggerFactory.getLogger(MyClass.class);
```

then you know that this code is fragile. If it's refactored to move into a superclass or subclass, the explicit class name would cause problems. With method handles, however, you can write this:

```
Logger lgr = LoggerFactory.getLogger(MethodHandles.lookup().lookupClass());
```

In this code, the `lookupClass()` expression can be thought of as an equivalent to `getClass()`, which can be used in a static context. This is particularly useful in situations such as dealing with logging frameworks, which typically have a logger per class.

> **NOTE** Method Handles has proved to be a very successful API. In fact, it's been so successful that in Java 18 (but not in 11 or 17), the implementing technology for reflection has been changed to rely on it, instead of the implementation we met in the last section.

With the technology of method handles in your toolbox of techniques, and armed with a working knowledge of bytecode from chapter 4, let's dive into the details of the `invokedynamic` opcode. It was introduced in Java 7 and (so far) is the only opcode ever to be added to the JVM's instruction set. The original use case of `invokedynamic` was to help non-Java languages get the most out of the JVM as a platform, but it has become a major agent of change within the platform, as we'll see.

17.4 *Invokedynamic*

This section deals with one of the most technically sophisticated new features of modern Java. But despite being enormously powerful, it isn't a feature that will necessarily be used directly by every working developer. Instead, this feature is mostly for frameworks developers and non-Java language implementors at present.

Therefore, it's OK to skip this section on first reading. To make best use of it, you will need to have read and understood the discussion of executing invoke instructions earlier in the chapter—it helps to know the rules that we are now about to break.

We'll cover the details of how invokedynamic works and look at some examples of decompiling a call site that makes use of the new bytecode. Note that it isn't necessary to fully understand this to use languages and frameworks that leverage invokedynamic, but this is the internals chapter, so we're going to get into the details.

As you might guess from the name, invokedynamic is a new type of invocation instruction, that is, it's used for making method calls. It's used to tell the JVM that it must defer figuring out which method to call until runtime.

This might not seem like much of a big deal—after all, invokevirtual and invokeinterface both decide at runtime which implementation is to be called. However, the target selection for those opcodes is subject to the constraints of the Java language inheritance rules and type system, so at least some *call target* information is known at compile time.

On the other hand, invokedynamic was created to relax these constraints, and it does so by calling a helper method (called a *bootstrap method,* or *BSM*) that makes the decision of which method ought to be called.

> **NOTE** The target method (call target) for an invokedynamic site does not have to fit into the rules of Java's inheritance hierarchy at all—it is a user-defined choice.

To allow for this flexibility, invokedynamic opcodes refer to a special section of the constant pool of the class that contains extended entries to support the dynamic nature of the call—the BSMs. These are a key part of invokedynamic, and all invokedynamic call sites have a corresponding constant pool entry for a BSM.

BSMs take in information about the call site and link the dynamic call. A BSM takes at least three arguments and returns a CallSite object. The standard arguments are of the following types:

- MethodHandles.Lookup—A lookup object on the class in which the call site occurs
- String—The name mentioned in the NameAndType
- MethodType—The resolved type descriptor of the NameAndType

Following these arguments are any additional arguments that are needed by the BSM. These are referred to as *additional static arguments* in the documentation. The returned call site holds a MethodHandle, which is the effect of calling the call site and will be executed as the actual invocation of the invokedynamic.

> **NOTE** To allow the association of a BSM to a specific invokedynamic call site, a new constant pool entry type, also called InvokeDynamic, was added to the classfile format.

The call site of the invokedynamic instruction is said to be "unlaced" at class loading time. This means that no target method has been associated with the call site and will not be until the call site is reached (i.e., when the JVM tries to link, and then execute, that specific invokedynamic instruction).

At this point, the BSM will be called to determine what method should actually be called. BSMs always return a CallSite object (which contains a MethodHandle), and it will be "laced" into the call site. With the CallSite linked, the actual method call can then be made—it's to the MethodHandle being held by the CallSite.

In the simplest case, when a ConstantCallSite is used, once the lookup has been done once, it will not be repeated. Instead, the target of the call site will be directly called on all future invocations without any further work. It behaves in a similar way to a CompletableFuture<CallSite>. In practice, this means that the call site is now stable and is, therefore, friendly to other JVM subsystems, such as the JIT compiler. More complex choices, such as a MutableCallSite (or even a VolatileCallSite), are also possible, and these allow for the possibility of relinking a call site so that it can point at a different target method over time.

A non-constant call site can have many different method handles as its target over the lifetime of a program. In fact, being able to change the method called at a particular call site is a technique that can be important for non-Java languages.

For example, in JavaScript or Ruby, an individual object of a particular type can have methods defined on it that are not present on other instances of the class. This is not possible in Java—the class defines a set of methods that are used to construct the vtable when the class is loaded, and all instances share the same vtable. The use of invokedynamic with mutable call sites can allow for this non-Java feature to be implemented efficiently.

We should point out that you can't make javac emit invokedynamic from a regular method invocation—a Java method call is always turned into one of the four "regular" invoke opcodes that we met in chapter 4. Instead, Java frameworks and libraries (including those in the JDK) use invokedynamic for a variety of purposes. Lambdas provide a great case study of one of these purposes. Let's take a closer look.

17.4.1 *Implementing lambda expressions*

Lambdas have become ubiquitous in Java programming, but many Java programmers don't really know how they're implemented. Let's find out, starting with the following simple example:

```
public class LambdaExample {
    private static final String HELLO = "Hello World!";

    public static void main(String[] args) throws Exception {
        Runnable r = () -> System.out.println(HELLO);
        Thread t = new Thread(r);
        t.start();
        t.join();
    }
}
```

You might guess that the lambda is really just syntactic sugar for an anonymous implementation of Runnable. However, if we compile the previous class, we can see that only a single file LambdaExample.class is generated—there is no second class file (which is where the inner class would be placed, as we discussed in chapter 8). So, there is more to the story, as we'll see.

Instead, if we decompile, then we can see the lambda body has in fact been compiled into a private static method that appears in the main class:

```
private static void lambda$main$0();
    Code:
        0: getstatic      #7    // Field
                                 // java/lang/System.out:Ljava/io/PrintStream;
        3: ldc            #9    // String Hello World!
        5: invokevirtual  #10   // Method java/io/PrintStream.println:
                                 // (Ljava/lang/String;)V
        8: return
```

and the main method looks like this:

```
public static void main(java.lang.String[]) throws java.lang.Exception;
    Code:
        0: invokedynamic #2,  0  // InvokeDynamic #0:run:
                                  // ()Ljava/lang/Runnable;
        5: astore_1
        6: new            #3     // class java/lang/Thread
        9: dup
       10: aload_1
       11: invokespecial  #4     // Method java/lang/Thread."<init>"
                                  // :(Ljava/lang/Runnable;)V
       14: astore_2
       15: aload_2
       16: invokevirtual  #5     // Method java/lang/Thread.start:()V
       19: aload_2
       20: invokevirtual  #6     // Method java/lang/Thread.join:()V
       23: return
```

The `invokedynamic` is acting as a call to an unusual form of factory method. The call returns an instance of some type that implements `Runnable`. The exact type is not specified in the bytecode, and it fundamentally does not matter. In fact, the actual returned type does not exist at compile time and will be created on demand at runtime.

We know that `invokedynamic` sites always have bootstrap methods associated with them. For our simple `Runnable` example, we have a single BSM in the appropriate section of the class file, as shown here:

```
BootstrapMethods:
  0: #28 REF_invokeStatic java/lang/invoke/LambdaMetafactory.metafactory:
         (Ljava/lang/invoke/MethodHandles$Lookup;Ljava/lang/String;
         Ljava/lang/invoke/MethodType;Ljava/lang/invoke/MethodType;
         Ljava/lang/invoke/MethodHandle;Ljava/lang/invoke/MethodType;)
         Ljava/lang/invoke/CallSite;
    Method arguments:
      #29 ()V
      #30 REF_invokeStatic LambdaExample.lambda$main$0:()V
      #29 ()V
```

This is a bit hard to read, so let's decode it. The bootstrap method for this call site is entry #28 in the constant pool—an entry of type `MethodHandle`. It points at a static factory method `LambdaMetafactory.metafactory()` in the package `java.lang.invoke`. The metafactory method takes quite a few arguments, but they're mostly supplied by the additional static arguments belonging to the BSM (entries #29 and #30).

A single lambda expression generates three static arguments that are passed to the BSM: the lambda's signature, the method handle for the actual final invocation target of the lambda (i.e., the lambda body), and the erased form of the signature.

Let's follow the code into `java.lang.invoke` and see how the platform uses *metafactories* to dynamically create the classes that actually implement the target types for our lambda expressions. The BSM (i.e., the call to the `metafactory` method) returns a call site object, as always. When the `invokedynamic` instruction is executed, the method handle contained in the call site will return an instance of a class that implements the lambda's target type.

NOTE If the `invokedynamic` instruction is never executed, the dynamically created class will never be created.

The source code for the `metafactory` method is relatively simple, as shown next:

```
public static CallSite metafactory(MethodHandles.Lookup caller,
                                   String invokedName,
                                   MethodType invokedType,
                                   MethodType samMethodType,
                                   MethodHandle implMethod,
                                   MethodType instantiatedMethodType)
          throws LambdaConversionException {
      AbstractValidatingLambdaMetafactory mf;
```

```
mf = new InnerClassLambdaMetafactory(caller, invokedType,
                                     invokedName, samMethodType,
                                     implMethod,
                                     instantiatedMethodType,
                                     false, EMPTY_CLASS_ARRAY,
                                     EMPTY_MT_ARRAY);
        mf.validateMetafactoryArgs();
        return mf.buildCallSite();
    }
```

The lookup object corresponds to the context where the invokedynamic instruction lives. In our case, that is the same class where the lambda was defined, so the lookup context will have the correct permissions to access the private method that the lambda body was compiled into.

The invoked name and type are provided by the JVM and are implementation details. The final three parameters are the additional static arguments from the BSM.

In the current implementation of lambdas, the metafactory delegates to code that uses an internal, shaded copy of the ASM bytecode libraries to spin up an inner class that implements the target type. This may change in the future.

Finally, we should note that it is perfectly possible to create a custom class that uses invokedynamic to do something special, but to construct such a class, you would have to use a bytecode manipulation library to produce a .class file with the invokedynamic instruction in it. One good choice for this is the ASM library(see http://asm.ow2.org/). We have mentioned this library a couple of times, and it's an industrial-strength library used in a wide range of well-known Java frameworks (including the JDK itself, as mentioned earlier). This marks the end of our discussion of invokedynamic, and it's time to move on to discuss some smaller, but still significant, changes to the internals.

17.5 Small internal changes

Sometimes small changes can have a big impact on a language. In this section, we're going to meet three small internal changes to the implementation that either help performance or correct an old piece of cruft in the platform. Let's start by talking about strings.

17.5.1 String concatenation

Remember that in Java, instances of String are effectively immutable. So, what happens when you concatenate two strings together with the + operator? The JVM must create a new String object, but there's more going on here than might be immediately apparent.

Consider a simple class with a main() method, as shown here:

```
public static void main(String[] args) {
  String str = "foo";
  if (args.length > 0) {
    str = args[0];
```

```
    }
    System.out.println("this is my string: " + str);
}
```

The Java 8 bytecode corresponding to this relatively simple method is as follows:

```
public static void main(java.lang.String[]);
Code:
    0: ldc          #17          // String foo
    2: astore_2
    3: aload_1
    4: arraylength              ┐ If the array is empty, jump
    5: ifle 12       ◁──────────┘ forward to instruction I2.
    8: aload_1
    9: iconst_0
   10: aaload
   11: astore_2
   12: getstatic     #19          // Field java/lang/System.out:    Loads System.out
                                  // Ljava/io/PrintStream;          onto the stack
   15: new           #25          // class java/lang/StringBuilder
   18: dup
   19: ldc           #27          // String this is my string:      Sets up
   21: invokespecial #29          // Method java/lang/               StringBuilder
                                  // StringBuilder."<init>"
                                  // :(Ljava/lang/String;)V
   24: aload_2
   25: invokevirtual #32          // Method java/lang/StringBuilder.append
                                  // (Ljava/lang/String;)Ljava/lang/StringBuilder;
   28: invokevirtual #36          // Method java/lang/              Creates a string
                                  // StringBuilder.toString:        from StringBuilder
                                  // ()Ljava/lang/String;
   31: invokevirtual #40          // Method java/io/
                                  // PrintStream.println:           Prints the string
                                  // (Ljava/lang/String;)V
   34: return
```

We have a few things to notice in this bytecode. In particular, the appearance of StringBuilder may be a little surprising—we asked for concatenation of some strings, but the bytecode is telling us that we're really creating additional objects and then calling append(), then toString() on them.

Instructions 15–23 show the object creation pattern (new, dup, invokespecial) for the temporary StringBuilder object, but in this case, construction also includes an ldc (load constant) after the dup. This variant pattern indicates that you're calling a non-void constructor—StringBuilder(String), in this case.

The reason behind all of this is that Java's strings are (effectively) immutable. We can't modify the string contents by concatenating it, so instead, we have to make a new object, and the StringBuilder is just one convenient way to do this.

The bytecode shape for Java 11 looks totally different, however:

```
public static void main(java.lang.String[]);
Code:
   0: ldc              #2        // String foo
   2: astore_1
   3: aload_0
   4: arraylength
   5: ifle             12
   8: aload_0
   9: iconst_0
  10: aaload
  11: astore_1
  12: getstatic        #3        // Field java/lang/System.out:
                                 // Ljava/io/PrintStream;
  15: aload_1
  16: invokedynamic #4,  0       // InvokeDynamic #0:makeConcatWithConstants:
                                 // (Ljava/lang/String;)Ljava/lang/String;
  21: invokevirtual #5           // Method java/io/PrintStream.println:
                                 // (Ljava/lang/String;)V
  24: return
```

The first 12 instructions are identical to the Java 8 case, but then things start to change. One obvious change is that the `StringBuilder` temporary is completely gone. Instead, there's an `invokedynamic` at instruction 16. This, of course, requires a bootstrap method:

```
BootstrapMethods:
  0: #23 REF_invokeStatic java/lang/invoke/StringConcatFactory.
     makeConcatWithConstants:(Ljava/lang/invoke/MethodHandles$Lookup;
     Ljava/lang/String;Ljava/lang/invoke/MethodType;
     Ljava/lang/String;[Ljava/lang/Object;)Ljava/lang/invoke/CallSite;
    Method arguments:
      #24 this is my string: \u0001
```

This is a dynamic invocation of a static factory method `makeConcatWithConstants()` that lives on a class called `StringConcatFactory` in the package `java.lang.invoke`. This factory method takes in a string—the concatenation *recipe* for these specific arguments—and produces a `CallSite`, which is linked to a customized method for this specific case.

In general, this is machinery that is deep inside the JVM's implementation code. Most ordinary Java code would never call these methods directly and instead would rely on JDK code and libraries/frameworks that would call it.

NOTE The static argument to the bootstrap method includes the character `\u0001` (Unicode point 0001), which represents an ordinary argument to be interpolated into the concatenation recipe.

The `invokedynamic` callsites can be reused and the implementing classes can be dynamically created if need be. The implementations also have access to private APIs—such as zero-copy `String` constructors—that it would not be possible to expose as a part of `StringBuilder`.

17.5.2 *Compact strings*

When you first learned Java, you were introduced to the primitive types, and you learned that a char is two bytes in Java. It isn't too difficult to guess that under the hood, a Java string is implemented using a char[] to hold the individual characters of the string.

However, this is not quite true. It is true that in Java 8 and earlier the contents of a String are represented as a char[]. However, this representation causes an inefficiency that may not be obvious, so let's dig into it a little.

Java's two-byte char (which represents a UTF-16 character) is wasteful for any string that contains only characters from Western European languages, because the first byte of each char is always zero for such strings. This wastes almost 50% of the storage of the string for those languages, and they're very common.

To address this issue, Java 9 introduced a performance optimization: it allows a per-string choice of (currently) two representations. Each string can be encoded as either Latin-1 (for Western European languages) or UTF-16 (the original representation).

> **NOTE** Latin-1 is also known by its standards number, ISO-8859-1. Try not to confuse it with ISO-8851, which is the international standard for determining the moisture content of butter.

Internally, the representation of a string has changed to a byte[], with a string of n characters being represented in n bytes if the string is Latin-1 or n * 2 bytes if not. The code in java.lang.String looks like this:

```
private final byte[] value;

/**
 * The identifier of the encoding used to encode the bytes in
 * {@code value}. The supported values in this implementation are
 *
 * LATIN1
 * UTF16
 *
 * @implNote This field is trusted by the VM, and is a subject to
 * constant folding if String instance is constant. Overwriting this
 * field after construction will cause problems.
 */
private final byte coder;

static final byte LATIN1 = 0;
static final byte UTF16  = 1;
```

Depending on the nature of the workload, this can cause significant savings in the common Latin-1 case. On the other hand, applications that deal primarily with text in, for example, one of the CJKV languages (Chinese, Japanese, Korean, and Vietnamese) will not see any space savings from this internal change.

In the field, applications using Western languages can see up to 30% or even 40% heap size savings when moving from Java 8 to 11, just from this change alone. Smaller heap sizes means smaller containers, and that can translate to a visible saving in the costs of cloud compute for your applications.

To conclude this discussion, a quick note about the performance impact of this change: it provides a great example of why we must treat performance as an experimental science and measure from the top down. The introduction of the two different `String` representations does involve more code being executed because string operations now need to have two separate implementations—one for Latin-1 and one for UTF-16—and so code needs to inspect `coder` and branch based on the result.

However, the key performance question is, "Does the extra code matter?" that is, do the benefits outweigh the cost of this additional "complexity tax"? The benefits of the change include the following:

- Smaller heap sizes
- Potentially faster GC times
- Better cache locality for Latin-1 strings

We can also question how much the additional comparison and branch operations really affect the amount of code actually executed—remember that the JIT compiler does a lot of nonobvious optimizations and can exploit the time spent waiting for cache misses, so the extra instructions needed by compact strings may actually come for free, essentially.

> **NOTE** In general, "counting instructions executed" is not a good way to reason about Java performance.

This picture of countervailing forces and trade-offs, the impact of which can be determined only by measurement of large-scale observables, is precisely the performance model that we discussed in chapter 7. In this specific case, the smaller heap size may translate directly into reduced cloud hosting costs because smaller containers can be used.

17.5.3 *Nestmates*

Nestmates were specified in JEP 181: Nest-Based Access Control, and the change essentially corrects an implementation hack that dates back all the way to Java 1.1 to do with inner classes. Let's look at an example and see the changes in bytecode that have been made to support nestmates:

```
public class Outer {
    private int i = 0;

    public class Inner {
        public int i() {
            return i;
```

```
        }
    }
}
```

If we compile this code, we will end up with two separate class files, whether we compile with Java 8 or 17. However, the bytecode is different in each case. We can use javap to look at the difference between the two cases. Here's Java 8:

```
Compiled from "Outer.java"
public class Outer {
  private int i;

  public Outer();
    Code:
        0: aload_0
        1: invokespecial #2        // Method java/lang/Object."<init>":()V
        4: aload_0
        5: iconst_0
        6: putfield      #1        // Field i:I
        9: return
```

> The compiler has inserted this "bridge" method.

```
  static int access$000(Outer);  ◄───┘
    Code:
        0: aload_0
        1: getfield      #1        // Field i:I
        4: ireturn
}
```

with the separate class file for the inner class:

```
Compiled from "Outer.java"
public class Outer$Inner {
  final Outer this$0;

  public Outer$Inner(Outer);
    Code:
        0: aload_0
        1: aload_1
        2: putfield      #1    // Field this$0:LOuter;
        5: aload_0
        6: invokespecial #2    // Method java/lang/Object."<init>":()V
        9: return

  public int i();
    Code:
        0: aload_0
        1: getfield      #1    // Field this$0:LOuter;
        4: invokestatic  #3    // Method                          ◄─────  The bridge method
                               // Outer.access$000:(LOuter;)I             used here
        7: ireturn
}
```

Note how the *synthetic* access method (or bridge method) `access$000()` has been added to the outer class to provide package-private access to the private field that we access in the inner class. Now let's see what happens to the bytecode if we recompile the source under Java 17 (or 11):

```
Compiled from "Outer.java"
public class Outer {
  private int i;

  public Outer();
    Code:
       0: aload_0
       1: invokespecial #2          // Method java/lang/Object."<init>":()V
       4: aload_0
       5: iconst_0
       6: putfield       #1         // Field i:I
       9: return
}
```

The synthetic accessor has completely disappeared. Instead, look at the inner class, shown here:

```
Compiled from "Outer.java"
public class Outer$Inner {
  final Outer this$0;

  public Outer$Inner(Outer);
    Code:
       0: aload_0
       1: aload_1
       2: putfield       #1         // Field this$0:LOuter;
       5: aload_0
       6: invokespecial #2          // Method java/lang/Object."<init>":()V
       9: return

  public int i();
    Code:
       0: aload_0
       1: getfield       #1         // Field this$0:LOuter;
       4: getfield       #3         // Field Outer.i:I
       7: ireturn
}
```

This is now direct access of a private field, as shown next:

```
SourceFile: "Outer.java"
NestMembers:
  Outer$Inner
InnerClasses:
  public #6= #5 of #3;              // Inner=class Outer$Inner of class Outer
```

Java 11 introduced the concept of *nests*, which are actually a generalization of the existing concept of nested classes. In previous versions of Java, to share the same access control context, the source code for one class had to be physically located inside the source code of another class. In the new concept, a group of class files can form a nest, in which *nestmates* share a common access control mechanism and have unrestricted direct (and reflective) access to each other—including to private members.

> **NOTE** The arrival of nestmates has subtly altered the meaning of `private`, as we saw earlier when we discussed `invokespecial`.

This change is indeed small, but it not only removes some less-than-perfect implementation cruft but is also needed for forthcoming changes in the platform. Let's move on from the small changes and discuss one of the major (and most notorious?) aspects of JVM internals: the `Unsafe` class.

17.6 *Unsafe*

In the Java platform, if some feature or behavior seems "magical," it is normally accomplished by using one of three primary mechanisms: reflection, class loading (including associated bytecode transformation), or `Unsafe`.

A power user of Java will seek to understand all three of these techniques, even if they resort to them only when necessary. The principle that "just because you *can* do something, it does not mean that you *should*" applies to our design choices in software as much as it does elsewhere.

Of the three, `Unsafe` is the most potentially dangerous (and powerful) because it provides a way to do certain things that are otherwise impossible and that break well-established rules of the platform. For example, `Unsafe` allows Java code to do the following:

- Directly access hardware CPU features
- Create an object but not run its constructor
- Create a truly anonymous class without the usual verification
- Manually manage off-heap memory
- Perform many other "impossible" things

The Java 8 `Unsafe` class, `sun.misc.Unsafe`, warns us of its very nature immediately—not only in the class name but also by the package in which it lives. The `sun.misc` package is an internal, implementation-specific location and not something that Java code should ever touch directly.

> **NOTE** In Java 9 and later versions, the danger of `Unsafe` is made even clearer, as the functionality has been moved to a module called `jdk.unsupported`.

Java libraries are, of course, not supposed to couple directly to these types of implementation details. Reinforcing this standpoint, the attitude of Java's platform maintainers has long been that end users who break the rules and link to internal details do so at their own risk.

However, the inconvenient truth is that this API, unsupported as it is, has widespread usage by library authors. It is not an official standard for Java, but it had become a dumping ground for nonstandard but necessary platform features of varying safety.

To illustrate this, let's take a look at a classic use of Unsafe: the use of the hardware feature known as "compare and swap," or CAS. This capability is present on virtually all modern CPUs but famously is not a part of Java's memory model (the JMM).

In our example, we'll recall the Account class we met back in chapter 5. For technical reasons, we'll assume the balance is an int rather than a double for this section. The Account interface is defined as follows:

```
public interface Account {
    boolean withdraw(int amount);

    void deposit(int amount);

    int getBalance();

    boolean transferTo(Account other, int amount);
}
```

We'll implement it in two different ways. First, we'll stick to the rules and use synchronization. Two of the methods on the interface look like this in SynchronizedAccount:

```
public class SynchronizedAccount implements Account {
    private int balance;

    public SynchronizedAccount(int openingBalance) {
        balance = openingBalance;
    }

    @Override
    public int getBalance() {
        synchronized (this) {
            return balance;
        }
    }

    @Override
    public void deposit(int amount) {
        // Check to see amount > 0, throw if not
        synchronized (this) {
            balance = balance + amount;
        }
    }
}
```

Now let's compare this to the atomic, Unsafe implementation, which contains significantly more boilerplate, due to having to access the Unsafe class reflectively:

```
public class AtomicAccount implements Account {
    private static final Unsafe unsafe;            ⟵   Our copy of the Unsafe object
    private static final long balanceOffset;       ⟵   The numeric value of the pointer
                                                        offset for the balance field relative
    private volatile int balance = 0;                   to the object start

    static {
        try {
            Field f = Unsafe.class.getDeclaredField("theUnsafe");
            f.setAccessible(true);
            unsafe = (Unsafe) f.get(null);
            balanceOffset = unsafe.objectFieldOffset(  ⟵  Computes the pointer offset
                                AtomicAccount.class
                                    .getDeclaredField("balance"));
        } catch (Exception ex) { throw new Error(ex); }
    }

    public AtomicAccount(int openingBalance) {
        balance = openingBalance;
    }

    @Override
    public double getBalance() {
        return balance;          ⟵   A volatile read of balance—no locks
    }

    @Override
    public void deposit(int amount) {
        // Check to see amount > 0, throw if not
        unsafe.getAndAddInt(this,
                    balanceOffset, amount);   ⟵  Updates the balance
    }                                             using CAS operations

    // ...
```

- **The actual balance field** (annotation pointing to `private volatile int balance = 0;`)
- **Looks up the Unsafe object reflectively** (annotation pointing to `unsafe = (Unsafe) f.get(null);`)

In this example, we are doing several things that are supposedly impossible in Java. First, we are computing a pointer offset (the offset where the field value lives relative to the start of AtomicAccount objects). There is no sequence of JVM bytecode instructions that can provide this—only native code that directly accesses the JVM's internal data structures can do it. The method objectFieldOffset() on the Unsafe object enables us to do that.

Second, we are performing a lock-free, atomic add on the balance. This is not possible within the terms of the JMM because volatile grants us only one operation (a read *or* a write) but addition requires both a read *and* a write. Let's look at the code in the getAndAddInt() method in Unsafe to see how this is done:

```
public final int getAndAddInt(Object o, long offset, int delta) {
    int v;
    do {
        v = getIntVolatile(o, offset);    ⟵  Programmatic
    } while (!compareAndSetInt(o, offset, v, v + delta));   volatile access
}                                                           ⟵  A low-level
                                                                CAS operation
```

```
        return v;
    }
```

In this code, we are choosing the memory access mode (in this case, volatile) instead of having that determined by how the variable was declared. We are also directly accessing memory via pointer offset, not by field indirection—another action that is impossible in normal Java.

NOTE The implementation in JDK 11+ uses an "internal Unsafe" object, for encapsulation reasons—it is this code that's shown here.

The semantics of the CAS method follows: on an object o, which has a field at a given offset from the start of the object header, as a single CPU operation:

1 Compare the current state of the memory location (four bytes) to an int v.
2 If the value of v matches, update it to v + delta.
3 Return true if the replacement succeeded; return false if it failed.

The replacement might fail because a thread that is actively running on another CPU has updated the memory location between the volatile read and the CAS. In this case, the method compareAndSetInt() returns false, and the do-while loop sends us around for another try.

So, these types of operations are lock-free but *not* loop-free. Highly contended fields that are being operated on by many threads may require us to spin around the loop for some time before the atomic addition eventually succeeds, but there is no possibility of Lost Update.

NOTE If we trace down into the code in the JDK, we can see that this implementation is pretty close to what the JDK actually does for AtomicInteger.

For the sake of completeness, let's have a look at the withdraw() implementation as well:

```
@Override
public boolean withdraw(int amount) {
    // Check to see amount > 0, throw if not
    var currBal = balance;                    ⟵——— A volatile read of balance
    var newBal = currBal - amount;
    if (newBal >= 0) {
        if (unsafe.compareAndSwapInt(this,    ⟵———┐
                            balanceOffset,          │ Attempts
                            currBal, newBal)) {     │ to update
                                                    │ balance via a
            return true;                            │ low-level CAS
        }
    }
    return false;
}
```

This case is a little bit different, because we are directly using the low-level API for the balance update. This is necessary, because we must maintain the constraint that the account balance must not become negative. This requires extra operations, such as the comparison on `newBal`.

For the case of a deposit, we can use the higher-level API, which loops until it succeeds. However, this is because money can always be deposited into an account, regardless of its state. If we used the same technique here, this withdrawal could spin indefinitely because there may not be enough money in the account to satisfy it.

Instead, we take the approach that we try once and fail the withdrawal if the CAS operation fails. This removes the race condition of two withdrawal operations attempting to claim the same funds but has the side effect that a withdrawal that *should* succeed can be spuriously failed because of a deposit occurring on another thread (which alters the balance after the volatile read).

> **NOTE** We could introduce a `for` loop to the withdrawal code to reduce the chance of spurious failures, but it must be a provably finite loop.

In benchmarks, the performance difference between these two approaches is quite considerable—the `Unsafe` implementation is roughly a factor of two to three times faster on modern hardware. However, you should not use techniques like this in your end user code. As already discussed, many (virtually all?) modern frameworks already use `Unsafe`. There is unlikely to be any performance benefit whatsoever in coding directly against `Unsafe` rather than using what your framework of choice provides.

More important, you are breaking the rules of the Java specification by doing this: using internal capabilities that do not necessarily follow the rules in the way that user code is supposed to. In the next section, we will discuss how recent versions of Java have tried to reduce this unsupported API and replace it with fully supported alternatives.

17.7 *Replacing Unsafe with supported APIs*

Recall that in chapter 2, we met Java modules. This encapsulation mechanism provides a strict exporting capability and removes the ability to call code in internal packages. How does this affect `Unsafe` and the code that uses it?

Given the number of frameworks and libraries that depend upon `Unsafe`, they would be unable to upgrade to versions of Java that do not permit reflective access to `Unsafe`.

> **NOTE** The `Unsafe` object must be accessed reflectively because the platform already prevents direct access to it for non-JDK code.

In Java 11+, the modules system provides the `jdk.unsupported` module. It is declared like this:

```
module jdk.unsupported {
    exports sun.misc;
    exports sun.reflect;
    exports com.sun.nio.file;

    opens sun.misc;
    opens sun.reflect;
}
```

This code provides access for any application that explicitly depends upon the unsupported module and—crucially—also provides unrestricted reflective access to sun.misc, the package containing Unsafe. Although this helps move Unsafe into a more module-friendly form, we may legitimately ask: for how long should this compromise access be maintained?

This is giving Unsafe a temporary pass for a short time only—the real solution is for the Java platform team to create new, supported APIs that can replace the "safe" features of sun.misc.Unsafe and then remove or close the jdk.unsupported module once Java library authors have had a chance to migrate to the new APIs.

> **NOTE** The closing of Unsafe affects everyone using a *very* wide range of frameworks—it's not an exaggeration to say that basically every nontrivial application in the Java ecosystem relies upon Unsafe indirectly in one way or another.

One of the major Unsafe APIs that needs to be removed is programmatic access modes for memory, such as getIntVolatile(). The replacement is the VarHandles API, which is the subject of our next section.

17.7.1 *VarHandles*

The VarHandles API, introduced in Java 9, looks to extend the Method Handles concept to provide similar functionality for fields and memory access. Recall that, as discussed in chapter 5, in the JMM, only two memory access modes are provided: normal access and volatile ("reread from main memory, disregarding CPU caches and stalling until read completes"). Not only that, but the Java language provides a way to express these modes only at the field level. All accesses are done in normal mode, unless a field is explicitly declared volatile, and in that case, *all* access to that field is done in volatile mode. What if these provisions are insufficient for modern applications?

> **NOTE** Volatile is a Java language fiction. Memory is just memory, and there are not separate banks of volatile-access and non-volatile-access memory chips.

One important goal of VarHandles is to allow new ways of accessing memory, that is, to provide a supported, and superior, alternative to Unsafe usage, such as alternative ways to perform CAS or general volatile access.

To see this in action, let's look at a quick example that shows how we might approach using VarHandles to replace `Unsafe` in the account class:

```
public class VHAccount implements Account {
    private static final VarHandle vh;
    private volatile int balance = 0;

    static {
        try {
            var l = MethodHandles.lookup();          ⟵──── Creates a Lookup object
            vh = l.findVarHandle(VHAccount.class,     ⟵──┐  Obtains a VarHandle
                             "balance", int.class);      │  for the balance, and
        } catch (Exception ex) { throw new Error(ex); }  │  caches it
    }

    @Override
    public void deposit(int amount) {                      Uses the VarHandle to access
        // Check to see amount > 0, throw if not           the field, using volatile memory
        vh.getAndAdd(this, amount);              ⟵──────┘  semantics
    }

    // ...
}
```

This is functionally equivalent to the version that uses `Unsafe`, but it now uses only fully supported APIs.

The use of `MethodHandles.Lookup` is an important change. Unlike reflection, which relies upon `setAccessible()` to access private fields, the lookup object has whatever permissions that the calling context has, which includes access to the private field `balance`.

The migration away from reflection and toward method and field handles means that a number of methods that were present in `Unsafe` in Java 8 can now be removed from the unsupported API, including the following:

- `compareAndSwapInt()`
- `compareAndSwapLong()`
- `compareAndSwapObject()`

The equivalents of these methods are found on `VarHandle`, along with useful accessor methods. There are also get and put methods for the primitive types and object, in both normal and volatile access modes, as well as methods for building efficient adders, such as:

- `getAndAddInt()`
- `getAndAddLong()`
- `getAndSetInt()`
- `getAndSetLong()`
- `getAndSetObject()`

Another key goal of VarHandles is to allow low-level access to the new memory order modes available in JDK 9 and later. These new concurrency barrier modes for Java 9 also require some rather modest updates to the JMM.

Overall, definite progress has been made in creating alternatives to the de facto APIs of Unsafe. For example, in addition to VarHandles, the getCallerClass() functionality from Unsafe is now available in the stack-walking API defined by JEP 259 (see https://openjdk.java.net/jeps/259). However, there is still more to do.

17.7.2 Hidden classes

Hidden classes are described in JEP 371 (see https://openjdk.java.net/jeps/371). This internal feature is designed for platform and framework authors. The JEP aims to provide a supported API for one of the most common usages of Unsafe: the desire to create on-the-fly classes that cannot be used directly by other classes (but can be handled indirectly).

These classes have sometimes been referred to as *anonymous classes*, and the method in Unsafe is called defineAnonymousClass(). However, that term is confusing to developers, because in the context of normal Java application code, it means a nested implementation of some interface that declares its static type to be the interface, like this:

```
public class Scratch {
    public void foo() {
        Runnable r = new Runnable() {
            @Override
            public void run() {
                System.out.println("Only way possible before lambdas!");
            }
        };
    }
}
```

This is usually called an "anonymous implementation of Runnable"; however, classes like this are not really anonymous—instead, the compiler will generate a class named something like Scratch$1, which is a genuine and usable Java class. Although the class name is not available to Java source code, the class can be found using that name and accessed reflectively and then used just like any other class.

A hidden class is not truly anonymous, either—it has a name that is available by directly invoking getName() on its Class object. This name can also show up in several other places, including diagnostic, JVM Tool Interface (JVMTI), or JDK Flight Recorder (JFR) events. However, hidden classes cannot be found using a class loader or in any way that regular classes can be found, including using reflection (e.g., via Class.forName()).

The intention is that hidden classes are named in a way that explicitly puts them in a different namespace from regular classes—the name has a sufficiently unusual form that it effectively makes the class invisible to all other classes.

The naming scheme exploits the fact that in the JVM classes typically have two forms of their name: the binary name (com.acme.Gadget), which is returned by calling getName() on a class object, and the internal form (com/acme/Gadget). Hidden classes are named in a way that does not fit this pattern. Instead, a name like com.acme.Gadget/1234 would be returned by calling getName() on the class object of a hidden class. This is neither a binary name nor an internal form, and any attempt to make a regular class that matches this name will fail. Let's have a quick look at an example of how to create a hidden class:

```
var fName = "/Users/ben/projects/books/resources/Ch15/ch15/Concat.class";
var buffy = Files.readAllBytes(Path.of(fName));
var lookup = MethodHandles.lookup();
var hiddenLookup = lookup.defineHiddenClass(buffy, true);
var klazz = hiddenLookup.lookupClass();
System.out.println(klazz.getName());
```

One advantage of this naming scheme (and differentiating hidden classes in this way) is that they need not be subject to the usual vigorous scrutiny of the JVM's class loading mechanism. This fits with the overall design that hidden classes are intended for use by framework authors and others who need capabilities that go beyond the usual bulletproof checks imposed on general Java classes.

> **NOTE** Hidden classes were delivered as part of Java 15 and are not available in Java 11.

In the context of Unsafe, JEP 371 aims to deprecate the defineAnonymousClass() method from Unsafe, with the overall goal being to remove it in a future release. This is a purely internal change—there is no suggestion that the arrival of hidden classes will change the Java programming language in any way, at least initially. However, the implementations of classes like LambdaMetaFactory, StringConcatFactory, and other "flexible factory" methods could well be updated to use the new APIs.

Summary

- Java provides features for runtime introspection not easily available in languages like C++.
  - Reflection
  - Method handles
  - invokedynamic
  - Unsafe

Future Java 18

This chapter covers developments in the Java language and platform since the release of Java 17, consisting of future updates that have not yet arrived. New directions in the Java language and platform are governed by JEPs, but those are descriptions of the implementations of specific features. At a higher level, there are several large, long-running projects within OpenJDK that are implementing the major changes that are currently in-flight and will be delivered over the coming years.

We're going to meet each project in turn and then Java 18. We're going to start with *Project Amber*, where we will hear more of the story of pattern matching and why it is such an important feature.

18.1   *Project Amber*

Of the current major projects in OpenJDK, Amber is the closest to completion. It also benefits from being relatively easy to understand in terms of a developer's day-to-day work. From the project's charter:

> *The goal of Project Amber is to explore and incubate smaller, productivity-oriented Java language features …*
>
> —Project Amber, https://openjdk.java.net/projects/amber/

The main goals of the project are

- Local Variable Type Inference (Delivered)
- Switch Expressions (Delivered)
- Records (Delivered)
- Sealed Types (Delivered)
- Pattern Matching

As you can see, a lot of these features have been delivered as of Java 17—and very useful they are, too!

The last major piece of Amber that is still outstanding is Pattern Matching. As we saw in chapter 3, it is arriving in increments, the first of which is the use of a type pattern in `instanceof`. We also met the preview version of patterns in `switch`.

It is reasonable to expect that patterns in `switch` will move through the same life-cycle that other Project Amber features have: a first and then a second preview, and then delivery as a standard feature after that.

Looking to the future, more JEPs are planned. Finalizing the basic form of Pattern Matching is not the only game in town—there are additional forms of pattern to add. This tells us that, with the change in the release cadence to an "LTS every two years" model, anything initially previewed in Java 18 or 19 would have time to fully graduate for the next expected LTS, Java 21, in September 2023.

For example, we've already seen how Sealed Types can be used to great effect in the current, preview version of Pattern Matching. Without Sealed Types, even the form of Pattern Matching we have now would not be as useful. In a similar fashion, some of the most important use cases for Records in patterns have yet to be delivered. In particular, *deconstruction patterns* will allow a Record to be broken up in to its components as part of a pattern.

> **NOTE** If you've programmed in Python or JS or other languages, you may be familiar with *destructuring*. The idea of deconstruction in Java is similar but is guided by Java's nominal type system.

This is possible because Records are defined by their semantics—a Record is literally nothing more than the sum of its parts. So, if a Record can be constructed only by stitching together its components, then it follows that it can be rendered down into its components with no semantic consequences.

At time of writing, this feature has not arrived into mainline JDK development, or even into the Amber-specific JDK repos. However, the syntax is expected to look like this:

```
FXOrder order = // ...

// WARNING This is preliminary syntax!!!

var isMarket = switch (order) {
    case MarketOrder(int units, CurrencyPair pair, Side side,
                     LocalDateTime sent, boolean allOrNothing) -> true;
    case LimitOrder(int units, CurrencyPair pair, Side side,
                     LocalDateTime sent double price, int ttl) -> false;
};
```

Note that this code contains explicit types for the Record components. It is also reasonable to expect that the types could also be inferred by the compiler.

It should also be possible to deconstruct arrays as well because they also act as element containers that do not have additional semantics. The syntax for that may look like this:

```
// WARNING This is preliminary syntax!!!

if (o instanceof String[] { String s1, String s2, ... }){
    System.out.println(s1 + s2);
}
```

Note that in both examples, we have not declared a binding for the element container, whether a Record or an array.

A side point that should be mentioned here is how Java serialization affects this feature. In general, Java serialization is a problem, because it violates some basic rules of how encapsulation is supposed to work in Java.

> *Serialization constitutes an invisible but public constructor, and an invisible but public set of accessors for your internal state.*

> —Brian Goetz

Fortunately, both Records and arrays are very simple: they are just transparent carriers for their contents, so there is no need to invoke the weirdness in the detail of the serialization mechanism. Instead, we can always use the public API and canonical constructor to serialize and deserialize records. Building upon this foundation, there are even suggestions that could be very far-reaching, such as removing the serialization mechanism partially or completely and extending deconstruction to some (or even all) Java classes.

Overall, the message from Amber is: if you're familiar with these features from other programming languages, then great. But, if not, then don't worry—they are being designed to fit with the Java language you already know and be easy to start using in your code.

Although some of the features are small and others larger, they can all have a positive impact on your code that is out of proportion with the size of the changes.

Once you've started using them, you'll likely find that they offer real benefit to your programs. Let's now turn to the next of the major projects, codenamed Panama.

18.2   *Project Panama*

Project Panama is, in the words of its project page, all about

> *improving and enriching the connections between the Java virtual machine and well-defined but "foreign" (non-Java) APIs, including many interfaces commonly used by C programmers.*

> —Project Panama, https://openjdk.org/projects/panama/

The name "Panama" comes from the idea of an *isthmus*—a narrow string of land connecting two larger landmasses—which in this analogy are understood to be the JVM and native code. It comprises JEPs in two main areas:

- Foreign Function and Memory API
- Vector API

Of these, we will discuss only the Foreign API in this section. The Vector API is not ready for a full treatment yet, for reasons that we will explain later in the chapter.

18.2.1   *Foreign Function and Memory API*

Java has had the Java Native Interface (JNI) for calling in to native code since Java 1.1, but it has long been recognized as having the following major problems:

- The JNI has a lot of ceremony and extra artifacts.
- The JNI really only interoperates well with libraries written in C and C++.
- The JNI does not do anything automatic to map the Java type system to the C type system.

The extra artifacts aspect is reasonably well understood by developers: as well as the Java API of `native` methods, JNI requires a C header (`.h`) file derived from the Java API and a C implementation file, which will call into the native library. Some of the other aspects are less well known, such as the fact that a native method cannot be used to invoke a function written in a language that uses a different calling convention than the one the JVM was built against.

In the intervening years since the JNI first arrived, a number of attempts have been made to provide a better alternative, such as JNA. However, other (non-JVM) languages have significantly better support for interoperating with native code. For example, Python's reputation as a good language for machine learning largely depends on the ease of packaging native libraries and making them available in Python code.

The Panama Foreign API is an attempt to close that gap, by allowing direct support in Java for the following:

- Foreign memory allocation
- Manipulation of structured foreign memory
- Lifecycle management of foreign resources
- Calling foreign functions

The API lives in the `jdk.incubator.foreign` package in the `jdk.incubator.foreign` module. It builds upon MethodHandles and VarHandles, which we met in chapter 17.

> **NOTE** The Foreign API is contained in an incubator module in Java 17. We discussed incubator modules and their significance way back in chapter 1. To get the code examples in this section to run, you will need to explicitly add the incubator module to your modulepath.

The first piece of the API relies on classes like `MemorySegment`, `MemoryAddress`, and `SegmentAllocator`. This provides access to allocation and handling of off-heap memory. The aim is to provide a better alternative to the use of both the ByteBuffer API and `Unsafe`. The Foreign API intends to avoid the limitations of `ByteBuffer`, such as performance, being limited to segments 2 GB in size and being not specifically designed for off-heap use. At the same time, it should be, well, safer than the use of `Unsafe`, which allows basically unrestricted memory access, making it very easy for bugs to crash the JVM.

> **NOTE** For the rest of this section, we assume that you are familiar with C language concepts, as well as building C/C++ programs from source and understand the phases of C compilation, linking, and so on.

Let's see it in action. To get started, you will need to download an early-access build of Panama from https://jdk.java.net/panama/. Although the incubator modules are present in JDK 17, the important `jextract` tool is not, and we'll need it for our example.

Once you have a Panama early-access install set up, test it with `jextract -h`. You should see output like this:

```
WARNING: Using incubator modules:
        jdk.incubator.jextract, jdk.incubator.foreign
Non-option arguments:
[String] -- header file

Option                          Description
------                          -----------
-?, -h, --help                  print help
-C <String>                     pass through argument for clang
-I <String>                     specify include files path
-d <String>                     specify where to place generated files
--dump-includes <String>        dump included symbols into specified file
--header-class-name <String>    name of the header class
--include-function <String>     name of function to include
--include-macro <String>        name of constant macro to include
--include-struct <String>       name of struct definition to include
--include-typedef <String>      name of type definition to include
--include-union <String>        name of union definition to include
--include-var <String>          name of global variable to include
-l <String>                     specify a library
--source                        generate java sources
-t, --target-package <String>   target package for specified header files
```

For our example, we're going to use a simple PNG library that's written in C: LibSPNG (https://libspng.org/).

EXAMPLE: LIBSPNG

We're going to start by using the `jextract` tool to get a set of base Java packages that we can use. The syntax looks like this:

```
$ jextract --source -t <target Java package> -l <library name> \
    -I <path to /usr/include> <path to header file>
```

On a Mac, this ends up being something like this:

```
$ jextract --source -t org.libspng \
    -I /Applications/Xcode.app/Contents/Developer/Platforms/MacOSX.platform/ \
        Developer/SDKs/MacOSX.sdk/usr/include \
    -l spng /Users/ben/projects/libspng/spng/spng.h
```

This may give some warnings, depending on exactly the version of the header file we're generating from, but providing it succeeds, it will create a directory structure in the current directory. This will contain a lot of Java classes in a package called `org.libspng`, which we'll be able to use from within our Java program later.

We also need to build a shared object to link against when we run our program. This is best accomplished following the project's build instructions at http://mng.bz/v6dJ.

The installation generates `libspng.dylib` locally within the project and installs it to a system-shared location. When running the project, you'll want to ensure that the file is somewhere in the paths listed by the system property `java.library.path`, or directly set that property to include your location. An example default directory on a Mac is `~/Library/Java/Extensions/`. With the code generation completed and the library installed, we can get on with some Java programming.

The aim of Panama is to provide Java static methods that match the names (and Java versions of the parameter types) of the symbols in the C library that we want to link against. So, the symbols in the generated Java code will follow C naming conventions and won't look much like Java names.

For the Java programmer, the overall impression is that we're calling the C functions directly (as far as possible). In reality, there's a certain amount of Panama magic that is happening under the hood, using techniques like method handles to hide the complexity. Under normal circumstances, most developers need not worry about the details of exactly how Panama works.

Let's take a look at an example: a program that uses a C library to read some basic data from a PNG file. We'll set up this code as a proper modular build. The module descriptor, `module-info.java`, looks like this:

```
module wgjd.png {
  exports wgjd.png;

  requires jdk.incubator.foreign;
}
```

The code comprises the packages org.libspng, which we autogenerated from the C code, and the single exported package, wgjd.png. It contains a single file, which we're showing in full as the imports and so on are important to understand what's happening:

```
package wgjd.png;

import jdk.incubator.foreign.MemoryAddress;
import jdk.incubator.foreign.MemorySegment;
import jdk.incubator.foreign.SegmentAllocator;
import org.libspng.spng_ihdr;

import static jdk.incubator.foreign.CLinker.toCString;
import static jdk.incubator.foreign.ResourceScope.newConfinedScope;
import static org.libspng.spng_h.*;

public class PngReader {
    public static void main(String[] args) {
        if (args.length < 1) {
            System.err.println("Usage: pngreader <fname>");
            System.exit(1);
        }

        try (var scope = newConfinedScope()) {
            var allocator = SegmentAllocator.ofScope(scope);

            MemoryAddress ctx = spng_ctx_new(0);
            MemorySegment ihdr = allocator.allocate(spng_ihdr.$LAYOUT());

            spng_set_crc_action(ctx, SPNG_CRC_USE(),
                                     SPNG_CRC_USE());

            int limit = 1024 * 1024 * 64;
            spng_set_chunk_limits(ctx, limit, limit);

            var cFname = toCString(args[0], scope);
            var cMode = toCString("rb", scope);
            var png = fopen(cFname, cMode);
            spng_set_png_file(ctx, png);

            int ret = spng_get_ihdr(ctx, ihdr);

            if (ret != 0) {
                System.out.println("spng_get_ihdr() error: " +
                                    spng_strerror(ret));
                System.exit(2);
            }

            final String colorTypeMsg;
            final byte colorType = spng_ihdr.color_type$get(ihdr);

            if (colorType ==
                    SPNG_COLOR_TYPE_GRAYSCALE()) {
                colorTypeMsg = "grayscale";
            } else if (colorType ==
```

Annotations in margin:

- **Panama classes for working with C-style memory management**
- **The Java wrapper for a C function in spng.h**
- **Reads data in 64 M chunks**
- **Copies contents of the Java string into a C string**
- **The Java wrapper for a C standard library function**
- **The Java wrapper for a C constant**

```
                        SPNG_COLOR_TYPE_TRUECOLOR()) {
                colorTypeMsg = "truecolor";
            } else if (colorType ==
                    SPNG_COLOR_TYPE_INDEXED()) {
                colorTypeMsg = "indexed color";
            } else if (colorType ==
                    SPNG_COLOR_TYPE_GRAYSCALE_ALPHA()) {
                colorTypeMsg = "grayscale with alpha";
            } else {
                colorTypeMsg = "truecolor with alpha";
            }

            System.out.println("File type: " + colorTypeMsg);
        }
    }
}
```

The Java wrapper for a C constant

This is built with a Gradle build script, shown here:

```
plugins {
  id("org.beryx.jlink") version("2.24.2")
}

repositories {
  mavenCentral()
}

application {
  mainModule.set("wgjd.png")
  mainClass.set("wgjd.png.PngReader")
}

java {
    modularity.inferModulePath.set(true)
}

sourceSets {
  main {
    java {
      setSrcDirs(listOf("src/main/java/org",
                        "src/main/java/wgjd.png"))
    }
  }
}

tasks.withType<JavaCompile> {
  options.compilerArgs = listOf()
}

tasks.jar {
  manifest {
    attributes("Main-Class" to application.mainClassName)
  }
}
```

And can be executed like this:

```
$ java --add-modules jdk.incubator.foreign \
   --enable-native-access=ALL-UNNAMED \
   -jar build/libs/Panama.jar <FILENAME>.png
```

This should produce some output providing basic metadata about our image file.

HANDLING NATIVE MEMORY IN PANAMA

One key aspect of handling memory is the question of the lifetime of native memory. C does not have a garbage collector, so all memory must be manually allocated and de-allocated. This is, of course, extremely error prone as well as being not at all natural for a Java programmer.

To work around this problem, Panama provides several classes that are used as Java handles for C memory management operations. The key is the `ResourceScope` class, which can be used to provide deterministic cleanup. This is handled in the usual Java way, via try-with-resources. For example, the previous code used a lexically scoped lifetime for the native memory handling:

```
try (var scope = newConfinedScope()) {
    var allocator = SegmentAllocator.ofScope(scope);

    // ...

}
```

The `allocator` object is an instance of an implementation of the `SegmentAllocator` interface. It is created from the scope via a factory method, and in turn we can create `MemorySegment` objects from the allocator.

Objects that implement the `MemorySegment` interface represent contiguous blocks of memory. Typically, these will be backed by blocks of native memory, but it is also possible to back memory segments with on-heap arrays. This is similar to the case of `ByteBuffer` in the Java NIO API.

> **NOTE** The Panama API also contains `MemoryAddress`, which is effectively a Java wrapper over a C pointer (expressed as a `long` value).

When the scope is autoclosed, the allocator will be called back to deterministically deallocate and release any resources that it had been holding. This is how the *Resource Acquisition Is Initialization* (or RAII) pattern, which is implemented in Java using try-with-resources, is carried into native code. The scope and allocator objects hold references to native resources and automatically free them when the TWR block exits.

Alternatively, this can be handled implicitly, with the native memory being cleaned up when a `MemorySegment` object is garbage-collected. This, of course, means that the cleanup happens nondeterministically, whenever the GC runs. In general, it is advisable to use explicit scopes, especially if you are not familiar with the potential pitfalls of handling off-heap memory.

At time of writing, `jextract` understands only C header files. This means that, at present, to use it from other native languages (e.g., Rust), you have to generate a C header first. Ideally, there would be an automatic tool to generate these, which would work like the `rust-bindgen` tool but in reverse.

More broadly, over time, `jextract` may get more support for other languages generally. The tool is based on LLVM, which is already language independent, so, theoretically, it should be extensible to any language LLVM knows and which can handle C function call conventions.

The Foreign API is about to see its second release as an Incubating feature (see way back in chapter 1 for the description of Incubating and Preview features) as part of Java 18. It is hoped that it will become a final, standardized feature as part of Java 19 in September 2022.

The Vector API is not as advanced, primarily because the API designers have decided that they would prefer to wait until the capabilities of Project Valhalla (see later in this chapter) are available. This API therefore will not move out of Incubating status until Valhalla is available as a standard feature.

18.3 *Project Loom*

In its own words, OpenJDK's *Project Loom* is about

> *easy-to-use, high-throughput lightweight concurrency and new programming models on the Java platform.*

> —Project Loom, https://wiki.openjdk.org/display/loom/Main

Why is this new approach to concurrency needed? Let's consider Java from a more historical perspective.

One interesting way of thinking about Java is that it is a late-1990s language and platform that made a number of opinionated, strategic bets about the direction of evolution of software. Those bets, from the perspective of 2022, have largely paid off (whether more by luck or by judgment is a matter for debate, of course).

As an example, consider threading. Java was the first mainstream programming platform to bake threads into the core language. Before threads, the state of the art was to use multiple processes and various unsatisfactory mechanisms (Unix shared memory, anyone?) to communicate between them.

At an operating system level, threads are independently scheduled execution units that belong to a process. Each thread has an execution instruction counter and a call stack, but shares a heap with every other thread in the same process.

Not only that, but the Java heap is just a single contiguous subset of the process heap (at least in the HotSpot implementation—other JVMs may differ), so the memory model of threads at an OS level carries over naturally to the Java language domain.

The concept of threads naturally leads to a notion of a lightweight context switch. It is cheaper to switch between two threads in the same process than otherwise. This is primarily because the mapping tables that convert from virtual memory addresses to physical ones are mostly the same for threads in the same process.

NOTE Creating a thread is also cheaper than creating a process. The exact extent to which this is true depends on the details of the operating system in question.

In our case, the Java specification does not mandate any particular mapping between Java threads and operating system (OS) threads (assuming that the host OS even has a suitable thread concept, which has not always been the case). In fact, in very early Java versions, the JVM threads were multiplexed onto OS (aka *platform*) threads in what were referred to as *green threads* or *M:1 threads* (because the implementation actually used only a single platform thread).

However, this practice died away around the Java 1.2/1.3 era (and slightly earlier on the Sun Solaris OS), and modern Java versions running on mainstream operating systems instead implement the rule that one Java thread == exactly one operating system thread. Calling `Thread.start()` calls the thread creation system call (e.g., `clone()` on Linux) and actually creates a new OS thread.

OpenJDK's Project Loom's primary goal is to enable new `Thread` objects that can execute code but do not correspond to dedicated OS threads, or, to put it another way, to create an execution model where an object that represents an execution context is not necessarily a thing that needs to be scheduled by the operating system.

So in some respects, Loom is a return to something similar to green threads. However, the world has changed a lot in the intervening years, and sometimes in computing, there are ideas that are ahead of their time.

For example, one could regard Enterprise Java Beans (EJBs) as a form of virtualized/restricted environment that overambitiously tried to virtualize the environment away. Can they perhaps be thought of as a prototypical form of the ideas that would later find favor in modern PaaS systems—and to a lesser extent in Docker/K8s?

So, if Loom is a (partial) return to the idea of green threads, then one way of approaching it might be via the query: "what has changed in the environment that makes it interesting to return to an old idea that was not found to be useful in the past?"

To explore this question a little, let's look at an example. Specifically, let's try to crash the JVM by creating too many threads. You should not run the code in this example unless you are prepared for a possible crash:

```
//
// Do not actually run this code... it may crash your JVM or laptop
//
public class CrashTheVM {
    private static void looper(int count) {
        var tid = Thread.currentThread().getId();
        if (count > 500) {
            return;
        }
        try {
            Thread.sleep(10);
            if (count % 100 == 0) {
```

```
            System.out.println("Thread id: "+ tid +" : "+ count);
        }
    } catch (InterruptedException e) {
        e.printStackTrace();
    }
    looper(count + 1);
}

public static Thread makeThread(Runnable r) {
    return new Thread(r);
}

public static void main(String[] args) {
    var threads = new ArrayList<Thread>();
    for (int i = 0; i < 20_000; i = i + 1) {
        var t = makeThread(() -> looper(1));
        t.start();
        threads.add(t);
        if (i % 1_000 == 0) {
            System.out.println(i + " thread started");
        }
    }
    // Join all the threads
    threads.forEach(t -> {
        try {
            t.join();
        } catch (InterruptedException e) {
            e.printStackTrace();
        }
    });
}
}
```

The code starts up 20,000 threads and does a minimal amount of processing in each one—or tries to. In practice, it will often die or lock up the machine long before that steady state is reached.

> **NOTE** It is possible to get the example to run through to completion if the machine or OS are throttled and can't create threads fast enough to induce the resource starvation.

Although it is obviously not completely representative, this example is intended to signpost what will happen to, for example, a web serving environment with one thread per connection. It is entirely reasonable for a modern high-performance web server to be expected to handle 20,000 concurrent connections, and yet this example clearly demonstrates the failure of a thread-per-connection architecture for that case.

> **NOTE** Another way to think about Loom is that a modern Java program may need to keep track of many more executable contexts than it can create threads for.

An alternative takeaway could be that threads are potentially much more expensive than we think and represent a scaling bottleneck for modern JVM applications. Developers have been trying to solve this problem for years, either by taming the cost of threads or by using a representation of execution contexts that aren't threads.

One way of trying to achieve this was the SEDA approach (Staged Event Driven Architecture)—roughly speaking, a system in which a domain object is moved from A to Z along a multistage pipeline with various different transformations happening along the way. This can be implemented in a distributed system using a messaging system or in a single process, using blocking queues and a thread pool for each stage.

At each step, the processing of the domain object is described by a Java object that contains code to implement the step transformation. For this to work correctly, the code must be guaranteed to terminate—no infinite loops—and this cannot be enforced by the framework.

This approach has some notable shortcomings—not least the discipline required by programmers to use the architecture effectively. Let's take a look at a better alternative.

18.3.1   *Virtual threads*

Project Loom aims to deliver a better experience for today's high-scale applications by adding the following new constructs to the JVM:

- Virtual threads
- Delimited continuations
- Tail-call elimination

The key aspect of this is *virtual threads*. These are designed to look to the programmer like "just threads." However, they are managed by the Java runtime and are *not* thin, one-to-one wrappers over OS threads. Instead, they are implemented in user space by the Java runtime. The major advantages that virtual threads are intended to bring include

- Creating and blocking them is cheap.
- Standard Java execution schedulers (threadpools) can be used.
- No OS-level data structures are needed for the stack.

The removal of the involvement of the operating system in the lifecycle of a virtual thread is what removes the scalability bottleneck. Our JVM applications can cope with having millions or even billions of objects—so why are we restricted to just a few thousand OS-schedulable objects (which is one way to think about what a thread is)? Shattering this limitation and unlocking new concurrent programming styles is the main aim of Project Loom.

Let's see virtual threads in action. Download a Loom beta (https://jdk.java.net/loom/), and spin up `jshell` (with Preview mode enabled to activate the Loom features) like this:

```
$ jshell --enable-preview
|  Welcome to JShell -- Version 18-loom
|  For an introduction type: /help intro
```

```
jshell> Thread.startVirtualThread(() -> {
   ...>      System.out.println("Hello World");
   ...> });
Hello World
$1 ==> VirtualThread[<unnamed>,<no carrier thread>]

jshell>
```

We can straightaway see the virtual thread construct in the output. We are also using a new static method `startVirtualThread()` to start the lambda in a new execution context, which is a virtual thread. Simple!

The general rule has to be that existing codebases must continue to run in exactly the way that they did until the advent of Loom. Or, to put it another way, using virtual threads must be opt-in. We must make the conservative assumption that all existing Java code genuinely needs the lightweight wrapper over OS threads that has been, until now, the only game in town.

The arrival of virtual threads opens up new horizons in other ways. Until now, the Java language has offered the following two primary ways of creating new threads:

- Subclass `java.lang.Thread`, and call the inherited `start()` method.
- Create an instance of `Runnable`, and pass it to a `Thread` constructor, then start the resulting object.

If the notion of what a thread *is* will be changing, then it makes sense to re-examine the methods we use to create threads as well. We have already met the new static factory method for *fire-and-forget* virtual threads, but the existing thread API needs to be improved in a few other ways as well.

18.3.2   *Thread builders*

One important new notion is the `Thread.Builder` class, which has been added as an inner class of `Thread`. Two new factory methods have been added to `Thread` to give access to builders for platform and virtual threads, shown here:

```
jshell> var tb = Thread.ofPlatform();
tb ==> java.lang.ThreadBuilders$PlatformThreadBuilder@312b1dae

jshell> var tb = Thread.ofVirtual();
tb ==> java.lang.ThreadBuilders$VirtualThreadBuilder@506e1b77
```

Let's see the builder in action by replacing the `makeThread()` method in our example with this code:

```
// Loom-specific code
public static Thread makeThread(Runnable r) {
    return Thread.ofVirtual().unstarted(r);
}
```

This calls the `ofVirtual()` method to explicitly create a virtual thread that will execute our `Runnable`. We could, of course, have used the `ofPlatform()` factory method instead, and we would have ended up with a traditional, OS-schedulable thread object. But where's the fun in that?

If we substitute the virtual version of `makeThread()` and recompile our example with a version of Java that supports Loom, then we can execute the resulting code. This time, the program runs to completion without an issue. This is a good example of the Loom philosophy in action—localizing the change applications need to make to just the code locations that create threads.

One way in which the new thread library encourages developers to move on from older paradigms is that subclasses of `Thread` cannot be virtual. Therefore, code that subclasses `Thread` will continue to be created using traditional OS threads.

> **NOTE** Over time, as virtual threads become more common and developers stop caring about the difference between virtual and OS threads, this should discourage the use of the subclassing mechanism because it will always create an OS-schedulable thread.

The intention is to protect existing code that uses subclasses of `Thread` and follow the principle of least surprise.

Various other parts of the thread library also need to be upgraded to better support Loom. For example `ThreadBuilder` can also build `ThreadFactory` instances that can be passed to various `Executors` like this:

```
jshell> var tb = Thread.ofVirtual();
tb ==> java.lang.ThreadBuilders$VirtualThreadBuilder@312b1dae

jshell> var tf = tb.factory();
tf ==> java.lang.ThreadBuilders$VirtualThreadFactory@506e1b77

jshell> var tb = Thread.ofPlatform();
tb ==> java.lang.ThreadBuilders$PlatformThreadBuilder@1ddc4ec2

jshell> var tf = tb.factory();
tf ==> java.lang.ThreadBuilders$PlatformThreadFactory@b1bc7ed
```

Virtual threads will need to be attached to an actual OS thread to execute. These OS threads upon which a virtual thread executes are called *carrier threads*. We have already seen carrier threads in some `jshell` output in one of our earlier examples. However, over its lifetime, a single virtual thread may run on several different carrier threads. This is somewhat reminiscent of the way that regular threads will execute on different physical CPU cores over time—both are examples of execution scheduling.

18.3.3 *Programming with virtual threads*

The arrival of virtual threads brings with it a change of mindset. Programmers who have written concurrent applications in Java as it exists today are used to having to deal (consciously or unconsciously) with the inherent scaling limitations of threads.

We are used to creating task objects, often based on `Runnable` or `Callable` and handing them off to executors, backed by thread pools, which exist to conserve our precious thread resources. What if all of that was suddenly different?

In essence, Project Loom tries to solve the scaling limitation of threads by introducing a new concept of a thread that is cheaper than existing notions and that doesn't directly map to an OS thread. However, this new capability still looks and behaves like a thread as Java programmers already understand it.

Rather than requiring developers to learn a completely new programming style (such as continuation-passing style or the Promise/Future approach or callbacks), the Loom runtime keeps the same programming model we know from today's threads for virtual threads; virtual threads are threads, at least as far as the programmer is concerned.

Virtual threads are *preemptive* because user code does not need to explicitly yield. Scheduling points are up to the virtual scheduler and the JDK. Users must make no assumptions on when they happen, because this is purely an implementation detail. However, it is worth understanding the basics of operating system theory that underlies scheduling to appreciate how virtual threads differ.

When the operating system schedules platform threads, it allocates a *timeslice* of CPU time to a thread. When the timeslice is up, a hardware interrupt is generated, and the kernel is able to resume control, remove the executing platform (user) thread, and replace it with another.

> **NOTE** This mechanism is how Unix (and assorted other operating systems) has been able to implement time-sharing of the processor among different tasks— even decades ago in the era when computers had only one processing core.

Virtual threads, however, are handled differently from platform threads. None of the existing schedulers for virtual threads uses timeslices to preempt virtual threads.

> **NOTE** Using timeslices for preemption of virtual threads would be possible, and the VM is already capable of taking control of executing Java threads—it does so at JVM safepoints, for example.

Instead, virtual threads automatically give up (or *yield*) their carrier thread when a blocking call (such as I/O) is made. This is handled by the library and runtime and is not under the explicit control of the programmer.

Thus, rather than forcing programmers to explicitly manage yielding, or relying upon the complexities of nonblocking or callback-based operations, Loom allows Java programmers to write code in traditional, thread-sequential style. This has additional benefits such as allowing debuggers and profilers to work in the usual way. Toolmakers and runtime engineers need to do a bit of extra work to support virtual threads, but that's better than forcing an additional cognitive burden onto end user Java developers. In particular, this approach differs from the `async`/`await` approach adopted by some other programming languages.

The designers of Loom expect that, because virtual threads need never be pooled, they *should* never be pooled, and instead the model is the unconstrained creation of virtual threads. For this purpose, an *unbounded executor* has been added. It can be accessed via a new factory method, `Executors.newVirtualThreadPerTaskExecutor()`. The default scheduler for virtual threads is the work-stealing scheduler introduced in `ForkJoinPool`.

> **NOTE** It is interesting how the work-stealing aspect of Fork/Join has become far more important than the recursive decomposition of tasks.

The design of Loom as it is today is predicated on the developer understanding the computational overhead that will be present on the different threads in their application. Simply put, if a vast number of threads all need a lot of CPU time constantly, your application has a resource crunch that clever scheduling can't help. On the other hand, if only a few threads are expected to become CPU-bound, these should be placed into a separate pool and provisioned with platform threads.

Virtual threads are also intended to work well in the case where there are many threads that are CPU-bound only occasionally. The intent is that the work-stealing scheduler will smooth out the CPU utilization and real-world code will eventually call an operation that passes a yield point (such as blocking I/O).

18.3.4 When will Project Loom arrive?

Loom development is taking place in a separate repo, not on the JDK mainline. Early-access binaries are available, but these still have some rough edges—crashes still occur but are becoming less common. The basic API is taking shape, but it is almost certainly not completely finalized yet.

JEP 425 (https://openjdk.java.net/jeps/425) has been filed to integrate virtual threads as a Preview feature, but at the time of writing, this JEP has not been targeted to any release yet. It is reasonable to suppose that if it is not included as Preview in Java 19, then a final version of the feature will not be available as part of Java 21 (which is likely to be the next LTS version of Java). There is still a lot of work to be done on the APIs that are being built on top of virtual threads, such as structured concurrency and other more advanced features.

One key question that developers always have is about performance, but this is always difficult to answer during the early stages of development of a new technology. For Loom, we are not yet at the point where meaningful comparisons can be made and the current performance is not thought to be really indicative of the final version.

As with other long-range projects within OpenJDK, the real answer is that it will be ready when it's ready. For now, there is enough of a prototype to start experimenting with it and get a first taste of what future development in Java might look like. Let's turn our attention to the last of the four major OpenJDK projects that we're discussing: Valhalla.

18.4 *Project Valhalla*

> *To align JVM memory layout behavior with the cost model of modern hardware.*
>
> —Brian Goetz

To understand where the current Java model of memory layout reaches its limits and starts to break down, let's start with an example. In figure 18.1, we can see an array of primitive ints. Because these values are primitive types and not objects, they are laid out at adjacent memory locations.

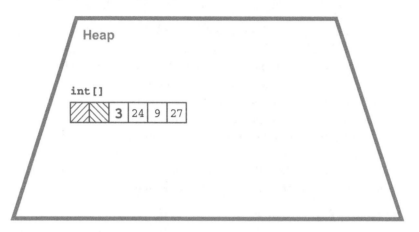

Figure 18.1   Array of primitive ints

To see the difference with object arrays, let's contrast this with the boxed integer case. An array of `Integer` objects will be an array of references, as shown in figure 18.2.

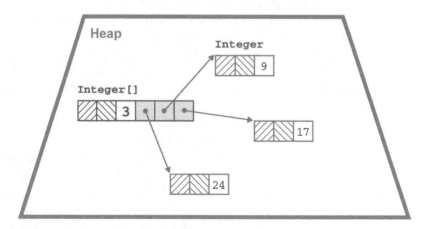

Figure 18.2   Array of `Integer` objects

Because each `Integer` is an object, it is required to have an object header, as we explained in the previous chapter. We sometimes say that each object is required to pay the "header tax" that comes with being a Java object.

For over 20 years, this memory layout pattern has been the way that the Java platform has functioned. It has the advantage of simplicity but has a performance trade-off: dealing with arrays of objects involves unavoidable pointer indirections and attendant cache misses.

As an example, consider a class that represents a point in three-dimensional space, a `Point3D` type. It really comprises only three spatial coordinates and, as of Java 17, can be represented as an object type with three fields (or an equivalent record) like this:

```
public final class Point3D {
    private final double x;
    private final double y;
    private final double z;

    public Point3D(double a, double b, double c) {
        x = a;
        y = b;
        c = z;
    }

    // Additional methods, e.g getters, toString() etc.
}
```

In HotSpot, an array of these point objects is laid out in memory, as shown in Figure 18.3.

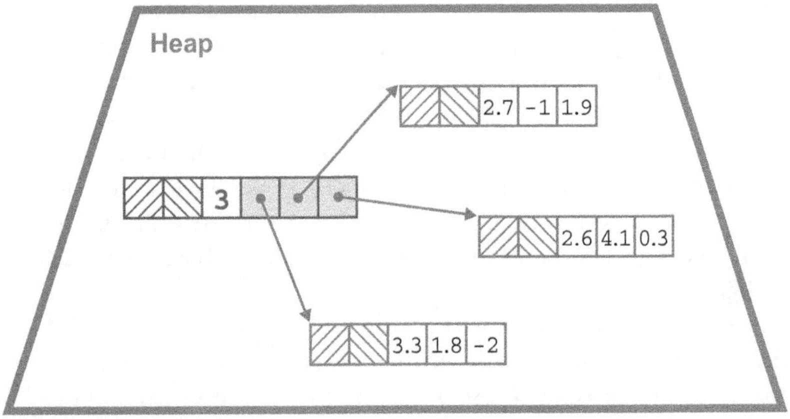

Figure 18.3   An array of `Point3D`

When processing this array, each element is accessed via an additional indirection to get the coordinates of each point. This causes a cache miss for each point in the array, degrading performance for no good reason.

For programmers who care a lot about performance, the ability to define types that can be laid out in memory more effectively would be very useful. We should also note that object identity has no real benefit for the programmer when working with `Point3D` values, because two points should be equal if and only if all their fields are equal.

This example demonstrates the following two separate programming concepts that are both enabled by the removal of object identity:

- *Heap flattening*—The removal of pointer indirection for identity-less objects resulting in higher memory density
- *Scalarization*—The ability to break up an identity-less object into fields and reconstitute it again elsewhere if needed

These separate properties will turn out to have consequences for the user model for identity-less objects.

> **NOTE** It turns out that scalarization—the ability of the VM to break up and reconstitute value objects as much as it likes—is surprisingly useful. The JVM contains a JIT technique called *escape analysis* that can greatly benefit from the freedom to split a value object into its individual fields and flow them through the code separately.

Keeping these properties in mind, we can also approach Valhalla starting from the question: "can we avoid paying the header tax?" Broadly, the answer is yes, provided the following:

- The objects don't need a concept of identity.
- The class is final, so all targets for method calls can be known at class loading time.

Basically, the first property removes the need for the mark word of the header, and the second greatly reduces the need for the klass word (see chapters 4 and 17 for more on the klass word).

The klass word is still required while the object is on the heap, unless it has been flattened as an instance field in another object or flattened as an element of array because the object field layout might need to be described—for example, so that the GC can walk the object graph. However, when the objects have been scalarized, we can drop the header.

From a developer's perspective, therefore, one of the main outcomes of Valhalla is the arrival of a new form of values in the Java ecosystem, referred to as *value objects*, which are instances of *value classes*. These new types are understood to be (usually) small, immutable, identity-less types.

> **NOTE** Value classes have been referred to by several different names during their development, including *primitive classes* and *inline types*. Naming things is hard, especially in a mature language that may well have used many of the common names for language concepts.

Example use cases for value classes include

- New varieties of numerics, such as unsigned bytes, 128-bit integers, and half-precision floats
- Complex numbers, colors, vectors, and other multidimensional numerical values
- Numbers with units: sizes, temperatures, velocity, cashflow, and so on
- Map entries, database rows, and types for multiple-return
- Immutable cursors, subarrays, intermediate streams, and other data structure view abstractions

There is also the possibility that some existing types could be retrofitted and evolve to become represented as value classes. For example, `Optional` and much of `java.time` are obvious candidates that could become value classes in a future release if it proves to be feasible.

> **NOTE** Records are not per se related to value classes, but it is highly likely that a number of Records will be aggregates that do not require identity, so the concept of a *value record* may be a very useful one.

If this new form of value can be implemented on the JVM, then for classes such as the spatial points we've been discussing, a flattened memory layout such as that shown in figure 18.4 would be far more efficient.

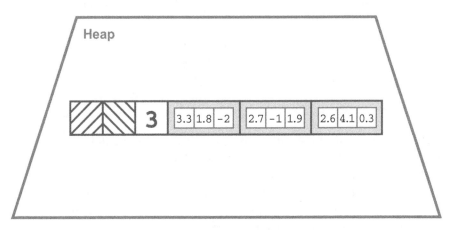

Figure 18.4   Array of inline points

This memory layout would be something close to what a C programmer would recognize as an array of `struct`, but without exposing the full dangers of low-level memory access. The flattened layout reduces not only memory footprint but also the load on garbage collectors.

18.4.1 *Changing the language model*

The biggest change that needs to be made is to modify the concept of `java.lang` `.Object` as a universal superclass because it has methods on it such as `wait()` and `notify()` that are inherently linked to object identity. Without the object header, there is no mark word to store the object's monitor and nothing to wait upon. The object does not really have a well-defined lifetime either because it can be freely copied and the resulting copies are indistinguishable. Instead, two new interfaces are defined in `java.lang`: `IdentityObject` and `ValueObject`. JEP 401 (see https:// openjdk.org/jeps/401) describes value objects in detail, but basically all value classes implicitly implement `ValueObject`.

All identity classes will implicitly implement `IdentityObject`, and all preexisting concrete classes are opted-in as identity classes. Existing interfaces and (most) abstract classes do not extend either of the new interfaces. API designers may wish to update their interfaces to explicitly extend `IdentityObject` if their capabilities are not compatible with the new semantics.

Value classes are `final` and may not be `abstract`. They may not implement (directly or indirectly) `IdentityObject`. An `instanceof` test can be used to check whether or not an object is a value object.

> **NOTE** As well as not being able to `wait()` or `notify()` on value objects, it will not be possible to have synchronized methods or blocks because value objects do not have a monitor.

The class `Object` itself will undergo some subtle repositioning because it will not implement either `IdentityObject` or `ValueObject` and will become more similar to an abstract class or interface. Code such as this

```
var o = new Object();
```

will also change meaning—it is anticipated that o will contain an instance of some anonymous subclass of `Object`, which for backward-compatibility reasons will be understood to be an identity class.

Although the initial aims of value classes seem clear, it turns out to have some far-reaching consequences. For the project to be successful, it is necessary to consider the logical conclusions of introducing a third form of value.

18.4.2 *Consequences of value objects*

Assignment of value objects has fairly obvious semantics: the bits are copied, just as they are for primitives (assignment of references also copies the bits, but in that case, we end up with two references to the same heap location). However, what happens if we need to construct a value object that is not completely identical to the original but is a modified copy?

Recall that value objects are immutable—they have only `final` fields. This means that their state cannot be changed by `putfield` operations. Instead, another mechanism is needed to produce a value object that has a different state than the original. To achieve this, some new bytecodes will be needed, shown next:

- `aconst_init`
- `withfield`

The new `withfield` instruction essentially acts as a bytecode-level equivalent to the use of wither methods (which we discussed in chapter 15).

The other new instruction, `aconst_init`, provides a default value for an instance of a value class. Let's take a closer look at why this is needed.

In Java to date, both primitives and object references are understood to have a default value that corresponds to "all bits zero," with `null` being understood to be the meaning of zero bits for references. However, when we try to extend these semantics to handle value objects, we find that there are two related issues:

- Some value classes do not have a good choice for default value.
- The possibility of *value tearing.*

The no-good-default issue really comes down to wanting to be able to say that the value object isn't really a value yet, but Java already has a way to do that: `null`. Furthermore, users are already used to dealing with `null` point exceptions (NPEs) when they have an uninitialized value.

The second problem, tearing, is really an old problem in a new guise. In older versions of Java, running on 32-bit hardware had some subtle potential problems when handling 64-bit values (such as longs). In particular, writes to longs were performed as two separate (32-bit) writes, and it was possible for a reading thread to observe a state where only one of the 32-bit writes had completed. This would allow the reading thread to observe a "torn" value for the long—one that was neither the before nor after state.

Value types have the possibility to reintroduce this issue. If values can be scalarized, then how can we guarantee the atomicity of writes?

The solution is to recognize that value classes represent not one new form of data but *two.* If we want to avoid tearing, we need to use a reference. This is the well-established idea that using a layer of indirection allows us to update values without tearing them.

Also, consider that some classes have no sensible default that could correspond to zero bits. For example, what would be the default of `LocalDate` after it has migrated to a value class? Some might argue that zero bits should be interpreted as zero offset from epoch (i.e., 1st Jan 1970), but this seems deeply error prone.

This bring us to the concept of *identity-free references*—basically, objects we have removed identity from. At a low level, this still allows calling convention optimizations in the JIT (e.g., scalarized passing of values) and scalarization in JIT code but gives up the memory improvements on the heap. These objects are always handled by reference, just as identity objects are, and they have a straightforward default of `null`. Setting a nontrivial default value for the object is then handled by the constructors or factory methods, just as it should be.

In addition, for advanced use cases, there are also *primitive value types.* These act more like the built-in "true primitives" and allow flattening in the heap as well as the scalarization allowed with value objects. The additional benefits come with associated costs, though—the requirement of accepting zero bits as the default value as well as the possibility of tearing under updates that might have data races.

> **NOTE** The intent is that primitive value types are really only meant for small values (64–128 bits or less on today's hardware) and will need additional care when programming with them.

Tearing does expose users to potential security problems, although it is tempting to say it is an issue only for "bad" programs that have data races. It is, in any case, a new form of possible concurrency bug and will require locking to properly defend against.

One other aspect of primitive value classes is that the runtime needs to know how to lay them out in memory. For this reason, it is not possible to create a field of a primitive value class that refers to (either directly or indirectly) the declaring class. In other words, instances of primitive value classes cannot contain a cyclic data structure of primitive value classes—they must have fixed-size layouts, so that they can be flattened in the heap. Overall, the expectation is that most users will want to use identity-free value objects and that the extended primitives will be used much more rarely.

To conclude this section, let's look at one other aspect of how value classes are represented in bytecode. Recall that way back in chapter 4, we met the concept of a type descriptor. Identity reference types are denoted in bytecode via *L-type descriptors* such as `Ljava/lang/String;` for a string.

To describe values of primitive classes, a new basic type is being added, the *Q-type descriptor.* A descriptor beginning with `Q` has the same structure as an L-descriptor (e.g., `QPoint3D;` for a primitive class `Point3D`). Both Q and L values are operated on by the same set of bytecodes, that is, those that start with a, such as `aload` or `astore`.

The values referred to via Q-descriptors (sometimes called "bare" objects) have the following major differences from references to value objects:

- References to value objects, like all object references, can be `null`, whereas bare values cannot.
- Loads and stores of references are atomic with respect to each other, whereas loads and stores of sufficiently large bare values may tear, as is the case for long and double on a 32-bit implementation.
- Object graphs may not be circular if linked via a path of Q-descriptors: a class `C` cannot reference `QC;` in its layout, either directly or indirectly.
- For technical reasons, the JVM is required to load classes named in Q-descriptors much earlier than those named by L-descriptors.

These properties are basically the bytecode-level encoding of some of the properties of value and primitive objects that we have already met.

There is one final piece of the puzzle that we should briefly consider before moving on from Valhalla: a need to revisit the subject of generic types. This arises quite naturally as a consequence of the introduction of value and primitive objects.

18.4.3 Generics revisited

If Java is to include value classes, the question naturally arises as to whether value classes can be used in generic types, for instance, as the value for a type parameter. If not, this would seem to greatly limit the usefulness of the feature. Therefore, the high-level design has always included the assumption that value classes will eventually be valid as values of type parameters in an enhanced form of generics.

Fortunately, the role of `Object` has subtly changed in Valhalla—it has been retrospectively altered to be the superclass of both value and identity objects. This allows us to include value objects within the realm of existing generics. However, the integration of primitive types into this model is also desirable.

The long-term intent is to be able to extend generics—to allow abstraction over all types, including value classes and the existing primitives (and `void`). If this project is to be successful, we need to be able to compatibly evolve existing libraries—especially the JDK libraries—to fully take advantage of these features.

Partially, this work would also involve updating the basic value types (`int`, `boolean`, etc.) to become primitive value classes, so that basic primitive values become primitive objects. This would also mean that the wrapper classes would be repurposed to fit into the primitive classes model.

This extension to generics will produce a form of *generic specialization* for the primitives. This brings in aspects of a generic programming system similar to that found in other languages, such as templates in C++. At time of writing, the generics work is still at an early stage, and all JEPs pertaining to it are still in Draft state.

18.5 Java 18

It is the nature of any text that attempts to be forward-looking that it will inevitably be out of date by the time it is read. At the time of writing, Java 17 has been delivered, and Java 18 was delivered in March 2022. The following JEPs were targeted at Java 18 and formed the content of the new release:

- JEP 400 UTF-8 by Default
- JEP 408 Simple Web Server
- JEP 413 Code Snippets in Java API Documentation
- JEP 416 Reimplement Core Reflection with Method Handles
- JEP 417 Vector API (Third Incubator)
- JEP 418 Internet-Address Resolution SPI

- JEP 419 Foreign Function and Memory API (Second Incubator)
- JEP 420 Pattern Matching for `switch` (Second Preview)
- JEP 421 Deprecate Finalization for Removal

Of these, the UTF-8 changes, the changes to Core Reflection, and the deprecation of finalization are internal changes that provide some tidying up and simplification of the internals that can be built on in future releases.

The Vector and Foreign API updates are the next milestone on the journey toward Panama, and the next iteration of Pattern Matching is the next step for Amber. Java 18 does not contain any JEPs that deliver any part of Loom or Valhalla. Nothing has been confirmed at time of writing, but it is rumored that the first version of Loom will be delivered as a Preview feature in Java 19 (expected in September 2022).

Summary

One of Java's original design principles was that the language should evolve carefully—that a language feature should not be implemented until the wider impact on the language as a whole was fully understood. Other languages can, and do, move faster than Java, which occasionally leads to complaints from developers that "Java needs to evolve faster." However, the flip side of this is that other languages may "advance at speed and repent at leisure." A flawed design, once integrated into the language, is essentially there forever.

Java's approach, on the other hand, is to proceed conservatively—to make sure that a feature is understood, including all of its consequences, before committing to it. Let other languages break new ground (or, the cynic might say, be first "over the top") and then see what conclusions can be drawn from their experimentation.

In fact, this sort of influence—the back-and-forth borrowing of language concepts—is a common feature of language design. It also provides a great example of the idea sometimes expressed as "Great artists steal." This quote is often attributed to Steve Jobs, but he did not invent it—he had merely borrowed (or stolen) it from other thinkers.

In actuality, this idea seems to have been invented multiple times, but one of the original forms of it that can be definitively traced is this one:

> *One of the surest of tests is the way in which a poet borrows. Immature poets imitate; mature poets steal; bad poets deface what they take, and good poets make it into something better, or at least something different.*

> —T. S. Eliot

Eliot's point applies as readily to language designers as it does to poets. Truly great programming languages (and language designers) borrow (or steal) from each other freely. Good ideas that are first expressed in one language do not remain solely confined there—in fact, that is one of the ways that we know the idea was good in the first place.

In this final chapter, we have met the four major ongoing projects within Open-JDK. Taken together, they aim to deliver a radically different version of future Java.

Some of these projects are very ambitious, others more modest. They will all be delivered as part of the regular cadence of Java releases. The Java we write in a year, or three, from now may well look quite unlike what we would write today.

The major aspects that we might guess will be reshaped include

- *The merger of object and functional programming*—Amber introduces new language features that converge these models.
- *Threading*—Loom will introduce a new model for threads that engage in I/O.
- *Memory layout*—Valhalla solves several problems at once, improving memory density as well as extending generics.
- *Better native interoperability*—Panama helps undo some of the design problems with JNI and other native technologies.
- *Ongoing cleanup of internals*—A series of JEPs to slowly remove aspects of the platform that are no longer needed.

The ultimate shape of future Java is still to be determined—the future is unwritten as of now. What is sure, however, is that after more than 25 years, Java is still a force to be reckoned with. It has already survived several major transitions in the world of software—a track record to be proud of, and one that bodes well for the future.

appendix A
Selecting your Java

With the changes to Oracle JDK distribution and support, there has been considerable uncertainty over the rights to use Oracle JDK versus Oracle OpenJDK builds versus OpenJDK builds from other providers. Various ways exist to get free updates (including security) and (new and existing) paid support models available from multiple vendors to consider. For a complete write-up of this topic, please see the seminal guide: "Java Is Still Free" at http://mng.bz/Qvdw by the Java Champions (https://dev.java/community/jcs/) community, an independent body of Java leaders in the industry.

A.1 Java is still free

You can still get OpenJDK builds by several providers (including Oracle) with complete freedom under the GPLv2+CE license (see https://openjdk.java.net/legal/gplv2+ce.html). Oracle JDK remains free (from cost) in some circumstances. See the rest of this section for the exact nuances of this.

A.1.1 Java SE/OpenJDK/Oracle OpenJDK Builds/Oracle JDK

The OpenJDK community creates and maintains the (GPLv2+CE) open source Reference Implementation (RI) of the Java SE Specification as governed by the Java Community Process (JCP) and defined through an umbrella Java Specification Request (JSR) for each feature release. Implementations (mostly OpenJDK-based) of Java SE are available from various providers such as Alibaba, Amazon, Azul, BellSoft, Eclipse Adoptium (successor to AdoptOpenJDK), IBM, Microsoft, Red Hat, Oracle, SAP, and others.

Oracle JDK 8 has gone through the "End of Public Updates" process, which means updates from April 2019 require a support contract for production use. As mentioned earlier, you can get entirely freely licensed OpenJDK 8, 11, and 17 builds from other providers. Oracle also provides zero-cost binaries for Oracle JDK 17. You have several options to get a JDK; this document focuses on Java SE 8, 11, and 17.

A.2   Staying with Java SE 8

Some people want to continue using Java SE 8 for various reasons:

1 Since the April 2019 update, Oracle JDK 8 has been under commercial use restrictions. To get an updated Java SE 8 binary, users can get a paid support plan for Oracle JDK 8 or use a Java SE 8/OpenJDK 8 binary from another provider.
2 If you are not using Oracle JDK 8, your current Java SE 8/OpenJDK 8 provider may offer updates or paid support plans.

A.2.1 $Free (as in beer) and free (as in use) Java SE 8

If you want free updates (including security) of Java SE 8, use an OpenJDK distribution that passes the TCK, such as Amazon, Azul, BellSoft, Eclipse Adoptium, IBM, Microsoft, Red Hat, SAP, and so on.

A.3   Getting Java SE 11

You can choose from the following options. Please read them carefully, especially how Oracle JDK manages releases and updates for Java SE 11:

1 For Java SE 11, Oracle provides their (OpenJDK based) JDKs via:
   a *Oracle OpenJDK 11 builds*—Under the GPLv2+CE license
   b *Oracle JDK*—Under a paid commercial license (but free for individual use, development, testing, prototyping, and demonstrating and with certain types of applications), for those who do not wish to use the GPLv2+CE or who are using an Oracle JDK with an Oracle product or service.
2 You can also get Java SE / OpenJDK binary distributions from a variety of other providers. These providers give you updates (including security) for a varying time but typically longer for an LTS version

A.3.1 $Free (as in beer) and free (as in use) Java SE 11

If you want free updates (including security) of Java SE 11, use an OpenJDK distribution that passes the TCK, such as, Amazon, Azul, BellSoft, Eclipse Adoptium, IBM, Microsoft, Red Hat, SAP, and so on.

A.4   Getting Java SE 17 (LTS)

You can choose from the following options. Please read them carefully, especially how Oracle JDK manages releases and updates for Java SE 17:

1 Starting with Java SE 17, Oracle provides their (OpenJDK-based) JDKs via:
   a *Oracle OpenJDK builds*—Under the GPLv2+CE license
   b *Oracle JDK*—Under the No-Fee Terms and Conditions (NFTC) license for three years and then a regular commercial license after that

2 You can also get Java SE/OpenJDK binary distributions from a variety of other providers. These providers give you updates (including security) for a varying time but typically longer for an LTS version.

NOTE The NFTC license has some restrictions on the free redistribution of Oracle JDK 17. Please make sure you read the license for details.

A.4.1 $Free (as in beer) and free (as in use) Java SE 17

If you want free updates (including security) of Java SE 17, use an OpenJDK distribution that passes the TCK, such as Amazon, Azul, BellSoft, Eclipse Adoptium, IBM, Microsoft, Red Hat, SAP, and so on.

A.5 Paid support

A wide range of paid support options exist for Java SE/OpenJDK 8, 11, and 17 binaries from Azul, BellSoft, IBM, Oracle, Red Hat, and so on. Azul also offers Medium-Term Support versions.

appendix B
Recap of streams in Java 8

This appendix is a refresher on Java 8 streams and the aspects of basic functional programming that are associated with them. If you are not familiar with the basic syntax of Java 8 lambda expressions, or the philosophy that underlies their design, you should read a basic text first to familiarize yourself with those concepts, such as *Modern Java in Action: Lambdas, Streams, Functional and Reactive Programming*, 2nd ed., by Raoul-Gabriel Urma, Mario Fusco, and Alan Mycroft (Manning, 2018). Java 8 introduced lambda expressions as part of *Project Lambda*, the overall goals of which can be summarized as follows:

- Allow developers to write cleaner and more concise code.
- Provide a modern upgrade to the Java Collections libraries.
- Introduce an abstraction that allows for convenient use of basic functional idioms.

In this appendix, we discuss the upgrades to the Collections libraries, default methods, and the `Stream` abstraction as a functional container type for data elements.

B.1 Backward compatibility

One of the most important concepts in the Java platform is that of backward compatibility. The guiding philosophy has always been that code that was written or compiled for an earlier version of the platform must continue to keep working with later releases of the platform. This principle allows developers to have a greater degree of confidence that an upgrade of their Java platform software will not impact currently working applications.

As a consequence of backward compatibility, limitations to the ways in which the platform can evolve exist—and these limitations affect developers.

NOTE To be backward compatible, the Java platform may not add additional methods to an existing interface within the JDK.

To see why this is the case, consider the following: if a new version of a certain interface `IFoo` were to add a new method `newWithPlatformReleaseN()` with release N of the Java platform, all previous implementations of `IFoo` that were compiled with platform version N–1 (or earlier) would be missing this new method, which would cause a failure to link old implementations of `IFoo` under Java platform version N.

This limitation was a serious concern for the JDK 8 implementation of lambda expressions because a primary design goal was to be able to upgrade standard JDK data structures to implement coding idioms from the functional school of programming. The intent was to add new methods that use lambda expressions to express functional ideas (such as `map()` and `filter()`) throughout the Java Collections libraries.

B.2 *Default methods*

To solve this problem, an entirely new mechanism was needed. The goal was to allow the upgrade of interfaces with new releases of the Java platform by adding *default methods*.

NOTE From Java 8 onward, a default method (sometimes called an optional method) can be added to any interface. This must include an implementation, called the *default implementation*, which is written inline in the interface definition. This change represents an evolution of the interface definition and does not break backward compatibility.

The rules governing default methods follow:

- Any implementation of the interface *may* (but is not required to) implement the default method.
- If an implementing class implements the default method, the implementation in the class is used.
- If an implementing class does *not* implement the default method, the default implementation (from the interface definition) is used.

Let's take a quick look at an example. One of the default methods that was added to `List` in JDK 8 is the `sort()` method. Its definition follows:

```
public default void sort(Comparator<? super E> c) {
    Collections.<E>sort(this, c);
}
```

This means that any `List` object has an instance method `sort()`, which can be used to sort the list in place using a suitable `Comparator`. Any implementation of `List` can provide its own override of the `sort()` behavior, but if it does not, this default, which falls back to the implementation provided in the `Collections` helper class, will be available.

The default methods mechanism works via class loading. When an implementation of an interface is being loaded, the class file is examined to see whether all of the optional methods are present. If they are, class loading continues normally. If not, the bytecode of the implementation is patched to add in the default implementation of the missing methods.

> **NOTE**   Default methods represent a fundamental change in Java's approach to object orientation. From Java 8 onward, interfaces can contain implementation code. Many developers see this as relaxing some of the rules of Java's strict single inheritance.

Developers should understand one detail of how default methods work: the possibility of *default implementation clash*, which has two parts. First, if an implementing class already has a method that has the same name and signature as a new default method, then the pre-existing implementation will always be used in preference to the default implementation.

Second, if a class implements two interfaces that both contain a default method with the same name and signature, the class must implement the method (and it can choose either to delegate to the interface default or to do something else entirely). This raises the possibility that adding a default method to an interface can break client code because if the client code is already implementing another interface that has a default method, the possibility of implementation clash exists. In practice, however, this situation is very rare, and this possibility is deemed a small price to pay for the other benefits that default methods bring.

B.3   *Streams*

Recall that one of the goals of Project Lambda was to provide the Java language with the ability to easily express techniques from functional programming. For example, this means that Java acquired simple ways to write `map()` and `filter()` idioms.

In the original design sketch for Java 8, these idioms were implemented by adding these methods directly to the classic Java Collections interfaces as additional default methods. However, this approach was unsatisfactory for several reasons.

For one thing, because `map()` and `filter()` are relatively common names, it was felt that the risk of existing implementations was too high—that many of the user-written implementations of the Collections would have existing methods that would not respect the intended semantics of the new methods.

Instead, a new abstraction, called a `Stream`, was invented. A `Stream` is a container type, which in some ways is analogous to an iterator for the more functional approach to handling collections and aggregate data.

The `Stream` interface is where all of the new *functionally orientated* methods have been placed, such as `map()`, `filter()`, `reduce()`, `forEach()`, and `flatMap()`. The methods on `Stream` make extensive use of functional interface types, such as lambda expressions as arguments.

A `Stream` is best viewed as a sequence of elements that is consumable. That means that after an element has been taken from a `Stream`, it is no longer available, in much the same way as for an `Iterator`.

> **NOTE** Because `Stream` objects are consumable, they should not be reused or stored in temporary variables. Assigning a `Stream` value to a local variable is almost always a code smell.

The original Collections classes, such as `List` and `Set`, have been given a new default method, called `stream()`. This returns a `Stream` object for the collection, in a similar fashion to how `iterator()` was used in code that uses the classic collections.

B.3.1   Example

This bit of code shows how we can use a `Stream` and a lambda expression to implement a filter idiom:

```
List<String> myStrings = getSomeStrings();
String search = getSearchString();

System.out.println(myStrings.stream()
                    .filter(s -> s.equals(search))
                    .collect(Collectors.toList()));
```

Note that we also need to call `collect()`—this is because `filter()` returns another `Stream`. To get a collection type back, after our filtering operation, we need to do something to actively convert the `Stream` to a `Collection`.

The overall approach looks like this:

```
        stream()  filter()   map()   collect()
Collection -> Stream -> Stream -> Stream -> Collection
```

The idea is for the developer to build up a "pipeline" of operations that need to be applied to the stream. The actual content of the operations will be expressed using a lambda expression for each operation. At the end of the pipeline, the results need to be materialized back into a collection, so the `collect()` method is used.

Let's look at part of the definition of the `Stream` interface (which defines the `map()` and `filter()` methods):

```
public interface Stream<T> extends BaseStream<T, Stream<T>> {
    Stream<T> filter(Predicate<? super T> predicate);

    <R> Stream<R> map(Function<? super T, ? extends R> mapper);

    // ...
}
```

NOTE   Don't worry about the scary-looking generics in those definitions. All the "? super" and "? extends" clauses mean is: "Do the right thing when the objects in the stream have subclasses."

These definitions involve two new interfaces: Predicate and Function. These can both be found in the java.util.function package. Both interfaces have only one method, which doesn't have a default. Therefore, we can write a lambda expression for them, which will be automatically converted into an instance of the correct type.

NOTE   Remember that conversion to the correct *functional interface* type (via type inference) is always what the Java platform does when it encounters a lambda expression.

Let's look at a code example. Suppose we're modeling otter populations. Some are wild, and some are in wildlife parks. We want to know how many caged otters are looked after by trainee zookeepers. With lambda expressions and streams, this is easy to do, as shown here:

```
Set<Otter> ots = getOtters();
System.out.println(ots.stream()
    .filter(o -> !o.isWild())
    .map(o -> o.getKeeper())
    .filter(k -> k.isTrainee())
    .collect(Collectors.toList())
    .size());
```

First, we filter the stream so that only captive otters are handled. Then, we perform a map() to get a stream of keepers, rather than the stream of otters (note that the type of this stream has changed from Stream<Otter> to Stream<Keeper>). Then, we filter again, to select only the trainee keepers, and then we materialize this into a concrete collection instance, using the static method Collectors.toList(). Finally, we use the familiar size() method to return the count from the concrete list.

In this example, we have transformed our otters into the keepers that are responsible for them. We didn't mutate any state of any otter to do so—this is sometimes called being *side-effect free*.

NOTE   In Java, the convention is that code inside map() and filter() expressions should always be side-effect free. However, this "rule" is not enforced by the Java runtime, so be careful. You should always follow this convention in your own code.

If our use case means that we need to mutate some external state, we could use one of two approaches, depending on what we want to achieve. First, if we want to build up aggregate state (e.g., a running total of the ages of otters), we could use a reduce(). Alternatively, if we want to perform a more general state transformation (e.g., transferring otters to a new keeper when the old one leaves), a forEach() is more appropriate.

Let's examine how we would calculate the otters average age using the `reduce()` method in the next code snippet:

```
var kate = new Keeper();
var bob = new Keeper();
var splash = new Otter();
splash.incAge();
splash.setKeeper(kate);
Set<Otter> ots = Set.of(splash);

double aveAge = ((double) ots.stream()
    .map(o -> o.getAge())
    .reduce(0, (x, y) -> {return x + y;} )) / ots.size();
System.out.println("Average age: "+ aveAge);
```

First of all we map from the otters to their ages. Next we use the `reduce()` method. It takes two arguments: the initial value (often called the *zero*) and a function to apply step by step. In our example, that is just a simple addition because we want to sum the ages of all the otters. Finally, we divide the total age by the number of otters we have.

Notice that the second argument to `reduce()` is a two-argument lambda. The simple way to think about this is that the first of those two arguments is the "running total" of the aggregate operation and the second is effectively the loop variable as we iterate over the collection.

Finally, let's turn to the case where we want to alter state. For this we will use the `forEach()` operation. In our example, we want to model the Keeper Kate going on holiday, so all her otters should be handed over to Bob for now. This is easily accomplished like this:

```
ots.stream()
.filter(o -> !o.isWild())
.filter(o -> o.getKeeper().equals(kate))
.forEach(o -> o.setKeeper(bob));
```

Notice that neither `reduce()` nor `forEach()` uses `collect()`. `reduce()` gathers up state as it runs over the stream, and `forEach()` is simply applying an action to everything on the stream, so, in both cases, there's no need to rematerialize the stream.

B.4   *The limits of collections*

Java's Collections have served the language extremely well. However, they are based on the idea that all of the elements of the collection exist and are represented somewhere in memory. This means that they are not capable of representing more general data, such as infinite sets.

Consider, for example, the set of all prime numbers. This cannot be modelled as `Set<Integer>` because we don't know what all the prime numbers are, and we certainly don't have enough heap space to represent them all. In early version of Java, this would have been a very difficult problem to solve within the standard collections.

It is possible to construct a view of data that works primarily with iterators and relegates the underlying collections to a supporting role. However, this requires discipline and is not an immediately obvious approach to the Java Collections. In the past, if the developer wanted to use this type of approach, they would typically depend on an external library that provided better support for this functionality.

Fortunately, Java `Streams` address this use case by introducing the `Stream` interface as an abstraction that is better suited to dealing with more general data structures than basic finite collections. This means that a `Stream` can be thought of as more general than an `Iterator` or a `Collection`.

> **NOTE** A `Stream` does not manage the storage for elements or provide a way to access individual elements directly from the stream.

However, a `Stream` is not really a data structure—instead, it's an abstraction for handling data, although the distinction between the two cases is somewhat subtle.

B.5   Infinite streams

Let's dig a little deeper into the concept of modeling an infinite sequence of numbers. Some consequences follow:

- We can't materialize the whole stream to a collection so methods like `collect()` won't be possible.
- We must operate by pulling the elements out of the stream.
- We need a bit of code that returns the next element as we need it.

This approach also means that the values of expressions are not computed until they are needed.

Up until Java 8, the value of an expression was always computed as soon as it was bound to a variable or passed into a function. This is called *eager evaluation*, and it is, of course, the default behavior for expression evaluation in most mainstream programming languages.

> **NOTE** With version 8, a new programming paradigm was introduced for Java—`Stream` uses *lazy evaluation* wherever possible.

This is an extremely powerful new feature and does take a bit of getting used to. We discuss lazy evaluation in more detail in chapter 15. The aim of lambda expressions in Java is to simplify life for the ordinary programmer, even if that requires extra complexity in the platform.

B.6   Handling primitives

One important aspect of the Stream API that we have glossed over until now is how to handle primitive types. Java's generics do not allow a primitive type to be used as a type parameter, so we cannot write `Stream<int>`. Fortunately, the `Streams` library comes with some tricks to help us work around this issue. Let's look at an example:

```
double totalAge = ((double) ots.stream()
                              .map(o -> o.getAge())
                              .reduce(0, (x, y) -> {return x + y;} ));

double aveAge = totalAge / ots.size();
System.out.println("Average age: "+ aveAge);
```

This actually uses primitive types over most of the pipeline, so let's unpack this a bit and see how the primitive types are used in code like this.

First off, don't be confused by the cast to `double`. This is just to ensure that Java does a proper average, instead of performing integer division.

The argument to `map()` is a lambda expression that takes in an `Otter` and returns an `int`. If we could write it using Java's generics, the lambda expression would be converted to an object that implements `Function<Otter, int>`. However, because Java's generics will not allow this, we need to encode the fact that the return type is `int` in a different way—by putting it in the name of the type, so, the type that is actually inferred is `ToIntFunction<Otter>`. This type is known as a *primitive specialization* of the function type and is used to avoid boxing and unboxing between `int` and `Integer`, which saves unnecessary generation of objects and allows us to use function types that are specific to the primitive type that's being used.

Let's break down the average calculation a little more. To take the age of each otter, we use this expression:

```
ots.stream().map(o -> o.getAge())
```

Let's look at the definition of the `map()` method that is being called, shown next:

```
IntStream map(ToIntFunction<? super T> mapper);
```

From this we can see that we are using the special function type `ToIntFunction`, and we're also using a specialized form of `Stream` to represent the stream of ints.

After this, we pass to `reduce()`, which is defined as follows:

```
int reduce(int identity, IntBinaryOperator op);
```

This is also a specialized form that also operates purely on ints and takes a two-argument lambda (both arguments are ints) to perform the reduction.

`reduce()` is a collecting operation (and, therefore, eager), so the pipeline is evaluated at that point and returns a single value, which is then cast to a double and turned into the overall average.

If you missed all of this detail about primitives, don't worry—it's one of the good things about type inferencing: most of these differences can be hidden from the developer most of the time.

Let's conclude by talking about a topic that's often misunderstood by developers: the support for parallel operations on streams.

B.7   *Parallel operations?*

In old versions of Java (7 and earlier), all operations on collections are serial. No matter how large the collection being operated on, only one CPU core will be used to execute the operation. As datasets get larger, this may become hugely wasteful, and one of the possible goals for Project Lambda was to upgrade Java's support for collections to allow efficient use of multicore processors.

> **NOTE**   The lazy evaluation approach for streams allows the lambda expression framework to provide support for parallel operations.

The primary assumption in the Stream API is that creating a stream object (whether from a collection or by some other means) should be cheap, but some operations in the pipeline could be expensive. This assumption allows us to characterize a parallel pipeline like this:

```
s.stream()
    .parallel()
    // sequence of stream operations
    .collect( ... );
```

The method `parallel()` converts a serial stream to parallel operations. The intent of this is to allow ordinary developers to rely on `parallel()` as the entry point to transparent parallelism and places the burden of providing parallel support onto the library writer rather than the end user.

This sounds great in theory, but in practice, implementation and other details end up detracting from the usefulness of the `parallel()` mechanism. Chapter 16 discusses this in more depth.

Due to these limitations, it is strongly recommended that you avoid parallel streams unless you can prove (using the methods of chapter 7) that your application will benefit from adding them. In practice, the authors have seen less than half-a-dozen cases in the wild where parallel streams are actually effective.

index

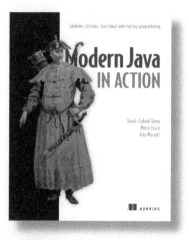

RELATED MANNING TITLES

Spring Start Here
Learn what you need and learn it well
by Laurențiu Spilcă

ISBN 9781617298691
416 pages, $49.99
September 2021

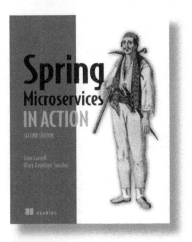

Spring Microservices in Action
Second Edition
by John Carnell, Illary Huaylupo Sánchez

ISBN 9781617296956
448 pages, $59.99
May 2021

Spring Security in Action
by Laurențiu Spilcă

ISBN 9781617297731
560 pages, $59.99
October 2020

For ordering information go to www.manning.com